ALSO BY SCOTT RITTER

Endgame:
Solving the Iraqi Problem Once and For All

War on Iraq:
What Team Bush Doesn't Want You to Know
(with William Rivers Pitt)

Frontier Justice:
WMD and the Bushwhacking of America

Iraq Confidential:
The Untold Story of America's Conspiracy
to Undermine the UN and Overthrow Saddam

Target Iran:
The Truth About the White House's
Plan for Regime Change

Waging Peace:
The Art of War for the Antiwar Movement

DANGEROUS GROUND

DANGEROUS GROUND

AMERICA'S FAILED ARMS CONTROL POLICY, FROM FDR TO OBAMA

SCOTT RITTER

NATION BOOKS
A Member of the Perseus Books Group
New York

Nation Books is a co-publishing venture of the Nation Institute and the Perseus Books Group.

Books published by Nation Books are available at special discounts for bulk purchases in the United States by corporations, institutions, and other organizations. For more information, please contact the Special Markets Department at the Perseus Books Group, 2300 Chestnut Street, Suite 200, Philadelphia, PA 19103, or call (800) 810-4145, ext. 5000, or e-mail special.markets@perseusbooks.com.

Designed by Pauline Brown
Typeset in 10.5 pt. Stemple Garamond by the Perseus Books Group

Library of Congress Cataloging-in-Publication Data

Ritter, Scott.
Dangerous ground : on the trail of America's failed arms control policy from FDR to Obama / by Scott Ritter.
p. cm.
Includes bibliographical references and index.
ISBN 978-1-56858-399-0 (alk. paper)
1. Arms control—United States—History—20th century. I. Title.
JZ5625.R58 2010
                                    327.1'740973—dc22

2009045065

10 9 8 7 6 5 4 3 2 1

To my daughters,
Patricia Nicole and Victoria Caroline,
may you raise your families in a world free of
the tyranny of nuclear weapons.

"I don't believe in peace - I
believe in War.
"Putin is on the right side of
history."
                    - Scott Ritter
                    12-22
                    Ann Arbor, M..

CONTENTS

FOREWORD

Scott Ritter has the great advantage of having "been there and experienced that" and so can bring the sharp edge of realism to the delicate task of separating fact from fiction. In this book he moves from the inspection mode that made him famous to introspection on the often obscure, usually veiled, and occasionally deliberate deceptions of high policy. The result is an engrossing account of fifty years of attempts, as he puts it, to put the "genie" of nuclear weapons back into some sort of bottle.

In some ways, Mr. Ritter's account parallels the study of McGeorge Bundy's *Danger and Survival: The Political History of the Nuclear Weapon,* but Mr. Ritter's work focuses more on what has been attempted to bring it under control.

Because of my own experience as a member of the "crisis management committee" during the Cuban missile crisis, I found particularly fascinating the parallels and contrasts Mr. Ritter draws between the Kennedy administration's attempt to find some basis for dealing with the Soviet Union and President Obama's venture with the Russians. The contrast—hopefully, since the results are not in—will be striking. John Kennedy was much more a child of the Cold War than many outsiders prefer to remember, whereas Barack Obama, who had little experience with it, seems determined to put the Cold War behind him. But the question that must concern us all is: Can he do it?

If we are to bequeath to our children and grandchildren a livable world, he must. As I had painfully engraved in my thoughts during the missile crisis, nuclear weapons anywhere are a danger to people everywhere. Yet, as Mr. Ritter makes clear:

The United States, President Obama will come to discover, is a nation addicted to nuclear weapons and the power and prestige, both real and illusory, that these weapons bring. Breaking this addiction will prove extremely difficult. This is especially true given the lack of having any real nuclear disarmament policy in place since the dawn of the nuclear age. The failure of the United States to formulate or to implement effective nuclear disarmament policy has placed America and the world on very dangerous ground. The longer America and the world continue to possess nuclear weapons, the greater the likelihood of nuclear weapons being used. The only way to prevent such a dire outcome is through the abolition, and not the reduction or control, of all nuclear weapons.

Mr. Ritter brings great personal experience to his task. Literally on the ground, he was charged with finding out the truth of the belief that Saddam Hussein was hiding nuclear weapons. His work was carried on under difficult and even dangerous circumstances and what he found was not what his patrons wanted him to find. With great intellectual courage, he reported what he found. He has carried that mindset into this book: he "tells it like it is," regardless of whose feet he steps on.

Dealing with the Russians has required more subtle ways than searching, and it sometimes came down to personal contacts, as it did with Paul Nitze's famous "walk in the woods" with his Russian counterpart. I had a somewhat similar encounter that I should contribute to his account. In 1968, I went to Moscow to lecture at the Soviet Academy of Sciences and visited the city then known as Leningrad with Yevgeny Primakov, who was at the time with the Academy and ultimately became prime minister of the USSR. We had a different sort of "walk in the woods." Ours was through the massive graveyard where the 900,000 victims of the Nazi onslaught were buried. We both were awed by the memory conjured by the graves, but at the end of our walk, Primakov turned to me and said simply, "We must not ever allow this to happen again." Those deaths, of course, occurred even before the dawn of the nuclear age: if the Germans had had nuclear weapons, no one would have been alive even to bury the dead.

It is, I believe, in this spirit that Mr. Ritter has approached his task: What should we have learned? How can we apply it to the fundamental task of keeping ourselves, our families, and indeed, our world alive?

On no subject, I believe, do we need the lesson of history so desperately as on Mr. Ritter's topic. This is an extraordinarily important book. It is technical where it needs to be, but it also addresses the broad political, military, and cultural aspects of arms control. Understanding the full dimensions of the danger and what we need to do to overcome it is an absolute necessity. We cannot afford to fail. To paraphrase the great English poet John Donne: if the bell ever tolls, it will toll for all of us. To help us perceive the danger of the sound, the first tremors of the "bell" before it is too late, Mr. Ritter's book gives us mental "hearing aids."

This book must be read and absorbed and become a part of our political thought and action.

— *William R. Polk*

GLOSSARY OF TERMS

A-35—Soviet ABM system

ABM—Anti-Ballistic Missile

ACDA—Arms Control and Disarmament Agency

AEC—Atomic Energy Commission

ALCM—Air-Launched Cruise Missile

Atlas—U.S. ICBM

B-1—U.S. swing-wing bomber

B-2—U.S. stealth bomber

B-29—U.S. World War Two–era heavy bomber

B-36—U.S. heavy bomber

B-47—U.S. medium bomber

B-52—U.S. heavy bomber

B-58—U.S. medium bomber

B-70—U.S. high-altitude bomber

Backfire—Soviet medium bomber, also known as the TU-22

BTWC—Biological and Toxins Weapons Convention

CargoScan—X-ray inspection equipment used in the INF treaty

CDM—Coalition for a Democratic Majority

CENTO—Central Treaty Organization

CFE—Conventional Forces in Europe Treaty

Corona—U.S. imagery satellite

CPD—Committee on the Present Danger

CSCE—Conference on Security and Cooperation in Europe

CTBT—Comprehensive Test Ban Treaty

CWC—Chemical Weapons Convention

DEFCON—Defense Condition

DIA—Defense Intelligence Agency

Discoverer—U.S. imagery satellite

DOD—Department of Defense

DPG—Defense Policy Guidance

ENDC—Eighteen-Nation Disarmament Committee

FB-111—U.S. tactical bomber

FBS—Forward Based Systems

Fencer—Soviet fighter-bomber, also known as the SU-24

FOBs—Fractional Orbiting Bombardment system

Foxtrot—Soviet class of submarine

GAC—General Advisory Committee

GLCM—Ground-Launched Cruise Missile

Golf—Soviet class of submarine

GRU—Glavnoye Razvedyvatel'noye Upravleniye, or Soviet Military Intelligence

IAEA—International Atomic Energy Agency

ICBM—Intercontinental Ballistic Missile

INF—Intermediate Nuclear Forces

JCS—Joint Chiefs of Staff

JSPS—Joint Strategic Planning Staff

Jupiter—U.S. intermediate-range missile

KGB—Kommitet Gosudarstvennoy Bezopasnosti, Soviet intelligence service

Lance—U.S. short-range ballistic missile

LTBT—Limited Test Ban Treaty, also known as the Partial Test Ban Treaty

M-4—Soviet medium bomber

MAD—Mutually Assured Destruction

MARV—Maneuvering Reentry Vehicle

MBFR—Mutual Bilateral Force Reductions

MC 14-3—NATO war plan

Minuteman—U.S. ICBM

MIRV—Multiple Independently Targeted Reentry Vehicle

MLF—Multilateral Force

MOA—Memorandum of Agreement, a special annex to the INF treaty

MPS—Multiple Protective Shelters

MRBM—Medium-Range Ballistic Missile

MRV—Multiple Reentry Vehicles

MX—U.S. ICBM, also known as the Peacekeeper

NCA—National Command Authority

NIE—National Intelligence Estimate

Nike—U.S. anti-aircraft missile

Nike Hercules—U.S. anti-ballistic missile

Nike X—U.S. anti-ballistic missile

Nike Zeus—U.S. anti-ballistic missile

NPT—Nuclear Non-Proliferation Treaty

NSAM—National Security Action Memorandum

NSC—National Security Council

NSC-30—U.S. Policy on Atomic Warfare (1948)

NSC-68—U.S. National Security Strategy (1950)

NSDD-13—U.S. Nuclear Weapons Employment Plan (1981)

NSDM—National Security Decision Memorandum

NSPD-4—National Security Presidential Directive 4 (1982)

NSPD-17—U.S. National Security Strategy Concerning Nuclear Weapons

NSTAP—National Strategic Targeting and Attack Policy

NTPR—Nuclear Target Policy Review

NUWEP—Nuclear Weapons Employment Plan

OPLAN-8022—U.S. Nuclear War Plan (2001)

OSIA—On-Site Inspection Agency

PD-18—Presidential Directive 18, U.S. National Security Strategy (1977)

PD-59—U.S. Nuclear Weapons Targeting Policy (1979)

Peacekeeper—U.S. ICBM, also known as the MX

Pershing 1a—U.S. medium-range missile

Pershing II—U.S. intermediate-range missile

PFIAB—President's Foreign Intelligence Advisory Board

PNW—Prevention of Nuclear War

Polaris—U.S. SLBM

Poseidon—U.S. SLBM

PRM-10—Presidential Review Memorandum 10, U.S. Guidance for Strategic Forces (1977)

PTBT—Partial Test Ban Treaty, also known as the Limited Test Ban Treaty

R-7—Soviet ICBM, also known as the SS-6

RAND—U.S. think tank affiliated with the U.S. Air Force

RDF—Rapid Deployment Force

Redstone—U.S. medium-range missile

RNEP—Robust Nuclear Earth Penetrator

RRW—Reliable Replacement Warhead

RS-24—Soviet MIRV ICBM, also known as the SS-29

RT-1—Soviet experimental ICBM

SAC—Strategic Air Command

SACEUR—Supreme Allied Commander, Europe

Safeguard—U.S. ABM system

SALT—Strategic Arms Limitation Talks

SALT I—Strategic Arms Limitation Interim Agreement

SALT II—Strategic Arms Limitation Treaty II

SDI—Strategic Defense Initiative, also known as Star Wars

SEATO—Southeast Asia Treaty Organization

Sentinel—U.S. ABM system

SIOP—Single Integrated Operational Plan

SLBM—Submarine-Launched Ballistic Missile

SLCM—Sea-Launched Cruise Missile

SNIE—Special National Intelligence Estimate

SORT—Strategic Offensive Reduction Treaty

Spartan—U.S. ABM missile

Sprint—U.S. ABM missile

Sputnik—Soviet satellite

SRF—Short-Range Nuclear Forces

SS-4—Soviet medium-range missile

SS-5—Soviet intermediate-range missile

SS-6—Soviet ICBM, also known as the R-7

SS-7—Soviet ICBM

SS-8—Soviet ICBM

SS-9—Soviet heavy ICBM

SS-11—Soviet ICBM

SS-13—Soviet experimental ICBM

SS-14—Soviet experimental road-mobile ICBM

SS-16—Soviet road-mobile ICBM

SS-17—Soviet ICBM

SS-18—Soviet heavy ICBM

SS-19—Soviet ICBM

SS-20—Soviet intermediate-range missile eliminated by the INF treaty

SS-24—Soviet heavy ICBM

SS-25—Soviet road-mobile ICBM

SS-27—SOVIET road-mobile ICBM, also known as the *Topol-M*

SS-29—Soviet MIRV ICBM, also known as the RS-24

START—Strategic Arms Reduction Treaty

Star Wars—Popular name for the Strategic Defense initiative, or SDI

SU-24—Soviet fighter bomber, also known as the Fencer

SVC—Special Verification Commission

Thor—U.S. intermediate-range missile

Titan—U.S. ICBM

Topol-M—Soviet road-mobile ICBM, also known as the SS-27

Trident—U.S. SLBM

TU-4—Soviet copy of the U.S. B-29 heavy bomber

TU-16—Soviet heavy bomber

TU-22—Soviet medium bomber, also known as the Backfire

TU-95—Soviet heavy bomber

U-2—U.S. high-altitude reconnaissance aircraft

Vela—U.S. seismic research project

INTRODUCTION

PRAGUE SPRING, REDUX
APRIL 5, 2009

Dressed in a dark suit, white shirt, and a subdued blue tie—a departure from the "power red" ties that were the mark of his predecessor—on the left lapel of his jacket an American flag pin, the symbol of the nation for which he served as chief executive. As he climbed onto the stage, he was accompanied by his wife, stylishly outfitted in a sleek black dress. Although her husband had been in office less than three months, her sense of fashion had already caught the attention of the media in both the United States and around the world. A clear sense of excitement filled the huge crowd that had gathered in Hradcany Square, in the center of the Czech Republic's capital, Prague. Barack Hussein Obama, the forty-fourth president of the United States of America, was about to deliver an address that was, by design, intended to capture the imagination of not just the audience in attendance but the entire world. After eight years of conservative administration marked by arrogance and unilateralism, Barack Obama's presence seemed to usher in a more liberal, open approach reminiscent of a different time, when people spoke of Camelot. The president was well aware of the comparisons that were being made, and he exploited them in humorous fashion. As his wife left his side in preparation for the start of his address, he told the adoring crowd that he was "proud to be the man who brought Michelle Obama to Prague." This statement was a clear reference to the famous statement made by John F. Kennedy during his May 1961 visit to Paris, when he told a similarly adoring crowd, "I do not think it altogether inappropriate to introduce myself . . . I am the man who accompanied Jacqueline Kennedy to Paris."[1]

The historic visit of the newly elected President Kennedy to Europe that Obama alluded to, a visit in which he toured Paris with his beautiful wife, involved business as well. This visit, in which Kennedy had a tense summit meeting in Vienna with Soviet Premier Nikita Khrushchev—where the two leaders discussed the comprehensive nuclear test ban and the Soviet–North Atlantic Treaty Organization, or NATO, standoff over Berlin—occurred months before America's forty-fourth president was even born. That Obama could make such a comparison, and have it be relevant in the context of his visit to Prague, underscored the reality that although nearly a half century separated the two visits, the circumstances under which they were taken remained similar.

The parallels between Kennedy and Obama were more than simply historical. The two presidents had to deal with a nearly identical adversary (Kennedy and the Soviets, Obama and the Russians). They had to do so under similar conditions: a deteriorating arms control environment (Kennedy had the comprehensive test ban treaty [CTBT] negotiations; Obama faced the looming expiration of the Strategic Arms Reduction Treaty, or START, which served as the foundation of the arms control verification agreements in place between the United States and Russia). These conditions were affected by serious disagreement over events taking place within the NATO sphere (Kennedy had the Berlin crisis; Obama faced the fallout over the short war between Georgia and Russia in August 2008, which continued to sour U.S.–Russian relations). The unifying factor that linked the situations, even though they were separated by nearly forty-eight years, was the reality that both sides possessed nuclear weapons that were capable of unleashing atomic Armageddon not only on themselves but also on the entire world.

While in Prague, Barack Obama was facing his own upcoming summit with the leader of Russia, scheduled for early July 2009, just three months away at that time. The START treaty, signed in July 1991, was due to expire in December 2009. Obama's predecessor had failed to establish a replacement framework of arms control and disarmament between the United States and Russia. The Strategic Offensive Reductions Treaty, or SORT, signed by President Bush and President Vladimir Putin in May 2002 and entered into force in June 2003, contained no verification mechanism or agreed-on benchmark for implementation. If START expired, there was real concern in both Moscow and Washington that the level of tension and mistrust that existed between Russia and the United States could trigger a new arms race. President Obama had inherited a planned missile defense shield in Europe (to be deployed on two bases, one in Poland, housing missile interceptors; and the other in the Czech Republic, housing the associated radar), to which Russia profoundly objected. Already Russia was hinting that it would deploy a new generation of intercontinental ballistic missiles (ICBMs) once START expired. Facing a massive budget deficit and an economy in crisis, the last thing President Obama wanted to embark on was a new and expensive arms race between these two nuclear powers.

One of his primary goals in coming to Prague was to blunt any talk of escalation between the two former Cold War adversaries. A month earlier, in March, Obama's secretary of state, Hillary Rodham Clinton, had presented the Russian foreign minister, Sergei Lavrov, with a symbolic reset button, symbolizing the new president's desire to move beyond the ideological tensions that existed during the Bush administration. In Prague, Obama planned to demonstrate that his administration would not operate in a "business as usual" mode when it came to the issue of nuclear weapons and disarmament. The new president wanted to usher in a similarly new beginning in regard to not only U.S.–Russian relations but indeed the entire world when it came to the issue of nuclear weapons.

Prague was an awkward location for President Obama to begin this journey. The Czech Republic retained a deep mistrust of Russia that recalled the time of the Soviet Union. Obama alluded to this reality early on in his speech, declaring, "When I was born, the world was divided, and our nations were faced with very different circumstances . . . few would have imagined that the Czech Republic would become a free nation, a member of NATO, a leader of a united Europe. Those ideas would have been dismissed as dreams." He spoke of the Velvet Revolution of 1989, which brought down the communist government in what was then Czechoslovakia. He also mentioned the Prague Spring, when from February to August 1968 the people of Prague, and indeed all of Czechoslovakia, sought to distance themselves from the oppressive nature of Soviet-style communism. The Prague Spring came to a crashing end in August 1968 when the Soviet Union crushed the Czechoslovakian effort to effect democratic-based political reform under the treads of hundreds of tanks. The defeat of the Prague Spring movement also destroyed any hope of implementing sweeping nuclear arms reduction measures being planned at the time by President Lyndon Johnson.

Moving to calm any fears among the Czechs that his administration might sacrifice the young republic in the name of improved relations with Russia, Obama hammered home the fact that the bond between the United States and the Czech Republic, cemented through the institutions of NATO, was unbreakable: an attack against one was an attack against all. There were new threats facing NATO, Obama said, and contingencies needed to be put in place. But as the United States, the Czech Republic, and NATO worked to confront these new threats, it was essential that they also ensure that the remnants of threats derived from the time of the Cold War, namely nuclear weapons, did not come back to haunt them.

"The existence of thousands of nuclear weapons is the most dangerous legacy of the Cold War," the president told the people assembled before him. "No nuclear war was fought between the United States and the Soviet Union, but generations lived with the knowledge that their world could be erased in a single flash of light. Cities like Prague that existed for centuries, that embodied the beauty and the talent of so much of humanity, would have ceased to exist." He continued:

Today, the Cold War has disappeared but thousands of those weapons have not. In a strange turn of history, the threat of global nuclear war has gone down, but the risk of a nuclear attack has gone up . . . one nuclear weapon exploded in one city—be it New York or Moscow, Islamabad or Mumbai, Tokyo or Tel Aviv, Paris or Prague—could kill hundreds of thousands of people. And no matter where it happens, there is no end to what the consequences might be—for our global safety, our security, our society, our economy, to our ultimate survival.

Some argue that the spread of these weapons cannot be stopped, cannot be checked—that we are destined to live in a world where more nations and more people possess the ultimate tools of destruction. Such fatalism is a deadly adversary, for if we believe that the spread of nuclear weapons is inevitable, then in some way we are admitting to ourselves that the use of nuclear weapons is inevitable.

Just as we stood for freedom in the 20th century, we must stand together for the right of people everywhere to live free from fear in the 21st century. And as nuclear power—as a nuclear power, as the only nuclear power to have used a nuclear weapon, the United States has a moral responsibility to act. We cannot succeed in this endeavor alone, but we can lead it, we can start it.

So today, I state clearly and with conviction America's commitment to seek the peace and security of a world without nuclear weapons. I'm not naive. This goal will not be reached quickly—perhaps not in my lifetime. It will take patience and persistence. But now we, too, must ignore the voices who tell us that the world cannot change. We have to insist, "Yes, we can."[2]

These were dramatic words announcing a bold vision. The challenges facing President Obama in following through on such a stark pronouncement were many. The president laid out the basic structure of a framework for moving forward with his vision—phased disarmament, improved nuclear nonproliferation measures, implementation of a comprehensive nuclear test ban. Yet what he did not raise in Prague, either through ignorance or wishful thinking, was the reality that the greatest obstacle facing the "zero nukes" vision comes not from Russia or the rest of the world but rather from the United States itself. The histories of post–World War II America and nuclear weapons are intertwined and inseparable. Nuclear weapons have become a fixture in that which defines the present-day United States, whether economically (via the massive multibillion-dollar-per-year research, development, manufacturing, maintenance, and storage infrastructure that has been established to handle the numerous requirements associated with these weapons), militarily (nuclear deterrence remains the cornerstone of American military strategy today, as it has been since 1945), or politically (having become addicted to the federal funding associated with maintaining Americas nuclear arsenal, and the perception of security possession of these weapons creates, few politicians dare support policies that would threaten either).

The United States, President Obama will come to discover, is a nation addicted to nuclear weapons and the power and prestige, both real and illusory, that these weapons bring. Breaking this addiction will prove extremely difficult. This is especially true given the lack of having any real nuclear disarmament policy in place since the dawn of the nuclear age. The failure of the United States to formulate or to implement effective nuclear disarmament policy has placed America and the world on very dangerous ground. The longer America and the world continue to possess nuclear weapons, the greater the likelihood of nuclear weapons being used. The only way to prevent such a dire outcome is through the abolition, and not the reduction or control, of all nuclear weapons.

President Obama, speaking before the crowd in Prague on that bright April morning, understood this. He was right in noting that in regard to the dream of nuclear abolition, the world should insist, "Yes, we can." But the reality is that being able to do something is no guarantee that it will actually be done. The president, the American people, and the world must know that in order for this dream to become reality, the motto must be changed from "Yes, we can," to "Yes, we must." This is the vision of a new Prague Spring. One can only hope that this dream will not be destroyed with American nuclear-fueled hubris playing the role of the Soviet tanks in crushing the life from what might be the world's last chance to free itself from the terror of nuclear war.

PROLOGUE

MISSILE CRISIS

On the morning of March 16, 1990, those Americans turning to the *Washington Post* for their news were in for a surprise. On page 23, underneath a dramatic headline proclaiming "Missile Crisis," noted political columnists Rowland Evans and Robert Novak reported on a March 10 confrontation between pistol-wielding Soviet officers and unarmed U.S. weapons inspectors outside a missile factory in the heart of the Soviet Union. "Soon after Soviet guards drew their pistols against unarmed U.S. technicians in a standoff at the Votkinsk missile plant last Sunday night," Evans and Novak wrote, "Ambassador Jack Matlock rushed to the Foreign Ministry near midnight in a crisis mood over relations with Moscow not felt since Mikhail Gorbachev took power."[1]

I was as surprised as any to read about this so-called missile crisis because on the morning of March 10, 1990, I was serving as part of the team of U.S. inspectors responsible for overseeing inspection operations in Votkinsk when the standoff occurred. Although Soviet troops were present, providing security for the sensitive shipment of intercontinental ballistic missiles (ICBMs) coming out of the Votkinsk Machine Building Plant, which served as the focal point of the standoff, their weapons (AK-74 automatic rifles, not pistols) were never unlimbered, and the inspectors were never threatened. Such was the difference between fact and fiction.

1

At the plant in question, the United States, operating in accordance with the provisions of the Intermediate-Range and Shorter-Range Nuclear Forces (INF) Treaty, had installed a portal monitoring verification facility where thirty inspectors maintained an around-the-clock vigil verifying Soviet treaty compliance. Under the terms of the INF treaty, the U.S. inspectors, myself included, were to monitor the shipment of materials out of the factory that approached the size of what was referred to as a "treaty limited item," or TLI. The item of greatest significance, and which defined the size of a TLI as far as Votkinsk was concerned, was the SS-20 intermediate-range ballistic missile. Capable of carrying three nuclear-tipped warheads, the SS-20—a missile that struck fear into the Western imagination in the early 1980s—was one of several missiles mandated by the INF treaty for elimination.

In addition to the SS-20, the Votkinsk factory also produced the SS-25, a road-mobile intercontinental ballistic missile that used a first stage similar in dimension to, but not interchangeable with, the first stage of the SS-20. The principal task of the U.S. inspectors was to verify that the SS-25 missiles being shipped from Votkinsk were in fact SS-25s and not prohibited SS-20s. We did this through a combination of visual inspections—we were prohibited from making physical contact with the missile or the container—and, with the help of a giant X-ray device known as Cargo-Scan, radiological imaging.

At first blush, the so-called missile crisis in Votkinsk had a very mundane genesis. On March 1, 1990, the U.S. inspection team received formal notification from their Soviet counterparts that one of the large, six-axle railcars used to transport SS-25 missiles would be exiting the Votkinsk Machine Building Plant. This was a normal treaty-associated activity that had been repeated more than a dozen times previously, all without incident. But this time there was a twist: we had recently certified the large CargoScan X-ray imaging system as fully operational and were intending to employ it for the first time in an official inspection capacity.

The INF treaty between the United States and the Soviet Union called for the use of this imaging system by inspectors within six months of the treaty entering force. The U.S. inspectors had been operating in Votkinsk since July 1988. However, installing the CargoScan system and bringing it up to full operational capability had dragged on for nearly twenty months. By February 1990 the entire system was in place and ready for operation. This, at least, was the position of our inspection team. From the Soviet point of view, CargoScan could not be deemed operational until additional questions about the capabilities and limitations of its radiological inspection system were better explained and documented. The Soviets were not convinced that the CargoScan system, as installed in Votkinsk, would neither harm the solid-fuel propellant used in its missiles nor give the U.S. inspectors design details about the SS-25 missile, the disclosure of which was not mandated by the INF treaty.

U.S. inspectors included military officers assigned to the On-Site Inspection Agency (OSIA), a Department of Defense organization specifically created for the purpose of implementing the INF treaty, and civilian employees of Hughes Technical Services Company, who were contracted to OSIA to install and operate the portal monitoring facility (including the CargoScan system). We were under considerable pressure from our overseers in Washington to get CargoScan up and running. The delays we faced were not the result of any lack of trying on our part. Nor were they the product of Soviet noncooperation. The reality was that the entire Votkinsk portal monitoring verification exercise, including CargoScan, had been an afterthought to the INF treaty, an add-on brought in after the majority of the treaty had been negotiated and agreed upon.

In October 1987, just two months before the INF treaty was signed by President Reagan and President Gorbachev, the Soviets notified the U.S. negotiators of a potential verification issue concerning the treaty as written: because there was an outward physical similarity between the first stages of the SS-25 and SS-20 missiles, some sort of inspection provision would need to be crafted in order to verify that the Soviets were only producing SS-25 missiles and not the soon-to-be prohibited SS-20s. The U.S. negotiators presented the concept of portal monitoring verification inspections to their Soviet counterparts, and the two sides hammered out generic language concerning the new portal inspection regime that was eventually included in the final treaty document. However, the complexity of portal monitoring inspections went far beyond the framework cobbled together in the body of the INF treaty, and both the United States and the Soviet Union agreed that the specifics of the inspection process, including all details surrounding the operational use of the CargoScan system, would be worked out in the form of a Memorandum of Agreement (MOA), which would be negotiated after the actual signing of the treaty document.

Given the legalities associated with the implementation of a complicated, groundbreaking arms control agreement such as the INF treaty, the United States and the Soviet Union agreed on the formation and operation of a body known as the Special Verification Commission, or SVC, which would oversee the resolution of any compliance issues and agree on measures to improve the treaty's effectiveness.

There should have been no problem with the implementation of inspection procedures agreed on in the MOA when the Soviets rolled out their missile on March 1, 1990. The reality was, however, that both the U.S. and the Soviet sides were aware that what had been negotiated in the MOA and what was actually in place at Votkinsk were not precisely in agreement with one another. Negotiators in the SVC made a decision in the fall of 1989 to have all technical problems involving portal monitoring implementation resolved on-site between the U.S. inspectors and the Soviet factory representatives. This decision meant that any unresolved discrepancies surrounding CargoScan would be put into diplomatic limbo. For some time the stage had been set for a decisive confrontation.

The heart of the Soviet refusal centered on what they considered a lack of documentation provided by the United States on the operation of the CargoScan system as well as documentation that had been provided showing that the system as installed was not in conformity with the procedures set forth in the MOA. As far as the Soviets were concerned, the way in which the CargoScan system was configured on March 1 allowed for the acquisition of technical information concerning the SS-25 missile that went beyond what was required by the INF treaty and as such constituted intelligence collection activities that would not be tolerated.

The Soviets were not the only ones who harbored distrust of their treaty opposites. Opponents of the INF treaty in the U.S. Senate, led by conservative Senator Jesse Helms (R–North Carolina), an influential member of the Senate Foreign Relations Committee, had been critical of the INF treaty from its inception. In January 1989, Senator Helms fired a parting shot at outgoing U.S. President Ronald Reagan, a fellow Republican who had embraced arms control in the final years of his presidency, decrying the fact that the Soviets had delayed the installation and operation of the CargoScan system so that the six-month period provided for by the INF treaty for bringing CargoScan into operation had passed with the X-ray system still not installed. "This prolonged Soviet failure to agree to allow US x-ray rights which under the provisions of the Treaty they are obliged to allow," Helms wrote, "constitutes the most serious Soviet violation of the INF Treaty so far," one which, in Helms's opinion, left the United States "totally unable to monitor effectively or verify whether the Soviets have continued to manufacture and deploy perhaps dozens of banned SS-20 missiles from the Votkinsk factory for the last eight months that the Treaty has been in force." Helms urged President Reagan, in his "final days" as president, to "advise the Senate about what your administration will do . . . to prevent the Soviets from continuing to exploit their potential to cheat at Votkinsk."[2]

The North Carolina Republican had tried his best to derail the INF treaty during the Senate ratification process and, having failed there, was looking to use the specter of Soviet cheating under INF as a vehicle to stop an even more ambitious disarmament effort being negotiated at that time between the United States and the Soviet Union. Helms used the lengthy process surrounding bringing CargoScan into operational capability as ammunition in his argument that the Soviets were cheating when it came to fulfilling their obligations under the INF treaty in Votkinsk.

On January 12, 1990, Senator Helms again wrote a letter, this time to newly elected President George H. W. Bush, designed to serve as a spoiler for disarmament. Helms cited as his chief complaint the failure on the part of the U.S. inspection team to get the CargoScan system up and running. Senator Helms reiterated that he had "long been concerned about the urgent need to install the US CargoScan x-ray system in the Soviet Union for monitoring the INF Treaty." Making reference to the ongoing Strategic Arms Reduction Treaty, or START, negotiations, which were well under way and viewed by the Bush administration as representing the cornerstone of its disarmament policy, Helms noted that "other similar systems [to CargoScan] will surely be required for monitoring a possible START Treaty." "I have just been reliably informed that despite my urgent and repeated exhortations," Helms wrote, boring in on his main point of argument, "the CargoScan system will not reach its initial operating capability until as late as February 14, 1990. I am also told that the main reason for this extraordinary tardiness is an endless series of questions raised by the Soviets about the CargoScan systems—questions designed to delay its operation." Helms closed his letter with a not-so-veiled threat: "I respectfully request that you expedite the operational capability of the INF Cargo-Scan.... These Soviet-inspired delays raise questions about Soviet intentions that could become issues in any START ratification process."[3]

Under political pressure to get CargoScan up and running, the U.S. inspection team brushed aside the Soviet concerns about the lack of documentation for CargoScan and the potential for the system to collect information that went beyond what was permitted by the INF treaty. Instead, the Americans sought to bring CargoScan into operational status by cobbling together a system of "local understanding" and interim procedures that avoided actual resolution of the problems vexing the Soviets. The U.S. inspectors pressed their Soviet counterparts in Votkinsk to "arrive at a mutually satisfactory timetable to come to an understanding on local procedures, implement them on an interim basis, and commence full operations," noting that it was the U.S. intention "that the first missile to exit the plant in February [1990] be subject to imaging" by CargoScan.[4] This was the official position of the U.S. government.

The Soviet side was not satisfied with the U.S. approach, and in a meeting held with U.S. inspectors on January 31, 1990, let it be known that, contrary to the U.S. position, the Soviets did not consider the CargoScan system to be operational, and that the Soviets would refuse to allow any SS-25 missile departing the Votkinsk factory to be so imaged until all of their concerns had been satisfied. In an effort to avoid any unnecessary confrontation over CargoScan, the Soviet side agreed, on February 5, to interim procedures drafted by U.S. inspectors regarding the operation of CargoScan, enabling the system to become fully operational on February 9. This agreement considered CargoScan as operational on that date and stated that the first railcar declared to contain a missile exiting the Votkinsk factory on or after that date would be imaged. The agreement noted that "both sides will continue seeking resolution through higher channels" about differences that existed regarding the outstanding technical issues and concluded that the agreed-on interim procedures would be in force until resolution of these issues was received through higher channels.[5]

Almost immediately after both sides in Votkinsk had agreed to these interim procedures, U.S. inspectors were informed, on February 6, that Washington objected to the February 9 start date and that all missiles exiting the Votkinsk factory from February 6 on would be subject to inspection, inclusive of CargoScan imaging. Stunned by the American about-face, on February 7 the Soviets declared CargoScan to be in violation of the MOA and demanded that the core concerns previously detailed be addressed prior to any operational use of CargoScan by the United States. The Soviets requested that the United States withdraw its unilateral declaration that CargoScan was in fact operational so that there would not be any "conflicting situation" when the Soviets decided to begin shipping missiles.[6] The stage was set for a showdown.

On February 28, 1990, the Soviets made one last effort to resolve the impasse. The senior Soviet factory representative met with U.S. inspectors and provided a list of on-site fixes that, from the Soviet point of view, would make CargoScan operational. But the U.S. side had boxed itself into a trap. Having declared CargoScan operational, the United States could not agree to any fixes. The unwillingness of the U.S. inspectors to budge frustrated their Soviet counterparts. In a state of exasperation, the senior Soviet representative cut off the discussions, noting that the two sides could not come to an agreement.[7]

At 2:20 PM on March 1, 1990, the Soviets provided U.S. inspectors with written notification of their intent to ship a missile on a railcar from the Votkinsk factory. Thirty minutes later the railcar exited the factory gates. By 3:00 PM the visual inspection of the missile canister was complete, and inspectors requested that the missile be imaged by CargoScan. The Soviets refused. At 4:00 PM U.S. inspectors held a meeting with the Soviets regarding the standoff. The results were predictable. Void of any instructions from U.S. and Soviet hierarchies, everyone simply repeated the same oft-spoken positions and then adjourned, awaiting orders. The Soviets asked for a second meeting at 6:00 PM, when they informed U.S. inspectors that if there were no resolution of the situation by 7:00 PM, then they would have no choice but to ship the missile. At 7:00 PM sharp, the Soviets dispatched a locomotive from the factory to be hooked up with the railcar.

As the duty officer in charge at the time, I refused to raise the traffic signal across the rail tracks, thus blocking the locomotive in place while other inspectors consulted with Washington. The Soviets waited for thirty minutes and then informed us that they would remove the railcar from the factory no matter what. Minutes before the Soviets would have had to force the traffic gate, we received instructions from OSIA to tell the Soviets that the White House was requesting a delay of forty-eight hours so that the issue might be worked out. The Soviets backed down. The forty-eight-hour delay passed, and there was no movement on either side. The U.S. ambassador to the Soviet Union, Jack Matlock, delivered a strongly worded démarche to the Soviet Ministry of Foreign Affairs, criticizing the Soviet actions in Votkinsk. The seriousness of the situation was noted in both Moscow and Washington, and a decision was made for a high-level delegation to be sent to Votkinsk to find a solution to the crisis. The date of the delegation's first meeting was set for March 11, 1990.

On March 9 at 6:55 PM, the Soviets shocked the U.S. inspection team by announcing that they intended to renew shipments of SS-25 missiles "immediately." By this time, I had rotated back to Washington and was monitoring the situation from my desk at OSIA headquarters. The U.S. inspectors contacted Washington, setting off frantic efforts to contact senior Soviet officials in order to prevent the Votkinsk factory from shipping the missiles. It was a Friday night, however, and therefore difficult to establish adequate communication. Also, whenever a Soviet official was contacted, he simply repeated the official line: CargoScan did not conform to the MOA, and therefore the Soviets were well within their treaty rights to ship missiles and not subject them to CargoScan imaging. The Soviets thus started shipping their missiles out of Votkinsk. The original missile, held in place since it attempted to exit the factory on March 1, was visually inspected by U.S. inspectors before departing the site under protest at 2:23 AM on March 10. Two additional missiles were shipped later that day, again under protest.

The U.S. delegation of experts soon arrived in Moscow and traveled to Votkinsk on March 12, where for the next four days the matter of the core issues regarding CargoScan compliance with the MOA was discussed. The U.S. delegation agreed to adopt all of the proposals for "fixing" the CargoScan system that had been proposed by the Soviet side. It was as close as the U.S. side would come to admitting that the Soviets were right.[8] On March 21, 1990, after all of the fixes were in place and thoroughly tested, the first operational use of CargoScan was carried out when a railcar carrying an SS-25 missile was imaged under the new agreed-on procedures. There were no issues noted, and CargoScan was finally declared by both sides to be operational. The Votkinsk missile crisis was over.

The success of the INF treaty, especially its unprecedented on-site inspection provisions, had withstood the test of time, and the verification procedures of the INF treaty were being absorbed into other, more far-reaching disarmament agreements, such as the Strategic Arms Reduction Treaty, or START. Far from signaling a failure of arms control, the Votkinsk missile crisis of March 1990 served as a demonstration of just how strong bilateral disarmament agreements could be when both sides were committed to achieving a common goal. For all of the differences of opinion that emerged throughout the period of CargoScan installation through to initial operation, compounded by the constant efforts by arms control opponents such as Senator Jesse Helms to undermine the treaty, neither the Soviet nor the U.S. side lost sight of the bigger picture, and in the end the intent of the INF treaty was carried out to the satisfaction of both parties.

This warming of relations between the United States and the Soviet Union threatened those inside the American body politic who had built their political careers off of the fear generated by the Cold War conflict between the United States and the "Evil Empire." Defense budgets had reached historic highs as a result of the Cold War, and those elected officials whose domestic political power bases were derived from the economic impact created by such high levels of spending were loath to have the calculus of fear driving their largesse suddenly done away with.

The American approach toward arms control had, by 1990, been driven almost exclusively by the engine of Soviet-American animosity. Since the dawn of the nuclear age in 1945, the United States and the Soviet Union had been engaged in an arms race built around the development of nuclear weapons and the means to deliver them to their designated targets. In Washington, policies of containment of the Soviet Union gave way to those espousing various forms of nuclear weapons–based deterrence bearing such titles as "assured destruction," "mutually assured destruction," "countervailing," and, more ominously, "prevailing." The massive effort required to sustain this arms race over the course of several decades had assumed its own critical mass, both economically and politically. "Arms control" was useful only insofar as it served to retard Soviet capabilities while preserving or enhancing those of the United States. Genuine arms control, of the sort promulgated under the INF treaty and which included on-site inspection-based verification regimes, was anathema to those Cold Warriors who cut their teeth in a world where a nuclear Armageddon was not simply theory, but reality. The rearguard actions carried out by disgruntled Cold War advocates within the administration of President George H. W. Bush, backed by their equally reactionary supporters in Congress, were singularly focused on preventing détente. But their efforts were very much toward a losing cause. As long as the Soviet Union and the United States maintained their collective course toward peaceful coexistence, meaningful arms control and disarmament were realities that even the most black-hearted of the anti-Soviet crowd could not deny.

But there was trouble looming on the horizon. The wave of reforms that had swept the Soviet Union in the form of glasnost—the groundbreaking policy of openness and transparency that had been implemented by Mikhail Gorbachev since the mid-1980s—had severely tested the bonds holding that nation together. Already there were cracks appearing in the once-impenetrable armor of the collective of Republics that constituted the Union. The previously daunting Warsaw Pact was crumbling. The Berlin Wall had fallen, and German reunification had become a reality.

While the United States maintained its focus firmly on the Soviet target, around the world developments were occurring that would shape the future of arms control and disarmament, and with it global security. In Pretoria, South Africa, the government of President P. W. Botha was engaged in a secret nuclear weapons program, inclusive of viable and deliverable devices, that had gone largely undetected by the rest of the world. In the spring of 1990, its nuclear weapons manufacturing team was preparing the seventh nuclear bomb for South Africa's arsenal. In Asia, North Korea—having signed the Nuclear Non-Proliferation Treaty (NPT) in 1985—had yet to enter into a safeguards inspection agreement with the International Atomic Energy Agency (IAEA). The country also was deeply involved in a cooperative arrangement with Iran involving the development of long-range ballistic missiles many feared could be armed with nuclear weapons.

Similar problems were emerging in South America, where regional rivals Argentina and Brazil were locked into competing nuclear programs, which were ostensibly for civilian energy use but contained military aspects related to the pursuit of viable nuclear weapons. Argentinean efforts to field a ballistic missile system, the Condor II, which was capable of delivering a nuclear warhead, were well under way at a secret military facility outside Cordoba. Brazil, in turn, began looking at expanding its nascent civilian satellite launch capability into one able to deliver a military payload. Brazil also wanted to expand the ballistic missile production capabilities of one industrial enterprise (Avibrás) while building another (Órbita Sistemas Aerospaciais) from scratch.

More ominous, in Iraq the government of Saddam Hussein was busy expanding its base of power in the aftermath of the end of the Iran-Iraq War. In secret factories throughout Iraq, scientists and engineers worked virtually nonstop on numerous programs dedicated to the manufacture of chemical and biological weapons and on long-range ballistic missiles to deliver them. Other scientists and physicists were hard at work on programs to manufacture a nuclear weapon, as well as to enrich uranium for such a weapon. Funded by more than $1 billion in U.S. financial assistance approved by the first Bush administration in the fall of 1989, Saddam Hussein flexed his regional muscle, threatening to "burn half of Israel" with Iraqi chemical weapons and bullying other regional nations, such as Kuwait.

The Votkinsk missile crisis marked the high-water mark for arms control for the United States. Unseen by the supporters and detractors of arms control alike, the United States had reached a critical juncture. America was treading on dangerous ground, its eyes fixed on a minefield of disarmament issues once solely defined by the Soviet threat, all the while blind to the numerous emerging disarmament issues that constituted a meaningful problem set of their own. The decisions that would be made by the United States in the coming months and years concerning arms control and disarmament would have a significant impact on the security of the United States and of the international community as a whole.

But decisions do not happen in a vacuum. Decisions are, by their very nature, solutions to problems that appear to manifest themselves in the moment but are in fact derived from events that have transpired over the course of a given time frame. The key to viable solutions rests not in the decisions from which they are derived but, more importantly, in the way in which the problem being solved has been defined. A solution to a problem that has been framed incorrectly or inaccurately is no solution at all. This is especially true when it comes to arms control and nuclear disarmament. There is no single school of disarmament or arms control theory in the United States from which solution sets are drawn. Rather, since the dawn of the nuclear age, there has been a wide range of personalities espousing philosophies that run the gamut from liberal to moderate, moderate to conservative, and even conservative to neoconservative.

People long relegated to the dustbin of history, such as John McCloy and J. Robert Oppenheimer—together with presidents dating back to Harry S. Truman, Dwight Eisenhower, John F. Kennedy, and Lyndon Johnson—have debated the same issues, under similar circumstances, as have more modern figures, such as Robert McNamara, Edward Teller, Richard Nixon, Gerald Ford, and Jimmy Carter. The debate over missile defense that rages today is very much the same debate, only with different players, that transpired in the 1960s, 1970s, and 1980s. The same holds true when discussing the fundamental essence of nuclear deterrence and the viability of nuclear weapons in shaping a national defense strategy. The advocates for nuclear disarmament today make identical arguments, as did the advocates for nuclear disarmament in 1945, such as John McCloy and many of the scientists involved in the building of the American atomic bomb, namely that nuclear weapons are too horrible to consider using and therefore should never be allowed to exist. In the same way, those who articulate in favor of nuclear deterrence and missile defense repeat the talking points of their predecessors, such as Leslie Groves and James Byrnes, who articulated that it is the very horror of the nuclear bomb that guarantees no nation would undertake any action that might prompt America to use this weapon in its defense. Nothing, in fact, is new when it comes to these issues. This ground has been covered again and again, always with the same result—the politics of fear trump factual reasoning.

Thus before one can appreciate the significance of the Votkinsk inspections and the INF treaty regime they were a part of, or the efforts of the United Nations in Iraq, Iran, and North Korea since then in terms of limiting the proliferation of nuclear weapons, one needs to go back to the beginning. One needs to retrace the history of America's relationship with the atomic bomb and the policies of arms control and disarmament that have been derived from this relationship. When this history and its nuances and insights are understood, one is equipped with the ability to recognize the true nature of the problem confronting the United States—and the world—when it comes to designing and implementing solutions that address the fundamental issues of arms control and disarmament. Understanding how the United States got to the critical policy junctures it faced during the nuclear era, and how and why it chose the policy paths it did, will go a long way in helping future policymakers choose effective arms control and disarmament policies that are to the benefit of both American national security and international peace and prosperity. In this subject, as in all others, the adage that those who forget the lessons of history are doomed to repeat the mistakes of the past applies. The biggest danger with the issue of nuclear disarmament and arms control is that if the mistakes of the past keep repeating themselves, there may be no future in which this history might be studied and appreciated. The failure of America's arms control policy has placed not only the people of the United States but indeed the entire world on very dangerous ground. One can only hope that the lessons of Votkinsk will be appreciated in time by those who are in a position to make a difference today.

CHAPTER 1

THE GENIE ESCAPES

Even by the heightened standards of a nation's capitol during wartime, the gathering of generals, admirals, and high government officials in the White House Cabinet Room on the afternoon of Monday, June 18, 1945, was impressive. Only one, however, could claim resident status—the newly sworn-in president of the United States, Harry S. Truman. A veteran of the First World War and a long-serving Democratic senator from the state of Missouri, Truman was an unlikely candidate for the job he now held. A compromise candidate for the office of vice president in 1944, Truman was no close confidant of President Roosevelt. Indeed, he had little insight into Roosevelt's thinking about postwar relations with the Soviet Union and no knowledge of the existence of a major program—the Manhattan Project—to produce an atomic bomb. In a series of meetings conducted shortly after being sworn in as president, Truman overcame this deficit, maintaining a pledge to adhere as closely as possible to the policy directions set forth by President Roosevelt. But some decisions would have to be taken by the new president, which is why he had convened the Cabinet Room meeting.

Joining Truman was General George Catlett Marshall, the distinguished sixty-four-year-old chief of staff of the U.S. Army. In addition to managing the problems associated with waging global war, General Marshall was also a member of a high-level committee (the Top Policy Group, formed in October 1941) overseeing the effort by the United States to construct an atomic bomb. Marshall had left most day-to-day decisions about the atomic bomb program in the hands of Major General Leslie Groves and had limited his own role to making sure Congress continued to underwrite the project financially and to a lesser extent policymaking about the use of an atomic weapon.

As recently as May 31, 1945, Marshall had told a gathering of atomic bomb scientists, administrators, and policymakers that he felt the United States would be in a stronger position in any postwar environment if it avoided using an atomic bomb against the Japanese. He also recommended that the United States invite the Soviet Union to attend tests of the atomic bomb. The majority attending that meeting ruled against Marshall, including soon-to-be secretary of state James Byrnes, who feared the United States would lose its lead over the Soviets in nuclear weapons if the Russians became a de facto partner through such cooperation.[1] In any event, Marshall viewed any decision to use or not use an atomic bomb, given the horrific ramifications, to be a purely political question, outside the purview of the military.[2]

Joining Marshall were two senior naval officers, Fleet Admiral Ernest J. King—the commander of the U.S. Fleet and chief of naval operations (the only person ever to hold such a joint command)—and Admiral William Leahy, the seventy-year-old chief of staff to the commander in chief, U.S. Army and Navy. Admiral King was an abrasive, hard-drinking man who openly disdained any use of American resources for purposes other than the total destruction of the Japanese. Unlike King, Admiral Leahy was a proponent of avoiding a bloodbath fighting the Japanese and was sympathetic toward the idea of reaching a negotiated surrender brought on by the combined pressure of an economic blockade of the Japanese islands and conventional aerial bombardment. Leahy was against any use of the atomic bomb against civilian targets, a concept he viewed as "barbaric."[3]

The Army Air Force was represented by Lieutenant General Ira C. Eaker. General Eaker had almost single-handedly made strategic bombing an accepted practice when, as the commander of the Eighth Air Force in Europe, he convinced British Prime Minister Winston Churchill to continue the controversial strategy, noting that "round the clock bombing" would "soften the Hun for land invasion and the kill."[4] Ira Eaker was standing in for the flamboyant chief of staff of the U.S. Army Air Force, General Henry Harley "Hap" Arnold. Sidelined by health issues, General Arnold was an unabashed proponent of strategic bombing and had, through sheer force of will, positioned the Army Air Force to carry out massive aerial bombardment campaigns against both Germany and Japan. Like Arnold, General Eaker carried the secret that it was the Twentieth Air Force, flying the B-29 "Superfortress" bomber, which would deliver the atomic bomb to a Japanese target should the president decide on its use.

Rounding out the meeting's attendees was a trio of civilians. At seventy-eight years old, Secretary of War Henry L. Stimson was by far the senior man present. Like General Marshall, Stimson was a member of the Top Policy Group overseeing the atomic bomb project. Stimson was the first official to brief President Truman about the existence of the atomic bomb, on April 25, 1945. At that meeting Stimson warned Truman that "with reference to this weapon, the question of sharing it with other nations and, if so shared, upon what terms, becomes a primary question of our foreign relations. Also our leadership in the war and in the development of this weapon has placed a certain moral responsibility upon us which we cannot shirk without very serious responsibility for any disaster to civilization which it would further."[5] From that meeting, Secretary Stimson, at the request of Truman, formed the Interim Committee, the purpose of which was to advise the president on the utility of using the atomic bomb. The Interim Committee's report, delivered on June 1, 1945, strongly advocated for the use of the atomic bomb against the Japanese. Unlike General Marshall, who also attended the Interim Committee's meetings, Stimson supported this decision.

Navy Secretary James Forrestal was also a member of the Interim Committee. Unlike Stimson, however, Forrestal believed that the United States should exhaust all alternatives to dropping the atomic bomb in order to get Japan to surrender. Forrestal's views were shaped more by his strong anticommunist position than they were out of any moral qualms about using the atomic bomb. He firmly believed that if a face-saving mechanism could be found to entice Japan into surrender, the geopolitical situation in the Pacific could be stabilized before the Soviet Union could shift its resources away from Europe.[6]

Accompanying Stimson and Forrestal was the junior civilian present, Assistant Secretary of War John J. McCloy. McCloy was a complex individual. A veteran of the First World War, McCloy served as a legal counsel for the German chemical company I. G. Farben. His links to Germany led him to be somewhat sympathetic to the rise of Adolf Hitler, whom McCloy was photographed sitting with at the 1936 Olympics in Berlin. However, his status as a lawyer and manager led to his appointment in 1941 as the assistant secretary of war.

For the bulk of the meeting, President Truman and his military chiefs wrestled with the decision to invade Japan. The battle for Okinawa was still raging, and U.S. forces there were taking upward of 35 percent losses. If this statistic held true for the initial invasion of Japan, an assault on the southern island of Kyushu, then the United States could expect to lose some 268,000 of the 766,000 troops earmarked for that operation. These statistics resonated with the president, who approved the invasion of Japan with a heavy heart.

McCloy had remained silent during the deliberations about invading Japan. Truman, who knew McCloy through his Senate work on wartime economic waste, turned to the quiet counselor and asked him to provide his opinion on these matters, especially if McCloy saw an alternative to invading Japan. McCloy responded by noting that the people in the meeting "should have our heads examined" if they didn't explore an alternative other than yet another island assault to ending the war with Japan.[7]

Truman asked McCloy to explain himself, and McCloy did so, emphasizing a diplomatic solution over the classic military endgame of "unconditional surrender." "Some communication to the Japanese government which would spell out the terms that we would settle for," McCloy told the president, "there would be a surrender. I wouldn't use again the term 'unconditional surrender,' but it would be a surrender that would mean that we would get all the important things that we were fighting for. . . . If we could accomplish our objectives without further bloodshed, there was no reason why we shouldn't attempt to do it."[8]

McCloy implored the president to find a way to remind the Japanese of America's overwhelming superiority in arms. He also suggested that the United States should show some flexibility when it came to allowing the Japanese to retain their traditional form of government, including the institution of the emperor. Then John McCloy said something that stunned everyone in the room: why not tell the Japanese that America had the atomic bomb? If Japan would not capitulate in the face of overwhelming military superiority and a diplomatic concession on the issue of the emperor, then surely they would surrender knowing the United States had the means and the will to destroy their cities with this new, horrible weapon.

McCloy's comments prompted President Truman to have the assistant secretary of war take his diplomatic concepts to the State Department for consideration by the secretary of state designate, James Byrnes. McCloy's intent was on how to avoid invading, as well as dropping the atom bomb on, Japan. But Byrnes had other concerns beyond Japan. In May 1945, while he awaited his formal appointment as secretary of state, Byrnes met with one of the Manhattan Project physicists, the Hungarian-born Leo Szilard. According to Szilard, Byrnes was concerned about the role of the Soviet Union in the postwar era. The Soviets' massive armies had already steamrolled into Eastern Europe, and America was faced with the difficult task of figuring out how to get them out of these nations after Hitler was defeated. Byrnes told Szilard "that Russia might be more manageable if impressed by American military might, and that a demonstration of the bomb might impress Russia."[9] Focused more on containing the Soviet Union than defeating Japan, Byrnes rejected McCloy's proposals about how best to proceed concerning the atomic bomb. Germany had surrendered, and Japan was on the verge of a similar capitulation. America's looming problem was Russia, and Byrnes wanted the atomic bomb up his sleeve when advising the president on that matter.

James Byrnes was appointed secretary of state on July 3, 1945. His first major task was to prepare President Truman for the upcoming Potsdam summit. Japan was not the first issue on his mind; Russia was. The basic decision as to whether an atomic bomb was to be dropped on Japan had already been made by early July 1945, prior to Byrnes being sworn in as secretary of state. McCloy had not succeeded in his efforts to dissuade the president from this course of action. An Interim Committee meeting held on July 6, 1945, noted that the matter of discussing the existence of an atomic bomb at the upcoming "Big 3" meeting was particularly urgent, given the short timeline between that meeting and the actual use of the weapon. According to the mindset of the Americans, the atomic bomb played a critical role in shaping the postwar world that was being planned in Potsdam.[10]

An undercurrent affecting the mood of the entire nation in the summer of 1945, unnoticed by many modern observers, was national exhaustion. Congressional pressure exerted in the aftermath of Germany's surrender in May 1945 resulted in not only 450,000 troops being demobilized in the European theater even while war raged in the Pacific but also an additional 30,000 being demobilized in the Pacific. America was having trouble in staying the course against Japan, let alone positioning itself to contain and control the Soviet Union in a postwar world. Only the secret of the atomic bomb changed the calculus of global power diplomacy.

McCloy and those assembled in the White House on June 18, 1945, were not the only ones in America concerned about the atomic bomb project and its impact on a world at war. In Los Alamos, the birthplace of the atomic bomb, many of the Manhattan Project scientists were likewise growing increasingly alarmed over the terrible weapon they were preparing to unleash on an unsuspecting people. As early as March 1944 these scientists were coming together in informal social gatherings held in their secret base of operations, where the issue of how best to use this new and terrible technology was discussed. One such meeting involved the Manhattan Project's military chief, General Groves. After a dinner with the head of the British mission to Los Alamos, James Chadwick, and Joseph Rotblat, a junior British physicist (and future founder of the Pugwash Conferences on disarmament, work that won him the Nobel Peace Prize in 1995), Groves offered his views on postwar Europe. As Rotblat recalled, Groves informed the two Brits that "the whole purpose of the project was to subdue the Russians."[11]

Rotblat wasn't the only scientist involved with the Manhattan Project who was concerned about the reality of an atomic bomb. At the University of Chicago, where Enrico Fermi first sustained a fission reaction, the "Chicago Scientists" formed several committees to study the implications of an atomic bomb. One of these, the Committee on Social and Political Implications, headed by James Franck, a German Jew distrustful of government control over science, published a report in June 1945 known as the "Franck Report," which detailed the consequences of embarking on policies that would lead to a nuclear arms race. The Franck Report cautioned against viewing the atomic bomb as a possible means of leverage against the Soviet Union, emphasizing that the United States could not "hope to avoid a nuclear armament race, either by keeping secret from the competing nations the basic scientific facts of nuclear power, or by cornering the raw materials required for such a race.... If no efficient international agreement is achieved, the race of nuclear armaments will be on in earnest not later than the morning after our first demonstration of the existence of nuclear weapons."[12]

Unfortunately for the Chicago Scientists, the die was already cast. At 5:45 AM on July 16, 1945, in a remote desert site near Alamogordo, New Mexico, the world's first atomic explosion occurred. "Trinity," as the test of the plutonium-core implosion device was known, proved the viability of the atomic bomb concept and in doing so forever changed the world. President Truman was already in Potsdam at the time of the Trinity test, awaiting the summit with Joseph Stalin and the British (Winston Churchill was initially present at Potsdam, but given the victory of Clement Atlee in the July British parliamentary elections, was replaced by the latter on July 27, 1945). The Potsdam conference was primarily designed to address the issue of postwar Europe, in particular how best to deal with a defeated Germany and how best to guide the recovery of Europe as a whole. On July 17, during their initial meeting, Stalin and Truman set forth their respective positions. Truman was not happy with the Soviet leader's hard-line stance on Poland and other Eastern European countries, but privately gloated about what he termed his own "dynamite" secret—the atomic bomb (Truman had been notified about Trinity on July 16).[13] Truman initially embraced the Russian decision to enter the war against Japan by August 15, but by the conference's end the president was hoping that the use of the atomic bomb against Japan might compel the Japanese to surrender before the Russians could initiate a land grab in Asia that rivaled the one under way in Europe.

On July 24, Truman mentioned to Stalin, in a very casual manner, that the United States "had a new weapon of unusual destructive force." According to Truman, "The Russian Premier showed no special interest. All he said was he was glad to hear it and hoped we would make 'good use of it against the Japanese.'"[14] To Truman and those who observed this exchange from the United States and Great Britain, it seemed that Stalin did not comprehend the enormity of what Truman had told him. Nothing could have been further from the truth. Regardless of the desires of the United States and Great Britain to keep the secret of the atomic bomb from Stalin and the Russians during the Second World War, the fact is that the Soviets were all too aware of what was transpiring inside the secret weapons plants in the United States and Britain. As early as 1942, the Soviet intelligence system had become aware of the existence of a nuclear weapons program. Armed with this intelligence, Louvrentiy Beria, Stalin's ruthless head of intelligence and security, was able to convince Stalin that Russia needed to embark on its own path toward acquiring the atomic bomb. In September 1942, Stalin concurred, and a handpicked team of Soviet physicists, led by Igor Kurchatov, set about constructing the Russian equivalent of Los Alamos at an abandoned monastery outside the city of Sarov, which would become known only by its postal code, Arzamas-16.[15]

Immediately upon his return to his quarters following his conversation with Truman, Stalin summoned Foreign Minister Vyacheslav Molotov and Marshal Georgy Zhukov and informed them of what Truman had said. Far from misunderstanding Truman, Stalin spoke of the atomic bomb and sent instructions to Kurchatov to "speed things up." Because of the work of Soviet intelligence, Stalin knew that the United States only had one or two atomic bombs in its possession. But even this limited arsenal was reason for the Soviet leader to be concerned. On July 25, the day after his conversation with Stalin, President Truman signed off on the final decision to drop the atomic bomb on Japan. On August 6, 1945, the B-29 "Superfortress" nicknamed the *Enola Gay* delivered its deadly cargo over the Japanese city of Hiroshima, immediately killing tens of thousands of Japanese, mostly civilians, and ushering in the age of atomic annihilation.

Stalin, fearful that the United States would seek to use its atomic monopoly to limit Soviet options in postwar Asia, immediately advanced the date of the Soviet declaration of war again Japan to August 8. The U.S. decision to bomb Japan a second time, also on August 8, resulting in the obliteration of the city of Nagasaki and tens of thousands of its citizens, further reinforced the Soviet paranoia that, as Marshall Zhukov noted, "the US Government intended to use the atomic weapon for the purpose of achieving its Imperialist goals from a position of strength in 'the cold war.'"[16]

In response, on August 20, 1945, Stalin ordered Lavrenti Beria to head up a Special Committee on the Atomic Bomb in order to build a Russian counter to the American bomb. Stalin's concerns about American abuse of the atomic bomb weren't born purely from paranoia. By August 30, 1945, a scant twenty-two days after the Japanese city of Hiroshima was subjected to nuclear holocaust, and ten days after Stalin ordered the acceleration of the Soviet bomb project, General Leslie Groves was presented with a document that listed Soviet cities and industrial facilities, along with a calculation as to how many atomic bombs would be required to destroy each targeted area (Moscow and Leningrad were each assigned six atomic bombs).[17] The atomic bomb created the illusion of "war made easy," even as some of the architects of the nuclear assault on Japan were getting a firsthand look at what destruction they had wrought.

Those who designed the atomic bomb made an effort to limit the damage brought on by their creation. J. Robert Oppenheimer, the director of Los Alamos, led the charge, arguing in a letter to Secretary of War Stimson that continued pursuit of the atomic bomb was folly, and that every effort should be made to capitalize on the horror of the new atomic weapon to outlaw war. Continued development of nuclear weapons, Oppenheimer argued, would only set off an arms race from which no side could emerge the victor. Oppenheimer's point of view was opposed by Secretary of State Byrnes, who cautioned that "in the present critical international situation" there was no choice but to move forward with the development of nuclear weapons.[18] Since both Germany and Japan had, by the time of this exchange (August 17, 1945), surrendered, Byrnes could only have been referring to Russia in the context of a situation worthy of nuclear weapons.

Secretary Stimson himself was having second thoughts about the wisdom of America having used the atomic bomb. Alarmed by the casualties inflicted on the Japanese, Stimson summoned his assistant, John McCloy, and instructed him to intervene with Byrnes for the purpose of forming a covenant between the United States, Great Britain, and the Soviet Union to foreswear nuclear weapons in the future, end all nuclear weapon development, and share the secret of the atom with the world for peaceful purposes. Byrnes disagreed with Stimson and told McCloy that "the Russians were only sensitive to power and all the world, including the Russians, were cognizant of the power of this bomb, and with it in his hip pocket he felt he was in a far better position to come back with tangible accomplishments even if he did not threaten anyone expressly with it." Byrnes attended a critical ministers' meeting in London on the future of postwar Europe. There, Byrnes followed through on his promise to use the atomic bomb as his "hip pocket" weapon to pressure the Soviets into backing down on their demands in Eastern Europe. Molotov, the Soviet foreign minister, was unmoved, at one point proclaiming to Byrnes that the Russians, too, had an atomic bomb. Though this was not actually the case, Byrnes chose to interpret Molotov's statement as future intent versus a pressing, ongoing reality.[19]

Secretary of State Byrnes had some strong allies of his own when it came to the issue of the atomic bomb and the Soviet Union—the U.S. Congress. Many senators had grown frustrated at what they viewed as President Truman's superficial treatment of Congress when it came to the issue of negotiating international treaties and agreements. Congress had taken a backseat to Roosevelt during the war, a courtesy that was extended to Truman, at least until the surrender of Japan in August 1945. The war over, Congress was in no mood to leave the governance in time of peace to the chief executive. Sharing the atomic bomb with Russia was unthinkable in the minds of many in Congress. Congressional views were heavily influenced by public opinion. In polls taken in August 1945, following the dropping of the atomic bomb on Japan, 85 percent of the U.S. public wanted America to retain its nuclear monopoly for as long as possible.[20]

Congress was also concerned about the question of domestic control of America's atomic program. A freshman senator from Connecticut, Brien McMahon, had submitted a proposal for the creation of a federal board to oversee America's nuclear program. The War Department opposed the McMahon proposal because it would give primacy of control to civilian, versus military, leadership. McMahon worked with Congress to craft legislation that proposed the creation of an Atomic Energy Commission dominated by the military, which would oversee all aspects of America's nuclear program. President Truman was also cognizant of the need for a rapid decision on how best to proceed with the issue of America's nuclear capability. Managed largely by the military in time of war, the Manhattan Project lacked a peacetime framework of law and legislation to govern its operations.[21]

On October 3, 1945, President Truman addressed Congress on the issue of the atomic bomb and America's nuclear capability. The president proposed legislation that would define U.S. nuclear policy and "give jurisdiction for these purposes to an atomic energy commission with members appointed by the President with the advice and consent of the Senate." The president voiced his opinion that there was a need for international agreements for "renunciation of the use and development of the atomic bomb, and directing and encouraging the use of atomic energy and all future scientific information toward peaceful and humanitarian ends." Respecting congressional sensitivities about sharing the secret of the atomic bomb, Truman proposed international cooperation not on weapons issues but rather on scientific and technical matters.[22] Congress acted on the president's advice and on October 22, 1945, passed legislation that created the Senate Special Committee on Atomic Energy. In keeping with Senate tradition, Senator Brien McMahon, the sponsor of the legislation, served as the chair of the new committee. The feeling in the Senate was that it was now time for the Congress of the United States to take a leading role in shaping American nuclear policy. Truman had suggested as much in his October 3 speech.

The difficulties faced by Truman in crafting an effective international policy approach to nuclear matters were many. Secretary of State Byrnes, freshly returned from his failed London summit, had no faith in the potential of diplomacy as a tool that could break through what he viewed as Russian intransigence. Byrnes argued against direct one-on-one discussions with the Soviets about the atomic bomb and nuclear policy. Looking for a multilateral solution to the atomic question, Truman, in preparation for a summit meeting with British Prime Minister Clement Atlee and Canadian Prime Minister McKenzie King, had Byrnes approach Vannevar Bush, the director of the Office of Scientific Research and Development, to draft a plan for achieving international control of nuclear material and capability, inclusive of the atomic bomb, via the United Nations.

Bush, who had supported Truman's decision to use the atomic bomb against Japan, recognized the new danger of an arms race with the Soviets and felt that although giving the Soviets the secret of the bomb directly was not wise, any effort to deny them access to the science involved would be futile in the face of Soviet espionage. Bush drafted a three-phased approach toward achieving international control, where all nations would open up their research facilities to foreign scientists. If this worked, then a free exchange of information on the use of atomic energy would be facilitated, inclusive of an inspection regime that would safeguard against any diversion of fissile material for use in manufacturing atomic bombs. The final stage would be an agreement among all nations only to use nuclear energy for peaceful purposes.[23] When Atlee and King arrived in the United States, Truman briefed them on the Bush plan, and the three issued a joint communiqué, the Washington Joint Declaration, on November 14, 1945, which endorsed this three-phased approach and called for the creation of a new UN commission to devise "effective safeguards by way of inspection and other means to protect complying states against the hazards of violations and evasions."[24]

In December 1945, Secretary of State Byrnes convened a meeting in Moscow between the United States, Great Britain, and Russia where the Washington Joint Declaration was presented to the Russians. To the surprise of Byrnes, Soviet Foreign Minister Molotov approved of the plan, with one exception: rather than go through the United Nations General Assembly, where the United States held sway, the Russians insisted that a United Nations Atomic Energy Commission be created that would report to the Security Council of the United Nations, where the Russian veto would serve to protect Russian interests. On December 27, 1945, Byrnes and Molotov agreed on a draft resolution for the creation of a UN commission to consider the atomic problem. On January 24, 1946, the General Assembly of the United Nations approved this resolution as its first official resolution.

Secretary of State Byrnes returned from Moscow emboldened by the prospect of a viable international agreement to control nuclear material. Byrnes possessed a disdainful attitude toward Soviet industrial capabilities and estimated that America could retain its atomic monopoly for up to twenty years. But even as Byrnes sat down with Molotov in Moscow, the Soviets were exploiting uranium deposits in then-Czechoslovakia and exploring new sources of uranium ore in territory recently captured from the Japanese in Asia. Near the Russian city of Kyshtym, plans were being implemented for the building of a giant plutonium processing plant, known as Chelyabinsk-40. Far from rolling over and submitting to the new American atomic monopoly, the Soviets were moving forward aggressively to achieve their own nuclear capability. The world was dangerously close to an all-out arms race of the sort feared by all involved in the creation of the atomic bomb.[25]

In the halls of Congress a political battle raged over the issue of the control of America's atomic energy programs. Senator McMahon's Special Committee on Atomic Energy held numerous meetings and hearings where the matter of civilian versus military control over America's atomic programs was discussed. Congress was hesitant to give too much control to the military, and the Senate approved legislation to that effect on June 1, 1946. The House approved it on July 20, and President Truman signed the new Atomic Energy Act of 1946 on August 1. The act called for the transfer of authority from the United States Army to the newly created United States Atomic Energy Commission (AEC). The Atomic Energy Act preserved the U.S. government's monopoly of atomic research and development while keeping America's atomic bomb arsenal under the control of civilian leadership. It also formalized a national nuclear weapons bureaucracy at a time when the United States was ostensibly leading the charge for the internationalization of nuclear activities and the banning of the atomic bomb.[26]

While Congress debated the future of American domestic nuclear policy, the Truman administration worked to put together a framework for international nuclear policy. Secretary of State Byrnes appointed his deputy, Dean Acheson, together with David Lilienthal, a senior official with the Manhattan Project, to form a panel of experts to craft a plan of action for international control of nuclear energy. Joining Acheson and Lilienthal were General Groves, Vannevar Bush, John McCloy, and J. Robert Oppenheimer, among others. The Acheson-Lilienthal panel, heavily influenced by Oppenheimer, rejected the three-phased approach that had been recommended by Bush. Inspections and police-like enforcement would not, in their opinion, work to bring the world together, especially the Soviets. Instead, the Acheson-Lilienthal panel proposed the creation of an International Atomic Energy Authority, which would control the entire stock of the world's fissile material and would release these materials as required to nations for the development of peaceful nuclear programs. The panel believed that the entire process involved in the manufacture of fissile material, from the mines onward, should be placed under international control. Perhaps most critically, the panel also recommended that the United States deal directly with the Soviet Union on the issue of atomic bombs, abandoning its monopoly by revealing all that it knew with regard to nuclear weapons in exchange for a mutual agreement against the development of additional atomic bombs. On March 16, 1946, the panel's findings, widely referred to as the Acheson-Lilienthal Report, were received by President Truman with general approval.[27]

Yet even as he accepted the recommendations of the Acheson-Lilienthal Report, President Truman set the groundwork for their ultimate rejection. Truman selected Bernard Baruch—a seventy-eight-year-old statesman who had served presidential administrations, Republican and Democrat alike, since the First World War—to represent the United States at the newly created United Nations Atomic Energy Commission. Baruch had served under James Byrnes during the Second World War when the latter headed the Economic Stabilization Office, and later the War Mobilization Board. Secretary of State Byrnes recommended Baruch to President Truman for the UN post, a decision based not on Baruch's credentials as a diplomat and international affairs specialist but rather on his role as a loyal Byrnes crony. Baruch's task was not to facilitate the success of the Acheson-Lilienthal Report but to ensure it never got off the ground.[28]

As Baruch prepared for his new task, the political environment in which he would be operating was being shaped by a growing American-Soviet animosity. In February 1946, the U.S. Department of the Treasury requested from the U.S. embassy in Moscow an assessment as to why the Soviets were opposed to the creation of a U.S.-sponsored World Bank and International Monetary Fund, designed to serve as the centerpiece of the U.S. plan for global postwar reconstruction. The Soviets instead created their own Council for Economic Aid (COMEON), which oversaw the economic reconstruction of those nations falling under Soviet control. The embassy's leading Soviet expert, George Kennan, who had been stationed in Moscow as a minister-counselor since 1944, responded with what is today known as "the long telegram."

Kennan put forward his thesis that the Soviet outlook on world affairs allowed for no chance for long-term peaceful coexistence between socialism and capitalism. The Soviets sought to advance the cause of socialism and viewed capitalist ideology as a threat to socialist ideals. It was this inherent conflict that made it impossible for the West to view the Soviet Union as a true partner in the postwar order. Rather, the Soviet Union was viewed as an opponent because it was Soviet policy not to cooperate but instead to exploit any weakness found in the Western approach toward international cooperation. Kennan's response was used by Truman and others to formulate a policy of "restraining and confining" Soviet power and influence.[29]

It wasn't just official policy that was affected by this reexamination of U.S.-Soviet relations but public opinion as well. On March 5, 1946, in Fulton, Missouri, former British prime minister Winston Churchill gave one of the defining speeches of his illustrious career, declaring that "from Stettin in the Baltic to Trieste in the Adriatic, an Iron Curtain has descended across the Continent. Behind that line lie all the capitals of the ancient states of Central and Eastern Europe. Warsaw, Berlin, Prague, Vienna,

Budapest, Belgrade, Bucharest and Sofia, all these famous cities and the populations around them lie in what I must call the Soviet sphere, and all are subject in one form or another, not only to Soviet influence but to a very high and, in many cases, increasing measure of control from Moscow."[30]

The specter of the Iron Curtain bore down heavily on the West. Efforts by the United States, led by Secretary of State Byrnes, to formalize a peace treaty in Europe ran afoul over the issue of Germany. The Russians were determined to recover from their war losses as quickly as possible and were intent on doing so at the expense of Germany. Stalin felt that Russia was well within its rights in dismantling German factories and industrial capability and shipping materials back to the war-torn Soviet Union. Stalin wanted a weakened Germany, and to accomplish this he wanted Germany not only disarmed but also economically eliminated as a nation capable of waging war.[31]

The United States was taking the opposite approach, seeking to rebuild Germany so that it could contribute to the overall European postwar economic recovery and thus reduce the economic drain on the United States. The Russians viewed the American policy with suspicion, believing the United States was positioning Germany to be part of a Western alliance poised against the Soviet Union. The United States felt that the Russians were making a power grab of their own. The inability to align the ambitions of Russia and the United States concerning a postwar Germany made disagreement, and the resulting misunderstanding of motivations, inevitable.

This was the underlying political context that surrounded the effort of the United States to pursue atomic disarmament and nuclear control under the supervision of a United Nations Atomic Energy Commission. The Acheson-Lilienthal Report had been drafted with the underlying assumption that there would be Soviet-American cooperation. Bernard Baruch, however, rewrote major aspects of the plan so that when he unveiled the American plan, it was quite different in almost every regard. A major change was Baruch's insistence that the United Nations should prohibit all members from using their veto powers to protect themselves from penalties brought on by any violation of the accord. In Baruch's opinion, a simple majority rule should decide the outcome of any decision as to whether or not penalties should be applied. This provision was designed to kill the deal because the Soviets would never surrender their veto power.[32]

The Soviet Union not only insisted upon retaining its United Nations veto but also argued that the abolition of atomic weapons should precede the establishment of any international authority; failure to do so, they thought, would leave the United States with a clear atomic bomb monopoly. From the Soviet perspective, all the Baruch plan did was ensure American nuclear dominance by keeping all bombs under American control and by eliminating the Soviet Union's own nuclear capabilities. The Soviets believed that in and of itself, the American atomic bomb monopoly gave it leverage over the rest of the world and that any meaningful negotiation on a matter of this importance should be conducted free of the pressures brought on by such a monopoly. In short, the United States wanted a mechanism of international control in place before it was willing to disarm; the Russians required that the United States disarm before it would submit to any system of international controls.

This was the poison pill of the Baruch Plan, one that its framer, working closely with Secretary of State Byrnes, knew existed from the very start. Six months after he presented his plan, Baruch forced a vote in the Security Council. The vote failed on a count of ten in favor and two (Russia and Poland) against (Security Council votes required a unanimous decision to become binding). The demise of the Baruch Plan has been viewed by many as one of the critical events in the history of the Cold War. The United States, convinced of Soviet perfidy, believed it had no choice but to exploit its atomic bomb monopoly to construct systems of Western security that could withstand Soviet pressure. By August 1946, the U.S. atomic bomb production line was pumping out bombs at a rate of two per week. Never again would the United States allow itself to be a nation void of a meaningful nuclear strike capability.[33]

Concerned by America's monopoly of atomic bombs, Stalin ordered a massive expansion of the Soviet Army, from a low of around 3.5 million men in 1946 to more than 5 million by 1947. This expansion of conventional military capability was seen as the only way to offset the American nuclear monopoly. President Truman responded in kind, implementing what has become known as the Truman Doctrine, which was spelled out in a speech before Congress on March 12, 1947. It is, President Truman said, "the policy of the United States to support free peoples who are resisting attempted subjugation by armed minorities or by outside pressures."[34]

The Truman Doctrine was followed in short order by the Marshall Plan, named after newly appointed Secretary of State George C. Marshall, the former chief of the army staff during the Second World War (James Byrnes, the former secretary of state, had resigned in January 1947). The Marshall Plan called for the rebuilding and revitalization of the countries and economies of Western Europe as a means of repelling the influences of communism. The Marshall Plan, like the Truman Doctrine, was a derivative of the new policy of containment on the Soviet Union that grew from George Kennan's "long telegram" of 1946.[35]

The Soviet Union rejected the Marshall Plan, viewing it as a mechanism for permanently dividing Europe into eastern and western blocs. The economic bloc created in Western Europe through the Marshall Plan went on to become the foundation of a military and political alliance first promulgated in the Treaty of Brussels in March 1947, when the United Kingdom, Belgium, the Netherlands, Luxembourg, and France set the groundwork for the creation of a Western European Union Defense Organization.

The situation in Europe worsened when, in February 1948, Stalin ordered the Red Army into Czechoslovakia when the Czech government attempted to take advantage of the Marshall Plan and gain access to American economic aid. At the same time, in London, the United States, Great Britain, and France agreed to bypass Soviet intransigence on German reintegration into Europe and fused the three Western-occupied zones into a single unified federal government. This action resulted in the Soviets declaring a military blockade of Berlin on June 12, 1948, which led to the Berlin Airlift, when a resupply of Berlin was effected by the U.S. and British air forces. The success of the airlift resulted in the Soviets lifting the blockade on May 12, 1949. However, the specter of Soviet military activism in Europe led to the creation of the North Atlantic Treaty Organization (NATO) in April 1948.

The Truman Doctrine, the Marshall Plan, and the creation of NATO served as a troika of events that manifested in American policy of containing the Soviet Union. But the final pillar of containment was put in place on September 16, 1948, when President Truman signed into effect NSC-30, the United States Policy on Atomic Warfare. The vacuum of nuclear policy that had existed since the end of the Second World War was now filled. NSC-30 stated that the United States must be ready to "utilize promptly and effectively all appropriate means available, including atomic weapons, in the interest of national security and must therefore plan accordingly."[36]

NSC-30 made it clear that the decision to use nuclear weapons was the sole responsibility of the president of the United States. President Truman was confident that the United States would maintain a monopoly in the area of atomic bombs for some time to come. The newly formed Central Intelligence Agency, in an assessment published in July 1949, estimated that the Soviet Union might be able to produce an atomic bomb no earlier than 1953. In direct contrast, the U.S. nuclear stockpile itself was improving. In April 1948, a series of nuclear tests on Eniwetok Atoll in the Marshall Islands validated a new atomic bomb design that achieved yields two times the size of the bombs used against Hiroshima and Nagasaki but that used less fissile material. In one fell swoop, the new design allowed the United States to increase the number of atomic bombs in its arsenal by 63 percent and the total yield available by 75 percent.[37] When signed, NSC-30 had real, not symbolic, teeth.

By May 1949, the Soviets had produced enough plutonium to manufacture a single weapon similar to the American bomb that had been tested at Trinity and dropped on Nagasaki. Stalin, concerned about a possible American response to a successful Soviet atomic bomb test, was anxious about testing a bomb without having at least one more in reserve. So the first operational test of a Soviet atomic bomb was put off until August, when enough plutonium had been produced for a second device. On August 29, 1949, on the steppes of Kazakhstan, some sixty miles northwest of the city of Semipalatinsk, Igor Kurchatov's team of Soviet physicists, under the direction of Beria himself, detonated a plutonium implosion device, the exact copy of the U.S. plutonium bomb design known as Fat Man, courtesy of Soviet intelligence. This device, nicknamed Little Joe in honor of Stalin, ended the American atomic bomb monopoly.[38]

On September 23, 1949, President Truman informed Congress, the Joint Chiefs of Staff, and the American public that the Soviets had joined the nuclear club. The Atomic Energy Commission went into emergency session. A range of options was discussed, from increasing the production of fissile material to the manufacture of a "Super Bomb"—a hydrogen fusion weapon. Such a bomb had been theorized for some time by American nuclear weapons designers, especially Edward Teller, an originally Hungarian physicist who had been pursuing the issue of a thermonuclear weapon. On October 5, 1949, barely five weeks after the Soviets detonated their first atomic device, the AEC made a recommendation that President Truman be approached about pushing forward with the development of an American hydrogen bomb. Teller had conducted calculations that showed that a thermonuclear device with a yield eight hundred times that of the Hiroshima bomb was feasible. On October 6, 1949, President Truman was briefed on the possibility of a hydrogen bomb, and he ordered the AEC to build one. Just as the original designers of the atomic bomb had feared, the nuclear genie was out of the bottle, and the world was now faced with an arms race that would threaten the very existence of humankind.[39]

CHAPTER 2

RED SCARE MYTHS

In addition to approving legislation on the creation of the Atomic Energy Commission (AEC), President Harry Truman oversaw a radical transformation of the national security establishment when he signed the National Security Act of 1947. This act created the National Security Council, the Central Intelligence Agency, the Department of Defense (a consolidation of the War Department with the Navy Department), and the establishment of the Joint Chiefs of Staff (JCS). In short, President Truman made permanent many of the changes to the U.S. defense bureaucracy that had occurred during the Second World War. America was organized to operate on a full-time war footing, even in times of peace.

Bureaucratic readiness to wage war, however, did not translate into physical readiness. The Soviet Union had rebuilt its conventional ground forces after the Second World War so that it had overwhelming power assembled in or around Eastern Europe. Conversely, the United States had rapidly demobilized so that its armed forces were but a mere shell of what had existed at the end of the Second World War. The advent of the nuclear age, and the monopoly of the atomic bomb possessed by the United States, led to an almost singular reliance upon the strategic bombing capability of the United States, and its nuclear delivery capability, as a counter to the perceived Soviet threat. Unfortunately for the United States, by 1947 the health of the strategic bomber force, like the rest of the military, was less than satisfactory. But America was enmeshed in a period of economic frugality, and President Truman had drawn the line on massive defense spending as a means of controlling the budget.

One of the theories behind the 1947 National Security Act was that with consolidation would come cost cuts. However, the transformation from the Department of War to the new National Military Establishment (later renamed the Department of Defense) was not without its problems, foremost of which would be the competition among the services for access to a reduced military budget. One of the staunchest opponents of the consolidation of services under the National Security Act of 1947 was the secretary of the Navy, James Forrestal. And yet when the position of the first secretary of defense needed to be filled, it was to Forrestal that President Truman turned. Forrestal came into his position a staunch anticommunist, and the fluid international situation would only reinforce this prejudice. From the Soviet invasion of Czechoslovakia in February 1948, through the Berlin Airlift (which began in June 1948), Forrestal's tenure was marked by a time of political turmoil and military uncertainty.

Forrestal had an able bureaucratic opponent in the person of Stuart Symington, a Missouri businessman who made a fortune during the Second World War selling gun turrets to the Army Air Force. In 1946 Symington was appointed the assistant secretary of war for air, and in 1947, with the consolidation of the armed forces, he was made the first secretary of the Air Force. One of the first problems faced by Secretary Symington was the budgetary battle, which Symington shaped as a matter of life and death not only for the new Air Force he headed but for the United States as well.

In July 1947, President Truman established a commission to draft a national air policy. Thomas Finletter, an attorney and economist who had served as an assistant to Secretary of State Cordell Hull during the Second World War, was selected to serve as chair of what came to be known as the President's Air Policy Commission. The commission finished its work on time, and on January 1, 1948, it sent to the president a report titled "Survival in the Air Age." This report was a major event in the formulation of national strategy, not only for air power but also for national defense, concluding that, "We believe that the defense of the United States must be based on air power. We need a much stronger air establishment than we now have."[1]

The United States, according to Finletter, "must have in being and ready [sic] for immediate action, a counteroffensive force built around a fleet of bombers, accompanying planes and long-range missiles which will serve notice on any nation which may think of attacking us that if it does, it will see its factories and cities destroyed and its war machine crushed. The strength of the counteroffensive force must be such that it will be able to make an aggressor pay a devastating price for attacking us. It must, if possible, be so strong that it will be able to silence the attack on the United States mainland and give us the time again to build up our industrial machines and our manpower to go on and win the war."[2]

The Finletter findings resonated with the Air Force, which was positioning itself as the principal peacetime military force in readiness. Historically this had been a U.S. Navy mission, but the Finletter Report emphasized that the change in technology, and the need for immediate, massive retaliation, dictated that the Air Force become the service of choice to take the lead in representing the American retaliatory strike capability in the nuclear age. The cornerstone of the new U.S. Air Force's atomic mission was the B-36 "Peacemaker" bomber, a six-engine (later expanded to ten engines) behemoth originally designed in 1941 to give the United States an intercontinental strike capability should England fall to the Germans.

The B-36 was a perfect fit for the new postwar military plans of the United States, which had relied on the B-29 bomber as its delivery system of choice for the atomic bomb, but in doing so had predicated the overseas deployment (and storage) of nuclear weapons, something the United States nuclear planners wanted to assiduously avoid. Only the B-36 bomber, with its more than 6,000-mile range and 72,000-pound payload (as compared to the B-29, with its 3,250-mile range and 22,000-pound payload), could accomplish the mission of intercontinental nuclear delivery from bases in the continental United States.

But the B-36 had problems. In the age of jet propulsion, there were concerns that the B-36 was vulnerable to interception by the new generation of Soviet fighters. There wasn't any viable alternative to the B-36 on the drawing board. The next generation bomber, the B-47, was a swept-wing, jet-powered modern aircraft, but with limited range. Development of the successor to the B-36 strategic bomber, the B-52, had been placed on hold in the summer of 1947 when it became clear that the design of that aircraft would be obsolete before the plane could be brought into production. The first versions of the B-36 to enter into operation, in November 1948, suffered from engine unreliability and other design flaws.

Technical difficulties aside, strategic atomic retaliation from the air became the foundation of the Truman nuclear defense posture, with the Air Force taking the lead. The Joint War Plans Committee of the Department of Defense also recognized that "the only weapon which the United States can employ to obtain decisive effects in the heart of the USSR is the atomic bomb delivered by long-range aircraft." It was estimated by the committee that 196 atomic bombs would cause "such destruction upon the industrial sources of military power in the USSR that a [military] decision could eventually be obtained."[3]

The Pentagon, however, had no detailed plan for executing an atomic attack on Russia, or anywhere else in the world. Atomic bombs were under the control of the AEC, and with the teams available in mid-1948, only two atomic bombs could be assembled per day, meaning the United States would need up to eighty days to prepare to deliver an atomic retaliation attack, not an ideal deterrence under any circumstance, especially when there were growing worries about the Russian capability to attack the United States.

The Russian threat, around which the increasing levels of American paranoia revolved, was almost totally illusory. Their only strategic bomber was a poor copy of an outdated American aircraft that was never produced in significant numbers. Whereas American bombers, operating from forward airfields in Europe and Asia, could hit targets throughout the Soviet Union, the United States was safe from any similar attack from the Soviet Union, whose bombers lacked the range. The reverse-engineered TU-4 bomber, a clone of the B-29, made its maiden flight in May 1947. On August 3, 1947, during the Aviation Day celebration at Tushino Airfield outside Moscow, Western observers were shocked to see four B-29 bomber look-alikes fly over the crowd.[4] With the Russians now possessing a strategic bomber capability, at least in theory, the United States had no choice but to press forward with its counter, which in 1947 was limited to the B-36 bomber. The Russian atomic bomb, far from creating a level playing field, only heightened the American paranoia that had seeped into the highest levels of decision making as well. Fear of the Russians "catching up" on the nuclear front drove a relentless push for the United States to contain Russia for as long as possible, prior to atomic equilibrium being reached. After the collapse of the Baruch Plan, nuclear disarmament as a policy was never considered by the Truman administration. In its stead was a push toward enlarging America's atomic arsenal, a policy that drove every aspect of the Truman diplomatic and military posturing.

While the Truman administration wrestled with the Berlin Airlift crisis and the new reality of the Russian atomic bomb, the United States was dealt yet another blow that only empowered those who viewed the world in terms of one gigantic communist plot. China had been the scene of a massive civil war pitting the nationalist forces of General Chiang Kai-shek against the Communist forces led by Mao Tse-tung. By 1949, Chiang's forces had been routed from mainland China, and on October 1, 1950, Mao declared the creation of the People's Republic of China, with Beijing as its capital. Chiang and nearly two million of his supporters fled to the island of Taiwan and established Taipei as the capital of the Republic of China.

The fall of China to the communists was viewed by many in the anti-communist establishment as a huge betrayal of the United States by those responsible for establishing and implementing Chinese policy. One senator in particular, the Democrat Pat McCarran of Nevada, placed the blame on alleged Soviet spies who had infiltrated the State Department.[5] Then, on February 9, 1950, a relatively unknown junior Republican senator from Wisconsin, Joseph McCarthy, gave a speech on Lincoln Day to the Republican Women's Club of Wheeling, West Virginia. Holding aloft a sheet of paper, McCarthy claimed that on that paper was a list of more than two hundred known communists who were working for the State Department, whose identities had been "made known to the Secretary of State as being members of the Communist Party and who nevertheless are still working and shaping policy in the State Department."[6] McCarthyism—a wave of reactionary anticommunism that swept over America—had reared its ugly head.

At this critical time, President Truman was wrestling with two decisions that would shape how America would function as a member of the world community in the coming decades. The first was the question of what the national security policy of the United States would be in the atomic age. The Truman administration had cobbled together pieces of policy that had come to be known as the Truman Doctrine. Although this doctrine created an ideological framework for American diplomacy, it did not establish hard-and-fast policy around which fundamental decisions could be reached with regard to military posture and economic priorities. Though NSC-30, the official document concerning atomic warfare that came into effect in 1948, had established a policy for using atomic weapons, there was no overarching nuclear weapons policy that was linked to a wider national security framework. The end result was a haphazard, inefficient approach toward policymaking, which exposed the Truman administration to political criticism that it was placing singularly economic concerns, centered on a balanced budget, ahead of legitimate national security concerns. Lacking an all-encompassing national security strategy, the Truman administration was ill-equipped to answer these charges.

This policy vacuum enabled the State Department to step in. Secretary of State Dean Acheson assembled a team of policy analysts, headed by the State Department's head of policy planning, Paul Nitze, and tasked them with crafting a policy that would overwhelm even the staunchest critic with its power and vision. The drafters of NSC-68, as this policy became known, could never be accused of being overly nuanced in their description of either the problem or the solution facing the United States. At the core of NSC-68 was the underlying assumption that, in the aftermath of the Second World War, the United States and the Soviet Union had inherited a bipolar world, where each was a respective center of power. Its framers also contended that the Soviet Union was driven by fanatical communist dogma to impose its absolute authority on the rest of the world.

Only the United States stood in the way of the Kremlin and its objectives, which meant that the United States was involved in a struggle for the survival of the free world. According to NSC-68, the Soviet Union viewed America as its only threat, and as such it had focused the totality of its society on organizing and equipping itself in order to destroy the integrity and vitality of the United States as a world power. NSC-68 assessed that the Soviets would have, by 1954, more than two hundred atomic bombs and a sufficient quantity of long-range bombers to deliver them in a surprise attack against the United States. The combination of this strategic nuclear strike capability and the massive conventional military force the Soviet Union had assembled in Europe would give the Soviets the ability to simultaneously overrun Western Europe, to neutralize Great Britain through aerial bombardment, and to attack the United States with atomic weapons.[7]

NSC-68 declared that the principal mission of the American national security establishment should be to assure the retention of national integrity and vitality of American society in the face of the Soviet threat. To achieve this end, the United States should seek to contain the Soviet Union to the greatest extent possible. Containment would not be passive but rather active, involving not only the confrontation of Soviet expansion but also the rollback of the control and influence of the Kremlin. It would identify and reinforce the seeds of destruction inherent in Soviet society so as to bring about a collapse of the Soviet Union, and with this collapse would occur a fundamental change in how the people and territory known as the Soviet Union would interact with the rest of the world, led of course by the United States.

To achieve this, NSC-68 called for a massive buildup of American political, economic, and military power so that American supremacy, with or without allies from like-minded nations, would reign unchallenged. In order to make sure that the policy of active containment was not viewed simply as a bluff, NSC-68 advocated a massive expansion of the American nuclear capability, including the manufacture and stockpiling of thermonuclear weapons. In order to ensure that American military options were not exclusively nuclear, NSC-68 also advocated for similarly massive increases in the conventional air, sea, and ground capabilities of the U.S. military.

Having defined the Soviet threat so starkly, and the remedy so clearly, NSC-68 then declared that the notion of negotiating with the Soviets should be rejected until the time when the Soviets had fundamentally altered their approach toward global interaction. NSC-68 rejected any notion that the United States would never use nuclear weapons first, stating that the potential of such a massive first use of nuclear weapons by the United States was, in and of itself, a means of deterrence. NSC-68 firmly underscored that its objectives were attainable at all levels—politically, economically, and militarily—and that all that stood in the way of achieving the goals and objectives of NSC-68 was a lack of will on the part of the administration and people of the United States.[8]

The Soviet threat postulated by NSC-68 was largely fictional. Not only did the Soviets lack a force capable of delivering a nuclear attack of the sort postulated by NSC-68, but they also lacked a deliverable weapon. A second test of a Russian atomic bomb was conducted on September 24, 1951, more than a year after NSC-68 was drafted. A month later, on October 18, 1951, the Russians tested a nuclear device delivered to the test site by a bomber, representing the first genuine Russian atomic weapon. However, even with a proven design in place, the Russian military did not receive its first atomic bomb until 1953. This was a far cry from Central Intelligence Agency estimates—supported by the U.S. Department of State, the U.S. military, and the Atomic Energy Commission—and cited by NSC-68, which gave the Soviet Union a production capability of 70–135 nuclear weapons by 1953.[9]

The principal thesis of NSC-68, that the Soviet Union sought to position itself as the undisputed world leader, was founded more on theory than reality. The argument that the Soviet Union was capable economically of implementing a plan for global domination of the sort outlined by NSC-68 was challenged by those in the Truman administration who felt that, rather than the Soviet Union gaining ground on the United States, the economic gap was widening. Even George Kennan, whose "long telegram" served as the ideological foundation of the NSC-68 thesis, disagreed with the document, primarily because of its calls for the massive rearmament of America.[10]

At first it looked like NSC-68 would not survive the bureaucratic realities of American politics. Truman wanted more clarification as to what the costs associated with NSC-68's implementation would be. He was already under pressure to do more for the military. In April 1950, Secretary of Defense Louis Johnson asked Congress for an additional $300 million to buy more aircraft for the Air Force. This and other appropriations requests raised the fiscal 1951 defense budget to $15.6 billion, from the $13 billion Truman had wanted to spend. His budget already under severe strain, President Truman was in no mood to embrace a policy direction that would triple or quadruple these expenditures, so he returned NSC-68 to its drafters unsigned. By June 1950, Paul Nitze, the principal author and coordinator of NSC-68, had given up hope of its ever being adopted.[11]

The development of a comprehensive national security strategy was but one of two major issues being addressed at the time. The second issue the Truman administration was focused on was the question of whether or not to proceed with creating a thermonuclear device, the so-called super or hydrogen bomb. President Truman had instructed the Atomic Energy Commission to proceed with these discussions on October 6, 1949, in the aftermath of his announcement that the Russians had exploded an atomic device. But authorizing a discussion and actually starting a national development program were two different matters. One of the biggest obstacles faced by the Truman administration in this regard was the opposition to the development of this weapon by many of the scientists who served as the core of the American atomic bomb program.

Not all scientists were opposed. Edward Teller, the Hungarian-born nuclear physicist, had been pushing for the development of a super bomb for several years. In April 1946, there was a gathering of scientists in Los Alamos, where Teller presented his calculations on harnessing fusion energy for a weapon. But this was a purely theoretical question, based upon advanced calculations that many scientists questioned, and Teller was compelled to put the super bomb on the back burner. Two of the biggest opponents to Teller's super bomb were J. Robert Oppenheimer and David Lilienthal, the head of the Atomic Energy Commission.

The detonation of the Russian atomic device changed the nature of the discussion. Simply enlarging the American stockpile of atomic bombs was no longer acceptable to many of the nuclear planners in America. Because the Russians had now demonstrated parity with the United States in the field of atomic bombs, it was imperative for the United States to establish its superiority by being the first nation to develop the hydrogen bomb. Three of the biggest proponents of this thought (besides Teller) were Lewis Strauss, a member of the AEC, and Ernest Lawrence and Louis Alvarez, two esteemed nuclear scientists. Alvarez had flown aboard the *Enola Gay* as the weapons officer responsible for final preparations for the first use of the atomic bomb over Hiroshima. In early October 1949, Lawrence and Alvarez met with Teller and then with Senator Brien McMahon to discuss the idea of moving forward with the super bomb. Their idea was met with extreme enthusiasm and support.[12]

The AEC called together the General Advisory Committee (GAC) at the end of October 1949 to further discuss the matter of the super bomb, and both Lawrence and Alvarez were brought in to make presentations. David Lilienthal was taken aback by their enthusiasm to pursue a weapon of such destructive potential. Besides the considerable technical hurdles that would need to be overcome, Lilienthal and others on the GAC were concerned about the moral questions of having a super bomb that had no military value and was simply a mechanism for the extermination of humankind. Having accurately predicted the atomic bomb arms race, Oppenheimer now feared an even greater sprint toward doomsday. The father of the American atomic bomb believed that not only should the United States not produce the hydrogen bomb but it should unilaterally announce a complete renunciation of fusion weapons. Even a demonstration of fusion technology should be prevented, especially, as Oppenheimer and others noted, "until the present climate of world opinion changes."[13] Other scientists believed that the United States should go even further and negotiate with the Russians and the rest of the world for a universal pledge of fusion renunciation.

The AEC as a body could not reach a unified decision. Three of the five members, including Lilienthal, were against going forward with the super bomb. Two voted in favor. But the overall tenor of the discussion was captured in the conclusion of the report they sent to President Truman on November 9, 1949: "The fact that no limits exist to the destructiveness of this weapon makes its very existence and the knowledge of its construction a danger to humanity as a whole. It is necessarily an evil thing considered in any light."[14]

The Joint Chiefs of Staff, in a report submitted to the president on November 23, 1949, urged the development of the super bomb, noting that even if the United States did not move forward with it as a weapon, America needed to understand the super bomb's characteristics so as to be in the position to understand how best to fight such a weapon. The issue of the super bomb was so controversial that when President Truman convened his Special Committee of the National Security Council (comprised of Louis Johnson, the secretary of defense, Dean Acheson, the secretary of state, and David Lilienthal, the AEC chair) to discuss the matter, it broke up after only one meeting, with Lilienthal and Louis unable to overcome their differences of opinion on the moral aspects of such a weapon. The GAC reconvened and passed a decision recommending against the development of the super bomb.[15]

Again the Joint Chiefs of Staff were approached and on January 13, 1950, they recommended that the United States pursue research into the technical feasibility of the super bomb, as well as an examination of how such a weapon would be delivered. The JCS stated that they believed that the possession of the super bomb by the United States would increase American national security. The possession of the thermonuclear weapon, in the mind of the JCS, was not inherently immoral but rather represented the only means for preservation of the free way of life enjoyed by the American people.[16]

Brien McMahon's Joint Congressional Committee on Atomic Energy recommended pursuing the feasibility of the thermonuclear concept but suggested that any final decision on whether to develop an actual weapon should be deferred until a comprehensive review of America's national security policy was completed. This recommendation was passed on to President Truman. In a last-ditch effort to prevent the development of the super bomb from going forward, David Lilienthal sought a meeting with President Truman so that he could better make his case. Truman was dismissive: "What the hell are we waiting for? Let's get on with it."[17] Later that day, January 31, 1950, the president announced to America and the world that he was instructing the "Atomic Energy Commission to continue its work on all forms of atomic weapons, including the so-called hydrogen or 'super' bomb."[18] A new arms race was under way.

Amid the internal wrestling within the Truman administration over the development of a national security strategy and the hydrogen bomb, world events once again intervened. On June 25, 1950, North Korea invaded South Korea, an act that caught the Truman administration completely off guard. An early agreement between the United States and the Soviet Union on the administration and eventual reunification of Korea fell apart, with the United States seeking to emplace the strong anticommunist leader Synghman Rhee through an election process that fell outside the framework of the original agreement.

Stalin was opposed to early North Korean requests to invade the south and end the crisis, not wanting to create a conflict with the United States.

However, in early 1950, Secretary of State Acheson indicated that Korea fell outside the defense perimeter established by the United States in the Pacific and that the Korean matter was one best handled by the United Nations. Based on a reassessment prompted by Acheson's speech, Stalin agreed to back a North Korean invasion of the south, and by April 1950, Stalin's final approval was granted.[19]

Stalin's decision was influenced by the victory of Mao and the Chinese communists against Chiang Kai-shek, as well as a new sense of confidence acquired in the aftermath of the successful Russian atomic test. Normally cautious on matters of diplomacy, Stalin began to feel more confident that the tide was turning in his favor. The Sino-Soviet Pact, signed on February 14, 1950, had Russia and China pledging to come to the aid of the other in case of a war with a third party. Stalin assessed that the United States would not respond energetically to a North Korean move against South Korea, a point the Acheson speech only reinforced.[20] Stalin was wrong.

President Truman was on vacation at his home in Independence, Missouri, when the news of the North Korean invasion arrived. He immediately flew back to the White House. The United States called for a meeting of the Security Council of the United Nations and pushed for a resolution calling for an immediate cease-fire. Two days later, the United States sponsored a resolution by the Security Council requesting member states to provide military forces to oppose the North Korean invasion. Russia, surprisingly, did not use its veto, under instructions from Stalin, who was not looking for a confrontation with the United States. Stalin assumed that the North Koreans would soon be in control of the entire Korean peninsula, and the matter would become moot.

The first U.S. ground forces, comprised of units from the Twenty-fourth Infantry Division, a garrison unit out of Japan, were committed to Korea in early July 1950. From July 5 to July 20, these forces fought a large, sustained action against the North Korean forces in and around the city of Taejon, where the Americans were routed with heavy casualties. America quickly found itself in a conventional shooting war where the outcome was quite uncertain. The U.S. Air Force, in particular the Strategic Air Command, was positioned to carry out a massive attack against the Soviet Union using atomic bombs, but there was no strategy for using nuclear weapons in a limited action such as Korea.

President Truman, upon his return to Washington, DC, instructed his senior planners to develop a nuclear response plan for the use of atomic weapons in Korea should the Russians get involved.[21] Shortly after the fighting began in the Taejon region, on July 9, 1950, General Douglas MacArthur sent a message to the Joint Chiefs of Staff in which he asked that consideration be given to making atomic bombs available for operations in direct support of ground combat. The United States possessed approximately 250 atomic bombs at that time, and the JCS chief of operations believed that 10–20 atomic bombs could be released to MacArthur without degrading the U.S. strategic capabilities worldwide. MacArthur wanted to use the atomic bombs to cut off lines of communication connecting North Korea with China and the Soviet Union.[22]

On August 1, 1950, the decision was made to send elements of the 9th Bomb Group to Guam as an atomic task force. Ten B-29s, loaded with unarmed (i.e., minus their nuclear capsules, which contained the fissile material) atomic bombs, were dispatched, but on August 5 one of the planes crashed during takeoff near San Francisco. The nine other planes reached Guam, where they went on standby duty until September 13, 1950, when the B-29 bombers were called back to the United States. The nine atomic bombs, together with their maintenance crews, remained in Guam.[23]

The war in Korea continued with seesaw ferocity. Pushed back to the confines of the Pusan perimeter, the American-led UN force finally held its ground. In September 1950, General MacArthur launched an amphibious assault into the North Korean rear area that compelled the North Koreans to retreat from the territory they had occupied in the south. By October, the UN forces had driven the North Koreans back across the 38th Parallel, which had served as the demarcation line between North and South Korea, and were pushing on toward the Chinese and Soviet borders.

The decision to cross the 38th Parallel and forcefully unify Korea was a direct by-product of the thinking that had gone into the creation of NSC-68. Prior to the North Korean invasion in June 1950, NSC-68 was for all purposes a dead document. The North Korean invasion, coupled with the acquisition of the atomic bomb by Russia and the victory of Mao and the Chinese communists, appeared to reinforce the worst fears set forth in the foundational framework around which NSC-68 was drafted. Faced with the need to act in the face of communist aggression, President Truman officially signed NSC-68 on September 30, 1950. Having embraced a policy that sought the rollback of communism around the world, the North Korean situation presented Truman with the opportunity to transform theory into reality. Truman's goal was not just to unify Korea but also to demonstrate that the tide of history had turned against communism. Truman wanted to make this demonstration not just for Mao and Stalin, but perhaps more importantly, for his domestic critics in the United States, who were blaming Truman for engaging in policies of appeasement that had enabled the communists to achieve victory in China and Korea and to acquire the atomic bomb.

Mao saw the American decision to push past the 38th Parallel in a similar light as the Truman administration, but from the opposite perspective. The decision of the Chinese to intervene in North Korea in the fall of 1950 was made on the principle that communism could not survive such a rollback and that China, as the Asian defender of communism, had no choice but to intervene. Even as American troops pushed into North Korean territory, the Chinese army started crossing into North Korea in large numbers to fight back against the Americans. The Chinese were supported by fighter aircraft provided by the Soviet air force. This cooperation was part of the Sino-Soviet mutual defense pact that placed the totality of Soviet defense capability at the disposal of China in the case of an American attack. Far from being simply a regional conflict, the war in Korea was threatening to explode into a global conflagration, capable of going nuclear at any moment.

By November 1950, the introduction of Chinese forces in North Korea had turned the tide once again against the UN force. General MacArthur renewed his requests for atomic bombs to break the back of the Chinese counteroffensives, but to no avail. Truman had stated in a press conference on November 30, 1950, that "there has always been active consideration" of nuclear weapons use in Korea, a statement that worried British Prime Minister Clement Atlee so much that he flew to Washington the next week for consultations. Truman assured Atlee that there were no plans to drop the bomb in Korea. He further told Atlee that he regarded the United Kingdom and the United States as "partners in this matter," and that Truman would not use the bomb without consulting London first, unless the United States was under attack.[24]

However, in March 1951, it looked as if the Russians and Chinese might be positioning themselves for a major escalation when U.S. intelligence detected a force of nearly 200 Soviet bombers being moved into bases in the Far East, well within striking distance of Japan, while the Chinese massed even more ground forces. This changed the entire strategic calculation. By April 1951, a plan for the use of the atomic bombs as a force of retaliation should the Russians and Chinese choose to escalate was drawn up. It was decided that nine nuclear capsules would be turned over to the U.S. military and deployed, along with a number of B-29 bombers, to Guam. In exchange for placing these weapons under direct U.S. military control, the president convinced the JCS to acquiesce on his decision to relieve General MacArthur as the commander in the Pacific.[25]

The reasons for Truman's decision to remove General MacArthur from command were numerous and complex, but one of the factors was that if the president were to turn over nuclear weapons to the military for use in

Korea, he wanted someone a bit more obedient at the helm. The bomb capsules and bombers were flown to Guam, where they remained until finally withdrawn from the theater in November 1951, again because of a lack of any viable targets. However, the capsules remained under military control, representing the first time that nuclear weapons fell outside the control of the Atomic Energy Commission.

The unfolding conflict in Korea only exacerbated a growing frenzy of anticommunist sentiment at home in America. In July 1950, while American soldiers were being slaughtered in Korea, America was further rocked by the arrests of Julius and Ethel Rosenberg, who were accused of passing atomic secrets to the Russians as part of the spy ring that had involved Klaus Fuchs, the German-born English nuclear physicist who passed nuclear design secrets to the Soviets while working at Los Alamos. The recent detonation of the atomic bomb by the Russians fueled the flames of anticommunist sentiment, and the political bodies in the United States acted accordingly.

American politicians started reacting to the perception that America was under the threat of imminent communist attack. In September 1950, Senator Patrick McCarran pushed through the Subversive Activities Control Act, part of a legislative package known as the Internal Security Act of 1950. This legislation required members of the American Communist Party to register with the U.S. government. President Truman opposed this act, stating that it betrayed the "finest traditions" of the United States by curbing "simple expression of opinion."[26] However, Congress overrode Truman's veto by large majorities. Before 1950 came to a close, McCarran oversaw the creation of the Senate Internal Security Subcommittee, which was empowered to carry out investigations in support of the Internal Security Act of 1950.

The Korean War placed President Truman in a difficult situation. On the one hand, the Truman administration was in the process of crafting a national security policy that defined the forces of communism, led by the Soviet Union, as the intractable enemy of the United States. At the same time, public opinion, mirrored in many respects by congressional sentiment, accepted the notion of Russia as a threat worthy of an American response. Truman knew he needed to spend more money on defense, but he also needed to keep the budget under control. The Korean War created conditions where certifying, even superficially, the warnings of NSC-68 as valid could have swept up the American public and Congress in war fever, leading to a military buildup and consequently a depletion of the budget. Such a circumstance would have put the United States on a dangerous path toward a decisive confrontation with the Soviet Union—an outcome undesirable for all parties involved.

By the end of November 1950, the scale of the Chinese intervention had become clear, with American divisions in full-scale retreat before Chinese human-wave attacks. On December 15, 1950, Truman delivered a "fireside speech" in which he told the American people that "Our homes, our nation, all the things we believe in, are in great danger," and that "this danger has been created by the rulers of the Soviet Union."[27] The next day President Truman signed a proclamation in the Oval Office, declaring a national state of emergency. Truman noted that communism constituted a threat to the freedoms guaranteed by the Bill of Rights and that these elements of a "full and rich life" would be lost if the communists won.[28]

On March 15, 1951, the trial of Ethel and Julius Rosenberg began in New York's Southern District federal court. The Rosenbergs were found guilty on March 29, 1951, of conspiracy to commit espionage. On April 5, 1951, the presiding judge in the case, Irving Kaufman, sentenced both Rosenbergs to death, stating that their "conduct in putting into the hands of the Russians the A-Bomb . . . caused, in my opinion, the Communist aggression in Korea, with the resultant casualties exceeding 50,000. . . . Indeed, by your betrayal you undoubtedly have altered the course of history to the disadvantage of our country. . . . We have evidence of your treachery all around us every day for the civilian defense activities throughout the nation are aimed at preparing us for an atom bomb attack."[29]

The public sentiment that fueled the fate of the Rosenbergs threatened in turn to provoke an all-out nuclear war between the United States, Russia, and China. But the Truman administration understood that whereas they needed the Korean War to enable them to undertake the sweeping transformation of America from a nation at peace to a nation operating under wartime footing, they had to act prudently in Korea while they gathered their strength and forged the alliances required to wage a wider war, at a time and place of America's choosing. A key element in the Truman plan was to position the United States to emerge victorious in a Cold War atmosphere, without ever having to exchange a shot with Russia. Thus even though the Korean War was used to justify an enormous buildup of U.S. military capabilities, very few of these capabilities were actually employed in Korea. The military budget expanded from the $15 billion per year Truman had been fighting to maintain to more than $50 billion. Only $5 billion of this was spent in Korea; the rest went to expanding American military capability worldwide.[30]

One area of this new worldwide focus was Europe. Since its creation in 1949, the North Atlantic Treaty Organization had functioned without either a political structure or a joint command. In fact, though the signatories to NATO had agreed to come to one another's aid in case of attack, there were no military forces earmarked for the defense of the alliance. The Korean War changed all of this. In 1949, there could be no talk of German membership in NATO because of the backlash that would come from the Soviet Union. With U.S.-Soviet tensions heightened because of the Korean conflict and America's global response, however, the idea of employing German troops gained ground. Such a use of the Germans could reinforce the overall capability of Western Europe to defend itself from Soviet aggression and became attractive to all in NATO but the French, who continued to harbor strong opposition to any notion of German rearmament only five years after the end of the Second World War.

As the situation in Korea deteriorated, and the probability of a Soviet attack on the West in Europe increased, NATO decided to create an integrated defense organization with common military structures that would include the Federal Republic of Germany. The United States appointed a man well qualified for the task of shaping this new NATO, General Dwight Eisenhower. Eisenhower had retired from the army in 1948 to become president of Columbia University. In December 1950, President Truman, at the request of the European members of NATO, recalled Eisenhower and appointed him the first Supreme Allied Commander, Europe. Eisenhower was able to work with the Europeans recovering from the ravages of war and assembled a viable military capability for NATO's common defense against the threat of communist aggression.

In January 1952, Eisenhower presided over the Lisbon Conference, where the NATO members pledged to undertake dramatic increases in the size of their military contributions to the NATO command. The Lisbon Conference called for an expansion to fifty divisions (twenty-five frontline, twenty-five in reserve) and 4,000 aircraft by the end of 1952. Eisenhower commented that this NATO commitment to arming assembled "such strength as the Communist world would never dare challenge."[31] In February 1952, NATO increased its membership by admitting both Turkey and Greece, two nations at the center of the Truman Doctrine in holding back the spread of communism.

The expansion of NATO into the global arena of U.S.-Soviet struggle brought with it the risk not only of a Soviet ground attack into Western Europe but also of a U.S. preemptive atomic attack. U.S. nuclear-capable B-36 bombers were deployed at seven bases on British territory. Since July 1950, President Truman had authorized the forward deployment of nuclear bombs, minus their nuclear capsule, to be stored on British territory (on December 6, 1950, President Truman endorsed the Joint Chiefs' request that nonnuclear components of atomic bombs be stocked on board the aircraft carrier, USS *Franklin Roosevelt*, stationed in the Mediterranean—the first naval deployment of atomic weapons).[32] The British were increasingly worried about the prospects of the United States ordering a nuclear attack against the Soviet Union from British bases, an action that would open up Great Britain to a nuclear retaliatory attack. The British sought a commitment that the United States would not order any nuclear strikes from those bases without their consent. A communiqué prepared in January 1952 stated that "the use of these bases in an emergency would be a matter for joint decision by His Majesty's Government and the United States Government in the light of the circumstances prevailing at the time."[33]

Whereas Great Britain may have had concerns about the U.S. nuclear arsenal operating on its shores, back in the United States the critical question was not how few, but rather how many, nuclear bombs to make. On September 18, 1951, Connecticut Senator Brien McMahon introduced Senate Concurrent Resolution 46, in which he argued that current nuclear expenditures were "unreasonably and imprudently small," noting that "the cost of military fire power based upon atomic bombs is hundreds of times cheaper, dollar for dollar, than conventional explosives" and that therefore the United States "must go all-out" to equip each military service with large numbers of nuclear weapons.[34]

One of the new nuclear weapons McMahon had in mind was the super, or hydrogen, bomb. Following the presidential decision to proceed with the development of the hydrogen bomb, the nuclear physicists assigned to the task, led by Edward Teller, had labored hard to turn theory into reality. Unfortunately for Teller, the basic calculations around which he had based his model for the super bomb had been proven wrong by his colleagues. A critical component in the design of the super bomb was the element tritium, which was required to kindle thermonuclear reactions at manageable temperatures. Tritium was a rare isotope and was manufactured in one place only in the United States, a special reactor in Hanford, Washington. In March 1950, President Truman authorized a "crash program," with a goal to create a program capable of producing ten super bombs per year, at a cost of nuclear material equivalent to between thirty and forty atomic bombs.[35] At a time when the U.S. military was pressing for more nuclear strike capability, this was a heavy sacrifice. Key to this calculation was the amount of tritium required to achieve this goal, about one kilogram. It turned out that Teller had underestimated the amount of tritium required. The actual amount was between three and five kilograms, which meant the United States would need three to five years to produce a single super bomb, at a cost of hundreds of atomic bombs that would not be manufactured because of the diversion of tritium. Suddenly, the super bomb did not look like a good bargain.[36]

A year later, in March 1951, the hydrogen bomb project was saved because of a dynamic new concept, "staging," which used a fission explosion from a classic atomic bomb as a means of initiating the fusion reaction needed for the thermonuclear reaction. Edward Teller, together with Stanislaw Ulam, came up with the concept. As the AEC moved forward on the super bomb project, however, the decision was made, largely based on Teller's brusque personality and his reputation as not being a strong team player, not to put Teller in charge of the program, prompting his angry resignation. In Teller's absence, a new design team, known as the Panda Committee, came together to turn the Teller-Ulam super concept into reality. By August 1952, the super bomb design had been finalized; the components had been produced; and the entire device, code-named "Mike," was being assembled on the Pacific island of Eniwetok.[37] It was at this juncture that three esteemed figures in the U.S. nuclear community intervened in an effort to stop the bomb from being tested. J. Robert Oppenheimer, the father of the atomic bomb; James Conant, the president of Harvard University and a long-serving member of the General Advisory Committee; and Vannevar Bush, the former head of the Office of Scientific Research and Development during the Second World War, had come to the mutual agreement that the timing of the Mike test, just days before a general election for the presidency of the United States, was a bad idea. They felt that a new administration should not be saddled with such a horrific reality as the detonation of a hydrogen bomb because it would be this new administration that would have to cope with the fallout of such a decision.[38]

Furthermore, all three believed that the Mike test provided one last chance to roll back the mad rush to nuclear armament in which the United States and the Soviet Union were engaged. If an agreement could be reached to stop all nuclear testing before Mike was detonated, then thermonuclear bombs would remain theoretical. Any breach of this testing ban would be immediately detectable, making inspection provisions virtually nonexistent. Truman was unimpressed with the last-second plea on the part of Oppenheimer, Conant, and Bush to unilaterally suspend the test of the super bomb, and he gave his permission to conduct the Mike test as scheduled, just before the election. On November 1, 1952, on the islet of Elugelab, the Mike device was detonated. It worked as designed, delivering a massive 10.4 megatons, 1,000 times more powerful than the bomb dropped on Hiroshima. Elugelab ceased to exist, replaced by a massive crater that scarred the former islet's lagoon. The strength of the explosion created by Mike was big enough, if dropped on New York City, to destroy all five boroughs.

Harry Truman had, with the death of President Roosevelt in 1945, inherited a world on the cusp of the nuclear era. Much had transpired since the Trinity test of July 1945. The United States went from a nation that used atomic weapons against Japan ostensibly to shorten a world war to one that sought to exploit its nuclear monopoly in order to maintain its strategic superiority over the Soviet Union in a new Cold War. Nuclear weapons had become an integral part of the American national security fabric, and any effort to contain these weapons was beaten back in the name of defending freedom in the face of the communist menace. The monopoly did not last long, and soon President Truman found himself facing a nuclear-armed Soviet Union, prompting a nuclear arms race that, though yielding to American scientists the horrific secrets of the hydrogen bomb, brought the United States no closer to the kind of genuine security possessing these weapons was supposed to bring. By the time President Truman left office in 1953, the United States was bogged down in a quagmire in Korea, fighting a determined communist foe who, having solved the atomic puzzle thanks to the combined efforts of its scientists and its spies, no longer had to back down in the face of American nuclear threats.

On November 7, 1952, Dwight D. Eisenhower was elected president of the United States. He inherited a world infinitely more dangerous at that time than even he could possibly comprehend. The competing issues of a nuclear arms race running out of control and a global confrontation between the United States and Russia made for their own critical mass that, if allowed to combine, could lead to the literal realization of the future imagined by J. Robert Oppenheimer when he quoted the classic Hindu scripture Song of God (perhaps better known as the Bhaghavad Gita), after seeing the result of his handiwork on July 16, 1945: "Now I am become death, the destroyer of worlds."[39]

CHAPTER 3

MASSIVE RETALIATION

Air Force General Curtis LeMay had his own private ideological plaything. Formed in the aftermath of the Second World War as an adjunct to the Douglas Aircraft Company, the RAND Institute was conceived as a think tank for the U.S. Air Force, an organization of intellectuals who would conceptualize on how the Air Force could fight, and win, future wars. LeMay, who after the war was named the deputy chief of Air Staff for Research and Development, not only forcefully pushed for the creation of RAND but in 1946 gave the fledgling organization its first mission: to research the feasibility of intercontinental ballistic missiles as a weapon for the Air Force. By mid-1946, RAND had produced a paper that postulated an orbiting spacecraft, the birth of the U.S. satellite program.

But LeMay had bigger fish to fry than the new frontiers of space. Ever the ideological warrior, LeMay was firmly focused on the Soviet Union as the greatest threat to American power and had become obsessed with positioning America and, in particular, the U.S. Air Force not only to contain the Soviet menace but ultimately to destroy it. In order to better predict Soviet behavior for the purpose of devising an appropriate American response, the analysts at RAND turned to "game theory" to prepare and test their various concepts. RAND undertook to transform the Russian-American relationship into a global game of power politics whereby each side became quantified into tidy collective "utility functions" that would permit cause-effect analysis to be performed on any number of given scenarios, including thermonuclear war. In this manner, the RAND analysts were able to transform the Soviet Union into an elegantly simplistic construct in which massive resource allocations were expended in a single-minded effort to achieve not only military supremacy over the United States but also global domination—thus creating the perfect enemy for LeMay.[1]

The RAND assessments, combined with national security documents such as NSC-68, postulated a real and imminent threat to the United States that demanded a capable response that, in the mind of LeMay and others, was best defined by the capabilities of the Strategic Air Command, or SAC. General LeMay built SAC in his own vision, and in doing so he created a military force designed to inundate the Soviet Union with more than seven hundred atomic bombs in a period of a few hours. Such an attack would transform the Soviet Union, in LeMay's own words, into "a nation infinitely poorer than China, less populated than the United States, and condemned to an agrarian existence perhaps for generations to come."[2]

LeMay sought to provoke a conflict that would enable the United States to obliterate the Soviet Union before that nation ever in fact threatened America. To wage this war, LeMay procured for SAC a new generation of high-altitude bombers, the jet-powered B-47 and B-52, capable of penetrating the great depth of the Soviet Union's landmass. These bombers were designed to deliver nuclear weapons to targets inside the Soviet Union. A target list was developed and a program established to build both the weapons needed to target these cities and the bombers needed to deliver these weapons. Following the detonation of a Russian atomic device in 1949, the Air Force dramatically increased its target list and in doing so correspondingly increased the number of nuclear bombs needed as well as the number of bombers to deliver them. In short, the Air Force was justifying its own dizzying growth through a strategy designed to counter the *potential* of the Soviet Union, not the *reality*. With the analysts at RAND prepared to manipulate data in a manner that quantified the Soviet Union as a grave threat, plenty of ideologically based ammunition was available to sustain the argument. By 1952, the U.S. Air Force had manipulated the politics of fear and uncertainty so as to achieve a 90 percent growth rate.

The new Eisenhower administration inherited a confusing mix of policies created by the Truman administration that had relied heavily on U.S. atomic superiority to back up the overarching Cold War containment of the Soviet Union. Developing a coherent defense plan, and with it a corresponding defense budget, was made difficult by the ongoing conflict in Korea. The Korean War had long since stopped being a struggle where the outcome was in doubt. Instead, the American-dominated UN forces had squared off against the Chinese-dominated communist forces roughly around the area of the 38th Parallel, the original demarcation line between North and South Korea, and were engaged in a struggle defined not by simply maneuvering troops on a battlefield but rather by killing each other in a bloody war of attrition. The costs in maintaining this kind of fight, in terms of both money and lives, were prohibitive, and President Eisenhower had made ending the war in Korea his top priority.

The United States was not the only nation struggling under the burden of the Korean War. China and North Korea recognized that the dream of forcefully unifying the two Koreas was over and that the best course of action would be to terminate the conflict and get on with economic reconstruction. The death of Joseph Stalin in March 1953 further pushed the Chinese toward seeking a cease-fire. Newly elected President Eisenhower worked with his national security team, led by Secretary of State John Foster Dulles, to formulate an approach toward the Korean conflict that would pressure the Chinese to sue for peace. In May 1953, Secretary of State Dulles, speaking through an Indian intermediary (India maintained relations with both the United States and China), hinted that the United States was prepared to use nuclear weapons if a settlement could not be reached in Korea. Whether this implied threat pushed the Chinese to accept peace, or whether the Chinese had already decided that peace was in their best interest, by July 1953, the fighting was over.[3]

President Eisenhower was determined to take advantage of the Korean War's end to fulfill his preelection promises of fiscal responsibility. The defense budget for 1954 had been devised with the war in Korea still a reality. The fighting now stopped, Eisenhower sought to cut drastically the defense budget and to reformulate national security policy in a manner that was not predicated on spending such high amounts of capital and that would also tame the spiraling upward trend of the defense budget during the last three years of the Truman administration.[4]

The U.S. Air Force, ever alert to any potential threat to the dominant position it had carved out for itself when it came to national defense, sought to preempt Eisenhower by defining the strategic situation along lines that precluded any significant deviation from the policy direction then embarked on (one that thoroughly favored the Air Force). As far back as 1950, General LeMay had identified the year 1954 as being particularly critical in terms of U.S.-Soviet strategic comparison, a time in which the United States must be prepared to "meet, and effectively counter, the full military force of the Soviet Union."[5] General LeMay had positioned SAC to be the premier American response to the Soviet threat during the Truman administration. Now, with 1954 looming in the immediate future, and the election of President Eisenhower bringing with it the potential for change, LeMay made a concerted effort to ensure that the civilian leadership of the United States never took its eye off the real threat posed by a nuclear-armed Russia and the critical role the Air Force played in dealing with this threat.

The Air Force helped orchestrate a special subcommittee of the National Security Council to which it reported, using data prepared by RAND, that the current defense posture of the United States was not enough to prevent, neutralize, or deter a Soviet nuclear surprise attack. Building upon this, the Air Force then convened its own special committee, headed by retired Air Force General James Doolittle, that proposed giving the Soviet Union a two-year deadline for coming to agreeable terms with the United States or else face a massive nuclear assault. By August 1953, the Air Force had rejected retaliation as a strategic concept, noting that in the nuclear age only the first strike mattered and that the United States should be preparing to do just that in the face of a growing Soviet threat.

Fears about a Soviet nuclear first strike were driving a series of RAND studies that would dominate U.S. strategic thinking for years to come. The first concept was put forward by a brilliant theorist named Bernard Brodie. In his treatise on atomic warfare, titled *The Absolute Weapon: Atomic Power and World Order*, Brodie noted that "thus far the chief purpose of our military establishment has been to win wars. From now on its chief purpose must be to avert them. It can have almost no other useful purpose."[6] "Deterrence Strategy," as Brodie's concept was known, required the reality of massive destruction in order to be viable. There was no more destructive force than the hydrogen bomb, so it was no surprise Brodie recommended that the United States stockpile as many hydrogen bombs as it could. The Soviet Union represented a far too unpredictable and belligerent adversary for any other course of action to be justified. To Brodie, the unimaginable devastation of the hydrogen bomb made nuclear war unthinkable. And yet, the destructiveness of these weapons made the concept of a preemptive first strike against a similarly armed enemy an all-too-tempting proposition. Brodie realized that the only true way to deter nuclear preemption by an enemy was to create a second strike capability, designed to survive any preemptive attack with enough striking power to ensure the destruction of the attacking power. In addition to building bigger thermonuclear weapons, Brodie recommended that the strategic infrastructure of the United States be dispersed so that a surprise decapitation attack (i.e., eliminating critical leadership and industrial targets in one blow) would be nearly impossible.[7]

While Bernard Brodie was ruminating on the issue of "second strike" and survivability, another RAND analyst was prepared to make his mark. Albert Wohlstetter was born and educated in New York City, having earned degrees in mathematics from both the City College of New York and Columbia University. After service on the War Production Board during the Second World War, Wohlstetter tried his hand at private industry before landing a job as a consultant with RAND in 1951. One of his first assignments was to put together an analysis of SAC's requirements for basing its bombers during the period between 1956 and 1960. In this analysis Wohlstetter was heavily influenced by a parallel study being done by his wife, Roberta, also an analyst at RAND. Roberta Wohlstetter was putting together a study of the Japanese surprise attack on Pearl Harbor. When considering SAC basing options, Wohlstetter's analysis was dominated by the notion of preventing a modern-day nuclear Pearl Harbor. He assessed that, across the board, SAC was lacking in real base security, noting that the Soviets would need only 120 atomic bombs of 40 kilotons each to be able to destroy up to 85 percent of SAC's European-based bomber force. Drawing on the influence of his wife's work, Wohlstetter's analysis made the SAC bombers in Europe the contemporary equivalent of the U.S. Navy's Pacific Fleet, noting that each was intended to contain the aggression of the Soviet Union and Japan, respectively. The Japanese chose to preemptively eliminate the American fleet by attacking Pearl Harbor. Wohlstetter opined that this was the logical course of action for the Soviets when it came to implementing their grand design in Europe.[8]

From the White House's point of view, studies such as Wohlstetter's were trending in the wrong fiscal direction. President Eisenhower was looking for ways to reduce, not increase, defense spending. In exchange for a reduction in military hardware and infrastructure, the Eisenhower administration constructed a national security strategy that emphasized regional alliances (such as NATO), covert operations carried out by the new Central Intelligence Agency, effective propaganda, and nuclear weapons. Nuclear weapons were deemed indispensable to national security, and it was assessed that as long as the United States maintained a sufficient stockpile of nuclear weapons, and the means to deliver them, the Soviet Union would be deterred from irresponsible aggression through the threat of "Massive Retaliation." In short, the fiscal frugality of the new Eisenhower defense budget was built on the back of a huge nuclear arsenal that the United States was willing to hold over the head of the world as a means of checking communist expansion. This strategy was dubbed the "New Look."

The New Look national security strategy of Eisenhower was unveiled to the world on January 12, 1954, at a speech given by Secretary of State Dulles before the Council on Foreign Relations in New York City. In addition to the established doctrine of deterrence, Dulles's speech introduced the new concept of Massive Retaliation as the centerpiece of U.S. strategic thinking. Local defenses, Dulles argued, were useless in the face of massive Soviet ground power and must therefore be backed up with massive retaliatory power. "A potential aggressor," Dulles noted, "must know that he cannot always prescribe battle conditions that suit him. The way to deter aggression is for the free community to be willing and able to respond vigorously at places and with means of its choosing." Dulles indicated that this was the approach being adopted by the Eisenhower administration. He pointed out that the recent conclusion of the Korean War ("on honorable terms") had only come about because the United States had threatened the Chinese with an expansion of the war beyond the limits China was comfortable with fighting (a reference to the implied threat of nuclear force by Eisenhower, which may or may not have influenced the eventual Chinese decision).[9]

Dulles's Massive Retaliation policy was not well received, within the United States or abroad. Under attack by the U.S. Senate and NATO allies alike, Dulles was forced to restate the New Look strategy, which he did in an article in *Foreign Affairs*, where he explained that the United States did not intend to rely upon massive strategic bombing as the sole means to deter and counter aggression. There was a role for local defense, as well, to manage and deter crisis. "The essential thing," Dulles wrote, "is that a potential aggressor should know in advance that he can and will be made to suffer for his aggression more than he can possible gain from it."[10]

Massive Retaliation may have worked in theory as a vehicle of deterrence, but when confronted by the reality of the real world, it failed to deliver on its promise. In Indochina, the French were entangled in a postcolonial war with an indigenous communist force known as the Viet Minh. In March 1954, the Viet Minh had succeeded in surrounding a large French military force in the valley of Dien Bien Phu. Unable to break the siege, France appealed to the United States for help. Options ranging from dropping nuclear weapons to carpet bombing Viet Minh positions with massive B-29 air strikes were considered, but in the end all were rejected.[11] The French garrison surrendered on May 7, 1954, paving the way for a total

French withdrawal from the region and the division of Vietnam into two parts, north and south. Far from being made to suffer their aggression, the communists in Vietnam emerged victorious and relatively unscathed. Massive Retaliation as a policy had failed its very first test.

The White House argued that any link between the Massive Retaliation deterrence of the New Look policy and the communist victory in Vietnam was specious. For Massive Retaliation to succeed, there first had to be in place a multilateral system of collective defense around which to rally. The situation in Vietnam, where the United States was asked to defend the fading vestiges of French colonialism, did not provide for the proper foundation required by a comprehensive policy such as the "New Look." Recognizing this shortfall, the Eisenhower administration began fashioning a series of treaty organizations that, like NATO in Europe, would foster the multilateral springboard for a policy of Massive Retaliation to deter against communist aggression and expansion.[12]

In September 1954, the United States brought together France, the United Kingdom, Australia, New Zealand, Thailand, the Philippines, and Pakistan to sign the Southeast Asia Collective Defense Treaty, which established the Southeast Asia Treaty Organization (SEATO), ostensibly to contain communist expansion in the region. This action was followed up in February 1955 with the creation of the Central Treaty Organization (CENTO), which linked Turkey, the United Kingdom, Iran, Iraq, and Pakistan in a mutual defense pact (the United States formally joined in 1958). Together, NATO, CENTO, and SEATO created a multilateral ring around the Soviet Union and China that formed the local defense "shield" that could be backed up by the thermonuclear "sword" of American Massive Retaliation.

While Eisenhower built his ring of alliances, the policy of Massive Retaliation was again tested in a crisis involving the Chinese islands of Quemoy and Matsu, the result being a policy fiasco. When Chiang Kai-shek and his nationalist forces withdrew to Taiwan from mainland China in 1949, they maintained a series of garrisons on coastal islands just off the Chinese coast, including Quemoy and Matsu, which were planned to be used as a springboard for the reconquest of China. In August 1954, Chiang Kai-shek dispatched 54,000 troops to Quemoy and another 15,000 to Matsu, prompting the Chinese communist forces to begin an artillery bombardment of the former island. The Eisenhower administration warned the Chinese against any attempt to liberate either Taiwan or any area controlled by the nationalist forces of Chiang Kai-shek. In keeping with his overall policy of building vehicles of containment of communism,

President Eisenhower pushed for a mutual defense treaty with Taiwan, which was signed in late 1954.[13]

There was increased talk in the Pentagon about using America's nuclear arsenal against China, either to disrupt ongoing Chinese attacks against nationalist-controlled islands such as Quemoy and Matsu or as part of a strategy that would help Chiang Kai-shek regain control of the Chinese mainland. On March 10, 1955, Secretary of State Dulles indicated that the United States was prepared to use nuclear weapons to defend Quemoy and Matsu. The very next day, President Eisenhower unleashed a stream of controversy when he stated that, in his opinion, atomic bombs were to be treated as just another piece of ammunition, "as you would use a bullet."[14] NATO ministers—concerned that any U.S. nuclear strike on China could escalate into a full-scale war with Russia, which would obliterate Europe—voiced their strong objection to any nuclear attack on China. Eisenhower himself understood the limited options available to him in this regard, telling the Joint Chiefs of Staff, who were pressing him to attack China, "We're not talking now about a limited, brush-fire war. . . . We're talking about going to the threshold of World War III. If we attack China, we're not going to impose limits on our military actions, as in Korea. Moreover, if we get into a general war, the logical enemy will be Russia and China, and we'll have to strike there."[15]

In the end, the Chinese communists backed down, stopping their bombardment of Quemoy and Matsu. It had become clear to the Chinese that the Soviets were not willing to be drawn into a larger conflict with the West over what amounted to a Chinese civil war, and the threat of nuclear attack by the United States proved too much of a price for China to pay for the liberation of two coastal islands. But once again the policy of Massive Retaliation had been tested and found wanting. The all-or-nothing approach such a policy entailed could not stand up to the realities of a limited conflict involving the peripheral interests of the United States.

The reality was that the policy of Massive Retaliation never had a chance of succeeding. Events in far-off Semipalatinsk, nestled in the midst of the steppes of Kazakhstan, were about to change the nuclear calculus forever. Andrei Sakharov, the brilliant Russian physicist, had overseen the manufacture of a "layered-cake" nuclear device that alternated layers of enriched uranium with lithium-6 deuteride. Nicknamed "Joe 4," Sakharov's device was detonated on August 12, 1953, achieving a yield of 400 kilotons.[16] Although crude by American standards, the Soviets had exploded a thermonuclear weapon, and in doing so, they actually pulled even with the United States in deliverable thermonuclear capability. Whereas the Mike test of November 1952 was a success, the device, dependent on huge cryogenic support facilities, was in no way near to being a deliverable system. When the Soviets detonated Joe 4, they were six months away from adapting the design to a form that could be delivered by an aerial bomb.

The scientists at the nuclear weapons laboratory in Lawrence Livermore, California, were scrambling to develop a smaller, lighter version of Mike that could be realistically weaponized. On March 1, 1954, this new device, weighing in at 23,000 pounds and designed to be delivered by a B-47 bomber, was tested. It was designed to achieve a yield of five megatons, more than twelve times more powerful than the Joe 4 device. A miscalculation led to the resulting explosion being much larger than anticipated, measuring some fifteen megatons. The Soviets would be able to produce a few Joe 4 bombs a year until their nuclear infrastructure was expanded for mass production. With the new, lighter-weight Mike design, known as Castle Bravo, the United States was able to produce hundreds of city-killers per year.[17] Even though the Soviets may have pulled even with the United States for a brief, fleeting moment, the United States quickly recovered and never again came close to yielding its overwhelming thermonuclear advantage.

The emergence of a Soviet thermonuclear capability, however minute, breathed new life into the growing paranoia that was sweeping the United States. This paranoia was perhaps best put on display when the anticommunist witch hunt turned on the father of the American atomic bomb, J. Robert Oppenheimer. Oppenheimer had grown increasingly disillusioned about the reality of the nuclear arms race between the United States and the Soviet Union, in particular the mad rush on the part of the United States to accumulate more and more nuclear weapons. In an article written for *Foreign Affairs* in the summer of 1953, Oppenheimer noted that there was little difference between 2,000 nuclear bombs and 20,000, that in the end the 2,001st bomb dropped would have accomplished all that was capable of being accomplished in terms of destructive capability. He likened the American and Soviet Union's rush to acquire nuclear weapons to "two scorpions in a bottle," each capable of destroying the other, but only at the risk of themselves being destroyed.[18]

This was not a message America's nuclear weapons designers wanted to hear. Indeed, many of these designers, including Edward Teller, viewed Oppenheimer's comments, and his track record of opposing the overall direction of the American nuclear weapons program, as bordering on treason. The chair of the Atomic Energy Commission, Lewis Strauss, likewise held a grudge against Oppenheimer because, in his mind, Oppenheimer helped delay the development of the hydrogen bomb. Strauss convinced

President Eisenhower that Oppenheimer was a threat to national security and succeeded in having Oppenheimer totally cut off from the nuclear weapons community. Edward Teller provided the FBI with testimony that reinforced Strauss's concerns that Oppenheimer was actively conspiring with the Soviets to delay the American development of the hydrogen bomb until the Soviets could catch up.[19]

On April 12, 1954, the Atomic Energy Commission initiated a formal hearing into J. Robert Oppenheimer in which his considerable service to the United States would come under direct attack. After hearing scores of witnesses—including Edward Teller, who condemned Oppenheimer not for any specific action or deed but rather for what he thought—the AEC found Oppenheimer to be a "loyal citizen," deserving of the nation's gratitude for his service. However, the AEC did revoke Oppenheimer's security clearances, and the father of the American atomic bomb was effectively excised from America's nuclear hierarchy.[20]

The public humiliation of Oppenheimer established a precedent that psychologically linked any philosophical approach opposing the expansion of nuclear weapons activity, such as arms control or disarmament, not only as being harmful to the national security of the United States but also as providing evidence of collusion with America's enemies, and therefore bordering on treason. Oppenheimer's security clearances had been revoked on a lesser, technical argument, and indeed he had been cleared of any wrongdoing in terms of either collaborating against the United States or working on behalf of the Soviet Union. Nevertheless, the mere fact that a man of Oppenheimer's stature could be so publicly crucified based on the mere allegation of impropriety served as a sobering brake to the development of any rational policy of nuclear constraint at the very moment in American history when such a policy was most needed.

The persecution of J. Robert Oppenheimer came at the high-water mark of the madness known as McCarthyism. By 1954, Senator Joe McCarthy's penchant for baseless attack had alienated many, including former supporters such as Stuart Symington. When McCarthy chose to take on the U.S. Army, he quickly found he had bitten off not only more than he could chew but, more importantly, more than the rest of the nation was willing to digest. When McCarthy attacked a colleague of the U.S. Army's chief counsel, Joseph Nye Welch, Welch eviscerated him before the Senate, and America, declaring that "You've done enough. Have you no sense of decency, sir, at long last? Have you left no sense of decency?"[21] By the end of 1954, America was done with McCarthy, and the Senate voted to censure their fellow senator.

But the demise of McCarthyism did not bring with it any reduction of anticommunist sentiment or any lessening of the paranoia regarding the Soviet Union. Massive Retaliation as a policy required weapons capable of achieving such unprecedented levels of destruction and of delivering them to their targets. Senator Stuart Symington may have railed against the excesses of Joe McCarthy, but he never once softened his position on the need for a powerful nuclear weapons–based counter to the perceived ongoing menace of the Soviet Union and communism. Symington had long-established relations with both the U.S. Air Force and a major defense contractor, Convair. Like Symington, Convair was convinced that long-range missiles were the weapon of the future, but it was having difficulty in getting the Air Force to invest in its ballistic missile design.[22]

Fortunately for Convair, at RAND there was a German-born mathematician and physicist named Bruno Augenstein who was a leading proponent of long-range missiles. Like many RAND associates, Augenstein believed that the Soviet Union was pressing ahead on all fronts, and he feared that the Soviets would soon take the lead in the field of intercontinental ballistic missiles (ICBM), which in the nuclear age meant the United States would be ceding nuclear supremacy. With the successful test of the hydrogen bomb, coupled with the efforts undertaken at Lawrence Livermore to reduce the size and weight of a hydrogen bomb, Augenstein argued that the stringent performance and accuracy requirements that had heretofore hindered the operational and fiscal (and thus political) viability of the ICBM as a weapon were no longer valid.

Smaller warheads meant that the ICBM could deliver them to their targets at greater ranges; moreover, the enormous destructive power of the hydrogen bomb dictated that accuracy requirements could likewise be significantly reduced. Convair had previously assessed that it would take until 1965 to field a viable, operational ICBM. Based on Augenstein's work, it now appeared as if Convair would be able to shorten this deadline to 1960. Bruno Augenstein detailed his analysis in a memorandum published in early 1954, titled *A Revised Development Program for Ballistic Missiles of Intercontinental Range*. In the memo, Augenstein encouraged the Air Force to throw its weight behind Convair and its ICBM missile concept, known as the *Atlas* missile, warning: "If the Soviet Union beat the United States in a race for the ICBM, the consequences would be catastrophic."[23]

The impact of the RAND/Augenstein Report resulted in the Air Force directing that a fully operational ICBM weapon system should be put into the hands of the Strategic Air Command within six years. The missile that would accomplish this mission was the *Atlas* ICBM, built by Convair. In 1954 the *Atlas* represented the height of ballistic missile technology, and yet no prototype had been flight-tested. Not willing to gamble everything on a single missile system, in October 1954, the Air Force contracted with the Martin Company to develop a second liquid-fueled ICBM, a more conventional two-stage design known as the *Titan*.[24]

Another analysis was conducted that pushed the case for an American ICBM. In March 1954, President Eisenhower had asked a panel headed by Massachusetts Institute of Technology president James R. Killian Jr. to consider the vulnerability of the United States to a surprise attack. The resultant product, known as the Killian Report, was released on February 14, 1955, and it warned of a growing disparity between the strategic capabilities of the United States and the Soviet Union, particularly in the field of ICBMs, which exposed North America to the risk of a surprise nuclear attack. Like the RAND/Augenstein Report that preceded it, the Killian Report recommended that the development of American ICBM capability become a national priority.[25]

While the Air Force wrestled with the issues surrounding the creation of a viable ICBM capability, the foundation of America's nuclear weapons delivery capability, Strategic Air Command's bomber fleet, was likewise undergoing a dramatic revision both in terms of its current composition and its vision for the future. Whereas the B-47 medium-range and B-52 long-range bombers were the mainstay of the SAC order of battle, both were deemed less than satisfactory—the B-47 because of its limited range, payload, and altitude and the B-52 because of its lack of speed and the fact that it was, in the minds of many, an already outdated platform (conceived and designed during the Second World War) by the time it entered service in 1955. The Air Force had its eyes on sleeker, more modern aircraft on the drawing board, such as the B-58 medium-range and B-70 long-range bombers.

For General LeMay and SAC, however, there was only one bomber in mind: the long-range, high-altitude, supersonic B-70. The B-70 was designed to penetrate Soviet airspace, flying higher and faster than any fighter the Soviets could bring to bear. For LeMay, the B-58 had the same lack of payload, range, and altitude that plagued the B-47. SAC didn't want the B-58, but the Air Force funded its development in 1954, naming SAC as the end user. LeMay took his dissatisfaction with that decision up the chain of command. In 1955, the Air Force concurred, dropping the B-58 as an operational bomber but agreeing to continue funding of the bomber as a research and design platform, with thirteen aircraft authorized at a cost of over $500 million.[26]

Politics then reared its ugly head. The huge Convair facility in Fort Worth, Texas, which had until recently been producing B-36 bombers, was now out of work. Convair was able to garner the support of former secretary of the Air Force (and longtime Convair friend) Stuart Symington, newly elected as a senator from the state of Missouri, as well as Texas's own Lyndon B. Johnson, a member of the powerful Senate Armed Services Committee. Pressure was building on the Air Force to reverse its decision regarding the B-58.

The supporters of the B-58 bomber, in and out of the Air Force, were able to build upon the growing paranoia that existed in the United States since the detonation of the Soviet hydrogen bomb in August 1953. Fears of falling behind the Soviet Union in any strategic capacity abounded. On May Day 1954, the Soviet Air Force displayed a new jet bomber, the M-4 Bison, in a flyover witnessed by Western observers. Until that time, the Soviets were thought only to have the TU-4, a B-29 copy. The M-4 bomber was intended to provide the Soviets with a true strategic bomber, capable of delivering a nuclear weapon against targets in the United States and then returning to the Soviet Union. In July 1955, the Soviets again displayed the M-4 in flight but this time had the aircraft keep flying past the reviewing stand, giving the impression that there were many more aircraft than actually existed. Some observers counted up to sixty M-4 bombers, when in fact all the Soviets had were eighteen. Furthermore, the M-4 was a sub-par aircraft, unable to achieve the range or payload specifications required. The Soviets were well aware of their weaknesses and perpetrated the fly-over hoax as a way of bluffing the United States into believing that the Soviets were more powerful than they really were.[27]

In this endeavor the Soviets were extremely successful. The CIA assessed the M-4 to be in full-scale mass production and estimated that there would be anywhere from 600 to 800 M-4 bombers in service by 1960. Soon Stuart Symington and others in Congress were announcing the existence of a "bomber gap" and were demanding that the appropriate measures be taken to build up America's capabilities, both in terms of matching the Soviets bomber for bomber but also in defending against the new threat of long-range, jet-powered, nuclear-capable M-4 bombers.[28] Convair benefited greatly from this new panic. The B-58 bomber was ordered into full production, and the flawed F-102 fighter-interceptor, in danger of being canceled, was likewise given the green light for full-scale production. Both aircraft were built by Convair.

The so-called bomber gap coincided with other developments internationally that fueled a growing animosity between the United States and the Soviet Union. In 1954, the Soviet Union, concerned over the growing capabilities of NATO, suggested that it should join the treaty organization in an effort to preserve peace in Europe. NATO and the United States rejected this advance, believing that it was merely a ploy designed to weaken the alliance. What the Soviet Union objected to the most, however, was a NATO decision to invite West Germany, which was formed out of the territory of former Nazi Germany that had been occupied by the United States, Great Britain, and France in 1949, into the alliance as a full member, which meant that the Russian nightmare of a rearmed Germany would become reality. NATO extended its invitation in 1954, and on May 9, 1955, West Germany was incorporated as a NATO member. The Soviet reaction was immediate, creating its own European defense alliance, the Warsaw Pact, which was signed into effect on May 14, 1955, and joined the Soviet Union together with Hungary, Czechoslovakia, Poland, Bulgaria, Romania, Albania, and East Germany (i.e., Soviet-occupied Germany, incororated as a separate state in 1949 following the creation of West Germany) in a Cold War counter to NATO.[29]

The Cold War was now a reality, with two military alliances ideologically opposed to one another facing off along the length of the entire European continent. Increased tension brought with it the paranoia of surprise military attacks. It was imperative that the United States gain access to high-quality intelligence information that would better define the Soviet capabilities when it came to manned bombers, the weapon the Soviet Union would use to deliver any new Pearl Harbor. The Lockheed Aircraft Company came up with a design for a high-altitude photographic reconnaissance aircraft, the U-2, which seemed to meet the bill. The first U-2 operational flights started in July 1956. One early mission, flown on July 4, 1956, flew over Engels Airfield near Saratov and photographed twenty M-4 Bison bombers sitting out on the ramp. At first CIA analysts thought that this was the normal complement of bombers for every Soviet airfield, and concerns grew anew about Soviet bomber supremacy. However, continued U-2 imaging missions showed that the July 4, 1956, mission had actually captured the entire M-4 Bison inventory for the Soviet Union, and soon it became clear that when it came to bombers, supremacy was overwhelmingly on the side of the United States.[30] Events just over the horizon, however, were about to make the issue of manned bombers, and with it any discussion of a so-called bomber gap, moot.

CHAPTER 4

MISSILE GAPS

In January 1956, the Eisenhower administration announced further cuts in the fiscal year 1957 defense budget as part of an overall austerity measure. Senator Stuart Symington and other Democrats cried foul, condemning Eisenhower for creating an atmosphere where "the security of the nation was being thrown into the marketplace for political advantage."[1] In April 1956, with the approval and support of Senate Armed Services Committee chair Richard B. Russell (D–Georgia), Symington formed the defense policy subcommittee, with himself as chair. Symington and fellow subcommittee member Henry "Scoop" Jackson (D–Washington) were vociferous in their condemnation of Eisenhower's budget cutting, declaring that the president's efforts to balance the budget had conceded the strategic advantage to the Soviet Union. What Stuart Symington wanted was for the Air Force to buy missiles, and more importantly, one in particular: the *Atlas* intercontinental ballistic missile.[2]

On October 4, 1957, the Soviets announced an achievement that dramatically affected America's perception of Soviet power. Using a two-stage R-7 rocket (known in the United States as the SS-6) and operating from the Tyuratam-5 space range in the Kazakh Soviet Socialist Republic, the Soviets lifted into geocentric orbit a small, hundred-kilogram sphere that contained a simple radio transmitter. This satellite, named *Sputnik-1*, captured the world's imagination. The Soviet launch planners had requested that the larger second-stage of the rocket be equipped with polished reflectors so that as it followed in trace of the smaller satellite, once the satellite separated from the stage, observers on the ground could see it with the naked eye in addition to monitoring the distinctive "beep-beep-beep" sound of the satellite's transmitter. While the Russians bragged about their accomplishment, and the rest of the world looked and listened in amazement, America went into deep shock. The Soviets now had a foothold in space, as well as a rocket system capable not only of placing a satellite in orbit but, more ominously, of delivering a nuclear warhead to American soil.[3]

President Eisenhower approached RAND's chair, H. Rowan Gaither, to form up a panel of experts—officially known as the Security Resources Panel but better known as the Gaither Panel—for the purpose of reviewing defense initiatives coming from RAND and elsewhere with an eye on their respective fiscal and operational viability in countering the new Soviet threat. Gaither fell deathly ill on the eve of the release of report, and the final draft was prepared by Paul Nitze, a key player in the formulation of NSC-68 in the waning months of the Truman administration.

The Gaither Panel's report, *Deterrence and Survival in the Nuclear Age*, continued the underlying assertion that the Soviet Union was an expansionist power that sought military advantage over the United States and the West. According to the report, the Soviets had the capacity to produce more than 1,500 nuclear weapons, and they were positioned to eliminate America's sole strategic deterrent, Strategic Air Command (SAC), with a surprise nuclear attack. The Gaither Panel recommended that the United States spend $44 billion on a crash nuclear shelter program to safeguard the American public from a nuclear attack and to disperse SAC bases and provide hardened shelters for SAC's bombers. The Soviet launch of *Sputnik* on the eve of the release of the Gaither Panel's report gave it even more credibility because the panel held that the Soviets were ahead of the United States in building and deploying missiles, something the Soviet rocket launch seemed to underscore.[4]

The Gaither Report was political dynamite. Leaked to the press a full two days prior to being sent to President Eisenhower, the report gave rise to one of the greatest intelligence failures in modern American history: the so-called missile gap. The passage in the Gaither Report that seemed to garner a great deal of attention was quite specific in terms of defining the threat: "By 1959, the USSR may be able to launch an attack with ICBMs carrying megaton warheads, against which SAC will be almost completely vulnerable under existing programs."[5]

The pessimistic tone of the Gaither Report was reinforced by the release of a series of reports by the CIA. The first, presented in October 1957, concluded that the United States was two to three years behind the Soviet Union in the field of ballistic missiles and that the Soviets could have a force of a dozen ICBMs deployed by the end of 1958.[6] Immediately following the release of the Gaither Report, the CIA published a National Intelligence Estimate (NIE) that assessed the Soviets as possibly having a force of ten ICBMs to deploy by 1959. A Special National Intelligence Estimate (SNIE), released two weeks later, dramatically altered this assessment, stating that a force of ten Soviet ICBMs would be operational in 1958, and that between 1959 and 1960, this number would be raised to a hundred ICBMs, growing to a force of five hundred ICBMs between 1960 and 1962. These numbers were backed up by the CIA in testimony given before the Preparedness Investigations Subcommittee of the Senate Armed Services Committee.[7]

Of the slew of interested parties delving into the issue of a so-called missile gap between the United States and the Soviet Union, one voice emerged as dominant in terms of not only influencing policy but also shaping a national mindset: RAND mathematician and nuclear strategist Albert Wohlstetter. Building on the reputation he established with his SAC basing study, in November 1958, Wohlstetter captured the schizophrenic reality of a nuclear-armed America with his essay "The Delicate Balance of Terror," published in *Foreign Affairs*. Wohlstetter believed that the United States had been lulled into a false sense of complacency and was once again using the concept of nuclear deterrence based upon the notion of Massive Retaliation as a crutch. This notion of nuclear deterrence, Wohlstetter stated, was merely wishful thinking. "Matching weapons," he wrote, "misconstrues the nature of the technological race. To deter an attack means being able to strike back in spite of it. It means, in other words, a capability to strike second."[8]

Terms such as *first strike* and *second strike* had been bandied around at RAND and within the circles of nuclear strategists for some time, but Wohlstetter held that few truly understood the implications behind the relationship between the two. The situation, according to Wohlstetter, was precarious. "A sober analysis of Soviet choice," Wohlstetter assessed, "from the standpoint of Soviet interest and the technical alternatives, and taking into account the uncertainties that a Russian planner would insure against, suggests that we must expect a vast increase in the weight of attack which the Soviets can deliver with little warning, and the growth of a significant Russian capability for an essentially warning-less attack. In short, the Soviets had the capability to be far better prepared to launch their first strike than America was to respond with its second strike, thereby eliminating any sense of deterrence."[9]

Deterrence, Wohlstetter argued, was aimed at a rational enemy. In the age of *Sputnik*, America no longer had the luxury of operating under the assumption that their enemy was, in fact, rational. Wohlstetter advocated in favor of what he termed a "protected retaliatory capability" that deterred against rational attack as well as created the conditions in which America could hope to fight, and win, a nuclear war. Arms control and disarmament measures, he argued, were not only fruitless but dangerous in that they invited "catastrophe and the loss of power to retaliate."[10]

Sputnik had, in one fell swoop, turned the world upside down. Fears of a missile gap combined with held-over anticommunist paranoia from the reign of terror of the McCarthy era created an environment of dread that was exploited by those in the defense industry, the military, and Congress who were proponents of massive defense spending. It was no longer a matter of matching the Soviets in capability, or even in achieving superiority. Wohlstetter and those who embraced his line of thinking were proponents of American supremacy.

President Eisenhower understood that he was standing on the edge of a nuclear abyss and tried to engage in policies that would help America, and the world, take a collective step back. On December 8, 1953, barely a month after authorizing his New Look defense posture that led to the publicly announced policy of Massive Retaliation, President Eisenhower stood before the General Assembly of the United Nations and delivered his famous "atoms for peace" speech. Reversing the policy trends of the Truman administration, which had sought to retain exclusive control over the technologies and means associated with nuclear power, and thus weapons, Dwight Eisenhower sought to partially embrace the call for sharing the secrets of the atom with the entire world in an effort to promote the peaceful, versus military, uses of nuclear energy.

"Today, the United States stockpile of atomic weapons, which, of course, increases daily, exceeds by many times the total explosive equivalent of the total of all bombs and all shells that came from every plane and every gun in every theatre of war in all the years of World War II," Eisenhower warned. Eisenhower pointed out the obvious, stating that "the secret is also known by the Soviet Union," and underscoring that "if at one time the United States possessed what might have been called a monopoly of atomic power, that monopoly ceased to exist several years ago."[11]

The solution President Eisenhower sought was nothing short of momentous: "The United States would seek more than the mere reduction or elimination of atomic materials for military purposes. It is not enough to take this weapon out of the hands of the soldiers. It must be put into the hands of those who will know how to strip its military casing and adapt it to the arts of peace."[12]

These weren't simply words from the president. Action was taken, and quickly. By August 1954, the Atomic Energy Act was rewritten so as to allow U.S. companies to export nuclear material and technology to recipient nations who undertook not to use them for military purposes. The giant flaw in the Eisenhower approach was that, in an effort to use the exportation of nuclear capability as a means of containing the Soviet Union, an emphasis was placed on getting the nuclear know-how and capability distributed. The critical aspect of safeguarding against any diversion of this capability away from its intended purpose was largely ignored. Eisenhower had designated southern Asia as a critical front in the Cold War, and nowhere more so than the subcontinent of India. The United States pushed nuclear technology into India, often without adequate safeguards, setting in motion the spread of nuclear know-how that would manifest itself decades later in a viral outbreak of nuclear weapons capability worldwide.

The creation of the International Atomic Energy Agency (IAEA), headquartered in Vienna, Austria, gave voice to the international aspect of Eisenhower's "atoms for peace" speech. But the reality was that when it came to nuclear politics in the 1950s, it was a two-player game: the United States and the Soviet Union (Great Britain, by 1954, had developed its own independent nuclear weapons capability, but it was, and would always be, overshadowed by the capabilities of the United States). The nuclear arms race between the United States and the Soviet Union had led to the open-air testing of dozens of nuclear and thermonuclear devices, so much so that by 1954 there was a growing frustration internationally about the widespread contamination the fallout from these tests was causing. Dealing with the political consequences of nuclear testing became a high priority for Eisenhower. The president personally favored a nuclear test moratorium but was held in check by deep divisions within his administration, especially from AEC chair Lewis Strauss and the Pentagon, who believed that only through continued testing could the United States maintain its nuclear superiority over the Soviet Union.[13]

In May 1954, Eisenhower, at a meeting of his National Security Council, proposed a halt to all nuclear testing.[14] Once again, the proponents of nuclear testing, citing in a large part Eisenhower's own New Look policy that had demanded a strong nuclear weapons capability, won out. It was therefore an embarrassment when the Soviet Union, on May 10, 1955, seized the diplomatic initiative by proposing, as part of its submission to the United Nations Disarmament Conference, a ban of all nuclear weapons testing. The United States rejected the Soviet initiative, largely on the grounds that it lacked any inspection mechanism from which any assurance of verification could be obtained.[15]

The ratcheting up of Cold War tensions brought about by the launch of *Sputnik* once again highlighted the issue of nuclear testing. Eisenhower's Presidential Scientific Advisory Council, flush with increased credibility in the aftermath of *Sputnik*, gave added gravitas to the concerns about nuclear testing, which continued to be expressed domestically and around the world. Eisenhower was inclined toward action, but once again the Soviets beat the United States to the punch, first by again proposing a moratorium on nuclear testing in early 1958, and then in March 1958, announcing that it was engaging in a unilateral cessation of nuclear weapons testing.[16]

Rather than rush into matching the Soviets moratorium for moratorium, President Eisenhower—together with British Prime Minister Harold MacMillan—was able to get Soviet Premier Nikita Khrushchev (who had emerged from the post-Stalin leadership muddle to take the helm at the Kremlin) to agree to an international conference of scientists and experts to discuss the technology and methodology of seismic monitoring and detection of nuclear tests. This conference, held in Geneva, Switzerland, in the summer of 1958, produced a report that provided a scientific blueprint for a monitoring regime. This blueprint could provide 90 percent certainty of detection of underground tests over five kilotons and could also detect any atmospheric test greater than one kiloton. Missing was any political agreement on how to implement this mechanism, as well as what would trigger any on-site inspection activity, how such an inspection would be carried out, and by whom.[17]

The Geneva meeting was successful enough to prompt President Eisenhower to announce that the United States, together with Great Britain, would likewise participate in a one-year moratorium on nuclear testing starting in October 1958. The United States, Great Britain, and the Soviet Union also agreed to begin formal test ban negotiations in Geneva at the end of October 1958. These negotiations were scheduled to last three years, during which time all parties involved agreed not to test nuclear weapons. If no progress toward an acceptable agreement governing a nuclear test ban was reached by that time, then the moratorium would automatically expire.[18]

In Geneva, the conference of scientists and experts had concluded that verification of a nuclear test ban was possible within specified limits. Thus armed with this information, the United States, Great Britain, and the Soviet Union began negotiating a comprehensive test ban in the fall of 1958. There was significant opposition in certain influential circles in the United States to a test ban, foremost of whom were many of the scientists involved in carrying out the tests themselves, and none more so than the father of the American hydrogen bomb, Edward Teller.

Teller cobbled together seismic test data derived from underground nuclear detonations carried out at the Nevada Test Site since 1951 and, together with a team of analysts from RAND, interpreted it to read that the threshold for detecting underground nuclear tests would be much higher than that agreed upon by the Geneva conference. Furthermore, Teller and the RAND analysts came up with cheating scenarios where they assessed how the Soviets could evade any monitoring regime, especially one constructed from the Geneva conference. These included conducting nuclear tests in outer space (on the far side of the moon, shielded from observation from Earth) and constructing giant holes in the ground that would "decouple," or muffle, the nuclear detonation, making it much more difficult to detect.[19] When the United States tried to introduce the new Teller-RAND data on remote testing, the Soviets balked, believing this to be a ploy to facilitate additional inspections, and with them intelligence collection. Although the Soviets had agreed upon the theory of inspections, they wanted to retain the ability to veto any inspection activity requested, a provision to which the United States would not agree.[20]

By April 1959, the United States put its diplomatic cards on the table, telling the Soviets that the United States would agree to a test ban if the Soviets backed down on their demands for a veto to inspections as well as accept an adequate frequency of inspections to detect underground nuclear activity. The Soviets refused to budge on the issue of inspections, and by December 1959, the Geneva talks had stalled. In January 1960, in an effort to get the talks back on track, the U.S. side raised the threshold concept, where all tests above a specific measurable seismic magnitude would be banned. The United States and the Soviet Union would engage in joint research to improve monitoring techniques and methods, and thus lower the agreed-upon threshold limits. In this way, the issue of inspection levels above that already agreed to would not need to be raised.[21]

The U.S. side was skeptical whether the Soviets would agree to this new approach and were thus surprised when, in March 1960, the Soviets announced that they were prepared to discuss a treaty based upon the threshold concept. But the Soviets added a caveat: they wanted a suspension of all tests above a 4.75 seismic magnitude, whereas the United States was only prepared to agree to a set moratorium period, during which time there would be more technical work to nail down an acceptable threshold level.[22] The shooting down of a CIA U-2 reconnaissance plane, flown by Gary Powers, over Soviet territory on May 1, 1960, soured U.S.-Soviet relations, and once again the test ban talks ended without reaching a conclusion.

An effort by the United States to propose a suspension of fissionable material during the ten-nation disarmament conference in March 1960 likewise met with disappointment when the Soviets walked out of the conference on June 27, 1960.[23] Other approaches to disarmament considered by the Eisenhower administration, including one that would subject the nuclear devices tested by all parties to a trilateral inspection regime (possibly conducted under the supervision of the United Nations), fell victim to election-year politics. Congress balked at any agreement that had U.S. nuclear devices inspected by the Soviets with little or nothing offered in return.[24] All effective talks between the Eisenhower administration and the Soviets hit an impasse when it became clear that the Soviets, frustrated by what they viewed as the inconsistencies of the U.S. negotiation position, were holding out for a new presidential administration before resuming discussions. Substantive arms control would have to await the arrival the next president in 1961.

Void of any confidence-building derived from meaningful disarmament talks, politics and paranoia soon seized Congress. This paranoia had been building for a number of years. On August 15, 1958, Senator Stuart Symington found that his position as the Senate's foremost critic of Eisenhower's defense priorities and as advocate of the looming threat of the so-called missile gap, was usurped by a new Democratic senator from the state of Massachusetts, John F. Kennedy. Like Symington, Kennedy was concerned about the state of affairs between the United States and the Soviet Union in the aftermath of *Sputnik*. Kennedy was an up-and-coming politician and had ingratiated himself with a number of Washington power brokers, including the syndicated columnist Joseph Alsop. Alsop authored a column published on August 1, 1958, that propelled the missile gap into the public eye. Alsop charged President Eisenhower with perpetuating a "gross untruth concerning the national defense of the United States," declaring that President Eisenhower himself had been either "consciously misleading" the American public, or had himself been misinformed about the reality of America's defenses.[25]

On January 16, 1959, Secretary of Defense Neil McElroy gave secret testimony to the Senate Foreign Relations Committee, in which he allegedly told the committee that the Soviet Union would have an edge of some 100 ICBMs over the United States by 1960.[26] McElroy's testimony was leaked to Alsop, who then wrote a column that opined that the real gap was actually in the area of 300 missiles.[27] In more than six columns starting on January 23, 1959, Joe Alsop laid out his case that the Soviets were well ahead of the United States in missile development. He built his argument on the premise that with 150 ICBMs attacking the United States, and a further 150 intermediate-range missiles firing on European targets, the Soviets could destroy all of NATO's nuclear weapons. He then set out to explain that if the Soviet missile factories were as efficient as the factory that produced the *Atlas* rockets, then the Soviets would have their 150 ICBMs in ten months' time.[28]

Eisenhower knew some things about the Soviet Union and its capabilities that Alsop and John Kennedy did not. The high-flying U-2 reconnaissance aircraft had not only debunked the so-called bomber gap but likewise provided a peek into the depths of the Soviet Union that provided facts for analysis about the true capabilities of the Soviets. During a four-year period, nearly twenty U-2 flights over Soviet territory were conducted, most of which were directed against the Soviet missile threat. But continued U-2 flights over Russia were growing increasingly risky in light of improved Soviet air defense systems. The CIA, which ran the U-2 missions, pressed for a surge in flights to collect against remaining information gaps, in particular rail lines in the Ural region where it was assessed that the Soviets might be establishing secret, heretofore undetected, missile launch sites.[29]

In May 1960, President Eisenhower was preparing for a crucial summit conference between Western nations and leaders of the Soviet Union in Paris, where disarmament was to be the main focus. On April 25, 1960, Eisenhower approved one last U-2 flight, again with Soviet ICBMs as the primary target. The CIA had detected, via intercepted communications, suspicious activity in and around the vicinity of Plesetsk. They wanted to fly one last U-2 mission to film the area and see if a missile launch site could be found. Eisenhower approved the mission with the caveat that the flight be completed no later than May 1, 1960.[30] Soviet-American relations were improving, and Eisenhower did not want to do anything that would undermine the potential thaw.

The formation of the Warsaw Pact in 1955, following the admission of West Germany into NATO, only increased the level of tension between the United States and the Soviet Union. Any notion of the Iron Curtain liberalizing in the aftermath of Stalinism was quickly dismissed after the Soviet crackdown in Hungary in 1956. East Germany was another hot spot. The Western enclave in Berlin served as a magnet for qualified East German laborers seeking a better life in the West. The "brain drain" was so severe that in November 1958, Nikita Khrushchev issued an ultimatum, calling for the withdrawal of all Allied occupation forces from West Berlin within a six-month period. Eisenhower rejected this demand, and tensions rose quickly.[31]

In August 1959, Vice President Richard Nixon, in an effort to help reduce the level of stress between the United States and the Soviet Union, visited the latter and engaged in a series of friendly debates with Khrushchev. In September 1959, Khrushchev returned the favor, touring the United States for a period of two weeks. After touring parts of America, including a farm in Iowa, Khrushchev visited with President Eisenhower at the presidential retreat in Camp David, Maryland. In a series of intimate discussions, the two leaders talked openly about the issue of Berlin as well as the reduction of nuclear weapons by both sides.

Khrushchev visited the United Nations on September 19, 1959, and in a major speech suggested that general and complete disarmament could be the best approach to peace. Khrushchev's statements were a preview of the document "Declaration of the Soviet Government on General and Complete Disarmament," which he delivered to the United Nations the next day.[32] Building on this momentum, on December 1, 1959, the United States and the Soviet Union, together with ten other nations, signed the Antarctic Treaty, which banned all weapons and military activities from Antarctica. Both Eisenhower and Khrushchev agreed to a major powers summit to be held in Paris in May 1960, when the ideas discussed at Camp David and in New York could be worked out in greater detail.

The Paris summit collapsed, however, after Gary Powers was shot down on May 1, 1960. At first the United States denied that there had been any reconnaissance flight, but when the Russians produced Gary Powers, alive and well, not only was Eisenhower deeply embarrassed, but on May 17, Premier Khrushchev stormed out of the summit after delivering a withering condemnation of American espionage. Khrushchev threatened to use force against American U-2 bases abroad, prompting the United States to raise its own defense condition level. Following the Powers incident, President Eisenhower brought an end to all U-2 operations over Russia.

Prior to the downing of Gary Powers, the CIA had recommended that the president authorize work on a follow-up system concerning imagery reconnaissance over the Soviet Union to replace the U-2. The CIA, with Eisenhower's approval, had begun work on a highly classified imaging satellite program known as Corona, which used reconnaissance satellites known as *Discoverer* that were launched into space. In August 1960, barely three months after the downing of the U-2 over Sverdlovsk, a *Discoverer* satellite was launched and successfully recovered, descending into the Pacific by parachute, enabling an orbiting U.S. Air Force plane to retrieve it before it splashed into the ocean. This flight, number 13, did not carry a camera. *Discoverer 14* did, however, and on August 19, 1960, it succeeded, in one mission, to image one-fifth of the landmass of the Soviet Union and Eastern Europe.[33]

The resolution of the *Discoverer 14* mission imagery was good enough to locate sites the size of Soviet missile launch facilities, including for the first time ever images of the new Soviet missile base at Plesetsk. The United States could now confirm that the Soviets had only two facilities (and another two under construction) capable of launching SS-6 rockets, one in Tyuratam with a single launch pad, and the other at Plesetsk with two launch pads operational. At best, the Soviets could launch three to five missiles, a far cry from the massive surprise attack envisioned by Albert Wohlstetter, Joseph Alsop, and others. Eisenhower now knew for certain that there was no missile gap, although he was unable to share the basis of his confidence with his detractors in politics and the media.

Even though Eisenhower had confidence—reinforced by the U-2 imagery and later the *Discoverer* photographs—that the missile gap was little more than a myth, he was beset by a panicked America that believed otherwise. The Soviets did not help quell this panic when they declared that their factories were churning out missiles "like sausages."[34] In the months following the launch of *Sputnik*, Eisenhower increased the budget for missile development by twenty times. Leading the charge were the *Atlas* and *Titan* missile programs. Like the Soviet SS-6, however, both the *Atlas* and *Titan* missiles were overly complex and fickle. Requiring long lead times to fuel and launch, neither system could be described as being a genuine "force in readiness." Albert Wohlstetter would have been correct in fearing that a Soviet decapitation attack, if one could have indeed been launched, might very well catch the American missiles sitting on their launch platforms, unable to be fired.

The Air Force's marriage to these complex liquid-fueled missiles was driven by the reality that, until the mid-1950s, the lack of advancement in the field of solid propellant had precluded an ICBM based on that technology. The Air Force was able to build on the progress made by the Navy in pursuing its *Polaris* missile and by August 1957, had come up with a simple three-stage missile design, known as *Weapon System Q*. This new system was capable of being mass-produced and stored, ready to launch, in hardened underground missile silos. By February 1958, the Department of Defense had approved the new missile, renamed the *Minuteman*.[35]

New ICBMs were not the only nuclear weapons the United States was capable of employing against the Soviet target. Medium-range *Redstone* missiles were approved for production in 1956, and by June 1958, the first fully operational *Redstone* unit had been deployed to West Germany. In October 1957, the first *Jupiter* intermediate-range ballistic missile (IRBM) was successfully launched, and by 1959, the United States had negotiated with Italy and Turkey for basing rights for this missile. The *Jupiter* joined the *Thor*, based in Great Britain since September 1958, as the other IRBM in Europe that targeted the Soviet Union.[36]

The *Redstone*, *Jupiter*, and *Thor* missiles were all liquid-fueled systems, possessing the same complexity and operational deficiencies as their liquid-fuel ICBM counterparts. But the solid-fuel revolution that made the *Minuteman* missile possible also paved the way for the design of a new, solid-fuel missile with a range of 750 miles. Begun in January 1958, the U.S. Army's *Pershing* missile, a two-stage system, was successfully launched in February 1960.

The revolution in missiles cut both ways. The surface-to-air missiles that brought down Gary Powers would likewise bring down any B-52 bomber attempting to enter Soviet airspace at high altitude (or any bomber, for that matter, including the controversial B-58). Not to be nullified, SAC sought to modify its aging B-47 and B-52 fleets to operate at low altitude, enabling them to slip in beneath Soviet radar coverage and reach their targets. The advent of the missile age meant that the Air Force needed to fight hard to come up with a viable mission for its nuclear bombers. Having finally received permission to wrest control of fully assembled operational nuclear weapons from the AEC so that they could be loaded onto bombers flying on nuclear standby missions, the Air Force did not want to see the nuclear bomber go the way of the dinosaur.

The B-47 simply wasn't up to the task of low-altitude penetration bombing, and fourteen aircraft were lost when the wings failed under the stress of the low-level flying. The B-52 did not fare much better, and when three were lost under similar circumstances, the entire B-52 fleet had to be modernized so that it could withstand low-level flight profiles. The advent of surface-to-surface missiles also represented the death knell for the B-70 bomber. Political gamesmanship, especially from Senator John F. Kennedy—who proclaimed his wholehearted support for the B-70— prevented Eisenhower from cutting off the funding for the B-70. However, the program survived on much-reduced expenditures, awaiting a new administration's final decision as to its fate.[37]

The U.S. Navy got into the nuclear game as well. In 1956, the Navy came up with the concept for a solid-fuel missile that could safely be launched from a submerged submarine. Named the *Polaris*, this missile was successfully flight-tested in 1959. In July 1960, it was launched without incident from the USS *George Washington*, the world's first submarine capable of launching ballistic missiles. The Navy had just officially become part of the national security nuclear retaliation force.

The massive amount of firepower the United States brought to bear against the Soviet Union in 1959 contradicted any real notion of there being a gap of any sort when it came to strategic capabilities in the nuclear arena. Senator Kennedy continued to blast the Eisenhower administration on the issue of the missile gap, charging that Eisenhower just didn't seem to grasp the gravity of the situation. In testimony before the Senate committee on which Kennedy sat, the chair of the Joint Chiefs of Staff, General Nathan Twining, became exasperated when continuously confronted with the idea of a missile gap. "Let's don't pick one system and call it a 'gap,'" Twining responded. He pointed out that in the face of a Soviet ICBM threat, the United States could respond with IRBMs based in Europe, which were more numerous and more accurate than anything the Soviets had, not to mention a sizable SAC bomber fleet based around the periphery of the Soviet Union. "We are surrounding them," he noted. "The only thing they can hit us with is the ICBM in the missile field, and we can hit them with all kinds of missiles."[38]

While Eisenhower pursued disarmament through diplomacy, he also recognized the need to bring the growing American nuclear arsenal under control through a coordinated nuclear targeting strategy to be used in case of a nuclear war. The fact that the United States had "all kinds of missiles," as General Twining put it, to hit the Soviet Union with dictated that there be some sort of coordinated approach to actually targeting these missiles. The plan approved by Eisenhower in August 1959 targeted a mix of industrial and urban centers, including the totality of the known Soviet nuclear infrastructure, especially all offensive weapons. This plan was designed to provide a 75 percent assurance that at least one nuclear weapon would detonate on each designated target. President Eisenhower made SAC the central authority for developing a nuclear target list. But when SAC tried, in August 1960, to implement its first integrated nuclear target plan, it ran into opposition from the U.S. Navy. Through its *Polaris* submarine-launched ballistic missile (SLBM) program, the Navy had assumed an important second strike retaliatory mission for which it wanted a larger degree of flexibility in planning and executing. President Eisenhower rejected the Navy's arguments and directed the secretary of defense to establish a Joint Strategic Planning Staff (JSPS) under the direction of SAC. By the end of 1960, the JSPS had developed what became known as the "Single Integrated Operational Plan," or SIOP. Even though he was satisfied with the consolidation of nuclear strike planning, President Eisenhower was dismayed at the level of nuclear overkill that existed in the SIOP, with the United States having far more nuclear weapons than targets.[39]

By 1960, time was running out on the *Atlas* missile program. Increased costs and overall system complexity made the *Atlas* ICBM, once embraced as the savior of the United States in the post-*Sputnik* era, seem more like a lemon. The *Titan* missile, its liquid-fuel competitor, was proving to be a more robust, simpler design, and the *Minuteman* missile, once theory, was rapidly becoming reality. The *Atlas*'s supporters in Congress, led by Senator Symington, attempted to parlay concerns about a Soviet missile advantage into a reason to provide even more funding for the beleaguered missile. Symington was so persistent on this point that he lost all objectivity on the matter. After one particularly aggressive pitch to both the president and the secretary of defense, which was turned down by both, Symington first leaked classified information to the press that argued for the existence of a missile gap with the Soviets, and then noted that this gap could be rapidly closed if the U.S. Air Force would simply buy more *Atlas* missiles.[40]

This brazen manipulation of U.S. national security in order to promote the economic well-being of a defense contractor by a U.S. senator was a wake-up call to President Eisenhower. At the end of his presidency, Eisenhower delivered one of the most memorable, and insightful, speeches of his term in office. His farewell address to the nation, delivered on January 17, 1961, has become better known as the "military-industrial complex" speech. President Eisenhower had originally planned to speak about the military-industrial-congressional complex, but politics interceded in the form of congressional objection, and the reference to the legislative branch of government was removed. But there can be no doubt as to the original intent, and therefore target, of his speech. And given the role played by Convair and Senator Stuart Symington in pushing the so-called missile gap, and with it the development and acquisition of the *Atlas* missile (and the bomber gap and the B-58 "Hustler" before that), the models Eisenhower drew on while drafting his speech are clear and by no means complimentary.

"Disarmament," Eisenhower noted, "with mutual honor and confidence, is a continuing imperative. Together we must learn how to compose differences, not with arms, but with intellect and decent purpose. Because this need is so sharp and apparent I confess that I lay down my official responsibilities in this field with a definite sense of disappointment." Issues such as the proliferation of nuclear-armed weapons and a SIOP to target them weighed heavily on the president. "As one who has witnessed the horror and the lingering sadness of war—as one who knows that another war could utterly destroy this civilization which has been so slowly and painfully built over thousands of years—I wish I could say tonight that a lasting peace is in sight."[41]

Dwight Eisenhower was unable to provide the American people with such assurance, noting that the reality of the present situation brought with it a "conjunction of an immense military establishment and a large arms industry" that was "new in the American experience." Eisenhower recognized the need for this situation but cautioned against its implications, which threatened the "very structure of our society."

In a statement that could have been aimed directly at Convair and Senator Symington, Eisenhower declared, "In the councils of government, we must guard against the acquisition of unwarranted influence, whether sought or unsought, by the military-industrial complex. The potential for the disastrous rise of misplaced power exists and will persist . . . we must never let the weight of this combination endanger our liberties or democratic processes. We should take nothing for granted. Only an alert and knowledgeable citizenry can compel the proper meshing of the huge industrial and military machinery of defense with our peaceful methods and goals, so that security and liberty may prosper together."

As President Eisenhower left office, the collective paranoia of the American people on all matters relating to the Soviet Union was fueled by the greed and ignorance of the military-industrial-congressional complex that hyped the Soviet threat at every opportunity, regardless of the lack of any supporting facts. In America in 1961, the citizenry was not overtly alert and knowledgeable. The only thing that could comfort Eisenhower was that the mechanics of nuclear war were perhaps too unwieldy, the weapons too complex and unreliable, for an all-out nuclear war to be a genuine threat. This, too, was about to change.

As 1960 came to a close, the first *Minuteman* missile was transported to Cape Canaveral, Florida, where it was to be flight-tested. Three solid-fuel stages were stacked, one on top of the other, each filled with a rubber-like mixture of solid fuel and oxidizer. A conical-shaped reentry vehicle, designed to carry a thermonuclear warhead, was mounted on top. At 11:00 AM on February 1, 1961, the *Minuteman* was launched. Unlike the slow, deliberate launch of the liquid-fueled *Atlas* or *Titan*, the *Minuteman* missile ignited with a loud bang before shooting into the sky like an arrow.

All stages performed flawlessly, and the inert warhead impacted in its designated target zone in the Atlantic Ocean, twenty-five minutes after lift-off, some 4,600 miles away. An engineer who witnessed the launch provided the most telling comment: "Brother," he said, "there goes the missile gap."[42]

CHAPTER 5

SIOP VERSUS "BIG IVAN"

It had been sixteen years since John McCloy cautioned against the use of the atomic bomb on Japanese cities. Since that time, the man known as the "Chairman of the Establishment" had served in a variety of positions, in and out of government, including a tour of duty as the president of the World Bank (1947–1949) and as the high commissioner for Germany (1949–1952). The Eisenhower years found McCloy engaged in a wide range of private and government-related service, from chair of Chase Bank, to chair of the Council for Foreign Relations, to service on a number of government panels. Following his election in November 1960, John F. Kennedy approached McCloy to become his special advisor for arms control, a position McCloy accepted.[1]

On January 22, 1961, McCloy convened a group of specialists in the field of arms control for a meeting at the prestigious Metropolitan Club in Washington, DC, to discuss how the executive branch of the government should be organized in relation to arms control and disarmament and where specifically this function should reside. The issue of a formal arms control and disarmament organization resident within the U.S. government was a matter that Kennedy had championed during his time in the Senate and that he, through McCloy, would continue to focus on. The Metropolitan Club meeting was designed to bring a focus to McCloy's arms control mission, with an emphasis on operations within the executive branch.[2]

McCloy had served as an advisor on disarmament affairs to the Eisenhower administration, offering his insights into such issues as a nuclear test ban. These insights were very influential at times, such as in a meeting on April 26, 1958, when McCloy and others were able to convince Secretary of State John Foster Dulles of the wisdom of the United States engaging in a unilateral nuclear test ban. U.S. participation in this ban would serve as a means of improving its image internationally, as well as providing pressure on the Soviet Union to accept a formal treaty banning all nuclear testing.[3] McCloy was well aware of the bureaucratic obstacles to a test ban treaty, especially from the Atomic Energy Commission and the U.S. military. The moratorium on nuclear testing was still in effect as President Kennedy took office, and McCloy had to come up with a recommendation to the new president as to whether the United States should continue the moratorium or pull out and resume nuclear testing.

From among those who attended the Metropolitan Club meeting, John McCloy assembled a panel of experts, chaired by the veteran negotiator and technical expert, James Fisk. Named the Fisk Panel, these experts studied the technical issues pertaining to any nuclear test ban and concluded that nuclear weapons development would be hindered by a ban. Yet this must be appraised in relation to other efforts to reduce the likelihood of war and to promote peace. A similar conclusion had been made by the Eisenhower administration when it agreed to implement the unilateral moratorium on nuclear testing.[4]

McCloy wasn't the only high-level personality drawn back into government service on behalf of John Kennedy. A 1922 graduate of West Point, Maxwell Taylor had gained fame as a paratrooper commander during World War II, first with the 82nd Airborne Division in Italy, and later as the commanding officer of the 101st Airborne Division, with whom he parachuted into Normandy in the early hours of June 6, 1944. He commanded U.S. forces in Berlin in postwar Germany and later led the U.S. 8th Army during the Korean War. No one could doubt his courage under fire, but perhaps his bravest act occurred in 1959. At that time U.S. Army chief of staff, General Taylor retired from service in protest over the refusal of the Eisenhower administration to consider adopting a "flexible response" posture rather than the inflexible (and unworkable, in Taylor's opinion) policy of Massive Retaliation.[5]

General Taylor felt that an overreliance on nuclear weapons had created a single-dimensional military incapable of carrying out missions other than full-scale nuclear warfare. He had pushed the Eisenhower military to fund a more adaptable Army, one capable of fighting—and winning—smaller, nonnuclear conflicts, but to no avail. Not content with simply walking away from a fight, Taylor articulated his argument in a book, *The Uncertain Trumpet*, which was published in 1960 to critical acclaim.[6] During the presidential election of 1960, John Kennedy had frequently referred to Taylor, his book, and the concept of flexible response when criticizing the policies of the Eisenhower administration. Shortly after being sworn in as president, Kennedy asked Taylor if he would be interested in serving as the ambassador to France. Citing personal reasons, Taylor declined.[7]

Disappointed at Taylor's decision, President Kennedy turned his attention to the "big three" issues that he had inherited from the Eisenhower administration: the Berlin crisis (derived from Khrushchev's 1958 threat to terminate the occupation of Berlin by the United States, Great Britain, and France); the growing crisis in Laos and Vietnam; and the developing situation in Cuba, where procommunist forces under Fidel Castro had overthrown the corrupt, pro-Western dictator Fulgencio Batista in 1958. Of these three, the situation in Cuba represented the most pressing matter. Kennedy had strongly criticized Eisenhower during the election for failing to deal aggressively with Castro, accusing the president of having "lost" Cuba.[8]

Shortly after the election, CIA head Allen Dulles briefed Kennedy on an ongoing CIA effort to train and equip a force of Cuban exile fighters who would invade Cuba and remove Castro from power. Eisenhower himself, on December 6, 1960, discussed the CIA's plans for ousting Castro with the president-elect. Both Dulles and Eisenhower stressed that the final decision to oust Castro would be Kennedy's alone but that the plan was far along in development and to cancel it outright could have serious repercussions.[9]

On January 11, 1961, little more than a week before Kennedy was to be sworn in, the Joint Chiefs of Staff were briefed for the first time about the CIA's plan, as were select members of Congress. There was an immediate negative reaction from almost every quarter, military and civilian alike. But Kennedy pressed forward, concerned that he needed to show Khrushchev that his administration was not going to simply roll over in the face of communist-inspired expansionism, especially when that expansionism was occurring in the Western Hemisphere. On April 15, 1961, CIA-backed Cuban counterrevolutionaries invaded Cuba, in what has become known as the Bay of Pigs. The Cubans were quickly routed by Castro's forces, and President Kennedy, fresh into his term as America's chief executive, had a major crisis (and personal embarrassment) on his hands.

Worse, the American-backed move on Cuba resonated darkly in the cor-
ridors of the Kremlin, where Khrushchev and others were watching Washington, looking for an indication of what kind of policy track the new
American president might take concerning U.S.-Soviet relations. The
strong anticommunist bias inherent in the Bay of Pigs fiasco did not bode
well for any hopes of a cooling down of tensions.[10]

In addition to Cuba, another of Kennedy's election-time points of attack against the Eisenhower administration was the issue of the so-called
missile gap. Then-senator Kennedy had stressed repeatedly that Eisenhower had done too little to counter the threat posed by Soviet missiles.
Because at that time Kennedy lacked the security clearances necessary to
have access to official government intelligence on the subject, he was compelled to turn to nongovernmental sources of information, such as the influential Special Studies Project underwritten by the Rockefeller Brothers
Fund. The Special Studies Project had an ambitious agenda, which included clarification of "national purposes and objectives," and among its
numerous recommendations was the need for the United States to undertake a massive arms buildup to counter perceived Soviet superiority in
the post-*Sputnik* era, including in the field of ballistic missiles. The Special Studies Project was chaired by Henry Kissinger, at that time a
scholar at Harvard University, and included such notables as Edward
Teller, Dean Rusk, John Gardner, and a New York lawyer and former
undersecretary of the Air Force under President Truman named Roswell
Gilpatric.[11] Gilpatric's presence on the Rockefellers' Special Studies Project caught Kennedy's attention; he then asked him to serve in his administration as the deputy secretary of defense, under Secretary of Defense
Robert McNamara.[12]

Gilpatric was a true believer in the reality of the missile gap and had
been a key advisor to Kennedy during the 1960 election where the gap was
used to attack Eisenhower, and by extension Nixon. Shortly after Kennedy
took office, Gilpatric and McNamara visited the Air Force intelligence office to review the available intelligence, primarily derived from U-2 and
Discoverer satellite imagery, concerning Soviet ballistic missile capabilities.
The Air Force continued to maintain that the Soviets were building an extensive network of well-camouflaged missile sites. Failing to find any hard
evidence of such sites, the Air Force went to extremes, designating a
Crimean War memorial and a medieval tower as examples of potential dis-
guises used by the Soviets.[13] The U.S. Army, however, took a more realistic
approach in making its assessments, noting that the SS-6 missile could only
be moved by railcars or large vehicles, traveling on specially constructed

military highways. The *Discoverer* satellites had imaged the majority of the Soviet rail and highway network, and no evidence had been found to substantiate any claim of a massive Soviet buildup in ballistic missile launch capability.[14]

All doubt regarding whether a missile gap existed was erased by July 1961, following two new *Discoverer* missions that had covered huge tracts of Soviet territory. Based on this imagery, the new intelligence held that Soviet ICBM strength was between 10 and 25 launchers, and it projected a force of between 75 and 125 operational ICBM launchers by 1963.[15] But even the *Discoverer* imagery could be misinterpreted. Sensitive intelligence provided by a Russian spy, Oleg Penkovsky, who was working jointly for British intelligence and the CIA, detailed the decision by Soviet authorities not to push forward with the SS-6 as a mainstream ICBM. Far from the ten to twenty-five launchers U.S. intelligence assessed as being operational in 1961, the reality was that the Soviets only had four.[16]

With the missile gap now discredited, McNamara wrestled with the issue of a viable national nuclear strategy. Kennedy was a proponent of Maxwell Taylor's flexible response theory, as was McNamara. The outgoing Eisenhower administration believed that it had positioned the United States well with regard to its ability to wage a limited war while preserving nuclear deterrence. The cornerstone of the Eisenhower deterrence package was a 1962 budget that funded the acquisition of 540 *Minuteman* missiles by 1964, together with 19 *Polaris* submarines.[17] However, the incoming Kennedy administration was not about to embrace an Eisenhower-era force structure and national strategy that had been called into question so vehemently during the 1960 presidential election.

The Kennedy national security transition team, headed by Paul Nitze (the author of NSC-68 who later became the assistant secretary of defense for International Security Affairs under Robert McNamara), operated from a particular premise. This premise held that the United States needed to reach a balance between attempting to follow "a politically meaningful 'win' capability in general war versus the creation of a secure retaliatory capability," concluding that "in addition to a secure deterrent posture, some mixture of possible 'win' capabilities is called for."[18] Massive Retaliation, and all that it entailed in terms of an inflexible nuclear response, was philosophically dead. The problem was that, in terms of U.S. nuclear strategy, Massive Retaliation was cemented in the Pentagon's war plans.

On February 4, 1961, McNamara was briefed by SAC on SIOP-62, the nuclear war plan. McNamara immediately recognized that there was a huge disconnect between the kind of flexibility he wanted to be able to provide the president in a time of grave crisis if it came to the utilization of nuclear weapons and the blunt instrument he was being briefed on. Any European crisis that resulted in a Soviet military attack would automatically trigger an American nuclear response involving more than 1,450 nuclear bombs targeting 654 targets in the Soviet Union, China, and Eastern Europe. This would occur even if the Soviets did not use nuclear weapons.

If the United States received information about a pending Soviet nuclear attack, it would then unleash a preemptive nuclear strike involving 3,423 nuclear weapons. It was estimated that the U.S. nuclear attack would kill around 285 million Soviets and Chinese and another 100 million Eastern Europeans. Another 100 million people in allied NATO nations would likely die, as would an additional 100 million neutral citizens around the world, all from radiation spread by the fallout from these attacks. Given the need to assure that a given target was hit, redundancy was built into the SIOP-62 plan, which had several nuclear weapons, in some instances between six and ten, assigned to each target. In short, the United States was committed to a plan of global destruction that could occur based simply on a perception of Soviet intent or out of a limited, nonnuclear conflict.[19]

McNamara was struggling to come to grips with the horrific reality of SIOP-62. Disappointed with both SAC and the Joint Chiefs for what he viewed as an unrealistic and unimaginative national nuclear war strategy, McNamara turned to a group of military outsiders for advice. One of the first people McNamara interviewed for his staff was an economist named Charles Hitch, formerly an Oxford University professor and since 1948 a senior analyst at RAND. In 1960 Hitch had written a book, *The Economics of Defense in the Nuclear Age*, that had attracted the interest of McNamara, who offered Hitch the position of assistant secretary of defense, serving as the comptroller.[20]

Hitch in turn created a new department, the Office of Systems Analysis, which he began to staff with a new generation of thinkers and analysts. The members of this office would seek to radically transform the American military bureaucracy, instilling business practices and management styles. Not surprising, Hitch turned to RAND as a vehicle to supply many of his new generation of systems analysts. To head the new office, Hitch selected a Rhodes scholar and MIT PhD named Alain Enthoven. While at RAND, Enthoven had worked very closely with Albert Wohlstetter in preparing the SAC basing study. Another MIT/Rhodes scholar/RAND alumnus was Henry Rowen, who was brought in as the deputy assistant secretary of defense for policy planning and national security affairs.

Rowen, like Enthoven, was an acolyte of Wohlstetter. Rowen brought with him a Harvard graduate and former U.S. Marines officer, Daniel Ellsberg. Collectively, these individuals, along with other mathematicians, political scientists, economists, and physicists, became known as the "Whiz Kids."[21]

Hitch and Enthoven were aware that McNamara was not satisfied with either SIOP-62 or the state of American nuclear strategic thinking. They arranged to have a fellow RAND analyst, William Kaufmann, deliver a briefing he had prepared based upon a synthesis of the works of Bernard Brodie and Albert Wohlstetter, a strategic philosophy Kaufmann called "Counterforce." Counterforce was a moral and intellectual response to Eisenhower's Massive Retaliation. As explained by Kaufmann, Counterforce replaced the all-out aspect of Massive Retaliation as manifested in SIOP-62 with a more discriminatory approach that allowed American leaders to allocate nuclear weapons, and to decide how they were targeted, to a given situation.[22]

The first thing Counterforce did was take civilian population centers off the target list—in short, creating what has become known as the No Cities strategy. Under Counterforce, the United States would maintain a highly survivable nuclear force that was capable of riding out a preemptive nuclear attack and then retaliating in a discriminatory fashion against an enemy's remaining nuclear strike capability and, if directed to do so, their military, industrial, and governmental centers. These attacks would be carried out primarily by ICBMs and a strategic bomber force. The U.S. Navy, with its less-accurate *Polaris* missiles, would be kept in reserve as a city-killing force in case the enemy began using nuclear weapons against American population centers. A key aspect to this strategy was the concept of being able to control the scope of the nuclear exchange so that the situation did not automatically result in the assured destruction of all involved.

McNamara embraced Kaufmann's Counterforce presentation and quickly established a list of priorities, the top three of which were a review of America's strategic nuclear war plans, a similar review of America's nonnuclear war fighting capabilities, and a review of America's tactical nuclear capabilities. To handle priority item number one, McNamara directed Rowen, who in turn tasked Ellsberg with the job of preparing a draft policy memorandum. The memo sought to revise the assumptions that influenced basic national security policy of the United States and to incorporate Kaufmann's Counterforce concepts. Ellsberg formalized Kaufman's briefing into a draft plan for the creation of a completely new SIOP, one that did not target enemy civilian population centers—focusing

instead on enemy nuclear weapons—and that maintained a significant reserve nuclear strike capability. This plan allowed for continued nuclear attacks against a wide range of target options. Ellsberg's draft was finished
by May 1961 and was submitted to the Joint Chiefs of Staff for use in
preparing SIOP-63.[23]

Another key aspect to Kaufmann's philosophy was to stress a nonnuclear solution to the problem of the large Soviet and Warsaw Pact forces
deployed opposite NATO forces. The standard scenario that led to a nuclear exchange between the United States and the Soviet Union started
with a Soviet/Warsaw Pact invasion of Western Europe, which in turn
would trigger a series of nuclear escalations because the NATO forces
lacked the strength to blunt the attack conventionally. The use of nuclear
weapons by NATO would lead to an all-out nuclear exchange between
the United States and the Soviet Union. Kaufmann held that the estimates
of Soviet/Warsaw Pact conventional capabilities were exaggerated and
that NATO and the United States should come up with a means to deal
with the Soviet/Warsaw Pact conventional forces in a nonnuclear manner.
McNamara was attracted to this concept because it melded perfectly with
his notion of flexible response and with it, less reliance upon nuclear
weapons and more reliance on America's conventional power.[24]

On the issue of a Counterforce-like strategy, McNamara had an ally in
the form of Maxwell Taylor. Recalled from retirement in April 1961 in the
aftermath of the CIA fiasco in Cuba, Taylor was appointed by President
Kennedy to head the Cuba Study Group, tasked with performing a post-
mortem on the Bay of Pigs operation. For the next six weeks, Taylor did
just that, producing a report that took the CIA and the U.S. military to
task for a lack of planning, coordination, and imagination. Kennedy was
so impressed with Taylor's report that he ordered the general back on active duty and appointed him to be the special representative for Military
Affairs, an unprecedented action and position that undercut the authority
and influence of the chair of the Joint Chiefs of Staff, who at that time was
Air Force General Lyman Lemnitzer.[25]

Under Eisenhower's New Look philosophy, the U.S. Army and NATO
were increasingly reliant on nuclear weapons as the tool of choice to stop
any Soviet/Warsaw Pact incursion into Western Europe. The U.S. Army
was simply not trained or equipped to fight and win a conventional war
in Europe. In contrast, the U.S. Army had a wide variety of tactical nuclear
weapons available to both it and NATO. U.S. Air Force units stationed
in Europe would also be able to unleash overwhelming nuclear firepower,
so much so that U.S. and NATO planners were confident that they could

stop a full forty-division attack by the Soviet and Warsaw Pact forces, even if they themselves made use of nuclear weapons. The problem was, as Taylor understood, once tactical nuclear weapons were used, there was nothing to stop the outbreak of general nuclear war. The U.S. Army needed to be retrained and reequipped to fight, sustain, and prevail in a conventional war in Europe, at least to stand toe-to-toe with the Soviets in a nonnuclear battle long enough for politicians on both sides to come to their senses and stop the fighting before an all-out nuclear war occurred.

In May 1961, no single location exemplified the dangers coming from Europe than the former capital of Hitler's Germany, Berlin. Jointly occupied by the four victorious allied powers (the United States, Great Britain, France, and the Soviet Union), Berlin was a living reminder not only of the unresolved issues held over from the end of the Second World War (for instance, a divided Germany, and no formal peace treaty between the four allied powers and Germany), but also of the heightened tensions between East and West brought on by the Cold War. If there was a danger of East-West conflict in Europe, its hair trigger was Berlin.

The reconciliation of West Germany with France, and the inclusion of West Germany into NATO, meant that the Soviet goal of a unified, neutral, and largely disarmed Germany was becoming a distant dream. The Soviet premier, Nikita Khrushchev, was not worried about West Germany as a military threat—the size of the Soviet Army and its possession of nuclear weapons effectively neutralized that possibility—but rather its economic strength. With more and more East Germans looking to West Germany for economic salvation, Khrushchev (and his communist allies in the East German government) feared a popular uprising that would present the Soviet Union with a *fait accompli*. Stabilizing East Germany became Khrushchev's number one priority.

In March 1961, at a meeting of Warsaw Pact nations, Khrushchev stated that he would conclude a separate peace treaty with East Germany if some sort of general settlement with the Western powers could not be reached.[26] Khrushchev hoped that he would be able to convince President Kennedy of the importance of the German question during their summit in Vienna on June 3, 1961. Immediately after his inauguration, Kennedy had been warned by Secretary of State Dean Rusk that Khrushchev would raise the Berlin issue in the near future. The U.S. ambassador to Moscow, Llewellyn Thompson, likewise warned Kennedy prior to the Vienna summit that Khrushchev would sign a separate peace treaty unless the United States came up with an acceptable alternative. Thompson, in a message written on May 27, 1961, cautioned Kennedy that, given Khrushchev's personal commitment to the issue of a peace treaty with Germany, if the United States continued its negative posture, "the chances of war or ignominious Western retreat are 50–50."[27]

Kennedy arrived in Vienna fresh from an official state visit to Paris, where French president Charles de Gaulle stated bluntly that the French would not, under any circumstances, accept a Soviet peace treaty with East Germany. When Kennedy met Khrushchev, the American president raised the issue of miscalculations, comparing the situation concerning Berlin then to the situation that existed in Europe in August 1914, warning that a simple spark could set off the powder keg of tension that currently existed. Khrushchev exploded, raising his voice at Kennedy, repeating the word "miscalculation" over and over. Khrushchev accused Kennedy of threatening him. The Soviet premier made it clear that he intended to sign a peace treaty with East Germany, which would result in East Germany blocking off Western access to Berlin via road or rail, before the year ended. "I want peace," Khrushchev said, "but if you want war, that's your problem."[28]

Khrushchev pressed his point, declaring that he would sign the peace treaty in December 1961 unless the United States endorsed an interim agreement. If this meant armed conflict, so be it: "Force will be met by force," the Soviet premier bluntly said. Kennedy refused to blink, responding to Khrushchev's threats, "Then, Mr. Chairman, there will be a war. It will be a cold, long winter."[29] The next day, after more discussion, Khrushchev handed Kennedy an ultimatum in the form of a memorandum, in which the goals of the Soviet Union regarding East Germany were spelled out in no uncertain terms. His tough rhetoric aside, the young American president was shaken to the core by the Vienna summit. Kennedy, in discussions with aides following the Vienna summit, believed that it represented a grave moral lapse to threaten the lives of millions of Americans simply to preserve Western access to West Berlin.[30]

For his part, Khrushchev continued to speak aggressively about a peace treaty with Germany and warned that anyone who opposed the consequences of this action (i.e., East Germany's closing down all road, rail, and air access into and out of Berlin) would receive a "proper rebuff."[31] Western saber-rattling, Khrushchev maintained, would no longer serve as a deterrent to the Soviet Union. On June 26, 1961, Khrushchev announced that the Soviet Union had sufficient military strength to enforce a German peace treaty. This reality was pounded home with typical bluntness when Khrushchev, at a Kremlin reception on July 2, 1961, told the British ambassador to the Soviet Union that "only six hydrogen bombs would be quite enough to annihilate the British Isles, and nine would take care of France."[32]

On February 17, 1961, Nikita Khrushchev wrote a letter to West German chancellor Konrad Adenauer, inviting the West Germans to join the four allied powers at the conference table to discuss the future of Germany. Adenauer, in close discussions with France's President de Gaulle, decided against participation because doing so would have implied that West Germany and the allies were willing to negotiate something away.[33] This was not the case from the standpoint of Great Britain and the United States, both leaning toward negotiations as a means of reducing East-West tensions.

Recognizing a growing split in the Western alliance, Kennedy turned to Dean Acheson (the former secretary of state under President Truman) to form an ad hoc advisory group. This group, which became known as the Acheson Review Group, was mandated to deal exclusively with the matter of Berlin. Acheson's advice to Kennedy was simple: do not negotiate with the Soviets, and be prepared to respond militarily to any Soviet efforts to block access on the part of the Western allies to Berlin. Acheson supported McNamara's call for increased conventional military forces but knew, as did McNamara, that the combined conventional forces of NATO were not capable of standing up to the military might of the Soviet Union. It was time, Acheson advised, for the president to think about what a Soviet military move against Berlin would mean to the Western alliance and to come to grips with the reality that the only force capable of stopping the Soviets was America's nuclear arsenal. Furthermore, Acheson noted, the only way this nuclear arsenal would work in deterring Soviet aggression against Berlin would be for the Soviets to be convinced that any move on Berlin would result in a state of general war with the United States, including the full use of America's nuclear arsenal.[34]

Arthur Schlesinger Jr., a special assistant to the president, responded afterward with a memo warning the president that Acheson's advice "hinges on our willingness to face nuclear war. But this option is undefined. Before you are asked to make the decision to go to nuclear war, you are entitled to know concretely what nuclear war is likely to mean. The Pentagon should be required to make an analysis of the possible levels and implications of nuclear warfare and the possible gradations of our own nuclear response."[35]

A general war with the Soviet Union meant the implementation of SIOP-62, with all of its consequences. At Harvard University, Henry Kissinger, who also consulted part-time for the National Security Council, reviewed the Acheson memorandum. He then followed up with a communication of his own to McGeorge Bundy, President Kennedy's national security advisor and a former political science professor at Harvard, where he was a close associate and friend of Kissinger. Kissinger warned Bundy that, in light of the growing tensions, the Kennedy administration should precisely define America's nuclear options before circumstances dictated a solution no one wanted. Kissinger was in contact with Henry Rowen, the deputy assistant secretary of defense, and Carl Kaysen, a former Harvard professor who was a deputy to Bundy at the National Security Council.[36]

Rowen had been communicating with William Kaufmann, still at RAND, regarding Kaufmann's analysis of the new *Discoverer* imagery of the Soviet Union, which was exposing not only the fallacies of the so-called bomber and missile gaps but also the reality that the Soviet Union was very much a paper tiger with an extremely small ICBM capability and an air defense network that could be penetrated at will by low-flying B-52 bombers. Kaufmann, a proponent of the nuclear Counterforce theory, now saw an opportunity for something new: a nuclear first strike that had a great chance of taking out the Soviet Union's entire strategic nuclear arsenal through a relatively limited nuclear attack, spearheaded by American bombers and leaving sufficient nuclear strike capacity in the form of ICBMs, uncommitted bombers, and *Polaris* submarines to finish off the Soviet Union should it press forward with aggression in Europe. Bundy thought enough of the idea that he recommended to President Kennedy that thought be given to developing a graduated program of nuclear weapon utilization as opposed to the all-or-nothing approach of SIOP-62.[37]

The last thing Kennedy wanted was to fight a war with the Soviet Union over the issue of Berlin. He agreed with Acheson that resolve needed to be demonstrated in the face of Khrushchev's threats, but he also recognized the importance of not backing Khrushchev into a corner. Preferring a war of nerves to a war of shooting, President Kennedy dramatically raised the stakes on Berlin, delivering a nationally televised address on July 25, 1961, when he attempted to walk the fine line that existed between these two positions. Kennedy noted that the United States needed "to have a wider choice than humiliation or all-out nuclear action," and as such proposed that Congress authorize nearly $3.25 billion in additional appropriations for the U.S. military. This would increase the Army's strength from 875,000 to some 1 million men, as well as increase the size of the Navy and Air Force as well. To meet these goals, Kennedy asked Congress to double and triple the draft calls in the coming months and to call to active duty certain reserve units. Recognizing "the possibilities of nuclear war in the missile age," Kennedy indicated he was pressing ahead aggressively on the issue of civil defense.[38]

Kennedy did not need to wait long for an official Soviet response. John McCloy, his special advisor for arms control and disarmament, happened to be in Moscow, working with his Soviet counterpart, Valeryan Zorin, on the framework for a larger disarmament agreement between the United States and the Soviet Union. (In the spring of 1961, Adlai Stevenson and his Soviet counterpart, Andrei Gromyko, had agreed that there should be an "exchange of views" between the United States and the Soviet Union in order to create the conditions for a renewal of disarmament negotiations. It was decided that John McCloy would travel to Moscow in the middle of July 1961 for this purpose.) McCloy and Zorin spent two weeks haggling back and forth on the issue of disarmament, with both eventually agreeing to consider the formulation of a basic statement of disarmament principles. With this achievement in hand, McCloy was preparing to return home when he was summoned by Nikita Khrushchev to his personal dacha in Pitsunda, in the Abkhazia region of Soviet Georgia.

McCloy arrived on July 25, the day of Kennedy's speech. Given the time difference, Kennedy had yet to deliver his message by the time the day ended, so the first day of the McCloy-Khrushchev meetings was spent on leisurely walks, informal discussions, and a swim in both Khrushchev's pool and the Black Sea. The next morning, the atmosphere changed dramatically. "The storm broke," McCloy subsequently reported to Kennedy.[39] Khrushchev bluntly stated that if East Germany were to exercise its right to control its borders, and if the Western allies attempted to force their way through, then war, thermonuclear war, would certainly break out. Khrushchev informed McCloy that the Soviet Union had the ability to deliver a hundred-megaton super bomb onto U.S. territory (indeed, Khrushchev's weapons designers had assembled such a terrible weapon, nicknamed "Big Ivan").[40]

Khrushchev was dismissive of McCloy's and Zorin's disarmament talks, noting that it seemed pointless to discuss disarmament at a time when Kennedy, through his speech, had "declared war on us and set down his conditions." McCloy provided an alternative explanation of Kennedy's speech, saying that instead of it being a declaration of war, it was a declaration of his readiness to negotiate a settlement. Khrushchev brushed this explanation aside, noting that the Americans seemed intent on trying to intimidate the Soviets. Khrushchev stated that although the Soviet Union would never start a war, nor would it back down. In very blunt language, Khrushchev stated that if President Kennedy started a war, then "he would probably become the last president of the United States of America." Khrushchev and McCloy took a break, during which time Khrushchev seemed to calm down. Certainly, he told McCloy, President Kennedy was too reasonable to actually fight for Berlin. Couldn't this problem be worked out between sensible people? McCloy returned to Moscow, where he fired off a cable to the president that reported his meetings with Khrushchev. Kennedy recalled McCloy to Washington, where everyone anxiously awaited the further unfolding of this drama.[41]

On July 27, 1961, the president convened a meeting of his top advisors, where the issues of how best to move forward on the issue of disarmament and a nuclear test ban were discussed. The president was actively considering ordering the resumption of nuclear testing and had requested that a study on the technical and scientific issues related to the resumption of testing be prepared. Wolfgang Panofsky, a physicist from Stanford University, authored a report in which he stated that the United States would retain a degree of technological superiority in nuclear weapons for some time even without tests. Panofsky could not offer an opinion on whether or not the Soviets were cheating on the test moratorium and testing in secret. Panofsky believed that any decision to resume testing was political, not technical, and therefore could only be answered by those who were involved in deliberations of that sort. Kennedy was having a hard time holding off the military and the Atomic Energy Commission on the issue of testing, but he believed strongly that the United States would suffer a huge blow in terms of negative world opinion if it proceeded with nuclear testing without at least one more concerted effort at achieving a test ban treaty.[42]

The president dispatched his disarmament negotiator, Arthur Dean, to Geneva in late August to spend a week trying to get meaningful Soviet movement in the way of a test ban agreement. Failing this, Kennedy would then personally address the United Nations General Assembly on the issue of disarmament, a speech designed more for softening the blow yet to come, namely the resumption of nuclear testing by the United States sometime in early 1962. Dean's mission was little more than diplomatic and political cover for a larger drive toward resuming the perfection of the nuclear bomb. Within a few days of the discussion of the Panofsky report, the Joint Chiefs of Staff were recommending moving forward with nuclear testing. Kennedy knew he had a major political problem, balancing the operational need to resume testing in the near future with the political requirement not to alienate the United Nations in the process.[43]

Khrushchev was likewise facing a difficult situation. At a Political Consultative Committee meeting held in Moscow at the end of March 1961,

the Soviet leadership recognized the need to link the increasingly deteriorating crisis surrounding Berlin with a military strategy designed to deal with the consequences of the crisis spinning out of control. If that happened, it would bring a state of war between NATO and the Warsaw Pact, and the United States and the Soviet Union. Ever since the end of the Second World War, the United States and its Western allies had worried about a perceived Soviet superiority in conventional ground forces in Europe. Much of NATO's military planning was based upon fears of a Soviet military thrust into Europe, and NATO devised strategies based upon the use of nuclear weapons to neutralize the specter of an omniscient Soviet ground army.[44]

But the reality was that the Soviet military, and the armed forces of its Warsaw Pact allies, was not nearly as powerful as NATO and the United States feared. Soviet military planners assumed that a decisive East-West conflict would be global in nature and would involve the massive use of nuclear weapons in its initial phases. The Soviets feared a preemptive nuclear attack by NATO forces that would neutralize Soviet ground forces. They therefore recognized that in order to adjust to this threat model, the Soviet Army (as well as the ground forces of the Warsaw Pact) would need not only to be organized and equipped to operate in a nuclear environment but also to rapidly go on the offensive in response to any NATO nuclear attack and to rapidly advance into NATO-held territory to destroy NATO's nuclear and conventional military capability.

Rather than ride out a preemptive nuclear attack, the Soviets would take the battle to NATO. New Soviet doctrine called for general nuclear war between the East and West in case of a war with NATO. A five-year plan was drawn up that called for an unprecedented expansion of Soviet and Warsaw Pact conventional military power. For the Soviets, there would be no "limited response." If a war broke out between the Soviet Union and the United States, the Soviets planned to be able to fight, and win, a large-scale combined nuclear and conventional war. But this ability was projected to only come online in 1965. Until then, the Soviet Union viewed itself as being in a position of strategic inferiority, and as such, vulnerable to Western aggression. Much of what drove Khrushchev's actions and words throughout the Berlin crisis of 1961 was a need to disguise the true state of affairs when it came to Soviet strategic military capabilities.[45]

On August 3, 1961, at an emergency meeting of the Warsaw Pact held in Moscow, Khrushchev gave a complete report of his dealings with McCloy in Pitsunda, as well as an assessment of where he stood on the issue of Berlin. Walter Ulbricht, the Communist Party leader of East Germany, started off the substantive portion of the meeting by demanding a consummation of the peace treaty, as well as an agreement about the Warsaw Pact's support of East Germany's comprehensive efforts to stem the flow of refugees into the West. Ulbricht stated that he intended to restrict all air traffic to set up a barrier sealing off West Berlin from the rest of the world. This is the first time Ulbricht had spoken openly about East Germany's plans to build a wall around West Berlin.

Khrushchev was next to speak. The Soviet premier stated that he would conclude a peace treaty with East Germany but that there was no rush. Now was not the time for decisive conflict, Khrushchev said. No one wanted war. Khrushchev indicated that there needed to be a cooling down period before relations between the United States and the Soviet Union could improve. Khrushchev gave the green light for Ulbricht to build his wall around West Berlin but for nothing more.[46]

Though behind the scenes the Soviet premier was the epitome of caution, his public face projected something completely different. On August 7, 1961, Khrushchev appeared on television to announce yet another Soviet victory in space: the successful orbiting of the Earth (seventeen times, in fact) by cosmonaut Gherman Titov. (Yuri Gagarin, back on April 12, 1961, had become the first man in space when he successfully completed one Earth orbit.) But Khrushchev had other achievements to announce as well. Having told the secret meeting of Warsaw Pact leaders about his meeting and conversations with John McCloy, Khrushchev now made similar pronouncements to the world, stating that the Soviet Union had enough hydrogen bombs to target every American military base in the world and that it had developed a superbomb capable of turning Germany into "dust" (a reference to Big Ivan). Khrushchev again reiterated his call for a roundtable discussion on the issue of Berlin between the Soviet Union and the three allied powers.[47]

At midnight on August 12, 1961, East Germany made its move. By day's end, West Berlin had been completely sealed off from the rest of the world, at first through the use of temporary barricades and barbed wire and then, systematically, through the installation of a massive concrete wall. These barriers, however, were used only to stop civilian traffic. U.S. and Allied military convoys could still transit to and from West Berlin. When it became clear that the East Germans were not shutting down either ground or air access to West Berlin for the Western allies, Secretary of State Rusk expressed great relief, noting that the matter seemed to be a local problem between East Germans and West Germans. The next day Rusk instructed George Kennan, by this time serving as the U.S. ambassador in Yugoslavia, to get in touch with his Soviet counterpart and inform him that the U.S. government wanted a peaceful resolution to the Berlin crisis. On August 19, 1961, Vice President Lyndon Johnson arrived in Berlin, where he informed the West Berliners of President Kennedy's intent to reinforce the American garrison and of the American commitment to defend West Berlin. Though his words were rousing and lifted the spirits of the West Berliners, what was more important was what went unsaid: that the United States formally condoned the division of East and West Berlin and with it, East and West Germany.[48]

Kennedy's arms control envoy, John McCloy, was engaged in frantic negotiations in New York and in the Soviet Union with Zorin over an agreement on a disarmament plan. During a visit to Sochi, McCloy was once again summoned to Pitsunda to meet with Khrushchev, who reiterated his position that there need not be a war over Berlin if both sides were open to meaningful negotiations. Khrushchev hinted that he was under heavy pressure from the Soviet military to resume nuclear testing, especially with regard to the giant 100-megaton bomb, which the Soviets viewed as the weapon of choice when dealing with American missile complexes. Such a weapon was needed by the Soviet Union, Khrushchev told McCloy, and would require numerous tests to prepare and perfect. Most Americans, including McCloy, brushed off Khrushchev's comments as simply continued bluster.[49]

But Khrushchev wasn't simply making noise. On July 10, 1961, the Soviet premier called together his top nuclear weapons scientists and told them that they must prepare for a resumption of nuclear testing. The tests had no technical justification but instead were politically motivated, a Soviet response to a deteriorating international situation. On September 1, 1961, the Soviets broke the moratorium on nuclear testing that had been in place since 1958. These tests began what was the largest nuclear test program in history, a crash program undertaken by the Soviet military to diversify and perfect its nuclear arsenal, enabling them to field nuclear weapons for both tactical and strategic use on land, in the air, underwater, or even in outer space.[50]

The Soviet resumption of testing was, in many ways, a gift for President Kennedy, who had been wrestling with the issue of resumed nuclear testing. In response to the Soviet action, Kennedy announced that the Soviet Union's decision presented a threat to the entire world by increasing "the dangers of a thermonuclear holocaust." Kennedy avoided any discussion of what the United States would do in response, noting that the present U.S. nuclear stockpile was capable of defending American interests in the free world. On September 3, 1961, Kennedy, together with Great Britain's

Prime Minister Harold Macmillan, issued a joint statement condemning the Soviet tests and called for an atmospheric test ban.[51]

Inside the Kennedy administration, the Soviet nuclear tests were widely seen as a mechanism of intimidation, designed not just for the ongoing Berlin crisis but beyond. Kennedy was still very much concerned about the court of international public opinion and was hesitant to give the Soviets any propaganda advantage by having the United States reply in kind. He was quickly dissuaded on this account by his advisors, typified by the comment of John McCloy: "World opinion? I don't believe in world opinion. The only thing that matters is power. What we have to do now is show that we are a powerful nation and not spend our time trailing after the phantom of world opinion."[52]

When John McCloy and Valeryan Zorin resumed their disarmament negotiations in September 1961, it wasn't just the venue that had changed (to New York) but also the approach. Both sides were maneuvering to win over international support in the United Nations within the context of the ongoing Berlin crisis as well as regarding the issue of nuclear testing and the general East-West ideological rift. With both the United States and the Soviet Union committed to the concept of disarmament within the framework of the United Nations, neither side wanted to give the other any political ammunition by being seen as obstructive, even if their cooperation was little more than superficial window dressing.

Disarmament was not the most politically attractive topic in Washington at that time. Cold War tensions, exacerbated by the ongoing Berlin crisis and the Soviet resumption of nuclear testing, made any discussion about disarmament appear to be a sign of national weakness, especially within the politically charged environment surrounding the executive branch. At this stage the Kennedy administration was ably assisted by the majority whip in the United States Senate, Hubert Humphrey, who backed the president's call for a major arms buildup while also calling for the creation of a formal bureaucracy dedicated to disarmament. Humphrey emphasized that presidential leadership was needed if the measure was ever to be pushed through an increasingly skeptical Congress.[53]

Despite Humphrey's assurances, Kennedy detected no great enthusiasm in Congress over the issue of disarmament. Humphrey's disarmament bill was floundering, and Kennedy was loath to throw his weight behind a losing cause. The president felt that the best political value he could extract from the disarmament issue was to use the continuing Soviet intransigence over the issue of inspections as a means to drive a wedge between the Soviet Union and the rest of the world at the United Nations. But he was cautioned against this approach by the U.S. ambassador to the UN, Adlai Stevenson, who pointed out that one cannot point an accusatory finger at the Soviets while likewise engaged in equivocation. "Your first decision, Mr. President," Stevenson advised, "must be to make sure that you yourself are genuinely for general and complete disarmament."[54]

Kennedy would need to be pushed in that direction. On September 5, 1961, Bundy's deputy, Carl Kaysen, had finally completed his review of SIOP-62, a task that grew from a July 21, 1961, NSC meeting dealing with Berlin response options. Kaysen's analysis, contained in a thirty-three-page document titled "Strategic Air Planning and Berlin," was conducted from the standpoint of adapting the SIOP to be able to carry out a more flexible nuclear response. Kaysen strongly believed that the United States should develop alternative plans that concentrated on military targets associated with eliminating the Soviet ICBM threat, including the inclusion of a first-strike option designed specifically for the Berlin crisis.[55]

On September 13, 1961, President Kennedy was briefed on SIOP-62 as it related to the Berlin Crisis. The plan had been approved in April 1961, and it targeted the Sino-Soviet Bloc as a whole entity. McNamara, who was present, had already been briefed on the plan, but this was Kennedy's first full exposure to the document. The chair of the Joint Chiefs of Staff, General Lyman Lemnitzer, went through the plan in great detail and told Kennedy that execution of SIOP-62, in his opinion, would permit the United States to prevail in a general nuclear war. He did say, however, that there was the likelihood of a few Soviet nuclear warheads slipping through American defenses and detonating over American targets. Kennedy was not pleased with what he heard from Lemnitzer. Mindful of Kennedy's unease over SIOP-62, General Taylor approached the president on September 19, 1961, with Kaysen's paper in its entirety.[56]

President Kennedy was simultaneously juggling several competing issues, all of them serious, exacerbated even further given the ongoing crisis in Berlin. Having made a decision to resume underground nuclear testing, the president was under pressure from the military and his nuclear weapons designers to authorize a renewed round of atmospheric testing deemed critical now that the Soviets had begun their own extensive program of testing. The tension surrounding a nuclear-armed superpower standoff in Europe was real. Congress was not in the mood for diplomacy or anything that hinted at a normalization of relations with the Soviet Union.

And yet, at this very time, Kennedy was about to announce one of his boldest moves in relation to disarmament. Having finally crafted an American position on comprehensive disarmament, the president wanted to keep the pressure on the Soviets in terms of international public opinion. With the able assistance of John McCloy and Hubert Humphrey, President Kennedy was able to complete two landmark agreements within the span of one month. On September 20, 1961, the same day Kennedy was meeting with his generals to discuss matters pertaining to strategic nuclear war, including the possibility of preemptive attack, McCloy and Zorin were meeting in New York, where they issued their long-awaited "Joint Statement of Agreed Principles for Disarmament Negotiations," better known as the McCloy-Zorin Agreement (or Accord).[57]

Five days after McCloy and Zorin signed into effect their agreement, President Kennedy addressed the UN General Assembly on the issue of disarmament. "Mankind must put an end to war—or war will put an end to mankind," Kennedy told the gathered diplomats and dignitaries. Disarmament, Kennedy said, must no longer be a dream, but rather had become a practical matter of life and death. Compared to the dangers of an arms race, the risks associated with disarmament were small. Building on the spirit of the McCloy-Zorin Accord, President Kennedy presented the American disarmament plan, *Freedom from War: The United States Program for General and Complete Disarmament in a Peaceful World*, and implored the United Nations that disarmament negotiations continue "without interruption until an entire program for general and complete disarmament has not only been agreed but has been actually achieved." The logical place to begin, Kennedy said, was with a test ban treaty. Kennedy concluded his speech by noting that the current generation would either be remembered for destroying the planet or for saving future generations from war. "Together we shall save our planet," he concluded, "or together we shall perish in its flames."[58]

The next day, in Washington, President Kennedy signed a law creating the United States Arms Control and Disarmament Agency (ACDA) as a bureaucratic entity working under the auspices of the secretary of state. Hubert Humphrey had delivered a statute for a "new disarmament agency." John McCloy had played no small part, both in terms of crafting the language of the act and in helping sell it to a skeptical Congress. William C. Foster, an industrialist who had served as a deputy secretary of commerce and deputy secretary of defense in the Truman administration, among many other government roles, was appointed as the first director for ACDA.[59]

Kennedy's speech before the UN General Assembly had been a great diplomatic and political success. But reality loomed in the form of an ongoing crisis concerning Berlin and the ever-present threat of a general nuclear war with the Soviet Union. On October 11, 1961, General Lemnitzer, the chair of the Joint Chiefs of Staff, sent General Taylor a memorandum that addressed SIOP-62 in relation to the Kaysen proposal on preemptive nuclear strikes. Whereas Lemnitzer acknowledged the need for greater flexibility when it came to employing America's strategic nuclear arsenal, he emphasized that SIOP-62 was the best plan available. A key factor in the lack of flexibility in the SIOP, Lemnitzer noted, was the lack of survivable forces, meaning that unless the United States used its strategic nuclear capability, it might very well lose it. Lemnitzer noted that SIOP-63, under development and which would be the first to factor in fully the new capabilities (including improved survivability) of the *Minuteman* missile, would contain important elements of flexibility. General Lemnitzer did not object to Kaysen's first-strike proposal because SIOP-62 already maintained that capability as one of its sixteen strike options. But Lemnitzer rejected any idea of a limited first-strike option, leaving President Kennedy with no choice other than the massive strikes set forth in SIOP-62 if he found himself at war with the Soviet Union.[60]

President Kennedy needed to send a signal to Khrushchev that the United States was not about to be intimidated by Soviet nuclear weapons. Kennedy authorized a speech by Deputy Secretary of Defense Roswell Gilpatric before the Business Council, an influential corporate advisory body, during its annual meeting in Hot Springs, Virginia. Gilpatric's speech was the most specific public reference by an American official up until that time not only to America's nuclear strategy, but also to America's nuclear supremacy. "The destructive power which the United States could bring to bear even after a Soviet surprise attack would be as great as—perhaps greater than—the total undamaged force which the enemy can threaten to launch against the United States in a first strike," Gilpatric declared. Kennedy's message had been delivered.[61]

Not to be outdone, in Moscow on October 17, 1961, Khrushchev convened the twenty-second Communist Party Congress. Khrushchev took advantage of this congress to again announce the existence of a giant hundred-megaton nuclear bomb (Big Ivan) as well as the intention of the Soviet Union to test the device before the month was out.[62] Consisting of three separate nuclear explosions, or stages, Big Ivan was, in fact, designed to attain a yield of a hundred megatons, hence its name. Because of fear of the radioactive fallout that such a device would generate, however, the natural uranium tamper for the third stage was replaced with lead, limiting the generation of neutrons, reducing the level of radioactive fallout, and in effect cutting Big Ivan's yield in half, to a mere fifty megatons. Weighing in at a massive twenty-seven tons, Big Ivan had to be transported to its test site onboard a specially modified TU-95 bomber where, at an altitude of approximately 34,500 feet, the bomb was released and a parachute deployed to retard its descent while the Soviet bomber made its getaway. At an altitude of some 13,000 feet, the device detonated.[63]

Khrushchev had given Kennedy his response to Gilpatric's speech. The detonation of Big Ivan was the fortieth nuclear test undertaken by the Soviets since testing resumed on September 1, 1961. These tests ranged in yields from very small (less than a kiloton) to the very large—Big Ivan's fifty-megaton yield. The tests included nuclear detonations conducted in the atmosphere, on the surface of the ground and water, underwater, underground, and even in outer space. There would be another twelve tests between October 31 and November 4, 1961. Berlin still loomed as a center of controversy. President Kennedy's efforts to contain Khrushchev had failed.

CHAPTER 6

ON THE EDGE OF
THE NUCLEAR ABYSS

The responsibility of breathing life and viability into the Arms Control and Disarmament Agency rested on the shoulders of its new director, William Chapman Foster. From the very outset of his tenure, Foster made it clear that neither he nor ACDA was expecting any sort of honeymoon period normally associated with new beginnings. Already familiar with the arms control and disarmament policy objectives of the Kennedy administration, Foster set about forming a policy study group, named the Foster Panel, to deal with the fundamental problem of heading off an arms race between the United States and the Soviet Union. One focus of the Foster Panel was to establish how many nuclear delivery vehicles represented enough — simply put, how much nuclear destruction was sufficient to enable effective deterrence to occur. Using a 50 percent level of guaranteed population annihilation as the benchmark for which nations would balk at going to war, the Foster Panel determined that a figure of 200 to 500 strategic nuclear delivery vehicles (missiles and bombers) was needed. To be on the safe side, the Foster Panel doubled the higher number and recommended to President Kennedy that he propose to the Soviets that a cap of 1,000 delivery vehicles be placed on the strategic nuclear arsenals of each nation.

Foster recognized that the United States and the Soviet Union stood on the edge of an arms race that would be economically prohibitive and,

given the heightened levels of tension between the two nations, potentially catastrophic. The Foster Panel recommendation had merit, and President Kennedy knew it. The problem was not so much getting the Soviets
to agree—there was no doubt that Khrushchev would have accepted any
solution that provided for parity between the two Cold War adversaries—
but rather the domestic opposition such a cap would generate from a Congress and Defense establishment still highly distrustful of Soviet intentions.

Secretary of Defense Robert McNamara had RAND calculate how many
nuclear warheads were needed to destroy 50 percent of the Soviet population, and the number was no more than 400, roughly what the Foster
Panel came up with. The day after Thanksgiving, 1961, Kennedy assembled his advisors at the Kennedy family retreat in Hyannis Port, where
the Foster Panel proposal was discussed. Although McNamara underscored the soundness of the proposal, he said that the Kennedy administration would be "politically murdered" by the Air Force and its supporters
in Congress—the Air Force had submitted requests for some 2,400 ICBMs.
McNamara, breaking with his military chiefs, believed he could get away
with building around 1,000 (the number favored by the Foster Panel), but
no less. Ted Sorenson, a close Kennedy advisor, warned Kennedy that
building that many missiles would lead to an arms race, but when McGeorge
Bundy labeled the Foster Panel plan "too radical," Kennedy concurred,
and the last chance to contain the buildup of American and Soviet nuclear
arsenals was missed.[1]

There was some fleeting progress in disarmament affairs on December
20, 1961, when the McCloy-Zorin Accord on General and Comprehensive
Disarmament was unanimously adopted by the United Nations General
Assembly. Capitalizing on the momentum created by the McCloy-Zorin
Accord, the United Nations established the Eighteen Nation Disarmament Committee (ENDC), comprising five nations from NATO, five nations from the Warsaw Pact, and eight nonaligned nations, which began
meeting in Geneva on March 14, 1962. One of the first acts of substantive
business for the ENDC was to create a subcommittee to consider a treaty
banning nuclear weapons tests.

But stopping nuclear war, not nuclear tests, dominated the agenda of
President Kennedy as 1961 drew to a close. The situation surrounding
Berlin remained tense. By the end of October 1961, President Kennedy
had signed off on National Security Action Memorandum (NSAM) 109,
a military plan of action on how to respond to any Soviet ground or air
blockade of Berlin. Divided into four phases, the plan called for a gradual
escalation of conventional responses before implementation of phase

four—general nuclear war as outlined in SIOP-62. NSAM 109 was hailed as the first genuine manifestation of a new flexible response strategy that had the United States relying on conventional forces initially before resorting to the use of nuclear weapons. But after all of the internal wrangling over creating a more flexible response capability, in the end the only nuclear fallback Kennedy had was total nuclear war.[2]

In order for NSAM 109 to have any credibility, there would need to be a massive increase in the conventional war fighting capabilities of NATO. But the members of NATO were extremely hesitant to commit to the massive fiscal outlays that such a military buildup would require of them, preferring instead to fall back on the security blanket afforded by America's nuclear umbrella. A critical factor in this thinking was that the United States would not divorce Europe from its overall approach to general, or nuclear, warfare, so the Soviets would know that any move on Europe would put the entire Soviet Union at risk. This, of course, was the exact opposite approach that was being pursued by the Kennedy administration under the precepts of flexible response. The United States was looking for the option to isolate and contain nuclear action without having to resort to general nuclear war. From Kennedy's perspective, the only legitimate reason for a massive buildup of American conventional military power in Europe was to protect Berlin. If the Soviets were to launch a military assault on Western Europe proper, the United States, together with the other Western European nations, simply did not have the conventional capacity to resist. President Kennedy was unwilling to expend the resources necessary to change that basic equation. In short, if the Soviets attacked Western Europe, nuclear weapons would be employed almost immediately.

The Kennedy administration had no desire to maintain a hands-off approach toward nuclear weapons and NATO. Given the consequences associated with any use of nuclear weapons by any NATO power, in particular the near certainty of a rapid escalation into a general strategic nuclear exchange between the United States and the Soviet Union, independent nuclear deterrent capability such as that being sought by Great Britain and France (which tested a nuclear device in the Sahara Desert on February 13, 1960) was a policy direction not supported by the United States. In an effort to appease Western European desires for an independent European nuclear force, the United States had, since the time of the Eisenhower administration, proposed the creation of a so-called multilateral force (MLF). This force would consist of *Polaris* missiles carried onboard naval ships, which would be jointly manned by NATO personnel (including West Germans, a measure strongly opposed by the Soviets) and operate under the command of NATO itself. In December 1960, the Eisenhower administration went one step further, recommending that the United States commit five nuclear submarines, armed with eighty *Polaris* missiles, to a NATO MLF. The question of European joint command and control over nuclear weapons continuously haunted the MLF concept. Even more critical, from the U.S. perspective, was the question of how any MLF nuclear capability would be integrated into a larger U.S. plan for nuclear war.[3]

But the Western Europeans had concerns of their own. The United States maintained a stockpile of approximately 5,000 tactical nuclear weapons in Europe. Even though there were a number of bilateral agreements between the United States and host nations ostensibly providing for a veto over the use of these weapons, in the end the United States, through its role as Supreme Allied Commander, Europe (SACEUR), had the real ability to use these weapons when and how it best saw fit. The American-proposed MLF was designed to assuage European sensibilities, but as of early 1962, it remained largely theoretical, and largely ignored. In the spring of 1962, NATO Secretary-General Dirk Stikker prepared a report that laid out a set of guidelines assuring NATO about what it wanted from the United States in terms of the availability of American nuclear weapons for NATO. It also proposed agreements NATO desired on the need for consultations between the United States and NATO prior to any decision being made about the use of nuclear weapons by NATO.[4]

But even though American nuclear strategy might have been influenced by Europe, ultimately it was driven by domestic American politics. By March 1962, it appeared that the driving force behind American defense posture was the struggling American economic situation. Both Kennedy and McNamara had ruled out a nuclear first-strike option, and neither was satisfied with the Eisenhower strategy of Massive Retaliation. Flexible response was the ideal concept, but McNamara's commitment toward producing a defense budget that met Kennedy's needs for fiscal constraint meant that the boost in American conventional military power overseas was not going to materialize.

McNamara was able to assuage the Department of Defense by authorizing money in the fiscal year 1963 budget to build a force of 1,000 *Minuteman* and 656 *Polaris* missiles by 1967.[5] These missiles were the heart of what McNamara was beginning to refer to as a strategy of Counterforce, in which the first salvo of nuclear weapons launched by the United States in retaliation against a Soviet nuclear attack would be targeted against Soviet military forces (missile silos, bomber bases, and so forth) instead of Soviet cities. A certain portion of U.S. nuclear launch capability would be held back for potential use against Soviet military, industrial, and civilian targets, if needed. The key to such a new strategy rested with survivable missile systems, such as the silo-based *Minuteman* and the submarine-launched *Polaris*. Counterforce became the U.S. nuclear doctrine, and the planning guidance for SIOP-63—which went into effect in June 1962—reflected this thinking.[6]

Having sold Congress on the fiscal merits of Counterforce, and having shaped U.S. nuclear targeting plans accordingly, McNamara now needed to sell his new concept to an increasingly worried and skeptical NATO audience. His opportunity came on May 5, 1962, at a meeting of NATO ministers held in Athens, Greece, where McNamara detailed the new Counterforce strategy. McNamara stated that the United States would not be targeting Soviet or Warsaw Pact cities in the event of a nuclear war. He also suggested that both the British and the French nuclear capabilities, unless appropriately targeted (i.e., integrated into an overall U.S.-controlled nuclear command and control framework), were counterproductive in so far as neither the British nor the French nuclear forces possessed the accuracy necessary for effective employment in a Counterforce mode. America, McNamara stated, was against small, independently targeted nuclear forces because they were outdated and lacked credibility as a deterrent. By extension, therefore, the United States was against the MLF. The key, McNamara noted, was that there was a much larger need for conventional forces, and Europe would have to do more in that regard.[7]

McNamara's Athens presentation was highly classified, presented behind closed doors to a limited audience. It wasn't until June 1962 that the crux of his new Counterforce thinking was presented publicly, when McNamara gave a redacted version as his commencement address to the University of Michigan in Ann Arbor. In this speech McNamara pointed out that the NATO alliance, inclusive of American power, had overall nuclear strength that was adequate to any challenge. Accordingly, McNamara told Ann Arbor, this nuclear strength not only reduced the likelihood of any major nuclear war but also provided for the development of a strategy that could limit the damage done to civil society in the case of a general nuclear war. To reduce the chances of nuclear war, and to deter any non-nuclear conflict, McNamara favored improving the conventional military power of the NATO alliance. The American secretary of defense noted that American nuclear supremacy made a surprise nuclear attack by any enemy an act of insanity, given the assured consequences. Likewise, McNamara told the graduates, it was highly unlikely for an enemy to initiate limited nuclear warfare as an outgrowth of a limited conventional conflict, either in Europe or elsewhere. Counterforce, McNamara argued (without actually naming it), made it official U.S. policy that in the event of a nuclear war, the principal military objective would be "the destruction of the enemy's forces, not of his civilian population." The robust nature of the U.S. and NATO nuclear capability provided sufficient "reserve striking power to destroy an enemy society if driven to it. In other words, we are giving a possible opponent the strongest imaginable incentive to refrain from striking our own cities."[8]

McNamara's presentation in Ann Arbor did not go over well in Moscow, where the Soviet premier, Nikita Khrushchev, alerted to the speech by the KGB, was furious over what he viewed as an American effort to make nuclear war more acceptable. Contrary to the vision of McNamara's No Cities strategy, Khrushchev angrily retorted that in any nuclear war between the United States and the Soviet Union, cities would be the first targets to be destroyed, and he warned President Kennedy not to embark on a "sinister competition as to who will be the first to start a war." Khrushchev's angst was not, as many believe, derived from his tendency toward knee-jerk reactions but was rather a consequence of a growing frustration that the United States was seeking to leverage its nuclear supremacy in a manner that constrained Soviet interests and, more important, national security.[9]

A critical aspect to this problem of U.S.-Soviet tension was the strategic imbalance that existed between the two nations in the arena of nuclear weapons and delivery systems. Even though there never had been a Soviet missile gap, there was in fact an American missile gap, one which the Soviets were painfully aware of and were doing their best to close. While the Soviets struggled to field a viable ICBM, they were able to deploy two extremely capable intermediate-range missiles, the SS-4 and the SS-5. In early 1962, the first regiments of SS-5 missiles were deployed to deal with targets in Western Europe from sites in the western Soviet Union. Like the SS-4, the SS-5 was considered a strategic asset and was deployed as part of the Strategic Rocket Forces. Yet both missiles lacked the range to threaten anything other than regional targets. Other than American forces stationed in Europe and Asia, the national territory of the United States at that time remained out of reach of any Soviet ballistic missile.[10]

The Soviet Union's only functional ICBM, the SS-6 missile, made use of unstable liquid fuel, reducing its viability as a military weapon. The logical follow-up to the SS-6 would either be a missile with stored-fuel capability or with a vastly improved handling system for the liquid oxygen oxidizer. In typical fashion, the Soviets chose to pursue both options. They soon began work on the SS-8 missile, which used a fully automated launch system that allowed the missile to be ready for firing within twenty minutes, enough time to guarantee it could be launched if the Soviets received early warning of an American preemptive attack. The other missile design, the SS-7, featured a storable fuel capability and could be fueled at the onset of any crisis and thus be maintained in a "ready launch" mode (able to be fired within six minutes) for up to thirty days. The survivability afforded to the Soviet ICBM force through the deployment of these two missiles was tremendous.[11]

But the deployment of the SS-7 and SS-8 missiles would take time. On March 9, and again on March 11, 1962, Khrushchev received sensitive reports from Soviet military intelligence (Glavnoye Razvedyvatel'noye Upravleniye, or GRU) that reported on the fictional deliberations within the Pentagon and the White House (purportedly happening in the summer and fall of 1961) about a preemptive nuclear strike against the Soviet Union. Khrushchev was troubled by these reports, especially when one considered the overall strategic balance that existed in early 1962. Even though the Soviet Union had sufficient nuclear strike capability to hit all of Western Europe, the United States was relatively secure from a Soviet nuclear threat. The Soviet Union had no long-range bomber capable of penetrating the air defenses of North America, and the SS-8 and SS-7 ICBM capability was small in numbers, slow to make operational, and thus vulnerable to preemption. The Golf-class submarine, although theoretically capable of intercontinental deployments, was not viewed as a survivable system because it would need to maneuver close to American shores, surface, raise its missiles, and then launch. The Soviet Union was able to flex its nuclear muscle against Western Europe but not the United States.[12]

And yet the United States was not in the same position. American strategic bombers not only were capable of penetrating Soviet air defenses at will but also were on active patrols over the Arctic, the Pacific, and Europe, ringing the Soviet homeland with the ever-present danger of a no-notice nuclear attack. The United States had 18 new *Titan* missiles deployed by May 1962, all of them in hardened underground silos. The *Titan* deployments were in addition to 129 *Atlas* missiles either already deployed or in the process of being deployed.[13] *George Washington*– and *Ethan Allen*–class nuclear-powered ballistic missile submarines, each armed with 16 *Polaris* missiles, were actively engaged in nuclear deterrence patrols based out of Holy Loch, Scotland, and were operating in arctic waters, placing Leningrad, Moscow, and much of the Soviet Union's European industrial and military infrastructure under imminent risk of military attack.[14]

The United States had deployed sixty *Thor* IRBMs to Great Britain between 1958 and 1959, where they could deliver a 1.4-megaton nuclear warhead to a target 1,500 miles away, with a total flight time of less than eighteen minutes. All of the Warsaw Pact nations, as well as the Soviet Union west of the Ural Mountains, were in range. The *Thor* missile took fifteen minutes to erect, fuel, and launch, making it a very difficult missile to neutralize with anything other than a surprise attack. The United States had also deployed *Jupiter* IRBMs to both Italy (thirty missiles) and, as of April 1962, Turkey (fifteen missiles). Like the *Thor*, the *Jupiter* missile had a range of 1,500 miles and carried a 1.4-megaton warhead. From its Turkish bases outside the city of Izmir, the *Jupiter* was capable of delivering a nuclear strike against Khrushchev's Pitsunda dacha in less than twenty minutes, something the Soviet premier was well aware of, and a fact that, after the receipt of the GRU intelligence on planning for an American preemptive nuclear attack, took on added significance.[15]

From Khrushchev's perspective, the Soviet Union faced an unacceptable national security situation. Europe, Khrushchev believed, could be stabilized if a German peace treaty could be obtained and the question of Berlin resolved. Soviet conventional military strength, backed up by theater-level (i.e., able to operate throughout Europe) nuclear weapons, would maintain a balance of power acceptable to Soviet interests. However, given the fact that Western Europe and the United States were integrated from a defense standpoint, the balance of power equation vis-à-vis the Soviet bloc and NATO was skewed unacceptably against the Soviet Union, especially when one factored in the imbalance between Soviet and American strategic nuclear capabilities. Matching the United States missile for missile was not an attractive option. Khrushchev faced severe economic problems at home. His agricultural reforms were failing, and overall the Soviet economy was growing at an unacceptably slow rate. In addition to the SS-7 and SS-8 missile development and deployment currently under way, the Soviet military was planning a new generation of missiles designed to match both the quick launch capabilities of the *Minuteman* ICBM and the hard-target kill capability of the *Titan* ICBM. To counter the American ICBM threat, the Soviet Union was designing advanced antiballistic missile (ABM) defenses, as well as new generations of ballistic missile submarines. Khrushchev was on the edge of embarking on an arms race that he knew would hold a distinct disadvantage for the Soviet Union because of the precariousness of its economic health.

Disarmament was the way out, Khrushchev believed, but the Soviet military and political bureaucracies would never concede the large number of on-site inspections that a genuine verification system would require, especially given the weak state of the Soviet strategic nuclear capability. Once disarmament was accomplished, and rough parity established, some form of limited inspection regime could be considered. A major problem, from the Soviet standpoint, was that America did not seem inclined toward genuine disarmament, which negated its strategic advantages. Khrushchev was left with two options: engage in a costly arms race until parity was achieved, or rearrange the strategic situation as it now stood to maximize available Soviet capabilities.

Khrushchev chose the former. In May 1962, he approached Soviet Defense Minister Rodion Malinovsky with an audacious plan of action: deploy Soviet medium-range and intermediate-range nuclear missiles to bases in Cuba. There they would be able to target U.S. cities and military-industrial facilities as far north as Atlanta, Georgia (for the medium-range missiles), and all of the U.S. bomber and missile bases in the midwestern part of America (for the intermediate-range missiles).[16]

On June 10, 1962, Khrushchev and Malinovsky briefed the Soviet presidium on the plan to place Soviet nuclear missiles in Cuba, code-named Operation Anadyr. In a follow-up meeting of the presidium held on July 1, 1962, Khrushchev linked Operation Anadyr with a new decision to resolve the ongoing Berlin crisis in the Soviet Union's favor. Khrushchev proposed a phasing out of the Allied occupation forces in Berlin over a two-year period, to be replaced by international troops under UN command. This proposal was to be the bottom-line position of the Soviets, which would be backed up by the new strategic nuclear reality of the Soviet missile force in Cuba. McNamara's Ann Arbor speech played a central role in pushing Khrushchev toward this decisive confrontation. Khrushchev knew that without the Cuban missile bases, the Soviet nuclear force was inferior to that of the United States. This massive American nuclear supremacy prevented any aggressive Soviet moves regarding Berlin. Operation Anadyr would, in Khrushchev's opinion, dramatically alter this equation.[17]

While Khrushchev put in place the pieces of his nuclear gambit in Cuba, U.S.-Soviet disarmament talks continued, albeit with almost zero progress. As of July 1962, talks in Geneva over the issue of a nuclear test ban remained stalled, primarily over the continued Soviet refusal to consider on-site inspections as a means of verification for any test ban agreement. The Soviets continued to be angry with what they viewed as American trickery concerning the technical issues surrounding seismic detection of any potential tests.

The Soviet point was reinforced, without their knowledge, in early July 1962, when the U.S. Air Force came in with some startling findings produced by Project Vela, which the Department of Defense had initiated in 1959. The project was set up to study seismic phenomena needed for nuclear test detection and treaty verification, spending some $30 million by 1961 in deploying a detection system known as the World Wide Standardized Seismographic Network. In reviewing Project Vela data relating to two underground nuclear tests (a Soviet test in Semipalatinsk conducted in February 1962 and a French test conducted in the Sahara Desert in May 1962), the Air Force determined that the Vela system was, in fact, capable of detecting seismic events 20 percent smaller than the current Geneva threshold of 4.75 kilotons. This meant that there would be a need for fewer on-site inspections because the seismic sensors would be able to detect the difference between a nuclear and nonnuclear seismic event.[18]

The Project Vela data set off a storm of debate inside Washington as to how best to proceed on the matter of a nuclear test ban treaty. Senator Henry "Scoop" Jackson made it clear that he regarded the new Vela data with great skepticism, informing the White House that in his view "there could be nothing more dangerous than to make a hasty change in the fundamental principle of arms control because of a preliminary scientific finding."[19] But there was a recognition that the Soviet insistence on zero inspections was the fundamental blockage in a comprehensive test ban treaty being negotiated, and the new Vela data threw open the question of whether or not inspections were even needed. In October 1961, the Indian government, in an effort to get ENDC talks back on track, had submitted a proposal for a test ban that excluded on-site inspections, and there was growing pressure on the part of the United Nations, both in terms of the General Assembly and the ENDC, for movement to be made. More and more, it was the United States, and not the Soviet Union, that was viewed as the impediment to progress in the field of disarmament.[20]

America's hands were no longer clean when it came to nuclear testing. When the Soviets resumed testing on September 1, 1961, Kennedy had responded with a series of underground tests. The weapons design laboratories had a number of atmospheric tests planned, however, many of which were high yield in nature and intended as weapons development tests. Under pressure from the military and nuclear laboratories, Kennedy had authorized U.S. atmospheric nuclear testing to resume on April 25, 1962.

Meanwhile, the situation in Cuba was growing more critical. By July 1962, the CIA was detecting evidence of a massive increase in the delivery of Soviet weapons to Cuba, including surface-to-air missiles. A month later, the evidence continued to grow, prompting an intervention on the part of U.S. Attorney General Robert Kennedy with the Soviet ambassador to the United States, Anatoliy Dobrynin, on September 4, 1962. Robert Kennedy expressed alarm over the scope and nature of the Soviet weapons' presence in Cuba, stating that although the current weapons appeared to be defensive in nature, if such shipments continued, what would prevent the Soviets from dispatching to Cuba offensive missiles armed with nuclear warheads? Dobrynin assured Robert Kennedy that the Soviet actions were defensive in nature and that the Soviet Union supported the nonproliferation of nuclear weapons.[21]

In Washington, President Kennedy was under increasing pressure from his Republican counterparts in the U.S. Senate, especially Senator Ken Keating of New York, who was expressing concern over the Soviet build-up in Cuba. The feeling was that the United States had to do something about Cuba. In discussions with his national security team and members of Congress, the idea of a naval blockade of Cuba was broached by the attendees. "Well, a blockade is a major military operation, too," the president responded. "It's an act of war." Kennedy meanwhile had his attention focused elsewhere—on Berlin. In his opinion, if the United States initiated a blockade against Cuba, "Berlin obviously would be blockaded also." Kennedy was searching for a sense of perspective. "I think Berlin is coming to some sort of climax this fall," he said. Cuba was, in his opinion, a distraction, a weapons buildup that, in Kennedy's opinion, "did not threaten America." For the moment, it seemed, the best option was to wait and observe. Under pressure from his national security team to ask Congress for an extension to the one-year call-up of reserves he had requested in July 1961, the president opted to ask for only 150,000 troops in an effort to downplay any suggestion of a crisis.[22]

On September 8, 1962, the Soviet freighter *Omsk* arrived in Cuba with the first shipment of SS-4 missiles, followed on September 15 by the freighter *Poltava* with the remaining ones. In response to Kennedy's decision to mobilize 150,000 reservists, Soviet Foreign Minister Andrei Gromyko, in a speech before the United Nations, warned that any American attack on Cuba could result in a war with the Soviet Union. On that same day, the Soviet news agency TASS issued a statement in which the Soviets declared all weapons sent to Cuba to be strictly defensive in nature. On September 13, 1962, President Kennedy, under increasing pressure from Republicans in Congress, again addressed the Cuba issue, stating that any talk of military action by the United States against Cuba was unjustified and not required. The main problem, so it seemed to the president, continued to be Berlin. The decision by Khrushchev to push Kennedy simultaneously on Berlin and Cuba left the president searching for a logical link between the two actions. Whereas the president was inclined toward striking a deal on Berlin, the domestic ramifications of the Soviet buildup in Cuba, exploited deftly by his Republican opponents, precluded any such action.

On October 14, 1962, a U.S. Air Force U-2 plane flew over Cuba and, taking advantage of a break in the clouds, imaged a portion of western Cuba where the SS-4 missiles were being deployed. By October 15, CIA photo analysts had assessed the images and confirmed the presence of the Soviet missiles in Cuba. Operation Anadyr had been uncovered by U.S. intelligence. The president was informed of the Soviet action on October 16, 1962, and immediately convened an executive committee of his closest advisors to discuss the issue. Early on in this meeting, President Kennedy had a telling exchange with his national security team. Speaking about a Soviet move to place missiles in Cuba, Kennedy noted that "it's as if we suddenly began to put a major number of MRBM's in Turkey. Now that'd be Goddam dangerous, I would think." McGeorge Bundy responded, "Well, we did, Mr. President." Alexis Johnson, a senior State Department official, added, "We did it. We did it in England." In a related conversation, General Maxwell Taylor speculated that the Soviet move might be designed to supplement their defective ICBM systems. Dean Rusk commented that the United States had fifteen *Jupiter* missiles installed in Turkey, noting that maybe Khrushchev "wants us to feel what it is like to live under medium-range missiles."[23]

Over the span of October 18 and 19, Kennedy and his advisors went back and forth about the consequences of any U.S. move against Cuba. Kennedy was concerned that if the United States attacked Cuba, then the Soviets would be compelled to take steps to end the Allied occupation of Berlin. Kennedy was adamant that the United States had no intention of invading Cuba, but noted that the Soviet missiles stationed there had created "the most dangerous situation since the end of World War II." Bundy urged the president to avoid any notion of trading Cuba for Berlin and suggested rather that the president stay focused on Berlin and maintain the U.S.-Western European alliance.[24]

On October 19, 1962, U.S. intelligence revealed that eight SS-4 missile sites in Cuba were operational, and eight more were approaching operational status. Sensitive intelligence from Colonel Oleg Penkovsky, a Soviet working for the CIA and British Intelligence, confirmed that the other system deployed to Cuba, and detected by U.S. intelligence on October 17, was the SS-5 intermediate-range missile. An associated nuclear warhead storage site was assessed to be six to eight weeks away from completion. Kennedy continued to hesitate on taking military action, again feeling that to do so would clear the way for the Soviets to move on Berlin. General Curtis LeMay, the Air Force chief of staff, believed that there really was no other choice but military action because if the United States waited three months and did nothing, the Soviets were, in his opinion, going to "squeeze us on Berlin." In LeMay's opinion, the Soviet missiles in Cuba increased the overall Soviet accuracy against the fifty critical targets inside the United States that had been assessed as capable of being struck by Soviet nuclear delivery systems.

On October 20, 1962, Kennedy decided to impose a naval blockade on Cuba. The military kept pressing Kennedy for a preemptive military attack, but he hesitated. President Kennedy was growing increasingly concerned about any Soviet preemption of the *Jupiter* missile bases in Turkey and Italy. The NATO European Defense Plan (EDP) called for the launching of the *Jupiter* missiles in the case of any Soviet nuclear attack against NATO. But the president felt that if the United States were to attack Soviet missiles in Cuba, then the Soviets would most logically launch "spot reprisals" against the *Jupiter* sites in Turkey and Italy. On October 22, 1962, Kennedy ordered General Taylor to make sure that no *Jupiter* missiles were to be fired without specific presidential authority. Taylor added that if any Soviet attack did occur, whether nuclear or nonnuclear, the U.S. custodians must destroy or make inoperable the nuclear warheads of the *Jupiter* missiles if any effort was made to fire them in order to prevent an escalation of nuclear conflict.[25]

Also that morning, Kennedy briefed members of Congress on the Soviet missile deployments. That night at 7:00 PM, President Kennedy broadcast a live message to the nation, and to the world: "This government, as promised, has maintained the closest surveillance of the Soviet military buildup on the island of Cuba. Within the past week, unmistakable evidence has established the fact that a series of offensive missile sites is now in preparation on that imprisoned island. The purpose of these bases can be none other than to provide a nuclear strike capability against the Western Hemisphere." Kennedy announced his intention to impose a naval quarantine around Cuba and demanded the withdrawal of the Soviet missiles from that island.[26]

In an opinion column published in the *New York Times* on October 23, 1962, the noted journalist Walter Lippmann, a friend and confidant of John Kennedy, had written that the presence of American *Jupiter* missiles in Turkey complicated President Kennedy's options when it came to Cuba.[27] This was indeed the case. But Kennedy did not have the flexibility of absolute authority when it came to the *Jupiter* missiles, which were ostensibly NATO assets and had been deployed under its auspices. Unilateral U.S. action to remove the *Jupiter* missiles from either Turkey or Italy, without coordinating this action through NATO and getting concurrence from the respective host nation, would greatly undermine the NATO alliance at a time when the crisis in Berlin mandated NATO unity and coherence.[28]

However, Kennedy no longer operated with the luxury of time, which was what diplomacy usually required. While the State Department floated the question of the utility of the *Jupiter* missiles in Turkey (the United States was prepared to offer Turkey *Polaris* nuclear submarines in their stead),[29] Robert Kennedy made use of an established secret back channel he had established with a Soviet intelligence officer, Georgi Bolshakov. Bypassing normal bureaucratic channels, Robert Kennedy turned to a reporter for the *Daily News*, Frank Holeman, to float the idea of a Turkey-Italy-Cuba missile swap. Holeman was careful to pass on Robert Kennedy's caveat to the proposal: such a deal could only be made once tensions had subsided.[30]

But tensions did not subside. In the frantic days that followed, both the United States and the Soviet Union increased their respective defense postures. Whereas the public rhetoric between the United States and the Soviet Union remained harsh, behind the scenes both sides were scrambling for a peaceful solution. Khrushchev ordered all Soviet ships involved in Operation Anadyr, with the exception of those carrying the remaining SS-5 missiles, to turn around and return to the Soviet Union. President Kennedy continued to fend off the pressure from the hawks at the Pentagon and within the Joint Chiefs of Staff to attack Cuba, all the while looking for the means to bring the crisis to a peaceful end. Kennedy was aware that the only way to give Khrushchev a face-saving way out of Cuba was to offer up the *Jupiter* missiles in Turkey.

Matters concerning Cuba were quickly coming to a head. On the evening of October 23, 1962, President Kennedy signed into effect a naval blockade of Cuba. By 10:00 AM on October 24, 1962, the U.S. Navy had sufficient ships in place to begin enforcing the blockade. The delay in ordering the blockade proved fortuitous because in the meantime the Soviet ship *Aleksandrovsk*, carrying the nuclear warheads for the SS-5 missiles, had slipped into Cuban coastal waters and had anchored off of the Cuban port city La Isabela. Because it avoided contact with the U.S. Navy vessels blockading Cuba, the prospect of a conflict arising over any attempt on the part of the U.S. Navy to seize Soviet nuclear warheads had passed. But the Soviets still had nineteen other ships sailing toward Cuba, two of these carrying the SS-5 IRBMs. Under orders from Khrushchev, sixteen of these ships turned around and returned to the Soviet Union. The two freighters carrying the SS-5 rockets, escorted by a single Soviet submarine, stopped short of the quarantine line. The Soviets sent an oil tanker forward, which was intercepted, boarded, and inspected by the U.S. Navy. Clearly the United States was intending to enforce the blockade. Khrushchev condemned the U.S. Navy's boarding of a Soviet vessel as a "pirate action."[31]

The next morning, U.S. intelligence detected continuing activity at the Soviet missile bases in Cuba, prompting Strategic Air Command's General Thomas Powers, acting without the authority of the president, to order his forces to Defense Condition (DEFCON) 2, one level below general war. His orders were deliberately broadcast unencrypted, to ensure that Soviet and Cuban signal intercept operators knew exactly what was happening.[32] The U.S. Army deployed three experimental radars along the southern border of the United States to detect any missile launch activity from Cuba. Kennedy signed National Security Action Memorandum 199, authorizing nuclear weapons to be loaded onto aircraft operating in Europe, because those would be the first to launch against the Soviet Union in case of any nuclear war. America was on a hair-trigger alert.

President Kennedy was becoming convinced that the only option available to rid Cuba of the Soviet missiles was an invasion. There was a growing recognition within the White House that any U.S. military action against Cuba would trigger a Soviet move on Berlin. The thinking was simple: bomb Cuba, kill Russians. Russians take Berlin, overrun American troops. "Then what do we do?" Robert Kennedy asked. Maxwell Taylor gave the answer no one wanted to hear: "We go to general war, if it is in the interest of ours." "You mean nuclear exchange?" Robert Kennedy said. "I guess you have to," Taylor affirmed. This reality persuaded the president to give diplomacy a final chance. But time was running out. If there was no change in the Soviet position by Sunday, October 28, then the president would order the U.S. military to move in the following day.[33]

A breakthrough in the Cuban crisis came from a totally unexpected source. On October 25, Alexandr Feklisov, the KGB resident agent at the Soviet embassy in Washington, invited the ABC News reporter John Scali, best known for hosting the program *Questions and Answers*, to lunch. During this lunch, Scali was asked by Feklisov if the United States might be interested in a deal where the Soviets would dismantle their missile bases in Cuba under UN supervision if the United States would undertake not to invade Cuba. Scali passed this proposal to a skeptical State Department.[34]

But the skeptics were proven wrong when, the very next day, Nikita Khrushchev wrote a letter to President Kennedy in which he agreed to the basic formula of a U.S.-Soviet deal over Cuba that had been floated during the meeting between Scali and Feklisov. In exchange for the Soviet agreement to withdraw their missiles from Cuba, the United States would agree not to invade Cuba. But then, on October 27, a second letter was received, this one linking the Soviet withdrawal from Cuba with an American withdrawal of *Jupiter* missiles from Turkey. The Kennedy administration chose to ignore the second Soviet communication and based its response upon the initial letter of October 26. This would represent the public face of diplomacy.[35]

Behind the scenes, President Kennedy provided assurances that U.S. *Jupiter* missiles in Turkey would be withdrawn in the near future, within four to five months. Robert Kennedy conveyed this to Soviet Ambassador Dobrynin during a meeting on Saturday, October 27, 1962. Robert Kennedy emphasized the need to keep the details of the missile trade confidential. Dobrynin passed Kennedy's message on to Khrushchev.[36] The next day, Khrushchev made a public announcement in which he explained the presence of Soviet missiles in Cuba to a Soviet public previously unaware of the bold, dangerous gambit. Khrushchev announced that these missiles would now be withdrawn, linked to an American agreement not to attack Cuba. No mention was made of the secret pact on the American pledge to close down its *Jupiter* missile bases in Turkey. Both America and the Soviet Union had come right to the edge of the nuclear abyss and, having peered over, collectively decided to step back.

CHAPTER 7

UNFULFILLED PROMISES

THE LIMITED TEST BAN TREATY AND NONPROLIFERATION

Even as President John Kennedy and Premier Nikita Khrushchev carried out their diplomatic maneuvering in an effort to avoid nuclear conflict in Cuba, both the United States and the Soviet Union continued to test their respective nuclear arsenals, using designs possessing ever-increasing yields detonated into the Earth's atmosphere. Both the American and Soviet nuclear weapons designers pursued programs dedicated to missile defense purposes. In fact, the final U.S. atmospheric nuclear test, conducted on November 4, 1962, made use of a *Nike Hercules* surface-to-air missile to test an antiballistic missile warhead over Johnston Island.[1]

The Soviets continued their testing program after the final U.S. blast, continuing through November 1962. With the exception of a single underground nuclear test conducted in February 1962, the Soviets had refrained from conducting nuclear tests until August 1, 1962. From that date until December 25 of that year, the Soviets conducted a total of seventy-four nuclear tests. These included three "weapons injurious tests" on October 22 and 28 and November 1, 1962, which consisted of a massive three-hundred-kiloton device exploded nearly three hundred kilometers up in a manner designed to knock out incoming missiles. These last three tests were of no small concern to the United States, which recognized the potential lethality of any Soviet weapon of that nature so employed against existing U.S. warheads.[2]

The nuclear arms race between the two nations continued unabated. Both sides were testing smaller, more efficient warheads that enabled missiles to carry their deadly cargos farther and with greater accuracy. The United States was testing warheads for a follow-up to the *Minuteman* I missile (which had achieved operational capability in December 1962), as well as a smaller warhead for the new *Polaris* A2 missile, enabling that missile to be the first armed with multiple warheads (the *Polaris* A2 would carry three). The Soviets themselves were working on smaller warheads designed to possess greater accuracy so that the *Minuteman* missile system might be more effectively targeted. More worrisome to the United States, the Soviets were making advances in an orbital weapons delivery system (known as the Fractional Orbital Bombardment System, or FOBS). This system would place a nuclear weapon in space as one would a satellite, enabling the weapon to be de-orbited at any time, increasing the strike capability of the weapon while making conventional missile detection and intercept ineffective.

The combined experiences of the Berlin crisis and the Cuban crisis had left both the United States and the Soviet Union disconcerted about how easily a crisis could spin out of control toward general nuclear war, and how undesirable such an outcome was for all parties concerned. The Cuban crisis in particular demonstrated the absolute importance of having a direct communications link between President Kennedy and Premier Khrushchev, and how unreliable and inefficient existing "backchannel" communications were. On December 12, 1962, the United States submitted a proposal to the Eighteen Nation Disarmament Committee that made certain recommendations designed to reduce the risk of war. Included in this proposal was the idea to establish a communications link between major world capitals to ensure quick and reliable communications during times of crisis. On June 30, 1963, the U.S. and Soviet representatives at the ENDC in Geneva signed the "Memorandum of Understanding Between the United States of America and the Union of Soviet Socialist Republics Regarding the Establishment of a Direct Communications Link." According to this memorandum, each nation would make arrangements within its own territory to ensure the continuous functioning of the communications link as well as the prompt delivery to the respective head of government of all communications so delivered.[3]

The establishment of a hotline between Washington, DC, and Moscow was especially important given the hair-trigger nature of each nation's developing nuclear arsenal. The quick-response capabilities of the *Minuteman* missile were being used to their utmost by the U.S. Air Force.

Although Secretary of Defense Robert McNamara's Counterforce strategy supposedly drove the targeting philosophy, the Air Force had almost exclusively tasked its *Minuteman* force with taking out some six hundred "time-urgent" targets inside the Soviet Union, primarily bomber bases and missile sites. The goal was to destroy these targets before they could threaten U.S. or allied territories. Beyond being a Counterforce capability, the *Minuteman* had taken on a quick response ("launch on warning") character, which approximated genuine first-strike capability.[4]

The Soviets were also developing their own rapid-response launch capability. Using a similar philosophy of "launch on warning," the Soviets could obtain the authority for the release of nuclear weapons within ten minutes from the premier, defense minister, or chief of the general staff. Given a flight time of some fifteen to twenty minutes for U.S. missiles to hit Soviet targets, there was not much buffer if an error were to occur that triggered any "launch on warning" response by either side. The new hotline was designed to help head off any such mistake. But there needed to be something more than simply establishing better communications between the United States and the Soviet Union if the threat of nuclear war was to be avoided. Both Kennedy and Khrushchev recognized this. Their final messages to each other at the end of the Cuban crisis reflected this knowledge as well as the desire on the part of both men to push forward on the issue of arms control. "We should like to continue the exchange of views on the prohibition of atomic and thermonuclear weapons," Khrushchev wrote, to which Kennedy responded, "Perhaps now, as we step back from danger, we can together make real progress in this vital field."[5]

Secretary of State Dean Rusk tried to make some advances in the area of nuclear nonproliferation, in particular the matter of the nontransfer of nuclear weapons. In December 1962, Rusk approached France, Great Britain, and Germany during a NATO meeting. Although the British were agreeable to the concept, both France and Germany expressed reservations.

But even in this effort the United States was sending mixed signals. The intimacy enjoyed between it and Great Britain in the area of nuclear weapons was underscored on December 18, 1962, with the signing of the Nassau Agreement between President Kennedy and Prime Minister Harold Macmillan. In this agreement, the United States was to provide Great Britain with nuclear-armed *Polaris* missiles in exchange for an American lease at the Holy Loch submarine base. Although technically this deal represented the very sort of transfer the United States was supposed to be trying to prevent, legally the British *Polaris* missiles were to be considered a NATO resource and could only be used independently by the British in the case of "supreme national interest."[6] This legal cover was thin, however, and the United States would be called to task for its seemingly contradictory approach toward nuclear nonproliferation.

The French, and in particular its volatile president, Charles de Gaulle, viewed the Nassau Agreement as a clear sign that the British were more interested in aligning themselves with the United States rather than with Europe. France under de Gaulle viewed the NATO organization as being too heavily influenced by the United States, and as such was interested in having its own independent nuclear capability. Since 1960, when France detonated its first atomic bomb in the Sahara Desert in Algeria, France had developed air-deliverable nuclear weapons and was developing warheads for use in ballistic missiles. Even though not yet capable of detonating a hydrogen bomb, France was well on its way to achieving that capability as well, an ambition only furthered by the Nassau Agreement.[7]

France was not the only nation concerned about the Nassau Agreement. The Soviets had received Dean Rusk's plan for limiting the proliferation of nuclear weapons with a degree of skepticism. Of the four nations possessing nuclear weapons in 1962, three (the United States, Great Britain, and France) were NATO nations. This reality prompted the Soviets to reject Rusk's initiative, noting that a nuclear-armed NATO was itself a contradiction of the stated goals and objectives of nuclear nonproliferation. Talks would continue on the nondiffusion (i.e., sharing) of nuclear weapons, but these talks would not bear fruit for years to come.

The primary area in which both the United States and the Soviet Union seemed to believe progress could be made was nuclear testing, and in particular a treaty banning nuclear tests. This policy path was not without controversy. President Kennedy viewed the issue of a test ban treaty not only in terms of reducing tensions between the Soviet Union and the United States but also as a vehicle to further the nonproliferation of nuclear weapons. In his opinion, a comprehensive test ban treaty would place tremendous international pressure on any nation that sought to acquire nuclear weapons. Even though President Kennedy believed there to be a link between a test ban treaty and the nonproliferation of nuclear weapons, this conclusion was not shared by many in his administration. The Arms Control and Disarmament Agency in particular believed that though a test ban treaty was of direct benefit to the United States, Great Britain, and the Soviet Union—and indirectly therefore in the NATO and Warsaw Pact nations whose military and national security interests were so linked— independent nuclear programs such as were ongoing in France and under development in China would create pressure for other, smaller nations to

develop their own nuclear weapons capabilities. Whereas a nation such as Sweden might be compelled to forgo nuclear weapons if the rest of Europe followed the same course, India could not be expected to remain still in the face of a Chinese nuclear weapon, nor Pakistan if confronted by an Indian nuclear capability. Likewise, should Israel decide to pursue nuclear weapons, the entire Arab world would be under pressure to do the same as a counter.[8]

The nation President Kennedy was most concerned about when it came to nuclear proliferation was China. China had been pursuing a nuclear weapons capability since January 1955, when the chairman of the Chinese Communist Party, Mao Tse-tung, approved a proposal put forward by Chinese Premier Zhou Enlai to build the infrastructure necessary for China to manufacture a nuclear weapon. The Chinese desire for a nuclear weapons capability was fueled by the Korean War experience, when the United States had repeatedly threatened China with nuclear weapons, as well as the clashes with Chiang Kai-shek over the islands of Quemoy and Matsu in 1954, in which the threat of U.S. nuclear weapons was again raised.

In January 1955, the Chinese had signed an agreement, the first of six, with the Soviet Union for the provision of assistance in peaceful atomic work. The pretense was shed in October 1957, when the Soviets and Chinese signed the New Defense Technical Accord, in which the Soviets promised to provide the Chinese with not only technical assistance in the development of a nuclear weapon but also fissile material and a sample atomic bomb. Within two years, however, the Soviet-Chinese relationship was falling apart, victim of an aggressive Chinese foreign policy posture vis-à-vis the West that the Soviets rejected as too confrontational. In the end, the Chinese were left with half-finished factories void of blueprints and equipment, no nuclear material, and no sample atomic bomb. If China were to have a bomb, it would be one developed completely on its own.[9]

When President Kennedy came into office in 1961, the U.S. intelligence community had assessed that China was a decade or more away from having a nuclear capability, unless there was major external assistance provided. With the Soviet Union out of the picture, the threat of a Chinese nuclear bomb being detonated anytime soon seemed remote. However, within months the analysis changed: imagery obtained from U-2 flights over China showed several massive construction projects that appeared to be nuclear-related. Suddenly the United States was confronted with having to deal with a nuclear-armed China. Although most policymakers were dismissive of any real military threat derived from a Chinese nuclear capability, the political consequences in terms of increased Chinese prestige and influence in the Far East were considerable. The State Department briefly considered pushing India to acquire a nuclear weapons capability to offset that of China, but in the end this proposal was rejected as being inconsistent with the overall U.S. policy objective of nonproliferation.[10]

President Kennedy was so concerned about the prospect of a nuclear-armed China that he considered approaching the Soviets with the possibility of a joint military action against the Chinese nuclear infrastructure. Khrushchev did not share Kennedy's alarm, however. The Joint Chiefs of Staff prepared an Air Force study on taking out the Chinese targets, but it became clear that the wide dispersal of the Chinese factories meant that the number of bomber sorties would be prohibitively large. As soon as the Air Force brought up the question of a preemptive nuclear attack, the matter was laid to rest. The Chinese nuclear program would have to be dealt with diplomatically.[11]

From the perspective of the Kennedy administration, this meant the passage of a nuclear test ban treaty. If the Soviet Union and the United States were able to conclude a nuclear test ban treaty, and China were still to go forward with a nuclear test, then the Kennedy administration would consider reapproaching the Soviets about the idea of a joint military operation against China's nuclear manufacturing capability. But the Soviet concerns over nuclear proliferation were geared more toward NATO and the proposed multilateral force (MLF). Fearful of any German acquisition of a nuclear weapons capability, the Soviets were hopeful that a nuclear test ban would stop the MLF before it started. In any event, though the United States and the Soviet Union had different concerns over the specific nations involved in the potential proliferation of nuclear weapons capability, they did share the basic desire to see the proliferation of these destructive weapons halted. Both sides wanted, and needed, a nuclear test ban treaty.

By the end of 1962, there looked to be a window of opportunity for movement on the issue of that treaty. In December, Arthur Dean, the chief U.S. negotiator in Geneva, engaged the Soviet deputy foreign minister, Valeryan Zorin, in discussions about on-site inspections. Zorin came away from the Dean meetings with the impression that the United States would accept a figure of two to four inspections a year. Interested in a breakthrough on the issue of nuclear tests, Khrushchev wrote to President Kennedy on December 19, 1962, saying that the Soviets were willing to accept Dean's offer. However, Kennedy told Khrushchev that the U.S. position had not changed and that the United States was still insisting on eight to ten inspections, not two to four. The two sides were back to square one.[12]

Khrushchev was angered by what he felt was American duplicity, telling the presidium that because of the reversal from the Dean offer, "once again I was made to look foolish. But I can tell you this: it won't happen again."[13] Secretary of State Rusk was likewise growing increasingly frustrated with the endless haggling over inspections. The Soviets had been intrigued by the possibility of using automatic seismic stations as a monitoring means, something brought up during discussions between U.S. and Soviet scientists at the Pugwash Conference in September 1962. The United States, however, would not allow the "black boxes" to serve as a substitute for on-site inspection. A comprehensive nuclear test ban seemed to be out of reach for the time being. Khrushchev was adamantly opposed to the presence of international inspectors on Soviet territory, fearing that "they would have discovered that we were in a relatively weak position."[14]

The U.S. insistence on inspections was driven not so much by science but rather by an irrational fear within the ranks of the U.S. military and nuclear weapons community over the possibility of Soviet cheating. Although both President Kennedy and Secretary of Defense McNamara believed that the United States was better off with a test ban treaty than without one, even given the potential of Soviet cheating, support in the U.S. Senate was shaky at best. In addition, strong testimony against a test ban treaty from either the Joint Chiefs of Staff or noted nuclear scientists such as Dr. Edward Teller would doom any agreement from ever being ratified. This reality was driven home on February 25, 1963, when senators Stuart Symington, Richard Russell, and Henry Jackson wrote a joint letter to Kennedy setting out their concerns about a test ban treaty that lacked adequate inspection mechanisms. The senators noted that they wanted to retain Democratic unity on national security but that they had no choice but to oppose the treaty as it currently existed. Frustratingly, U.S. efforts to seek a limited test ban treaty, one which encompassed atmospheric and underwater testing, were rejected outright by Nikita Khrushchev, who insisted on a total test ban, without on-site inspections.[15]

Kennedy tried to break the impasse and dispatched a series of letters to Khrushchev in April 1963, an effort which initially appeared to backfire; Khrushchev continued to publicly complain about the American reneging on inspection numbers. In the final correspondence to Khrushchev, on April 24, 1963, Kennedy, together with British Prime Minister Macmillan, suggested that the test ban negotiations be resumed, either in Geneva or in Moscow, with Khrushchev's direct participation. Khrushchev chose Moscow. Kennedy now needed to create the conditions for a successful meeting.[16]

President Kennedy had been scheduled for some time to deliver the commencement address at American University, to be held on June 10, 1963. Kennedy had decided that he would deliver a groundbreaking speech that looked forward, not backward. The importance of this stance was underscored when, two days before he was scheduled to deliver his talk, a letter was received from Nikita Khrushchev that set the date of the Moscow test ban talks as July 15, 1963. Kennedy now had a window of opportunity with which to directly influence the talks, and he took full advantage of it.

As soon as he started to speak, it was clear that this commencement speech was going to be different. Gone was the standard meat-and-potatoes fare normally associated with major policy speeches concerning the Soviet Union—threats of nuclear destruction, Soviet duplicity and treachery, and American superiority of arms. "Total war makes no sense in an age when great powers can maintain large and relatively invulnerable nuclear forces and refuse to surrender without resort to those forces. It makes no sense in an age when a single nuclear weapon contains almost ten times the explosive force delivered by all the Allied air forces in the Second World War. It makes no sense in an age when the deadly poisons produced by a nuclear exchange would be carried by wind and water and soil and seed to the far corners of the globe and to generations yet unborn."[17]

Having set the stage, Kennedy then moved to close the deal. "The one major area of these negotiations where the end is in sight, yet where a fresh start is badly needed, is in a treaty to outlaw nuclear tests. The conclusion of such a treaty, so near and yet so far, would check the spiraling arms race in one of its most dangerous areas. It would place the nuclear powers in a position to deal more effectively with one of the greatest hazards which man faces in 1963, the further spread of nuclear arms. It would increase our security—it would decrease the prospects of war. Surely this goal is sufficiently important to require our steady pursuit, yielding neither to the temptation to give up the whole effort nor the temptation to give up our insistence on vital and responsible safeguards."

Kennedy's speech was a tremendous success in Moscow. The Soviets allowed the speech to be rebroadcast in its entirety and had it translated and published throughout the Soviet Union. Khrushchev himself referred to the American University address as "the best speech by any president since Roosevelt."[18]

On June 14, 1963, the president convened a meeting of the Principles Committee (a senior consultative body consisting of the members of the Cabinet and select high officials, usually at the secretary level), in which the goals and objectives of the Moscow summit were discussed. Secretary of State Rusk felt that the U.S. delegation should be prepared to move forward using the April 1 draft treaty. The Joint Chiefs had been heavily influenced by the concerns of Dr. Teller and other Atomic Energy Commission scientists who viewed a test ban treaty as being detrimental to the national security interests of the United States and who were citing as a major point of contention against any treaty the issue of potential cheating on the part of the Soviets. The Joint Chiefs were scheduled to testify before the U.S. Senate, and they did not want to be in a position of testifying against government policy, thereby raising the ugly spectacle of the government debating itself in front of Congress.[19]

Congress, which through the House of Representatives controls national spending and through the Senate oversees national policy via the process of oversight and advise, was in a bind. There was little support in Congress for a comprehensive test ban treaty, both from an ideological (few were willing to trust the Soviets) and an economic (the U.S. nuclear weapons program was too big to be done away with without economic, and thus political, ramifications) point of view. However, since the Cuban missile crisis, President Kennedy had accrued considerable political capital, and few were willing to decisively confront him on a major foreign policy issue while his political stock was so high. In May 1963, Senator Joseph Clark, a Democrat from Pennsylvania who was sympathetic toward the president's policies pursuing a comprehensive nuclear test ban treaty, conducted a private poll of his colleagues. The results showed the president to be ten votes shy of what was needed for ratification of a treaty. Based upon Clark's survey, Senators Hubert Humphrey and Thomas Dodd, a staunch anticommunist Democrat from Connecticut, came together to push forward a nonbinding resolution. Cosponsored by thirty-two other senators, the resolution advocated a limited test ban treaty, one which prohibited nuclear testing in the atmosphere and water. As recently as April 1963, Dodd had been against any treaty limiting nuclear testing, but after a series of exchanges with ACDA director William Chapman Foster (and considerable arm twisting by Senator Humphrey), Dodd reversed course and advocated support for a limited test ban.[20]

On July 2, 1963, Nikita Khrushchev closed the door on any hope of reaching an agreement for a comprehensive test ban when, during a speech in East Berlin, he accused the West of trying to facilitate espionage against the Soviet Union by insisting on on-site inspections. Khrushchev was frustrated by President Kennedy's recent visit to Berlin, where on June 26, 1963, he delivered his memorable "Ich Bin Ein Berliner" speech. But although one door was closed, another was opened. In the same speech, Khrushchev announced that the Soviet Union was prepared to conclude a limited test ban agreement, one which banned testing in the atmosphere, underwater, and in outer space. Khrushchev linked such an agreement with the signing of a nonaggression pact between NATO and the Warsaw Pact. Though such a pact was a nonstarter as far as the Kennedy administration was concerned, it was believed that Khrushchev's condition could be worked around. What was clear was that the Moscow meeting was poised to deliver a major arms control agreement, one that had been years in the making. Though not as meaningful as a comprehensive test ban, a limited test ban was a major step forward and could be used as a stepping-stone for later, more meaningful disarmament measures.[21]

Khrushchev had hoped that President Kennedy himself would lead the delegation to Moscow, giving the two leaders a chance to repair the damage created during their disastrous initial summit in Vienna in 1961. Kennedy did not believe the time was right for such a summit. He was, however, very serious about bringing to closure a test ban treaty, and so he selected the veteran American politician and diplomat, Averill Harriman, to head the U.S. delegation. Harriman was a former ambassador to Moscow and Great Britain as well as secretary of commerce during the Truman administration. He made two unsuccessful attempts at the presidency himself, in 1952 and in 1956, and from 1954 until 1958 he served as the governor of New York. An experienced diplomat with a keen political acumen, Harriman brought a sense of gravitas to the test ban negotiations, which more than offset President Kennedy's absence.

Harriman, together with his British counterpart, Lord Hailsham (the former Quinton Hogg), arrived in Moscow on July 14, 1963, in an atmosphere of great expectations. After nearly ten days of sometimes contentious negotiations, Harriman and his Soviet counterparts (Khrushchev and Andrei Gromyko) were able to come to agreement on a final treaty text. On July 25, 1963, Harriman, Lord Hailsham, and Gromyko conducted a formal ceremony, where three leather-bound copies of the treaty document were initialed, signifying final agreement on the treaty text. The next day, President Kennedy delivered a nationally televised address in which he announced the agreement on a treaty he believed represented "an important first step—a step toward peace, a step toward reason, a step away from war."[22]

Khrushchev, in his own statement, praised the treaty but encouraged the American president to move quickly to resolve others issues that would bring about an end to the Cold War. The French were circumspect, allowing that the treaty was useful only if it served as a launching point for more comprehensive disarmament. Charles de Gaulle pledged that France would continue to conduct nuclear weapons tests. The Chinese were outraged by the Soviet action in concluding this agreement with the West. Calling the treaty a "dirty fake" and a "fraud," the Chinese condemned any effort by the Soviets, or any party, to limit Chinese freedom of action when it came to developing a nuclear weapon.[23]

Kennedy still had to win over a skeptical Congress. He knew the key to doing this would be to have the support of his military chiefs. Even prior to the treaty being signed, the president met with the Joint Chiefs of Staff as a body, pressing on them to weigh both the military and political aspects of the treaty before passing final judgment. In the course of these discussions, the president assured the Joint Chiefs that he would strongly support additional safeguard measures that they felt critical for their support of even a limited test ban treaty. These included the continuation of a robust underground nuclear testing program designed to ensure the United States retained its edge in terms of nuclear weapons design and function.[24]

This support would guarantee that the United States would retain a robust nuclear testing capability that would also maintain the viability of the AEC nuclear laboratories and manufacturing plants, keep the current nuclear scientific community fully employed, and allow for the rapid resumption of nuclear testing in the atmosphere if the Soviets abrogated their treaty responsibilities. The Joint Chiefs also insisted that the United States further its intelligence collection capabilities targeting the Soviet Union not only for the purposes of treaty verification but also to make sure that America remained abreast of what the Soviet Union was up to in the field of nuclear weapons. During heated testimony and debate in the U.S. Senate throughout the month of September 1963, the tipping point for many senators on whether or not to support ratification hinged on these four safeguards. The Senate voted to ratify the limited test ban treaty, 80–19, on September 24, 1963. On October 5, President Kennedy signed the treaty into law, and five days later, the treaty went into effect, the articles of ratification being exchanged in ceremonies taking place in Washington, London, and Moscow.[25]

With the limited test ban treaty finally nailed down, President Kennedy and his advisors began to turn their attention to other pressing issues. The growing conflict in Vietnam was attracting focus, as was the ever-increasing level of American military involvement there. The link of the escalating U.S. military involvement in Vietnam to an overall policy of confronting and containing so-called communist aggression worldwide made any dramatic moves to de-escalate Soviet-American tension difficult. For all the work done to bring about a limited test ban treaty, the arms race between the Soviet Union and the United States was very much a reality. From the initialing of the limited test ban treaty in July until the end of October 1963, eleven underground nuclear weapons tests were conducted by the United States at the Nevada Test Site. Another six would be conducted before year's end. In sharp contrast, the Soviet Union conducted no nuclear tests in all of 1963.

Another issue was that of ballistic missile deployments, in particular the *Minuteman* missile. The U.S. Air Force initially had been pushing for 10,000 missiles, but this was rejected out of hand by McNamara. The Air Force chief of staff in turn reduced the request to 3,000 missiles, but McNamara had drawn the line at 1,000. The logic that drove McNamara's calculations was built around his second-strike principle. Given that it would take seven years to design, manufacture, and completely field the *Minuteman* missile, McNamara and his analysts projected where the Soviet Union was expected to be in terms of its strategic capability. They then calculated how many *Minuteman* missiles would be required to maintain a credible second-strike capability, which McNamara maintained was the foundation of deterrence. McNamara never intended the *Minuteman* as a first-strike weapon, a situation that fielding a force of 3,000 to 10,000 missiles would have created.[26]

In asking for 10,000 *Minuteman* missiles, the Air Force wasn't trying to directly circumvent the McNamara Counterforce strategy. Rather, the Air Force was trying to achieve the ability to launch a credible preemptive or launch-on-warning attack as well as to maintain a viable second-strike capability. In doing so, the Air Force kept reworking an increasing number of Soviet targets, and in turn asked for an increasing number of missiles and bombers to strike these targets.

McNamara himself began asking his staff, "How much is enough?" Not satisfied with the ever-changing calculus of destruction his question elicited, McNamara brought in Alain Enthoven and broke the U.S. nuclear strike capability down into three "legs," representing land-based ICBMs, submarine-launched missiles, and nuclear-capable bombers. The two strategists determined that each leg should be capable of delivering the equivalent of four hundred megatons of nuclear explosive power. By establishing this cap, the question of the numbers of delivery systems to procure became manageable.

Thus was born the concept of the nuclear triad, which became the foundation of America's nuclear posture. Driven not by what threat it was supposed to deter or defeat but rather by the need to cap internal defense spending, the triad in turn drove the Single Integrated Operational Plan to the extent that megatons were shifted around a targeting map like chips on a gaming table, allocating so many here, and so many there, until the megaton cap was reached.[27]

The key to preventing a Soviet surprise attack lay not with possessing the ability to strike first, which would logically necessitate the Soviets in turn to be thinking about preempting the preemption, but rather with building a survivable nuclear force that, after absorbing everything the Soviets could deliver, would be able to assure the destruction of the Soviet Union. McNamara described the ideal deterrent strategy, based upon the principle of "assured destruction," as being "the ability to destroy, after a well-planned and executed Soviet surprise attack on our Strategic Nuclear Forces, the Soviet government and military controls, plus a large percentage of their population and economy." However, McNamara noted that "this calculation of the effectiveness of U.S. forces is not a reflection of our actual targeting doctrine in the event deterrence fails." In a move that addressed long-standing Air Force concerns, McNamara continued to invest in Counterforce, or "damage-limiting," nuclear strike capability. However, the secretary of defense never considered developing a genuine first-strike capability.[28]

McGeorge Bundy shared McNamara's concern about the illogical nature of U.S. nuclear strategy. Whereas in 1961 there might have been a chance to pull off a genuine nuclear decapitation by delivering a devastating nuclear first strike against the Soviet Union, with the Soviets' development of a new generation of silo-based missiles and their fleet of oceangoing ballistic missile submarines, it was no longer viable to speak of a fully effective preemption. Some Soviet missiles would get through.

Pentagon planners would calculate that the United States could launch a "force limiting" preemptive nuclear strike against Soviet nuclear targets, killing some 100 million people and limiting the Soviet response to a reduced number of attacks that would "only" kill 30 million Americans. Besides the practical downfalls of such an attack, there were the moral and political realities of embracing a doctrine that made the attack on Pearl Harbor pale in comparison and that would subject the American people to a level of devastation unknown in their history. In reviewing the nuclear war plans in September 1963, President Kennedy was concerned that the United States was engaged in a dangerous game of "overkill," one that ended up promoting a preemptive nuclear attack, either by creating the ability to do so, or by inviting a Soviet counter-buildup that could become so strong as to invite preemption. When confronted with the horrific reality of the massive U.S. losses that would result from an American preemptive nuclear attack on the Soviet Union, President Kennedy told his advisors that such a strike option was "not possible for us."[29]

The combined effects of the Berlin crisis and the Cuban missile crisis seemed to have matured Kennedy as president. The success of the limited test ban treaty created the potential for Kennedy to act more forcefully on the concepts he had spelled out in his address at American University in June 1963. In conversations with Ambassador Dobrynin, Kennedy spoke of the need to move forward with agreements that would help prevent surprise attacks and to ban weapons from outer space. On November 15, 1963, Robert Kennedy was brainstorming with Dobrynin about the need for a new summit between Kennedy and Khrushchev, where the two leaders could redefine U.S.-Soviet relations. There was an atmosphere of great promise. But on November 22, 1963, the hope died when an assassin's bullets took the life of President Kennedy in Dallas, Texas.[30]

Nikita Khrushchev received the news of Kennedy's death while at his home in Moscow. The death of Kennedy was devastating to Khrushchev. After a tumultuous relationship that had brought the two leaders to the brink of nuclear war, Khrushchev had grown to trust Kennedy and was looking forward to building a lasting and fruitful peace with the United States. The KGB briefed Khrushchev on the character and politics of Lyndon Johnson, the American vice president and successor to Kennedy. Johnson was described as being "conservative" and "reactionary." Khrushchev was prepared to take risks with President Kennedy in order to promote peace. With Johnson, he was not.[31]

Secretary of Defense McNamara and Secretary of State Rusk were given the opportunity to fill in the newly sworn-in President Johnson on the status of U.S.-Soviet relations at a National Security Council meeting convened on December 5, 1963. Johnson opened the meeting by reading from a prepared statement. "The greatest single requirement," Johnson said, "is that we find a way to ensure the survival of civilization in the nuclear age. A nuclear war would be the death of all our hopes and it is our task to see that it does not happen."[32]

McNamara briefed Johnson on the enormous strategic advantage the United States enjoyed in nuclear strike capability, especially for a first strike. However, McNamara echoed Johnson in saying that there would be no winner in any nuclear exchange between the two powers. Rusk was insistent that the United States remain vigilant in containing Soviet expansion, noting that under Khrushchev the Soviets had made marked efforts in improving both its economy and its strategic military capabilities. Johnson was anxious to continue to build on the success of the Kennedy-Khrushchev relationship, and in January 1964, he instructed that the Soviets be approached concerning a freeze on the deployment of ballistic missiles and a reduction in the manufacture of plutonium.[33]

But the time was not right for the Soviets to embrace a major arms-control initiative that would only cement their inferiority. As proposed by the United States, the Strategic Nuclear Delivery Vehicle, or SNDV, freeze would have required extensive on-site verification inspections that went well beyond that which had already been rejected by Khrushchev in regard to a comprehensive test ban treaty. A proposal by the United States for the elimination of medium bombers was likewise rejected by the Soviets, who were not impressed with an American proposal that had the United States scrapping bombers (the B-47) it had already unilaterally decided to do away with while asking the Soviets to eliminate bombers (the TU-16) that served as the mainstay of their strategic aviation force.

The first two forays into disarmament by the Johnson administration were failures. For the Soviets, it was becoming clear that the United States was more interested in cementing its strategic superiority than it was in meaningful arms reductions. The one area where there was some agreement was in the reduction of military spending. The United States had announced military spending reductions in late 1963 and had asked the Soviets to do the same. Khrushchev made an announcement on December 16, 1963, declaring the Soviet intention of reducing its defense budget. But this was a risky policy. Although it was in the best interests of the new Johnson administration to seek to curtail runaway military spending that had created the current strategic superiority, the Soviets were just beginning to respond with a new generation of nuclear missiles in development that would bring the Soviets on level with the United States. Khrushchev's announcement put him at odds with many in the Soviet military and deepened a split within the Soviet political hierarchy, which would prove to be politically fatal to the Soviet premier.[34]

A critical aspect of the U.S.-Soviet relationship centered on the issue of Germany. Tensions were still high over Berlin, and the refusal of President Kennedy to entertain a nonaggression pact between NATO and the Warsaw Pact was a sore subject with Khrushchev. But President Johnson was not inclined to seek rapid change in regard to Germany. With 300,000 American troops and thousands of nuclear weapons stationed in Europe, the United States had a significant investment in West Germany and NATO that the Johnson administration was expecting to pay dividends. As a major economic partner in both civilian and military terms, West Germany's status as a creditor and buyer of American goods helped offset America's ongoing problems with balance of payment deficits. West Germany was the key to maintaining NATO, and NATO was the anchor of America's relationship with Europe. As the leader of NATO, the United States was able to dictate policy direction in a manner that was most beneficial to the United States, militarily, politically, and economically.

Nonproliferation was another major issue confronting the new Johnson administration. The new president had to deal not only with the emerging reality of a Chinese nuclear weapon but also with the fact that the nuclear weapons secret was about to expand beyond the borders of the major powers and into what was euphemistically referred to as the "N-th" countries— small nations possessing the intellectual and industrial capability to produce nuclear weapons. Central among these N-th countries was Israel. Israel had been pursuing a nuclear program ever since the Suez crisis in 1956, when it acted, together with Britain and France, to attack Egypt for the purpose of regaining control of the Suez Canal after Egypt nationalized it. With secret assistance from France, Israel began construction of a nuclear reactor in the Negev Desert in 1957. However, it wasn't until 1960, in the waning moments of the Eisenhower administration, that the Israeli nuclear reactor, located in Dimona, was identified by U.S. intelligence.

One of the major problems confronting the United States when it came to containing Israel's nuclear ambitions was the absence of any international framework for the control of nuclear proliferation. The only leverage the United States had was in the form of bilateral agreements. Yet these were notoriously flawed, as was shown by the initial intervention on the part of President Kennedy in May 1961, when two American scientists visited Dimona, under heavy Israeli escort, to inspect the facility following a meeting between Kennedy and Israeli Prime Minister David Ben-Gurion. The inspectors found nothing that indicated the reactor was being used for purposes other than its declared peaceful purpose, a finding Kennedy was compelled to accept, given that it was derived from his intervention with Ben-Gurion. Later, in 1963, U.S. inspectors again visited and likewise concluded that there was no evidence of a nuclear weapons program. Although inspections were recommended on an annual basis, under Johnson these inspections were not continued. The Israeli nuclear program threatened to derail the Kennedy administration's efforts on nonproliferation. The cornerstone of the Kennedy administration's approach toward nonproliferation was the concept that any meaningful agreement would stem from an initial U.S.-Soviet agreement.[35]

In April 1963, the United States presented the Soviet Union with a draft of what was called the "Non-Transfer Declaration," in which signatory

nations pledged "not [to] transfer any nuclear weapons directly or indirectly through a military alliance, into the national control of individual states currently not possessing such weapons, and that they will not assist such states in the manufacturing of such weapons." The only problem was that the United States sought to exclude the MLF from such an arrangement, something the Soviet Union would not accept. NATO, the Soviets noted, was a military alliance, and in any event, the MLF would provide nuclear weapons to West Germany, something the Soviets were adamantly opposed to. By July 1963, on the eve of the test ban negotiations in Moscow, President Kennedy was still trying to bring together an understanding of how the United States would approach allied nations such as Israel and West Germany who were seeking to acquire nuclear weapons, in hopes that such a model would be employed by the Soviets toward its allies, such as China.[36]

The Kennedy administration had been following China's march toward acquisition of a nuclear bomb with great interest and concern. In January 1964, the Johnson administration received alarming intelligence that indicated China was preparing to detonate its first nuclear device in October of that year. By April 1964, U.S. satellite imagery showed that a tower had been constructed at the Chinese nuclear test facility in Lop Nor, an action that clearly indicated preparations for an impending test.[37]

The Chinese actions were viewed in Washington as extremely destabilizing, not only from the standpoint of American influence in Asia but also for what such Chinese acquisition of a nuclear bomb would do to the overall issue of nuclear nonproliferation. If China developed a nuclear weapon, then its neighbor and rival, India, would feel compelled to do so as well. Already in India the Cambridge-educated physicist, Homi Bhabha—who since 1948 had served as the chair of the Indian Atomic Energy Commission—was spearheading India's acquisition of the capability to produce a nuclear weapon. In 1954, India had created the Department of Atomic Energy, with Bhabha serving as its secretary, and it soon was involved in an ambitious program of nuclear reactor construction, including a Canadian-built heavy water reactor that produced significant amounts of plutonium. In 1961, the Indians had built a plutonium extraction plant that operated free of any safeguards inspections.[38]

Although Indian Prime Minister Jawaharlal Nehru continuously advocated for the peaceful use of atomic energy and stated that as being the sole reason for India's ambitious nuclear program, Bhabha always held that India should be prepared to acquire a nuclear weapons capability, especially in light of China's march toward the bomb. In early 1964, Bhabha openly argued that nuclear weapons would provide India with a means of deterring a larger nation such as China. India was still reeling under the ignominy of its military defeat during the Sino-Indian conflict of 1962. Even though Nehru continued to advocate for peaceful nuclear uses, the pressure China was placing on India when it came to developing a nuclear answer to the Chinese nuclear problem was real. And the pressure wasn't being felt only by India.

Around the world, nations were examining the global situation vis-à-vis nuclear weapons and deciding that their best interests may in fact lie in acquiring an independent nuclear deterrent of their own. In Europe, Sweden, Switzerland, and Italy were researching military nuclear programs. Israel was well on the way to acquiring nuclear weapons capability. Taiwan (the Republic of China) was alarmed by the events on the Chinese mainland and was making moves of its own to acquire a nuclear weapon. And as each of these nations progressed toward their own nuclear weapons capability, then the pressure was felt by others to do the same. Neither the United States nor the rest of the world had a plan on how to prevent this proliferation of nuclear weapons from occurring.

The assassination of President Kennedy created a vacuum in policy progression on disarmament and nonproliferation, which could not have come at a worse time. American domestic politics made 1964 a "lost year" when it came to pursuing meaningful arms control and disarmament. The signing of the limited test ban treaty in August 1963 had created a wave of momentum not only for the control of nuclear weapons among the major powers but also for nonproliferation in general. President Kennedy's death brought this momentum to a sudden halt. President Johnson retained the entirety of Kennedy's cabinet, out of respect for the fact that though he had inherited the mantle of leadership, he did not yet possess a mandate for change. But even though the staff was the same, the executive was not; Johnson did not share Kennedy's passion and experience concerning the control of nuclear weapons. The reality was that 1964 was an election year, and Johnson needed to turn his attention to getting elected. As a result, the critical window of opportunity that had been created in the last months of the Kennedy administration to achieve lasting and meaningful results in the fields of arms control and nonproliferation closed.

Nothing signified this loss of imagination and opportunity more than how the Johnson administration responded to a major policy initiative from the Soviets in late summer 1964. During a visit to London in August 1964, Nikita Khrushchev announced that he was ready for meaningful disarmament agreements with the West. "A new initiative would be welcome," Khrushchev said. For the first time, Khrushchev stated that if an agreement could be reached, then he would reverse his long-standing opposition to on-site inspections. "If we make a disarmament agreement and a start is actually made on disarmament, then we will allow free inspections as part of the specific program—and close inspections, too, so no one cheats."[39] Khrushchev indicated that he was willing to personally attend a disarmament conference in early 1965 to make good on his offer. In Washington, Khrushchev's comments fell on deaf ears. With a presidential election looming in November, Johnson was reluctant to make any commitments about attending a future international conference.

Fear of doing anything controversial in a political year also drove Johnson's approach toward China. Throughout the summer of 1964, the U.S. intelligence community watched as China prepared for its first nuclear test. Johnson was engaged in a fierce political fight with the Republican Party nominee, Senator Barry Goldwater, an archconservative from Arizona. An ardent anticommunist, Goldwater had opposed the limited test ban treaty as well as any form of disarmament, having stated quite clearly in 1961, "I have no faith in disarmament. There is always one S.O.B. in the world who won't go along with it."[40] The issue of nuclear weapons and nuclear war was on display front and center in an increasingly contentious and ideologically driven political season.

Another issue was the conflict in Vietnam, which was escalating dramatically, with two American aircraft carriers being dispatched off the coast of North Vietnam in the spring of 1964 in response to North Vietnamese incursions into Laos. In August 1964, the situation in Vietnam spiraled out of control, when U.S.-backed commando operations in North Vietnam led to a confusing situation when the commander of a U.S. destroyer, the USS *Maddox*, claimed (and later recanted) that he had been attacked by North Vietnamese torpedo boats. President Johnson ordered a naval air strike in retaliation, and two U.S. jets were shot down. Three days later, under pressure from Johnson, Congress passed the Gulf of Tonkin resolution, authorizing the president to take whatever means necessary to defend Southeast Asia.

As the Republican candidate, Goldwater had put America, and the world, on notice when, during his acceptance speech delivered at the Republican Convention in 1964, he declared, "I would remind you that extremism in the defense of liberty is no vice. And let me remind you also that moderation in the pursuit of justice is no virtue."[41] The Johnson campaign had capitalized on Goldwater's oftentimes less-than-politic comments, and a number of controversial, yet extremely effective, television advertisements were run by the Johnson campaign (including the famous

"Daisy Girl" spot, which featured a little girl picking flowers before being blotted out by a nuclear explosion) that depicted Goldwater as a man whose finger would too quickly push the nuclear button.[42]

The Johnson campaign did not want to participate in any activity that would provide political ammunition to the Goldwater campaign. It was in this light that Khrushchev's initiative on disarmament was left to hang unanswered. And in the case of China, with a potentially politically explosive nuclear test looming on the horizon, the Johnson administration was compelled to assume a posture of inaction. The best the Johnson team could come up with was a statement issued by Secretary of State Dean Rusk, on September 29, 1964, that made clear the United States was fully aware of an impending Chinese nuclear test and was not alarmed by it.[43]

Early in the morning of October 14, 1964, in the desert test facility of Lop Nur, a team of technicians working under the supervision of a Yale-educated Chinese physicist named Chen Nengkuan assembled a nuclear device made from enriched uranium 235. After hoisting the device to the top of the test tower that had been photographed by the United States the previous spring, the Chinese detonated, at precisely 3:00 PM, a twenty-kiloton nuclear device. The Chinese were quick to announce their achievement, but the United States, through its worldwide network of seismic stations, was able to detect, isolate, and characterize the Chinese event.[44] President Johnson decried the Chinese test as a "tragedy for the Chinese people," but privately noted that China was a long way from having a deliverable weapon and that the specter of a nuclear-armed China was a problem that would be faced by a future president. Somewhat surprisingly, Johnson's Republican challenger professed similar sentiments, telling a political rally that China was not a nuclear threat and that the nuclear device had no military value unless it could be delivered "from here to there."[45]

A reaction from the Kremlin was not immediately forthcoming. While Khrushchev vacationed at his dacha in Pitsunda, in Moscow his political rivals gathered. Frustrated by Khrushchev's disastrous economic policies, and embarrassed by what they believed to be his ill-advised reconciliation with the United States, presidium members Nikolai Podgorny and Leonid Brezhnev, backed by former KGB chief Aleksandr Shelepin, plotted to remove the seventy-year-old Soviet premier from power. When Khrushchev returned to Moscow on October 14, he was taken immediately to the Kremlin, where he was confronted by an openly hostile presidium. What transpired over the next two days was nothing short of a complete repudiation of the policies of Nikita Khrushchev by his fellow communists.[46]

Khrushchev's gamble in Cuba in 1962 was in particular harshly criticized. More telling were the criticisms of Khrushchev's outreach to the

United States in the form of disarmament. The assassination of President Kennedy made it clear to Khrushchev's critics the fragile nature of national agreements made on the strength of individual charisma. By October 15, 1964, the deed was done. Khrushchev was forced to resign from all of his positions of authority. Brezhnev was appointed party first secretary, with Aleksei Kosygin named prime minister and Anastas Mikoyan named president. In removing Khrushchev, the new Soviet leaders had made it clear that, though not seeking confrontation with the United States and the West, they were definitely breaking with the policies of détente that had been so aggressively pursued by the former Soviet leader.[47]

On November 3, 1964, the American people voted for their thirty-sixth president. Any concerns over the Chinese going nuclear, or uncertainty coming out of Moscow due to the removal of Khrushchev from power, were offset by fears, justified or not, of nuclear war. Barry Goldwater, who during the campaign joked that the United States should "lob one [a nuclear bomb] into the men's room of the Kremlin," was defeated by Lyndon Johnson in one of the largest landslides in American presidential election history, larger than Franklin Roosevelt's 1936 victory.[48] Johnson had been concerned that he lacked a mandate to govern in his own right. He no longer needed to be concerned about that. Lyndon Johnson chose Hubert Humphrey, the champion of arms control and disarmament, as his vice president. President Johnson was congratulated by Soviet Prime Minister Kosygin and President Mikoyan. Moscow Radio, expressing a relief that was felt not only in the Soviet Union but also in Europe and the world as a whole, broadcast that the American people had chosen the "more moderate and sober policy" toward East-West relations. On the cusp of a time of historical change, President Johnson's implementation of this "moderate and sober" mandate would dictate the course of the Cold War for decades to come.

CHAPTER 8

MISSED OPPORTUNITIES

The historic victory of Lyndon Johnson in the 1964 presidential election paved the way for a number of important policy initiatives to be undertaken, most of which involved critical domestic issues pertaining to civil rights and poverty. However, there were a number of pressing foreign policy matters that needed attention as well. The growing conflict in Vietnam loomed large, as did the question of how the Johnson administration was going to deal with China, given that nation's newfound status as a nuclear power. Whereas the simplistic politics of presidential elections precluded sharp and decisive action at the time of the August 1964 Chinese nuclear test, after the election, Johnson was liberated by a mandate only a sweeping electoral victory could provide.

The Chinese acquisition of the atomic bomb highlighted the growing threat presented by the proliferation of nuclear weapons technology, a threat that had been identified by President Kennedy prior to his death and yet pushed to the side by Johnson during the run-up to the 1964 election. With the election finished, Johnson could assemble a high-level committee that he tasked with exploring "the widest range of measures that the United States might undertake in conjunction with other governments or by itself" when it came to the limitation of the spread of nuclear weapons.[1] This committee became known as the Gilpatric Committee, named after its chair, Roswell Gilpatric, the former deputy secretary of defense, who left his government job in January 1964 to take a position with a Wall Street law firm.

The Gilpatric Committee was composed of some of the most experienced men in government and industry, including the veteran diplomat and arms control specialist John McCloy; another veteran diplomat and arms control negotiator, Arthur Dean; former White House science advisor George Kistiakowsky; former CIA director Allen Dulles; the chair of IBM, Arthur Watson; and the former NATO commander, General Alfred Gruenther. The committee was served by a strong and experienced staff, including Spurgeon Keeney of the National Security Council as well as Henry Rowen and George Rathjens. The committee also consulted with officials in and out of government.[2]

The Gilpatric Committee made its report to President Johnson on January 21, 1965, the day following the president's inauguration. The report set forth three pillars of policy guidance around which, in its opinion, a successful American nonproliferation policy must be built. First and foremost, the committee emphasized the paramount importance of the need for the United States to take the lead in the negotiation of formal multilateral agreements on the issue of nonproliferation. The second pillar was the need for the application of influence by the United States, and other like-minded nations, on individual nations considering nuclear weapons acquisition. And the final pillar, which was perhaps the most critical, was the need for the United States to set the example through its own policies and actions.[3]

Time, the Gilpatric Committee believed, was in short supply. "The world is fast approaching the point of no return," the report warned ominously, "in the prospects of controlling the spread of nuclear weapons."[4] Though not the original intent of Eisenhower's "atom's for peace" program, the fact of the matter was that the proliferation of nuclear power programs had succeeded in placing the "knowledge, equipment and materials for making nuclear weapons" in the hands of numerous nations.[5] The Chinese nuclear test in October 1964, as with the French nuclear test before it, brought with it the impression that possession of a nuclear weapon awarded it automatic status as a regional, if not world, power.

If the United States was to have any success in preventing the spread of nuclear weapons, the committee noted, there must be immediate concerted and intensified effort. All policies were interlinked in this regard, including foreign relations abroad, the deployment of nuclear weapons at home and abroad, peaceful atomic energy, and commercial relations. Although other issues were important, the Gilpatric Committee noted, nonproliferation was going to need to be emphasized to a much greater degree than had been the case in the past.[6]

There could be no effective nonproliferation policy without the full involvement of the Soviet Union. This meant that the Cold War–inspired arms race had to be brought to an end because, as the committee underscored, "it is unlikely that others can be induced to abstain indefinitely from acquiring nuclear weapons if the Soviet Union and the United States continue in a nuclear arms race. Therefore, lessened emphasis by the United States and the Soviet Union on nuclear weapons, and agreements on broader arms control measures, must be recognized as important components in the overall program to prevent nuclear proliferation."[7] The Soviets, the committee stated, have a shared perception of the problem. The recent change in Soviet leadership, combined with a possible review of Soviet nuclear policies, could very well provide immediate opportunities for joint or parallel action by both the United States and the Soviet Union to stop the spread of nuclear weapons. The cornerstone of any nonproliferation regime, the committee held, was the need for an improvement in U.S.-Soviet relations, with an emphasis on strengthening arms control through new agreements. The Gilpatric Committee viewed the ongoing pursuit of a multilateral force (MLF) by the United States and NATO as inherently contradictory to the overall U.S. nonproliferation objectives, so they argued strongly for the MLF to be dropped.[8]

In perhaps its most controversial finding, the Gilpatric Committee recommended that the United States de-emphasize nuclear weapons as a tool of military and national power. This was, the committee believed, the only way to prevent giving other nations around the world any incentive to develop nuclear weapons. Not only would U.S. strategy need to be reworked but also the strategy of NATO, since tactical nuclear weapons played such an important role in its overall military defense posture. Even though the committee concurred that some tactical nuclear weapons capability needed to be retained within NATO for the purposes of preserving a viable deterrent, strategic flexibility, and overall credibility, the reliance on the part of NATO on tactical nuclear weapons needed to be significantly reduced.[9]

The Gilpatric Committee's report challenged numerous aspects of U.S. policy in effect at the time, including arms control, relations with NATO, and the integration of nuclear weapons in overall U.S. military strategy. Upon conclusion of the committee's verbal report, Johnson expressed some frustration, noting that to him it seemed like the implementation of the committee's findings would be "a very unpleasant undertaking."[10] Johnson then ordered a complete embargo of the committee's written report, to include prohibiting the attendees from even mentioning the fact that the committee had produced a written report. The suppression of the committee's report and findings left many committee members, including Gilpatric himself, angry and critical of the president and his advisors, especially Secretary of State Dean Rusk, who was singled out as being particularly inflexible when it came to altering U.S. foreign policy priorities.

President Johnson was confronted with two major foreign policy issues early on in his administration, both of which he had reflected on in his State of the Union speech delivered on January 4, 1965. The first was the issue with Soviet Union, to which the president said, "With the Soviet Union we seek peaceful understandings that can lessen the danger to freedom. Last fall I asked the American people to choose that course. I will carry forward their command. If we are to live together in peace, we must come to know each other better."[11] The Gilpatric Committee had provided President Johnson, through its report, with as big an incentive as possible for an immediate improvement in U.S.-Soviet relations, namely the need to jointly confront what was, in its opinion, the greatest threat faced by America, that being the proliferation of nuclear weapons.

But President Johnson was wrestling with another foreign policy demon, this one in Vietnam. While arguing for better US-Soviet relations, Johnson noted: "In Asia, communism wears a more aggressive face. We see that in Vietnam." As if debating himself, Johnson asked the question, "Why are we there?" His answer provided insight into the direction Johnson was heading concerning U.S. involvement in that nation. "We are there, first, because a friendly nation has asked us for help against the communist aggression."[12] The U.S. military action in Vietnam damaged relations between the United States and the Soviet Union and, more critically, between Soviet Premier Aleksei Kosygin and President Johnson, at a critical time. Following the ascension to power of Kosygin and Brezhnev in the Soviet Union in October 1964, and the election of President Johnson in the United States in November 1964, efforts had been made by all parties to seek to repair relations between the world's two superpowers, with particular attention being paid to the field of disarmament and proliferation. Johnson and Kosygin exchanged letters to that effect.

But radical changes in disarmament policy were not part of the Johnson agenda. McGeorge Bundy, having helped created the Gilpatric Committee, was now leading the charge to undermine its findings. Neither Johnson nor Bundy had embraced any of the committee's conclusions, or even its

basic philosophy of arms control and nonproliferation. Overseeing the drafting of a new National Security Action Memorandum on arms control, Bundy emphasized to Johnson that the new review would "bring the issues up clear and clean where you can see them and hear the arguments of the different parties of interest," a clear slap at the Gilpatric Committee, which Bundy viewed as being composed of "outsiders."[13] Bundy informed both McNamara and Rusk that the Gilpatric Committee report was "unbalanced in its apparent feeling that immediate progress is possible in these areas."[14] Rather than sweeping arms control proposals and initiatives, Bundy preferred that both the State and Defense Departments simply seek to "reaffirm our basic support for the principle of non-dissemination and the principle of a comprehensive test ban treaty."[15] Such limited thinking was designed to keep policy from becoming "unbalanced in the other direction," this despite protests from Bundy's NSC staff not "to sweep the [Gilpatric] report under the rug."[16]

On June 28, 1965, Johnson authorized the issuing of National Security Action Memorandum 335, "Preparation of Arms Control Program." Prepared by McGeorge Bundy, NSAM 335 directed the Arms Control and Disarmament Agency to draft "a proposed new program of arms control and disarmament, including a proposed program for preventing the spread of nuclear weapons." The end product of these efforts would be a new U.S. negotiating posture designed to reinvigorate the regularly scheduled meeting of the Eighteen Nation Disarmament Conference in Geneva, which would be "brought to the attention of the President in a timely and orderly manner in order to permit a decision by him at the appropriate time."[17] The lack of specific direction in the body of NSAM 335 reflected Bundy's prejudice against the Gilpatric Committee's finding. A few days after issuing NSAM 335, Bundy wrote Johnson that "in light of the fact that the Gilpatric Committee has not worked out to your satisfaction, I want to be quite sure that our next efforts in this critically important field are along lines you approve." President Johnson checked the "approve" box on the bottom of the page, indicating his concurrence with Bundy's motives.[18]

Given Bundy's stance on the Gilpatric Committee's report, and Rusk's continued embrace of the MLF, there was no hope for any meaningful progress on the issue of nonproliferation in Geneva. The Gilpatric Committee's report, especially its findings on placing a nonproliferation treaty ahead of any agreement on MLF, was in direct opposition to the positions of President Johnson and Secretary of State Rusk, who were both heavily committed to the MLF. The Soviet Union continued to view the MLF as being incompatible with a nonproliferation treaty. Rusk, in particular, continued to embrace the MLF as the best means to ensure West Germany did not pursue an independent nuclear capability. Any prospects of the Gilpatric Committee's findings concerning MLF and NATO being widely embraced were further damaged by a National Intelligence Estimate published in April 1965, which warned that failure to achieve adequate nuclear sharing arrangements with Germany "may lead them to eventually consider alternative nuclear policies."[19] Upcoming German elections in September 1965 prompted the Germans to request the United States to remain low-key on MLF, out of fear of influencing German elections. But the MLF was destined to become a major issue after that time.

Hobbled by the lack of creativity on the part of Bundy and Rusk, and lacking any bold direction from the president, the best ACDA could produce was a draft nonproliferation treaty that was submitted at the ENDC on August 17, 1965. Predictably, the Soviets responded on September 24, 1965, noting that the greatest threat to proliferation was the MLF, and because the U.S. draft treaty continued not to address these issues, there would be no acceptable treaty text. All work toward achieving a viable nonproliferation treaty was stalled.[20]

By failing to act decisively on the issue of proliferation, the United States continued to operate as if the status quo ante of U.S.-Soviet nuclear deterrence models was still viable. This may have been the case in a bipolar world, but the development of nuclear weapons capability in France and China meant that these nations, operating outside the framework of U.S.-Soviet–dominated nuclear policy, would be developing their own nuclear deterrence models. Thereby a model of independent national security policy would be created that other nations could then seek to emulate. This was something the Gilpatric Committee both had predicted and had rightly labeled as inherently destabilizing.

While the United States sought to continue American control of nuclear ambition in the West through its pursuit of an MLF, France (and in particular its volatile leader, Charles de Gaulle) viewed such an integration of nuclear capability as an unacceptable limitation on European political sovereignty. Europe circa 1965 was, in the mind of de Gaulle, far removed from the period immediately following the end of the Second World War. Europe had recovered from the ravages of war, and the implementation of European institutions such as the European Community meant that there was no longer a pressing need for U.S. leadership. The Soviet Union had not emerged as a viable model for social, economic, and political development, and as such any bipolar framework such as that being pushed by the United States was outdated. America no longer enjoyed a nuclear monopoly, and the ongoing war in Vietnam was damaging America's role as a moral world leader. Not only was a U.S. guarantee of nuclear security no longer credible, but in fact, as many in France and Europe believed, it was also morally questionable.

Although France believed that an alliance with the United States was desirable, military integration, especially involving nuclear weapons, was not. France under de Gaulle would never cede the subordination of French security to another. By December 1960, the French Parliament had voted to fund a bomber force of thirty-six *Mirage* IV aircraft, as well as a nuclear missile–armed submarine force. An interim force of eighteen intermediate-range missiles was likewise funded as an interim measure until France's submarine-launched missile force could be fielded. French nuclear deterrence went from being a theory to being a reality which the entire world, including the United States, had to deal with. Whether or not any direct American effort targeting France and its nuclear weapons program, as recommended by the Gilpatric Committee, could have succeeded in reversing the French nuclear effort will never be known. What is certain is that the uncertainty and instability created by an unconstrained French independent nuclear capability was unleashed on the world, creating a model that promoted nuclear proliferation as opposed to constraining it.[21]

As the Gilpatric Committee warned, the world was on the cusp of viral proliferation. By 1965, South Africa was discussing the need to build a nuclear weapon for "prestige purposes." At the inauguration of the Safari reactor in 1965, Prime Minister H. F. Verwoerd spoke of the duty of South Africa to consider the military applications of nuclear power.[22] On November 2, 1966, another nation flirting with nuclear weapons status took a giant step in that direction. Israel conducted a test which brought it closer to having viable nuclear weapon. Although Israel would never formally admit having a nuclear weapon (the official Israeli policy of nuclear ambiguity was in play), the November 1966 test, believed to have involved the use of high explosives compressing a core of natural uranium, also known as a "cold test," is often cited as representing the start point of Israel's actual, versus theoretical, nuclear capability.[23]

The question of China and its nuclear capability continued to loom large in the minds of the Johnson administration. In addition to the Gilpatric Committee, the Johnson administration had commissioned a number of panels and committees to examine the Chinese nuclear program and American policy responses. The fact of the matter was that China's nuclear capability did not immediately manifest itself into a direct threat against the United States. Indirectly, China, by fielding a number of intermediate-range ballistic missiles, was able to extend its nuclear coverage over parts of the Soviet Union, Japan, and South Korea. While China possessed intermediate-range missiles, any Chinese intercontinental capability was at least a decade away. The biggest threat China posed in the short term was serving as an impetus for an Indian nuclear weapons program.

A January 1965 meeting between Undersecretary of State George Ball and the head of India's Atomic Energy Commission, Homi Bhabha, provided critical insight into India's thinking regarding nuclear weapons and nuclear proliferation. The successful Chinese test of a nuclear device in October 1964 sent shockwaves through India, and Bhabha himself believed that China had positioned itself advantageously vis-à-vis India when it came to prestige and influence among Asian and nonaligned nations. In Bhabha's opinion, the Chinese could not have progressed as rapidly and as effectively as they had on a nuclear device without extensive help from the Soviet Union, including, according to Bhabha's unfounded assertion, China's receipt of a complete set of blueprints from the Soviets for making a nuclear weapon. Bhabha pressed Ball for similar support on the part of the United States to India, support that would enable India to manufacture a nuclear weapon in less than six months.[24]

From the American perspective, the loss of prestige India would suffer having been exposed both as a fraud and a proxy of the United States would far offset any gains that might be gained by being seen as the nuclear equal of China. India would thus be better served by promoting the merits of nuclear nonproliferation as opposed to becoming a proliferator itself. Bhabha's nuclear dreams came to a tragic end when, on January 24, 1966, he died in a plane wreck in Europe. Bhabha's death slowed, but did not stop, India's progress toward nuclear weapons.

The Chinese nuclear threat, or perceptions thereof, played a major role in propelling the United States down one of the more controversial arms acquisition paths of the nuclear age, one which continues to this day: ballistic missile defense. The Soviet missile threat was seen as being too massive to be viably countered by any system of surface-based missile interceptors. But the Chinese missile threat, comprised of a much smaller number of missiles, was a different story. The Sino-Soviet schism, which came to a head in the late 1950s, allowed the United States to begin viewing these two communist nations seperately when it came to threat analysis. As such, building a ballistic missile defense system that was Chinese-specific was considered plausible, even after most U.S. defense analysts agreed that trying to put in place a similar system to counter the Soviets would be ineffective and cost-prohibitive.

The allure of a ballistic missile defense system had been around since the dawn of the missile age. In 1955, the U.S. Army began research and development work on the *Nike Zeus* antiballistic missile (ABM), but it was never deployed. President Eisenhower decided in 1959 to keep the *Nike Zeus* program alive as a pure research-and-development effort, which by January 1963 had evolved into what was known as the *Nike X* system. But whereas *Nike X* represented a viable ABM response based upon Soviet strike capabilities that existed pre-ABM, it was not a system that took into account what the Soviets would do to counter it. It was this cause-and-effect relationship between defensive and offensive weapons that led two top-level Pentagon scientists, Jack Ruina and Murray Gell-Man, to write a 1964 paper titled "BMD and the Arms Race." The main thesis of the Ruina/Gel-Man paper was that ABM systems were inherently destabilizing and should not be pursued. The best way to control the arms race between the Soviet Union and the United States, the paper stated, was to limit ABMs. Secretary of Defense Robert McNamara concurred, concluding that ABMs undermined arms control and encouraged an arms race because ABMs by their very nature called into question the assured destruction capabilities of the other side, leading to a massive arms race as each side increased its offensive strike capability to overcome the defensive characteristics of a given ABM system.[25]

In the early 1960s, the Soviets had been making strides toward fielding a viable ABM system of their own. In early 1961, a V-1000 missile was used to shoot down a SS-4 intermediate-range missile using a conventional high-explosive warhead, marking the first time in the world that a genuine anti-ICBM capability had been tested. The Soviets began installing V-1000 sites around the Estonian capital of Tallinn, and later around Leningrad, with installation completed in 1962. However, these sites were dismantled in 1964, when the Soviets began fielding the A-35 ABM system around Moscow.[26] Designed to protect the Soviet capital from single-warhead *Titan II* and *Minutemen II* missiles, the ABM-1 was a three-stage missile with a three-hundred-kiloton warhead possessing a range of some three hundred kilometers. The system's manually directed radars reduced its efficiency, and it soon became obvious to Soviet military planners that the A-35 ABM system as designed was ineffective.[27]

The perception of a growing Soviet ABM capability had led to McNamara's Counterforce strategy as set forth in the Athens's Doctrine, coming under closer scrutiny from none other than McNamara himself. Misperceptions existed in the public sector that the No Cities targeting approach of the Counterforce strategy somehow made nuclear war more feasible. Furthermore, as the Air Force expanded the number of targets it needed to strike in order to achieve a genuine Counterforce capability, it began to demand even more nuclear weapons and vehicles to deploy them. The Counterforce strategy brought with it an assumption that there would need to be an even larger air defense capability (to defend against Soviet bombers ostensibly launched on their own "counterforce" sorties) and missile defense (to defend against Soviet ICBMs targeting American nuclear forces).

All of this led to increased military spending, which the Johnson administration could ill afford. When combined with the ongoing negative reaction to the Athens's Doctrine from the Soviets and America's NATO allies, McNamara had no choice but to turn to a strategic deterrence strategy of "Assured Destruction," defined by McNamara as "to deter deliberate nuclear attack upon the United States and its allies by maintaining a highly reliable ability to inflict an unacceptable degree of damage upon any single aggressor, or combination of aggressors, even after absorbing a surprise first strike."[28] In short, Assured Destruction existed when the United States maintained the capability to absorb the full brunt of a Soviet nuclear surprise attack and still retaliate with a force guaranteed to destroy 20 to 25 percent of the Soviet Union's population and 50 percent of its industrial capacity.[29]

Assured Destruction, which soon morphed into Mutually Assured Destruction, or MAD, retained as a working principle the concept of "damage limitation." This concept had American nuclear forces targeted in such a manner as to reduce the damage any Soviet nuclear attack might inflict on American population and industrial centers by attacking and diminishing the strategic offensive nuclear forces of the Soviet Union. But even this concession to the original Athens's Doctrine was soon de-emphasized by McNamara out of concern that the Air Force would turn damage limitation into a genuine first-strike capability.

By the end of 1964, McNamara had set the strategic missile strength of the United States at 1,054 missiles (1,000 *Minuteman* missiles and 54 *Titan II* missiles) and 656 *Polaris* missiles on 41 submarines.[30] As the *Minuteman* capability stood up, the original workhorse of the U.S. ICBM force, the *Atlas* missile, began to be phased out. The Air Force was not pleased with the limitation on a *Minuteman* force it once envisioned as being 10,000 in number.

However, technology soon intervened in a way that forever changed the calculus of mass destruction. Ironically, it was the Navy, and not the Air Force, that was initially responsible for the innovation in question: multiple reentry vehicles (MRVs) in which a single delivery system, or missile, could carry more than one warhead. The accuracy of the *Polaris*

A-3 at its maximum range of 2,500 miles was such that it was only useful as an area weapon. In order to increase kill probability, and to saturate any ABM system that might be deployed around a given target, the *Polaris* A-3 missile was deployed with a clamshell multiple reentry vehicle system, which carried three warheads underneath a reentry shroud. Each warhead would be ejected by use of a small rocket motor, allowing for a given target area to be covered by three overlapping explosions. When the USS *Daniel Webster* took up its initial operational patrol in the Atlantic Ocean on September 28, 1964, the *Polaris* A-3 MRV was operational. This was followed on December 25, 1964, when the USS *Daniel Boone* began its Pacific Ocean patrol. The Soviet landmass was now fully covered by the *Polaris* A-3 missile, making it a critical component of the U.S. deterrent arsenal.[31]

Although the three-warhead MRV of the *Polaris* A-3 was designed to saturate a given defense, it still was operated on the premise of one target, one missile. In order to increase the effectiveness of an MRV missile, one would need to add what were known as penetration aids, or missile decoys. But even this did not change the one missile, one target equation. Missile designers experimented with the idea of maneuvering the "bus," or vehicle that held the warheads. By doing this, and by controlling the timing of each warhead's release, each warhead could be independently targeted. Thus was born the concept of the MIRV, or multiple independently targeted reentry vehicle. Now each MIRV-capable missile became a force-multiplier, the missile-equivalent of however many MIRVs with which it was equipped.[32] MIRVs were not developed as a response to Soviet ABMs, but once the capability to overwhelm ABM defenses was identified, the MIRV became the perfect weapons system. However, though MIRVs were seen as a proper response to a Soviet nationwide ABM system, there was in fact no need for MIRVs if the Soviets didn't have a viable ABM system, which was the case in 1965.

Secretary of Defense McNamara understood that if American MIRVs could overwhelm a Soviet ABM defense, then in due time Soviet MIRVs would likewise overwhelm any American ABM defense.[33] However, MIRVs became the weapon of choice for everyone involved in the strategic targeting business. For the Air Force and Navy, the limitations imposed by McNamara's 1,054/656 missile cap were now meaningless because MIRVs allowed the number of deliverable warheads to be increased without changing those numbers. As MIRVs became more accurate, each warhead could be targeted on a single missile silo, creating not only a potent Counterforce capability but in actuality a viable first-strike weapon as well. As MIRVs made land-based systems more vulnerable, they in turn enhanced the importance of submarine-launched ballistic missiles, not only as a retaliatory force but also as a backup to the Counterforce/first-strike capability of ICBMs. During the period 1965–1966, MIRVs were very much a theoretical weapon. However, the ascension of MIRVs as the new "wonder weapon" drove the strategic planning for future weapons acquisitions, and as such pushed the Soviet Union and the United States closer to the edge of a new expensive, and dangerous, phase of the arms race.[34]

McNamara commissioned a study concerning ABM employment and viability under the direction of Army Major General Austin Betts. The Betts Panel examined potential *Nike X* deployment locations, production schedules and costs, system effectiveness, national strategic objectives, and cost-effectiveness in terms of both the current Soviet ICBM threat as well as any potential improvements the Soviets might make in response to an American ABM system. The critical factor behind whether or not the *Nike X* was deemed a viable system was the degree to which it reduced the Assured Destruction aspect of the Soviet strategic nuclear force. If the *Nike X* could prevent the Soviets from achieving the criteria set forth by McNamara for Assured Destruction (i.e., preserving more than 75 percent of the U.S. population and more than 50 percent of America's industrial capacity), then the United States would emerge with strategic dominance because it would, theoretically at least, emerge from a full-scale nuclear exchange with the Soviet Union in a superior position.[35]

McNamara had earlier commissioned a study to be conducted by the Office of Research and Engineering. Air Force Brigadier General Glen Kent headed the study. Kent organized his study so that two factors could be assessed: first, what the damage to the United States would be from a determined and adaptive Soviet attack; and second, what would constitute a proper allocation of resources among various entities (civil defense, *Nike X* ABM, Counterforce attacks by *Minuteman* missiles, antisubmarine warfare targeting Soviet missile submarines, and air defense against Soviet bombers) in order to limit damage against the United States.

Kent's study concluded that in order to obtain a 70 percent survival rate for the American population against then-current Soviet forces, the United States would need to spend $28 billion. However, if the Soviets then responded to the American damage-limiting actions by deploying more ICBMs and SLBMs, then the United States would need to expend even more money to sustain the 70 percent survivability factor, at a cost of some $2 dollars spent on defense to every $1 spent on offense. Because a 70 percent survivability rate meant that some 60 million Americans were destined to die, this tack was politically unacceptable. Yet when efforts were made to improve the survivability factor to 90 percent, it was found that the exchange ratio (the amount the United States would have to spend to limit damage compared to the amount the Soviets would have to spend to create damage) rose to 6:1 in favor of the Soviets.[36]

In short, Kent concluded, it was always cheaper to create damage than it was to limit damage. The destruction generated by nuclear weapons, combined with the vulnerability of modern urban-industrial society, meant that neither the United States nor the Soviet Union could avoid national destruction in the event of an all-out nuclear conflict. This was even further underscored when one factored in that an attacker was able to modify its weapons and tactics after the defender had invested and deployed its defenses. McNamara, thanks in no small part to Kent's study, determined that damage limitation as a national strategy simply would not work.[37] Instead of seeking to unilaterally limit damage through new weapons and strategies, the best option for both the United States and the Soviet Union would be to enter into negotiated treaties to curtail nationwide ABM defenses and limit the deployment of offensive nuclear forces.[38]

But, as was far too often the case, national security considerations alone did not suffice to make the case. Politics reared its ugly head. Michigan Governor George Romney, by 1966 considered a leading Republican challenger to Lyndon Johnson in 1968, was being very vocal about the existence of an "ABM gap," hoping to repeat the success that the so-called missile gap had created for John Kennedy in 1960. Romney made a point of the ABM gap during an interview on *Meet the Press*. Melvin Laird, head of the GOP Congressional Committee, was likewise making it clear that the ABM issue would be a focus of the Republican Party challenge to the national security policies of the Johnson administration.[39]

Romney and Laird had support from hawks in the U.S. Senate, such as Republican Strom Thurmond, but also including a number of prominent Democrats (e.g., Henry "Scoop" Jackson and Richard Russell) when it came to the early deployment of an ABM system. Both Thurman and Russell had long records of supporting a strong defense against a Soviet threat, whether real or perceived. Jackson's motivations were more complicated: as the senator from Washington State, Jackson had become known as "the senator from Boeing" as a result of his unwavering support of the Seattle, Washington–based company. Boeing was a major contractor involved in the ABM system.

Secretary of Defense McNamara had opened the door for congressional action when, in his annual military posture statement presented to the House of Representatives in early 1966, he noted that a small ABM system could provide a "highly effective defense" against any ballistic missile attack launched from China. McNamara had made this statement in order to head off congressional pressure, noting that there was no rush to field such an ABM system because any viable Chinese missile threat would not materialize for many years.[40] Congress was considering three options for an ABM system: a "thick" nationwide system, costing some $40 billion and designed to provide maximum protection against a Soviet missile attack; a missile protection option designed to defend ICBM bases; and a "thin" nationwide system designed to protect against a Chinese-style attack and projected to cost around $5 billion.[41] Based upon the work done by General Kent, McNamara was strongly opposed to either the thick defense or the equally expensive ICBM base defense, primarily because he believed the Soviets would be able to easily overwhelm these defenses with missiles then in development.

However, the Joint Chiefs of Staff, alarmed by intelligence reports detailing the deployment of Soviet ABM systems around Tallinn, Leningrad, and Moscow, together with other reports indicating the Soviets were modernizing their ICBM force, believed that the national security could not brook a continued delay in fielding a national ABM defense. In 1966, Congress, against the desires of the Johnson administration but with the full support of the JCS, had authorized and appropriated some $167.9 million for the production of the *Nike X* ABM. President Johnson and Secretary McNamara had, by the end of 1966, refused to spend these funds.[42]

But the political pressure on Johnson was starting to heat up. The JCS desires for immediate deployment of an ABM system were about to be made public by the Republicans in Congress, as was the intelligence about the deployment of a Soviet ABM system. Lyndon Johnson could ill afford to continue to delay on the issue of fielding an American ABM system. It looked as if McNamara was going to be overruled on this issue. Then, showing considerable political savvy, McNamara maneuvered back. In a series of meetings with Lyndon Johnson, held at the Johnson ranch in Austin, Texas, on November 3 and 10, 1966, McNamara pressed home his case that an ABM system simply would not work, was excessively expensive, and would dangerously destabilize the strategic balance between the Soviet Union and the United States. Following the November 10 meeting, McNamara preempted the Republicans in Congress by holding a press conference at which he revealed details about the Soviet deployment of an ABM system and his own belief that ongoing U.S. efforts to improve its offensive nuclear capabilities, namely the deployment of the *Minuteman III* ICBM and the new *Poseidon* SLBM, would represent a more-than-adequate response.[43]

McNamara again traveled to Johnson's Austin ranch on December 6, 1966, this time joined by Deputy Secretary of Defense Cyrus Vance; the president's special assistant for national security affairs, Walt Rostow (McGeorge Bundy, frustrated by the ever-escalating conflict in Vietnam, had resigned from the position in March 1966); and the Joint Chiefs of Staff. The ostensible purpose of the meeting was to review the 1968 defense budget, due to be presented to Congress in February 1967. But the centerpiece of discussion was the issue of funding for the production of an ABM system. The JCS were pressing hard for the funding and were equally opposed by McNamara and Vance. Rostow took the side of the Joint Chiefs, and it looked for a moment as if Johnson was going to overrule his secretary of defense.[44]

McNamara interceded one last time, stating unequivocally that building an ABM system was absolutely the worst decision the United States could make at this juncture. The proper course of action was to expand the offensive strike capability of the United States in order to overwhelm the Soviet ABM system. This would obviate the Soviet defense (at great expense to the Soviets) while at the same time making sure the United States did not make the same blunder. Recognizing that Congress had already approved funding for the ABM system, McNamara proposed that the 1968 budget allow for a small amount of money for ABM procurement. However, McNamara then wanted to inform Congress that none of this money would be spent, and no final decision would be made about deploying an ABM system, until the United States made every possible effort to negotiate an arms control agreement with the Soviets that banned ABMs and limited offensive nuclear forces.[45]

Johnson agreed to this compromise approach. He directed Secretary of State Dean Rusk to begin outreach to the Soviets for the purpose of initiating dialogue on arms reductions and limitations. The president even tried to assist this effort when he revealed in a March 1967 meeting with educators in Nashville, Tennessee, that the United States had an extensive satellite reconnaissance program and that from it the United States was able to know exactly how many ICBMs the Soviets had. "I wouldn't want to be quoted on this," Lyndon Johnson said, knowing full well he would be quoted, "but we've spent thirty-five or forty billion dollars on the space program. And if nothing else had come out of it except the knowledge we've gained from space photography, it would be worth ten times what the whole program has cost. Because tonight we know how many missiles the enemy has and, it turned out, our guesses were way off. We were doing things we didn't need to do. We were building things we didn't need to build. We were harboring fears we didn't need to harbor."[46] But even this "slip of the tongue" did not produce results; the Soviets simply refused to talk about arms reductions.

There were several reasons behind the Soviet obstinacy over arms limitations talks. First, the United States was still not seen as an honest partner when it came to arms reduction talks. The Soviets continued to be frustrated by the insistence of the United States to support the MLF, which in the eyes of the Soviets meant giving their arch-nemesis, Germany, access to nuclear weapons. President Johnson had supported a *Polaris*-armed surface fleet but was opposed on this by the British. Prime Minister Harold Wilson in turn proposed his own compromise, termed the Allied Nuclear Force (ANF), consisting of a partnership between U.S. and British submarines with a loose attachment to NATO. This concept was also rejected. The United States continued to push for an MLF out of concerns that in opposing this force, the Soviets were really trying to undermine NATO.

In March 1966, the United States submitted a draft nonproliferation treaty text that prohibited transfer or control of nuclear weapons to nonnuclear weapon states or to an association of nonnuclear weapon states. The United States was bound to this language by the MLF. The planned deployment of *Polaris*-armed ships within NATO territories would not constitute a violation under the interpretation that because France, the United Kingdom, and the United States were already in possession of nuclear weapons, and were NATO members, NATO could not be defined as an association of nonnuclear weapon states. However, by this time it was becoming clear to President Johnson that the MLF was a dead issue. It was also clear that Johnson was hesitant about moving forward with a nonproliferation treaty that would alienate Germany.

Adrian Fisher, the ACDA deputy director, conducted some deft political maneuvering, getting Senator John Pastore, the chair of the Joint Committee on Atomic Energy, to submit a resolution in May 1966 that commended President Johnson for his work in pursuing a nonproliferation treaty and encouraged additional effort by the president to bring such a treaty to fruition. There was no mention of the role of the MLF in sidelining work on nonproliferation. However, hearings conducted in support of this resolution, in which McNamara and others testified, highlighted the reality that America's efforts over the course of two years on the MLF had not only harmed efforts concerning a nonproliferation treaty but also failed to achieve any sort of viable agreement within NATO about the MLF. Pastore, a close friend and political ally of Johnson, made it clear to the president that his committee would not amend the Atomic Energy Act as required by the MLF to permit the transfer of U.S. nuclear weapons to German, or any other nation's, control. The MLF was officially dead. Johnson responded as Adrian Fisher and Senator Pastore had hoped he might: on June 13, 1966, the president wrote Pastore a letter in which he noted that ACDA was being instructed to "renew our urgent pursuit of a treaty."[47]

President Johnson was preoccupied with the growing escalation in Vietnam and the negative reaction that war was generating at home. Realizing that a nonproliferation treaty might improve his slumping public approval ratings, Johnson pressed Secretary of State Rusk to start looking for common ground with the Soviets on treaty language. On July 5, 1966, Johnson held a press conference in which he formally announced his desire for "an acceptable compromise" on treaty language that would allow the Soviet Union and the United States to move forward.[48]

The opportunity for movement came in September 1966, when Soviet Foreign Minister Andrei Gromyko again restated the Soviet position that any nonproliferation treaty must contain language that prohibited nonnuclear countries from producing or obtaining nuclear weapons from any means, including an alliance. The Americans, by this time souring on the MLF, altered their negotiating position with the Soviets, proposing a counterprovision prohibiting the five nations then in possession of nuclear weapons (China, France, the Soviet Union, the United Kingdom, and the United States) from transferring control over any of their nuclear weapons to anyone. At the same time the American proposal kept the door open for preserving current "dual-key" control of U.S. nuclear weapons stationed in NATO countries.

Rusk and Gromyko chaired a series of working groups in New York, where the specifics of an agreement on treaty language were hammered out. Further negotiations between the United States and West Germany resulted in the Germans accepting their status as a nonnuclear nation, meaning that there was no longer any need for the MLF, and a nonproliferation treaty would therefore be acceptable to the Soviets. Although this quid pro quo arrangement managed to breathe new life into a nonproliferation treaty, it did so at the expense of a genuine multilateral undertaking. The nonproliferation treaty had become very much a bilateral affair, to be negotiated between the United States and the Soviet Union, and only after that to be considered by the rest of the world.[49]

On June 17, 1967, China successfully exploded its first hydrogen bomb in western China. The explosive power was 150 times that of the atomic bomb used by the United States against Hiroshima during the Second World War. However, China's ongoing Cultural Revolution, which had paralyzed the nation since April 1966, almost derailed the test. Through sheer force of will, China's nuclear design team was able to overcome an extremely chaotic political environment that had manifested itself in numerous management and logistical problems and to execute the test successfully and on time. Despite the success of the test, the Cultural Revolution was to wreck China for nearly a decade to come, detrimentally affecting China's overall strategic nuclear programs. It was because of these ongoing internal domestic problems that China's test passed virtually unnoticed by either the United States or Soviet Union.[50]

China, however, was not viewed by either the Soviet Union or the United States as being a major problem in the summer of 1967. Vietnam continued to dominate the news, and a new conflict in the Middle East likewise seized the attention of the United States and the Soviet Union alike. On the morning of June 5, 1967, the Israeli air force launched a surprise attack against Egypt and Syria. Six days later, Israeli forces were in control of the Golan Heights, had completely occupied the Sinai Peninsula, and had reclaimed Jerusalem, together with all of the Jordanian-controlled West Bank. The Middle East would never again be the same. The 1967 Six-Day War, as it became known, also marked the point when Israel transitioned from a nation capable of having nuclear weapons to a nuclear weapons–possessing state, having assembled at least one, and probably more, viable nuclear weapons during the height of the conflict.

On June 19, 1967, Soviet Premier Aleksei Kosygin delivered an address to the General Assembly of the United Nations in which he presented a draft Soviet-sponsored resolution condemning the Israeli actions. Kosygin was in New York to attend an emergency session of the UN Security Council convened to address the consequences of the Six-Day War. Once these meetings were finished, Soviet and American officials conspired to organize an unplanned summit between President Johnson and Premier Kosygin. The Americans preferred a meeting held in Washington, while the Soviets preferred New York City. As a compromise, a decision was made to meet at Glassboro State College, in New Jersey, a location almost exactly halfway in between.

The meeting was intended to provide a forum for the discussion of serious arms control issues. At the initial introductory meeting on June 23, 1967, President Johnson told Kosygin that in the three years he (Johnson) had been in office, there were no new arms control treaties between the two nations. Johnson's primary purpose in convening the Glassboro Summit was to engage the Soviets in a meaningful dialogue on arms control in an effort to head off a spiraling arms race. The issue of ABMs was addressed in detail. But ultimately Kosygin saw little hope of genuine discussions so long as the Vietnam War continued and the situation in the Middle East remained unresolved. The Glassboro Summit ended shortly thereafter with nothing having been accomplished.[51]

The lack of results from the Glassboro Summit represented a setback to the Johnson administration's ambitions to pursue a meaningful arms control agenda. There were almost immediate consequences for this failure. Upon their return to Washington, Johnson and McNamara met with the Joint Chiefs of Staff, where it was agreed that in the face of the Soviet refusal to discuss the ABM issue, the United States would initiate immediate action to expand its offensive strike capability. The cheapest and most effective way to do this was to move forward with the development and deployment of MIRVs. However, McNamara recognized that this measure had inherent risks, namely that if the Soviets followed suit and deployed its own MIRV capability, then the United States would find itself on the receiving end of a more potent Soviet arsenal, magnified by the reality of the larger throw-weight (i.e., how heavy of a payload it could carry) capability of the Soviet missiles. Therefore, even though the United States would develop a MIRV capability, a final decision to deploy MIRVs would be withheld pending a renewed effort at negotiating a treaty to ban ABM defenses. If such a treaty could be implemented, then the MIRV program would be terminated.[52]

Like the United States, the Soviets were assessing their potential enemy's strategic capabilities and making their own adjustments. The Soviets were following the deployment of the *Minuteman* missile with great interest. They knew that the *Minuteman* operated as a wing of 150 missiles. Each wing consisted of three squadrons, each composed of five flights containing 10 missiles each stored in an unmanned launch facility, or silo. The silos were separated from one another by a distance of three miles, which also represented the distance the silos were from their respective launch control centers (LCC). In order to successfully target the *Minuteman* missile complex, the Soviets would either have to saturate the area with huge warheads in the large megaton range, hoping to collapse the silos, or target each silo independently with smaller warheads requiring a much greater degree of accuracy.

The Soviets soon realized that the weak link in the *Minuteman* system was the LCC. If the LCC could be taken out, then one achieved the same effect of taking out ten missiles in their silos. If the Soviets were to embark on a Counterforce strategy of their own, then they would need a missile capable of carrying a warhead large enough to defeat a hardened LCC and accurate enough to get within half a nautical mile of the target—a circular error of probability, or CEP, of about 925 meters. From this operational requirement, imposed on the Soviets by the reality of the *Minuteman* missile, came the SS-9.[53] The SS-9 was an "ampulised" missile, meaning that it would be loaded into its missile silo as a sealed round of ammunition, completely fueled and ready to fire. In this mode, the SS-9 could guarantee being able to launch for a period of at least five years. It would be transported to its silo, loaded in, fueled, and then sealed and left unattended. Like the *Minuteman*, the SS-9 silos were to be separated from one another by a distance of eight to ten kilometers, making them difficult to target.[54]

Whereas the SS-9 ICBM was designed as a *Minuteman*-killer, the Soviets still needed an equivalent ICBM to match the *Minuteman* in performance (i.e., the ability to be quickly launched). The answer came from the design bureau of Vladimir Chelomei in the form of the SS-11, a lightweight ICBM that ultimately would be deployed in more numbers than any other Soviet ICBM. The SS-11 was designed to be silo-launched as a certified round of ammunition and was able to be stored, fully fueled and ready to launch, for up to five years. The Soviet Union was in such a hurry to match the *Minuteman* capability of the United States that secret survey teams were already constructing silo locations for the SS-11 even before the missile was initially tested. The SS-11 carried a 1.1-megaton warhead, but its accuracy was so poor as to limit its effectiveness to "soft" targets, like cities and major industrial areas.[55]

In the midst of a growing U.S.-Soviet arms race, there was some progress being made in arms control. By the spring of 1967, the nonproliferation treaty, having broken free of its MLF-imposed chains, was in the final stages of negotiation. Concerted U.S.-Soviet negotiations, conducted throughout the fall and winter of 1966, had produced a draft treaty text in which most major problems had been rectified. New West German elections had produced a coalition government that endorsed improved relations with the Soviet Union. Willy Brandt, the new German foreign minister, gave final approval to the termination of any potential for a future German nuclear weapon. There was widespread support for a nonproliferation treaty around the world, although not from all corners, or without reservations.[56]

By August 1967, separate but identical U.S.-Soviet treaty texts were submitted to the ENDC in Geneva for consultation and consideration. On December 19, 1967, the General Assembly of the United Nations adopted a resolution calling for the ENDC to present a full report on the status of the nonproliferation treaty by March 1968. By January 1968, the United States and the Soviet Union had agreed on a treaty text that was then subjected to debate within the ENDC until March 1968. Then, with some final tinkering of language conserning safeguards and the right to pursue atomic energy, a nonproliferation treaty was finally a reality. On June 12, 1968, the General Assembly of the United Nations commended the draft treaty, and on July 1, 1968, the treaty was opened for signature and was signed on that date by the United States, Great Britain, the Soviet Union, and fifty-nine other countries. China, along with France, did not sign the nonproliferation treaty, instead denouncing it as a "conspiracy concocted by the USSR and the US to maintain their nuclear monopoly."[57] But Chinese opinion circa 1968 did not carry much weight in Washington, and on July 9, 1968, Lyndon Johnson submitted the nonproliferation treaty to the U.S. Senate for ratification. The president finally had his long-sought arms control agreement.

It was a moment that Lyndon Johnson would not be able to share with his longtime secretary of defense, Robert McNamara. Since 1966, McNamara had become more and more controversial in the face of his opposition to both the president and the Joint Chiefs of Staff about the war in Vietnam. McNamara's resistance to an ABM system also alienated him from his military counterparts. On November 29, 1967, with a contentious political season approaching, President Johnson had pulled the plug, announcing that McNamara would be resigning from his position as secretary of defense and moving on to become president of the World Bank. McNamara left office on February 29, 1968. For his seven years of dedicated service, President Johnson awarded him both the Medal of Freedom and the Distinguished Service Medal.[58] McNamara was replaced by Clark Clifford, who took over in March 1968. Unlike McNamara, Clifford was not a proponent of arms control; he wanted to limit any initial steps involved in arms negotiations to simple administrative and procedural functions and await a specific Soviet proposal. Clifford viewed any commitment made by the United States up front as concessions preceding the negotiations, something he contended was never a wise move in the field of diplomacy.[59]

But Lyndon Johnson wanted more. His time as president was running out. Because he had not been elected president in 1960, Johnson was not affected by the Twenty-Second Amendment to the United States Constitution, limiting a president to two terms in office. It was widely assumed that Johnson, despite being heavily criticized over the conduct of the Vietnam War, would seek reelection. However, a strong showing by antiwar candidate Eugene McCarthy during the New Hampshire primary on March 12, 1968, followed four days later by Robert Kennedy's announcement that he would challenge Johnson for the nomination of the Democratic Party, compelled Johnson to rethink his ambition. (Bobby Kennedy's bid for election was tragically cut short by an assassin's bullet on June 5, 1968.)

On March 31, 1968, Lyndon Johnson addressed the American people in a live televised speech, during which he announced that he was ordering the suspension of aerial bombing attacks on North Vietnam in favor of peace negotiations. Johnson concluded his presentation with a stunning statement: "I shall not seek, and I will not accept, the nomination of my party for another term as your President."[60] Johnson was in poor health, and he and his family were very concerned that he might not survive another term in office. Thus liberated from the constraints of a national election, Lyndon Johnson turned to thoughts of his legacy. Worn down by Vietnam, Johnson had been rejuvenated by the success of the nonproliferation treaty and was intent on closing out his tenure as president with even more far-reaching arms limitation agreements.

Lyndon Johnson sought arms control treaties even prior to his decision not to seek a second term. On January 22, 1968, Johnson had sent a letter to Soviet Premier Kosygin in which he proposed early talks on strategic missile controls.[61] Having not heard back from the Soviets, on March 16, 1968, Secretary of State Rusk instructed the U.S. embassy in Moscow to seek a favorable response to the president's letter. The U.S. ambassador to the Soviet Union, Llewellyn Thompson, met with Soviet Foreign Minister Andrei Gromyko on March 26, 1968, to discuss Johnson's proposal, only to be told that the Soviet government, though attaching great importance to the idea, was still studying the proposal.

By May 2, 1968, the continued Soviet silence prompted President Johnson to write another letter, noting his concern over the "necessity to initiate meaningful discussion as soon as possible," noting that "each passing month increases the difficulty of reaching agreement on this matter as, from a technical and military point of view, it is becoming more complex."[62] Concerned about possible problems in the general assembly over the opening of the nonproliferation treaty for signature, Johnson told Kosygin that "it is important that our two governments do everything possible to give the greatest impetus to world sentiment favorable to opening the treaty for signature at an early date," and to this end proposed that "our two governments announce early . . . they have agreed to commence bilateral negotiations on an agreement to limit strategic offensive and defensive missiles within a specific time from the date of the announcement."[63]

On May 17, 1968, the Soviets responded indirectly, having a diplomat state that Moscow was still considering the U.S. proposal that talks begin. Then, on June 21, 1968, Aleksei Kosygin finally responded in a letter of his own to Johnson. The Soviet premier told Johnson that the Soviets "attach great importance to these questions, having in mind that they should be considered together, systems for delivery of offensive strategic nuclear weapons as well as systems for defense against ballistic missiles. All aspects of this complex problem are now being carefully examined by us, and we hope that before long it will be possible more concretely to exchange views with regard to further ways of discussing this problem, if of course the general world situation does not hinder this."[64]

But the success of the nonproliferation treaty did not, in any way, slow down the nuclear arms race then under way between the Soviet Union and the United States. On July 1, 1968, following the opening of the nonproliferation treaty for signatures, both nations simultaneously announced that they were in agreement to meet in the "nearest future" to discuss strategic nuclear arms limitations, as well as limitations on ballistic missile defense. Johnson decided he would up the ante by increasing the pressure on the Soviets to come to the negotiation table. On July 2, Dean Rusk met with Soviet ambassador to the United States Anatoliy Dobrynin and informed him that President Johnson wanted another summit meeting with his Soviet counterpart in the near future.[65]

President Johnson's desires for an arms control agreement did not, however, directly translate into an agreed upon position within the U.S. national security hierarchy. Secretary of Defense Clifford was concerned about on-site inspection and verification regimes that would be associated with any such agreements. Others wanted to preserve the ability to maintain qualitative force improvements, both for a nuclear warhead for the *Sentinel* ABM but also for any future MIRV warhead. Under pressure from the White House, a policy paper was prepared on July 31, 1968, that outlined the basics of an agreed-on U.S. position on strategic arms limitations: a freeze on ICBM, MRBM, and SLBM submarines; a ban on deploying mobile ICBM systems; a ban on mobile ABM systems; and an agreement to limit any ABM system to a specific number of fixed launchers and associated radars.[66]

A final meeting of the principal players tasked with drafting a U.S. position was held on August 7, 1968. It soon became clear that there were many issues that lacked resolution. The Joint Chiefs were very concerned about cheating scenarios involving mobile ICBMs. Dr. Ivan Selin, representing Clifford, responded that the Soviets would only be able to field 200–300 mobile ICBMs without being detected, and the U.S. nuclear force was able to withstand a surprise attack from thousands of nuclear warheads. This kind of cheating scenario, in Selin's opinion, made no sense. "Our forces are so large and diverse," he stated, "that our assured destruction capability is relatively insensitive to most forms of qualitative improvements, cheating or abrogation scenarios."[67] In his opinion, MIRVs represented a far greater threat than mobile ICBMs.

At this point, Adrian Fisher of ACDA interjected that he thought the Soviets might seek to ban MIRVs, a possibility that Selin conceded had not been considered by the Pentagon. The two MIRV systems being considered by the United States, the *Minuteman* III and the *Poseidon*, were due to be flight-tested in mid-August. Secretary of State Rusk asked if these flight tests should be postponed until after the arms limitations talks were held. However, the consensus among attendees was that the tests should go forward as scheduled. This was a critical decision because, by agreeing to flight tests of an MIRV capability, the United States had made it all but impossible to ban MIRVs once negotiations began. The final U.S. position was submitted to the president on August 15, 1968. In covering memorandums, both Rusk and Clark offered their support of the position paper, noting that the United States would maintain its deterrent posture, leave no doubt as to the adequacy of the deterrent, be confident that the deterrent could not be eroded by one or more powers alone or in combination, maintain a damage-limiting capability, and be able to prevent other (non-Soviet) nuclear powers from threatening the agreement.[68]

All that was needed was a summit. Presidential politics intervened, in the form of the Republican nominee, Richard Nixon, having asked to be received in Moscow. The Soviets agreed, prompting Secretary of State Rusk to ask Moscow if the Soviets might likewise agree to meet the man who was still the president.[69] The Soviets postponed the meeting with Nixon. Then, on August 19, the Soviets finally agreed to receive Johnson in Moscow on October 15, or any other date close to that time.[70] Elated, President Johnson prepared to make an announcement concerning his trip and the goals of limiting strategic arms through reduction talks.

At this portentous moment, unexpected events intervened. On August 20, 1968, Soviet tanks rolled into Czechoslovakia. The series of reforms initiated in the country since Alexander Dubček had replaced the Czechoslovakian Communist Party leader, Antonin Novotny, in the spring of 1968 had proven to be too much for the Soviet leadership. Czechoslovakia's neighbors, East Germany and Hungary, were nervous about the liberalization of what was being called "Prague Spring" and were pressuring the Soviets to do something. On July 14 and 15, the Soviets hosted a Warsaw Pact meeting, without Czech involvement, followed on July 23 with the Soviets announcing a large military exercise, "Nieman," which served as a cover for the deployment of hundreds of thousands of troops and more than 7,000 tanks to the Czech border regions. The final decision to

invade Czechoslovakia was made between August 15 and 17, with Soviet Communist Party chair Leonid Brezhnev sending a letter to Dubček on August 19, the same date the Soviets extended the invitation to Johnson to visit Moscow.[71]

On August 20, President Johnson convened a cabinet meeting to discuss the status of the strategic arms reduction talks. The National Security Council agreed with Johnson's calling the Soviet invasion an "aggression" and agreed that thus there could be no summit with the Soviets on arms reduction, noting that such a meeting might be interpreted by the Soviets and others as the United States condoning the Soviet action. Ambassador Dobrynin was summoned by Rusk, who informed him of the president's decision.[72]

There was some effort to restart the talks, with the Soviets agreeing to a meeting in mid-September 1968 to set out an agenda. But Johnson had taken the Soviet invasion of Czechoslovakia as an insult. As Rusk told Ambassador Dobrynin on September 20, 1968, during a lunch meeting, "the coincidence of actions [the invasion of Czechoslovakia and agreeing to arms reduction talks] was like throwing a dead fish in the face of the President of the United States."[73] Time had run out on the Johnson administration for accomplishing meaningful arms control with the Soviets.

The presidential elections of November 5, 1968, saw the Republican Richard Nixon defeat Vice President Hubert Humphrey. With a new administration due to take power, there was no incentive for the Soviets to sit down and talk, even on an issue as important as arms reductions. The nonproliferation treaty notwithstanding, from his rejection of the Gilpatric Committee report in 1964, to the demise of the strategic arms reduction talks in the face of the Soviet invasion of Czechoslovakia in 1968, President Johnson had presided over a period of history where so much could have been accomplished in the field of disarmament, and so little was.

CHAPTER 9

PEACE THROUGH STRENGTH

Foreign policy was destined to be the foundation upon which any Nixon administration would be built. Richard Nixon, never one to mince words (or disguise prejudices), once stated that he didn't want foreign policy run by "striped-pants faggots in Foggy Bottom."[1] Nixon was determined to consolidate control of foreign policy within the White House. To do this he needed a strong national security advisor. He found that in Henry Kissinger, an esteemed Harvard professor who had advised previous administrations on issues pertaining to national security. Nixon appointed Kissinger *before* making his selections for either secretary of state or secretary of defense.

With Kissinger onboard, Nixon went on to select as his secretary of state William Rogers, an experienced Washington lawyer. Rogers had served in the Navy with Nixon back at the end of World War II, had previously served as U.S. attorney general under President Eisenhower, and in 1967 had served as the U.S. representative to the United Nations. Melvin Laird, an eight-term Republican congressman from Wisconsin, who at the time of his appointment was chair of the House Republican Caucus, was Nixon's choice for secretary of defense. But both Rogers and Laird were to be frustrated by Kissinger.

Though the Vietnam War was the principal focus of the Nixon administration and would dominate its actions as it had the Johnson administration before it, there were other critical matters that needed to be addressed, some of which would, on occasion, seize center stage. One of these was nuclear strategy. In Henry Kissinger, Nixon had picked a man who was intellectually capable of grasping the nuances and complexities of nuclear war and nuclear strategy. In 1957, he had published an acclaimed book on the subject, *Nuclear Weapons and Foreign Policy*, based upon discussions he had chaired as the study director for nuclear weapons and foreign policy with the Council on Foreign Relations. In this book Kissinger argued that the American tradition of absolute victory in times of war had created a trap of sorts in the nuclear age, namely Massive Retaliation. Such a policy, Kissinger believed, was a dead end. Kissinger had rejected the Eisenhower approach toward nuclear strategy and was instead a proponent of the Kennedy embrace of "limited war."[2]

The Soviet Union, Kissinger believed, was America's main opponent in international affairs, and as such needed to be confronted. Kissinger, however, respected the Soviet Union's status as a nuclear superpower and therefore sought to limit confrontation in a way that avoided the zero-sum approaches of the past. Together with Thomas Schelling, the MIT games theorist and strategist, Kissinger developed the so-called Charles River Doctrine (named for the Charles River that runs through the Cambridge neighborhoods containing both Harvard and MIT). This doctrine made the case that the purpose of arms control was not disarmament but rather stability by controlling the respective arsenals based on qualitative, versus quantitative, factors for the purpose of precluding a surprise-attack capability.[3] Simply counting missiles, and equating parity based on the number of missiles possessed by either side, ignored the reality that no two missiles were exactly alike. Nor were the procurement systems, missile design requirements, or warhead capabilities. Thus, although the United States might have put a premium on the quick-launch capabilities of the lighter *Minuteman* missile system, the Soviets instead emphasized the heavy-lift capabilities of the SS-9. By focusing on the true capabilities and requirements of a given side (i.e., qualitative) rather than simply counting numbers of missiles (i.e., quantitative), a true measure of capability could be taken. In this manner the quick-strike capability of the *Minuteman* could be used as a factor to offset the massive-strike capability of the SS-9.

"For the first time, because the people of the world want peace, and the leaders of the world are afraid of war, the times are on the side of peace." These were the words of Richard Nixon, delivering his inaugural address on January 20, 1969, moments after being sworn in as the president of the United States of America. "The greatest honor history can bestow is the title of peacemaker. This honor now beckons America—the chance to help lead the world at last out of the valley of turmoil, and onto that high ground of peace that man has dreamed of since the dawn of civilization." Nixon had been elected largely on a platform that was built around the concept of getting America out of Vietnam. Peace, as such, was a major theme in how Nixon chose to introduce his administration to the American people and the world. "Let us take as our goal: where peace is unknown, make it welcome; where peace is fragile, make it strong; where peace is temporary, make it permanent."[4]

Nixon had others in mind too as he spoke: the Soviet Union and Communist China. "After a period of confrontation, we are entering an era of negotiation," Nixon stated. "Let all nations know that during this administration our lines of communication will be open." Understanding the need to balance peace and strength, Nixon sought to balance his message. "With those who are willing to join, let us cooperate to reduce the burden of arms, to strengthen the structure of peace, to lift up the poor and the hungry . . . but to all those who would be tempted by weakness, let us leave no doubt that we will be as strong as we need to be for as long as we need to be."[5]

The reaction to Nixon's address, at least from the standpoint of his major international targets, couldn't have been better. In Moscow, the Soviet Foreign Ministry called a rare press conference stating that the Soviet Union was ready to start a serious exchange of views concerning the control of nuclear weapons. And in China, Mao Tse-tung ordered Nixon's entire speech to be translated and published on the front page of the *People's Daily*. Nixon had previously hinted, through an article that appeared in *Foreign Affairs* in 1967, that continuing to ignore China was unwise, noting that America "simply cannot afford to leave China forever outside the family of nations, there to nurture its fantasies, cherish its hates, and threaten its neighbors."[6] On February 1, 1969, less than one month into his presidency, Nixon wrote a confidential memorandum to Kissinger instructing his national security advisor to make the opening of relations with China a high priority, but only as long as it could be done out of the public eye.[7]

Making contact with the Chinese would prove to be a challenge. On November 26, 1968, the Chinese informed the U.S. ambassador to China that they would like to have a meeting on February 20, 1969. The Chinese stated that Nixon's article in *Foreign Affairs* had created a positive impression that they would be interested in following up. The United States and China had used Warsaw as a venue for low-level (i.e., ambassadorial) meetings since 1954, with 134 sessions being held through the end of 1968. With the advent of the Cultural Revolution, the frequency of meetings had subsided, with only one meeting held in all of 1968. However, the defection of a Chinese diplomat in the Netherlands, an action China accused the United States of facilitating, strained relations and prompted the Chinese to cancel the February meeting.[8]

Meeting with the Soviets proved to be less problematic. On February 17, 1969, Soviet ambassador Anatoliy Dobrynin met with President Nixon and informed him that the Soviet Union was prepared to enter into wide-ranging negotiations on a number of issues. The Soviet objectives for such talks were to enforce the nonproliferation treaty, end the war in Vietnam, settle the conflict in the Middle East, recognize the status quo in Europe, and curb the arms race through strategic arms reductions. Dobrynin asked Nixon when the United States would be ready to begin these talks. Nixon was noncommittal, saying arms reduction discussions in particular required considerable preparation. The president, bypassing the secretary of state (whose job it usually would be), asked Dobrynin to bring up the issue of talks with his national security advisor instead. So began the Dobrynin-Kissinger channel, a highly confidential mechanism for a candid "exchange of opinions" between the United States and the Soviet Union. Once Kissinger and Dobrynin could agree in principle about the issues in question, the problem would then be turned over to the appropriate diplomatic channel for a "detailed working review."[9]

On the issue of arms control negotiations, the problem at hand was one of timing, Kissinger explained to Dobrynin. The key matter was the link between when such talks should begin and the deployment of an antiballistic missile (ABM) system by the United States. Kissinger stressed that there were differences between the State and Defense Departments over this—State wanted talks to begin as soon as possible and not be subject to military constraints, whereas Defense believed practical decisions about the deployment of an ABM system should not be made contingent upon arms control talks.[10]

Kissinger was surprisingly honest and open with Dobrynin about how much time it would take to get arms reduction talks on track. But he had been less so when it came to attributing the reasons for this delay. Kissinger had long viewed the Soviet push for arms reductions talks as a device used by Moscow to regain credibility lost after their move against Czechoslovakia in August 1968. Kissinger also believed that the Soviets intended to use such talks as a means to divide NATO, in addition to stabilizing the strategic balance. Both Nixon and Kissinger believed in the principle of linkage, where one policy objective would be linked with others—not treated in isolation—when it came to foreign policy. In the case of arms reduction talks, both Nixon and Kissinger believed that they should not be pursued in isolation but rather be linked to the Soviet Union's ability to assist the United States in Vietnam and the Middle East.

The war in Vietnam was an ever-present reality as well as a source of policy frustration for the Nixon administration. The year 1968 had been the bloodiest one yet for the American forces fighting in Southeast Asia, and Nixon was determined to bring the war to a close. Within the Nixon administration, many policy advisors blamed the continued Soviet military, political, and economic support of the North Vietnamese government for the difficulty the United States faced in South Vietnam. Using his linkage philosophy, in mid-April 1969, Kissinger told Ambassador Dobrynin that U.S.-Soviet relations were at a critical phase and that Vietnam was the key to resolving differences in other areas, such as arms control. Kissinger proposed sending Cyrus Vance—who had been leading the U.S. delegation to the Paris peace talks since 1968—to Moscow to initiate arms reduction talks and, at the same time, open discussions with the North Vietnamese. Dobrynin was evasive, and Vance never made the trip.[11]

The Soviets, however, continued to send signals that they were prepared for arms reduction negotiations. On May 1, 1969, the Soviets canceled their usual military parade. Instead, Leonid Brezhnev spoke from atop Vladimir Lenin's tomb, calling for peaceful coexistence with the West. On July 10, 1969, Foreign Minister Andrei Gromyko addressed the Supreme Soviet, calling for closer relations with the United States, declaring, "We for our part are ready."[12] This was the best the Soviet Union could do. Domestically, Brezhnev was in the midst of a bitter power struggle with Aleksei Kosygin. Kosygin had attempted to implement economic reforms in the post-Khrushchev era by shifting the emphasis in the Soviet economy from heavy industry and military production to light industry and the production of consumer goods. Brezhnev did not support this policy and stymied Kosygin's reforms. He was also concerned about Kosygin's preeminence in foreign affairs and was gradually trying to insert himself in that arena. By the end of the decade, Brezhnev would become the unquestioned leader of the Soviet Union, but in the first half of 1969, he was not in a position to make bold moves. Signaling his resolve to meet an American initiative was the best he could do.[13]

Linkage wasn't the only issue that hindered movement on arms reduction talks. For President Nixon, American military strength was the basis of a successful negotiation. As such, the United States could ill afford to enter into any meaningful negotiations from a position of real or perceived weakness but rather was required to "look tough." As had been the case when the Johnson administration had begun constructing a unified position on arms reduction talks, two issues proved to be particularly sticky when it came to achieving consensus on how best to proceed: multiple independently targeted reentry vehicles (MIRVs) and antiballistic missile defense.

The United States had a significant lead over the Soviet Union when it came to MIRVs. Initial testing of an MIRV-equipped missile had begun in August 1968, and the Navy and Air Force were scheduled to undergo final testing in May 1969 for both the *Minuteman* and *Poseidon* missiles. These tests were scheduled to be completed by July 1969.[14] The Soviets lagged behind, having tested an MRV-equipped missile for the first time in September 1968. However, the Soviets had fielded the giant SS-9 missile, which with its ability to deliver large payloads (defined in arms control terms as "throw weight") meant that if the Soviets were to develop and test their own MIRV capability, they would soon be able to overwhelm the United States in terms of the numbers of nuclear warheads it could deliver, even if the number of missiles remained unchanged.[15] This fact had not gone unnoticed by analysts in the United States. In a June 1969 memo, George Rathjens and Jack Ruina warned Kissinger that a decision to go ahead with MIRV tests "probably also implies the eventual abandonment of the *Minuteman* missiles by the United States," because the United States would need to replace the small *Minuteman* with a missile possessing a throw weight equal to or exceeding the SS-9.[16] This was the arms race everyone feared.

Both the Department of Defense and the Joint Chiefs of Staff supported the development and deployment of MIRVs. American strategic nuclear targeting centered on having the MIRV-equipped *Minuteman* III missile (which would carry three MIRVs) and the new *Poseidon* missile (which would carry twelve MIRVs). Instead of banning MIRVs, the Department of Defense wanted U.S. arms reduction talks to focus on limiting missile throw weight, thereby limiting future Soviet MIRV potential. The president came down on the side of having MIRVs. Nixon released secret information about Soviet MRV tests, claiming that analysis conducted by the United States concerning impact patterns of the missiles showed that they were being optimized to strike U.S. *Minuteman* silos.[17] Survivability of the U.S. deterrent, therefore, hinged on the United States equipping its own forces with MIRVs to ensure that enough retaliatory capability survived any Soviet attack.

By summer 1969, the Air Force awarded a contract for the manufacture of thirty-eight MIRV missiles. From an arms control perspective, this was a critical move. Any ban of MIRV testing would be relatively easy to verify—since satellite imagery and electronic intercepts would suffice as a means of monitoring. A ban on MIRV deployment, on the other hand, would require intrusive on-site inspection-based verification measures neither the Soviets nor the Americans would agree to. Committing to the testing of MIRVs all but assured that they would be deployed.[18]

Although MIRVs as a weapons system impacted any future arms reduction talks, so did the manner in which the United States planned to utilize nuclear weapons in any conflict, MIRVs or no MIRVs. On January 27, 1969, Nixon and Kissinger—joined by Secretary of Defense Laird and chair of the Joint Chiefs of Staff Earle Wheeler—traveled to the Pentagon, where they were briefed on SIOP-4, the latest version of America's nuclear war plan. SIOP-4, which had basically remained unchanged in operating philosophy since mid-1966, consisted of five nuclear attack options, retaliatory or preemptive in nature, depending on the amount of warning time available to the decision-maker. There was also a launch-on-warning capability. All strike options involved thousands of nuclear weapons hitting Soviet military, economic, and population centers. Helmut Sonnenfeldt, an NSC staffer who was present at the briefing, reported that President Nixon was "appalled" at the prospect of a nuclear conflict that would kill some 80 million Soviets, and at least that many Americans, as well as the fact that he, as the American chief executive, had so few choices when it came to responding to a major crisis between the United States and the Soviet Union.[19]

The basic guidance behind the creation of the SIOP was known as the National Strategic Targeting and Attack Policy (NSTAP), which established the three core objectives of waging strategic nuclear war as being (1) to destroy nuclear threats to the United States and its allies in order to limit damage to them; (2) to destroy a comprehensive set of nonnuclear military targets; and (3) to destroy war-supporting urban and industrial targets so that 30 percent of the enemy's population would be killed together with 70 percent of their war-fighting industry. Following along strategic thinking in place since the Berlin crisis of 1961, the SIOP was designed to "maximize U.S. power" and "attain and maintain a strategic superiority which will lead to an early termination of the war on terms favorable to the United States and our allies." Derived from McNamara's No Cities philosophy contained in his Athens's Doctrine, SIOP-4 was simply a repackaging of SIOP-3, providing options for nuclear targets only;

military targets only; and all targets, including urban areas. Kissinger was obviously frustrated by the lack of flexibility inherent in the SIOP, and shortly after receiving the briefing, called up McNamara and asked of the military, "Is this the best [you] can do?"[20]

By the time Nixon assumed office, the United States and the Soviet Union had achieved strategic parity, and McNamara's Assured Destruction had become Mutually Assured Destruction—MAD was its famous acronym. Both Kissinger and Nixon, after reviewing American nuclear strategy, were concerned that the Soviets in fact had achieved a greater ability to inflict harm on the United States than the United States could inflict on the Soviet Union. They also worried that this fact would embolden the Soviets when it came to confronting the United States and its allies on foreign policy matters worldwide. Nixon and Kissinger were so concerned over the Soviet Union's potential to stand up to the United States in Europe that the president, at a meeting of the NSC on February 19, 1969, declared that "the nuclear umbrella in NATO is a lot of crap."[21]

Kissinger was also concerned about other hypothetical crisis options that might present themselves, such as a Soviet attack on Tel Aviv, Israel, in response to any renewed conflict in the Middle East. He asked General Wheeler, the chair of the JCS, if there was a way to selectively engage the SIOP so that an appropriate response to such a scenario could be crafted. Wheeler stated that breaking up the SIOP into smaller packages was not an option but that the United States could fall back on the General Strike Plan of the supreme Allied commander in Europe, which provided for major attacks against the Warsaw Pact and the Soviet Union separate from the SIOP. By March 1969, nothing of substance had been accomplished along these lines, and Secretary of Defense Laird suggested that Kissinger request the Department of Defense to study "sub-SIOP options."[22]

While Kissinger wrestled with American nuclear strike plans, he was in fact satisfied with the level of American nuclear forces. Having defined the Nixon nuclear strategic doctrine as being based on the concept of "strategic sufficiency," Kissinger believed that the current force levels based upon the existing nuclear triad (1,054 ICBMs, 656 SLBMs, and a substantial strategic bomber force), together with a viable ABM system, were sufficient to deter a Soviet attack. In this philosophy, Kissinger in effect supported the underpinnings of the McNamara nuclear posture of Assured Destruction without actually embracing the term. However, Kissinger took the argument to a new level, asking if the Soviets operated on an all-or-nothing approach (zero nuclear weapons or massive attack), or if they might themselves have an option where they could fire off a limited nuclear attack, knowing that the United States would hesitate to respond because the result would be the destruction of American cities. Although his advisors argued that this was not a likely course of action for the Soviets, Kissinger believed that the United States should be in a position to place the Soviets in a similar quandary. Kissinger wanted to be able to use discriminating nuclear attacks as a means of getting the Soviets to back down in a crisis.[23]

An outgrowth of these internal debates and discussions was the formal definition, in the form of National Security Decision Memorandum (NSDM) 16, "Strategic Sufficiency," published on June 24, 1969. In it, Kissinger stated that strategic sufficiency was defined as being assured that the U.S. second-strike capability was sufficient to deter an enemy surprise attack, thus insuring the Soviets had no incentive to strike the United States first in a crisis. A key aspect to this was possessing the capability to ensure that the United States could deny the Soviets the ability to cause more damage to America in a nuclear exchange than America could cause to the Soviet Union.[24]

This guidance underscored the emphasis both Nixon and Kissinger were placing on an ABM capability and underscored why ABM was playing such a major role (bigger than MIRVs or the SIOP) in shaping a Nixon arms control policy. It is not that Nixon conceived ABM, or even initiated its deployment; he had done neither. The decision to deploy ABM was made during the Johnson administration. On September 18, 1967, then-Secretary of Defense McNamara had announced that the United States would begin deployment of a "thin" ABM system, known as *Sentinel*, intended to defeat a limited Chinese missile attack. *Sentinel* was also intended to reinforce American security assurances to its allies by demonstrating its deterrent capability and to protect against "the improbable but possible accidental launch of an intercontinental missile by one of the nuclear powers." In making his announcement, McNamara had stated that the "decision to go ahead with a limited ABM deployment in no way indicates that we feel an agreement with the Soviet Union on the limitation of strategic nuclear offensive and defensive forces is in any way less urgent or desirable."[25]

But McNamara only initiated the political process of an ABM deployment. By the time Nixon assumed office, *Sentinel* was still a plan, not a reality. One factor McNamara could not have considered when making his announcement in September 1967 was the fundamental difference between the ninetieth Congress, which had so aggressively funded ABM even when McNamara and Johnson didn't ask for funds, and the ninety-first Congress, elected alongside Nixon, which was a product of increasing skepticism of all things military thanks to the ongoing debacle in Vietnam. Money had been allocated for *Sentinel*, but the new Congress was not necessarily so inclined to spend it.[26]

On March 5, 1969, Kissinger provided Nixon with a new modified *Sentinel* ABM proposal designed to ease congressional concerns. First, Kissinger noted that the modified *Sentinel* program was not designed with modern Soviet threats in mind, namely submarine-launched ballistic missiles (SLBM) and a new threat, known as the fractional orbital bombardment system, or FOBs. The SLBM, being launched close to American shores as opposed to launched from fixed bases in the Soviet Union, had a much shorter flight time (three to fifteen minutes) that made interception by a *Sentinel*-type system unlikely unless the individual crews of the *Spartan* and *Sprint* missiles were given authority at all times (i.e., pre-delegation) to launch nuclear missiles over American soil. Given the possibility of an accident, such pre-delegation was politically impossible.

FOBs presented a completely different problem set: in short, there was no defense. The goal of FOBs was to place a large nuclear warhead equipped with a de-orbited rocket stage into low Earth orbit (approximately 90 miles altitude). The warhead could theoretically approach the United States from any direction, below the altitude of any tracking radar, and be de-orbited at will, meaning no one would know when it might strike. The Outer Space Treaty, implemented in 1967, banned orbiting nuclear weapons, but it did not ban systems capable of orbiting nuclear weapons, so the Soviets exploited that loophole by never testing FOBs with a live warhead. Likewise, the Soviets never allowed the system to complete an orbit, de-orbiting the test warhead prior to one complete revolution around the Earth (hence the name "fractional orbiter").

Another problem lay in the nature of the interceptor missiles themselves. Kissinger noted that atmospheric detonation by a *Spartan* missile would more than likely "black out" the critical U.S. target acquisition radars, meaning that additional intercepts would be impossible. Thus, the modified *Sentinel* system would be committing suicide as soon as it was employed. Likewise (especially where ABM was employed to protect ICBM bases), an exploding *Spartan* or *Sprint* missile could knock out *Minuteman* and *Titan* missiles being launched in retaliation for any Soviet attack. This could not be compensated with anything less than a costly coordination system or restrictive operational procedures.

The ABM system was designed to operate in one of three modes, with command and control being conducted locally, regionally, or nationally through automation. All three modes had major disadvantages. Ultimately, the ability of the ABM system to work depended on its ability to destroy incoming warheads. "Kill assessments" were being made relative to how "hard" a Soviet warhead was (meaning its ability to withstand a nuclear blast). This in turn affected how close an interceptor needed to be to guarantee a kill. Kissinger noted that if the assumptions were wrong, then the system wouldn't work. And finally, Kissinger had to concede that the modified *Sentinel* ABM could easily be overwhelmed by a concentrated nuclear bombardment, especially if penetration aids were employed. In short, the system's effectiveness against a Soviet attack was nil.[27]

Kissinger acknowledged that the U.S. nuclear retaliatory capability was not threatened by any realistic intelligence estimate that extended through the decade of the 1970s. However, the Department of Defense utilized what was known as "greater than expected" threat analysis in determining U.S. defense requirements, and if these data were applied, then the U.S. retaliatory capability would come under risk by 1976 as the Soviets deployed an increased number of larger missiles equipped with MIRVs. For this reason, the concept of deploying an ABM capability designed to ensure a minimum of 300 *Minuteman* missiles survived any Soviet nuclear attack was an attractive idea, especially for the Department of Defense and the Joint Chiefs of Staff.[28]

But focusing an ABM system on a Soviet threat ran against the initial justification of the *Sentinel* program to begin with, namely defending against a Chinese threat. The problem was, if the United States placed too much emphasis on the Chinese threat, then ABM could not be factored into any meaningful arms reduction talks. Nixon, in speaking out in defense of ABM, had placed considerable emphasis on China, more than Kissinger would have preferred. But in the end, Nixon appeared to have been swayed by Kissinger's Soviet-centric approach, supporting a focus on *Minuteman* ICBM defense that reflected the fact that the Soviets had closed the gap when it came to strategic parity as well as Nixon's desire that the gap not be widened on the other side, which required that any threat to *Minuteman* be reduced. ABM, in Nixon's mind, accomplished this.[29]

On March 14, 1969, President Nixon announced his decision concerning the future of the *Sentinel* ABM system. Recognizing that the system as designed required modification, Nixon directed that a new, modified ABM system, using many of the same components and designs as *Sentinel*, be constructed. Nixon highlighted the "unmistakable" defensive nature of the new ABM system, noting that it was designed to protect U.S. land-based retaliatory forces against a direct attack by the Soviet Union, to defend the American people against the kind of nuclear attack that

Communist China was likely to be able to mount within the decade, and to protect against the possibility of accidental attacks from any source. Nixon said that the new ABM system was not designed to protect American cities from nuclear attack, noting that it was not feasible to do so, and that any effort in this direction "might look to an opponent like the prelude to an offensive strategy threatening the Soviet deterrent."[30]

In arguing in favor of an American ABM system, Nixon highlighted Soviet capabilities—namely that the Soviets already had a functioning ABM system that they were continuing to improve. Using the briefing provided by Kissinger back in early March, Nixon pointed out that the Soviets were also continuing to deploy large ICBMs that possessed the ability to destroy silo-based *Minuteman* ICBMs, as well as substantially increasing the size of its SLBM fleet. Nixon referred to the Soviet development of a "semi-orbital nuclear weapon system" (i.e., FOBs), without detailing what such a system entailed. Nixon also highlighted an ABM's value against any Chinese nuclear threat or an accidental nuclear missile launch from any direction.

Sentinel thus became *Safeguard*. But Nixon's speech, rather than putting the ABM debate to bed, only breathed new life into those who opposed any ABM deployment. The scene was set for a major showdown in Congress, where the fate of the *Safeguard* ABM system was linked to a Senate funding bill authorizing appropriations for fiscal year 1970 for military procurement, research, and development. The total amount involved in *Safeguard* was more than $20 billion, but the matter being debated dealt with only the $759.1 million required for the initial deployment of the *Safeguard* ABM system. The Senate split 50–50 on the vote on August 7, 1969. Vice President Spiro Agnew was called in as the president of the Senate to cast the decisive fifty-first vote in favor of the bill.[31]

President Nixon and Henry Kissinger were handed a foreign policy challenge, and the beginnings of an opportunity, when on March 2, 1969, Chinese troops attacked Soviet border guards along the Ussuri River straddling China and the Soviet Union. Tensions between the two former allies had been high ever since the Soviet Union withdrew its strategic support in the late 1950s. The March 1969 border clashes between the two nuclear powers raised the prospect of a nuclear war. Despite some attempt at rapprochement in May, by June 1969, the Chinese media was making claims of Soviet war preparations, including nuclear weapons, and instructing the Chinese people to prepare for conflict. Sino-Soviet tensions would ease considerably when, on September 11, 1969, Aleksei Kosygin met with Chinese Premier Zhou Enlai in Beijing. There they settled on the framework of an agreement that maintained the status quo of the Sino-Soviet border; halted armed conflict and sought to disengage the armed forces of both sides in the disputed areas along the border; and agreed on negotiations, which were initiated in October 1969, for the settlement of the border question.

Intrigued by the possibilities presented by a Sino-Soviet split, Nixon tried to signal the Chinese that he was interested in opening up relations between the two nations. On April 21, 1969, Secretary of State William Rogers announced a new "two Chinas" policy in the United States, accepting the existence of a Communist China mainland and a Nationalist China entity on Taiwan as a "fact of life." In July 1969, the United States eased visa restrictions and partially lifted a ban on bringing Chinese-made goods into America. And later that month, in a speech that set forth what has become known as the "Nixon Doctrine," the president announced that America would never again serve as the world's police officer (a reference to Vietnam) and that instead the United States would provide nations, especially those in East Asia, with the means of defending themselves.[32]

Arms control and arms reductions were still very much on the foreign policy agenda of the Nixon administration. As his point person for America's arms control effort, the president chose the new director of ACDA, Gerard Smith, a veteran State Department official with experience in the Truman, Eisenhower, Kennedy, and Johnson administrations. In an effort to get arms control back on the agenda with the Soviets, President Nixon (with Kissinger present) met with Soviet ambassador Dobrynin at the White House on October 20, 1969. The ambassador opened the meeting by presenting Nixon with a brief announcement concerning arms reduction talks. The Soviets were interested in beginning a preliminary round of discussions on November 17, 1969, and were suggesting Helsinki, Finland, as the venue.[33]

On October 25, 1969, both Moscow and Washington announced their mutual intent to begin what were being referred to as "Strategic Arms Limitation Talks," or SALT. On November 13, 1969, Secretary of State Rogers made a public announcement on the eve of the U.S. SALT delegation's departure for Helsinki, in which he underscored his belief that the ultimate question SALT would confront was "whether societies with the advanced intellect to develop these awesome weapons of mass destruction have the combined wisdom to control and curtail them."[34]

The two delegations sat down on November 17, 1969, and for the next five weeks probed one another as to the seriousness in which the respective parties were pursuing the issue of arms reductions. One of the areas in which there appeared to be considerable differences of opinion lay in what constituted "strategic weapons." The Soviets insisted on including U.S. aircraft carriers and nuclear-capable aircraft stationed in Europe because these weapons could target the Soviet homeland. On the other hand, the Soviets wanted to exclude their medium- and intermediate-range missiles, which only targeted Europe, because these weapons did not threaten America. The Soviets were pushing for either no ABM deployment or a very low level of ABM deployment and a loose verification regime based on national technical means (a euphemism for satellite-based imagery). The Soviets proposed a halt, or even reversal of, ABM development, indicating that a flight test ban represented the easiest means of verification. Noting that with zero or low ABM deployment, the Soviets underscored that MIRVs became unimportant and could be banned with no significant risk. The Soviets stated that if their concerns over ABM and MIRVs were met, then they would be amenable to considering a mutual halt to the construction of offensive missiles and launchers. Although there were many areas of disagreement, the two sides were finally talking about limiting strategic arms. On December 22, 1969, the preliminary discussions on SALT were recessed, with both sides agreeing to reconvene in Vienna, Austria, in April 1970.[35]

On April 9, 1970, Kissinger met with Dobrynin, informing the Soviet diplomat that the United States was preparing comprehensive alternative proposals for a ban on MIRVs and arms reductions. However, Kissinger noted that if the Soviets were interested in a more limited agreement, then the United States might consider that as well. What Kissinger didn't tell Dobrynin was that there were two conditions to these proposals, both of which were designed to make the Soviets balk. The first was a requirement for on-site inspection, insisted on by the Pentagon, and the second was a loophole permitting the production of MIRVs. The Soviet Union would never approve any intrusive on-site inspection regime, and a clause permitting the manufacture of MIRVs, but not their testing, meant the United States would lock itself into a strategic advantage because the Soviets had yet to conduct MIRV testing.[36]

The Vienna round of talks began on April 16, 1970. Early on in these talks, when Gerard Smith started reading the U.S. proposal, the Soviets took extensive notes. However, as soon as Smith got to the provision concerning on-site inspection, his Soviet counterpart put down his pen. "We had been hoping you would make a serious MIRV proposal," he said once Smith had finished. No sooner had they begun than the Vienna talks were stalled.[37] Over the course of the next weeks, the Soviets countered with a proposal of their own that permitted MIRV testing but prohibited manufacture and deployment of the systems. This proposal was, perhaps intentionally, just as absurd as the American proposal, and it too was rejected. Recognizing that time was running out on any possibility of containing the MIRV problem, Smith wrote back to Washington, proposing an outright MIRV ban; Kissinger rejected this initiative.[38]

When it came to defining the limits for each side in terms of strategic weapons, Smith came up with the "Vienna Option," proposing limits of 1,900 launchers on each side, 1,710 in missile launchers, and 250 in modern heavy missiles (the Soviet SS-9, a major concern for the MIRV-sensitive United States). This was passed back to Kissinger for review. The Soviets also accepted a U.S. proposal limiting ABMs to one site protecting each nation's capital. This decision guaranteed an expensive and dangerous MIRV-based arms race between the United States and Soviet Union because it locked in the numbers of missiles but with no limit on the number of warheads.[39]

It also created a huge domestic problem for Kissinger. The Senate had voted 51–50 to approve the deployment of *Safeguard*, a two-site system. Construction had already begun on *Safeguard* at the North Forks Air Force Base in North Dakota and was scheduled to begin in June 1970 at Malstrom Air Force Base in Montana. Many prominent senators from both parties had thrown their support behind *Safeguard*, and now it looked as if Kissinger and Nixon were negotiating the ABM system away. Setting the stage for a confrontation with Congress, Nixon's promise in the summer of 1969 to conduct an annual review of the ABM program created a second opportunity for congressional opponents of *Safeguard* to try to kill the system. In early March 1970, while Gerard Smith was formulating a U.S. SALT negotiating position, Defense Secretary Laird had gone to Congress to request funding for a "Modified Phase 2" *Safeguard* system. This system comprised a third *Safeguard* site to be constructed at Whiteman Air Force Base in Montana, with additional missiles for the first two sites, and the appropriation of land for five more *Safeguard* bases, for a total budget increase of $1.5 billion on top of the $759 million Congress appropriated in 1969. As envisioned by Laird, the planned *Safeguard* system would comprise fourteen sites. Laird argued before Congress that the Soviets "are continuing the rapid deployment of major strategic offensive-weapons systems at a rate that could, by the mid-1970s, place us in a second-rate strategic position with regard to the future security of the free world." Despite continued opposition in Congress, the funding request was passed.[40]

The strategic balance between the United States and the Soviet Union appeared to have reached parity. By June 1970, the Soviets had deployed some 1,300 ICBMs and 270 SLBMs. The American number had remained unchanged, at 1,054 and 646, respectively. But the United States deployed its first MIRV-equipped *Minuteman* III in June 1970, and *Poseidon* MIRVs were due to be in place in January 1971. Thus, by the end of 1972, though the number of strategic missiles would be roughly 2,000 on each side, the United States would have 4,000 deliverable warheads, double that of the Soviets. As feared by many opponents of the MIRV, the Soviets had no choice but to push for their own MIRV capability and thus had no motive to freeze offensive weapons. Kissinger's allowing ABM to be de-linked from force limitations severely damaged the U.S. negotiating effort during this phase of the SALT talks.

Meanwhile, the situation in Southeast Asia was worsening, with U.S. troops invading Cambodia in early 1970, prompting massive demonstrations throughout the United States. Nixon was desperate for an opportunity to distract the American public away from Cambodia. He therefore sought a U.S.-Soviet summit, preferably in the fall of 1970, in time to influence congressional elections. Nixon broached the idea with Kissinger, and on April 7, 1970, Kissinger met with Ambassador Dobrynin and raised the idea of a summit. Dobrynin agreed that the fall was the ideal time for such a summit, in time for the United Nations twenty-fifth anniversary celebration. Kissinger emphasized that such a summit should be linked with the SALT discussions.[41]

A major issue facing any potential summit was the problems the Soviets were having in the course of their twenty-fourth Party Conference. For the first time in its history, the Soviets were unable to come up with a Five Year Plan, a reflection of the severe economic stress they were facing. Much of this stress was caused by the extreme burden placed on the Soviet economy to support the ongoing arms buildup. The Brezhnev-Kosygin struggle for power was likewise coming to a head. Having heard nothing back by June 1970, Nixon had Kissinger make another push for a summit. The Soviets responded, first by trying to link any such summit with a comprehensive Middle East peace plan. Nixon rejected this. The second Soviet response was to offer an early agreement on ABM systems, to be finalized at a summit, in exchange for a joint U.S.-Soviet agreement on cooperative response to any attack on one party by a third party. This proposal was raised in Vienna, to Gerard Smith, who forwarded it to Kissinger in July. Again, this proposal was rejected.[42]

Void of any potential of a radical departure from the ongoing SALT negotiations that a U.S.-Soviet summit would offer, Kissinger circulated new negotiating instructions to Smith and his delegation, which represented, in fact, an official embrace of Smith's Vienna Option. In it, Kissinger stated that the limitations goals for the United States included capping the aggregate number of ICBMs, SLBMs, and strategic bombers at 1,900 for each side, with an added condition that heavy missiles produced after 1965 could not number more than 250. Within the agreed total, the aggregate number of ICBMs and SLBMs should be limited to 1,710. After any transition period to allow for both sides to reach the agreed-upon arms cap, the United States would then propose a ban on mobile ICBMs and new missile silo construction. The U.S. definition of "strategic weapons" would remain unchanged from that put forward in earlier instructions.[43]

Kissinger also put forward two negotiating positions concerning ABM, the first limiting deployment to a single site protecting a national capital (the National Command Authority, or NCA, option), the second a "zero" option banning all ABMs. The negotiating instructions concluded by noting that "the United States continues to support a comprehensive agreement, along the lines of either of the approaches already outlined and that we will seek to have an initial agreement followed by further agreements, including if possible controls on multiple independently targeted re-entry vehicles."[44]

The Soviets surprised the Americans by immediately agreeing to the NCA option for ABM deployment. Kissinger had agreed to put this on the table because he assumed the Soviets would reject it and ask for a more robust ABM defense. However, the remainder of the negotiating points became deadlocked. By insisting on the old interpretation of strategic weapons, the United States failed to address the Soviet concerns of what they termed "forward-based systems," or FBS—namely, U.S. aircraft carriers and European-based tactical aircraft that could strike the Soviet Union. The Vienna round of SALT discussions was scheduled to come to an end on August 14, 1970, and the late release of the new negotiating instructions made any hope of doing anything other than simply transmitting the new U.S. position fruitless. Progress would have to wait until the delegations reconvened in Helsinki on November 2, 1970.[45]

SALT wasn't the only arms control effort undertaken by the Nixon administration during this time. Upon assuming office, President Nixon still had to confront the issue of the nonproliferation treaty, ratification of which had been held up in 1968 following the Soviet invasion of Czechoslovakia. On March 13, 1969, President Nixon handed the nonproliferation treaty over to the Senate for ratification, and on November 24, 1969, it was finally ratified by the United States. Another problem the Nixon administration faced was the issue of American ratification of the 1925 Geneva Protocol, which banned the use of chemical weapons and biological weapons. However, the United States never ratified the protocol, and President Truman formally withdrew it from the Senate after World War II. Scant attention was paid to the protocol until 1966, when the United States came under criticism for using tear gas and herbicides in Vietnam. When Hungary, in the General Assembly of the United Nations, charged that U.S. practice violated the Geneva Protocol, the United States responded by introducing amendments to the Hungarian resolution that would have made the use of any chemical and bacteriological weapons an international crime. The United States called for "strict observance by all states of the principles and objectives" of the protocol.[46]

However, it was politically difficult for the United States to refer to a protocol that it itself had yet to ratify. Therefore, President Nixon announced on November 25, 1969, that he would resubmit the protocol to the Senate. In doing so, Nixon reaffirmed America's long-held position that it would not use chemical weapons first in any conflict, and he also renounced the use of all biological weapons. Nixon resubmitted the 1925 Geneva Protocol to the Senate for ratification on August 11, 1970, and in doing so reaffirmed the position held by his administration that the protocol did not apply to the use in war of riot-control agents and herbicides. The Senate Foreign Relations Committee did not agree with Nixon's interpretation regarding riot-control agents and herbicides, and the matter soon became bogged down in the Senate, where there was growing angst over the continued involvement of the United States in Vietnam. Such issues as the U.S. use of herbicides and riot-control agents in the Vietnam conflict thus became political fodder.

The delay in getting a U.S.-Soviet summit under way, brought on largely by the Kissinger-driven insistence on policy linkage between such issues as Vietnam and SALT, created opportunities for others to take center stage in terms of influencing East-West relations. On August 12, 1970, West Germany's newly elected leader, Willy Brandt, traveled to Moscow, where he signed a West German–Soviet treaty that recognized both East Germany and the special status of Berlin. Responding to his critics, Brandt noted that "with this treaty nothing has been lost that had not long since been gambled away."[47] This move gave the Soviets what they had been seeking for some time, namely closure on the issue of World War II–era hostilities with Germany. A major irritant to East-West relations, and the source of some the most serious confrontations between the United States and the Soviet Union, had been done away with. While publicly praising the Brandt initiative, privately Kissinger and Nixon fumed because it introduced a complicating feature (i.e., West German acquiescence on a peace treaty) into the overall approach the president was pursuing regarding U.S.-Soviet détente.[48]

While the Nixon administration and the rest of the world came to grips with the reality of Brandt's bold Ostpolitik ("East Politics," his focus on improving relations with East Germany and the Soviet Union), the U.S. and Soviet SALT delegations assembled in Helsinki on November 2, 1970, to resume their stalled negotiations. They quickly found themselves stymied on the issue of what constituted strategic forces. Frustrated, by December 1970, the Soviets proposed de-linking an ABM agreement from an overall agreement on force limitations. Gerard Smith was attracted to the proposal, but Kissinger continued to insist on a comprehensive agreement based upon the August 1970 negotiating instructions. The main problem was that the U.S. proposals were not designed to succeed, and this was painfully obvious to all involved. The fact that the Soviets knew, via the back-channel talks between Kissinger and the Soviets, that Kissinger was open to a de-linking of ABM from reductions talks meant that Smith and his colleagues kept defending a process that ultimately had no chance of success. The Helsinki talks were wrapped up on December 18, 1970, no further along toward an agreement than when they had convened six weeks earlier. The talks were scheduled to resume in Vienna on March 15, 1971.[49]

Time was running out for President Nixon if he was to accomplish any meaningful breakthrough in arms control during his first term as president. Elections were coming up in 1972, and Nixon was experiencing severe domestic political repercussions over his handling of the Vietnam War. Faced with pressure from the president, Kissinger worked to establish the foundation for success in the coming SALT negotiations. At a luncheon with Dobrynin, the two discussed the status of the negotiations. Dobrynin expressed some frustration at the pace of the talks, noting that the Soviets had made an offer concerning ABM and that the U.S. delegation had not only rejected it but let it be known that the Soviet initiative had been personally rejected by Kissinger. Kissinger informed the ambassador that the United States was prepared to enter into a separate ABM agreement, provided such an agreement was coupled with an understanding that both sides would continue working on arms reductions talks, and agree to a "freeze" on any new offensive land-based missiles during the period of these negotiations.[50]

Nixon and Kissinger were now faced with a dilemma. Having agreed in principle, via the back channel, to a separate ABM agreement, they were confronted with the fact that the United States had proposed, and the Soviets had accepted, a single antiballistic missile defense base that would defend each respective nation's capital city. Nixon was under considerable political pressure from senators "Scoop" Jackson and John Stennis, both of whom were concerned that the ABM system they had fought so hard for was being negotiated away. If this was the case, they told Nixon, then they would begin to attack the SALT talks themselves. In order to maintain the appearance of pushing for a strong ABM system, Nixon instructed Smith to chair a new proposal on ABM, the so-called four-to-one proposal, in which the United States would have four ABM sites (the three sites defending ICBM silos funded in 1970, together with a new NCA site around Washington). The proposal never had a chance. The Soviets rejected it as absurd and questioned Smith and his team as to why the United States would not stick with the NCA proposal that had already been agreed to.[51]

In early May 1971, the head of the Soviet delegation, Deputy Foreign Minister Vladimir Semenov, hinted to Smith that the Soviets might be willing to link a separate ABM agreement with an understanding on strategic force limitations. This, of course, was the same understanding that had been reached between Kissinger and Dobrynin, but Smith, intentionally kept ignorant of the back channel by Kissinger, who wanted to remain in control of the negotiations, knew nothing about it. Smith reported Semenov's discussion back to Kissinger via official channels, requesting instructions.[52]

Building on this breakthrough, Nixon made an announcement that the United States and the Soviet Union had agreed to work together in seeking an ABM agreement and simultaneously "certain measures with respect to the limitation of offensive strategic weapons." Nixon described this agreement as a "significant development in breaking the deadlock" that had gripped the SALT negotiations. However, Nixon noted that "intensive negotiations will be required to translate this understanding into a concrete understanding." For the first time since the talks began, Smith had very defined marching orders: to negotiate an ABM agreement and an interim freeze of strategic forces.[53]

Drafting an ABM agreement was to prove more difficult than imagined. There was still a divergence on the issue of the number of ABM sites that would be permitted. The Soviets continued to insist on the previously agreed-on NCA solution. Realizing that the four-to-one option was a nonstarter, Kissinger authorized Smith to propose a three-to-one option (two ICBM sites and one NCA site for the United States, and one NCA site for the Soviets), and when this was rejected, a two-to-one option. The Soviets held fast to their position.[54]

While the talks dragged on in Vienna, events unfolded elsewhere that would influence not only the SALT negotiations but also U.S.-Soviet relations in general. The war in Southeast Asia continued to plague Nixon. The president needed a major event to occur that would shift public attention away from the Vietnam War. Henry Kissinger gave it to him in the way of a dramatic opening of relations between the United States and China. Following a secret visit by Henry Kissinger to Beijing in early June 1971, President Nixon went on national television on July 15, 1971, to announce his intention to visit China in the future. A new element had been added to an already complex U.S.-Soviet relationship.

The SALT negotiations in Vienna continued through the summer of 1971, with minimal progress. A major issue still unresolved was the question of future ABM systems. On September 24, 1971, just as the talks were preparing to adjourn for a recess, the two sides were able to prepare a joint ABM agreement text that, though containing numerous points of contention, appeared to move closer on one critical issue: the number of ABM sites that would be allowed. The United States by this time was proposing that each side be permitted either two missile defense sites or one NCA site; the Soviets had responded by proposing one missile defense site and one NCA site for each side. These positions remained unchanged for the rest of the year.[55]

While the SALT talks continued to be hindered, there was some progress made toward achieving an elusive summit between Nixon and the Soviet leadership. Back in June 1971, Kissinger had pressed Dobrynin for a deadline on announcing a summit date for the fall of 1971. In September 1971, it was agreed that a summit would take place during the second half of May 1972 in Moscow. When the SALT negotiations reconvened in Helsinki in early January 1972, both sides knew they were laboring under the clock to get an agreement in time for the scheduled May 1972 summit in Moscow. On January 7, 1972, Gerard Smith sought clarity by asking his Soviet counterpart if the U.S.-Soviet agreement on ABMs should be drafted in treaty form. The Soviets concurred. The Soviets continued to push to limit ABM deployments to one missile defense site and one NCA site, something to which the United States was not yet prepared to agree. However, the Soviets began to budge on the issue of future ABM systems; by the end of January they had come around to accepting the merits of the U.S. proposal, which would permit future systems so long as before any side deployed such a new system, both sides would have to agree on the systems involved. The issue of how many, and what type of, ABM sites each side could have was not settled until mid-April 1972, when U.S. and Soviet negotiators agreed to allow one missile defense site and one NCA site for each country, or a two-for-two solution. The last of the major outstanding issues concerning ABM had been resolved.[56]

From February 21 to 28, 1972, President Richard Nixon made history by visiting China. This remarkable trip was widely publicized, and the photographs of the onetime communist-baiting California congressman seated smiling next to Chairman Mao Tse-tung enthralled the world. It was a great moment for Nixon, the United States, and China—and indeed the world. The Shanghai Communiqué, which grew from this visit, established the intent of both nations to normalize diplomatic relations with one another. Although the Soviet reaction to Nixon's Beijing visit was generally negative, the end result was for the Soviets to push even harder for a May summit in Moscow and to seek not only an ABM agreement but also one on strategic arms limitations that could serve as the basis for even more far-reaching agreements. It was in Moscow's interest to bring America even closer to its breast than Beijing could.

The Moscow summit was less than a month away when Henry Kissinger engaged in yet another secret diplomatic journey, this time to Moscow itself, where he was tasked with preparing for the upcoming Nixon-Brezhnev meeting. Two issues stood between Kissinger and a successful summit: final agreement on what would constitute an ABM treaty and the issue of Soviet submarine-launched ballistic missiles (SLBMs) that would be permitted under any arms limitation agreement. In a series of meetings with Brezhnev and Foreign Minister Gromyko, Kissinger was able to solidify the basis of not only an ABM treaty but also an agreement on arms limitations. On ABM, the two-for-two proposal that had been worked out in Helsinki was formally agreed to by both Kissinger and Brezhnev. Brezhnev next settled the issue of SLBMs by proposing Kissinger's own suggestion, made via the back channel with Dobrynin, that the Soviets be permitted to build up to sixty-two SLBM submarines equipped with 950 launchers.[57]

Kissinger returned to the United States and began the process of preparing Nixon for the summit. There would be two major documents at play, the first being the ABM treaty, and the second an interim agreement on strategic arms limitations. Both agreements were dependent on the other. The interim agreement could only enter into force when the United States and the Soviet Union formally accepted the ABM treaty, and either side could withdraw from the ABM treaty if, in the words of Gerard Smith, "an agreement providing for more complete strategic offensive arms limitations were not achieved within five years."[58]

On May 22, 1972, President Nixon arrived in Moscow. Nixon was taken by motorcade to the Kremlin, where he met with Leonid Brezhnev, the Stars and Stripes flying for the first time over the Kremlin's Grand Palace. Lesser agreements were signed over the course of the first few days of Nixon's Moscow visit, but the heart of the Moscow summit was the signing of the ABM treaty and the interim agreement on SALT. Shortly before midnight on Friday, May 26, President Nixon, together with Leonid Brezhnev, assembled in the Hall of Saint Vladimir inside the Kremlin's Grand Palace to jointly sign the two agreements that would set their respective nations down a path of peaceful cooperation. In doing so they would reduce the prospects of global nuclear holocaust that had terrorized the world since the dawn of the nuclear age, some thirty-seven years earlier.

In the aftermath of this momentous occasion, both men were joined by their assistants and colleagues in toasting to their success. It was a grand moment for Nixon. A presidential election was to be held in 1972, and the Moscow summit, with its arms control successes, stood as a symbol of Nixon's commitment to improving superpower relations, easily offsetting any political problems Nixon might face concerning the difficult disengagement from Vietnam. That year saw Nixon break all ideological barriers by visiting China and then by following that up with his successful Moscow summit. It had all the makings of a great year in the life of an American president. And yet, less than a month later, on June 17, 1972, in the Watergate Apartment complex in Washington, events would unfold that would not only bring down President Nixon but also threaten the very foundation of security he had helped build through his presence in Moscow on that glorious May evening.

CHAPTER 10

THE END
OF DÉTENTE

The Moscow summit of May 1972 was, on the surface, a grand display of diplomacy and a great success for the Nixon-Kissinger team. However, behind the scenes, the reality of how Kissinger had weakened the final agreements through his meddling back-channel diplomacy was well known to those closest to the negotiations. One of those most upset by the turn of events was the architect of the ABM treaty and SALT interim agreement, ACDA Director Gerard Smith, who believed Kissinger's interference had undermined his effectiveness as a negotiator. The last-minute agreement between Kissinger and Brezhnev on SLBM numbers was an unpleasant surprise for Smith, who believed the numbers agreed on were far too high and could have easily been negotiated downward.[1] Smith had been planning to retire after the SALT agreement was signed but then was considering extending his tenure in order to be involved in the SALT II negotiations, scheduled for the fall of 1972. Though he did stay on as ACDA director for the remainder of Nixon's first term, Smith submitted his resignation as arms reduction negotiator after the interim agreement was signed. America had lost an able champion of effective arms control.

Gerard Smith was a true arms control expert who believed that the specifics of an agreement were best left to those who understood the nuances and complexities of the technical realities of the weapons and weapons systems being discussed. As such, he placed high value on the role he and his Soviet counterparts were expected to play in negotiating any arms control agreement. Kissinger was more interested in the art and process of policy formulation, and its role in the grand scheme of national security, than he was in the esoteric, sometimes mundane details that were being mulled over by Smith and his colleagues. Kissinger was also very much one who did not like to relinquish control of anything to others, especially when dealing with such a high-profile topic as arms control. Kissinger repeatedly undercut Smith's negotiating efforts through his use of the back channel with Dobrynin. It was a mark of Smith's professionalism that he stayed on as long as he did given the reality of the working conditions he faced under Kissinger.

The May 1972 Moscow summit, and its resulting ABM treaty and SALT interim agreement, triggered opposition from Senator Henry "Scoop" Jackson, a Democrat from Washington State, who had a strong record of anticommunism and anti–arms control and was adamantly against any arms control treaties with communists. Scoop Jackson was also a man of considerable political ambition, especially during the 1972 presidential race. Jackson had announced his candidacy for the Democratic nomination, and although a long shot (Jackson withdrew early on in the primary campaign), the senator from Washington recognized the importance of seizing the national spotlight, operating as he was with an eye on the 1976 presidential contest. In March 1972, when it had become apparent that Kissinger was leaning toward a separate ABM agreement, Jackson held several informal hearings in which he staked out his position on *Safeguard* and the need for a viable ABM system. Now, with an ABM treaty signed, linked as it was to the SALT interim agreement, Jackson (heavily influenced by his new staff member, Richard Perle) began leveraging his political clout not so much to oppose the existing agreements but rather to ensure that any future arms control proceedings would be conducted in a manner that he found acceptable. In order to make sure events unfolded to his liking, Jackson put his sights on ACDA, seeking to limit the influence and effectiveness of that agency.[2]

One of the fatal flaws of the détente that emerged from the Moscow summit was that rather than being based on a solid foundation of negotiated principles mutually agreeable to both parties, it became captured by domestic politics and as such subjected to the vagaries of politicized public opinion. Nixon had instructed Kissinger to have the Moscow summit serve as a stage upon which he, Nixon, would emerge the star in time to influence the 1972 presidential election. Kissinger had accomplished this task, but in doing so had set up the policy of détente, inclusive of arms control, to be attacked by Nixon's political opponents, led by the indefatigable Jackson. The last thing Nixon needed was a long, drawn-out congressional battle over ratification. Knowing that the president had invested immense political capital in the ABM treaty and SALT interim agreement, Jackson was able to exploit the numerous fundamental weaknesses in the two agreements to pursue his own objective of limiting the role and functionality of arms control.

The first thing Scoop Jackson did was use the administration's own arguments in a manner that reinforced the argument in favor of specific weapons programs Jackson supported. In his testimony before Congress on SALT, Secretary of Defense Laird stressed the importance of taking advantage of the SALT agreement to pursue permitted upgrades to the U.S. strategic nuclear deterrent, namely a new SLBM, the *Trident*, and a new bomber, the B-1.[3] In this he had, of course, a strong advocate in Jackson, who not only pushed for the *Trident* and B-1 programs on behalf of Boeing, the Seattle-based defense contractor heavily involved in both projects, but also was able to parlay his conditional support of the ABM and SALT agreements into a concession from Laird that moved the home base of a future U.S. Navy *Trident* SLBM force from the East Coast to Washington State.[4]

There were arguments put forward in the debate defending the SALT agreement's concepts of "sufficiency," which focused on qualitative aspects of a nation's nuclear arsenal (i.e., what was sufficient to meet a national security objective), as opposed to a more quantitative-based approach, which used simple missile counts as a means of expressing "equality." But these arguments did not satisfy Senator Jackson, who used his position as the chair of the Arms Control Subcommittee of the Armed Forces Committee to drive the debate in the direction he wanted, namely a rejection of sufficiency and an embrace of equality. Jackson slammed Kissinger and others on the ambiguous nature of the SALT agreement, in particular the fact that whereas Kissinger had committed the United States to a specific number of ICBMs, there was no such specific limitation for the Soviets because they could exchange ICBMs and SLBMs and strategic bombers within an overall "cap" that was not system-specific. Jackson rejected the concept of overall ceilings; instead, he wanted a specified Soviet limit that matched the specified U.S. limit. In an effort to bring Jackson's assaults on SALT to an end, Kissinger brokered several deals that would heavily affect the future of U.S.–Soviet arms control.[5]

The first deal was the "Jackson Amendment" to the Joint Congressional Resolution expressing support for the SALT interim agreement (SALT was not a treaty, and as such did not require formal ratification). The language of the amendment "urge[d] and request[ed] that the President seek a future treaty that, inter alia, would not limit the United States to levels of intercontinental strategic forces inferior to the limits provided by the Soviet Union."[6] This amendment was incorporated into the ABM ratification process, and on August 3, 1972, the ABM treaty was ratified by the U.S. Senate.

The Jackson Amendment may have hobbled future U.S.-Soviet arms control negotiations by placing stringent conditions on force levels in advance of the actual negotiation, but the second deal between Kissinger and Jackson was much more nefarious. Jackson was appalled at the idea of détente with the Soviet Union. He viewed arms control not only as a mechanism of surrendering American military superiority to the Soviets but also as a vehicle that facilitated détente. To Jackson, arms control for arms control's sake was the enemy, and as such the principal agency responsible for formulating and implementing American arms control policy, the ACDA, became his foremost target.

Kissinger had once noted that "ACDA isn't an agency, it's a lobby." His own clashes with Gerard Smith and the SALT negotiating team left him only too willing to cooperate with the powerful Democratic senator in orchestrating ACDA's demise. Thus, when Jackson demanded that the ACDA be purged of all those who were active proponents of arms control, its ranks significantly reduced in numbers, and those senior positions that remained staffed by people personally approved by Jackson, Kissinger was only too willing to oblige. In November 1972, Richard Nixon won his bid for reelection. Immediately afterward, he called for the resignation of all senior staff. Though usually a pro forma procedure conducted for the symbolism of presidential control, in the case of ACDA Kissinger was quick to make these resignations reality.

The earlier resignation of Smith made Kissinger's actions easier. Although Smith was a Republican, he had retained within ACDA fifteen senior holdovers from the Kennedy-Johnson administration in order to provide continuity in the ongoing arms reduction discussions between the United States and the Soviet Union. Jackson insisted that these personnel be replaced with people to his personal liking, and by the end of the year fourteen of the staff were fired, including Smith's deputy, Ray Garthoff, and his military advisor, General Royal Allison.[7]

In their place, Jackson signed off on the appointments of Owen Zurhellen, a State Department officer who specialized in East Asia affairs, as the ACDA deputy (replacing the veteran arms control specialist, Phil Farley), as well as inserting his own protégé, Paul Wolfowitz, onto the ACDA roster.[8] Jackson even went so far as to pressure the Pentagon into assigning, as General Allison's replacement, Lieutenant General Edward Rowny, a decorated combat veteran of World War II, Korea, and Vietnam. Rowny, a son of Polish immigrants, was very conservative and not surprisingly (given his background) strongly anti-Soviet. Naming Rowny to replace Allison was the price Jackson extracted for his continued support of the ABM treaty. Out of a staff of 230, some 50 positions were cut, and fully one-third of the ACDA budget was eliminated.[9]

In addition to its shrinking size, ACDA also lost its influence over arms control. Jackson had pressed the White House to reduce the role of ACDA for the second round of SALT negotiations, scheduled to begin again in March 1973. Kissinger got Nixon to agree to removing the responsibility for conducting negotiations from the ACDA director. Instead Nixon appointed U. Alexis Johnson, a career diplomat and former undersecretary of state who had previously represented the United States at the ENDC talks in Geneva, to take over responsibility for the SALT II negotiations. The director of ACDA became responsible solely for conducting research and planning arms strategy.[10]

The downsizing of ACDA occurred at a time when the future of America's strategic nuclear policy was in the balance. The Scoop Jackson–driven purge of American arms controllers meant that any discussion involving the composition of, and policy framework for, America's nuclear arsenal would be in an environment unconstrained by meaningful arms reduction pressures. There represented no surer formula for encouraging a massive increase in defense spending, and as a result, unleashing the very sort of arms race the arms controllers had been trying to stem. The genesis of this policy debate is well known: Nixon and Kissinger's revulsion over the current SIOP, especially the lack of flexibility it provided the commander in chief when it came to employing nuclear weapons in a time of crisis. Ironically, what was meant to bring a sense of sanity to U.S. nuclear strategy achieved the exact opposite.

On January 19, 1972, Secretary of Defense Melvin Laird had formed a panel for the purpose of reviewing American policy for employing strategic nuclear weapons, partly in response to Kissinger's dissatisfaction with the SIOP. The Foster Panel, named after its chair, John Foster (a former nuclear weapons scientist at Livermore and at the time of his appointment the director of defense research and engineering), examined the best ways to give the American national command authority the widest possible choices when it came to controlling the escalation of nuclear war. It took the existing SIOP attack options and categorized them as "major attacks." Then, in an effort to limit the destructiveness of nuclear war, the panel proposed two new categories of targets, known as "selective options" and "limited options."

Limited option strikes were designed to stop any nuclear war quickly and thus limit the level of destruction. If limited option attacks failed to prevent escalation, then the United States could exercise selective option attacks, which were designed "to minimize the enemy's residual military power and recovery capability and not just destroy his population and industry." These last two categories were precisely the kind of "sub-SIOP" plans Kissinger had been looking for. The Foster Panel, however, was simply reviewing nuclear weapons tasking and not the actual selection of targets. That could only occur if the panel's recommendations were accepted as formal policy guidance, and the Pentagon and Joint Chiefs of Staff were instructed to comply.[11]

Henry Kissinger had asked the National Security Council to work on issues similar to those being investigated by the Foster Panel. The Foster Panel had been organized as a Department of Defense–only entity and was doing its work void of any outside input or knowledge of its existence. However, in July 1972, Henry Kissinger became cognizant of the Foster Panel's efforts and immediately transformed the Pentagon-only group into an interagency effort headed by NSC staffer Philip Odeen, who melded the work being done by the NSC with the Foster Panel.

Within a few months, Odeen distilled the work of the Foster Panel into a twenty-page document known as the Nuclear Weapons Employment Plan, or NUWEP. It incorporated the three main strike options of the Foster Panel (major nuclear attack, selective nuclear attack, and limited nuclear attack) and added a fourth—regional nuclear attack. Going beyond simply establishing nuclear attack options, Odeen's NUWEP also set forth the parameters for what was called Damage Expectancy, or DE. Each target would be given a DE percentage (most were set at 90 percent, some even higher), which meant more often than not more than one nuclear weapon was required to be assigned to achieve the DE requirement. This was a departure from the previous targeting guidance associated with the SIOP, which simply dealt with what was known as a Designated Ground Zero, or DGZ, to which a designated allocation of nuclear weapons would be assigned.

The SIOP had been simply a matter of assigning weapon X to target Y. Under NUWEP, however, Odeen was seeking to apply a qualitative aspect to what had previously only been a quantitative task. This represented a paradigm shift in thinking when it came to nuclear targeting. The consequences of this approach from an arms-control perspective were not insignificant because a qualitative approach in targeting meant more targeting options, which required a greater flexibility in terms of the types of U.S. nuclear weapons as well as their means of delivery. As such, NUWEP created pressures to increase the size of the U.S. nuclear arsenal.[12]

At the same time the United States was refining its instrument of nuclear war (SIOP), it was dismantling its instrument of nuclear disarmament (ACDA). The termination of ACDA as a meaningful arms control agency was assured when, in April 1973 (three months after Gerard Smith left the directorship), President Nixon appointed Smith's replacement, Fred Iklé. Iklé was an experienced nuclear strategist who had devised the "permissive action link," which made it physically impossible to arm a nuclear weapon without proper authority. Iklé rejected the nuclear strategy options calling for preemptive or first-strike capability, believing that in order to be able to launch quickly, ICBMs themselves became vulnerable to attack. In his view, any enemy who became concerned about a U.S. first-strike capability would be more inclined to launch its own preemptive attack. Instead, Iklé proposed to bury ICBMs into deep, super-hardened silos that all but assured their survival in case of a surprise attack, thereby guaranteeing a retaliatory capacity, and thus ensuring deterrence. Iklé was also ideologically in tune with the direction Scoop Jackson wanted to pursue when it came to U.S. nuclear strategy. In an article published in the January 1973 issue of *Foreign Affairs*, titled "Can Nuclear Deterrence Last Out the Century?" Iklé rejected the then-current dogma of Assured Destruction or Mutually Assured Destruction and instead embraced a strategy that promoted the concept of Counterforce, where American nuclear weapons targeted the Soviet military but not its cities.[13] Such a strategy embraced other concepts, such as MIRVs, increased accuracy for ICBMs and SLBMs, new manned bombers and of course ABMs—everything Jackson wanted for the military and his friends at Boeing.

The second half of 1972 was noted for more than just a burglary at the Watergate Hotel, Senate debates over arms control, and President Nixon's reelection. In early October 1972, the North Vietnamese agreed to meet with the United States in Paris, and by January 1973, the two sides had hammered out the framework of a peace accord. Within twenty-four hours of signing the agreement, U.S. prisoners of war began to return home, and the complete withdrawal of all U.S. forces from South Vietnam had begun. "Peace with honor" had been, in the eyes of the Nixon administration, at last achieved. Finally free of the Vietnam War, Kissinger immediately turned to the task of tying in the politics of détente with China and the Soviet Union within the framework of U.S.-European relations.

In April 1973, Kissinger announced that 1973 was to be "the Year of Europe." He had high hopes. The Moscow summit had opened the door for other arms reduction venues: the Conference on Security and Cooperation in Europe (CSCE), a priority of the Soviets, and Mutual Bi-Lateral Force Reduction talks (MBFR), something America's NATO allies were interested in. Nixon, at the time under pressure from Congress to achieve reductions in the defense budget, realized that he couldn't pursue the drawdown of U.S. troops in Europe without viable MBFR talks, and the Soviets would never agree to such talks unless the United States agreed to CSCE talks. Kissinger's task was to breathe life into both.[14]

Under normal circumstances, Kissinger's ambitious undertaking would have been difficult. But given the circumstances of the time, the Year of Europe was doomed from the very start. Kissinger needed significant support from a strong executive to make the Year of Europe happen, coupled with a broad range of cooperation between the executive and Congress. But the executive Kissinger so depended on was in the midst of a process of self-immolation known as Watergate. By May 1973, some seventeen associates of the president were under investigation in relation to a break-in at the Democratic National Committee headquarters during the 1972 presidential election. Soon many of them began testifying before Congress, breathing life into accusations that the president himself was involved in covering up their actions.

On May 4, 1973, Kissinger traveled to Moscow, where he met with Leonid Brezhnev for the purposes of shaping the agenda for a June summit in the United States. Brezhnev made it quite clear that one of his priorities in such a summit was to sign an agreement on the Prevention of Nuclear War (PNW), making sure that SALT II would incorporate talks designed to control or eliminate MIRVs and to improve economic ties between the two countries. The Soviets were pushing for a PNW treaty, in part because they hoped such a sweeping agreement between the world's two nuclear superpowers would align the United States more closely with Soviet goals in Europe and with China, namely reducing American influence by diminishing the American nuclear umbrella.[15]

Kissinger, understanding the importance of PNW in terms of a successful U.S. summit (something Nixon deemed critical, given his need to divert public attention away from the growing Watergate scandal), negotiated a compromise. This compromise extended the PNW treaty's language to include not only a nonuse clause concerning the Soviet Union and the

United States but third parties as well, a move designed to lessen European and Chinese concerns over any U.S.-Soviet agreement that excluded their respective roles. Kissinger's goal for a treaty was to assist in creating a web of conditions that prevented the Soviets from turning on either NATO or China. Brezhnev was also anxious to move forward on the matter of U.S.-Soviet trade, driven largely by growing economic difficulties inside the Soviet Union.[16]

On June 16, 1973, Brezhnev and his Soviet delegation arrived in the United States. The U.S. summit lacked the drama of the Moscow summit the year before, and very little of substance emerged beyond the signing of the PNW treaty. Several other minor agreements were signed between the two leaders, and a broad range of issues discussed, including SALT II, U.S.-China relations, most-favored trading nation status for the Soviet Union, and the ongoing situations in Vietnam and the Middle East. However, there were to be no major breakthroughs when it came to U.S.-Soviet relations. Concerning SALT, the best the two leaders could do was agree upon a basic set of principles, which were so vague as to be useless. They did, however, create a political imperative, transferred to both negotiating teams, that some sort of progress had to be achieved by the end of 1974. Court testimony implicating Richard Nixon in the Watergate scandal pushed the U.S.-Soviet summit off the front pages of America's newspapers, denying the president even that small political boost.[17]

The only significant result of the U.S. summit was the signing of the PNW treaty. Kissinger had touted the PNW treaty, claiming that had such an agreement existed a decade ago, there never would have been a crisis over Berlin. "The West," Kissinger had announced in April 1973, "no longer holds the nuclear predominance that permitted it in the '50s and '60s to rely almost solely on a strategy of massive nuclear retaliation. Because under conditions of nuclear parity such a strategy invites mutual suicide, the Alliance must have other choices."[18]

These other choices involved repackaging total nuclear conflict into smaller, more acceptable options. The NUWEP paper being prepared by Phil Odeen at the NSC had, by the end of the summer of 1973, been reviewed by every involved department and agency. The product of this effort was National Security Decision Memorandum 242 (NSDM 242), "Planning the Employment of Nuclear Weapons." Kissinger used NSDM 242 to instruct the Pentagon to develop the "different options that the President could absorb before a crisis develops and he is called upon to make a decision." NSDM 242 was ready for the president's signature by the end of August 1973. Kissinger had always been concerned that events might transpire that would confront an American president with the need to consider the employment of nuclear weapons, with the president then to be faced with the horrific reality of there being no option but the worst: all-out nuclear war. NSDM 242 was designed to answer this concern.[19]

Those in the Nixon administration opposed to détente with the Soviet Union embraced the absolute necessity to revise American nuclear strategy so that meaningful deterrence capability existed to offset any potential Soviet power grab, whether in the Middle East, Europe, or elsewhere. That the Soviets had not demonstrated interest in such a power grab, or better, had demonstrated the exact opposite, was not a factor in the thinking of these hard-liners. What they were worried about was the *potential* for Soviet action and the demonstrated inability of the United States to effectively deter, and if necessary, respond to any such Soviet provocation with anything other than total nuclear Armageddon.

Kissinger thought he had a solution ready and waiting in the NSDM 242 document. Kissinger (who had been selected to receive, along with Le Duc Tho of North Vietnam, the 1973 Nobel Peace Prize) was now preparing to present to Nixon a document that would guide the development within the U.S. military of a "broad range of limited options aimed at terminating [nuclear] war on terms acceptable to the U.S. at the lowest levels of conflict feasible." The United States retained the capability to launch massive nuclear strikes against the Soviet Union and Communist China, if escalation of any nuclear conflict could not be controlled. However, Kissinger told the president that the goals of U.S. nuclear strategy had changed, and rather than seeking to achieve the "wholesale destruction of Soviet military forces, people, and industry," the United States now possessed the option for "inhibiting the early return of the Soviet Union to major power status by systematic attacks on Soviet military, economic, and political structures." Kissinger presented the NSDM 294 document to President Nixon in early January 1974.[20]

Nixon was, by this time, fighting a rearguard action for his own political survival. The dramatic revelation that the White House had secret voice recording capability led to the subpoena of all private conversations the president had conducted in the oval office. Nixon refused to surrender the tapes of these conversations, citing executive privilege. Under pressure from a special prosecutor he himself had directed to be appointed, Nixon ordered his attorney general, Elliot Richardson, to fire that same special prosecutor. He refused, and Nixon promptly fired Richardson, leading off a series of firings and threatened firings that became known as the "Saturday Night Massacre." Nixon was reduced to pathetically commenting to the press, unprompted, that "I am not a crook." By January 1974, the fight for access to the Nixon tapes had taken on constitutional proportions, with the involvement of the United States Supreme Court. Thus distracted, Nixon signed NSDM 294, one of the most far-reaching and important documents in the history of U.S. nuclear strategy.[21]

Only a few months after the dissemination of NSDM 242, Secretary of Defense James Schlesinger, who had taken over the job from Elliot Richardson, who had been appointed by Nixon as attorney general in August 1973, signed off on guidelines that came to be known as NUWEP, borrowing liberally from Phil Odeen's paper of the same name. The advent of NDSM 242 and the new NUWEP doctrine gave the Defense Department great latitude with the technological means to implement the new strategic nuclear targeting guidelines. The Pentagon turned its attention to the U.S. Navy's new SLBM program, intent on creating an SLBM that possessed the accuracy of a *Minuteman* III ICBM.[22]

Back in September 1971, the Defense Department had approved a long-term modernization plan that called for a new, larger submarine and a new, longer-range missile while preserving a nearer-term option to develop an extended-range *Poseidon* missile. The Navy had become increasingly concerned over the vulnerability of its SLBM submarines to improved Soviet antisubmarine warfare capabilities, which became more lethal the closer a U.S. submarine came to the Soviet coastline. The greater the range of an SLBM, the greater the safety would be for the U.S. submarine launching it. The *Poseidon* missile had a range of 2,000 miles. The goal for the new Navy missile, named *Trident*, was to have a missile possessing the same accuracy and MIRV capability of the *Poseidon*, but possessing a range of 4,000 miles. The *Trident* missile was designed to be retrofitted into the existing *Poseidon*-class SLBM submarine fleet and was designed to carry up to eight MIRV 100-kiloton warheads possessing an accuracy of 1,250 feet. An even newer missile, the *Trident II*, having a greater range, payload, and accuracy than the *Trident*, was also to be developed for service in a new class of *Trident* SLBM submarines. It was the *Trident II* missile that the Pentagon wanted to convert from a weapon of retaliation into a weapon of preemption that possessed hard-kill, first-strike capability.[23]

NSDM 242 also directed the CIA to prepare a report assessing the Soviet and Chinese reactions to the new nuclear policies of the United States. This tasking led the CIA to speculate that the Soviet Union might seek to develop its own range of limited nuclear strike options for Europe or the Middle East, or in a regional conflict with China. The CIA noted that the current trend for Soviet nuclear planning appeared to emphasize "massive strikes" for both regional and intercontinental nuclear conflict. But the CIA conjectured that the Soviets might very well be influenced by the new U.S. nuclear policy to enhance their own version of limited nuclear attack, whether or not the Soviets viewed such moves as feasible. Rather than adopt similar flexibility for intercontinental nuclear strikes, the CIA believed that the Soviets would instead seek ways to avoid nuclear escalation. The CIA noted that it possessed little information about Chinese nuclear strategy but speculated that the Chinese might also develop a limited nuclear strike option to counter the new American strategy.[24]

The one hope the United States had in averting this rush toward nuclear insanity was through the ongoing SALT II negotiations. In the fall of 1973, the Soviets presented the U.S. delegation with a draft SALT II treaty text that maintained the unequal limits on missile launchers set forth in the interim agreement and that provided for an unspecified limit on MIRVs. The Soviet proposal was based upon the sufficiency model of qualitative factors that had been vehemently rejected by opponents of arms control, such as Scoop Jackson, who insisted on strict quantitative equality formulas. U. Alexis Johnson, hobbled by the constraints of the Jackson Amendment, was only able to respond with the standard U.S. position insisting on numerical equality, which would require the Soviets to cut the numbers of their missiles while securing for the United States a qualitative advantage.

It wasn't until February 1974 that the United States began to get serious about the SALT II negotiations. On February 19, 1974, Kissinger issued a formal SALT II negotiating position that set 2,350 as the overall aggregate number of ICBMs, SLBMs, and strategic bombers each side could possess. The position also established that both sides would be limited to an equal number of ICBM MIRVs determined by throw weight, as opposed to capping the total number of MIRVs that could be deployed.[25]

This was a ploy to limit the number of missiles on which the Soviet Union could deploy MIRVs, while giving the United States the option to deploy as many MIRVs as it wanted on its own ICBM force. The Soviets rejected this, but by March, again through extensive use of the back channel with Soviet Ambassador Anatoliy Dobrynin, Kissinger had crafted a compromise, acceptable to the National Security Council, that had the United States accepting unequal aggregate numbers of launchers and bombers on the part of the Soviet Union in exchange for the Soviets accepting an unequal number of MIRVs on the part of the United States.[26]

The U.S. position on MIRVs, based as it was on the issue of throw weight, placed the Soviets at a significant disadvantage, minimizing the one major advantage they enjoyed over the United States. The Soviet counterproposal was to insist on maintaining the unequal aggregate of launchers through 1980 but to provide the United States with a 1,100:1,000 edge over missiles armed with MIRVs, using numbers instead of throw weight as the limiting feature. The Soviets also proposed limiting the ABM deployment on both sides to one site each, instead of the two agreed upon in the ABM treaty. Kissinger met with Soviet Foreign Minister Andrei Gromyko twice in April 1974 to try to break the impasse. Kissinger proposed accepting the unequal aggregate numbers through 1980 but limiting the MIRV-equipped missiles to 1,100 for the United States and just 850 for the Soviet Union. This proposal was rejected by the Soviets.[27]

Simultaneously with the SALT II talks, the Soviets were pursuing the issue of a comprehensive nuclear test ban treaty. The Soviets wanted the two major powers to conclude a comprehensive ban at the summit and then pressure the other nuclear powers (Great Britain, France, and China) into accepting it. This would put the United States in the position of alienating both China and France, something it was unwilling to do. In March 1974, Brezhnev brought up the possibility of a limited threshold ban, which would limit a nuclear test to a specified size. Advances in seismic detection capability had made a threshold ban viable, and because the Soviets did not insist on other nuclear powers' participation, Kissinger responded optimistically, and the issue began to be discussed in earnest at the ongoing test ban talks in Geneva. An acceptable agreement was made that set the threshold for nuclear tests at 150 kilotons.[28]

But the United States and the world soon had a new nuclear test–based crisis, this one stemming from the Indian subcontinent. On May 14, 1974, India successfully tested a nuclear device, the so-called Smiling Buddha event. The test had been planned since 1972, when Indian prime minister Indira Gandhi gave her approval for the Indian Atomic Energy Agency to undertake activities specifically intended for the manufacture of a nuclear device. The Indians were quick to declare that their test was not that of a nuclear weapon but rather a "peaceful nuclear explosion." The "N-th" factor, so long anticipated concerning nuclear proliferation, had just emerged. The implications of the Indian test were considerable, especially in regard to Pakistan, but also concerning the viability of the NPT. With a nonproliferation treaty review conference coming up in 1975, the Indian test made it difficult for the United States to argue about the credibility of the NPT. However, at a time when events screamed for American leadership, Henry Kissinger, overwhelmed with Watergate and Moscow, noted that the official U.S. reaction to the test was to be "limited," stressing only America's continued commitment to nonproliferation.[29]

Kissinger continued to struggle to shape a coherent and unified SALT policy but was set back by a high-profile resignation. Paul Nitze, the veteran diplomat and one of the senior Department of Defense representatives serving on the SALT II delegation, resigned from his position on June 14, 1974. Nitze was growing increasingly concerned that Kissinger was under pressure from the White House to come up with a dramatic foreign policy breakthrough at the Moscow summit involving SALT in order to divert attention away from the president's growing Watergate problems. His concerns were shared by Admiral Elmo Zumwalt (the chair of the Joint Chiefs of Staff) and Secretary of Defense Schlesinger. Nitze resigned largely because of the Kissinger back channel, concerned that it provoked a lack of confidence between the negotiating team and the executive branch of government. "Excessive suspicion of people down the line," Nitze testified before Jackson's subcommittee on June 23, 1974, destroyed the "relationship of trust" that needed to exist for a negotiation to be successful.[30] It should also be noted that Nitze, like Zumwalt and Schlesinger, was no fan of détente and was fundamentally opposed to strategic arms reductions of any sort that put limits on the American military.

A major problem that confronted the SALT delegation was how to convert the SALT interim agreement into a permanent agreement, per the Gerard Smith provision that limited the interim agreement to just five years' duration. Two years closer to this deadline, both sides were deadlocked over some very fundamental issues. Perhaps the biggest issue dealt with the difference in definitions between Soviet requirements for "equal security and no unilateral advantage" and American needs for "essential equivalence" in strategic weapons. The Soviets alleged that certain "asymmetries" existed in technological, geographic, and strategic factors that warranted their side being permitted greater aggregate numbers. Of particular concern to Secretary of Defense Schlesinger (and Jackson as well because his military industrial constituent Boeing would be affected) was the Soviet demand that the B-1 bomber and the *Trident* missile programs be terminated so that these asymmetries would not be further exacerbated.[31]

There were also issues over how to apply both quantitative and qualitative controls for MIRVs on an equitable basis, as well as how to deal with U.S. forward-based systems (i.e., tactical nuclear weapons and aircraft stationed in Europe). As a way of demonstrating the rather esoteric nature of the debate taking place, the Soviets were said to have 6.5 million pounds of missile throw weight, compared to 3.8 million for the United States. However, U.S. bombers had 16.7 million pounds of weapons deliverable weight (adding up missile and bomber capabilities), whereas the Soviets had 5.6 million. These were the sort of asymmetries the Soviets were concerned about. The Standing Consultative Committee (SCC), composed of both U.S. and Soviet negotiators, had finalized agreed procedures for implementation of the SALT interim agreement prior to Nixon's visit to Moscow in late June 1974, and there was concern that Nixon might agree to similar rushed procedures in order to secure a last-minute compromise on SALT that did not meet with the approval of either the JCS or the secretary of defense.[32]

The Soviets were developing two new missiles, the SS-19 (a two-stage, storable liquid–fueled missile designed to be the Soviet Union's first MIRV-capable missile, able to carry six warheads) and the SS-17 (likewise a two-stage, storable liquid–fueled missile designed to carry four MIRVs). The Soviets were also working on a giant follow-up to the SS-9 missile (which had proven inadaptable to MIRV configuration), the SS-18, a mammoth, two-stage, storable liquid–fueled missile capable of carrying up to ten MIRVs (although only planned to carry eight). The SS-18 was to be deployed in completely retrofitted SS-9 silos, superhardened to resist all but a direct hit from a nuclear weapon.

These three missiles were to become the bane of the U.S. strategic nuclear forces. They were the living manifestation of the myopic vision of those in the United States, like Scoop Jackson, who argued strenuously for a continuation of U.S. MIRV testing and fielding back in 1968 and 1970. The American insistence on preserving a short-term MIRV superiority had created the conditions for not only Soviet sufficiency in MIRV capability but even the potential for Soviet supremacy.[33]

Nixon's visit to Moscow, which took place from June 25 to July 3, 1974, did not produce the career-saving diplomatic breakthrough he had wished for. Kissinger and Nixon were hoping that they would be able to obtain Soviet agreement on basic guidelines for the negotiation of MIRV limits, as well as a temporary extension of the five-year deadline imposed on the SALT interim agreement. Nixon was unable to gain any concessions from the Soviets and was likewise unable to present any new initiatives of his own. As a result, neither a permanent SALT agreement nor a temporary extension to the interim agreement could be achieved. The one agreement of substance that was signed concerned the ABM treaty, in which both sides agreed to limit the total number of ABM sites to one per country, meaning the Soviets would keep their Moscow ABM site, and the United States would keep the one under construction at Grand Forks (the Malstrom ABM site was abandoned).[34]

Richard Nixon returned to the United States from Moscow on July 3, 1974. By July 8, 1974, the Supreme Court heard arguments on the *United States of America* v. *Richard M. Nixon* concerning the release of the secret tapes. On July 24, the Supreme Court, in a unanimous judgment (there was one abstention) ruled against President Nixon. Soon thereafter, the House Judiciary Committee voted to pursue three articles of impeachment against Nixon. Faced with the reality of being convicted, on August 8, 1974, Richard Nixon resigned the office of the presidency. (Earlier, on October 10, 1973, Vice President Spiro Agnew, who had been accused of tax evasion and money laundering, had resigned his office. Gerald Ford, a Republican representative from Michigan, was nominated by Congress, under the Twenty-Fifth Amendment, to serve as vice president and was sworn in on December 6, 1973.) On August 9, 1974, Vice President Gerald Ford was sworn in as the president of the United States. On September 8, President Ford pardoned Richard Nixon, declaring that the Watergate scandal "is an American tragedy in which we all have played a part. It could go on and on and on, or someone must write the end to it. I have concluded that only I can do that, and if I can, I must."[35]

President Ford did his best to restore credibility and viability to a presidency shaken to its core by the criminal actions of Richard Nixon. He was, however, fighting an uphill battle. The American economy was being ravaged by a recession largely brought on by the collapse of the dollar and an oil embargo imposed by Arab oil-producing nations against the United States for its support of Israel in the 1973 Yom Kippur War. Détente was not the priority of anyone in Congress, and Gerald Ford was being urged by many to keep as his priorities the pressing problems of the domestic scene and not get diverted by any foreign policy adventure, least of all détente with the Soviet Union.[36]

President Ford first met with Soviet Foreign Minister Gromyko in Washington on September 20, 1974. Gromyko informed the new president that he was optimistic that the Soviets could work with the Ford administration to achieve the kinds of concessions required to build a new arms limitation agreement. Based upon Gromyko's optimism, Ford decided to dispatch Kissinger to Moscow in October 1974 to settle on the terms of a new SALT II accord, the negotiations of which had been reconvened in Geneva on September 18, 1974. However, given the fact that the United States did not have a unified position, the delegation was instructed not to make any new proposals or to receive any new proposals from the Soviets. If there was to be any breakthrough, it would be done via the back channel. Kissinger continued to articulate in favor of unequal aggregates of delivery vehicles, accepting the Soviet position that asymmetries in American technological superiority, especially concerning MIRVs, could only be offset by increased Soviet numbers.[37]

This position was opposed by Secretary of Defense Schlesinger, who argued for equal arms caps. Schlesinger prevailed, and in mid-October 1974 Kissinger met with Ambassador Dobrynin, when he proposed a new American position that entailed equal overall numbers of missile launchers at 2,200 per side, of which 1,320 could have MIRVs (a number picked by the United States based upon Navy concerns that they be given some leeway when it came to developing the *Trident* missile). There would be a further limit of 250 set for heavy missiles (SS-9) and bombers. Furthermore, the SS-9s could not be armed with MIRVs, and each side could not modernize its missile force at a rate greater than 175 per year. To Kissinger's surprise, the Soviets did not reject the American proposal and instead indicated that they would be willing to use it as the basis of a meaningful negotiation. Kissinger called Ford, who instructed the secretary of state to agree to a summit with the Soviets in late November 1974 to solidify a SALT agreement. This summit was to be held in the Soviet far eastern city of Vladivostok.[38]

On November 23, 1974, President Ford traveled to Vladivostok where, over two days, he and Soviet leader Leonid Brezhnev met to discuss a range of issues, the most pressing of which was the SALT II accords. Both leaders were looking for a successful summit, and in the end they were able to craft a SALT II agreement that provided for equal aggregates of 2,400 launchers, of which 1,320 could be armed with MIRVs. Ford and Brezhnev issued a joint communiqué, which framed the agreement in general terms. The technical details were left to be hammered out by the military experts. This was anticipated to take but a few days, but it wasn't until December 10, 1974, that a text could be agreed upon, and by this time a new controversy had emerged over air-launched cruise missiles. The Soviets insisted that any strategic bomber, if equipped with missiles having a range of six hundred kilometers or more, would have to count each missile individually as part of the 2,400 aggregate. The United States instead said that only ballistic missiles should be counted, and since the U.S. missiles were cruise missiles, they should not be counted. In order to gain an agreed-on text, the United States dropped the term *ballistic* from the text, although insisting on their intent when interpreting the passage. The United States had also raised a new issue, that being whether or not the new Soviet TU-22M "Backfire" bomber should be counted as a medium-heavy bomber. Kissinger (in Moscow and Vladivostok) and Ford (in Vladivostok) had left the impression with the Soviets that they agreed with Leonid Brezhnev that the "Backfire" was a medium bomber and not to be counted. However, the Joint Chiefs of Staff and the Secretary of Defense believed that it must be counted as a strategic system.[39]

The failure of President Ford and Leonid Brezhnev to depart Vladivostok with a solid, mutually agreed-upon understanding of what constituted the new SALT II accord proved to be a fatal flaw. Kissinger, upon his return to the United States, warned Congress that a failure to support SALT II could significantly damage U.S.-Soviet relations, as the Soviets would have no choice but to conclude that "a political détente with us faces domestic difficulties of an insuperable nature in the United States."[40] In January and February of 1975, both houses of Congress passed resolutions supporting the Vladivostok accord. However, there was still no formal agreement for the Senate to ratify.

In Geneva, during this same time, the U.S. and Soviet delegations squared off to hammer out their differences, but it soon became clear that not only were the existing gaps proving impossible to close, but new ones kept springing up. The United States delegation, under pressure from the Pentagon and the JCS, stressed the need for verification procedures regarding the MIRV limits, whereas the Soviets believed there was no such need. Not only did the two sides continue to disagree on the definition of *air-launched missile*, as well as how to categorize the "Backfire" bomber, but the Soviets raised a new issue, arguing that sea-launched cruise missiles with a range greater than six hundred kilometers should be counted in the same manner as those launched from the air. Rather than moving forward, the SALT II negotiations were backing up. This failure to close the deal created a window of opportunity for opponents of the SALT II negotiations to intervene.[41]

One of these opponents was Albert Wohlstetter, the esteemed nuclear strategist. Wohlstetter had been alarmed by Nitze's resignation and subsequent disclosures about what he viewed to be serious shortcomings in American arms control policy vis-à-vis the Soviet Union. Like Nitze, Wohlstetter was concerned about the quality of the threat assessment being produced by the CIA on the Soviet Union, an assessment that Wohlstetter and others believed to be much too benign in nature. Wohlstetter articulated his concerns in a writing campaign that saw his views prominently featured in the *Wall Street Journal*, *Foreign Policy* magazine, and *Strategic Review*. Wohlstetter's criticism caught the attention of the President's Foreign Intelligence Advisory Board, or PFIAB, a panel of outside experts created by President Eisenhower for the purpose of providing an independent review of U.S. intelligence estimates. The PFIAB during the Ford administration was chaired by retired Admiral George

Anderson and was staffed by a number of conservative thinkers affiliated with RAND, including John Foster (of the Foster Panel), Edward Teller, and George Shultz. Anderson and his fellow members of PFIAB had for some time rejected what it viewed as the CIA's overly soft approach toward the Soviet Union, rejecting the CIA's assessment that the Soviets were only seeking rough parity with the United States, and instead put forward a counterassessment that found the Soviets on the path toward nuclear superiority.[42]

The specific point of contention was National Intelligence Estimate (NIE) 11–3/8–74, "Soviet Forces for Intercontinental Conflict Through 1985." Of all the NIEs produced by the CIA during the Cold War, NIE 11–3/8, which dealt with Soviet strategic nuclear capability, was by far the most important, and most influential, in the formulation of U.S. national security policy. NIE 11–3/8 was produced on an annual basis (the final numerical sequence was the year the NIE was published). Given its overall importance, it came as no surprise that the findings contained within would become highly politicized.[43]

During the contentious debates over MIRVs and ABMs, the findings of NIE 11–3/8 were attacked over and over again by those who advocated for programs and systems threatened by the analysis contained therein. For example, when NIE 11–3/8–69 published its finding that the Soviet SS-9 missile was not armed with MIRVs, it contradicted the public pronouncements of Secretary of Defense Melvin Laird, who had stated that an MIRV-equipped SS-9 missile threatened survivability of the *Minuteman* force, reinforcing the need for a viable ABM system. Many prominent defense officials, including John Foster, attacked that NIE, going on record with their strong pronouncements of Soviet capability that flew in the face of the U.S. intelligence community. Even when they were proven wrong (and they almost always were; by 1974 it was clear the SS-9 was not MIRV-capable, just as the CIA had said), these critics remained unapologetic, noting they had a responsibility to look for the "worst case" that they believed the CIA too often ignored. (This tendency on the part of the anti-arms controllers to second-guess the CIA by providing manufactured intelligence as a replacement for professional assessments derived from a systematic approach toward intelligence analysis would be repeated again in 2002. Then, some of the same personalities involved in opposing NIE 11–3/8 would be involved in manufacturing their own case for war with Iraq, using flawed data concluding that the Iraqi government continued to possess viable weapons of mass destruction at a time when the United Nations and the CIA was far more guarded on the subject.)[44]

With Anderson's approval, Edward Teller drafted an alternative estimate, dated June 18, 1975, which he presented to the NSC and Henry Kissinger. The NSC rejected Teller's effort, noting that "Teller's technique is to take propositions that can neither be proved nor disproved at this time. Nevertheless, his consistent suggestion that every proposition will unfold in a worse case situation for the U.S. undermines the overall credibility of his 'alternative' National Intelligence estimate." Teller, together with Foster, then held a meeting with the CIA on August 8, 1975, when they expressed their fundamental disagreement with the CIA's "net assessment" of Soviet capabilities. Foster recommended that the PFIAB set up an adversarial assessment team, which would review the CIA's body of work when it came to assessing Soviet strategic power. The CIA was opposed to this concept.[45]

The argument between Wohlstetter and CIA Director William Colby had caught the attention of Anderson, who subsequently supported Teller's alternative estimate. Anderson waited two days and then wrote a letter to President Ford that questioned the validity of the CIA's estimates and recommended that the president appoint a so-called Team B. This team would be composed purely of outside experts who would review the same classified information as the CIA and come up with their own estimates. CIA Director Colby responded to Anderson's letter with a scathing rebuttal that debunked almost every claim Anderson had made. However, President Ford was not in a position to reject out of hand the suggestions put forward by such a high-powered body as PFIAB and directed Kissinger to respond to the PFIAB's concerns.[46]

On September 8, 1975, Kissinger oversaw the preparation of a draft presidential directive instructing the CIA to undertake a new, three-phased process for preparing estimates on Soviet air defense and Soviet missile accuracy, which included the preparation of an estimate void of any net assessment, a separate net assessment document, and then an adversarial estimate prepared by an independent group of experts. On September 11, 1975, Kissinger convened a meeting between the CIA and PFIAB, in which this directive was discussed. In a rather heated session, the CIA let it be known that it was opposed to this new approach. The CIA also noted that PFIAB was sabotaging the CIA's efforts by trying to create a separate team that would promote the conclusions sought by PFIAB. Kissinger nonetheless directed the CIA to respond to the PFIAB concern.[47]

On November 21, 1975, CIA Director Colby delivered a five-page letter to President Ford, noting that NIEs were the most important documents prepared by the intelligence community. Colby was satisfied that the estimate in question, NIE 11–3/8–74, was the product of the best information, and best analysis, America had to offer. The entire intelligence community supported Colby's contention that a Team-B assessment not only was unnecessary but also would be counterproductive and even damaging to U.S. intelligence analytical efforts. There the matter should have rested. Unfortunately for Colby and the CIA, Colby was forced to resign as the CIA director in November 1975. He was singled out in particular due to the ongoing U.S. Senate investigations, known as the Church Commission, into CIA activities and abuses, during which Colby honestly and openly answered the commission's questions, often to the detriment of the CIA and the embarrassment of the U.S. government. Ford picked George H. W. Bush, the former U.S. ambassador to the United Nations, and at the time of his appointment the chief U.S. diplomat in China, to head the CIA. This was more of a political appointment than a practical one. Bush was not an intelligence professional and was not in a position to effectively dismiss the efforts of Anderson, Teller, Foster, and PFIAB to elbow their way into the production of U.S. intelligence analysis.[48]

Bureaucratic obstruction from both the secretary of defense and the Joint Chiefs of Staff ground the SALT II negotiation process to a near halt because absent an agreed-upon negotiating position, there could be nothing to negotiate. Frustrated by the lack of progress in Geneva, Henry Kissinger reactivated back-channel communications with Dobrynin in May 1975, beginning an exchange of positions that led to Kissinger meeting with Soviet foreign minister Gromyko in Geneva on July 10–11, 1975. Kissinger was trying to sell a concept to the Soviets which involved "class counting," which counted as an MIRV-capable missile any system that had been previously flight-tested with an MIRV. However, the two sides struggled with how to define what a heavy missile was, as well as what constituted an allowable silo modification.[49]

The issue of the "Backfire" bomber, and whether it should be classified as a strategic or medium bomber, was likewise a source of ongoing friction. In an effort to bring the matter to a close, President Ford and Henry Kissinger met with Leonid Brezhnev and Andrei Gromyko in Helsinki on July 30 and August 2, 1975. In their first meeting, Ford confronted Brezhnev with U.S. intelligence about the capabilities of the "Backfire," which had led the United States to conclude it was a strategic system. After asking for a break to gather his own information, Brezhnev came back with a briefing of his own, in which he presented detailed technical information about the "Backfire" bomber to Ford that upheld the Soviet contention that the "Backfire" was only a medium bomber. This unprecedented openness between U.S. and Soviet leaders, with each side sharing a level of intelligence and technical military information previously unheard of, created an atmosphere of mutual trust and, with it, hopes of a breakthrough in the stalled SALT II talks. Andrei Gromyko met again with President Ford and Henry Kissinger in Washington on September 18, 1975, and it was agreed that the United States would soon propose a major new policy position for the Soviets to consider.[50]

However, the secretary of defense, together with the Joint Chiefs of Staff, would not permit any radical departure from their previously held stance. When Kissinger met with Gromyko in New York on September 21, 1975, all he did was submit a new proposal, based upon Schlesinger's demands. This proposal created a new category of limits (300) in addition to the 2,400 aggregate already agreed to that covered FB-111 bombers (a U.S. equivalent to the "Backfire") and sea-launched cruise missiles (SLCMs) having a range of 600 to 2,000 kilometers for the United States, and the "Backfire" bomber and SLCMs with the same range for the Soviets. This was very much a one-sided proposition that would have given the United States an ability to deploy up to 270 SLCMs with no cost to any other forces (because the United States only deployed 70 FB-111 aircraft), while either forcing the Soviets to cut back on "Backfire" bombers or not to deploy any SLCMs because the Soviets already had 300 "Backfire" bombers scheduled for deployment. In addition to a verbal presentation of the proposal, Kissinger gave Gromyko a letter from President Ford, urging Brezhnev to accept the new proposal. Brezhnev rejected the American proposal in his own letter to Ford on October 27, 1975.[51]

Gerald Ford was growing extremely frustrated by the inability of his administration to effectively deal with a growing list of problems, including arms control. Acting on the advice of his inner circle of advisors and friends, the so-called Kitchen Cabinet, and with an eye on the 1976 presidential elections, Ford ordered a top-to-bottom purging of his administration on October 25, 1975, in what became known as the Halloween Massacre. Among the major changes were the removal of Henry Kissinger as national security advisor (he did stay on as secretary of state), in which position he was replaced by his deputy, Brent Scowcroft. Ford also fired Secretary of Defense James Schlesinger and appointed in his stead White House Chief of Staff Donald Rumsfeld (who was in turn replaced by Richard Cheney, a former congressman from Wyoming).[52]

Henry Kissinger tried to take advantage of the Halloween Massacre to get movement on SALT II. Kissinger convinced President Ford to allow him to travel to Moscow for another round of talks with the Soviets concerning SALT II. With Schlesinger gone, Kissinger redrafted a U.S. proposal to make it more acceptable to the Soviets. Back in Washington, Secretary of Defense Rumsfeld became aware of Kissinger's plan. Rumsfeld conferred with Scoop Jackson, who then instructed his aide, Richard Perle, to leak classified information to the noted and influential columnists, Rowland Evans and Robert Novak. On December 6, 1975, Evans and Novak wrote that several Ford administration officials were "outraged" at Kissinger's "drafting top secret proposals for major concessions to Moscow" without consultation with Rumsfeld and others.[53] Rumsfeld then waited until Kissinger's arrival in Moscow, at which time, on January 21, 1976, he requested, together with the Joint Chiefs of Staff, that the National Security Council be convened. In a two-hour meeting described by National Security Advisor Scowcroft as "surreal," the Pentagon withdrew its support for the proposals Kissinger was preparing to make in Moscow concerning SALT II. President Ford was furious at the Pentagon's "total inconsistency with previous defense positions." However, Ford would not overrule the Pentagon and JCS in an election year, and Kissinger was left stranded in Moscow with no instructions on how to proceed.[54]

This intervention by Donald Rumsfeld effectively killed SALT II, at least until after the elections in November 1976. But it did far more than that. Ford and Brezhnev had announced in Vladivostok that there would be a follow-up summit meeting between the two leaders in the United States. As the delay in closing the deal on SALT II dragged on, the summit was pushed off, first from the fall of 1974 to the spring of 1975, then to June, and later September 1975, then to 1976. Finally, following Kissinger's embarrassment in Moscow, the summit was canceled altogether. Détente had become a bad word and with it the policies of arms control and constraint that it represented. With presidential elections looming, détente as a policy and concept was dead. Ford refused even to utter the word, whereas his political opponents, Republican and Democratic alike, did so only in a derogatory fashion as part of their attacks on the president and his policies. At a time when the world was joining the United States in celebration of its bicentennial, and American leadership was so vital in creating the conditions for peace, once again domestic American political discord, coupled with ideologically driven malfeasance, had conspired to shut the door on any hope of progress in this direction.[55]

The age of détente was, for all intents and purposes, effectively over.

CHAPTER 11

THE COLD WAR
BEGINS ANEW

By the end of January 1976, public confidence in détente was deteriorating rapidly. Quick to exploit this domestic political environment was a challenger to President Ford for the Republican Party nomination, the two-time governor of California, Ronald Reagan. When Reagan announced his challenge to Ford for the Republican nomination in early 1976, Ford enjoyed a twenty-three-point lead in the polls. Within a month Reagan had taken an eight-point lead, largely on the strength of his attacks against the Ford-Kissinger policy of détente. "The overriding reality of our time," Reagan reminded Americans, "is the expansion of Soviet power in the world."[1]

Ford carried with him the power of incumbency and was able to narrowly win a bitter political battle for the nomination, edging out Reagan at the Republican convention. Ford may have won the nomination, but it was clear that the base of the Republican Party was with Ronald Reagan and his conservative views. Reagan accepted the political reality of the convention's nominating process, noting that his one true regret was that he would not be able to reject, in the near future, any arms control propositions put forward by the Soviets.[2]

The battle for the White House in 1976 severely hobbled the Ford administration's ability to make any meaningful foreign policy initiatives. The SALT II negotiations were left languishing, leading to charges leveled by Leonid Brezhnev that whereas the Soviets were reaffirming their support for détente, the Americans were sacrificing this policy, and the SALT, for domestic political reasons. The Soviets had a valid case. President Ford himself stopped using the term détente when defining U.S.-Soviet relations, instead speaking of "peace through strength" and the need to bolster American military capabilities. Congress followed up on this about-face, passing a resolution on May 5, 1976, that reaffirmed the principles of SALT but rejected détente in favor of a renewed emphasis on American military strength. Ford's actions were a direct result of the pressures he felt from Ronald Reagan and had little to do with the reality of U.S.-Soviet relations. In September and October 1976, Soviet Foreign Minister Andrei Gromyko met with both President Ford and Henry Kissinger in an effort to achieve progress on the SALT negotiations, but domestic political considerations prevented any movement on the part of the Americans.[3]

Although Ford had overcome the challenge to his presidency posed by Ronald Reagan, he was struggling on the national scene to rise up to the Democratic challenger, a relatively unknown governor from Georgia named Jimmy Carter. Carter was successful at creating the image of Ford as a do-nothing president held prisoner by the Machiavellian policies of Henry Kissinger. Ford was never able to recover political traction, and Carter won the 1976 presidential election by a narrow margin. Even though Brezhnev had committed publicly to forward, positive momentum with whoever emerged victorious from the election, nonetheless, at a critical time in U.S.-Soviet relations, the Soviets had to adjust to a new American administration, replete with new policies and new policymakers.

As much as President-elect Carter may have wanted to begin his presidency with a clean slate in terms of policy options, he was soon to discover that the conservative backlash against détente was to outlast the Ford-Kissinger years. On December 26, 1976, the New York Times ran a story titled "New CIA Estimate Finds Soviets Seek Superiority in Arms." This article disclosed in greater detail what earlier press stories, published in October 1976, had already alluded to: the existence of Team B, the alternative CIA that had been proposed by Edward Teller and John Foster back in November 1975 and that had been so decisively rejected by the CIA. But William Colby, the CIA director who had stood up to the Team B concept, was gone, and in his place the new CIA director, George H. W. Bush, proved unable or unwilling to stand up to the intellectual assault coming from the American political Right.[4]

The resurrection of Team B came at the behest of an anti-Soviet group known as the Coalition for a Democratic Majority (CDM), formed in

1972 by Senator Henry "Scoop" Jackson and other like-minded Democrats and Republicans and dedicated to promoting policy that had at its core a belief that the Soviet Union represented a great evil. Thus the coalition believed that the Soviet Union had to be opposed by those who not only recognized the threat but sought its eradication in the name of global democracy. Led by Eugene Rostow, a number of CDM hard-liners decided that the time was right to resurrect the Committee on the Present Danger (CPD), an organization originally formed in 1941 to raise public awareness of the dangers posed by Nazi Germany.[5]

The CPD had a high-placed ally in the form of Secretary of Defense Donald Rumsfeld, who was opposed to the policies of détente being pursued by Henry Kissinger. Rumsfeld, like the CPD, was not satisfied with the CIA estimates of Soviet strategic strength and therefore placed pressure on the new CIA director to initiate a review of the CIA's work. Bush, against the advice of his own agency, sought and received White House approval to create a Team B of outside experts who would review the same intelligence used by the CIA and then prepare its own estimate of Soviet capabilities. The concept was approved on May 26, 1976.[6]

The Team B concept was originally designed to evaluate the Soviet triad of strategic capabilities — missiles, bombers, and submarines. However, the chief of naval operations, Admiral Bobby Inman, refused to release to the CIA any data relating to the operational deployments of U.S. SLBM submarines, which made any assessment of their vulnerability to Soviet antisubmarine warfare capabilities impossible to obtain. As a result, the third assessment topic was changed to Soviet strategic objectives. Richard Pipes, a Harvard professor of Russian and Soviet history, was selected to head this third panel, which included Paul Wolfowitz, Paul Nitze, and William van Cleave, among others.[7]

The Team B report was due to be released in December 1976. Prior to its release, Pipes and his team met with their CIA and Defense Intelligence Agency (DIA) counterparts (the so-called Team A) to discuss and debate their findings. Led by Nitze, the Team B experts grilled their CIA counterparts on every aspect of the earlier national intelligence estimates (NIEs), calling into question the methodology of analysis as well as the facts. Whereas the CIA took into account a broad spectrum of possibilities, Team B would only consider the worst-case scenarios. If facts did not lend themselves to a particular conclusion sought by Team B, then they would proceed as if the lack of evidence in and of itself constituted proof that something did in fact exist. The CIA derided the Team B approach, and it soon became clear to the latter that their product was doomed to be sidelined as inaccurate and irrelevant.[8]

Determined to prevent this from happening, Team B orchestrated a series of leaks to the press that reinforced the more alarmist conclusions they were drawing. Team B held that Soviet defense spending was at least twice the rate reported by the CIA, citing its own methodology, which held that because the Soviet Union was a dictatorship, standard models of economic evaluation could not apply. Assumptions on Soviet missile accuracy, based on speculation as opposed to hard data, led Team B to conclude that the Soviets were planning a first-strike capability. The Soviets were assessed as having expanded capability in mobile ICBMs, air defense, antisubmarine warfare, strategic bombers, and antiballistic missile defense (including an advanced laser research and development capability).[9]

The CIA disagreed with every aspect of the Team B report (in retrospect, Team B was in fact wrong on every account). But effective leaks to the media, coupled by high-level support in Congress and the Pentagon, assured the Team B report a level of influence it did not deserve. CIA Director Bush noted that the Team B report "lends itself to manipulation for purposes other than estimative accuracy," whereas Kissinger accurately stated that its only purpose was to undermine détente and destroy arms control. But Secretary of Defense Rumsfeld took the opposite approach, applauding the Team B report as credible and worthy of concern. Rumsfeld's support all but assured that the alarmist and incredibly inaccurate pronouncements of Team B would influence the incoming Carter administration more so than any competing, sound analysis produced by the CIA.[10]

In the midst of this controversy over Soviet capability, President Jimmy Carter worked to assemble a diverse and capable national security team that would have to confront this issue and others. Harold Brown, a longtime national security specialist who had served during the Eisenhower, Kennedy, and Johnson administrations, was appointed secretary of defense. His last post, under Johnson, was as the secretary of the Air Force, a position he held until Nixon was elected president. From 1969 until 1977, Brown was the president of the California Institute of Technology. Brown became the first scientist ever to hold the position of secretary of defense, a status that some believed made him the most qualified secretary of defense up until that time. Carter selected a fellow Navy veteran, Cyrus Vance, as his secretary of state. Like Brown, Vance possessed vast experience dating back to the Kennedy administration, in which he served as the secretary of the Army under Kennedy and deputy secretary of defense under Johnson. Vance was a supporter of negotiations (he had led the U.S. team at the Paris peace talks in 1968–1969) and of arms control.

Perhaps his most controversial move was to appoint the Polish-born, anti-Soviet academic Zbigniew Brzezinski as his national security advisor. The hawkish Brzezinski had written many articles and books on the Soviet Union and Eastern Europe and in 1975 had been asked by then-governor Jimmy Carter to serve as his foreign policy advisor on his presidential campaign. A proponent of an aggressive human rights policy, Brzezinski was instrumental in shaping President Carter's attitudes and opinions toward the Soviet Union at a critical time in the U.S.-Soviet relationship. Rounding out the ranks of critical appointments were Admiral Stansfield Turner, a Naval Academy classmate of Carter's, as the director of the CIA and Paul Warnke, an advocate of arms control who had served in the Defense Department during the Johnson administration, as the director of the Arms Control and Disarmament Agency and the senior U.S. negotiator for SALT II. Warnke's appointment in particular was interesting, signaling as it did a new emphasis by the White House on the role expected to be played by ACDA in bringing the SALT II accord to fruition.

The Committee on the Present Danger, fresh from its Team B intrusion into strategic policymaking, submitted fifty-three names of experts for President-elect Carter to consider for foreign policy appointments. Carter refused them all. Unable to take full control of the CIA's assessment of the Soviet Union, the CPD sent its Team B members to the media, where they began a strident campaign designed to strike fear in the hearts and minds of Americans about the looming Soviet threat and in doing so influence Congress to increase spending on defense.[11]

One appointment in particular came under withering attack from the CPD, that of Paul Warnke as the director of ACDA. Nitze, the veteran arms control negotiator who was the heart and soul of the CPD anti-Soviet effort, testified at Warnke's Senate confirmation hearings that Warnke's views were "absolutely asinine." Scoop Jackson followed suit, publicly warning Carter that if Warnke were confirmed by anything fewer than sixty votes, it spelled doom for any arms control agreement Carter might attempt to get ratified by the Senate. Due in large part to Jackson's withering assaults, Warnke was confirmed by a vote of 58–40.[12]

Warnke's confirmation difficulties were unwelcome developments for a president who had placed such a strong emphasis on arms control and disarmament. In his inaugural address, Carter noted: "The world is still engaged in a massive armaments race designed to ensure continuing equivalent strength among potential adversaries. We pledge perseverance and wisdom in our efforts to limit the world's armaments to those necessary for each nation's own domestic safety. And we will move this year a step toward our ultimate goal—the elimination of all nuclear weapons from this Earth. We urge all other people to join us, for success can mean life instead of death."[13] Six days after his inaugural address, Carter wrote a letter to Brezhnev, following up on January 30, 1977, with a meeting with Soviet Ambassador Anatoliy Dobrynin. In this meeting Carter emphasized his desire to move forward with U.S.-Soviet relations as well as for an early consummation of a comprehensive test ban treaty and a SALT agreement.[14]

The president had high hopes for a new SALT agreement, but the problems with the confirmation of Warnke as ACDA director, coupled with a track record of negotiation difficulties experienced in the recent round of the SALT negotiations (the Scoop Jackson–appointed replacement for General Royal Allison, Lieutenant General Ed Rowny, had proven to be so intractable and inflexible that the Soviets simply refused to do any business with him, much to Jackson's delight) prompted Carter to seek to circumvent the normal negotiation processes. Instead, Carter sought to jump-start a new SALT II process in March 1977 by sending Secretary of State Cyrus Vance, armed with a new set of U.S. proposals, to Moscow. These proposals not only deviated from the SALT II positions the United States had agreed to during the previous administration but also were presented to the Soviets outside of the normal negotiating channels and in a highly publicized manner. The Soviets had grown accustomed to the diplomatic rhythms of Henry Kissinger and were naturally leery of the sudden shift on the part of the United States in both substance and style when it came to arms control.[15]

A broad consensus existed within the NSC that the best course of action would be to conclude a SALT II agreement based on the Vladivostok accords and then begin work on a more ambitious SALT III agreement. This track was favored by Vance. However, Secretary of Defense Brown and National Security Advisor Brzezinski were opposed to accepting a SALT II agreement they viewed as too favorable to the Soviets. Carter went along with Brown and Brzezinski. The major point of contention centered on so-called MIRV counting, which allowed both sides to spread out their MIRVs among a range of delivery options. The main U.S. concern was that the Soviets would concentrate their MIRVs among its heavy missile population and thus create a decapitating first-strike capability against U.S. *Minuteman* missiles. These concerns were shared by Scoop Jackson, who after the inauguration had lunch with the president, urging him to move away from the SALT II agreement of Nixon-Ford and to adopt a more stringent set of limitations that would meet Jackson's concerns.[16]

Carter was intimidated by Jackson's heavy-handed approach and, not wanting a fight in Congress over ratification of any future SALT agreement, instructed Brzezinski that a completely new approach toward SALT be taken. Such an approach should meet the concerns of Jackson and should break with the agreed framework that had been hammered out by Henry Kissinger. In early March 1976, Brzezinski chaired a special coordination committee, which prepared a new negotiating option known as the "Comprehensive Proposal." The Comprehensive Proposal limited Soviet MIRV-capable ICBMs to 550, a level equal to that on the American side. It also sought to reduce the number of strategic nuclear delivery vehicles to 1,800 to 2,000 on each side and limit the number of MIRVs on each side to 1,100 to 1,200. The proposal also sought to cut the Soviet heavy missile force in half, to 150, and to ban all cruise missiles on air, land, and sea possessing ranges of more than 1,500 miles.[17]

In exchange for the Soviet commitment to cut its heavy missile force, Carter was prepared to halt all new ICBM developments, including *Minuteman* upgrades and the new MX missile. The United States also sought a ban on mobile ICBMs. More specifically, they pushed for the Soviet Union to abandon the deployment and further development of the new SS-16 mobile ICBM, as well as to work with the United States to develop the means of differentiating between the newly developed SS-16 ICBM and SS-20 intermediate range missiles. In exchange, the United States was willing to accept the Soviet position on the "Backfire" bomber, that it was not a strategic bomber with intercontinental range. The United States also pushed for a satisfactory resolution of the issue of MIRV verification.

Secretary Vance was nervous about such a decisive break from the Vladivostok accord and asked President Carter if he would permit Vance to propose a fallback proposal, based on Vladivostok, that would allow the unresolved issues such as the "Backfire" bomber and cruise missiles to be covered by a future SALT III agreement. Carter approved, on the condition that Vance would make sure that the Soviets knew the comprehensive proposal was the preferred U.S. position. Vance then communicated this new position to Dobrynin on the eve of his departure for the Soviet Union. Dobrynin warned Vance that any deviation from the Vladivostok accord would not be received well in Moscow.[18]

Vance arrived in Moscow on March 27, 1977, and almost immediately was put on notice by the Soviet leadership that Dobrynin had not spoken idly. Brezhnev reemphasized the importance of the Vladivostok accord to the Soviets, and Foreign Minister Gromyko, aware of Vance's negotiating position from communications with Dobrynin, let Vance know in advance that if this was indeed the U.S. intention, then the Soviets would reject the proposal. Vance proceeded undeterred, believing that if the Soviets did in fact go through with their threat to reject the Comprehensive Proposal, they would undoubtedly respond with a counterproposal.[19]

The Soviets, however, rejected the Comprehensive Proposal out of hand and snubbed Vance's fallback proposal. The Soviets viewed the Vance proposals as very much a one-sided deal in which the Soviets were being asked to make huge concessions while the United States gave up nothing. Gromyko declared the proposals "outrageous." Vance had no choice but to concede publicly that the negotiations were a failure, and he departed Moscow. Vance's mission was savaged by Gromyko, who belittled the U.S. effort as a "cheap and shady maneuver" seeking American "unilateral advantage." Rather than emerging from Moscow with a SALT II agreement in hand, Vance and the Carter administration were left with a SALT strategy that lay in ruins.[20]

Another major arms control policy initiative President Carter sought to achieve early on was a comprehensive test ban on nuclear weapons. Carter called for a preliminary analysis to be conducted on the problems associated with verifying a complete ban on nuclear testing for both military and peaceful purposes by the United States, the Soviet Union, and other nuclear powers. Carter was interested in what effect a U.S. ban on testing might have on the Soviet Union and directed that several diplomatic options be considered, including a unilateral U.S. testing moratorium, a bilateral U.S.-Soviet moratorium, and approaches to other nuclear powers to join in such a moratorium. It soon became clear, however, that neither the Joint Chiefs of Staff nor the weapons designers from the Atomic Energy Commission would support the cessation of underground nuclear testing, even if the Soviets agreed to follow suit. (The AEC was soon to be reorganized under the auspices of the Department of Energy, created by President Carter on August 4, 1977, in order to consolidate all national energy-related activities so as to best deal with the ongoing energy crisis.) President Carter was hoping to make a comprehensive test ban treaty the centerpiece of his nonproliferation efforts, but the bureaucratic resistance within the U.S. national security system stymied this effort.[21]

While President Carter and his national security team worked to pick up the pieces of their shattered arms control policy, they also struggled to define their national security policy, in particular the nuclear strategy that would serve in juxtaposition to any arms control strategy they might eventually be able to resurrect. The Carter administration had inherited the most up-to-date version of the SIOP, the SIOP-5, a derivative of the process put in place by Kissinger and Schlesinger via NDSM-242 and NUWEP. It was put into effect in early 1976. Although both President Carter and Secretary of Defense Brown were uncomfortable with NDSM-242, in particular the emphasis it placed on destroying so-called economic recovery targets, they had no formal policy guidance available to replace it.

To provide interim guidance, President Carter released Presidential Directive 18 (PD-18), which reaffirmed NDSM-242 and NUWEP as policy as well as retained SIOP-5 as the nuclear strike plan. PD-18 did not represent a drastic change from the policies elaborated in NDSM-242 and NUWEP insofar that it continued to affirm deterrence, damage limitation, and escalation control as the foundation of U.S. nuclear strategy. PD-18 simply superseded NDSM-242 and NUWEP, allowing the Carter administration to claim its own imprint on national security strategy.[22]

PD-18, however, was a temporary measure. Formal policy guidance was needed, and in January 1977, President Carter signed Presidential Review Memorandum 10 (PRM-10), the president's initial guidance for strategic forces. PRM-10 provided the basic guidelines for nuclear weapons employment and the basis for targeting within SIOP-5, as well as providing guidance for future weapons procurement and deployment. It reaffirmed that nuclear strategy policy would continue to be formulated via the PD-18/NDSM-242/NUWEP model. It also established fundamental criteria for U.S. nuclear strategy, focusing on the maintenance of "essential equivalence" between the Soviet Union and the United States, with an understanding that America would never accept a strategically inferior position vis-à-vis any nation or group of nations. PRM-10 established that there would be no U.S. policy of conducting a disarming first strike unless Soviets opted to establish a similar policy first. PRM-10 also directed that the United States would maintain a secure nuclear reserve force and the forces and command, control, and communications capability to ensure the ability to carry out limited nuclear attack options, as well as an adequate attack warning and assessment capability. The fundamental strategic objective behind PRM-10 was to achieve what the Carter national security team termed "flexible nuclear response."[23]

Carter and Brown, in releasing PRM-10, recognized the evolutionary nature of nuclear deterrence. Though Assured Destruction may have been a viable posture once the United States established a secure nuclear retaliation capability in the 1960s, a policy of large-scale retaliation eroded the confidence of U.S. allies—especially in NATO—when it came to deterrence. In the minds of European allies, all the U.S. policy did was limit nuclear war to the European continent. Likewise, within the United States itself, the perceived rise in Soviet nuclear strike capability had resulted in declining confidence in the ability of the *Minuteman* Counterforce to keep the damage in the United States low in the case of nuclear war. This, coupled with a lack of a viable ABM defense, meant that Massive Retaliation as a strategy had run its course.

President Carter was simultaneously confronted with an emerging Soviet nuclear capability that threatened U.S. nuclear deterrence as well as a collapsing arms control mechanism to contain this threat. The Soviets had waited until 1977 to get a SALT agreement they felt had been all but assured. The failure of the Vance mission to Moscow further complicated matters. The health of Leonid Brezhnev was declining, and there were concerns that any future Soviet leadership would not be receptive to arms control. President Carter needed to act quickly to secure a meaningful arms control agreement with the Soviets, but he also needed to move forward to secure credible American nuclear deterrence in the face of both declining prospects for SALT and increased Soviet strategic nuclear capability.

Complicating this situation was the fact that the Soviet Union was, itself, going through a period of political transformation. The position of relative unchallenged authority that Leonid Brezhnev had been enjoying since having pushed Aleksei Kosygin from the inner circle was coming to an end. As Brezhnev grew older and more unpredictable in his health and behavior, he was increasingly challenged by a growing clique of senior officials, including Andrei Gromyko, the foreign minister; Yuri Andropov, KGB chair; Dmitri Ustinov, representing the Communist Party Central Committee; and Marshal Andrei Grechko, the minister of defense.

Lacking the ability to limit Soviet nuclear power through arms control–induced agreements, President Carter had no choice but to reach out to a new generation of American nuclear weapons delivery systems. Carter had to provide the United States not only the assurance of national survival through nuclear deterrence but also the ability to successfully implement the flexibility mandated by the new nuclear targeting guidance. President Carter turned to his secretary of defense, Harold Brown, for input on how best to shape the American nuclear arsenal. A critical aspect of U.S. nuclear deterrence was the survivability of the American nuclear arsenal. The foundation of U.S. nuclear strategy lay in its embrace of the triad of nuclear delivery systems—land-based ICBMs, sea-based SLBMs, and manned bombers. Since the end of the 1960s, the United States had been planning follow-up weapons systems to replace the *Minuteman-Titan* ICBMs, *Poseidon* SLBMs, and B-52 bombers, the three of which constituted the triad as of 1977. The Carter administration, criticized for supporting arms control policies perceived to be solidifying not only a Soviet quantitative advantage but a qualitative one as well, was under considerable political pressure to push funding for a new generation of nuclear delivery systems through a hesitant Congress. This funding would tilt the qualitative factor back in favor of the United States. Key among the weapons being proposed was a new generation of ICBM, the MX missile, designed to deliver ten MIRV warheads with greater accuracy than the current *Minuteman* III arsenal. Carter was also interested in pursuing the *Trident* submarine, capable of carrying twenty-four *Trident* II missiles, each armed with eight MIRVs.[24]

President Carter was under tremendous pressure to approve a new generation of manned U.S. bomber, the B-1. Although he had initially campaigned for the presidency pledging to cut the B-1 bomber, which Carter viewed as too expensive and obsolete, members of Congress in whose districts the B-1 was scheduled to be built lobbied hard to keep the B-1 alive. Nevertheless, at a price tag of more than $100 million per aircraft, President Carter found it hard to justify producing the B-1. He had already been briefed on the existence of new stealth technology that would allow for the production of a more viable manned bomber for penetration missions into the Soviet Union and other highly defended territories. Furthermore, the Air Force was in the process of procuring advanced, air-launched cruise missiles that could be retrofitted onto the existing B-52 fleet at a fraction of the cost of building the B-1. A single B-52 bomber could be equipped with up to twenty of these advanced missiles, making each bomber the equivalent of an SLBM-equipped submarine on patrol. In July 1977, facing considerable criticism from the political right wing, President Carter announced that he was canceling the B-1 bomber program, opting for the cruise missile–armed B-52 bomber instead.[25]

The next system to come under scrutiny by the Carter administration was the *Trident* submarine program. Viewed as a key part of a revamped nuclear delivery capability that gave teeth to the NDSM-242 flexible response concept, the *Trident* program had been slowed by political opposition from a combination of antinuclear domestic advocacy groups, arms control proponents, and an increasingly frugal Congress. The U.S. Navy's fleet of ballistic missile submarines was equipped, as of 1977, with *Poseidon* C-3 missiles, possessing a range of more than 2,500 miles and an accuracy of 25 miles. Capable of carrying up to fourteen MIRV warheads (but deployed with only six, to increase range), the *Poseidon* C-3 was a devastating weapon. The deployment of the *Poseidon* C-3 was a driving factor behind the pressure to revamp the SIOP because suddenly the

Pentagon had more deliverable warheads than actual targets. Yet the *Poseidon* C-3 was a controversial missile because its accuracy limitations fell short of true hard-target capability but exceeded simple assured destruction requirements. Its MIRV capability created a political problem as well, with its large MIRV capacity eating into arms control–driven MIRV caps.[26]

The U.S. Navy had been working on a follow-up to the *Poseidon* SLBM program, known as the *Trident* C-4, or *Trident* I. It possessed similar capabilities as the *Poseidon* C-3 in terms of accuracy and payload but had far greater range, up to 4,000 miles, thus increasing the survivability of the submarine launch platform. The *Trident* I missile was designed to be retrofitted into existing *Poseidon*-capable submarines. There was also a program for a new class of large ballistic missile submarines, the *Ohio* (which was capable of carrying twenty-four versus sixteen missiles), as well as a completely new missile, the *Trident* D-5, or *Trident* II, which had even greater range, accuracy, and genuine hard-target kill capability than *Trident* I.[27]

The Carter administration was disenchanted with the *Trident* submarine program, in large part because of its cost overruns and limited value when compared to the *Trident* I missile–equipped *Poseidon* submarines. Prior to being sworn in as president, Carter had queried the Pentagon as to what constituted "minimum deterrence" and had requested a study on the viability of reducing the number of SLBMs in the U.S. inventory down to between 200 and 250 as a means of promoting strategic arms reductions. In addition to their concerns about excessive costs, both President Carter and Secretary of Defense Brown remained skeptical about the overall viability of the *Trident* submarine as part of the U.S. nuclear deterrence capability.[28]

Another weapons system under scrutiny by the Carter administration was the Air Force's MX missile. Designed as a follow-up to the *Minuteman* III ICBM, the MX missile was supposed to provide increased survivability and hard-target kill capability, both advantageous capabilities in the face of a perceived Soviet first-strike capability and the new Counterforce emphasis created by the policy combination of NDSM-242 and PD-18. The MX missile was a larger missile than the *Minuteman* III and was designed to carry twelve MIRVs if armed with the same 335-kiloton Mk-12a warhead carried by the most up-to-date version of the *Minuteman* III. The original *Minuteman* I missile had been phased out of service by 1974, replaced by the *Minuteman* II, which possessed a giant 1.2-megaton warhead, and the MIRV-capable *Minuteman* III, the final missile of which was deployed by 1976. A total of 450 *Minuteman* II missiles were deployed, along with 550 *Minuteman* III missiles, which together with the 54 *Titan* II missiles still in the U.S. inventory comprised the 1,054 U.S. ICBMs in service.[29]

One of the main reasons the MX was being promoted was the perceived vulnerability of the silo-based *Minuteman* missiles to a Soviet preemptive attack. By 1976, Congress had rejected a plan to base the MX missile in silos because such a move defeated the purpose of the MX to begin with. Two ground-basing schemes were considered. The first was a so-called trench system, which involved a trench five feet below the ground, ten to fifteen miles in length, and covered by five inches of concrete and earth. A transport erector launcher (TEL) would transverse the trench, and if a launch was required, would raise a launch canister that would break through the concrete, allowing the missile to be launched.[30]

The second option under consideration was known as Multiple Protective Shelters (MPS). MPS called for two hundred missiles that were randomly moved between 4,600 "soft" (not hardened against nuclear blasts) shelters spread out among sites located in the deserts of the American Southwest. Both options were expensive, and both had issues in terms of the viability of their survival in case of an attack. As a result, shortly after he assumed office, President Carter put the MX missile program on hold, reducing the funding level for MX deployment by 85 percent. One of his reasons for doing so was that he hoped to get the Soviets to agree to a ban on mobile missiles as part of the SALT II agreement.[31]

The Soviets had been experimenting with mobile ICBM concepts since the early 1960s. A critical aspect to effective mobility was the need for a solid-fuel system, like the *Minuteman*. The first Soviet effort at a solid-fuel ICBM was the experimental RT-1 system. It was flight-tested between 1962 and 1963, with mixed results. A follow-up system, the SS-13, was tested in 1966 and initially deployed in 1968. The SS-13 missile was adapted as a mobile ICBM, known as the SS-14, using the two upper stages of the SS-13 missile. This system was extensively tested but never deployed, in large part because the Soviets had begun work on the SS-16 solid-fuel ICBM.[32]

Development of the SS-16 began in 1969 and was flight-tested in 1972. The SS-16 was developed in tandem with the SS-20 intermediate-range missile, designed as a mobile replacement for the SS-4 and SS-5 liquid-fueled missiles of Cuban missile crisis infamy. The SS-20 used the first two stages of the SS-16 and as such represented a nightmare system for the United States in terms of arms control and for Europe in terms of its overall security. NATO had grown comfortable with its ability to target and interdict the older SS-4 and SS-5 missiles, and the introduction of a mobile missile with quick reaction/launch capability threw NATO targeting into flux. Moreover, the SS-20 was armed with three MIRV warheads, meaning that the Soviet nuclear strike capability against NATO had improved not only in terms of response time but also in overall strike capability, since one missile could now hit three targets.

By 1977, units equipped with the SS-20 missile began deploying to operational sites in the western Soviet Union, where they could target NATO sites. This caught the attention of NATO—West Germany in particular. On October 28, 1977, during a speech delivered in London on the dangers of an escalating arms race, West German Chancellor Helmut Schmidt emphasized the SS-20 deployment and specifically requested President Carter to come up with a response to this development, which had assumed crisis proportions in Europe.[33]

The fielding of the SS-16 and the SS-20 presented two challenges to the Carter administration. The first was military in nature: having to deal with how best to respond to the new operational realities created by the SS-20. The second dealt primarily with the field of arms control and centered on not only banning mobile ICBMs as a practical matter but also the specific verification problems arising with the SS-20 and the SS-16 missile systems, which used identical first and second stages. Given the stalled status of SALT II, the most immediate problem was how best to respond militarily to the SS-20 deployments.

In 1977, the United States maintained three battalions of *Pershing* 1a medium-range (460 miles) missiles, consisting of thirty-six missile launchers each. The German Luftwaffe had had two similarly equipped *Pershing* 1a units. The *Pershing* 1a was a capable system, but its lack of range meant that it was useless as a counter to the SS-20 missile. Another problem was that, as a tactical nuclear weapon, the *Pershing* 1a's four-hundred-kiloton nuclear warhead was larger than all U.S. strategic systems, with the exception of the *Titan* II and the *Minuteman* II. Since 1973, the United States had been developing a follow-up system, the *Pershing* II, possessing a smaller warhead (a variable five- to fifty-kiloton weapon) with improved accuracy (making use of a maneuvering reentry vehicle, or MARV).[34]

Originally, the goal was to place the new MARV on the *Pershing* 1a missile. By 1977, however, the overall military posture of the Soviet Union in Europe had changed dramatically. The Soviet Union/Warsaw Pact maintained not only an overwhelming conventional force advantage but also a major modernization program, which included the fielding of advanced TU-22 "Backfire" bombers and SU-24 "Fencer" attack aircraft in addition to the SS-20 missile. The balance of power in Europe between NATO and the Warsaw Pact had shifted dramatically in favor of the latter. A new weapon would be needed, and the *Pershing* II missile was redesigned with completely new rocket motors that gave it a range of 1,100 miles. This redesign meant that *Pershing* II deployment would be delayed by at least five years.[35]

In addition to the *Pershing* II missile, the United States was looking at a new generation of weapon, the ground-launched cruise missile (GLCM), to counter the growing Soviet theater nuclear capability in Europe. The GLCM was an outgrowth of the air-launched cruise missile (ALCM) program that had been conceived in the 1960s under Secretary of Defense Robert McNamara and pursued in the 1970s by Secretary of Defense James Schlesinger as the ideal weapon for flexibility in nuclear war. ICBMs and SLBMs were armed with large-yield nuclear weapons possessing accuracy limitations that made them effective against large targets but less so against smaller, more discriminatory targets. Even if used in a discriminating Counterforce role, an ICBM strike would result in the deaths of millions of civilians.

A cruise missile, on the other hand, was capable of achieving accuracies of thirty meters or better. The need for flexibility in designing a nuclear response short of total war dictated a weapon possessing the accuracy offered by the cruise missile. The concept of flexibility in a nuclear conflict meant that nuclear war would become a protracted event as opposed to a single spasm of apocalyptic destruction. The goal in such a conflict was to keep any nuclear exchange confined to the lowest level possible and to prevent nuclear conflict from escalating to the next level. The weapons sought for use in this environment were conceived so as to obtain what became known as "escalation dominance," meaning that any potential enemy would be deterred from taking the next step in escalating a given conflict.[36]

The U.S. Air Force and Navy had been working on separate cruise missile programs. In 1974, they had been ordered to cooperate on their respective technologies, with the Air Force providing its propulsion system and the Navy its guidance system. The Navy's version surpassed that of the Air Force in demonstrated capability, prompting a congressional threat to cut funding for the Air Force system. By early 1977, a Joint Service Cruise Missile Project was created, requiring as much commonality between the two programs as possible. The Air Force version became known as the air-launched cruise missile, or ALCM. The Navy's version was not only brought into service as the ship-launched cruise missile, or SLCM (launched from ships and submarines), but also finding a new life as a ground-launched cruise missile (GLCM) operated by the U.S. Air Force.

Suddenly, cruise missiles were the weapon of choice. The cancellation of the B-1 bomber by President Carter created an even greater necessity for the deployment of the air-launched cruise missile as a way of extending the viability of the aging B-52 bomber. And the Soviet deployment of the SS-20 missile made the ground-launched cruise missile that much more vital as a counter in the European theater.[37]

Cruise missiles were formally integrated into the overall U.S. approach toward helping NATO shape a military response to the Soviet threat. Official NATO strategy was expressed in the MC 14–3 plan, adopted in 1967 and embracing the notion of flexible response. NATO strategy was designed to deter and counter a limited nonnuclear attack and to deter any large nuclear attack. This plan presented a large enough conventional military capability that any attacker would have to know that engaging this force meant the prospects of an escalation to general nuclear war were real. The ambiguity of this strategic posture had permitted the United States to push NATO for a stronger conventional military capability while allowing NATO to shield itself with an American nuclear umbrella.

The deterrence chain that held MC 14–3 together called for a large conventional military capability that was designed not to defeat the Soviet Union/Warsaw Pact but rather set the requirement for any Soviet/Warsaw Pact conventional military attack so high as to guarantee an escalation of hostilities into the realm of nuclear conflict. A jump straight from conventional conflict in Europe to general nuclear war between the Soviet Union and the United States was not desirable, especially within Europe, because of the concern that the relative equality of the U.S.-Soviet strategic nuclear capability would prompt the United States to abandon Europe in the face of Soviet aggression as a means of self-preservation. This was the primary reason why NATO opposed the concept of Assured Destruction.

The flexible response strategy instead required an ability to viably escalate any NATO conflict with the Soviet Union/Warsaw Pact into the realm of nuclear exchange short of general nuclear war. As such, there had to be a balance of capabilities between the theater nuclear forces of NATO and those of the Soviet Union/Warsaw Pact. The fielding of the SS-20 mobile missile, together with the deployment of the "Backfire" and "Fencer," tipped the balance of power of theater nuclear forces decisively in favor of the Soviet Union/Warsaw Pact by providing the Soviet Union with so-called escalation dominance. This escalation dominance meant that in any conflict between NATO and the Soviet Union, the advantage in terms of nuclear strike capability would lie with the Soviets at every phase of the conflict (low-level through all-out war), creating pressure to avoid any escalation because there would be no advantage to NATO in doing so.

This reduced the likelihood of NATO use of nuclear weapons, thereby keeping any conflict in Europe confined to conventional forces. The SS-20, with its mobility, multiple warheads, and longer range (meaning it could operate effectively from deeper inside Soviet territory), represented a true revolution in military affairs for the Soviets. The combination of its capabilities and NATO's inability to counter it effectively created a genuine feeling of fear and concern in the West. The deterrence chain, from the perspective of NATO, was broken. With NATO nuclear deterrence thus nullified, the Soviets were able to begin work on a radical new approach to a conventional ground war in Europe designed to have Soviet/Warsaw Pact forces reaching the English Channel without any need to escalate to nuclear weapons. The challenge for President Carter was to construct a combination of military response and arms control measures that restored equilibrium to the deterrence chain.[38]

Following the March debacle in Moscow, President Carter found himself making greater efforts to getting the SALT negotiations back on track. Carter maintained that the United States should try adhering closely to the comprehensive proposal pushed by Cyrus Vance in Moscow, while at the same time making limited concessions based upon Vance's fallback position and known Soviet concerns. The NSC worked throughout April to meld these three positions into a single, coherent position, which was presented to Carter on April 23, 1977, with Brzezinski, Brown, Vance, Vice President Walter Mondale, and ACDA Director Warnke in attendance.

Based upon this briefing, Carter instructed Vance, on April 25, 1977, to reach out to the Soviets with the new compromise position. Vance reopened the back channel with Soviet Ambassador Dobrynin, who received the proposals in a positive light. Carter was under pressure to achieve a breakthrough because the SALT I agreement was due to expire on October 3, 1977. With this deadline in mind, the president dispatched Vance to Geneva for meetings on May 18, 1977, with Soviet Foreign Minister Gromyko.[39]

After ten hours of intense negotiations spread out over three days of meetings, Gromyko and Vance were able to indicate, in a joint statement released on May 21, 1977, that a thaw in relations, strained since March, had been achieved, and that the differences between the two sides on SALT had been "narrowed." Vance and Gromyko were aided by the work of their respective SALT negotiators, ACDA Director Warnke and his Soviet counterpart Vladimir Semyonov, who had hammered out the particulars of the so-called secondary issues that could have interfered with any broader understanding.

President Carter had agreed to a three-tiered approach to framing any SALT agreement. In a major concession to the Soviets, Vance had agreed that for the first tier, the SALT II formula would follow the 1974 Vladivostok agreement, at the same time getting a Soviet agreement that both sides would work to lower the numbers of aggregate launchers for any final treaty. Both sides agreed that any SALT II agreement would be effective through 1985. The second tier involved the Soviets agreeing to a statement of general principles regarding any future SALT III agreement that committed the Soviets to pursuing the deeper cuts desired by President Carter. Two of the most contentious issues facing the United States and Soviet Union—cruise missiles and the "Backfire" bomber—were moved out of any formal agreement and instead were to be dealt with in a separate protocol that ran parallel with a SALT II agreement: the third tier of the negotiation.[40]

While the two sides were still some distance from reaching a final agreement—Gromyko cautioned the press that "major and serious difficulties remain"—the fact was that the United States and the Soviet Union had found a formula for discussions that seemed to work. Key to this was the return to Kissinger-like secrecy on the part of the United States, not only in terms of reopening the back-channel line of communication but also in terms of telling the press as little as possible about the status of negotiations. (In Moscow back in March, Vance had undertaken a very high-profile relationship with the press, providing daily briefings that detailed the minutia of the talks, much to the ire of the Soviets.)[41]

When Vance and Gromyko departed Geneva, they left behind their respective negotiators (Warnke and Semyonov) to continue their work in the shadows, crafting a final agreed draft treaty text. The tenuous nature of the framework supporting the SALT negotiations was underscored by the fact that just as Vance and Gromyko were working hard toward the thaw in U.S.-Soviet relations in Geneva, the U.S. Congress voted for a $35.9 billion defense budget. This budget included funding for new strategic weapons, including cruise missiles and a new, highly accurate guidance system for the *Minuteman* III missile, one that would give it true hard-target kill capability. This congressional action led to heated criticism from the Soviet media, which accused the Pentagon of trying to stir up a new arms race between the two nations.[42]

Vance and Gromyko had left Geneva with an understanding that the two sides would meet a few months later with the goal of trying to conclude a final agreement by early fall 1977. Hardly had Vance returned to Washington, however, than it became obvious that serious divisions existed within the Carter national security team with regard to the details of a SALT agreement. Throughout the summer of 1977, Zbigniew Brzezinski had clashed with Secretary of Defense Brown and Cyrus Vance on the specifics of a formal U.S. SALT negotiating position. In many instances, President Carter himself was called on to mediate. By August 30, Brzezinski forced the issue by establishing a deadline of September 6 for a U.S. negotiating position to be finalized in time for an NSC meeting—with the president in attendance—scheduled for that date. A critical issue centered on whether or not the United States should allow ALCM-equipped heavy bombers to count in the overall 1,320 delivery system total in exchange for a raised MIRV ceiling.[43]

The United States also needed a public assurance from the Soviets that the "Backfire" bomber would not be adapted for intercontinental use. On September 9, 1977, Vance was directed to use the back channel with Dobrynin to communicate U.S. expectations of the Soviets. At the upcoming meeting between Vance and Gromyko scheduled for September 22 in Washington, America expected the Soviets to address the issue of reducing the Vladivostok ceilings, limiting the numbers of heavy ICBMs that would be permitted, and imposing a subceiling on MIRV-equipped ICBMs.[44]

Any expectations for a major breakthrough to emerge from the September 22 meeting between Gromyko and Vance were quickly dashed, as the Soviets refused to budge from their insistence that any SALT II accord adhere as closely to the 1974 Vladivostok agreement as possible. Gromyko continued to hold a hard line during his meeting with President Carter the next day. Then, on September 27, Gromyko requested a meeting with Carter and Vance, this time armed with a Soviet proposal that had been approved by the Politburo, the most senior Soviet decision-making body. The September 22–23 meetings had been an effort to ascertain the seriousness of the United States when it came to defending its position. Seeing no room for flexibility, and conscious of the need to make progress, the Soviets relented on their hard-line stance concerning the Vladivostok numbers, agreeing in principle to lower the aggregates by as much as 10 percent and accepting the U.S. limit of 1,320 MIRVs.[45]

In another concession to the United States, the Soviets agreed that there could be an "allowance" for ALCM-equipped bombers within "the context" of an overall MIRV limit. The issue of ALCM range would be addressed outside the framework of any formal SALT II treaty, with a separate protocol restricting the ALCM range for a period of three years, after which the United States could field a longer-range version. The Soviets continued to resist having any limits placed on the numbers of SS-18 ICBMs, preferring that these be counted against the overall launcher ceiling. The Soviets also agreed in principle to a banning of telemetry encryption—the practice of encoding the electronic data sent by a missile to ground stations during test flights in order to assess a missile's performance in flight—as a means of verification, meaning that all flight tests would be able to be monitored in detail by the electronic surveillance systems of the other side. President Carter hailed the Washington meeting as a "conceptual breakthrough," but the fact remained that the details of any SALT II agreement still needed to be hammered out by the U.S. and Soviet SALT negotiating teams in Geneva. One positive achievement was that both the United States and the Soviet Union agreed to honor the SALT interim agreement until a SALT II accord could be finalized.[46]

The September conceptual breakthrough, though not bringing full closure to the SALT II issue, did manage to get the United States back on track to fulfilling President Carter's goals and objectives in the field of arms control. The president was at the same time dealing with yet another contentious issue: whether to go forward with the development and deployment of the so-called enhanced radiation weapons, better known as the neutron bomb, in Europe. Given the conventional military superiority enjoyed by the Soviet Union/Warsaw Pact forces, and the almost certain collapse of NATO's conventional defenses in the case of any conventional attack, which would result in the employment of tactical nuclear weapons, the desirability of enhanced radiation weapons was high. The employment of such weapons would kill Soviet/Warsaw Pact forces with minimal damage and significantly reduce radiation contamination do to the efficiency of these weapons, which produced little or no nuclear fallout. The NATO military leadership was very much in favor of the weapon. On the other hand, the political leadership of the various NATO members opposed such an action, including the British, basing the decision on whether to go forward with enhanced radiation weapons on the success of future arms control agreements, especially SALT. But the Dutch, in early 1978, voted against the deployment of enhanced radiation weapons, regardless of the success or failure of ongoing arms control talks, putting the United States in the position of developing a weapon whose utility was limited to the European theater of operations but which the Europeans did not want to deploy. In the end, Carter deferred the final decision, instead modernizing the U.S. tactical nuclear arsenal in Europe so that each weapon could be upgraded with enhanced radiation warheads if the decision was made to go forward.[47]

If Carter had been hoping for significant progress in the aftermath of his September 1977 meetings with Andrei Gromyko, he was sadly disappointed. On his return to Washington Carter authorized his national security team to conduct a series of closed-door briefings for selected senators, including Scoop Jackson. Because the details of the negotiations were classified, Jackson was unable to directly and publicly confront the Carter administration armed with facts. Instead, he began selectively leaking information to the press—using his aide Richard Perle as the conduit—for the purpose of shaping public opinion against any SALT II accord. The message Jackson was doing his best to send was that the Carter administration had conceded too much to the Soviets, and as a result American national security had been endangered. Jackson was incensed at the willingness of the U.S. side to barter away the cruise missile without gaining Soviet concessions on the "Backfire" issue or reductions of SS-18 missiles. Jackson also made effective use of Paul Nitze, who publicly proclaimed that the Carter administration had locked the United States into a position of strategic inferiority vis-à-vis the Soviets. It was clear that Carter had his work cut out for him in terms of crafting an agreement that would not only be workable with the Soviet Union but also pass muster in the Senate.[48]

The negotiations in Geneva dragged on inconclusively, emerging from the summer of 1978 with little to show in the way of progress. On September 30, 1978, in an effort to breathe life into the stalled talks, President Carter had lunch with Gromyko and Vance at the White House. Carter agreed that the best policy for the United States and the Soviet Union was to pursue a SALT II treaty first, followed by a comprehensive test ban. Knowing there were numerous unresolved issues, Carter highlighted the matter of encrypted telemetry as the most pressing. He also pointed out that a key aspect of any arms control agreement is its ability to be verified. Neither the Soviets nor the Americans were in favor of intrusive on-site inspections, and in any event, the task of confirming every technical detail of an accord such as SALT was beyond the capability of any human-based verification organization.[49]

Both sides, however, had enough confidence in their understanding of the capabilities of each other's current arsenal of strategic weapons. In order to maintain this level of confidence, and to ensure that future weapons systems were in compliance, it was necessary to monitor the technical data related to a given system's operation while in flight, either as part of a research and development program or as in-service testing. Each time a missile was flown for testing purposes, a whole range of technical data was monitored by onboard sensors, which then transmitted these data to receiving stations on Earth. These data were known as telemetry. In order to protect the specific technical capabilities of the system being tested, both the United States and the Soviet Union encrypted these signals, so even if they were intercepted by another party, they would be useless. The Americans were insisting that the Soviets cease encrypting their telemetry so that the United States would be able to confirm that any missile tested by the Soviets did not exceed performance limitations (for instance, MIRV deployment) imposed by the SALT accord.

Despite Carter's personal intervention, Gromyko was noncommittal on the issue of telemetry. He did, however, indicate that the Soviets would back down on their insistence that cruise missiles possess a range less than 2,500 kilometers, if the United States would agree to limit the number of cruise missiles that could be deployed on a given aircraft to twenty. Buoyed by this development, Carter sent Vance to Moscow again, in October 1978, with high hopes that a decisive breakthrough could be obtained that would finally permit closure on a SALT II treaty. The talks mired down over the issue of MIRV counting, although the Soviets did finally give in on the point that the MX missile could be armed with ten MIRVs—a huge political victory for Carter, who could now inform Congress that the United States, under a SALT agreement, would possess an equivalent ICBM to the SS-18.[50]

President Carter instructed Vance to work with Dobrynin via the back channel to get the SALT talks back on track toward an early resolution of the outstanding issues. The two met repeatedly throughout November and into early December, covering and recovering the same ground as before in an effort to reach some sort of compromise language acceptable to both sides. Thanks to the work of Vance and Gromyko in Washington and the teams of SALT negotiators in Geneva, dates were set, December 21–23, 1978, for Vance and Gromyko to meet in Geneva to settle on a final draft of a SALT II treaty that then could be signed during a summit between President Carter and Leonid Brezhnev to be held in Washington in January 1979.

On December 15, while SALT was wrapping up, President Carter, in a surprising move, announced plans to normalize diplomatic relations with China effective January 1, 1979, and to host the Chinese leader in the United States later that same month. A week later, Vance and Gromyko met in Geneva, in what was supposed to be a final meeting that would conclude the SALT II agreement. President Carter was optimistic that his announcement on China would not damage the prospects of a SALT II agreement, and indeed the initial meetings in Geneva seemed to back up his view. The breaking point in the talks came, however, with the issue of encryption of telemetry. The Soviets were against any banning of encrypted telemetry. As a compromise, Vance had been able to get Gromyko to accept a broad principle that held that encryption would not be permitted in any manner affecting the other side's ability to verify treaty limitations, but it would not be banned outright. This meant that the Soviets would leave unencrypted those signals they believed were related to measuring missile performance characteristics related to an arms control treaty, but continue to encrypt those signals it deemed outside the framework of any such agreement.

This set off a firestorm, especially among those in the arms control community who were inherently distrustful of the Soviets. Both technically and legally, the Soviet position was defensible. However, for those on the U.S. side who were inherently distrustful of the Soviet Union, to allow any encryption of telemetry not only was a major compromise in terms of principle but also opened the door for the potential of Soviet contravention of any arms control agreement it might enter into with the United States. Lieutenant General Edward Rowny, the Pentagon's senior representative on the U.S. SALT delegation, resigned in protest. Back in Washington, Carter was besieged by Stansfield Turner, the CIA director, as well as Brzezinski, Brown, and General Jones, the chair of the Joint Chiefs of Staff, who insisted that there be no encryption permitted whatsoever.[51]

Carter personally directed Vance to inform Gromyko that the Soviet definition of what constituted compliance was too vague. To illustrate his point, Vance brought up a recent Soviet test of a SS-18 missile, conducted back on July 29, 1978, and told the Soviets that the encryption undertaken during that test would be viewed as a violation of the SALT II agreement. To make matters worse, the Soviets conducted a similar test of the same missile type on December 21, 1978, in which the telemetry was encrypted in the same manner as the July test. Gromyko was visibly angered by the U.S. position, especially the references made to specific Soviet missile tests. There would be no final agreement. The Geneva talks ended in the same manner as those that had preceded it—failure.[52]

While the outstanding differences over critical aspects of the agreement, such as telemetry, appeared to represent the primary reason for the failure of the December meeting in Geneva, the fact was Carter's precipitous announcement concerning U.S.-Sino relations may have been the real reason behind the undoing of the negotiation. Brezhnev had no desire to sign a SALT II treaty in the United States only to be overshadowed by Deng Xiaopeng's visit. For this reason, the SALT process was deliberately slowed down by renewed Soviet intransigence on positions on which there previously had been what was believed to be an agreement.[53]

While President Carter believed that the opening of U.S.-Sino relations would damage neither SALT nor U.S.-Soviet relations, Brezhnev cautioned otherwise, stating that "the Soviet Union will most closely follow what the development of American-Chinese relations will be in practice." Moscow likewise sought to shift the blame for the collapse of the talks onto the United States, accusing the American side of continuing to seek "supremacy in strategic armaments, thus obtaining unilateral advantages." The Soviets could look to the fiscal year 1980 military budget for evidence in this regard, with the Carter administration asking Congress for $123 billion, a $10 billion increase since Carter took office.[54]

Events elsewhere in the world further damaged the prospects for a SALT agreement. Throughout 1978, one of America's closest allies in the Middle East, Mohammed Reza Pahlavi, the shah of Iran, had been coping with an increased level of unrest stemming from the brutal and authoritarian nature of his reign. Iran was strategically vital to the interests of the United States, in part because of its status as a major producer of oil, in part because of its long border with the Soviet Union. The United States maintained a series of electronic monitoring stations along the Iranian border with the Soviet Union that provided outstanding coverage of Soviet missile launches from Kapustin Yar and Baikonur. Faced with unrest verging on the brink of civil war, the shah was forced to flee Iran in January 1979. On February 1, 1979, the Shi'a religious leader Ayatollah Khomeini left Paris and returned to Tehran, where he was greeted as a hero. On April 1, 1979, Iran was declared an Islamic republic.

The loss of the Iranian monitoring stations provided new ammunition to the anti-SALT forces in Congress, in particular Jackson, who used his position as the chair of the Arms Control subcommittee as a platform to declare the harm done by the loss of the Iranian facilities to America's ability to monitor and verify a SALT agreement as "irreparable." Carter and Brown both responded by declaring that the United States would regain its complete coverage of the Soviet target within a year's time. Under the direction of the president, measures were taken to field new satellites that would be able to monitor Soviet missile launches.[55]

January 1979 brought other problems for President Carter. That month he met with French President Giscard D'Estaing, British Prime Minister James Callaghan, and German Chancellor Schmidt, all three of whom were extremely concerned about deterioration of U.S.-Soviet détente. The ongoing deployment of Soviet SS-20 missiles was a major issue for the Europeans. Carter expressed his frustration that his NATO allies didn't want any of the weapons systems the United States was proposing as a counter to the Soviet deployments, namely enhanced radiation weapons, the *Pershing* II, or GLCM. D'Estaing supported the development of these new weapons—but only as a bargaining chip to be able to negotiate away the SS-20. Callaghan wanted the United States to press forward with SALT II, so that the issue of intermediate nuclear forces could be handled as part of a SALT III treaty. Schmidt didn't want any new nuclear weapons on German soil unless other NATO nations were willing to take some as well. Carter reminded Schmidt that it was his speech in December 1977, in which Germany asked for U.S. intervention in the face of the Soviet deployment of SS-20 missiles, that started the whole affair. The NATO leaders had touched on what Carter knew was true: There had to be a breakthrough on SALT II soon, or the entire fragile framework of arms control between the United States and NATO, on one hand, and the Soviet Union and the Warsaw Pact, on the other, would fall apart.[56]

President Carter summoned Soviet Ambassador Dobrynin to the White House on February 27, 1979, informing him that both the United States and the Soviet Union needed to immediately initiate corrective action to repair their relations, or they were in danger of threatening not only SALT but détente as a whole. Carter's message got through to the Kremlin. Within a few days, on March 2, Brezhnev publicly announced his support of the SALT II process. This announcement met with a burst of progress in Geneva, where Soviet negotiators suddenly agreed to the U.S. conditions concerning the encryption of telemetry, as well as the U.S. definition of what constituted a "new" missile, namely the 5 percent size difference.[57]

One by one, the obstacles that previously dogged the negotiations fell to the side, as pressure from Brezhnev swept aside any remaining Soviet reticence concerning the SALT negotiation process. The Soviets agreed to provide a statement that committed them to capping production of the "Backfire" bomber at the current rate of thirty per year. The Soviets accepted a compromise of cruise missiles that limited the total number that could be carried to twenty on heavy bombers and twenty-eight on other types of aircraft. On May 7, the United States made the final concession, agreeing that no more than three MIRVs would be mounted on the *Minuteman* III missile. On May 11, the United States and the Soviet Union formally announced that President Carter would meet with Brezhnev in a summit to be held in Vienna, Austria (the same location as the historic summit between President Kennedy and Soviet Premier Khrushchev back in 1961), on June 15–18, 1979, for the purpose of signing the SALT II treaty.[58]

The lengthy negotiating process had created a tricky political environment that President Carter had to navigate with care. In a risky move that could have undermined his chances for a successful summit, Carter announced on June 8 that he was pushing forward with the deployment of two hundred MX missiles. This move was designed to simultaneously appease those in Congress who were concerned that the SALT II agreement would put the United States in a disadvantageous position vis-à-vis the Soviets and create leverage in any future negotiations with the Soviets on force reductions.[59]

Carter and Brezhnev arrived in Vienna on June 15, ahead of the treaty they were supposed to be signing. In a marathon negotiating session, the U.S. and Soviet delegations in Geneva hammered out the final details of what was the most technically arcane agreement in arms control history. The final detail to be smoothed over was the fate of the eighteen Fractional-Orbit Bombardment (FOB) systems the Soviets had developed back in the 1960s. Outdated, inaccurate, and ineffective, these missiles were confined to a single missile field outside Tyuratom, Kazakhstan. The United States wanted these missiles counted as part of the heavy-missile ceiling, while the Soviets claimed that they were used for testing purposes only. In the end, the Soviets agreed to dismantle twelve of the missiles and clearly mark the remaining six silos as being used for tests only.[60]

In his first meeting with President Carter, held on June 16, Brezhnev set the stage for a successful summit by calling the SALT II treaty "mutually acceptable, adequately balanced, and acceptable." As part of the elaborate diplomatic process that involved both sides providing "statements" that would serve as understandings outside the body of the treaty text, President Carter read statements on cruise missile limits and the *Minuteman* missile MIRV limit. Brezhnev was supposed to do the same about "Backfire" production being kept to thirty per year, but he only said he would not dispute any U.S. claim that the production rate was thirty a year.[61]

Brezhnev stated that SALT II would not go into effect until ratified, which deviated from past practice, which had both parties adhere upon signing. He also said that any future arms control agreement would have to take into account British and French weapons, and those of the Chinese as well. Likewise, in a clear message to the United States that the SALT II negotiations were over, Brezhnev stated that the Soviet Union would not accept any unilateral amendments from the U.S. Senate. Remarking on Carter's announcement on June 8 about the MX missile, Brezhnev expressed concern over the basing option for the MX, saying more than one silo per missile was a violation of the SALT II treaty.[62]

President Carter, somewhat taken aback, responded that this issue had already been discussed between the United States and Soviet sides. The two leaders concluded the first day's session by exchanging statements that no encrypting of telemetry of weapons systems covered by SALT II would be allowed and that there would be no interference with national means of verification operating in support of the treaty. Despite the bumpy nature of the discussions, Brezhnev remained positive, telling President Carter that both sides had no choice but to go forward.[63]

The next day, and again on the morning of June 18, the two leaders discussed issues pertaining to future arms control agreements, and the Soviets pressed the United States for a formal statement pledging no first use of nuclear weapons. However, the situation in Europe, in which NATO faced off against a superior Soviet/Warsaw Pact conventional force, meant that the first use of nuclear weapons on the part of the United States and NATO represented the only true deterrent to a Soviet attack. What Carter was able to agree to in the end was a statement in which the United States pledged to no first use of military force. And to clear up the issue of Soviet "Backfire" production, Carter was able to get Brezhnev to formally state that "the Soviet Union will not produce more than 30 Backfire bombers per year," which was accepted by the United States in lieu of a written statement. Before the two leaders wrapped up their meeting, Carter again pressed Brezhnev on the importance of an early SALT III accord that sought deep reductions in the strategic arsenals of both nations.[64]

The meetings between Brezhnev and Carter were anticlimactic. With no firm agenda at play save signing the SALT II treaty, all that was left to do was complete the act. The SALT II treaty itself was signed in a short ceremony held in the magnificent gold and white ballroom of the Redoutensaal, part of the Vienna Hofburg Palace Complex. The two leaders exchanged a few words beforehand, and then the treaty documents were signed. Within ten minutes the deed was done, and President Carter said his farewells to Leonid Brezhnev. The two would never again meet.

For Brezhnev, the fight was over: The Soviet position as expressed in the treaty text represented a formal government decision. For Carter, however, the battle was just beginning, with a long and difficult fight expected with Congress and others over treaty ratification. President Carter flew home on the afternoon of June 18, 1979, and later that night he addressed a joint session of Congress on the SALT II treaty, repeating the practice of Richard Nixon after he had signed the SALT I agreement in 1972. In his speech, Carter tried to shape the coming debate on SALT II by making clear what was at stake. "The truth of the nuclear age is that the United States and the Soviet Union must live in peace, or we may not live at all,"

Carter warned. "Between nations armed with thousands of thermonuclear weapons—each one capable of causing unimaginable destruction—there can be no more cycles of both war and peace. There can only be peace."[65]

Carter's political foes, in particular the Committee for the Present Danger (CPD), wasted no time in responding. The CPD sent delegations around America armed with maps showing American cities that would be destroyed by warheads carried on the SS-18 missiles the CPD accused Carter of allowing the Soviets to retain in an unconstrained fashion. Paul Nitze was a principal player in this effort, both in terms of his participating in the delegations as well as through his testimony savaging the SALT treaty. The irony was that the Carter administration had expended a tremendous amount of energy and time consulting with Nitze about the state of the negotiations, and the vast majority of the issues Nitze had expressed concern over had in fact been addressed in a manner that resolved the basis for his concern. Nevertheless, as a central part of the CPD team, Nitze had to stay on message in order to help promote the principal underlying political objective of the CPD, which was to get President Carter out of office in 1981 and replace him with someone more in line with the CPD's ideology.[66]

The principal candidate for that task was former California governor Ronald Reagan, who had challenged Gerald Ford in 1976 and was poised to make another run at the White House in 1980. Reagan had been openly proselytizing for the CPD and its anti-SALT campaign, and in March 1979 he began receiving polling data from the CPD designed to counter mainstream polls, which had more than 60 percent of the American public supporting a SALT agreement. In his radio broadcast of March 27, 1979, Reagan used CPD data to ask questions in a manner that exposed not the flaws of the SALT agreement but rather the ignorance of the American people about SALT. He pointed out that one could really only make an argument that slightly more than 20 percent of Americans truly supported the SALT process and that the majority of Americans had no idea about the specifics of what SALT represented. Reagan continued his radio attacks on SALT II, weighing in negatively during the midst of the Senate debate on ratification. Reagan was more than simply a mouthpiece for the CPD—in 1979, he joined the ranks of the CPD as a member of its executive committee.[67]

The Senate Foreign Relations Committee held hearings throughout the summer of 1979 on the issue of SALT. The committee chair, Frank Church, did his best to keep the discussion balanced, but in the end the opponents of the treaty were many and could not be ignored. The underlying thesis of the conservative opposition to the SALT II treaty was that the Soviet Union was a threat that could not be contained by either détente or arms control. They maintained that the SALT II treaty was an unequal treaty that conceded an unacceptable strategic advantage to the Soviets at the very time the Soviet Union was engaged in expansionistic intervention around the world—in Africa, Asia, and even America's own backyard, the Caribbean. They also attacked the verifiability of the treaty, focusing on General Rowny's contention that the treaty language opened the door for Soviet selective encryption of telemetry, which would enable them to mask treaty violations. Finally, they asserted that the SALT II treaty weakened NATO by limiting weapons systems needed to counter the growing Soviet threat presented by both the SS-20 missile and the "Backfire" bomber, without limiting these Soviet systems at all.[68]

The Senate Foreign Relations Committee wrapped up its hearing in August 1979. The Senate Armed Services Committee conducted its own, separate hearings, as did the Intelligence Committee. The Foreign Relations Committee convened on October 15 to formally consider the SALT II treaty. The debate was hot and contentious, and lasted through November 8. However, on that date, the Foreign Relations Committee voted 9 to 6 to send the articles of ratification to the Senate floor. It looked as if President Carter might get his treaty after all.

But outside events conspired against the U.S.-Soviet arms accord. On October 1, reflecting both the sensitivity of U.S. national security relating to the Middle East and southwest Asia and the need to be seen as tough in the face of perceived Soviet expansion, President Carter announced before a television audience the creation of the so-called Rapid Deployment Force, or RDF, a mobile combat capability designed to respond rapidly to crisis around the world but focused on the Middle East. The goal of the RDF was to use U.S.-only forces in a manner that precluded any drawdown on forces committed to the defense of NATO.[69]

Soon after his announcement of the creation of the RDF, Carter found himself facing a full-scale crisis in the Persian Gulf. In October 1979 the United States admitted the exiled shah of Iran into the country for cancer treatment. Immediately, elements in Iran, including its leadership, began calling for the extradition of the shah to face trial and judgment. The United States refused, and the shah soon left for Egypt, where he and his family were offered exile by Anwar Sadat. On November 4, hundreds of Iranian militants, primarily university students angry at the United States for letting the shah go, stormed the U.S. embassy in Teheran, seizing fifty-two American diplomats. Images of blindfolded diplomats and U.S. Marines (who guarded the embassy) were soon broadcast around the world.

December proved to be an even more contentious month for the em-battled Carter administration. In mid-December, NATO voted to accept 464 GLCMs and 108 *Pershing* IIs, with deployment scheduled to begin in 1983. In addition to deploying these new weapons, and as a measure to offset the public outcry expected in Europe over this escalation of arma-ments, NATO linked its approval to deploy these weapons with a U.S. agreement to approach the Soviets for the purpose of entering negotiations designed to reduce the numbers of intermediate-range nuclear forces (INF) on both sides. This policy, referred to as the "dual track" (for both the deployment of weapons and negotiations to reduce weapons), repre-sented an amalgamation of the French, British, and German positions briefed to President Carter during his January 1979 meetings with the leaders of the three nations. NATO was looking to the U.S.-Soviet INF talks to generate equal ceilings for both sides. Carter also moved at this time to convince moderate senators, like Sam Nunn of Georgia, that he was not soft on defense, putting forward a defense budget for fiscal year 1981 that was 5.6 percent larger than the previous year's.[70]

The dual-track NATO decision was viewed by the Carter administra-tion as a positive action regarding the SALT II ratification process, and it, together with Carter's commitment to increase defense spending, was seen to offset some of the more negative attention the SALT II treaty was getting, including the unanimous vote (10–0, with 7 abstentions) against SALT II on December 20 by the Senate Armed Services Commit-tee, whose chair, Senator Barry Goldwater, proclaimed that the treaty, as it stood, "was not in the national security interest of the United States of America." Nevertheless, the SALT II treaty was scheduled to go before the Senate for a vote on ratification sometime in January 1980, and Pres-ident Carter was optimistic that it would (barely) pass the ratification process.[71]

Then disaster struck. On December 24, 1979, the Soviet Union invaded Afghanistan, crossing in from Afghanistan in order to—formally—assist the Afghan military in confronting Islamic fundamentalists opposed to Afghanistan's socialist government, but in reality to oppose the regime of Hafizullah Amin, who had ousted a pro-Soviet Afghan faction in a coup in September 1979. On December 25, Soviet paratroopers began landing in Kabul. On December 27, Soviet special operations forces launched an assault on the Afghan presidential palace, killing Amin, who was replaced as prime minister by Babrak Kamal. Kamal immediately asked for Soviet military assistance, and by the end of December Soviet troops were pour-ing into Afghanistan.

More than anyone, President Carter was aware of the realities associated with the Soviet action in Afghanistan, and he knew that what the Soviets were doing was not part of a major grab for regional and global power, but rather a limited reaction to a pressing regional crisis that was threatening to spill over into the Soviet Union itself. Unfortunately, the realities of American politics trumped fact and reason, and Carter was forced to take a hard line in response to the Soviet actions. On January 1, 1980, Carter announced he was considering boycotting the 1980 Summer Olympics, scheduled to be held in Moscow. The next day he withdrew the U.S. ambassador to the Soviet Union in protest of the Soviet action in Afghanistan and convened a meeting of the National Security Council to discuss additional measures that could be taken against the Soviet Union.

One clear casualty was the SALT II treaty. Carter was approached by Senator Robert Byrd, the Senate majority leader, who informed him that the SALT II treaty had no chance of passing the Senate given the Soviet invasion of Afghanistan. Byrd advised that to avoid defeat on the Senate floor, and the embarrassment of withdrawing the treaty, the best course of action would be to keep the treaty in the Foreign Affairs Committee, postpone the Senate action, and then subsequently work with the Soviets to keep the provisions of the treaty adhered to until ratification could be reconsidered. On January 3, President Carter wrote a letter to Senator Byrd, informing him that "in light of the Soviet invasion of Afghanistan, I request that you delay consideration of the SALT II Treaty on the Senate floor. The purpose of this request is not to withdraw the Treaty from consideration, but to defer the debate so that the Congress and I as President can assess Soviet actions and intentions, and devote our primary attention to the legislative and other measures required to respond to this crisis. As you know, I continue to share your view that the SALT II Treaty is in the national security interest."[72]

The next day, President Carter addressed the American people about the Soviet invasion of Afghanistan, informing them of his decision to "defer further consideration of the SALT II treaty so that Congress and I can assess Soviet actions." He stated that, given the Soviet action in Afghanistan, the United States could no longer conduct "business as usual with the Soviet Union," and that the United States would severely restrict trade with the Soviets. Diplomatic interaction would be curtailed. In short, U.S.-Soviet détente was dead, and along with it the prospect for meaningful arms control in the foreseeable future.[73]

CHAPTER 12

THREE MINUTES UNTIL MIDNIGHT

In 1945 a Russian-born biophysicist named Eugene Rabinowitch, together with fellow Manhattan Project alumnus Hyman Goldsmith, created a newsletter called the *Bulletin of the Atomic Scientists*. Its purpose, according to the founders, "was to awaken the public to full understanding of the horrendous reality of nuclear weapons and of their far-reaching implications for the future of mankind; to warn of the inevitability of other nations acquiring nuclear weapons within a few years, and of the futility of relying on America's possession of the 'secret' of the bomb." In 1947 the *Bulletin*, recognizing that their efforts to halt the atomic arms race were failing, developed a symbol of the legacy of nuclear weapons known as the "Doomsday Clock." Originally set at seven minutes to midnight, the Doomsday Clock has tracked the progress of humankind's efforts to contain nuclear weapons' menace since 1947, with its time being changed when circumstances warranted.[1]

In 1953, as a result of the Soviet Union's continued testing of nuclear weapons, the Doomsday Clock was set at two minutes to midnight, the closest to the end it ever reached in its history to date. After a period of fluctuation, in 1972 the clock was set at twelve minutes to midnight as a result of détente and the signing of the SALT accords. This setting matched the best result up until that time, achieved when President Kennedy and

Soviet Premier Khrushchev signed the limited test ban treaty in 1963. The testing of a nuclear device by India in 1974, followed by the demise of the SALT II treaty in 1980, combined to put the clock back to its original setting, seven minutes to midnight. This was the clock's reading when President James Earl Carter entered the fourth year of his presidency.[2]

On January 23, 1980, President Carter delivered his State of the Union address to the American people with an eye on defining his response to the ongoing situations in Iran and Afghanistan. Carter addressed the hostage crisis in Iran and the Soviet invasion of Afghanistan as the two major problems facing the United States, before outlining the history of U.S. efforts to contain Soviet power since the end of the Second World War. The president noted that the United States had, throughout this period,

> maintained two commitments: to be ready to meet any challenge by Soviet military power, and to develop ways to resolve disputes and to keep the peace.
>
> Preventing nuclear war is the foremost responsibility of the two superpowers. That's why we've negotiated the strategic arms limitation treaties—SALT I and SALT II. Especially now, in a time of great tension, observing the mutual constraints imposed by the terms of these treaties will be in the best interest of both countries and will help to preserve world peace. I will consult very closely with the Congress on this matter as we strive to control nuclear weapons. That effort to control nuclear weapons will not be abandoned.[3]

It was an election year, and the issues of arms control took second seat to matters that resonated in a more serious fashion on the domestic front. When the Iranian militants had originally taken over the U.S. embassy in Teheran, President Carter had seen his popularity rise among an American public who tended to rally around the flag, so to speak, in times of military crisis. However, as time moved on and Carter had shown no inclination to break the impasse that had become the Iran hostage crisis, his popularity began to plummet. Such negative poll results carried considerable political weight, especially in an election year.

Under pressure to be seen as doing something, Carter authorized the U.S. military to implement a bold rescue mission to free the hostages. On April 24, 1980, the mission was aborted after a fiery crash involving rescue aircraft, and the next day President Carter made a televised address to the American people in which he informed them about the rescue attempt and its failure. The "Desert One" fiasco, as the rescue became known, further damaged Carter's political fortunes. Carter's image wasn't helped when his secretary of state, Cyrus Vance, resigned in protest of Carter's decision to go forward with the rescue attempt.

While Carter wrestled with the issues of Iran and Afghanistan, he also focused on the difficult problem of strategic nuclear deterrence and deciding what form American nuclear war plans would take. The decisions he ultimately made ended up being some of the least understood, and yet most controversial, of his administration, culminating in his signing Presidential Directive 59 (PD-59), "United States Nuclear Weapons Targeting Policy." PD-59 grew out of the Nuclear Targeting Policy Review (NTPR), ordered as a result of PRM-10, the president's initial guidance for strategic forces. The person responsible for putting the NTPR together was Leon Sloss, a veteran State Department bureaucrat who had previously served as the deputy director of the Bureau of Political-Military Affairs (from 1973 to 1975) and as the assistant director of ACDA from 1976 to 1978. It was in this latter capacity that he was assigned the task of preparing the NTPR.[4]

The NTPR, also known as the "Sloss Panel Report," was conducted in two parts, the first dealing with nuclear targeting and the second with a strategic reserve force. The first part of the study was completed in December 1978. Sloss and his fellow planners stopped evaluating the Soviets from the mind-set of America when it came to establishing deterrence criteria. Rather, they focused on what the Soviets would be concerned about most in terms of American nuclear targeting, and planned accordingly. In doing so, Sloss took into account political targets that, if struck, could lead to the unraveling of Soviet power in non-Russian republics, and thus the dismantling of the Soviet Union itself. Such sites, known as "counter-control" targets, were also referred to as "ethnic targets," given their focus on non-Russian nationalities.[5]

At the heart of the targeting philosophy contained in the NTPR was the concept that the best way to deter the Soviet Union from engaging in a nuclear war was not only to demonstrate an American will to retaliate if attacked but also to put the Soviets on notice that any American nuclear response would be designed not simply to punish the Soviet Union but rather to defeat the Soviet Union by ensuring that the chaos and disruption that would ensue from a nuclear strike would destroy the Soviet system of government and compel the Soviet Union to surrender. Originally the targeting of the Soviet political machinery was labeled as Counterforce targeting. However, in order to differentiate between the targeting of

Soviet missiles and the Soviet political apparatus, a new term was coined: *Countervailing*.

The key to a Countervailing strategy was the notion that if the Soviets chose to start a nuclear war, not only would they lose, but the United States would win. This represented a key departure from the Assured Destruction philosophy that had governed U.S. nuclear deterrence up until that time. According to the drafters of the NTPR, the Soviets believed that nuclear war could be waged in a protracted fashion and that military targets, not civilian or industrial, would be the first targets of any such war. The Soviets also sought to wage nuclear war in a manner that guranteed the survival of the Soviet regime and produced a Soviet victory. In order to be effective, U.S. deterrence capability had to be able not only to counter the Soviet model of nuclear warfare but also to prevail, for only by knowing that they would fail in the event of a nuclear war would the Soviets be truly detered from engaging in a nuclear conflict. The "Sloss Panel Report" and its Countervailing strategy were initially supported only by Zbigniew Brzezinski, but eventually Harold Brown and the Joint Chiefs of Staff were brought on board (the State Department was kept out of the deliberations over the Sloss report). Brzezinski had a Presidential Directive drafted, and on July 25, 1980, President Carter signed PD-59, America's new nuclear war strategy.[6]

Carter's embrace of the MX missile, and a new advanced-technology strategic bomber that made the canceled B-1 bomber moot, as well as his support for the *Trident* II missile and submarine program, when combined with his approval of PD-59, pointed to a hard-line position on defense that had not been seen since the 1960s. But the public thought otherwise. Some 60 percent of Americans believed that the United States needed to be spending even more on defense, despite the fact that Carter had increased defense spending by a substantial amount. The combined effects of a terrible economy and ongoing hostage crisis with Iran proved to be Carter's undoing. On November 4, 1980, Ronald Reagan defeated Jimmy Carter in a landslide, winning 489 electoral votes to Carter's 49 and beating Carter by almost 10 percentage points of the popular vote.

One issue that the new president would not have to address was that of the Americans held hostage in Iran. The combined impact of the death of the shah of Iran from cancer while in exile, on July 27, 1980, and the Iraqi invasion of Iran in September 1980, helped push Iran toward being receptive to ending the crisis. President Carter desperately wanted to have the hostages released while he was still in office. Finally, through the use of an Algerian diplomat as an intermediary, the United States and Iran were able to enter into what was known as the Algerian Accords, which called for the release of the U.S. hostages in exchange for the United States to unfreeze some $8 billion in Iranian assets. In a parting insult to President Carter, the Iranians delayed the release of the hostages until right after Ronald Reagan was sworn in as president. Former President Carter was able to meet the hostages when they landed in Rhein-Main Air Base in West Germany.

In his inaugural address, President Reagan did not mention the Soviet Union once. He spoke about the strength of American democracy and the importance of his vision of governance, one in which the government served the people and not the other way around. He spoke about the symbols of American democracy and the price paid by those who died defending it. It was an uplifting, optimistic speech, full of dignity and hope but with little substance. One of the criticisms leveled against Ronald Reagan during the 1980 presidential election was that he was very much a lightweight when it came to the details of governance. His first inaugural address set forth a broad vision, but it would be up to him and his team of advisors to turn that vision into reality.[7]

Reagan had selected as his vice president George H. W. Bush, a man seasoned in foreign policy, national security, and the inner workings of Washington in every way that Reagan was not. Bush and Reagan had been bitter political rivals, and it was almost a foregone conclusion that Vice President Bush would not be a major player in the formulation and implementation of policy in the Reagan White House. While a weak vice president was nothing new in Washington, the concept of a weak national security advisor was, especially given the past practices of the three previous administrations. Reagan picked Richard Allen, a longtime Washington insider and former Nixon administration official (Allen had served on the National Security Council), to serve in the diminished role of national security "counselor," a position that lacked direct access to the president and required Allen to report to Ed Meese, the White House general counsel.[8]

Allen, like Reagan, was a member of the Committee for the Present Danger (CPD). Such membership appeared to play a major role in determining the makeup of the Reagan administration national security team. All in all thirty-two members of the CPD were given appointments in the Reagan administration. One of the cofounders of the CPD, Eugene Rostow, was appointed to head ACDA. Paul Nitze, the entrenched foe of arms control, became the chief negotiator for theater nuclear forces (INF) in Europe. William Casey took over the CIA. Jeane Kirkpatrick, a lifelong, albeit hawkish, Democrat, was picked as the U.S. ambassador to the United Nations. Richard Pipes moved to the NSC, where he served as the leading Soviet specialist, and Richard Perle became the assistant secretary of defense for international security policy. The elevation of so many CPD members to positions of responsibility resulted in an immediate change in the tone emerging from within the Reagan administration concerning the Soviet Union. Reagan may not have mentioned the Soviet Union in his inaugural address, but within days Washington was awash in CPD-driven rhetoric, which repudiated détente, denigrated arms control, and called for a massive increase in defense spending.[9]

The man who would oversee the defense budget, as well as the entire American defense bureacracy, as secretary of defense under Reagan was Caspar "Cap" Weinberger. Weinberger served the Nixon administration as director of the Office of Management and Budget, and as secretary of health, education, and welfare. His tenure as OMB director earned him the nickname of "Cap the Knife" for his efforts to cut government spending. What Weinberger lacked in defense experience was, in Reagan's mind, more than adequately compensated for by both his management skills and his dedicated anticommunist stance. Picking up on the mantra of the CPD, shortly after assuming his post as secretary of defense, Weinberger quickly began advocating for a dramatic increase in defense spending. By March 1981, President Reagan—with Weinberger's input and approval—submitted a $228 billion defense budget for fiscal year 1983, a $33.8 billion increase. Reagan also proposed a 7 percent increase in defense spending per year through 1985, totaling almost a trillion dollars. Weinberger's nickname was changed in some circles to "Cap the Shovel" in reference to these, and later other, increases in military spending. Reagan's pick for secretary of state, Alexander Haig, possessed impressive credentials, including working in the White House under presidents Nixon and Ford. Ronald Reagan selected Haig to lead the State Department in January 1981 and gave Haig every assurance that he would play a pivotal role in formulating and implementing foreign policy.[10]

On January 29, 1981, President Reagan gave his first press conference, in which the issue of arms control was featured. Reagan told the reporters that he was in favor of a negotiated agreement that achieved "an actual reduction in the numbers of nuclear weapons," as long as this was verifiable. Arms control could not be conducted in a vacuum, however, and the president noted that his administration would work on the basis of "linkage," which took into account "other things that are going on." Détente, Reagan said, had so far been "a one-way street that the Soviet Union has used to pursue its own aims," which were, according to Reagan, "the promotion of world revolution and a one-world Socialist or Communist state" that reserved "unto themselves the right to commit any crime, to lie, to cheat, in order to attain that," something the United States had to keep in mind when seeking to do business with the Soviets.[11]

This was harsh talk, which was well received by the CPD-dominated members of the Reagan administration. But before the new administration could organize itself effectively with regard to a unified approach toward arms control, President Reagan was shot, on March 30, 1981, by would-be assassin John Hinckley. In addition to producing a made-for-television moment when the president joked with his wife about "forgetting to duck," Reagan's brush with mortality also led to his reflecting on the state of U.S.-Soviet relations and in particular about the consequences of a nuclear war between the two nuclear powers. While in the hospital, he reflected that God may have spared his life in order for him to "reduce the threat of nuclear war." Reagan then proceeded to write a letter to Brezhnev in which he called for renewed efforts at disarmament and elimination of nuclear weapons. While Reagan's inner circle was able to rewrite specific passages of the letter calling for a reduction in nuclear weapons before sending the letter to Brezhnev, there could be no doubt that the president's position on the issue of nuclear weapons became heavily influenced by his near-death experience. While many of Reagan's closest advisors were shocked by the tone and content of the letter, there was nothing they could do to alter this newfound passion for a world free of nuclear weapons.[12]

The president's new view of arms control had no policy outlet. Haig would continue to articulate publicly about arms control with the Soviet Union, noting in April 1981 that any future arms control effort would be linked with Soviet behavior, declaring that it served "no useful purpose" to negotiate with the Soviets while they engaged in "imperialist policies."[13] Later, in July 1981, Haig appeared on ABC News's "Issues and Answers," where he said that "arms control is no longer the centerpiece of US-Soviet relations. The centerpiece must be what contributes to the security of the American people, to international peace and stability."[14] But other players were emerging from within the Reagan administration that would have a say in what direction U.S. policy would take vis-à-vis arms control, and lacking the ability to control the issue via a supreme bureaucratic position, Haig saw the issue slip further and further from his grasp.

One of the other players was Eugene Rostow, nominated to head ACDA. During his Senate confirmation hearings, in June 1981, Rostow belittled the very cause he was supposed to be championing, declaring that "arms control thinking drives out sound thinking."[15] Unlike his predecessors, who seemed to understand that the role of ACDA was to help prevent nuclear war, Rostow took an opposite point of view, telling the Senate that the United States could fight and win a nuclear war with the Soviet Union, and even flourish in the aftermath of a global conflict that killed between 10 million and 100 million people, citing the "resilience" of the human race. Rostow staffed ACDA with like-minded persons who believed that the United States could fight and win a nuclear war if it were prepared to fight one. Arms control, in their collective opinion, was the antithesis of war preparation.[16]

The lack of a central bureaucratic framework for arms control policy would play havoc with the Reagan administration's early efforts to organize in a cohesive manner. Rostow's ACDA ostensibly operated under the aegis of Haig's State Department but in fact possessed a great deal of independence. Nonetheless, where in the past ACDA had exercised control over the process of negotiating arms control agreements (through either the director himself or his deputy), under Reagan the job of negotiating with the Soviets was given to independent negotiators, who reported directly to the White House. The job of negotiating strategic arms reductions was given to retired Lieutenant General Ed Rowny, who had resigned his position on the SALT II negotiation team in December 1979 and had spent most of 1980 testifying against the SALT II treaty. With strategic arms reduction talks in limbo, the selection of Rowny as the man to head them up on behalf of the United States was a clear sign that the Reagan administration was in no hurry to jump-start the process, as Carter had been back in 1977.

The Reagan administration had inherited the "dual-track" policy concerning theater nuclear forces. This policy had the United States promising to seek to negotiate with the Soviets about reducing or eliminating INF in Europe while at the same time preparing to deploy a new generation of theater nuclear weapons, the *Pershing* II and GLCM, as counters to the Soviet SS-20. The individual chosen to head up the INF talks was Paul Nitze, the founding father of America's Cold War policy of containing the Soviet Union and, like Rowny, a vociferous opponent of the SALT II treaty and arms control in general. The selection of these two men to head up the respective negotiations was an ominous beginning for a process so many hopes were based on.[17]

Before the Reagan administration could embark on a fresh approach toward negotiating any arms control agreement with the Soviets, there needed to be an understanding about what the strategic nuclear posture of the United States would be in terms of nuclear weapons employment and the related nuclear weapons delivery systems. Much of this work had been recently done by the Sloss Panel in preparing the NTPR for President Carter, which led to the promulgation of PD-59. Rather than subject the national security mechanisms of the United States to a new top-to-bottom study, the Reagan administration convened a panel for the purpose of refining PD-59. This work was done over the summer of 1981 and had the input of many who would be involved in formulating the arms control policies of the Reagan administration, including Rowny, Nitze, Rostow, and others. The end result of this effort was the issuing of NSDD-13 on October 19, 1981, the "Nuclear Weapons Employment Plan of the United States." Unlike the massive PD-59 that preceded it, NSDD-13 was a slim document that set forth some basic guidelines, further amplifying the work of PD-59. First, the United States would no longer operate under a Countervailing policy, but rather a Prevailing policy: Nuclear war would be waged with the goal from the outset being American victory in any protracted nuclear exchange lasting up to 180 days in duration.[18]

NSDD-13 represented the final philosophical victory for nuclear strategist Albert Wohstetter. Not only did he advise on its creation, but his adherents, including Andrew Marshall, were central contributors to its content. Wohlstetter had long viewed the concept of Assured Destruction as immoral, given its focus on destruction inflicted on civilian populations. The paralysis created by Assured Destruction, or its corallary, Mutually Assured Destruction, was also ineffective, since it neutralized a nuclear arsenal that cost so much to build. Wohlstetter proposed a concept of Graduated Nuclear Deterrence, which accepted the reality of a limited nuclear war, utilizing precision nuclear weapons to destroy an enemy's military and command capability. As such, Wohlstetter was adamantly opposed to arms control, which he viewed as self-constraining, since it limited the technological advantage enjoyed by the United States. Instead, he advocated the creation of highly accurate weapons, nuclear and nonnuclear alike, whose mere existence would suffice to deter any potential enemy because, if needed, they would in fact be used, as opposed to the massive city-killers of the past, which no prudent leader would ever seek to unleash. NSDD-13 represented a full embrace by the United States of Wohstetter's theories, capping a long and distinguished (if controversial) career. (Wohstetter retired from the University of Chicago in 1980.)[19]

President Reagan had campaigned vigorously on the concept of America's "window of vulnerability" vis-à-vis the Soviet Union. He had promised to close this window if elected, and now that he was commander in Chief, he faced the political problem of being seen as fulfilling one of the cornerstone objectives of his administration. The rhetoric regarding the scope of the threat faced by the Soviet Union existed, thanks to Wohlstetter and Pipe's pronouncements. Now what was needed was substance. NSDD-13 directed that the United States be able to wage and persevere in a nuclear conflict with the Soviet Union lasting up to 180 days in length. The arsenal necessary to accomplish this, however, did not exist. The *Trident* II submarine (and its D-5 missile) was years away from being deployed; so, too, was the advanced technology "stealth" bomber. The B-1 bomber had been canceled by President Carter, and the MX missile, while ready for production, lacked a coherent basing strategy.

On October 3, 1981, President Reagan stood side by side with Defense Secretary Weinberger and announced that not only was he bringing the B-1 bomber back into production, but he was also going ahead with the production of a hundred MX missiles. There was a catch, however: Reagan was scrapping the "race track" concept that had been the cornerstone of the MX employment concept under President Carter. Instead, he proposed placing thirty-six MX missiles into "superhardened" *Titan* II missile silos and exploring other options for the remaining sixty-four missiles, including deploying them on large aircraft, protecting them with a new ABM system, or burying them in extra-deep silos dug into the sides of mountains. The window of vulnerability was closed, Reagan said, although his actions to accomplish this closure represented more of an illusion than substance. The Reagan-Weinberger MX plan did nothing to alter the underlying assessment that U.S. silo-based missiles were vulnerable to a Soviet first strike, and on November 5, 1981, Caspar Weinberger himself testified before Congress that the B-1 bomber's ability to penetrate Soviet air defenses past 1988 was assessed as limited. A week later he reversed himself in a letter written jointly with CIA Director Bill Casey: The two men stated that the B-1 was viable as a penetration bomber well past 1990. Congress, focusing on the MX missile issue, failed to muster enough votes to override the president's stated desires, and the B-1 bomber program became official.[20]

With a strategic nuclear posture cobbled together, however haphazardly, the Reagan administration was positioned to set in motion its arms control strategy. Having labeled SALT II as being "fatally flawed," Reagan had, since before the 1980 election, promised to enter into a new round of negotiations for a SALT III treaty, promising reductions in nuclear arms, not just limitations. But the rhetoric of the Reagan team often took on the tenor of nuclear machismo, which seemed to represent the antithesis of arms reductions, focusing instead on arms employment. Weinberger announced publicly that the United States would be seeking to build and deploy enhanced radiation weapons (the "neutron bomb"), only to be contradicted by Secretary of State Haig, who stated that no decision had been made to deploy the weapon. Reversing course, Haig touted a NATO contingency plan to detonate a tactical nuclear "shot across the bow" of any Soviet conventional assault on Europe, only to be contradicted by Weinberger, who expressed ignorance of any such policy.[21]

The rift between the State Department and the Defense Department extended into the field of arms control policy, with Foggy Bottom advocating an immediate push for Intermediate Nuclear Forces (INF) talks in order to placate a growing antinuclear movement in Europe, while the Pentagon pushed for the continued deployment of the *Pershing* II and GLCM weapons systems, void of any arms control constraints. The negative political fallout from the Carter-era decision to deploy new INF weapons into Europe had, by the time Ronald Reagan took office, expanded into a full-blown peace movement of considerable political clout. The heavy-handed rhetoric of the Reagan national security team only made matters worse. Far from seeing the deployment of the *Pershing* II and GLCM missiles as a means of countering the Soviet deployment of SS-20 missiles, many Europeans viewed the new missiles as representing targets for the Soviet weapons, targets that were located in their own backyard. Hundreds of thousands of protesters took to the streets to protest the deployment of weapons systems that represented, in the eyes of the antinuclear movement and much of the general European population, the ultimate taboo: the mass annihilation of civilians in an avoidable nuclear holocaust.[22]

The structure of the INF policy debate was twofold. On the side of the State Department was the newly appointed head of the Bureau of European Affairs, Richard Burt. A former reporter for the *New York Times*, Burt was on record commenting, shortly before Reagan took office, that "there are strong reasons for believing that arms control is unlikely to possess much utility in the coming decade."[23] On assuming his office, however, Burt was confronted with the reality of the European antinuclear movement and its opposition to the deployment of the *Pershing* II and GLCM missiles. This opposition was especially strong in West Germany and the Netherlands, two nations slated to receive the new U.S. weapons systems. Burt carried out a series of meetings with European leaders, including several with West German Chancellor Helmut Schmidt, whose appeal to President Carter for an American response to the Soviet SS-20 deployment was responsible for initiating this entire crisis. Burt soon found himself articulating strongly in favor of an early initiation of INF talks between the United States and the Soviet Union with the goal of significantly reducing the numbers of INF systems to be deployed by either side. In addition to appreciating the European perspective, Burt recognized the dangerous linkage between the planned deployment of INF weapons and the threat of all-out general nuclear war between the United States and the Soviet Union, noting that "the emplacement of long-range U.S. cruise and ballistic missiles in Europe makes escalation of any nuclear war to involve an intercontinental exchange more likely, not less."[24]

Burt's concerns were brushed aside by his counterpart within the Defense Department, Assistant Secretary of Defense Richard Perle, who represented the other half of the INF policy debate. Perle had assumed his post straight from his position on Senator Scoop Jackson's staff, where he had become a vociferous foe of both the Soviet Union and arms control. To Perle, the linkage between the INF deployment and the escalation to general nuclear warfare was precisely the intended result. An adherent of Wohlstetter's philosophy on nuclear deterrence, Perle believed that only by linking NATO's nuclear capability with the strategic nuclear forces of the United States could one truly deter a Soviet military assault on Europe, either conventional or nuclear. The numbers of planned U.S. INF forces, and their ability to disperse to remote deployment areas, meant that the Soviets would have to expend a considerable percentage of their nuclear arsenal in any decapitation strike against NATO-affiliated INF, knowing that scores of U.S. weapons would survive to strike back against targets inside Soviet territory. Once U.S. nuclear weapons detonated inside the Soviet Union, there would be nothing to stop a general Soviet attack against the United States. NSDD-13 anticipated this, with its commitment to "controlled escalation" and the ability to wage a protracted nuclear conflict. Of course, the intention was not to promote nuclear warfare but rather to deter it by demonstrating a genuine willingness to use nuclear weapons and prevail, if Soviet actions warranted it. Perle was opposed to any effort to engage the Soviets directly on INF. It was his belief that any effort to reduce U.S.-Soviet differences to a system of treaty-imposed constraints that would then need to be complied with represented a fundamentally flawed point of view. Perle was joined in his opposition to any INF negotiations by National Security Counsellor Allen, who viewed such talks as little more than "blackmail." Defense Secretary Weinberger and Secretary of State Haig both supported the INF deployments at the earliest possible time.[25]

Haig was confronted with the reality of the scope and breadth of European opposition, and as such he was cognizant of the need to hold INF talks, if for no other reason than to be seen as being sympathetic to the concerns of America's NATO allies. Under pressure from Burt, the State Department began aggressively pushing for the initiation of INF talks at the earliest possible moment. Following a visit by Helmut Schmidt to Washington in May 1981, President Reagan agreed to fully prosecute the dual-track policies of the December 1979 INF agreement, giving equal weighting to both the deployment of INF weapons and the conduct of arms control talks designed to reduce their numbers. Confronted with this reality, Richard Perle executed a brilliant political maneuver, proposing what became known as the "Zero Option": the removal of all Soviet SS-20 missiles from Europe and Asia, in exchange for U.S. agreement not to deploy the *Pershing* II and GLCM missiles. Both Burt and Haig rejected Perle's initiative as unworkable in terms of selling it to the Soviets and its impact on the overall U.S. military buildup, creating as it would the suspicion that American efforts were an exercise in propaganda, easily dismissed as merely a negotiating ploy.[26]

Perle's boss, Caspar Weinberger, was initially skeptical, fearful that the Soviets might actually accept the offer. But it became more and more clear that the Zero Option was, from an anti–arms control point of view, perfect: There was no chance the Soviets would accept the elimination of one of their most effective weapons systems in Europe and Asia, a weapon that was actually deployed, in exchange for the United States not deploying weapons that had yet to be built, let alone deployed. The Zero Option, by playing into European demands for a reduction of nuclear weapons, virtually guaranteed that the *Pershing* II and GLCM missiles would be deployed into Europe on schedule on the strength of the anticipated Soviet rejection.[27]

On December 18, 1981, Ronald Reagan officially unveiled the Zero Option INF proposal in remarks made before the National Press Club in Washington, DC. Calling his proposal a "simple, straightforward yet historic message," Reagan sought to assuage European leaders' concerns over American intentions toward the Soviet Union, which Reagan maintained were purely peaceful, while maintaining pressure on the Soviet Union for some sort of meaningful arms control. Declaring the scheduled deployment of *Pershing* II and GLCM missiles as a "reaction" to ongoing Soviet INF buildup, Reagan touted the Zero Option as the ideal solution to European peace and stability. Any INF agreement, Reagan underscored, would have to be fully verifiable based on the precepts of "openness and creativity rather than the secrecy and suspicion which have undermined confidence in arms control in the past."[28]

Reagan's presentation got exactly the reaction that was hoped for in Europe. While several leaders were skeptical of the real policy objectives of the Reagan administration, the Zero Option proposal created an environment of hope not only for meaningful INF talks but also for a resumption of strategic arms limitation talks with the Soviets. Brezhnev was in West Germany when Reagan delivered his speech, immediately putting the Soviets on the defensive at a time when, because of the antinuclear peace efforts in Europe, Moscow felt it had the upper hand diplomatically. Some in Europe recognized that the Zero Option was designed with failure in mind. However, short-term domestic political considerations trumped long-term strategic issues. Reagan's appointee as the U.S. INF negotiator, Paul Nitze, was bringing a hard-liner's perspective to the table in Geneva. Reagan's instructions to Nitze were simple: "Hang tough."[29]

At a time when the Reagan administration needed stability in terms of its national security policy formulation, it instead was delivered a shattering blow when National Security Counsellor Allen was forced to resign his position in January 1982 after allegations surfaced about a $1,000 gratuity paid to Nancy Reagan by a Japanese magazine that ended up in Allen's safe, unreported. An investigation also uncovered the existence of three expensive watches Allen had accepted as personal gifts from other Japanese associates. To replace Allen Ronald Reagan turned to a close friend, Deputy Secretary of State William Clark. Unlike Allen, who had to report to Reagan through Edwin Meese, Clark was given direct access to the president.

One of the first crises faced by newly appointed National Security *Advisor* (a change in status from Allen, who had been called "counsellor") Clark was, not surprisingly, related to the issue of INF. In February 1982 the Soviets, true to form, rejected the Zero Option, incredulous that the United States would seriously seek such a major deviation from the existing SALT accords, which had left the Soviet INF systems untouched. Now the Americans were attempting to have the Soviets do away with all of their INF systems, proposing in exchange not to deploy a new family of weapons still under development, while leaving intact the "forward based systems" (FBS) comprised of the large number of nuclear-capable U.S. military aircraft based in Europe and on U.S. aircraft carriers. Richard Perle had been correct: The Zero Option was an offer the Soviets simply could not accept. In March 1982 the Soviets responded with a counterproposal, calling for a phased reduction in NATO and Warsaw Pact medium-range missiles and nuclear-armed aircraft to six hundred systems by 1985 and three hundred by 1990. Leonid I. Brezhnev, in an effort to appease the concerns over the deployments of the SS-20, announced a moratorium on the deployment of any additional SS-20s in Europe. April and May came and went, with the stalemate in Geneva over INF talks in place.[30]

In early May 1982 President Reagan attempted to break the deadlock in strategic arms talks by announcing a major new arms control initiative that sought not simply limitations on strategic nuclear forces but actual reductions. Such talks had been envisioned since the Carter administration, under the guise of SALT III. Reagan viewed the SALT title as political poison, however, and instead unveiled a new name to accompany his new proposal: strategic arms reductions treaty, or START. In a speech delivered on the campus of his alma mater, Eureka College, the president stated that he would like to begin the new START talks as early as June 1982 and that he was open to having a meeting with Brezhnev when the Soviet leader visited the United Nations, also in June. Reagan had to strike a fine balance in his speech between alleviating the political pressure being brought to bear by the European antinuclear protests and acknowledging the disdain among his core supporters for anything associated with arms control. He proposed a two-phased approach toward disarmament, the first phase reducing the strategic arms of both sides by 33 percent, and even deeper cuts—some 50 percent—by the end of the second phase. The START proposal represented dramatic cuts and was designed to have each side possessing the same numbers of nuclear weapon delivery systems. But the proposed cuts were also designed to cut the heavy ICBMs, which represented the core strength of the Soviet strategic arsenal.[31]

As was the case with the Zero Option INF proposal, Reagan's START initiative was very much one-sided, calling for the Soviet Union to make significant cuts in its ICBM force while leaving untouched two of the three major components of the U.S. strategic nuclear arsenal, submarines and heavy bombers. Likewise, the United States was asking the Soviets to make cuts in forces that actually existed, while promising not to deploy new weapons systems, like the MX missile. The START proposal was, it seemed, designed to fail. But in fact Reagan and his advisors were serious about making START work. Despite his criticism of the SALT II treaty, Reagan reluctantly agreed to observe the treaty, although it had not been ratified by the U.S. Senate, as well as to adhere to the 1972 SALT interim agreement, so long as the Soviets did the same. A major concern, especially among members of the Joint Chiefs of Staff, was that if the SALT accords broke down, then the Soviets would be in a prime position to build up their missile forces more rapidly than the United States could make other plans for. Reagan viewed START as a legitimate exercise in arms control. The question was whether the Soviets would share this same view.[32]

Even as the Reagan administration put together its combined strategic nuclear strategy and arms control policy, the policy team itself underwent a dramatic transformation in July 1982 with the resignation of Secretary of State Haig. Haig had been under fire from the beginning of his tenure. His inability to establish firm control of American foreign and national security policy had led to numerous bureaucratic clashes with Defense Secretary Weinberger and his further alienation from Reagan's inner circle. The departure of Allen as the "national security counselor," and his replacement with Clark, who took over an upgraded national security advisor position that further diluted Haig's influence, only exacerbated matters. Haig submitted his resignation in early July 1982. Reagan accepted it and replaced Haig with George P. Shultz, the former treasury secretary under Richard Nixon and, until his appointment as secretary of state, an executive at Bechtel, a leading international engineering and construction firm. Shultz was also a member of the CPD, and his appointment brought the State Department, on paper at least, into ideological alignment with the rest of the CPD-dominated Reagan administration.[33]

The vacuum caused by the shuffle of leadership at the State Department created a window of opportunity for the most unlikely of initiatives from the most unlikely source. Paul Nitze, the INF chief negotiator, had grown increasingly frustrated by the lack of progress in the INF talks, caused largely by the Zero Option policy and his inability to deviate from its strictures in his dealings with the Soviets. He was joined in his frustration by his Soviet counterpart, Yuli Kvitsinsky. Kvitsinsky had indicated to Nitze that the Soviets were undergoing a major review of their whole approach to INF, and unless the deadlock in negotiations was broken soon, this review would happen in a manner detrimental to the goals and objectives of the INF process. The United States was on the verge of beginning its controversial deployment of *Pershing* II and GLCM missiles into Europe, and the Soviets were threatening to walk out of the talks if this occurred. In a moment of brilliant improvisation, Nitze and Kvitsinsky went on what has become famously known as "the walk in the woods," where the two negotiators, on their own and without instructions, sought to create a proposal that could serve as the foundation of a Reagan-Brezhnev summit meeting. Recognizing that both sides needed to make concessions in order for their gambit to succeed, Nitze and Kvitsinsky came up with a proposal that would have the Soviets agree to reduce the number of SS-20 missiles deployed against Europe to seventy-five and the United States in turn forgo the deployment of the *Pershing* II missile, which worried the Soviets greatly, given its ability to strike targets in the western Soviet Union, and limit its deployment of GLCMs into Europe to seventy-five.[34]

When Nitze brought the proposal to Reagan and his inner circle, it was initially met with approval and excitement. Kvitsinsky had told Nitze that he would communicate the Soviet response to the proposal via the Soviet embassy in Washington, DC. But while Washington waited for Moscow, Moscow was likewise waiting for a sign from Washington that the "walk in the woods" proposal was acceptable to the Americans. Kvitsinsky was a direct representative of Andrei Gromyko, the foreign minister, and as such spoke with his authority. Gromyko had decided to go out on a limb. With Brezhnev's mental health deteriorating, and Aleksei Kosygin and Mikhail Suslov already dead, Gromyko had permitted Kvitsinsky to go forward without a formal blessing from the central authorities. Yuri Andropov, the head of the KGB, was making a political move to replace Brezhnev, and Gromyko had filled the vacuum by freelancing on INF. In order for the initiative to succeed, however, it would require the Americans to be seen making the first move.[35]

In Washington, as reports of Nitze's bold proposal began circulating among the national security apparatus, a wave of protest swelled against the compromises Nitze and Kvitsinsky had crafted. Richard Perle and his allies were aghast at any deviation from the Zero Option stance. The Joint Chiefs of Staff rightfully concluded from the compromise that the Soviets were fearful of the *Pershing* II missile, and as such they were loath to voluntarily surrender such a weapon. Secretary of Defense Weinberger wanted to use the *Pershing* II missiles to pressure the Soviets into eliminating the SS-20 missiles deployed against Asia, on the grounds that these systems could be rapidly transferred to the European theater in a time of crisis, making the proposed cuts in European-based systems meaningless. But ultimately the proposal was shot down by the new secretary of state, George Shultz, who criticized Nitze for unauthorized "freelancing." Once it became clear that Nitze had not been speaking with the authority of the secretary of state, Gromyko had no choice but to reject the "walk in the woods" proposal, which he did formally in September 1982. Gromyko chastised Kvitsinsky, noting that in the future all back-channel dealings with Nitze needed to have the backing of Secretary of State Shultz prior to any discussion taking place.[36]

While the INF talks stalled, the newly named START talks sputtered. Led by chief negotiator Ed Rowny, the U.S. negotiating team seemed to place a premium on making it clear to their Soviet counterparts that these talks were not to be a repeat of the SALT process, but rather something quite different. Rowny did not have much leeway when it came to negotiating any aspect of a START agreement. The foundation of the U.S. position on START was spelled out in May 1982, stating that the U.S. goal in

START was to achieve significant reductions in strategic arms yet retain viable deterrence. The focus would be placed on missiles, with the goal of eliminating Soviet advantage in heavy throw-weight systems. The Reagan administration wanted to shift both sides away from ballistic missiles as the key delivery system and rather embrace what it viewed as the less-destabilizing cruise missile, which the United States viewed more as a second-strike system. Additional guidance, released in a document that same month, directed that the United States would comply with the SALT II treaty—and in doing so take no action that would undercut existing arms control agreements with the Soviet Union—and made it clear that SALT II was not an adequate foundation for arms control and that any action the United States might take to ensure the survivability of its existing strategic weapons was justified. Likewise, this document declared that the United States would take no position on the issue of mobile missiles, thereby retaining flexibility when it came to basing concepts for the MX missile.[37]

The actual START talks began in June 1982. The first specific guidance Rowny and his team received for START established equal caps of 850 total ballistic missiles per side, with a sub-limit of 210 medium to heavy missiles, of which 110 could be heavy missiles. There would be a ban on any new heavy missiles in order to make moot the Soviet advantage in throw-weight capability, a proposed limit on the weight of any new re-entry vehicles of two hundred kilograms, and a limit on the number of MIRVs per ICBM to 10, and 14 for SLBMs. A new issue the U.S. START delegation was authorized to discuss was that of nondeployed missiles and their use in any potential "break out" scenario. Nondeployed missiles were those missiles—spares or reserve stock—that were not deployed with frontline units. With cuts scheduled to take place in both the Soviet and US arsenals, there was a concern that the missiles removed from operational status might be held in reserve, only to be rapidly brought back into service in times of crisis, creating a strategic advantage. The U.S. negotiation position, although based on a singular entity, was actually divided into two distinct phases. Phase 1 had the United States seeking equality through the reduction of actual missiles; phase 2 would focus on the issue of achieving equality in terms of throw weight.[38]

In mid-August the Soviets made a surprise move, providing a comprehensive counterproposal that offered to reduce U.S. and Soviet strategic forces to 1,800 long-range missiles and bombers each. The Soviet proposal was very similar to that put forward by President Carter in March 1977. The Soviets also asked for curbs on new classes of ballistic missile submarines (the *Ohio* for the Americans and the *Typhoon* for the Soviets) and a ban on cruise missiles. The fact that the Soviets did not reject the U.S. START position out of hand, but rather responded in the traditional manner of putting forward a counteroffer, indicated that despite the animosity created by the Reagan administration's harsh anti-Soviet rhetoric, the Soviets remained committed to conducting serious arms control negotiations. That commitment notwithstanding, there was a massive gulf between the U.S. opening proposal and the Soviet counterproposal, derived as they were from fundamentally different approaches toward what would constitute a fair agreement based on the notion of equality.[39]

In September 1982 Rowny received a new negotiating guidance that addressed the issue of verification and underscored the need for on-site inspection, both in terms of an active and a passive presence, in any such verification arrangement. This on-site presence was sought not only at specific sites related to treaty activity but also in the areas around ICBM complexes to make sure there were no nondeployed missiles present; there was a provision for challenge inspections of other areas as well. The Soviets viewed the American numbers concerning missiles as a useful starting point for discussion, even if they were by and of themselves unacceptable (the Soviets specifically noted that the U.S. position was not "comprehensive" in nature, refusing, for instance, to discuss the matter of heavy bombers). The demands for on-site inspection, as always, were rejected out of hand.[40]

"I intend to search for peace along two parallel paths—deterrence and arms reductions."[41] These were the words of President Reagan as he introduced his basing plan for the MX missile in a speech on November 22, 1982. The Reagan approach was simple: In order to get the Soviets to agree to sweeping arms reductions, America had first to rearm itself so that it no longer operated from a position of strategic inferiority. This, the president argued, was the only way to generate fair and equitable force reductions through any arms control effort. The Reagan administration had already initiated its arms control agenda, via the INF and START talks. Now he tackled the issue of deterrence through the vehicle of rearmament by announcing his decision to deploy a hundred advanced MX missiles, deployed in what he termed the "Dense Pack" configuration: The missiles were to be deployed in a line 14 miles long and 1.5 miles wide, buried in superhardened silos spaced 1,800 feet apart, so not only would a single Soviet warhead be able to take out only one missile, but also the explosion of the Soviet warhead would destroy any additional incoming Soviet warheads without degrading the surviving MX missiles' ability to launch. This theory of "fratricide" was untested. If it were viable, more than half of the deployed MX missiles would survive a surprise Soviet attack. If it weren't, then Reagan was putting all of his strategic eggs in one basket, not exactly the model of strategic survivability called for in the U.S. deterrence strategy.[42]

The Dense Pack concept was quickly criticized by many members of Congress as a $26 billion negotiating ploy. Less than a month after Reagan proposed Dense Pack, Congress killed it. Reagan, disappointed by the failure of Congress to give him the missile system he wanted, responded on January 3, 1983, by appointing a special panel, headed by former Lieutenant General Brent Scowcroft, to review U.S. strategic missile options, including options for the MX. It wasn't just Congress that was troubled by Reagan's MX plan. The Soviets were apoplectic. The day after Reagan's speech the Soviet Union blasted the Dense Pack proposal as a "new dangerous step" toward an all-out arms race. Within a week the Soviets expanded on their concerns, calling Dense Pack a violation of the SALT II treaty, which banned the construction of additional fixed missile launchers. The START talks adjourned in early December 1982, with Soviet Defense Minister Dmitri Ustinov warning ominously that the Soviets would respond to what they viewed as a violation of an existing arms control agreement by fielding a new missile of their own.[43]

Complicating the overall environment of U.S.-Soviet relations was the death of Soviet leader Leonid Brezhnev on November 10, 1982. Brezhnev was replaced by Yuri Andropov, the former head of the KGB. Andropov was immediately faced with the controversy created by Reagan's Dense Pack speech and the need to be seen as responding in an appropriate fashion, resulting in Ustinov's strongly worded warning. But confrontation was not the path he desired. The new Soviet leader let it be known that Moscow favored a return to the time of détente. Andropov—who as head of the KGB was well acquainted with the reality of Soviet daily life beyond the gloss of Soviet propaganda—had a keen interest in reviving the moribund Soviet economy and understood better than most that a renewed arms race with the United States would have devastating consequences for his country. But the Soviet defense ministry, and in particular Defense Minister Ustinov, were increasingly alarmed by what they viewed as a relentless U.S. effort to achieve world supremacy.[44]

With the passing of Brezhnev, Andropov was interested in measures that would instill East-West stability and facilitate Soviet economic recovery. Avoiding an arms race with the United States was a large factor in this equation, and early in 1983 the new Soviet leader fielded his own arms control initiative, unilaterally reducing Soviet warhead levels in Europe to those of the French (ninety-eight weapons) and British (sixty-four weapons), thereby achieving the lowest level of nuclear weapons in Europe since 1978. This was real arms control, but Andropov's effort went unrewarded by a Reagan administration caught in its own rhetorical insanity.[45]

For all of his talk of the need for arms control, Ronald Reagan and his administration had no viable arms control policy. Right-wing ideology had crafted positions so rigid and one-sided as to make them virtually worthless. At ACDA, Eugene Rostow had become increasingly frustrated over the constraints being imposed on negotiations by anti–arms controllers, such as Richard Perle in the Defense Department, and started demanding that he be given more flexibility in crafting a workable arms control policy. This stance cost him his job, and in January 1983 President Reagan replaced Rostow with Kenneth Adelman, an archconservative neophyte on arms control. Rostow's dismissal, and his replacement by Adelman, only reinforced the concern in Moscow that Reagan was utterly confused about how to approach the issue of restricting the arms race.[46]

If the dismissal of Rostow sent tremors of concern through Moscow, what Reagan did next had to register as the policy equivalent of an earthquake. On March 8, 1983, in a speech delivered before the National Association of Evangelicals, Ronald Reagan lashed out at a Soviet leadership he called the "focus of evil in the world," and labeled the entire Soviet Union an "evil empire." Clearly the Reagan administration was not positioning itself to build a sound relationship with Andropov in the aftermath of Brezhnev's passing. Instead, building on the concept of mistrust, Reagan himself injected a new initiative that sought not only to undermine any residual goodwill that might exist beween the United States and the Soviet Union, but also to shred one of the foundational documents of the modern arms control experience: the ABM treaty.[47]

On March 23, 1983, President Reagan delivered a second speech, famously referred to as the "Star Wars" speech, in which he unveiled his administration's intentions to deploy what was termed the Strategic Defense Initiative (SDI). In a move directly challenging the foundation of conventional nuclear deterrence, Reagan announced the need for American defensive measures capable of rendering Soviet ballistic missiles obsolete. While Reagan claimed otherwise, the SDI initiative represented a direct attack on the ABM treaty and on the concept of equality when comparing U.S.-Soviet strategic power. Although purely theoretical at this stage, this initiative meant that the White House, through the release of NSDD-85, "Eliminating the Threat from Ballistic Missiles," was committing the

United States down a path of long-range research and development for a ballistic missile defense program.[48]

Reagan followed up his "Star Wars" speech with another prime-time television appearance, this time to announce the findings of the Scowcroft Commission on ballistic missile options for the United States. Scowcroft, together with commission members such as Donald Rumsfeld, recommended that the United States deploy a hundred MX missiles, renamed *Peacekeeper*, in existing *Minuteman* silos in Wyoming. This was seen as an interim measure until the United States could develop a more survivable basing mode for the *Peacekeeper*.[49]

The combined effects of the "Evil Empire" and "Star Wars" speeches served to convince the Soviet leadership that the Reagan administration was serious about only one thing: the total domination of the United States over the entire world, including the Soviet Union. Andropov called the Reagan policies "madness" and warned that Reagan was walking an "extremely dangerous path." The Soviets were growing increasingly concerned about the stalled INF and START talks, and they feared that the Americans were using the talks as a vehicle to achieve a first-strike capability, concerns reinforced by Reagan's pursuit of SDI. Secretary of State Shultz spent the summer of 1983 trying to repair U.S.-Soviet relations, and there was some minor progress actually made in terms of increased grain shipments and talks on the opening of new consulates. All of this was undone on the night of August 31–September 1, 1983, when the Soviet Air Force shot down Korean Air flight 007, a Boeing 747 aircraft that had strayed deep into Soviet air space, killing all 269 persons onboard. Immediately the Reagan administration reacted, not only condemning the act itself but also questioning the viability of dialogue with a nation capable of committing such an act. Information available today appears to defend the Soviet contention that they viewed KAL 007 as a U.S. reconnaissance aircraft, refuting the charges made by the Reagan administration that this was a deliberate act of murder. But Reagan himself kept upping the rhetoric, labeling the shoot-down as an act of "barbarism," "savagery," and "a crime against humanity." When George Shultz met with Andrei Gromyko on September 8, 1983, in Madrid, Spain, what was supposed to be a time to celebrate a new direction for U.S.-Soviet relations quickly turned into a bitter exchange between the two senior diplomats.[50]

The attention of America was soon diverted by the deaths of 241 U.S. service members in Beirut, killed when a suicide bomber blew up a barracks housing U.S. Marines, and by the U.S. invasion of Grenada a few days later, ostensibly to free American medical students trapped on the island in the aftermath of a socialist coup d'état, but in fact intended to eliminate a secret Cuban military base alleged to be under construction there. Shortly after the Grenada operation, President Reagan spoke before the Heritage Foundation, a conservative think tank, and unveiled a new policy direction toward the Soviet Union, one that envisioned "rolling back" socialism around the world. The Grenada operation, although small in scale, clearly demonstrated in the eyes of the Soviet Union that the anti-Soviet stance taken by Reagan went beyond rhetoric and had assumed an actively militaristic posture. Andropov condemned the Reagan administration's policies as representing a "serious threat to peace." The Soviets, Andropov said, had given up on the possibility of serious negotiations with the United States so long as these anti-Soviet policies were in place.[51]

In November the Soviet Union submitted one last proposal at the INF talks in Geneva, offering to reduce the number of SS-20 missiles facing Europe to even lower numbers than they had agreed to under the moratorium. The U.S. delegation, still operating under the inflexibility of the Zero Option policy, rejected the Soviet offer, and shortly thereafter the United States began the deployment of *Pershing* II and GLCM missiles to Europe. The Soviets immediately withdrew from the INF talks. In an effort to keep the START talks alive, Brent Scowcroft drafted a proposal calling for both the Soviet Union and the United States to reduce their nuclear arsenals according to the concept of equivalence, based on the disparities between the strategic forces of each side. This represented a departure from the previous Reagan demand of strict equality. Ed Rowny, the START negotiator, was opposed to the new proposal and misrepresented it to the Soviets in Geneva, reinforcing to his Soviet counterparts that the "basic position of this administration has not changed." The Soviets in turn refused to deal with Rowny and walked out of the START talks when they concluded in December 1983 without setting a date for their resumption.[52] U.S.-Soviet relations were frozen. Andropov, his health failing, condemned the U.S. actions in deploying INF to Europe, somewhat ominously warning about the "dangerous consequences of that course." Later, in a December 1983 speech to Soviet war veterans, Soviet Defense Minister Ustinov accused the United States of breaking the military-strategic balance between the United States and the Soviet Union, something he said the Soviet Union was "determined not to allow."[53]

In January 1984, the *Bulletin of the Atomic Scientists* reset the Doomsday Clock to three minutes before midnight, citing the total collapse of arms control dialogue between the United States and the Soviet Union. The Cold War not only had grown colder but was in greater danger of becoming a "hot" war than any time since the Cuban missile crisis of 1962.

CHAPTER 13

THE TRIUMPH
OF REASON

In Washington, DC, Soviet Ambassador Anatoliy Dobrynin joked that he should apply for unemployment benefits, given the fact that there was little or no work to be done in the way of U.S.-Soviet diplomacy. The collapse of the INF and START talks was symptomatic of an overall freeze in U.S.-Soviet relations. But there was no worse time than the end of 1983 for these two superpowers not to be talking to one another. The decision by President Reagan to deploy INF to Europe in the fall of 1983, in particular the *Pershing* II missile, left the Soviet leadership concerned that the United States was pushing to acquire, and perhaps employ, a legitimate nuclear first-strike capability against the Soviet Union. In response, the Soviets began an intelligence collection effort designed to detect advanced warning of any U.S./NATO first-strike attack, and they put together an operational plan designed to preempt any such attack.

The Soviet intelligence effort was geared toward collecting indicators of any impending attack. Thus, in early November 1983, when the United States held a full-scale rehearsal for nuclear war in Europe, code-named Able Archer 83, it appeared to the Soviets that the United States was moving forward with a first-strike attack against the Soviet Union. Soviet nuclear forces were put on the highest alert and needed only a simple order from the ailing Yuri Andropov to launch a preemptive strike that would have triggered a nuclear holocaust. Exercise Able Archer 83 ended by mid-November 1983, and the crisis soon passed. Nevertheless, the deep underlying suspicion on both sides about one another's intent still existed.[1]

Much of the work for creating a strong anti-Soviet bias in the policies of the Reagan administration up until late 1983 was done by National Security Advisor William Clark, who had ready access to the president on a daily basis. Operating away from the spotlight, Clark carefully controlled the information the president had access to, helping color his judgments and, ultimately, his decisions. The incoherence of the Reagan arms control philosophy was, by the fall of 1983, being harshly criticized in the press. When the media, in August 1983, began suggesting that it was Clark, and not Reagan, who was calling the shots in the White House, it was simply a matter of time before Clark was asked to step down. The assault on Clark, orchestrated by White House Chief of Staff James Baker and supported by Nancy Reagan, resulted in his resignation on October 13, 1983. He was rewarded for his loyalty to the president by being appointed secretary of the interior. Clark's replacement as national security advisor was Robert McFarlane, a former Marine Corps officer who had served in the White House on and off since the early 1970s.[2]

McFarlane did not share Clark's "Evil Empire" approach toward the Soviet Union. While McFarlane had been one of the principal authors of Reagan's 1983 "Star Wars" speech, his actions were motivated by a perceived need to break free of the previous patterns of behavior that propelled the United States and Soviet Union on a collision course. With McFarlane installed as national security advisor, an opportunity was created for a more pragmatic shift in the direction of U.S.-Soviet relations. McFarlane was quick to act when U.S. intelligence reported, in January 1984, on the Soviet reaction to the Able Archer exercise. When Reagan found out how serious the situation had been in terms of a Soviet overreaction to the exercise, he was disturbed and soon thereafter made a speech, influenced by McFarlane, in which he declared that the top priority between the United States and the Soviet Union must be reducing the potential for nuclear war and likewise reducing their respective nuclear arsenals.[3]

On February 9, 1984, after only fifteen months in office, Soviet leader Yuri Andropov died. While Andropov had indicated that his successor should be Mikhail Gorbachev, the minister of agriculture, the Soviet Central Committee instead chose Konstantin Chernenko as general secretary. Chernenko was a protégé of Brezhnev, and his selection as general secretary represented a return to the hard-line policies of that era. While promising that the Soviet Union had "no need for military superiority," Chernenko promised that he would seek the right level of defense to "cool the hot heads of bellicose adventurists." Soon after assuming the mantle of leadership, Chernenko sent a letter to President Reagan in which he embraced the "opportunity to put our relations on a more positive track."[4]

The National Security Council and State Department both began a move to renew serious dialogue with the Soviets. The continued deployment of INF missiles into Europe was a source of tension with the Soviets, who refused to engage in any renewed dialogue with the United States under these conditions. By the summer of 1984 Chernenko had rejected all American overtures on any resumption of arms control talks as election year tactics (1984 was a U.S. presidential election year) and demanded that the United States back up its words with concrete action.[5] None was forthcoming. Instead, the Soviets were treated to a continuation of campaign-induced hard-line rhetoric and gaffes, including one by President Reagan in August 1984, when an open microphone caught him joking about signing legislation that would "outlaw Russia forever" and concluding with "We begin bombing in five minutes."[6]

In the fall of 1984, the Soviet Union announced its first major defense budget increase in several years. Proclaiming that this move was a reaction to the massive defense spending undertaken by the Reagan administration, Soviet leaders, including Chernenko, Gromyko, and Ustinov, stressed the defensive character of their military buildup, although a major part of the funding increase went to testing and fielding a new generation of mobile ICBMs, including the SS-24, armed with ten MIRVs and capable of being launched from a standard silo or on special railcars, which gave it strategic mobility, and the SS-25 road-mobile ICBM, armed with a single nuclear warhead.[7] While some in the Soviet military pushed for even greater defense spending, Chernenko refused, unwilling to stress an already fragile civilian economic sector. In order to reinforce his decision to cap defense spending, Chernenko began a move toward improved diplomatic relations with the United States, starting in late September 1984 with a meeting between Andrei Gromyko and President Reagan. In October 1984 Secretary of State George Shultz met with Soviet Ambassador Dobrynin, and later Gromyko met with the U.S. ambassador to the Soviet Union, Arthur Hartman. By November 1984 both sides were discussing the possibility of a Shultz-Gromyko meeting in early 1985 for the purpose of jump-starting nuclear and space arms talks.[8]

But any major breakthrough in U.S.-Soviet relations was hampered by uncertainties about Soviet leadership. While the elections of November

1984 cemented Reagan's position as the leader of the United States for the next four years, the failing health of Konstantin Chernenko led to a behind-the-scenes power struggle that boiled down to two men: Mikhail Gorbachev and Grigory Romanov. Romanov was linked to the Soviet defense industry and represented old-style Soviet leadership reminiscent of the Brezhnev era. Gorbachev had already made his mark as a reformist with new ideas about the direction the Soviet Union needed to take. In a speech delivered in November 1984, Gorbachev had already raised two concepts—perestroika (rebuilding) and glasnost (openness)—that would later change the Soviet Union and the world. But Chernenko's succession, as of the end of 1984, was very much in doubt, and this lack of certainty impeded any rapid improvement in U.S.-Soviet relations. Chernenko's declining health worsened by the end of 1984, and the Soviet leader was confined to bed in a Moscow sanatorium for the final months of his life, finally passing away on March 10, 1985.[9]

The issue of Soviet succession wasn't the only arms problem facing the American president. When Reagan assumed office in 1981, his administration articulated strong support for the Nuclear Non-Proliferation Treaty (NPT) and the overall issue of nuclear nonproliferation. In particular, Reagan called upon U.S. allies to join the United States in requiring comprehensive safeguards from all nonnuclear weapons states before they would be permitted to import significant quantities of nuclear material. However, the Reagan administration was facing a situation in which the theory of the proliferation of nuclear weapons was being replaced by the reality of nuclear weapons programs in the hands of nations operating outside the framework of the NPT.

India's "peaceful" nuclear test of 1974 had sent shockwaves through the nonproliferation community. Even while the nuclear supplier nations struggled to develop export-import control mechanisms, the proliferation of nuclear weapons capability continued unabated. In September 1979 a U.S. surveillance satellite detected evidence of a possible nuclear detonation over the Indian Ocean, in the vicinity of South Africa's Prince Edward Island. Data collected indicated a low altitude explosion of some three kilotons. The possibility of a nuclear weapons test that implicated either Israel or South Africa created enormous political problems for the United States. The Carter administration convened a panel of experts to review the data related to the September event; the panel concluded that the activity in question was "probably not from a nuclear explosion," although it could not be ruled out. While the September 1979 "nuclear" event over the Indian Ocean continues to be in dispute, what was clear was that both South Africa and Israel were working on nuclear weapons programs, and that the two nations were providing assistance to one another in this regard.[10]

By the time Ronald Reagan assumed the presidency, the list of non-NPT nations engaged in nuclear weapons–related activities had grown by one more: Pakistan. In 1981 the State Department was reporting that Pakistan was actively seeking to acquire a nuclear weapons capability. This report was updated in 1983, citing "unambiguous evidence" of Pakistan's nuclear weapons ambition. Pakistan's leadership acknowledged in 1984 that it had acquired a "very modest" nuclear enrichment capability, but that it was for "peaceful purposes" only. Nonetheless, President Reagan warned Pakistan's government that there would be "grave consequences" if Pakistan enriched uranium above 5 percent, the level needed to fuel a nuclear reactor.[11]

In confronting the nuclear proliferation taking place in Israel, South Africa, and Pakistan, the Reagan administration was running head-on into its own Cold War–driven policies of containment of the Soviet Union. Israel was a major U.S. ally in the Middle East, where the United States sought to block the spread of Soviet influence among the Arab nations there. South Africa, despite its policy of apartheid, was allied with the United States in confronting Soviet-supported activities in Angola and Mozambique. And Pakistan served as America's principal interlocutor with the anti-Soviet mujahadeen in Afghanistan. The Reagan administration had to tread carefully in an effort to strike a balance between not insulting critical allies and trying to craft meaningful nonproliferation policy.

The United States was able to proclaim a nonproliferation victory of sorts when, in April 1984, a U.S.-Sino trade pact was signed following China's agreement to join the International Atomic Energy Agency (IAEA) and to accept IAEA inspection of all nuclear equipment and material being exported by China.[12] But the issue of dual standards continued to haunt the Reagan administration. Secretary of State Shultz tried to address this matter on November 1, 1984, when he spoke before the United Nations Association of the United States. Although he cited America's strong commitment to nonproliferation, Shultz noted that the United States makes "rational distinctions between close friends and allies who pose no great proliferation risk, and those areas of the world where we have real concerns about the spread of nuclear weapons."[13] In short, the United States wanted to be able to make its own judgment call, free of the constraints of safeguards imposed by the NPT, with which it would share nuclear technology.

The Third NPT Review Conference, held in Geneva from August 27 through September 21, 1985, again illustrated the differences of opinion on the implementation of the NPT between, on the one hand, the United States and the developed nuclear powers and, on the other hand, those lesser developed nations who sought to acquire nuclear power. A major point of discussion was the unsafeguarded nuclear facilities in Israel and South Africa, which many Middle Eastern and African nations pointed to as an example of how Western double standards actually promoted the horizontal proliferation of nuclear weapons. As had been the case in the first two Review Conferences, the nuclear weapons states (NWS) came under harsh criticism for failing to make any significant progress in the field of nuclear disarmament, especially on the issue of a comprehensive nuclear test ban treaty. The issue of guarantees of protection for safeguarded nuclear facilities also arose in light of Israel's 1981 bombing of Iraq's Osirak reactor, and Iraq's repeated attacks against Iranian nuclear facilities under construction. These two issues hampered the issuing of a final declaration. In the end, the conference's final document reiterated the widespread support of the NPT while citing shortfalls in the area of nuclear disarmament. In a hopeful move, however, the NPT added a new member in December 1985, when North Korea joined, agreeing to open a nuclear research reactor to IAEA inspections and safeguards.[14]

The Third NPT Review Conference underscored the need for a renewed dialogue between the United States and the Soviet Union on the issue of nuclear disarmament. When Gorbachev emerged as the new Soviet leader in March 1985, he repeated the trend of the previous two Soviet leaders in writing a letter to President Reagan reaffirming his "personal commitment . . . to serious negotiations."[15] The difference this time was that Gorbachev, unlike his predecessors, would follow up on his commitment. He was assisted by the reality that by 1985 the Soviets no longer needed the SS-20. Soviet strategic forces, equipped with new, mobile SS-24 and SS-25 missiles in addition to the existing ICBM and SLBM launchers, were so large and diverse that SS-20 had become a redundant system.

Gorbachev was assisted by the diplomacy that had been conducted in the last months of Andropov's rule. In the fall of 1984 both the United States and the Soviet Union had expressed an interest in entering into "umbrella" negotiations encompassing defense and space systems, START and INF. These talks began on March 12, 1985, in Geneva. With the advent of these talks, the Reagan administration installed a new team of negotiators. Gone was Ed Rowny, the hard-liner whose antics had so alienated his Soviet counterparts. His replacement was Max Kampelman, a member of the

CPD who had previously served as the U.S. ambassador to the Conference on Security and Cooperation in Europe (CSCE) from 1980 to 1983. Also gone was Paul Nitze, largely because of the animosity created within the ranks of the Reagan administration hard-liners over his "walk in the woods" initiative. Nitze was replaced by his deputy, Maynard Glitman. Both Nitze and Rowny were offered opportunities to stay on as advisors to the president on arms control.[16]

Little progress was made in these new talks, mainly as a result of the demand by the Soviet Union that the ABM treaty be strictly adhered to and the efforts by the United States to seek as broad an interpretation of the ABM treaty as possible so as to permit ongoing work on SDI. Secretary of State Caspar Weinberger and his assistant deputy, Richard Perle, sought to undermine the ABM treaty while opposing any new talks designed to impede SDI. Their work ran counter to the efforts of Secretary of State Shultz and National Security Advisor McFarlane, both of whom were keen on getting serious arms control talks with the Soviets back on track.[17]

In an effort to help reduce tensions with Europe and the United States, Mikhail Gorbachev initiated a unilateral moratorium on the deployment of INF into Europe, which was scheduled to last until December 1985, by which time there was hope that a U.S.-Soviet summit could occur that would produce a more thorough blueprint for disarmament action. Gorbachev's moratorium reduced the number of SS-20s in the western Soviet Union to levels that existed when the INF talks broke off in 1983. Talk of an early summit in 1985 cooled in April 1985, when an American officer, Major Arthur Nicholson, was shot and killed by a Soviet soldier while carrying out his duties as part of the Military Liaison Mission in Potsdam, East Germany.[18]

The stalemated talks in Geneva began to frustrate both Moscow and Washington. Hard-liners such as Weinberger and Perle continued to oppose any effort at negotiations between the United States and the Soviet Union. Since 1984 President Reagan had been presented with intelligence analysis pushed by Perle that asserted that the Soviet Union had violated its political commitment to adhere to the provisions of the SALT II treaty. Reagan had, since 1982, committed the United States to a path of adherence with the SALT II treaty, even though he was personally opposed to the treaty. In June 1985, confronted with evidence that Perle and others contended proved the Soviets to be noncompliant in their agreements, President Reagan announced that the United States would continue to abide by the SALT II treaty so long as the Soviet Union demonstrated comparable restraint and provided that the Soviets pursue in good faith the ongoing arms reduction talks in Geneva.[19]

Reagan's position incensed Gorbachev, who accused the president of acting in bad faith by framing a scenario that was inconsistent with the facts. "One cannot dispute the fact that the American side created an ambiguous situation whereby the SALT II Treaty, one of the pillars of our relationship in the security sphere, was turned into a semi-functioning document that the U.S., moreover, is now threatening to nullify step by step," Gorbachev wrote in a letter to President Reagan on June 10, 1985. "Your approach is determined by the fact that the strategic programs being carried out by the United States are about to collide with the limitations established by the SALT II Treaty, and the choice is being made not in favor of the Treaty, but in favor of these programs."[20]

It became clear to both Reagan and Gorbachev that the atmosphere in Geneva was not conducive to sound negotiations, and on the joint recommendation of Secretary of State Shultz and the new Soviet foreign minister, Eduard Shevardnadze, it was agreed in October 1985 that a back channel of communications would be established to bypass the usual diplomatic processes. Once again, the Soviets turned to their ambassador in Washington, Anatoli Dobrynin, to carry out this function. Through this back channel, and in subsequent dialogue between Shultz and Shevardnadze, Reagan and Gorbachev began to discuss a mutual understanding concerning the "inadmissibility of nuclear war." Both sides started working toward organizing a summit between the two leaders before the end of 1985.[21]

Critical to the success of any summit was the need by both sides to break free of the impasse that existed in Geneva over the issue of arms reductions. On September 27, 1985, Shevardnadze presented President Reagan and Secretary of State Shultz, during a meeting in New York City, with a new Soviet proposal on strategic arms reductions which proposed a 50 percent reduction in strategic arms by both sides as well as a "cap" of 6,000 nuclear warheads per side. Further more, no basing mode (ICBM, SLBM, bombers) could contain more than 60 percent of the warhead total.[22] On November 1 the United States responded with a counterproposal that continued to reflect the U.S. focus on missile throw weight as a unit of measuring strategic capability. The United States proposed a 50 percent reduction in the highest overall ballistic missile throw weight, in addition to limiting reentry vehicles to 4,500 for each side, with a sub-limit of 3,000 reentry vehicles on ICBMs and a further sub-limit of 1,500 reentry vehicles on heavy ICBMs. The desire for an early summit provided an opportunity for both sides to bridge their differences and bring their positions closer together.[23]

Secretary of State Shultz traveled to Moscow in early November 1985 to meet with Shevardnadze and Gorbachev in order to help pave the way for the summit scheduled later that month. Back in Washington, Shultz was being supported by Richard Burt, the head of the Political-Military Affairs Bureau. Burt was pushing for a successful summit defined by a meaningful agreement in the field of arms control. Opposing Burt was Richard Perle, who, together with Secretary of Defense Weinberger, was concerned that in their rush to have a good summit, Shultz and Burt were positioning the president to make too many compromises to the Soviets. Perle drafted a memorandum that warned the president not to give in on issues of principle, especially SDI, even if the Soviets appeared to be making concessions elsewhere. The Soviets, Perle claimed, had a history of violating every arms control agreement they had entered into. According to Perle, Gorbachev, despite his new style of open leadership, was no different from any other previous Soviet leader in that regard. In the end, Perle warned, no matter what the United States commits to, Gorbachev and the Soviets will cheat.[24]

On November 19, President Reagan and General Secretary Gorbachev finally met face to face in Geneva, the first such meeting between U.S. and Soviet leaders in six years. Gorbachev pushed early for "a substantive agreement . . . which would increase peoples' hope and would not destroy their view of the future with respect to the question of war and peace."[25] In the discussions that followed, Gorbachev lectured the U.S. delegation that twenty years ago America had four times as many nuclear weapons as the Soviet Union. What would the United States have done if the situation had been reversed? Gorbachev asked. His answer: the same thing the Soviets did—seek parity. Today, Gorbachev noted, parity exists. The Soviets do not seek any advantage but rather would like to see strategic nuclear parity at a lower level than today. The main problem was SDI, which Gorbachev contended could only lead to a renewed arms race inclusive of space weapons. SDI made no sense to the Soviets, who considered that its only utility lay in its potential to defend against a retaliatory strike. This, Gorbachev stated, was unacceptable. If the United States went forward with SDI, then there could be no reduction in strategic nuclear weapons, and the Soviets would be compelled to pursue a similar program of its own.[26]

President Reagan responded by declaring that SDI was not a threat, since it was not linked to any offensive military capability. The U.S. pursuit of SDI, Reagan contended, should not be viewed by the Soviets as a threat and therefore should not trigger an arms race. Offensive weapons can and should be reduced, even with SDI. Gorbachev then asked Reagan what he thought they should tell their negotiators in Geneva, to which Reagan responded that guidelines seeking a 50 percent reduction in strategic arms would be acceptable, with some flexibility provided based upon the differing structure of U.S. and Soviet forces. But the sticking point continued to be SDI. Gorbachev pounded away on the issue, and it became clear that while the United States believed the principal destabilizing factor in U.S.-Soviet relations to be offensive nuclear weapons, the Soviets believed the same about SDI.[27]

Shultz, in a side conversation with Shevardnadze, argued that the closer the two sides could get to zero nuclear weapons, the more viable SDI became in terms of eliminating the threat from offensive nuclear missiles. Shevardnadze responded by noting that if both sides were serious about eliminating nuclear weapons, and could get other nations to participate in their overall reduction, there would be no need for a defensive shield. These conversations were repeated, in one form or another, over the course of two days. In the end, the Geneva summit collapsed under the weight of Reagan's SDI program and the refusal by Gorbachev and the Soviets to accept it as legitimate. The good news was that, after a six-year hiatus, the leaders of the Soviet Union and the United States had finally met and had come away from that meeting with a mutual recognition of the need for continued dialogue between the world's two largest nuclear powers on the issue of the world's most dangerous weapons.[28]

While Gorbachev was dismayed with President Reagan's close-minded embrace of SDI, his overall assessment of the American leader, and his policies, clashed with previous analysis from the Soviet Union, which held that the United States was seeking unilateral nuclear supremacy with the goal of being able to launch a preemptive nuclear first strike. Reagan had no intention of launching such an attack. Gorbachev's challenge was to convey this understanding to a Politburo that was disappointed with the lack of discernible results from the summit. The major problem with SDI, from Gorbachev's perspective, was political. Soviet scientists had studied the American concepts and concluded that SDI was fanciful, expensive, and unrealistic as a legitimate defense shield. The Soviets would be able to overcome any SDI shield with little or no problem, but at great expense, especially if Soviet defense interests insisted on building a similar shield in the name of "parity." Gorbachev had a good understanding of the poor economic state of the Soviet Union and realized that the reforms he wanted to embark on could not survive in the climate of a new arms race. At the Geneva summit Gorbachev had linked any movement in arms reductions with the United States dropping SDI. Now, post-Geneva, Gorbachev began to articulate disarmament policy options that accepted SDI as an unpleasant reality.[29]

In January 1986 Gorbachev tried to jump-start arms control by proposing a three-phased deal that would scrap SDI, reduce each side's strategic nuclear arsenal by 50 percent, and, in a move that took everyone by surprise, accepted the Zero Option when it came to INF. When the INF proposal bogged down in Geneva over the issue of linkage with SDI, Gorbachev made it clear, in a February 1986 meeting with Senator Edward Kennedy, that an INF agreement could be considered separate from strategic arms reductions and SDI. In order to sell this position to his own side, Gorbachev moved to downplay the importance of SDI, telling the Politburo in March 1986, "Maybe we should just stop being afraid of the SDI."[30] Gorbachev stressed that the Soviets could not ignore SDI but needed to recognize that hard-liners in the U.S. administration—namely Weinberger and Perle—were using SDI as a vehicle to push the Soviets into an arms race that would economically exhaust them. The secretary of defense and his hawkish assistant deputy were likewise now thrust into a position of opposing the very Zero Option on INF they had proposed back in 1981, because Gorbachev had done what neither of them thought any Soviet leader would ever do: accept the Zero Option disarmament proposal.

Gorbachev's analysis was accurate. Back in Washington, both Weinberger and Perle, historically staunch opponents of arms control, were tentatively jumping on the arms control bandwagon. Their goal was not to create a viable arms control agreement, but rather just the opposite: to ensure that whatever arms control initiative went forward would be couched in a manner that was unacceptable to the Soviet Union. Accordingly, Weinberger and Perle, assisted by Perle's boss, Fred Iklé, and the new ACDA chief, Kenneth Adelman, launched a frontal assault on the two major pillars of U.S.-Soviet arms control, the ABM treaty and the SALT II treaty. For the ABM treaty, the Department of Defense hired a lawyer with no arms control experience to craft a legal reinterpretation of the ABM treaty that would allow for ongoing work in SDI. So expansive was this interpretation that even the State Department rejected it. The goal wasn't to create a legal justification for SDI, but rather to push the Soviets into scrapping the ABM treaty altogether, something Gorbachev was loath to do.[31]

The next target was the SALT II treaty. Perle was able to oversee the production of a series of reports and studies that purported to document ongoing Soviet noncompliance with the SALT II treaty. Based on these reports, and under pressure from hard-liners in Congress (led by Republican Senator Jesse Helms of North Carolina, who had filled the ideological gap created with the death of Scoop Jackson in September 1983), Reagan, on May 26, 1986, declared that the United States would no longer be constrained by the limits imposed by the SALT II treaty but rather would "base decisions regarding its strategic force structure on the nature and magnitude of the threat posed by Soviet strategic forces." The United States, Reagan declared, would "continue to exercise the utmost restraint, while protecting strategic deterrence, in order to help foster the necessary atmosphere for significant reductions in the strategic arsenals of both sides," and he called upon the Soviet Union to work with the United States to establish a framework of "truly mutual restraint."[32]

INF was another issue for which Weinberger and Perle sought to craft an adequate American response. Having pushed for the Zero Option, Perle now had to try to explain why it might not be the ideal solution after all. A major problem was that, in selling the deployment of *Pershing* II and GLCM missiles to its NATO allies, the United States had emphasized the importance of linking INF in Europe to American strategic nuclear forces in order to make nuclear deterrence viable. Now, if the United States was to go forward with any INF Zero Option, it would be reversing course on the concept of a European "trip wire" linking the U.S. nuclear arsenal to the defense of Europe. Also, while the United States would be withdrawing INF missiles from Europe, the availability of the SS-25 road-mobile ICBM as an alternative to the SS-20 missile meant that Europe would still be covered by a Soviet nuclear threat without any European-based U.S. counter. Another problem was that the Soviet proposal only covered INF in Europe; there were still nearly a hundred SS-20 missiles deployed in Asia.[33]

Weinberger and Perle were able to operate with a level of bureaucratic impunity because of a major shake-up within the Reagan national security team, which saw the pragmatic Robert McFarlane replaced by the indifferent (at least when it came to issues pertaining to arms control) John Poindexter. McFarlane's resignation came as a result of a growing scandal concerning U.S. covert assistance to anticommunist forces in Nicaragua (the so-called *Contras*) in violation of congressional prohibitions, as well as a controversial arms-for-hostages deal involving Iran. These issues merged as part of a larger Iran-*Contra* affair that was beginning to distract the Reagan administration from other matters, including arms control. With McFarlane out of the way, Weinberger and Perle were free to push their hard-line positions void of any significant interference from the National Security Council.

Gorbachev was wrestling with serious matters on the domestic front at that time. In April 1986, a horrific accident at a Soviet nuclear power reactor in Chernobyl killed scores of people and caused widespread contamination not only in the area surrounding Chernobyl and the Soviet Union but throughout Europe as well. The Soviet reaction to the Chernobyl disaster led Gorbachev to conclude that there was an acute need for more openness within the Soviet Union and that the scourge of nuclear weapons needed to be addressed once and for all.[34] Chernobyl was to Gorbachev what the made-for-television film *The Day After* was for Ronald Reagan. In that movie, which Reagan watched when it was aired in November 1983, American citizens struggle to survive in a post–nuclear war environment. Reagan was so moved by the movie that he became personally committed to the elimination of nuclear weapons, even if that goal seemed to run counter to the overall policy direction of his administration.[35] Now, in Chernobyl, Gorbachev faced a real-life example of the horror of nuclear contamination. Chernobyl became a seminal point in the Soviet leader's evolution as a nuclear abolitionist.

In a move that surprised the hard-liners in Washington, Gorbachev broke from his previous insistence, articulated during the Geneva summit in November 1985, that any arms reduction effort must be linked to an American renouncement of SDI. Instead, Gorbachev submitted a new proposal on May 29, 1986, that called for a two-phased approach toward disarmament. The first phase called for a cap of 8,000 nuclear devices for each side and a ceiling of 1,600 nuclear delivery vehicles each. Most telling, the Gorbachev proposal excluded the so-called Forward Based Systems comprising U.S. aircraft stationed in Europe and on aircraft carriers. The second phase would provide for "interim" reductions in strategic nuclear forces contingent upon both sides agreeing not to withdraw from the ABM treaty for a period of fifteen to twenty years.[36]

These were serious proposals, but they were largely ignored in Washington, DC. Instead, the U.S. response was to return to a formula that differed little from what had been proposed in the past, including the insistence that the Soviet Union cut its throw-weight capability by 50 percent. Perle and Iklé also proposed a treaty to limit all ballistic missiles, noting that if there were no ballistic missiles, then there could be no U.S. nuclear first strike, meaning that the Soviets had nothing to fear from SDI. Countering the Soviet argument that if there were no ballistic missiles, there would be no need for SDI, the Reagan administration fell back on the "mad man" argument, noting that the United States, and the world, needed a defense against the potential actions of a rogue state and/or leader.[37] Recognizing that the negotiations on strategic arms and SDI were, for the time being, stalled, in September 1986 the Soviets proposed an INF-only deal, de-linked from any other agreement, in which both sides would be held to one hundred missiles each in Europe (none of these could be *Pershing* II missiles) and a freeze would be placed on Soviet SS-20 deployments in Asia. The United States responded with a counterproposal that accepted the hundred-missile cap but insisted that some of these missiles be *Pershing* II's. The United States also insisted that Soviet SS-20 missiles in Asia count toward this total.[38]

The atmosphere between the United States and the Soviet Union deteriorated when, on September 2, 1986, the Soviet KGB arrested a U.S. journalist, Nicholas Daniloff, on charges of espionage. Daniloff's arrest was in apparent retaliation for the U.S. arrest in late August of Gennadi Zakharov, an employee of the Soviet mission to the United Nations in New York. While a deal was struck that allowed for the release of both Daniloff and Zakharov, the arrests received widespread attention in the media and led to a toughening of rhetoric in Washington about the Soviet Union.[39] Fearful that matters might spiral out of control, Gorbachev dispatched Shevardnadze to Washington, where he delivered a personal letter to President Reagan in which Gorbachev proposed a "quick one-on-one meeting, let us say in Iceland," the goal of which would be to produce instructions to their respective negotiating teams in Geneva on "two or three very specific questions" that could then be signed as formal agreements when Gorbachev visited the United States.[40]

Many in the Reagan administration, including Weinberger and Perle, were against the idea of a Reagan-Gorbachev get-together, feeling that meetings held at this level assumed a stature that mandated formal agreements, and that there might develop pressures to seek agreement for agreement's sake. Shultz and others in the State Department rejected this, noting that in their opinion the Soviets were seeking to pave the way for a future summit in which arms control reductions might be discussed. Shultz was wrong, however.[41] In Moscow, Gorbachev sat down with the Politburo and emphasized the importance of the Soviet Union taking the lead in making dramatic proposals in the area of arms control. Final U.S. briefings provided to Reagan on the eve of his meeting with Gorbachev in Iceland predicted that the Soviet leader would be "coy" about the prospects of a future U.S. summit and that Reagan would have to press Gorbachev for action. The best the United States could hope for, the briefers told Reagan, was an agreement to limit the number of strategic nuclear warheads to something between the U.S. proposed cap of 5,500 and the Soviet position of 6,400.[42]

The two leaders met in Reykjavik, Iceland, in a home formerly used by the French as a consulate, on October 11, 1986. After an initial exchange of greetings and general remarks, during which Reagan chided Gorbachev for the Soviet Union not responding to the U.S. proposal calling for a 50 percent reduction in strategic nuclear arms ("perhaps the Soviets would agree to initial reductions to a level of 5,500 warheads," Reagan prodded), the two leaders were joined by Shultz and Shevardnadze, and Gorbachev dropped his bombshell proposal: the Soviets were seeking nothing less than a 50 percent reduction in strategic nuclear arms, not tied to INF or any other negotiation, which would call for substantial reductions in Soviet heavy missiles. This proposal, Gorbachev noted, took into account U.S. concerns. In exchange, Gorbachev asked for the United States to show some flexibility with regard to American SLBM forces, which consisted of some 6,500 warheads.[43]

On INF, the Soviets proposed a complete elimination of U.S. and Soviet INF missiles in Europe, separate from the issue of French and British nuclear forces. The Soviets proposed that the matter of Soviet SS-20 missiles in Asia be put aside until all INF systems had been removed from Europe. The Soviets also proposed a freeze on the deployment of short-range nuclear missiles in Europe (possessing a range of less than 1,000 kilometers) and indicated a willingness to discuss the reduction of these missiles in future arms control discussions. Gorbachev also brought up the issue of the ABM treaty, in which he proposed that both sides agree to a ten-year period during which they could not withdraw from the treaty and a period of negotiations (three to five years) in which they would discuss how to proceed from that point. Gorbachev also proposed a ban on antisatellite weapons and a comprehensive nuclear test ban.[44]

Reagan had little of substance to offer in response to the dramatic proposals outlined by Gorbachev. During a break in the meeting, evidence of a split in the U.S. delegation emerged, as Paul Nitze embraced the Soviet proposals as the most sweeping he had seen in over twenty years, while Richard Perle downplayed them as flawed and nothing new. Shultz was inclined to accept the Soviet proposal concerning the ABM treaty, citing the fact that since SDI was in its infancy, there could be no realistic discussion of fielding a system prior to that. As such, the United States lost nothing by agreeing. Reagan, however, refused to budge on the issue of SDI. This was to prove critical to the prospects of success in Reykjavik.[45]

As the talks progressed, Shultz placed Nitze in charge of the expert-level discussions. Nitze's counterpart was Marshall Akhromeyev, the senior Soviet military commander—his presence underscored the seriousness which the Soviets attached to these talks. Akhromeyev proposed a 50 percent reduction in strategic nuclear forces across the board, and in an effort to accede to U.S. sensitivities, he agreed that these cuts would be done in a manner that would allow neither side any discernible advantage. He also agreed that bombers would be counted as a single delivery system, whether or not they carried cruise missiles. The Soviets agreed to eliminate their SS-20 missiles in Europe in exchange for the Americans agreeing to eliminate the *Pershing* II. The Soviets would keep their SS-20 missiles in Asia, and the United States would be able to position a similar number of missiles in Alaska aimed at the Soviet Union.[46]

The U.S. counterproposal, written with the heavy influence of Richard Perle, proposed a 50 percent cut in strategic nuclear weapons and a five-year agreement to limit SDI to research while abiding by the ABM treaty, which the United States continued to interpret in widely divergent ways. However, Perle was not able to hold back the tide for more sweeping arms control, which had gripped both delegations in Reykjavik. By the afternoon of October 12, President Reagan presented the Soviets with an offer to reduce each side's strategic ballistic missile force by 50 percent in a five-year period, followed by complete elimination in a second five-year period. Both sides would agree to adhere to the ABM treaty during this time and not seek to withdraw. The Soviets soon agreed to this formula, with one major exception: SDI research would, during this ten-year term, be limited to the laboratory, and there could be no testing of operational components outside of the laboratory or in outer space. Reagan would not accept this limitation, and Gorbachev refused to drop it. As a result, an opportunity for the Soviet Union and the United States to get rid of all strategic nuclear weapons was missed, defeated by a program, SDI, that was more theory than reality and that no one outside Ronald Reagan and a handful of advisors thought would ever be deployed. Reykjavik ended with both sides conceding that there had been no agreement reached on disarmament.[47]

After Reykjavik, both the Soviet Union and the United States conducted postmortems designed to extract "lessons learned" from what appeared to be a failed summit. Back home in Washington, Reagan ran into a wall of criticism, as Congress and the Joint Chiefs of Staff confronted the reality that the nation's chief executive almost negotiated away all strategic offensive nuclear weapons without first consulting them. Reagan found that he was soon compelled by domestic pressure to back away from some of the commitments made in Reykjavik. The irony was that, at the same time Reagan began retreating from full nuclear disarmament, Gorbachev began to make concessions on the issue of SDI. Gorbachev seemed motivated by the words of Andrei Sakharov, the Soviet nuclear physicist who designed the first Soviet hydrogen bomb. Under house arrest in the city of Gorky since his dissent of the 1960s, Sakharov was released on the personal orders of Gorbachev. In his first public appearance, Sakharov chided Gorbachev for failing to embrace an opportunity to get rid of all nuclear weapons by seeking to restrict a concept, SDI, that would never work. Gorbachev listened to Sakharov and soon was crafting compromise language that would allow the United States to test SDI outside of the laboratory, but not in outer space.[48]

But it was too late. On November 3, 1986, Reagan signed NSDD-250, "Post-Reykjavik Follow-up." In it the president directed that all options be considered, including one that saw the elimination of all ballistic missiles. He instructed military planners to examine NSDD-13, for the employment of nuclear weapons, as well as MC 14/3, the NATO war plan. Reagan was confident that both NSDD-13 and MC 14/3 could be implemented effectively in a ballistic missile–free world. Nevertheless, the Joint Chiefs of Staff responded with a briefing to the president in December 1986 in which they argued that any effort to eliminate ballistic missiles would require the U.S. Army to increase its number of divisions, the Air Force to expand air defense capabilities in the United States, and the Navy to acquire more ships and more sea-launched cruise missiles. The Pentagon, working with the JCS, began to formulate a counter to the concept of eliminating strategic nuclear weapons, stating that it would cost the United States more to build up its conventional military capability in order to fill the defense vacuum created than it would to retain its nuclear arsenal. This was a specious argument, pulled together on the spur of the moment, but it resonated in Congress. Largely because of pressure brought to bear by hard-liners in the Pentagon and in Congress, there would be no return to the moment that had occurred in Reykjavik, where an American president and a Soviet general secretary had agreed, in simple terms, to rid the world of nuclear weapons.[49]

While SDI stymied strategic arms talks and threatened the ABM treaty, the one area both the Soviets and the Americans recognized as being open for agreement was that of INF. The two sides had agreed to the concept of the Zero Option in Europe. The stumbling block centered on the Soviet INF deployed in Asia. The Soviets, like the United States, reshuffled their delegation in Geneva, and the new chief negotiator, Yuli Vorontsov, arrived with instructions from Gorbachev to achieve a breakthrough in INF. In February 1987 Vorontsov informed his counterpart, Max Kampelman, that the Soviets were formally de-linking INF from START and SDI, and were willing to proceed along the lines of the original U.S. Zero Option. Under pressure from Perle and others in the Pentagon, Kampelman pressed Vorontsov on the importance of eliminating not just INF in Europe but also all short-range ballistic missiles and INF throughout the entire Soviet Union.[50]

Another sticking point was verification. Any agreement would require the strictest form of verification, including on-site inspection, something the Soviets had never before agreed to. The United States had produced a draft INF treaty in early March 1987 that proposed the elimination of all INF in Europe and established a ceiling of a hundred INF systems for each side worldwide. However, the United States made it clear that a global Zero Option was the preferred position. This was followed up with an additional proposal in mid-March that addressed the issue of verification, with the United States laying out its position on on-site inspections, including both regular and "challenge" inspections. Perle viewed these provisions as showstoppers, in particular the requirement for on-site inspection.[51]

There was still enough ideological fervor within the Reagan administration to usher forth some made-for-television grandstanding by the "Great Communicator" himself. On June 12, 1987, Ronald Reagan traveled to West Berlin, where, in the shadow of the Berlin Wall, which symbolized much of the Cold War antagonism between the United States and the Soviet Union, he delivered a fervent address not only to the citizens of West Berlin but also to those residing in East Berlin and, by design, to the Kremlin itself. Pointing out that there could be no freedom so long as walls and barriers divided Europe, Reagan dramatically proclaimed, "General Secretary Gorbachev, if you seek peace, if you seek prosperity for the Soviet Union and Eastern Europe, if you seek liberalization: Come here to this gate! Mr. Gorbachev, open this gate! Mr. Gorbachev, tear down this wall!"[52]

In the past, such an outburst during a critical juncture in sensitive negotiations might have derailed the talks. But Gorbachev had attuned himself to the ideology of Reagan's core constituency and was able to see past the rhetoric to the larger objective of arms reductions, a goal he believed was shared by President Reagan. Little by little, the Soviets began to accede to U.S. demands with regard to the structure of an INF agreement.

In April 1987, during a visit to Moscow by Secretary of State Shultz, Gorbachev agreed that any INF agreement would include all short-range
missiles as well. The Soviets at this time also produced a draft INF treaty
text that reflected the basis of the U.S. March text. In June 1987 the United
States followed up on Gorbachev's comments in March to Shultz and
modified its proposal to include not only all short-range nuclear missiles
but also a "double global zero," meaning that any treaty would cover all
INF and short-range missiles operated by both the Soviet Union and the
United States worldwide. In July, much to the surprise of many in the Pentagon, including Richard Perle, the Soviets accepted the "double global
zero" proposal.[53]

The final facilitation of an INF agreement came when German Chancellor Kohl announced in August 1987 that he would eliminate all of West
Germany's seventeen *Pershing* 1a missiles once the INF treaty was implemented, and that the nuclear warheads loaded on those missiles would be
returned to U.S. custody and removed from Europe.[54] And in September
the Americans submitted, and the Soviets accepted, a proposed inspection
protocol that incorporated on-site inspection to an unprecedented level,
inclusive of "challenge" inspections. The United States and Soviet Union
also agreed to establish "nuclear risk reduction centers," equipped with
special hotline phones and staffed twenty-four hours a day, in order to
guard against any accidental conflict. These new centers would also serve
as the means of exchanging information pertaining to arms control and
inspections.[55] All that remained was to sign a treaty document. On December 8, 1987, Soviet General Secretary Mikhail Gorbachev flew to
Washington, DC, where he and President Ronald Reagan signed the
*Treaty on the Elimination of Intermediate-Range and Shorter-Range Mis-
siles*, or the INF treaty. The agreement called for the elimination of all INF
and short-range nuclear missiles (that is, missiles possessing a range between 500 and 5,500 kilometers) within a period of eighteen months, covering some 2,692 weapons in all.

In January 1988 the Department of Defense, tasked with the implementation of the INF treaty, created the On-Site Inspection Agency, or OSIA.
The mission of OSIA was to conduct inspections inside the Soviet Union
(and select Warsaw Pact nations) as well as to facilitate Soviet inspections
in the United States and select NATO nations for the purposes of verifying
compliance with the terms of the treaty. OSIA represented the new face
of the Pentagon. Gone from the mix was Richard Perle, the extraordinarily
influential assistant secretary of defense who had made a career opposing
arms control. Perle was indifferent to the issue of an INF agreement but

remained adamantly opposed to any sweeping arms control agenda, which, at the time of his resignation in March 1987, appeared to be the path the Reagan administration was headed down. Another casualty was Kenneth Adelman, the anti–arms control head of ACDA, who submitted his resignation at the end of July 1987. Like Perle, Adelman resigned over the direction the Reagan administration was taking on the matter of arms control. Unable to stop the progress toward arms control, Adelman chose not to be a part of it. But perhaps the biggest casualty of the INF treaty was the secretary of defense himself, Casper Weinberger, who tendered his resignation on November 21, 1987. Under fire from the growing Iran-*Contra* scandal, Weinberger had decided that he could no longer function effectively as secretary of defense. The pending INF treaty was simply the last straw for a hard-liner who had consistently opposed arms control agreements between the United States and the Soviet Union.[56]

With the hard-liners in the Pentagon removed, the only obstacle remaining for the INF treaty was ratification by the Senate. The Senate began hearings on the INF treaty in January 1988, with President Reagan urging a quick ratification process. The treaty was attacked by the right wing of the Republican Party, led by Jesse Helms, which condemned it on the grounds that it seriously undermined national security, in particular America's commitment to its NATO allies. Helms questioned the viability of the verification regime, continuously pointing out the extensive track record (according to Helms) of Soviet noncompliance with arms control agreements. Helms accused Reagan of "appeasement" and likened the American president to Neville Chamberlain, the British prime minister who caved in to Hitler on the issue of Czechoslovakia in 1939. Despite Helms's efforts, the outcome was never in question, as the Senate voted to approve the INF treaty, 93–5, on May 27, 1988.[57]

At the end of May President Reagan took the ratified INF treaty with him to Moscow, where he and Mikhail Gorbachev met for their fourth summit. In addition to overseeing the depositing of the articles of ratification for the INF treaty, both leaders had hoped that this summit could have witnessed the signing of a new START treaty as well. They had agreed at the December 1987 summit in Washington that they should have a goal of finalizing a START treaty before Reagan left office. However, two new members of Reagan's national security team, Defense Secretary Frank Carlucci and National Security Advisor Colin Powell, were not inclined to support a rush toward a START treaty. Although not as openly hostile to arms control as Weinberger and Poindexter, both Carlucci and Powell promoted a "go slower" approach that dismayed Secretary of State

Shultz and led Reagan, in February 1988, to conclude that a START treaty would not happen during his time as president. Shevardnadze would continue to press Shultz on the issue of START, but a sticking point had developed over the issue of sea-launched cruise missiles, with the U.S. Navy opposing any effort to limit these systems in a nuclear role.[58]

Stymied on START, Gorbachev began focusing on the issue of conventional weapons in Europe, pressuring his military to come up with a formula that would permit significant cuts in its size. This was a particularly sensitive time for Gorbachev, who had decided to terminate the Soviet involvement in Afghanistan from the beginning of his term as general secretary. He was coming under increasing pressure from within the power structures of the Soviet Union. In February 1988, during the Party Plenum, he was put on the defensive regarding his policies of glasnost and perestroika. The decision to withdraw from Afghanistan, announced in July 1987, was seen as an extension of these policies. When the initial Soviet contingents began crossing back into the Soviet Union in May 1988, Gorbachev felt particularly vulnerable to accusations of being weak. President Reagan, flush with what he perceived to be a U.S. victory in light of the significant support his administration had provided the Afghan mujahadeen, did not help Gorbachev's situation by delivering a series of speeches in which he gloated over the Soviet defeat in Afghanistan. Gorbachev complained vigorously to Secretary of State Shultz and National Security Advisor Powell. Both downplayed the president's speeches, stating that Reagan's words during the Washington summit in December 1987 should serve as a guide to where he stood on U.S.-Soviet relations. But even without the issue of Afghanistan, Reagan continued to pressure Gorbachev and the Soviets on the issue of human rights. This would serve as a sensitive issue up through the Moscow summit.[59]

In the end, the Moscow summit was more ceremony than substance. Unable to come to an agreement on START, the two leaders engaged in a series of cultural activities, including attending the Bolshoi Theater. On May 31, 1988, Ronald Reagan spoke before the students and teachers of Moscow State University, where he addressed the issue of arms control between the United States and the Soviet Union, and in particular the stalled START talks. "We had hoped that maybe, like the INF Treaty, we would have been able to sign it [a START treaty] here at this summit meeting," Reagan said. "We are both hopeful that it can be finished before I leave office which is in the coming January. But I assure you, that if it isn't, I assure that I will impress upon my successor that we must carry on until it is signed. My dream has always been that once we've started down this road, we can look forward to a day, you can look forward to a day, when there will be no more nuclear weapons in the world at all." Reagan's time in Moscow exposed him to the Russian people for the first time, and he was impressed by the experience. When someone asked him if he still believed that the Soviets were part of an "Evil Empire," Reagan responded, "No, I was talking about another time, another era."[60]

In many ways the Moscow summit marked the end of the Reagan era. His second term was up in January 1989, and soon domestic American politics would require him to pass the torch of leadership to his successor in the Republican Party, Vice President George H. W. Bush. Bush, concerned about the conservative backlash that was growing in response to Reagan's change of pace on all things Soviet, did his best to distance himself from Reagan's rosy characterizations of the Moscow summit. The vice president did not attend the summit and, shortly after the summit ended, made headlines by declaring that "the Cold War is not over."[61] Gorbachev recognized that if there were to be any major move in U.S.-Soviet relations, it would have to come from Moscow. Gorbachev facilitated this by shoring up his political base at the nineteenth All-Union Conference of the Communist Party of the Soviet Union, during which the general secretary of the Communist Party maneuvered himself to become the president of the Soviet Union.[62] President Gorbachev then turned to the Soviet military and requested that they look into the matter of unilateral military cuts of up to a million men. Gorbachev was able to consider such cuts in light of a new defensive doctrine implemented in 1987 that broke free of the former strategy of rapidly overrunning Western Europe with conventional forces in case of a war with NATO. Gorbachev had declared that such a conflict was unthinkable and was now prepared to back up his words with action.[63]

In a speech to the United Nations General Assembly on December 7, 1988, the first by a Soviet leader since Nikita Khrushchev had pounded his shoe on the podium in 1960, Gorbachev announced that the Soviet Union would begin the unilateral reduction of conventional forces by cutting 500,000 men from the ranks of the Soviet military. These were real cuts, resulting in the elimination of six tank divisions stationed in Central Europe, totalling 50,000 men and 5,000 tanks. All in all, Gorbachev would reduce the Soviet forces in Europe by 10,000 tanks, 8,500 artillery pieces, and over 800 aircraft in phased withdrawals scheduled to take place over the course of the next two years. To Gorbachev, this speech signaled an end to the Cold War and the beginning of a new era, when the Soviet Union would seek to interact with its neighbors and the world based on a foundation of ideas, not imposed by armed might.[64]

Gorbachev viewed his speech as groundbreaking, and it was. He was widely acclaimed as a visionary by the Western media and many Western politicians. But the speech was designed to influence one particular audience, the new president-elect, George H. W. Bush. Here, Gorbachev would be disappointed. Prior to delivering his speech, Gorbachev had requested an opportunity to meet with President Reagan and President-elect Bush in what amounted to a fifth summit meeting. The three leaders met on Governor's Island, in the harbor of New York City, following Gorbachev's speech. While Reagan found the ideas put forward by Gorbachev appealling, Bush was less enthusiastic, telling a disappointed Gorbachev that while he "would like to build on what President Reagan had done," he would "need a little time to review the issues" before he would be able to commit to any given course of action. Gorbachev was pushing hard for an early summit meeting between himself and Bush in order to finalize a START agreement. But Bush and his new team of advisors, including Brent Scowcroft as his national security advisor, were not so keen on an early meeting. The new president, sworn in on January 20, 1989, wanted to create a gap between the "euphoria" of the Reagan administration and the "reality" of his own.[65]

President Bush had assembled his national security team, led by Secretary of State Baker, an experienced Washington insider who had recently served under President Reagan; National Security Advisor Scowcroft, another Washington insider with Reagan administration credentials; and Secretary of Defense Richard Cheney, a conservative Republican who had served as White House chief of staff under Gerald Ford before becoming a congressman representing the state of Wyoming (Cheney's appointment actually came in April 1989, following the refusal by the Senate to confirm Bush's first choice, Texas congressman John Tower, because of allegations of misconduct). Right from the start this team refused to buy into any notion of a "new era" of U.S.-Soviet relations and instead defined policy objectives in classic Cold War terms. One of the most pressing issues facing the new Bush team, at least from its own internal point of view, was how to deal with the fallout of the INF treaty. American nuclear weapons in Europe had traditionally represented the physical manifestation of the linkage between European security and the American strategic nuclear umbrella. With INF now removed from Europe, there was a concern among many European nations that the United States was considering the complete withdrawal of nuclear weapons from Europe, thereby challenging the nuclear deterrence status quo and disrupting the basis of European security.

In order to offset European concerns, the Bush administration embarked on a program of modernizing the eighty-eight *Lance* short-range nuclear missiles stationed in West Germany. This effort was strongly criticized by Gorbachev, who was pushing for an agreement to eliminate even these short-range nuclear missiles. Rather than engage the Soviets in a discussion on short-range missiles, the Bush team decided to announce a new sweeping arms control initiative of its own, calling for the total withdrawal of all U.S. and Soviet ground forces from Europe. The Soviets countered by proposing that both sides set an equal cap on military hardware in Europe and seek to reduce their respective ground forces by 25 percent. The Soviets pointed out that cuts in conventional forces of this level required a basis of trust that would be undermined if the United States went forward with the *Lance* missile upgrade. In contrast to the momentum created during the final years of the Reagan administration, the Bush administration had brought U.S.-Soviet relations to a standstill when it came to meaningful arms control.[66]

A critical ingredient to getting U.S.-Soviet relations back on track was the need for a policy review process that would define in precise terms what the Bush administration's policy objectives were vis-à-vis the Soviet Union. A first cut at such a review, circulated in late March 1989, was rejected by Scowcroft and Baker as "unimaginative." The lack of a viable "policy review" was seen by Gorbachev as a deliberate "braking mechanism" designed to slow the pace of progress between the United States and Soviet Union. At the same time, George Kennan, the father of the containment policy targeting the Soviet Union and perhaps the most respected Sovietologist alive, testified that the Bush administration was being unresponsive to the recent spate of "encouraging" overtures from the Soviet Union, noting that the time for viewing the Soviet Union as a military threat "has clearly passed." Even former president Reagan fretted to the media about the lack of decisiveness within the Bush administration when it came to the Soviet Union.[67]

Brent Scowcroft did not see the need for any bold moves with regard to U.S.-Soviet relations. In an appearance on ABC's *Meet the Press*, the national security advisor declared that the recent developments involving the Soviet Union underscored the fact that "the West had won" the Cold War. As such, there was no need for any "dramatic change" in U.S. policy toward the Soviet Union. Shortly after Scowcroft made that statement, the Soviet Union began its gradual slide toward oblivion. On April 9, 1989, Soviet troops violently suppressed a demonstration by over 10,000 Georgians in the streets of Tbilisi. Over 200 people were injured, and 19 were killed. While Gorbachev wrestled with this development, the Warsaw Pact began to display cracks in its foundation, as the Polish government recognized the labor movement Solidarity, led by Lech Walensa, and began collaborating with the Polish dissident to reform the Polish economy and political system. In this sea of turbulence all the United States could offer was a policy of "wait and see."

Gorbachev wasn't in a "wait and see" mode. In early May Secretary of State Baker flew to Moscow, where he met with Foreign Minister Shevardnadze and, later, President Gorbachev. With Gorbachev was the former Soviet chief of staff, Marshall Sergei Akhromeyev, who now served as Gorbachev's principal military advisor. Gorbachev proceeded to unveil a dramatic new unilateral action, a decision to remove five hundred short-range nuclear missiles from Europe. This move placed the United States in a difficult political position vis-à-vis NATO, and in particular West Germany. NATO was moving toward the deployment of upgraded *Lance* missiles, something Germany opposed, since if these missiles were ever used in time of war, they would be detonated on German soil. Void of any formal policy guidance, Baker was unable to adequately articulate a response to Gorbachev's announcement, again creating the perception of an obstructive America in the face of Soviet efforts at genuine disarmament.[68]

The Bush administration's policy review was finally completed on May 12, 1989, in the form of a seven-page document known as National Security Directive 23, or NSD-23. While the document itself wasn't signed by Bush until September, its main theme was the notion that "containment" of the Soviet Union was never viewed as an end in itself and that the United States now had to look "beyond containment" in an effort to help integrate the Soviet Union into the international system. "Beyond containment" compelled the Bush team to formulate a dramatic proposal of its own to counter the unilateral moves put forward by Gorbachev on conventional force and short-range missile reductions. NATO was deadlocked on the issue of *Lance* modernization. Bush refused to be pushed into accepting a so-called Third Zero, meaning an agreement to eliminate short-range nuclear missiles, because of the damage it would do to NATO at a time when, with the fracturing of Eastern Europe, the United States needed a strong, unified alliance in Europe. At a NATO summit meeting in late May, President Bush announced his own proposal, which called for 20 percent cuts in the ground forces of both the Soviet Union and the United States in Europe and an agreement to delay the modernization of the *Lance* force as well as to discuss short-range missile force reductions, but not elimination. Bush also called for a conventional forces treaty to be negotiated within six months and implemented no later than 1993. Bush's proposal was met with acclaim by the

NATO members, a good start to the era of "postcontainment" relations with the Soviet Union.[69]

The postcontainment era was more than simple rhetoric. The reality was that the state of affairs that had governed Cold War relations between East and West was rapidly changing, creating conditions for events that were unpredictable and heavy with consequence. In March 1989 student demonstrations broke out throughout China, culminating in tens of thousands of students seizing control of Tiananmen Square in Beijing. By May the Chinese authorities had declared martial law and ordered the Red Army to regain control of the square. On June 3, the Red Army did just that, sending armored units against the students in a violent crackdown resulting in the deaths of hundreds of Chinese demonstrators. The crackdown on dissent in China was widely condemned by the United States. It was also viewed by many in Eastern Europe as a warning as to how far they would be able to push the old communist system before it, too, turned on them.

In June 1989, President Bush announced a new set of proposals designed to help create the conditions under which a START agreement might be finalized between the United States and the Soviet Union. Known as the Verification and Stability Initiative, the proposal called for on-site inspection at missile production facilities involved in the manufacture of strategic missiles (similar to the kind of inspections already underway as part of the INF treaty), an exchange of data on the strategic missile forces of each side, the banning of all encryption of telemetry relating to missile tests, and other confidence-building measures that could be incorporated into a later treaty document.[70]

However, the atmosphere in which arms control negotiations normally were conducted, amid Cold War–inspired superpower stability, no longer existed. Events in Poland and Hungary, two Warsaw Pact nations, were progressing to the point that President Bush was able to visit both nations in July 1989 and was greeted by hundreds of thousands of people anxious for change. In August 1989, the Lithuanian parliament declared the 1940 Soviet annexation of the Baltic States illegal, setting the stage for the declaration of independence of the Baltic States (Lithuania, Latvia, and Estonia) from the Soviet Union. That same month, after a personal intervention from Gorbachev, the Polish government announced the formation of a coalition government that included Lech Walesa's Solidarity movement.

In an effort to maintain the momentum needed for a successful arms control negotiation, Secretary of State Baker invited Soviet Foreign Minister Shevardnadze to his vacation home in Jackson Hole, Wyoming, for a summit. There Shevardnadze dropped the previous Soviet linkage between SDI and START, although he warned that the Soviets might withdraw from a START agreement if the United States did not abide by the ABM treaty (this was a warning about any attempt on the part of the United States to interpret the ABM treaty in any manner that permitted the deployment of SDI). The United States also dropped its insistence that all mobile missiles be banned under START, contingent on the Soviets agreeing to specific verification measures specifically for mobile missiles. Two of the major hurdles concerning a START agreement were thus overcome. And in respect to President Bush's Verification and Stability Initiative, Baker and Shevardnadze signed an agreement on the principles of implementation of the proposal. But the main thrust of the Jackson Hole meeting was the issue of change in Eastern Europe and the Soviet Union. The two men verbally sparred over the situation in the Baltics, in Germany, and inside the Soviet Union itself, where thousands of coal miners had paralyzed Soviet industry by holding a massive strike unprecedented in modern Soviet history. Baker told Shevardnadze that change was coming, perhaps faster than any of them could possibly know, and that it was important to manage this change without violence.[71]

Mikhail Gorbachev shared Baker's concerns about violence. Having already intervened in Poland to facilitate the peaceful transition of power from a communist government to a coalition government containing noncommunists, Gorbachev next turned his attentions to Germany and the vexing issue of unification. In early October 1989 Gorbachev visited East Berlin, where he announced that policy with regard to East Germany was made in Berlin, not Moscow. On November 9, following weeks of demonstrations and protests, the East German government announced that its citizens were free to visit West Germany and West Berlin. Soon East German citizens were scaling the Berlin Wall, greeted on the other side by crowds of enthusiastic West Berliners. Over the next weeks, the Berlin Wall was dismantled, and the process of German unification began. On November 28, taking matters into his own hands, German Chancellor Helmut Kohl unveiled a plan for German reunification. The issue of Germany's future, and indeed the future of all of Europe, took center stage when, on December 2, 1989, Gorbachev and Bush met for their first summit meeting in Malta. While the two leaders discussed the importance of moving forward on both a START (with Gorbachev again raising the issue of sea-launched cruise missiles as being of particular interest to the Soviets) and a conventional forces reduction in Europe (CFE) treaty, arms control was pushed aside as the leaders of the world's two largest nuclear arsenals instead discussed the end of the Cold War and the peaceful dismantling of the Warsaw Pact and, to a lesser extent, the Soviet Union.

Even as Bush and Gorbachev met, events continued to unfold in Europe at a rapid pace. On December 5, Czechoslovakia announced the formation of a noncommunist government. The next day the East German leadership resigned. On December 20 the Lithuanian Communist Party declared its independence from Moscow, and on December 25, following a revolution in Romania, the Romanian leader, Nicolae Ceausescu, was executed in what was to be the only violent change of government to occur in Europe.[72]

As the Soviet Union and United States entered 1990, the issue of arms control continued to languish in the face of the tremendous change sweeping over Europe. Whereas agreements like START and CFE once dominated the relations of these two nations, compelling armies of bureaucrats and diplomats to contend with the complexities associated with missile throw weights and MIRVs, the context of a postcontainment Soviet Union pushed such discussions to the sidelines. It was not as if either side wanted to ignore START or CFE. Rather, these issues began to pale when compared with the looming crisis of national survival faced by Gorbachev when it came to the future of the Soviet Union. The focus of attention was on the situation in the Baltics, where the three republics were clamoring for independence, and on the issue of German unification, which was threatening to rip apart decades of European balance-of-power issues defined by NATO and the Warsaw Pact. And in August 1990 a new complicating factor was added when Saddam Hussein, the president of Iraq, ordered his troops to invade and occupy neighboring Kuwait, threatening global energy supplies. Representatives from the United States and the Soviet Union actively cooperated on all these issues, but it was becoming increasingly apparent that the Soviet Union no longer carried the same clout as before. America was emerging as the dominant world power.

In September 1990, as U.S. forces began flowing into the Middle East to confront Saddam, Baker and Shevardnadze tried their best to finalize a CFE agreement (START was left off the agenda as being "too difficult"). But even as they wrestled with Cold War–era formulations, the world around them changed forever. On October 3, West and East Germany united, bringing Germany together for the first time since the end of the Second World War. The Warsaw Pact was collapsing. When presidents Bush and Gorbachev finally sat down in Paris on November 19 to sign the CFE treaty (together with representatives from NATO and the Warsaw Pact), each knew he was entering into an agreement that had been largely overcome by events. Europe was no longer the center of the world's attention. That claim was now held by the Middle East, where a coalition of nations, acting under the Charter of the United Nations, faced off against Iraq.

On January 17, 1991, the United States and its allies initiated military action against Iraq. By the end of February, the fighting was over. Iraq had been decisively defeated, and Kuwait had been liberated. The world was now confronted with the reality that the United States stood alone as the sole remaining superpower. Although the Soviet Union was still physically intact, the war with Iraq demonstrated the clear limits of its influence, both military and political. While the issue of nuclear arms reductions between the United States and the Soviet Union was still of paramount importance, new problems, symbolized by Iraq's arsenal of weapons of mass destruction (chemical and biological weapons, as well as a nascent nuclear weapons program), were capturing the imagination of the world. The United Nations Security Council, in April 1991, passed a resolution calling for the disarmament of Iraq's WMD and dispatching international inspectors into Iraq to carry out that mission. On May 10, President Bush, spurred into action by the conflict with Iraq, which highlighted the threat posed by chemical weapons, pushed for the conclusion of a Chemical Weapons Convention (CWC) by the end of 1991 and committed the United States to the unconditional destruction of all of its chemical weapons stocks and production facilities within a ten-year period.

This new focus on chemical weapons did not mean that the Bush administration no longer cared about START or CFE. The main problem with START rested in the minutia of details that bogged down the negotiations. The U.S. side, in particular, was seeking exemptions for a new class of nonnuclear ALCMs, arcane accounting rules for ALCM-equipped heavy bombers, and a cap on SLCMs combined with a mutually binding procedure by which each side would declare what kinds of ships and submarines carried SLCMs. The United States also sought on-site inspection-based verification for what it termed "nondeployed" mobile missiles, focusing on missile stage production facilities, and a cap of 800 to 1,200 on warheads permitted to be carried on mobile missiles, as well as a renewed focus on "heavy" missiles, limiting the Soviets to 1,540 warheads mounted on 154 missiles. Just how entrenched the U.S. negotiating position was in terms of old-school thinking was reflected by the continued interest in the "Backfire" bomber, with the United States seeking new Soviet assurances that this bomber would not be converted for strategic use.[73]

The inconsistency between the events unfolding in Europe and the Soviet Union and the hard-line positions taken by the United States on arms control was rooted in decades of mistrust and paranoia. It wasn't just arms control policy that was influenced, but also how the United States planned to use nuclear weapons. A review of the nuclear weapons employment plan by the Bush administration brought about little change to the Prevailing strategy set forth in the Reagan-era NSDD-13, other than to reduce the number of targets in the Soviet Union in anticipation of proposed cuts in strategic missiles expected to take place as result of a START agreement. Regardless of the rhetoric of goodwill generated by the leaders of the United States and the Soviet Union, America was still positioned to wage total nuclear war with the Soviet Union on the same level that existed a decade prior, at the height of the Cold War. A study completed in March 1990 called on the United States to focus on non-Soviet threats emerging in the Third World, particularly in the arena of WMD, and used this emerging threat not only to justify the continued possession of nuclear weapons by the United States but also to develop a new range of nuclear weapons designed to deal with it.[74]

After the Gulf War, in the spring of 1991, Secretary of Defense Cheney issued a new Nuclear Weapons Employment Plan, which began to shift nuclear targeting away from the Soviet Union and onto Third World nations suspected of possessing WMD capabilities. Building on this new direction, the U.S. nuclear weapons design labs began submitting proposals for the development of a new generation of smaller nuclear weapons designed for these threats, as opposed to the old Soviet threat. These recommendations were backed by a high-level study group commissioned by the U.S. Air Force's Strategic Air Command in the summer of 1991, the so-called Reed Panel (named after former secretary of the Air Force Thomas Reed, who headed the study). The Reed Panel called for a new targeting strategy that had the United States shift its nuclear targeting to Third World nations deemed either to possess or capable of possessing WMD. The panel also recommended that the United States consider the adoption of a principle of nuclear preemption in situations in which U.S. conventional forces were threatened with defeat. Recognizing that the massive nuclear weapons currently in the U.S. arsenal were not useful in this new strategy, the Reed Panel called for the creation of an entirely new generation of sub-kiloton nuclear weapons that could readily be used anywhere in the world without fear of widespread nuclear contamination.[75]

Fortunately, President Bush chose a more pragmatic approach to the issue of nuclear weapons. The path was not an easy one, however. By the end of 1990, the START talks were once again bogged down, this time over the issue of warhead "downloading," which involved reducing the number of warheads carried by a specific missile type. After years of struggling with the issue of MIRVs, the Soviet Union finally agreed to drastically cut back on the number of warheads its missiles carried. As such, an SLBM originally designed to carry seven warheads would now be downloaded to three, or an ICBM designed to carry three warheads would be downloaded to carry one. Skeptics in the Bush administration, led by National Security Advisor Scowcroft, were concerned about a potential "breakout" scenario in which the Soviets would suddenly rearm by "uploading" their missiles with previously downloaded warheads. Scowcroft wanted specific limits on the missile types that could be subjected to downloading; all other missiles would be counted against their existing warhead capability. Scowcroft's hard-line position compelled the U.S. START negotiator, Richard Burt, to resign in frustration in January 1991 after he tried, and failed, to jump-start the negotiations by seeking a specific limit on the number of warheads that could be downloaded.[76]

In discussions with Bush administration officials in Washington in May 1991, Foreign Minister Primakov acknowledged that a "new" Soviet Union would in fact be a smaller Soviet Union, since the complete secession of six republics—the Baltics, Georgia, Armenia, and Moldova—was all but certain. And the election of a major Gorbachev rival, Boris Yeltsin, as the president of Russia on June 12 further eroded the viability of a strong, viable Soviet Union. The "Grand Bargain" sought by the Bush administration was threatening to tear the Soviet Union apart. By the end of June, former foreign minister Shevardnadze was warning American visitors to Moscow of the real danger of a coup in which hard-liners would seize control of the government and assume emergency powers in order to reverse the chaos that prevailed throughout the Soviet Union.[77]

Under pressure to complete a START agreement in time for a U.S.-Soviet summit in Moscow scheduled for the end of July 1991, Scowcroft finally conceded on the issue of downloading, allowing for multiple missile types but a limited number of warheads. This good news was offset by an embarrassing development in London, where the G-7 economic summit turned down the Soviet Union's application for membership. When President Bush traveled to Moscow on July 29, he was confronted with a growing schism between Russian President Boris Yeltsin and Gorbachev. Bush and Gorbachev were able to stage one last meeting in the grand style of past summits involving momentous arms control agreements, signing the START treaty in the spectacular setting of Saint Vladimir's Hall in the Kremlin in a ceremony on July 31, which saw each leader using a pen crafted from metal taken from missiles destroyed as part of the INF treaty.[78]

Less than three weeks later, on August 18, while Gorbachev was on vacation in the Crimea, a group of hard-liners led by Vice President Gennadi

Yanayev seized control of the Soviet government and announced the creation of a State Committee for the State of Emergency. Russian President Boris Yeltsin immediately denounced the coup. Soviet troops were called out but were met by hundreds of thousands of protesters. Brief clashes killed three demonstrators before the troops were pulled back. In a matter of days the coup collapsed, and Gorbachev returned to Moscow. However, the situation in Moscow, and indeed throughout all of Russia and the Soviet Union, was forever changed. Yeltsin had emerged as the key player, and it was clear that Gorbachev's days as head of state were numbered.

In an effort to help strengthen Gorbachev's standing with the Soviet defense industry, Bush pushed for a new round of arms reductions. On September 27, 1991, Bush announced that the United States would eliminate all of its ground-based tactical nuclear weapons. This involved withdrawing all ground-launched, short-range weapons deployed overseas, including tactical nuclear weapons deployed on U.S. Navy surface ships, attack submarines, and land-based naval aircraft. Bush did reserve the right to redeploy these weapons if a crisis unfolded that warranted such an action. He had hoped his action would spur a similar response from Gorbachev, and he was not disappointed. On October 5, the Soviet leader announced his own cuts in tactical nuclear weapons, declaring his intention to eliminate all nuclear artillery munitions, nuclear warheads for tactical missiles, and nuclear mines; remove all tactical nuclear weapons from Soviet surface ships and multipurpose (non-SLBM) submarines; and separate nuclear warheads from air defense missiles, putting the warheads in central storage.[79]

But these measures proved to be too little, too late to save the beleagured Soviet economy and, with it, the political system. By the end of October 1991 the Soviet Union was bankrupt, fiscally and politically. One by one, the republics that comprised the Soviet Union voted to secede. On December 1, Ukraine voted to leave the Union. On December 8, Boris Yeltsin met with the leaders of Ukraine and Belarus in Minsk and announced the creation of the Commonwealth of Independent States. Gorbachev resigned as the president of the Soviet Union on December 25, 1991. The Soviet Union was finished. In its place was an almagamation of newly independent states, many of which possessed nuclear weapons and none of which had a coherent foreign or national security policy in place to effectively deal with a situation that could easily spin out of control. After years of striving to contain Soviet power, the United States now found itself face to face with the difficult problem of managing the absence of Soviet power. As one commentator warned, "We will miss the Cold War." How America and its leaders would deal with this problem would define global security issues for decades to come.

CHAPTER 14

NEGLECT
AND DECAY

New Year's Day 1992 found a world radically transformed and yet very much the same. No longer were the world's leaders operating in a bipolar environment, pulled by competing centers of gravity in Washington and Moscow. There was no longer talk of containment or postcontainment. There was no longer a Soviet Union. The sole remaining superpower, the United States, was left basking in the glow of ideological "total victory." But the flush of victory faded fast as the reality of a post-Soviet world set in. The nuclear weapons that existed in the Soviet Union in 1991 still existed in 1992, but this time under even more uncertain political leadership. Moscow no longer served as the single address for resolving arms control issues. The collapse of the Soviet Union left strategic nuclear weapons under the control of not only Moscow but Kiev (Ukraine), Minsk (Belarus), and Alma Ata (Kazakhstan). Tactical nuclear weapons by the thousands were scattered across the fourteen time zones that had been the Soviet Union. And nuclear weapons were not the only threat present. The considerable chemical and biological warfare resources of the Soviet Union were likewise fractured, and in the political atmosphere of the post–Gulf War era, these weapons categories were assuming a new importance when it came to disarmament and nonproliferation.

With the Soviet "forest" now removed, America was able to see what lay under the canopy of the global nonproliferation problem. Nuclear issues loomed large, leading off with the matter of controlling the former Soviet Union's massive arsenal. Mikhail Gorbachev had worked closely with Russian President Boris Yeltsin in the final months of the Soviet Union's existence to ensure a safe and orderly transfer of control over the Soviet nuclear weapons in Russia. While similar arrangements were made with political leaders in both Ukraine and Belarus, it was the intention of both Russia and the United States to see all former Soviet strategic weapons located outside the territory of Russia either destroyed or transferred to the control of Russia. The U.S. Congress passed legislation in the fall of 1991, the Cooperative Threat Reduction (CTR) Act (also known as the Nunn-Lugar Act, so named after the two senators who sponsored the legislation).[1] Operating on a budget of $400 million, which was funding previously allocated to the Pentagon, the CTR program focused on weapon destruction and security in the former Soviet Union. By early 1992 an ambitious plan had been drafted that had the United States, in cooperation with the former Soviet Republics, undertake a five-step program designed to inventory and secure all nuclear, chemical, and biological weapons in the former Soviet Union, dismantle the weapons, place the relevant materials in storage, and clean up the facilities involved in the manufacturing of these weapons.

The Russian government early on reaffirmed its commitment to nuclear disarmament. On January 29, 1992, President Yeltsin expanded on former Soviet president Gorbachev's reduction in tactical nuclear weapons, promising to eliminate one-third of Russia's sea-based tactical nuclear weapons and one-half of its surface-to-air nuclear warheads. Yeltsin also committed to eliminating one-half of Russia's aerial tactical nuclear weapons (bombs and missile warheads) and, if the United States responded in kind, stated that Russia was willing to remove the other half and place it in central storage facilities. It seemed that the drawdown of tactical nuclear weapons by the United States and Russia was going smoothly. By the end of 1992, the United States had completed its promised reductions and withdrawals. Likewise, by July 1992 all tactical nuclear weapons deployed in the Republics of the former Soviet Union had been returned to Russia and Russian control.[2]

During the drawn-out collapse of the Soviet Union, President Bush and Secretary of State James Baker had repeatedly assured Gorbachev that the United States would be sensitive to Russia's concerns during this period, especially when it came to matters of national security. Gorbachev's commitment to not only a unified Germany but also its inclusion as a member of NATO was of critical importance to the success of that sensitive process. But with Gorbachev's support came an implicit understanding that the United States would not exploit Russian weakness, either by seeking unilateral strategic advantage or by expanding NATO in a manner that threatened Russia or Russian interests. President Bush had convinced Gorbachev that the United States was a benign superpower, without territorial ambition or ideological objectives beyond encouraging the kind of freedoms and reforms that Gorbachev himself espoused. Maintaining this image was of vital importance for the future of U.S.-Russian relations.[3]

On January 28, 1992, President Bush delivered his State of the Union address to Congress. He spoke of a "dramatic and deeply promising time in our history and in the history of man on Earth"—the death of communism—and, moreover, "the biggest thing that has happened in the world in my life. . . . By the grace of God, America won the cold war." Bush emphasized that point on several occasions: "the cold war didn't end; it was won." He spoke of American victory, while the loser in the conflict was portrayed in stark terms: "imperial communism," "avowed enemy," and a "failed system." Even as the Soviet Union faded away into history, Bush continued to push Congress for funding of a Cold War relic, SDI, citing "new threats." America, the president declared, was the undisputed leader of the world and therefore must continue to behave as such.[4]

Gorbachev and, to a lesser extent, Yeltsin became concerned when they heard the president's speech. By defining the U.S.-Russian relationship in terms of winners and losers at such an early stage, Bush was creating the conditions for a Russian backlash. Already there were indications that the Russians were not so willing to concede defeat. On the issue of the CFE treaty, which entered into force in July 1992, Russia had concerns because the treaty was designed to deal with two equal "blocs" (NATO and the Warsaw Pact), but upon implementation, there was only one bloc (NATO), an ill-defined mess that was the former Warsaw Pact (many of whose members were making their desire to join NATO known), and Russia. Russia, especially its military, was extremely sensitive to the issue of NATO expansion and was looking to Washington for some sign of restraint. Bush's "victory" speech was not the sign they were looking for. Likewise, the one-sided American victory in Iraq further highlighted the difference between the modern U.S. military and its frazzled Russian counterpart. Many Russian officers were already looking back on the former Soviet era as a time of pride and strength.[5]

Although taking a backseat to economic and democratic reforms, arms control remained on the agenda of U.S.-Russian relations. In his State of the Union address, President Bush had outlined a plan for reductions in

U.S. and Russian strategic nuclear arsenals of up to 50 percent. In a reversal on past policy, Boris Yeltsin indicated that Russia would be supportive of joint work in missile defense, removing a critical obstacle in the way of Bush's vision of deploying a viable SDI (although many U.S. defense analysts questioned the utility of sharing SDI with the Russians). On June 17, 1992, President Bush and President Yeltsin met in the first U.S.-Russian summit since the collapse of the Soviet Union. Held in Washington, DC, the summit had an ambitious agenda, which included the two leaders agreeing on a joint text of a START follow-on that sought the elimination of MIRVs and deeper cuts in strategic missiles. The goal was to eliminate all heavy missiles, reduce the numbers of SLBMs to around 1,700, and lower the number of nuclear warheads on each side to between 2,000 and 2,500.[6]

By July 1992 the United States was able to present to the Russians a draft treaty text for a follow-on START, known as START-2. The Russians responded to these proposals in September 1992, noting some concerns about what Russia was being asked to do (namely, eliminate all of its heavy missiles). In November, after a series of high-level consultations between U.S. and Russian officials, which addressed Russia's concerns (the heavy missiles would be eliminated as planned, but the United States would also "download" its MIRV-capable ICBMs and SLBMs so as to avoid any issue of retained superior capability), the Russians turned over to the United States their own version of a draft treaty text. In a series of meetings held in Geneva in December, the draft treaty text was turned into a joint agreed text, and on January 3, 1993, President Bush met with Boris Yeltsin in Moscow, where they signed the START-2, which mandated the elimination of all MIRVs and sought deep cuts in the number of nuclear warheads on each side. The rapid pace of the treaty process, from conceptualization in June 1992 to treaty signature in January 1993, was stunning when compared to the drawn-out processes of the past. On January 15, 1993, President Bush submitted START-2 to the Senate for ratification.[7]

The START-2 was a great success for proponents of arms control. Nevertheless, there were other challenges that needed addressing, including the issue of nuclear testing. During the era of superpower-driven nuclear deterrence, the concept of a comprehensive nuclear test ban had been floated repeatedly, only to be sunk by those in the nuclear weapons bureaucracy of both the United States and the Soviet Union who insisted on being able to continue nuclear tests for the purposes of maintaining the viability and reliability of the current nuclear weapons arsenal, as well as designing new generations of nuclear weapons optimized for an ever-changing global environment. Thus, when former Soviet President Mikhail Gorbachev announced a unilateral nuclear test ban moratorium in August 1985, on the fortieth anniversary of the dropping of the atomic bomb on Japan by the United States, there was no reciprocal move on the part of the Reagan administration. The Soviet moratorium lasted until October 1987, when under pressure from Soviet weapons designers, Gorbachev permitted renewed testing.[8] When Reagan left office, Gorbachev again launched a unilateral moratorium on nuclear testing, this time from November 1989 to October 1990, and again met with no response from President Bush, who had authorized a series of over eighty nuclear weapons tests extending into 1992. Even when Gorbachev stopped Soviet nuclear testing for good (the last test was conducted on October 24, 1990), the United States continued its own nuclear tests.[9]

President Bush was careful to ensure that all U.S. testing conformed with America's treaty obligations under the Partial Test-Ban Treaty (PTBT). The PTBT sought "the discontinuance of all test explosions of nuclear weapons for all time," but the continued nuclear testing by the United States (a signatory member), and France and China, neither of whom had signed the treaty, made it difficult to achieve this goal. However, on August 5, 1988, on the twenty-fifth anniversary of the PTBT, an initiative was taken by several nonnuclear weapons states to amend the PTBT into a comprehensive test ban treaty. Bush and Gorbachev had discussed such a treaty on a bilateral basis, but now it was being pursued in a multilateral forum. By May 1989 a total of forty-one nations, including India and Pakistan, were asking for the convening of an amendment conference, and in January 1991 it took place in New York City. Gorbachev took advantage of this stage to press home his desire for a comprehensive test ban treaty. Only the United States and the United Kingdom, both of whom had veto power over any amendments proposed, were opposed.[10]

The United States and the United Kingdom were looking forward to a successful NPT Review Conference in September 1990. The NPT itself was coming up for extension in 1995. Past NPT Review Conferences had confronted the issue of Article VI noncompliance by the nuclear weapons states. Given the success in disarmament that took place between 1985 and 1990 (the INF treaty and work toward a START), the Bush administration believed it was well positioned to shore up the Article VI problems and help make a push for a successful NPT renewal process in 1995. The PTBT amendment process, highlighting as it did the reality of a U.S.-U.K. nuclear weapons program seeking to entrench itself through continued testing, threatened the NPT Review Conference. Indeed, when the conference convened in September 1990, there was recognition given for the important disarmament work that had been conducted by the United States and the Soviet Union. But the NPT Review Conference was decidedly split over the issue of a comprehensive test ban treaty, just as the Bush administration had feared. The failure to resolve that issue loomed large as the 1995 NPT extension deadline approached.[11]

The pressures brought to bear by the amendment conference (which was recessed due to U.S.-U.K. intransigence) prompted both France and China to announce their respective moratoriums on nuclear testing. Indeed, France and China had attended the 1990 NPT Review Conference as observers, signaling their respective interest in nuclear nonproliferation.[12] While the Bush administration remained indifferent to this international maneuvering, the U.S. Congress did not. In September 1992 Congress cut all funding for nuclear testing from the U.S. budget, thereby halting nuclear tests by both the United States and the United Kingdom (who used U.S. facilities). Bush threatened to veto this legislation but held off until after the 1992 presidential election. As 1992 came to a close, there was no nuclear test program in place anywhere in the world, but there was also no treaty vehicle to monitor and enforce this ban. The lack of such a treaty threatened the one vehicle that existed to combat nuclear proliferation: the NPT.

The news on the nuclear nonproliferation front wasn't all bad. Back in September 1989, South African President F. W. de Klerk ordered the dismantling of not only apartheid but also South Africa's covert nuclear weapons program, which had managed to produce a half dozen uranium-type bombs in great secrecy (although many nations suspected it). A year later, in September 1990, Brazil's President de Mello closed down a site in Brazil that was intended for use as a nuclear test facility. The next month, the Brazilian leader formally declared that Brazil had been pursuing nuclear weapons but that the program was being shut down. On November 28 Brazil and Argentina signed the second Foz do Iguacu declaration, in which both nations committed to carrying out nuclear work that was exclusively civilian in nature.[13]

In June 1991 France announced that it would join the NPT as a nuclear weapons state. June also witnessed the full dismantling of South Africa's nuclear weapons program under IAEA supervision. On July 10 South Africa joined the NPT as a nonnuclear weapons state, the first former nuclear power to do so. In July 1991 Brazil and Argentina established a joint agency for the control of nuclear materials and followed this action by entering into an agreement with the IAEA to allow full-scope safeguards inspections for Brazilian and Argentinean nuclear facilities. On August 10, 1991, China announced that it, too, would join the NPT as a nuclear weapons state, and in January 1992 North Korea joined the NPT, agreeing to allow IAEA safeguard inspections of its nuclear facilities. On May 23, 1992, the Lisbon Protocol to the START was signed by Belarus, Kazakhstan, Russia, and Ukraine (all representing the nuclear-armed successor states to the Soviet Union) and by the United States. The Protocol required Belarus, Kazakhstan, and Ukraine to come into compliance with the NPT as nonnuclear weapons states as soon as possible.[14]

This positive momentum notwithstanding, the IAEA and the NPT safeguards system had suffered a setback over the issue of Iraq, which had carried out an expansive nuclear weapons program, including several nuclear enrichment efforts, while being monitored by the IAEA. Israel continued to operate outside the framework of the NPT, all the while expanding its secret nuclear weapons program, a source of constant tension in the volatile Middle East. Pakistan and India were also posing a serious proliferation problem. After stealing nuclear enrichment designs from Europe, Pakistan had, by 1983, successfully "cold tested" (meaning no fissile material was used) a nuclear weapons design, and by 1992 both Pakistan and India had small but growing nuclear arsenals that were aimed at one another.[15]

The Iran-Iraq War of the 1980s highlighted the continued threat posed by chemical weapons. Even though chemical weapons were not used by Iraq during the 1991 Gulf War, their existence, together with Iraq's biological and nuclear weapons programs, led to the creation of an inspection regime, the United Nations Special Commission (UNSCOM), tasked with accounting for and destroying Iraq's proscribed weapons and their associated programs. But the mandate of UNSCOM only covered Iraq. There was a pressing need for a more global chemical disarmament regime. Superpower politics had complicated any meaningful movement toward a global chemical weapons ban, but with the Soviet Union dissolved, the United Nations Conference on Disarmament, which had been working on the issue since 1968 (organized at that time as the Eighteen-Nation Disarmament Committee), was able to submit a draft chemical weapons treaty (Convention on the Prohibition of the Development, Production, Stockpiling and Use of Chemical Weapons and on Their Destruction) to the UN General Assembly in September 1992. The General Assembly approved the treaty in November 1992, and on January 13, 1993, the Chemical Weapons Convention (CWC) was opened for signature in Paris. The CWC was a more substantive arms control and verification vehicle than its counterpart, the Biological and Toxin Weapons Convention (BWTC), which was signed in 1972 and entered into force in 1975. Unlike the BWTC, the CWC had a significant on-site inspection capability that allowed for both scheduled and challenge ("surprise") inspections. With the signing of the CWC, there was hope that the BWTC could be amended so that it, too, would have a meaningful verification regime.[16]

In addition to the arms control mechanisms for nuclear, chemical, and biological weapons, attention had also been given to their means of delivery, in particular ballistic missiles. In 1987 seven leading industrial nations agreed to create a mechanism for curbing the proliferation of "unmanned delivery vehicles," a euphemism for ballistic missiles and remotely piloted aircraft capable of delivering nuclear weapons, focusing on the capability to deliver a five-hundred-kilogram payload (deemed to be the lower threshold for a viable nuclear device) distances over five hundred kilometers (a range these nations determined to represent strategic, as opposed to battlefield, capability). The United States, Great Britain, France, Canada, Japan, Italy, and West Germany were all parties to this agreement, known as the Missile Technology Control Regime (MTCR). The MTCR was successful early on in helping curb nascent military missile programs in Egypt, Argentina, Brazil, South Africa, South Korea, and Taiwan. In July 1992 the MTCR expanded its scope, largely because of the 1991 Iraq War, to include all "unmanned" aerial vehicles capable of carrying any weapon of mass destruction, including nuclear, chemical, or biological, regardless of range or payload restrictions.[17]

America, and the world, emerged from the demise of the Soviet Union with an arsenal of nonproliferation tools. As the world's sole remaining superpower, America had assumed a leadership role for issues pertaining to arms control, disarmament, and nonproliferation. The administration of President George H. W. Bush was struggling with how best to respond to this new era of post–Cold War complexity. That the United States would assume a major leadership role was without dispute. The question of whether this leadership position would be unilateral, with the United States filling the void created by the end of the Soviet Union, or multilateral, with the United States working with other nations to share roles and responsibilities, was at the center of an internal policy review conducted by the Bush administration following the Gulf War of 1991.

The Pentagon took the lead in formulating policy guidance and in February 1992 put forward a draft document entitled "FY [Fiscal Year] 94–99 Defense Planning Guidance," or DPG. The DPG had been requested by Secretary of Defense Cheney and was drafted by two of his deputies, "Scooter" Libby and Paul Wolfowitz. The document started out by acknowledging the new reality of a post-Soviet world, noting that the United States and the West no longer faced a substantive threat from the former republics of the Soviet Union, including Russia, and that no threat was likely to reemerge within a period of several years, and then not without considerable warning beforehand. The DPG noted that the demise of the Soviet Union might encourage other regional powers around the world to become more aggressive, but in a somewhat self-congratulatory tone dismissed these concerns by underscoring America's dominant post–Gulf War military strength as a likely source of deterrence.[18]

The goal of the United States, the DPG stated, was to prevent the emergence of any new "global competitor" by dominating regions critical to American interests and meeting any emerging threat at a lower level of conflict than the United States had been preparing for during the Cold War. The U.S. military would be used to prevent the domination of key regions by a hostile power. With regard to the former Soviet Union, the DPG stated, the United States should support the development of democratic institutions while hedging against the possibility that democracy would fail and other, potentially hostile forms of government would emerge instead. The key element in containing any post-Soviet power, whether from Russia alone or in conjunction with other former Soviet republics, would be to maintain NATO as a viable organization. This would serve two goals. First, NATO would act as a bulwark against any potential hostile nation or group of nations coming out of Eurasia. Second, NATO would serve to undermine any effort at creating a "Europe-only" security arrangement. The United States needed NATO, especially its American-dominated integrated command structure, to guarantee American political, military, and economic influence in Europe in the new post-Soviet era. Ominously, the DPG concluded that should there reemerge a threat from a post-Soviet Eurasia, NATO should seek to defend itself in Eastern Europe and not wait for any direct threat against Western Europe.[19]

The DPG also outlined U.S. goals in the Middle East ("to remain the predominant outside power in the region and preserve US and Western access to the region's oil"), Korea ("prevent the emergence of a vacuum or regional hegemon"), and southwest Asia (India and Pakistan). Weapons of mass destruction and nonproliferation were likewise examined by the DPG, with a mind toward developing preemptive strategies to deal with these issues. The DPG also talked about humanitarian intervention by the United States, especially if such intervention served the interests of the United States. The draft DPG was leaked to the press in March 1992 and immediately came under attack from Congress and the public, who took umbrage at the underlying theme of world domination. Cheney withdrew the DPG and had it redrafted in a manner that took into account public sensitivities while preserving the direction and intent of the February 1992 draft.[20]

The goal of the DPG was to serve as a guideline for the development of national security policy for a second Bush term. However, a sluggish economy, combined with a Republican president who struggled to effectively communicate his ideas for solving the economic difficulties faced by the American people, created a political window of opportunity for the Democratic Party challenger, Arkansas governor Bill Clinton, to oust President Bush in the November 1992 presidential election. Instead of having an experienced foreign policy figure at the wheel of the ship of state, tempered by the challenges of managing the collapse of the Soviet Union, the unification of Germany, regional crises such as Iraq, and a host of arms control and nonproliferation matters, the United States instead had as its new chief executive a man with little foreign policy experience whose almost singular focus was on issues pertaining to domestic policy and the economy. America, basking in the afterglow of the post–Cold War, post–Gulf War experience, was desirous of a "peace dividend," and was looking to President Clinton to deliver it.

Clinton's domestic priorities were on full display as he selected his national security team, one of the least impressive assembled in the post–Second World War era in terms of experience and credibility. Warren Christopher, a former deputy secretary of state under President Carter, was selected to serve as Clinton's secretary of state. Les Aspin, an outspoken and very liberal congressman from Wisconsin, was picked to be secretary of defense, and Anthony Lake, a former NSC staff member under Richard Nixon who resigned in protest over the U.S. invasion of Cambodia, was made national security advisor. The one person with a résumé befitting a national position was Clinton's choice for CIA director, James Woolsey, who had served previously on the SALT delegation, as counsel to the Senate Armed Services Committee, undersecretary of the Navy, a delegate at large for the START talks, and the U.S. ambassador to the CFE talks. Woolsey was the token hard-liner in an otherwise liberal national security team.[21]

President Clinton, in his inaugural address, spoke of the challenges faced as "a generation raised in the shadows of the Cold War assumes new responsibilities in a world warmed by the sunshine of freedom but threatened still by ancient hatreds and new plagues." But Clinton made it clear that "there is no longer division between what is foreign and what is domestic—the world economy, the world environment, the world AIDS crisis, the world arms race—they affect us all." The president spoke of the need for American leadership in this new environment, which, according to him, blurred foreign and domestic priorities into one.[22]

As with the past practices of previous administrations, the new Clinton team undertook a "bottom-up" policy review before committing to any specific course of action on arms control and national security. But the world does not stop for policy reviews. In February 1993 the United Nations Special Commission, together with the IAEA, announced that it had completely dismantled Iraq's nuclear weapons program. This news was a boost for the IAEA, which had its reputation damaged when Iraq violated its safeguards agreement while assembling its nuclear program. In reviewing the Iraqi actions, the IAEA concluded that its current safeguards regime was virtually powerless to prevent future violations by nonnuclear states. The IAEA director general, Hans Blix, began pushing for a revamped safeguards program that possessed greater verification capabilities, including the right to conduct surprise inspections of nonsafeguarded facilities.[23]

The issue of surprise IAEA inspections came into play early on in the Clinton administration, not in Iraq, but rather in North Korea. North Korea had signed the NPT in 1985 and entered into a safeguards agreement with the IAEA in June 1992. This safeguards agreement allowed for the conduct of "surprise inspections," and the IAEA used this tool on at least two occasions in 1992 without difficulty. U.S. intelligence reports, however, indicated that North Korea was pursuing a covert nuclear weapons program and using its membership in the IAEA as a means of acquiring needed technological support under the guise of legitimate civilian use. As tensions between the United States and North Korea increased, the United States announced the resumption of joint military exercises with South Korea. These exercises had been suspended in 1992, and their resumption was viewed by the North Koreans as a serious provocation. In early 1993 the IAEA announced that it wanted to carry out a new round of "surprise inspections," targeting North Korean nuclear reactors. The North Koreans accused the IAEA of collaborating with the CIA in an effort to use inspections as a vehicle to spy on North Korea, and they refused to allow the IAEA inspectors to carry out the inspections. In March 1993, North Korea announced its intention to withdraw from the NPT, precipitating a serious crisis for the new Clinton administration.[24]

Complicating matters even more, in April 1993 the Kuwaiti government announced that it had uncovered an Iraqi plot to assassinate former president George Bush while he was visiting Kuwait City that same month. A perfunctory investigation was carried out by the FBI, and the Clinton administration accepted a finding of Iraqi complicity. In June 1993 President Clinton ordered the U.S. military to launch a cruise missile attack against the headquarters of the Iraqi intelligence service in retaliation, thereby cementing the assassination attempt as fact, even though there was no hard evidence linking Iraq to the Kuwaiti claims. Once Clinton branded the government of Saddam Hussein as being associated with a plot on the life of a former president, the nature of the U.S. relationship with Iraq was dramatically altered.[25]

While the Bush administration had, in October 1992, authorized the CIA to undertake covert operations against Iraq with the goal of removing Saddam Hussein from power, Clinton had put those plans on hold while the "policy review" was taking place. After June 1993, however, the policy of the Clinton administration became one of removing Saddam Hussein from office. This policy, which made use of UN-imposed economic sanctions against Iraq as the best means of containing and undermining Saddam's regime, ran counter to the goals and objectives of the UN inspectors in Iraq, who were seeking to verify Iraqi compliance with its disarmament obligations so that economic sanctions, linked to this disarmament, might be lifted. Disarmament became the enemy of U.S. policy in Iraq, and the United States began pushing more for inspections that sought to maintain the perception of a noncompliant Iraq than for inspections that sought to discover the genuine status of Iraq's proscribed WMD programs.[26]

The Clinton administration had inherited two major regional crises, in addition to Iraq and North Korea, that dominated in 1993. The first was the civil war in the former Yugoslavia, which had been raging since 1990. By 1993 the fighting had converged on the Muslim area of Bosnia-Herzegovina, with ethnic cleansing and massive human rights violations occurring on a scale not seen in Europe since the Second World War. The United Nations dispatched peacekeeping forces, but these proved unable to stop the fighting. The Clinton administration, working with its NATO allies, declared a "no-fly" zone over the territory of Bosnia-Herzegovina and threatened the use of force to enforce it. This military commitment represented a departure from the defensive focus of NATO during the Cold War and was reflective of both American and European interest in defining a new role for NATO in the post-Soviet era.[27]

The second crisis was in the African nation of Somalia. Civil unrest in Somalia, where rival militias fought for control of cities and neighborhoods, led to a serious humanitarian disaster in which millions of civilians were put at risk from lack of food, water, and medicine. UN humanitarian relief groups were unable to operate safely, and militias were stealing international aid shipments before they could be distributed to those in need. In December 1992 President Bush ordered the U.S. military to intervene in order to provide security and engender stability so that a humanitarian disaster might be averted. These efforts were initially a success, but soon the United States found itself embroiled in a classic regional conflict. Forced to choose sides, the United States opted to confront a powerful Somali warlord, Mohammed Farid Aideed. These clashes turned increasingly more violent, culminating on the night of October 3–4, 1993, in a massive street battle in the capital city of Mogadishu between Aideed's militia and U.S. Army forces, resulting in nineteen American soldiers killed, nearly a hundred more wounded, and the images of American dead being dragged through the streets. This battle proved to be a major political embarrassment for President Clinton and his administration, resulting in the resignation of Defense Secretary Les Aspin, who was replaced by his deputy, William Perry.[28]

In the midst of this, the Clinton administration completed its bottom-up review of U.S. policy in September, leading to an announcement that the Department of Defense would be conducting a comprehensive review of America's nuclear posture, known as the Nuclear Policy Review, or NPR. The bottom-up review had determined that U.S. nuclear strategy should shift away from war fighting, which had been the U.S. posture since President Carter signed PD-59 in 1980, making Countervailing the official policy (and expanded when President Reagan signed NSDD-13 in 1981, changing Countervailing to Prevailing), and instead return to the classic role of nuclear-based deterrence. How this shift would be executed was to be determined by the NPR. Heading up a five-person steering committee was Assistant Secretary of Defense Ashton Carter, who had publicly committed to achieving a U.S. defense posture that did not include nuclear, chemical, or biological weapons but rather a conventional military force able to prevail under any circumstance.[29]

This vision was in direct opposition to the views of America's military leadership, which continued to see U.S. nuclear weapons as an essential element of national security. While the generals and admirals who comprised the Joint Chiefs of Staff and commanded U.S. strategic forces recognized the need for downsizing and change in the aftermath of the demise of the Soviet Union, they did not believe a world with a nuclear-free America was viable. Continued concerns about Russia and China, combined with the new focus on rogue regimes such as Iraq and North Korea, not only made the maintenance of the classic TRIAD-based strategic nuclear capability essential, but also dictated that America seek to acquire a new nuclear capability that was specifically molded for employment in the scaled-down world of the post–Cold War era. In this the military was more in line with the thinking of former Defense Secretary Cheney than the new national security team of President Clinton.

The NPR examined six specific roles played by nuclear weapons in U.S. national security strategy: nuclear force structure, nuclear force operations, nuclear safety and security, the relationship between nuclear posture and counter-proliferation policy, and the relationship between nuclear posture and threat reduction policy with the former Soviet Union. Ashton Carter initially pushed for a deadline of February 1994, but this was rejected by the military chiefs as too rushed. One of the main concerns of the military was the concept being pushed by Carter that would remove ICBMs and strategic bombers from the U.S. strategic nuclear force, leaving some 1,500 warheads loaded on a reduced number of SLBMs. This concept directly threatened the established TRIAD structure, which had been in place since the 1960s, and the associated military structures and bureaucracies that had grown and solidified since then.[30]

The February 1994 deadline for finishing the NPR came and went, and in April 1994 the military revolted, appealing directly to Congress to stop the radical proposals Carter was trying to foist on the NPR. As the NPR process collapsed, the military stepped in and pushed its own program, preparing several papers and studies that were justified as "interim measures" pending a final NPR. These concepts served as the basis of the final NPR, released in September 1994. The TRIAD structure was retained, with the NPR recommending a force structure that included twenty B-2 bombers, seventy-six B-52 bombers, and a nonnuclear role for the B-1 bomber. The U.S. Navy would retain fourteen *Trident* submarines, all equipped with the new D-5 missile, deployed in two bases, one on the Atlantic Ocean and the other on the Pacific. The U.S. Air Force would also deploy a force of five hundred *Minuteman* III missiles, all downloaded from three warheads to one warhead (using the ultra-accurate warheads developed for the MX missile).[31]

The publishing of the NPR cleared the way for the conduct of the traditional planning process associated with U.S. nuclear weapons. The Defense Department would take the force structure as approved and develop a nuclear weapons employment plan (NUWEP), which would define the targeting requirements of the nuclear force. Then, using the NUWEP, the successor organization to Strategic Air Command, known as U.S.

Strategic Command (formed in June 1992 and combining U.S. and Navy nuclear forces under a single command structure), would develop an integrated target plan, or SIOP.

Three major factors influenced the thinking of the Clinton administration when it came to developing a nuclear weapons employment strategy. The first, and perhaps most significant, was the U.S. relationship with Russia. The second was the growing recognition of China as an emerging superpower, and thus the need to look at China as a potential adversary. And the third was the problem of nonsuperpower nuclear proliferation, in particular nations such as Iraq and North Korea, but also nations such as India and Pakistan. Of the three factors, the relationship with Russia was the most problematic.

Ever since President Bush and President Yeltsin signed the START-2 in January 1993, the treaty had been languishing, awaiting ratification in the U.S. Senate and Russian parliament. The new Russian democracy, however, was not about to rubber-stamp a treaty many viewed as unfavorable to Russia. While the START-2 was on the surface a document that sought parity when it came to the U.S.-Russian strategic nuclear arsenals, the reality was that the treaty required Russia to eliminate more systems than the United States, and while the United States would not need to produce any new systems to replace those being eliminated, the same could not be said of Russia, which would need to continue manufacturing new SS-25 ICBMs and SS-N-20 SLBMs to replace the older systems being taken out of service if the treaty went into force. Given the poor state of the Russian economy, this was an expense the Russian parliament was not willing to bear. The same held true on matters pertaining to the dismantlement and destruction of missiles, silos, bombers, and submarines eliminated under the treaty. Such elimination was a very expensive proposition, one that could not be adequately funded by Russia. Efforts were made by the United States, using money provided by the Nunn-Lugar Act, to help offset these costs, but the intrusive nature of American oversight and management of these funds offended many Russians, already sensitive to their reduced status in the world after the fall of the Soviet Union.[32]

Finally, the Russians had a legitimate national security concern. The United States continued to fund missile defense research, which the Russians viewed as a potential violation of the 1972 ABM treaty. Although the Clinton administration had announced the termination of Reagan's SDI in July 1993, it only cut the space-based portion of the massive missile defense effort. Ground-based missile defense was still part of the U.S. strategic future. The ABM treaty was viewed by the Russians as a foundational agreement that was essential for all future arms control efforts. The Russians were extremely sensitive to the idea of the United States putting in place a missile defense shield the Russians could not hope to match in the foreseeable future, while at the same time they were reducing their arsenals of missiles.[33]

Furthermore, Russia was getting rid of its larger systems, including the SS-18. The remaining ICBMs and SLBMs had a much-reduced payload capability, with the SS-25 operating as a single warhead system and the SS-N-20 carrying four warheads instead of eight. The United States, on the other hand, was retaining the *Minuteman* III and *Trident* D-5. While these missiles were downloaded from their Cold War capabilities, with the *Minuteman* III carrying one warhead instead of three, and the D-5 carrying eight warheads instead of fourteen, the Russians were concerned about a potential "breakout" scenario that had the United States deploying a limited SDI system and then uploading its *Minuteman* III and D-5 SLBMs to their maximum ability, achieving a first-strike capability backed up by a significant nuclear strike reserve and missile defense shield that would deter any Russian retaliation effort.[34]

President Clinton tried to allay Russian concerns when he met with President Yeltsin in Moscow on January 14, 1994. The original START could not enter into force until the issue of transferring and/or eliminating the strategic nuclear weapons that had been based in Belarus, Ukraine, and Kazakhstan was resolved. Both leaders agreed that the sooner they could get START up and running, the better chance they would have at getting START-2 ratified, since START would engender a better sense of confidence on both sides. On December 5, 1994, Russia, Ukraine, Belarus, and Kazakhstan exchanged articles of ratification for the START with the United States in a ceremony held in Budapest, Hungary, the site of the CSCE Summit. START baseline inspections began in March 1995. It looked as if U.S. arms control policy was back on track and with it a chance to restructure America's nuclear arsenal accordingly.[35]

Another issue that needed to be addressed when structuring America's nuclear weapons employment strategy was America's relationship with China. When Clinton came into office in 1993, tension still existed because of the massacre of demonstrators in Tiananmen Square in 1989. Nevertheless, the Clinton administration made it clear that it sought to normalize and expand U.S.-Chinese relations, with an eye toward increased economic interaction. China wanted U.S. technology, and the United States wanted to open up China's markets. Human rights issues were pushed to the side as both nations focused on more tangible, and less controversial, matters.

China was a nuclear weapons state. It had agreed to join the NPT in 1992 as a nuclear weapons state. However, in the era of U.S.-Soviet arms control, no meaningful effort was ever undertaken to engage China in any arms control discussions. This was largely due to the fact that China's nuclear arsenal was so small as to be militarily insignificant in any global nuclear conflict. But this didn't mean that there wasn't nuclear tension between the United States and China. Under Richard Nixon the United States started withholding a strategic nuclear reserve for the purpose of deterring a nuclear-armed China in the aftermath of a U.S.-Soviet nuclear war, and this remained U.S. policy up until the time Clinton took office.

For its part, China had developed a policy of nuclear deterrence based on the concept of no first use. China's nuclear arsenal was purely a retaliatory force, designed from the outset to deter any potential attacker with the certainty of a devastating nuclear response. Chinese missiles were outdated liquid-fueled systems known as the DF-5A. Capable of delivering a five-megaton warhead to ranges of up to 13,000 kilometers, the DF-5A could threaten cities in western Russia and the United States. But by 1994 the Chinese had fielded only about twenty DF-5As. These missiles were stored horizontally in tunnels bored into the sides of mountains in central China. The missiles had to be removed from the tunnel and have the warhead mated, raised, and fueled before being fired, a process that took up to two hours. Chinese nuclear policy was such that no missile was assigned a target until placed on alert. As such, there was no "launch on warning" capability, or the potential for an accidental launch. China had a single SLBM-capable submarine, outfitted with twelve JL-1 missiles possessing a range of 2,500 kilometers. This submarine was largely confined to a hardened bunker on Hainan Island. The bottom line for the Clinton administration was that China posed no significant threat to the United States, and current nuclear targeting strategies were deemed sufficient.[36]

But regional issues did affect U.S. nuclear posture with respect to China. The most serious of these was the situation regarding Taiwan. The Chinese government continued to insist that Taiwan was an integral part of China and threatened to use force if necessary to bring Taipei back under the fold of Beijing. While the Clinton administration announced a "one China" policy that was little more than a continuation of U.S. policy since the Nixon administration, it made it clear to Beijing that the United States would not tolerate the use of military force to resolve the Taiwan issue. Despite the effort to achieve a thaw in relations through improved economic relations, highlighted by Clinton's decision in 1994 to grant China most-favored nation (MFN) trade status, thus paving the way for a trading relationship estimated to be worth $38 billion a year, friction still existed between China and the United States over human rights and Taiwan.[37]

China also came into play on the issue of North Korea. Prior to the 1994 MFN decision, China had been hesitant to weigh in on the issue of North Korea's nuclear program. However, with North Korea threatening to withdraw from the NPT and, once IAEA safeguards ended, withdraw nuclear fuel rods from its nuclear reactor in order to extract plutonium that could be used to manufacture a nuclear bomb, the United States needed China's help more than ever to bring North Korea back into the embrace of the NPT. The spring of 1994 found the United States preparing for war with North Korea. Plans were drawn up to bomb the North Korean nuclear reactor at Yongbon and to fight a ground war on the Korean peninsula in case North Korea lashed out in retaliation. Diplomacy won out in the end, with the United States and North Korea signing what became known as the Agreed Framework, which had North Korea remaining in the NPT and agreeing to install light water nuclear reactors incapable of producing plutonium, in exchange for the dismantling of its Yongbon reactor and a promise by the United States to provide oil for heating and electricity production while North Korea shut down its banned reactor and installed the new ones.[38]

Iraq also continued to loom large in the national security picture for the Clinton administration. UN inspections in 1993 and 1994 went further in accounting for Iraq's WMD programs. They faced a confused situation in Iraq, where documents and facilities were destroyed and/or damaged during the 1991 war, as well as hidden as part of Iraqi efforts to retain proscribed WMD capability. Even when Iraq was forthcoming on an issue, the lack of documentation and hard physical evidence impeded UN efforts at verification. The UN inspectors were, however, able to install a comprehensive monitoring and verification system that blanketed Iraq's industrial infrastructure, and in doing so found neither evidence of a retained WMD capability nor any indication of an effort to reconstitute any former WMD programs.

In August 1995, Saddam Hussein's son-in-law, Hussein Kamal, defected to Jordan, bringing with him intelligence information about Saddam Hussein's WMD programs (which Hussein Kamal had headed up in the 1980s), including data pertaining to the concealment of WMD-related documents and activities. While none of this led to the uncovering of any viable weapons, the Iraqis were compelled to disclose the existence of a massive archive of documents relating to Iraq's past WMD programs. The new disclosures uncovered programs for the manufacture of chemical, biological, and nuclear weapons, along with long-range missiles, that went beyond what the UN inspectors had previously known about. From a technical standpoint these disclosures brought the UN closer to a full understanding of the scope and scale of Iraq's WMD effort, and with it an accounting of what happened to it all. Nevertheless, it was a political setback for the inspection effort: the Hussein Kamal revelations helped sustain the perception of a defiant, noncompliant Saddam Hussein.

Frustrated by the inability to bring about the demise of Saddam's regime through sanctions and external pressure, President Clinton ordered the CIA to undertake covert action designed to remove the Iraqi president from office, including the use of lethal force. Arms control and disarmament efforts became subordinated to the unilateral policy objectives of the Clinton administration. These objectives were driven more by domestic political considerations than they were from any real threat to national security. Saddam's continued survival had become a political embarrassment to the Clinton administration, and eliminating this political problem trumped meaningful arms control. The UN experience in Iraq had produced a viable model of multilateral disarmament that had proven technically capable of accomplishing its mission. However, the political reality of America's newfound status as the world's sole remaining superpower trumped multilateral-based arms control, especially when the domestic political stakes were so high.[39]

The first two years of the Clinton administration had provoked a strong backlash of anger and resentment from the Republican Party, especially on the issue of national security. The 1994 midterm elections saw the Republican Party win back the House of Representatives for the first time since the 1954 elections. Led by Representative Newt Gingrich from Georgia, the Republicans launched a program of reform, the so-called Contract with America, a series of legislative acts designed to reverse the policies of the Clinton administration. Included in this legislative push was the National Security Restoration Act, which targeted the use of U.S. troops in a UN role and pushed for the voluntary integration of former Warsaw Pact nations into NATO.[40]

The issue of the future of NATO was a key factor in shaping the new post–Cold War U.S.-European relationship. With the demise of the Warsaw Pact and the Soviet Union, and the reunification of Germany, the justification for the existence of NATO was no longer viable (as the first NATO secretary general, Lord Ismay, once remarked, NATO's purpose was "to keep the Russians out, the Americans in and the Germans down").[41] Indeed, the post–Cold War situation in Europe reflected many elements of Ismay's simplified mission statement. With Germany now unified, NATO served as a vehicle to constrain German ambition. France rejoined the NATO Military Committee in 1995 largely out of a desire to better coordinate with Germany on economic and security issues. As Europe flexed its post–Cold War muscles, there was also recognition that NATO provided a safety net against a recurrence of American isolationism by keeping America involved in European affairs. And Europe continued to be concerned about Russia, given the poor state of the post-Soviet economy; the seeming instability of its leader, Boris Yeltsin; a growing nationalism in the Russian parliament; and the reemergence of Russia as a nation capable of military adventure. Fears about the violent breakup of the non-Russian parts of the Russian Federation were for the most part not realized by events. The one major exception was in the Caucasus Republic of Chechnya.

In 1991 Chechnya declared its intent to become a sovereign nation, and in 1993 it declared its independence. This action led to a decision by the Russian government to dispatch troops into Chechnya in December 1994 in order to restore "constitutional authority." The result was a disastrous conflict for both sides, with Russia suffering numerous military setbacks and defeats and the Chechen population being subjected to horrific aerial bombardment and shelling. Tens of thousands of people died on both sides. The deployment of Russian troops into Chechnya and the surrounding regions created a situation in which Russia was in violation of regional troop caps established by the CFE treaty. This unnerved several NATO members, who believed Russia could use the issue of internal unrest to redeploy its ground forces in a manner that threatened Eastern Europe. Pressure was building inside NATO to begin inviting the former Warsaw Pact members to join the organization as a means of containing Russian expansionism, despite the fact that verbal exchanges between Mikhail Gorbachev and the administration of President Bush (including the president himself) precluded any such expansion. Any effort undertaken to expand NATO would be viewed in a negative light by the Russians.

But Russia was not the Soviet Union, and by 1995 many Americans had stopped viewing Russia as a global power worthy of concern. The disastrous state of the Russian economy had prompted massive Western investment and intervention to the point that at times it seemed that Russia had become a third-world nation managed by benevolent Western benefactors. American auditors and technicians oversaw Russian disarmament efforts through the Nunn-Lugar Act, while Harvard economists directed Russian economic reforms, and other academics managed Russian efforts at democratization. Arms control was no longer viewed in life-or-death terms. Hard-line Republicans in the U.S. Senate, led by Trent Lott and Jesse Helms, downplayed concerns over the Russian nuclear arsenal, noting that, with or without a START-2, the collapsing Russian economy would mandate a reduction in Russian strategic forces.[42] The problem was no longer Russia, but rather North Korea, Iraq, and Iran. Rogue nations, such as Saddam Hussein's Iraq, were the new threat, and the Republicans were not supportive of an arms control agreement with Russia that they viewed as superfluous, holding American security hostage by placing a national missile defense system, which many Republicans actively supported, at risk.

Proponents of START-2 shared the view that Russia's worsening economy would force strategic arms reductions out of necessity, but underscored the importance of START-2 in shaping the structure and doctrine of America's nuclear arsenal. The U.S. Senate finally voted to ratify START-2 on January 26, 1996, but the treaty continued to be held up in the Russian parliament, where concerns existed over a perceived U.S. global power-grab. This mindset was fueled by the actions of NATO in the former Yugoslavia, where NATO aircraft were patrolling the sky over Bosnia and shooting down Serbian aircraft that strayed into the no-fly zone. In August, NATO began a major aerial bombardment campaign against the Bosnian Serbs in retaliation for their ongoing campaign of ethnic cleansing and murder of Bosnian Muslims, including attacks on UN-designated "safe areas." These "safe areas" were created in the aftermath of the July 1995 slaughter of 8,000 Bosnians by Serb forces in and around the town of Srebrenica.[43]

NATO troops were deployed in Bosnia in December 1995 to implement an EU-sponsored peace plan. The Implementation Force, or IFOR, represented the first major NATO ground action since its founding. This expansion of the NATO role and mission had many in Russia concerned about what the future would hold regarding NATO expansion. NATO had already created several forums, such as the Partnership for Peace (in which former Warsaw Pact nations, including Russia, worked to establish a relationship built on trust in the post–Cold War era), the Mediterranean Dialogue Initiative (designed to foster dialogue and goodwill between NATO and its Mediterranean neighbors), and the Europe-Atlantic Partnership Council (in which NATO reached out to non-NATO European and Asian countries in order to foster better relations). To many Russians, rather than seeking to maintain the status quo, NATO was aggressively expanding its regional and global reach. It was only a matter of time, they believed, before NATO turned its sights on expanding its membership by inviting former Warsaw Pact nations to join the organization.[44]

Russia did not have to wait long for this fear to materialize. On July 8, 1997, the countries of Hungary, the Czech Republic, and Poland were issued formal invitations to join NATO. When the United States first approached Russia on the issue of expanding NATO, they were met with outright hostility to the idea. While NATO viewed the expansion as a vehicle for promoting democracy and stability, the prospective new members, each of whom had suffered from Soviet aggression in one form or another during the Cold War, clearly viewed their membership as a vehicle to protect them from future threats out of Moscow. Far from building a bridge between East and West, the expansion of NATO threatened to build a new wall separating the two blocs, only this time the wall would be right on Russia's borders. The promise of increased economic aid mollified the Russians somewhat, however, and by early 1997 Yeltsin had indicated Russia's willingness to accept the inevitable.

While the United States and Russia wrestled over the issue of NATO expansion, there were still arms control issues that needed to be resolved, including a comprehensive nuclear test ban treaty (CTBT). The United States was running up against a deadline of early 1995 to resolve the impasse on the issue of nuclear testing. On October 2, 1992, President Bush had announced that the United States would undertake a unilateral moratorium on nuclear weapons testing, largely as a result of congressional pressure. This moratorium was extended by President Clinton in July 1993 to March 1994, when it was extended again through September 1995. The test moratorium was done in an effort to facilitate a positive outcome from the Review and Extension Conference of the NPT, scheduled for April–May 1995. This conference would conduct a review of the implementation processes of the NPT, as well as make a recommendation on whether to extend the NPT and, if so, for how long.[45]

In the end, the conference voted to seek improvements in the IAEA safeguards regime, with a focus on a more comprehensive, inspection-based verification system, and to continue to push for more effective disarmament among the nuclear weapons states. In particular, the conference called on the United States and Russia to ratify START-2, and for all parties to facilitate the negotiation of a comprehensive test ban treaty. In addition to expressing concern over the nuclear programs of Iraq and North Korea, which were being addressed by the IAEA through enhanced safeguards inspections, the conference also singled out Israel, Pakistan, and India as nations where nuclear weapons proliferation was occurring outside the framework of the NPT. Likewise, the conference voted to extend the NPT indefinitely, which represented a great success for the cause of nuclear nonproliferation.[46]

The CTBT was held up within the Conference on Disarmament in Geneva for nearly three years of negotiations, from 1993 until 1996, without consensus being reached on a draft text. While the CTBT was being negotiated, France announced that it would conduct eight nuclear tests between June 1995 and May 1996, after which time it would be prepared to sign a CTBT. This move was widely criticized by the United States and other nations. Fearful that the French action might set off a chain reaction of nuclear testing (China also conducted a nuclear test on July 29, 1996, after which it announced a moratorium on nuclear testing), the impasse was broken at the Conference on Disarmament, and a draft treaty was submitted to the United Nations General Assembly, which approved the treaty on September 10, 1996.[47]

For its part, the Clinton administration did all it could to facilitate the signing of the CTBT. In addition to pushing for U.S. Senate ratification of START-2 in January 1996, the president pushed for a Nuclear Safety Summit, which was held in April 1996 in Moscow. The attendees were the major economic powers of the West (the so-called G-7), Russia, and Ukraine. They reiterated their collective desire for a CTBT, as well as a universally binding fissile material production ban and improved safety for both peaceful and military nuclear programs.[48]

President Clinton signed the Test Ban Treaty on September 24, 1996, as did the leaders of Russia, France, China, and the United Kingdom, committing these declared nuclear weapons states to never again test nuclear weapons. By November 1996 the treaty signatories adopted a resolution creating the CTBT Organization (CTBTO), to be based in Vienna, Austria, which would be tasked with establishing a verification regime capable of meeting the requirements of the CTBT. This verification capability was put forward in the form of the International Monitoring System (IMS), a global monitoring capability that integrated seismic, hydro-acoustic, radionuclide, and infrasound sensors into a single comprehensive verification system. The IMS also provided the ability to conduct on-site inspection as required when the CTBT entered into force.[49]

In addition to the CTBT, the Clinton administration was also focused on getting the Chemical Weapons Convention (CWC) up and running. On October 31, 1996, Hungary became the sixty-fifth nation to ratify the CWC, thereby initiating an automatic 180-day process for the treaty to enter into force, which it did on April 29, 1997.[50] The CWC had been held up in the U.S. Senate, where hard-line Republican senators opposed its ratification. President Clinton had pulled the treaty from ratification consideration in 1996, not wanting to politicize the process during an election year. But Hungary's ratification forced the Clinton administration's hand,

and it began a high-profile campaign to push for Senate ratification before the CWC entered into force. The arguments made were effective: not ratifying the CWC would put the United States in the same company as Libya, Iran, and North Korea, and the best way to pressure Russia to ratify the CWC, and thus take Russian chemical weapons out of play, would be for the United States to ratify the convention.

Ratification was a difficult process. Led by Senator Jesse Helms, the chair of the Foreign Relations Committee, the Republicans derided the CWC as being "worse than nothing."[51] In the end, the Senate voted to ratify the CWC, but not without the Clinton administration paying a heavy cost. As part of the trade-off the Clinton administration agreed to terminate the existence of the Arms Control and Disarmament Agency, rolling its functions into the bureaucracy of the State Department. Hard-line Republicans had been opposed to the role and mission of the ACDA since the 1970s, believing that the agency advocated on behalf of arms control at the expense of U.S. national security. While President Clinton viewed the compromise as a necessary sacrifice in the name of maintaining momentum on arms control, Republican senators led by Jesse Helms viewed the trading of ratification of the CWC for the demise of ACDA as part of a larger plan to bring arms control to a standstill. To these senators, through the CWC America was sacrificing a historical opportunity to assert itself as the undisputed world leader; it was allowing its military strength to be hobbled by arms control agreements that contained too many loopholes for its potential enemies, thereby creating a situation in which it might have to confront a foe armed with the very weapons America foreswore.[52]

President Clinton ended his first term in office with a mixed record on national security and arms control. The debacle of Mogadishu still haunted him, and the unresolved situation in Iraq only furthered the notion that the Clinton administration was weak on defense. The president had inherited a difficult world situation and was forced to shape policy in a post–Cold War era that was without precedent. Clinton had also inherited a promising arms control agenda, with a START-2 and CFE treaty signed and awaiting ratification. By 1996, CFE was under way, but START-2 still floundered, impeded largely by Clinton's continued support of a missile defense shield system that threatened the ABM treaty. The sacrifice of ACDA in order to secure Senate ratification of the CWC treaty did not bode well for a second term, when issues such as a comprehensive test ban treaty, resolving the START-2 impasse, and modifying the ABM treaty to permit the fielding of a viable missile defense without killing the agreement were very much on the agenda.

Clinton easily won his bid for reelection and, in an effort to shore up his national security credentials, conducted a major reshuffling of his national security team. Gone were Secretary of State Warren Christopher and Defense Secretary William Perry. Madeleine Albright, the U.S. ambassador to the United Nations, replaced Christopher, and William Cohen, a recently retired Republican senator from Maine, was moved to Defense in the name of bipartisanship. How this new team would deal with the myriad of serious issues confronting it would determine whether the United States was going to manage the post–Cold War period in a way that moved the world toward peace and security or further down the path of chaos and instability.

A showdown was looming in the Senate over two major arms control initiatives: the CTBT and amendments to the 1972 ABM treaty that sought to bring Russia, Belarus, Ukraine, and Kazakhstan into the treaty as successor states to the former Soviet Union. A 1996 Memorandum of Understanding on the issue of ABM succession was stalled, however, because of an ongoing struggle between Russia and the United States over the definition of the differences between a "theater missile defense" system and the "strategic missile defense" systems covered by the ABM treaty. The defining characteristics of concern, worked out between the United States and Russia in June 1996, involved the speed of the interceptor missiles. "Low-speed" interceptors, up to and including velocities of three kilometers per second, were to be defined as theater missile defense systems and permitted, while "high-speed" interceptors (anything above the threshold velocity) were deemed "strategic" and subject to the ABM treaty restrictions. However, differences of opinion on how to precisely demarcate "high-speed" interceptors led to the collapse of the negotiations without reaching a final agreement in October 1996.[53]

In January 1997 the Republicans in the Senate, led by Trent Lott of Mississippi, introduced the National Missile Defense Act of 1997, which mandated the creation of a theater missile defense system by the year 2003. This was more of a political maneuver than a sincere effort at legislation, for although the bill made it out of the U.S. Armed Services Committee in April 1997, it went no further.[54] However, the Senate action provided enough pressure to compel Clinton and Boris Yeltsin to meet, in March 21, 1997, in Helsinki, where both leaders agreed to the original demarcation agreement of June 1996. They also agreed to immediately begin negotiations on a START-3, designed to limit each side to 2,000 to 2,500 deployed strategic warheads by the end of 2007, following Russian ratification of START-2.[55] By September 1997 Russia and the United States had agreed to a framework that expanded the ABM treaty to include Belarus, Ukraine, and Kazakhstan, in addition to Russia, and to define parameters for both low-velocity and high-velocity missile interceptors as part of a permitted theater missile defense system. In April 1998, Boris Yeltsin submitted the ABM MOU agreement, together with START-2, to the Russian parliament for ratification, paving the way for a more solid framework of arms control agreements between the two nuclear-armed nations.[56]

While Russia and the United States worked out their differences on the ABM treaty and a potential START-3, President Clinton moved to bring closure on the issue of a comprehensive test ban treaty. The president sent the CTBT to the Senate in September 1997 for its advice and consent to ratification. In his January 19, 1998, State of the Union address, President Clinton called on the Senate to ratify the CTBT during the coming year in order to "make it harder for other nations to develop nuclear arms, and to make sure we can end nuclear testing forever."[57] Consideration of the CTBT was immediately sabotaged, however, by Senator Jesse Helms, the chair of the Armed Services Committee, who refused to review the CTBT until the Clinton administration addressed other arms control issues, in particular the ABM treaty.

While these political maneuverings were ongoing in Washington, the Clinton administration finally released, in September 1997, its new guidelines for the targeting of U.S. nuclear weapons. Entitled Presidential Decision Directive 60 (PDD-60), "The U.S. Strategic Nuclear Doctrine," the new guidelines terminated the previous Prevailing strategy of the Reagan and Bush administrations and instead directed the Pentagon and the Joint Chiefs of Staff to return to a more classic deterrence posture, which had the United States deterring any use of nuclear weapons against the United States or its allies by threatening a devastating response. The United States would no longer plan to fight a protracted nuclear war. However, PDD-60 did retain established options for launching nuclear attacks against military and civilian targets inside Russia, reflecting the opinion of many in the Clinton administration that despite all that had transpired since the fall of the Soviet Union, Russia still represented the major nuclear threat to the United States. PDD-60 also contained instructions regarding the nuclear targeting of China, as well as any nonnuclear enemy that employed chemical or biological weapons against the United States or its allies.[58]

From a practical point of view, PDD-60 facilitated the direction the Clinton administration was taking with regard to arms control. By rejecting a protracted nuclear war strategy, the United States no longer was required to maintain a significant nuclear reserve. These weapons could now be eliminated as part of any new arms reductions agreement, without adversely affecting the still powerful nuclear deterrent represented by the reduced force structure. The TRIAD would be retained, but at a reduced size. PPD-60 required that the Department of Defense conduct a review of its nuclear weapons employment plan (NUWEP) and nuclear targeting plan (SIOP) to take into account the new guidance. While the Clinton administration claimed that PDD-60 underscored the reality that nuclear weapons played a smaller role in the U.S. national security strategy than at any time in the nuclear era, this was not actually the case.

While PDD-60 focused on deterrence, and not on waging nuclear war, it did retain the U.S. ability to conduct "launch on warning" attacks as well as the ability to conduct preemptive nuclear strikes where deemed necessary. PDD-60 also retained the requirement that any nuclear targeting plan derived from these guidelines should offer the president a wide range of possible options, ranging from a limited use of nuclear weapons in a regional conflict to all-out general nuclear war. Special consideration was given to developing a range of options with regard to China, as well as other nations, such as Iraq, Iran, and North Korea, that could be targeted by U.S. nuclear weapons in case of a regional conflict or crisis. The targeting of nonnuclear states was deemed controversial by some in the Clinton administration. However, in the post–Gulf War environment, with controversy surrounding the work of the UN inspectors in that country, in particular about the status of Iraq's actual level of disarmament, there was greater sensitivity to the threats posed by chemical and biological weapons. According to the PDD-60 guidelines, any nation that used WMD against America or its allies forfeited its protection, extended in the form of a "no first use" pledge by President Clinton in 1995, from nuclear attack by the United States.[59]

While the Clinton administration worked to balance a new nuclear weapons strategy with the demands of arms control and disarmament, a movement was gaining momentum internationally to strengthen the nuclear nonproliferation capabilities of the IAEA. Building on the experience obtained in Iraq following the 1991 Gulf War, and in North Korea during the 1990s, the IAEA Board of Governors, in May 1997, approved a robust regime of "Additional Protocol" safeguards designed to improve the verification of a signatory nation with its compliance to the NPT. While voluntary, any nation that adopted the Additional Protocol regime provided the IAEA with the legal basis for implementing intrusive inspections designed to detect undeclared nuclear activity.[60]

The need for the Additional Protocol was underscored in May 1998, when first India (on May 11 and 13) and later Pakistan (on May 28 and May 30) conducted a series of nuclear weapons tests (five for India, six for

Pakistan). The Indian tests were purported to include a thermonuclear device, a standard fission-type weapon of about the same size as the atomic bomb dropped on Japan, a "low-yield" device, and two "sub-kiloton" devices, demonstrating India's ability to employ nuclear weapons across the entire spectrum of the modern battlefield. Pakistan responded by detonating five forty-kiloton devices on May 28, followed by a similarly sized device on May 30. A more worrisome aspect of the Pakistani test of May 30, 1998, was the reported presence of a senior North Korean official who was heavily involved in North Korea's nuclear weapons program. The fact that the sixth Pakistani device was determined to be a plutonium-based weapon only heightened the concern that in addition to testing a Pakistani device, Pakistan may have helped validate a North Korean plutonium weapon design.[61]

While the Clinton administration immediately condemned both the Indian and the Pakistani tests, and imposed stiff economic sanctions against both New Delhi and Islamabad, it interpreted the exchange of nuclear tests in Southwest Asia as underscoring the importance of early U.S. ratification of the CTBT. India was always a wild card in the CTBT entry-into-force equation, having pulled out of the final negotiations on the CTBT in 1996, prior to the treaty having been approved by the United Nations. The CTBT could not enter into force unless India, along with all of the other nations possessing nuclear power reactors, signed and ratified the treaty. However, India was focused on a nuclear-armed China collaborating with a nuclear-armed Pakistan to surround India with nuclear threats. Faced with this problem, India believed it had no choice but to withdraw from the CTBT process (even though it was India that originally championed the idea of a nuclear test ban back in 1954) and demonstrate the reality of the Indian nuclear deterrent.[62]

The Indian and Pakistani nuclear tests were used by the opponents of the CTBT to mock not only the notion of a verifiable nuclear test ban (the Indian test took the CIA completely by surprise) but also the concept of America putting its weight behind a treaty process that, because of India's intransigence and resistance from other nations, including Pakistan and North Korea, had little viability. If the United States ratified the CTBT, then it would be constraining its nuclear capability at a time when potential threats were expanding theirs. Given the reality of Indian and Pakistani nuclear weapons programs, and the possibility of nuclear programs existing in other nations such as North Korea, Iran, Libya, and Syria, the opponents of the CTBT believed that the last thing the United States should do is agree to a permanent cessation of nuclear testing. Ensuring that the U.S. nuclear arsenal remained safe, robust, and reliable seemed more critical than at any time since the end of the Cold War. The need for an American nuclear deterrence was not diminishing, and as such the need to be able to rely on nuclear testing as a means of verifying the reliability and safety of America's nuclear arsenal had become, if anything, more crucial.[63]

The Clinton administration continued to press aggressively for Senate ratification of the CTBT, believing that, having conducted their tests, both India and Pakistan might be lured into joining the CTBT by the example of U.S. leadership. Indeed, in dialogue with Washington, both India and Pakistan undertook to adhere to the CTBT in the future, as long as the other party did so as well. In January 1999, in his State of the Union address, Clinton implored the U.S. Senate to seek early ratification of the CTBT. Clinton's call resulted in increased pressure by the supporters of the CTBT, both in Congress and among the public, on Senator Helms to get the CTBT out of the Senate Armed Services Committee and onto the floor of the Senate for debate and a vote. This pressure built throughout the summer of 1999, and by September the White House and the Senate Democrats were working on a resolution aimed at forcing the issue. In a surprise move, the Senate majority leader, Trent Lott, together with Jesse Helms, agreed to move toward a quick vote on the CTBT in early October 1999. After three hearings before the Senate Armed Services Committee, and fourteen hours of debate on the Senate floor, the Senate voted against ratifying the CTBT, sending the Clinton administration a shocking political defeat and setting back the issue of arms control around the world.[64]

Arms control as a theme was no longer in vogue politically in Washington, DC. Instead, there was a rush to highlight the concept of "emerging threats" and the need to confront them. In early 1998 the Clinton administration impaneled (at the urging of the Republican-controlled Congress) the Commission to Assess the Ballistic Missile Threat to the United States, more commonly referred to as the Rumsfeld Commission, after its chair, former secretary of defense (under President Ford) Donald Rumsfeld, who was nominated for the post by conservative Republicans in Congress. Meeting from January through July 1998, the Rumsfeld Commission issued its report on July 15, declaring that the ballistic missile threat to the United States was so great that "the United States might have little or no warning before operational deployment." The report highlighted the missile threats from "rogue regimes" in Iraq, Iran, and North Korea, noting that the United States would be vulnerable to a missile attack from these nations within a ten- to fifteen-year period.[65]

Having created the Rumsfeld Commission, the Clinton administration could not ignore its findings. Not surprisingly, the commission's report was used by opponents of the ABM treaty to justify the need for a missile defense shield. Under pressure to be seen as responding to the threat postulated by the Rumsfeld Commission report, Clinton approached Russian President Yeltsin in January 1999 with a proposal that would allow for a modification of the ABM treaty to provide for a limited theater missile defense system that would protect the United States from potential rogue states. U.S.-Russian relations were strained by the December 1998 U.S. decision to order UN inspectors out of Iraq before launching an aerial bombardment ostensibly designed to degrade Iraqi WMD programs kept hidden from UN inspectors, but in reality a final effort to remove Saddam Hussein from power. This abandonment of the multilateral disarmament process in Iraq was but the beginning of the complete unraveling of the Clinton administration's arms control policy. As a result of the December action against Iraq, the Russian parliament pulled back START-2 from consideration for ratification.[66]

U.S.-Russian relations were further strained when, in March 1999, NATO unleashed an eleven-week bombing campaign against Yugoslavia in an effort to stop a Serbian-led crackdown in the province of Kosovo. NATO troops were deployed to Albania, where they threatened to intervene directly in Kosovo. Russia condemned the NATO action against Yugoslavia, and the Russian parliament, only recently in receipt of a new ratification bill for Start-2 from President Yeltsin, again recommended that ratification be delayed in light of the NATO action. Alarmed by the turn of events, Russian Prime Minister Primakov warned the parliament that a Russian failure to ratify START-2 could result in the United States withdrawing from the ABM treaty, thus triggering a new arms race. The continued NATO bombardment of Yugoslavia, however, made ratification politically impossible at that time.[67]

In June 1999, following the end of military operations against Yugoslavia, President Clinton and Boris Yeltsin met in Cologne, Germany, where they agreed to put the Kosovo experience behind them and begin focusing on a new round of discussions concerning the ABM treaty and a START-3 agreement. Both presidents knew that they were up against the end of their respective terms in office and that a breakthrough was needed if there were to be any hope of completing an agreement before the end of 2000. Yeltsin agreed to honor President Clinton's request for Russia to reconsider its opposition to any modification of the ABM treaty but was unable to translate this agreement into anything substantive. On July 23, 1999, President Clinton signed the Missile Defense Act of 1999, which put the United States on the track of deploying an active missile defense system. This action, conducted outside of any discussion with the Russians, caused the Russians to rescind Yeltsin's commitment when U.S. and Russian negotiators met in Moscow in August 1999.[68]

In late August 1999 another conflict broke out, further straining U.S.-Russian relations. Russia had fought a bloody two-year conflict in Chechnya from 1994 until 1996. That conflict ended with a cease-fire agreement that gave the Chechens de facto independence from Russia. In August 1999, reacting to a series of attacks on Russian territory attributed to Chechen separatists, Boris Yeltsin again ordered Russian troops into Chechnya. By September Russian forces were laying siege to the Chechen capital of Grozny, and the Russian bombardment of civilians in that city and elsewhere drew widespread condemnation from around the world, including the United States. The Russian military operation also brought into question Russian compliance with the CFE treaty. Even before the August offensive, Russian military deployments in the Caucasus exceeded the caps permitted under the CFE treaty. These caps were completely disregarded after August, as Russia poured in tens of thousands of troops and thousands of tanks and armored vehicles.[69]

In the midst of the Chechen conflict, the thirty nations party to the CFE treaty signed a treaty adaptation agreement on November 19, 1999, that sought to overhaul the Cold War–era framework of the original treaty by allowing for a more flexible distribution of ground forces in recognition of the reality that there no longer was a Warsaw Pact. Even with these new structures in place, Russia remained noncompliant in the Caucasus region, not only in Chechnya but also in regard to force deployments in Georgia and Moldova. Ratification of this new agreement hinged on Russia coming into compliance, something that was not likely so long as fighting raged in Chechnya. The conflict in Chechnya led to deteriorating personal relations between President Clinton and Boris Yeltsin: at a November meeting of the Organization for Security and Cooperation in Europe, Clinton demanded that Yeltsin stop the aerial bombardment of civilians in Grozny. Yeltsin immediately left the conference, and in December, during a state visit to China, he declared that Clinton had "forgotten that Russia has a full arsenal of nuclear weapons." Before relations could further deteriorate, however, Boris Yeltsin surprised everyone when, on December 31, he announced his resignation as president of Russia. Yeltsin appointed Prime Minister Vladimir Putin to take over as acting president until elections could be called in March 2000. Putin was a previously unknown former KGB official who had risen to post-Soviet political prominence in St. Petersburg before becoming prime minister in early August 1999.[70]

The surprise resignation of Boris Yeltsin put a freeze on U.S.-Russian relations, as both nations sought to take stock. Vladimir Putin was a relative unknown, and his interim status made meaningful negotiations problematic. Putin's reputation in Russia was rooted in his strong handling of the Chechen conflict. Shortly after becoming acting president, Putin conducted a tour of Russian troops in Chechnya, cementing his reputation as a tough leader. His standing, however, was somewhat tarnished when, in his first act of official business, Putin gave Yeltsin and his family immunity from prosecution for any crimes that may have been committed while Yeltsin was president (Yeltsin was under investigation at the time of his resignation on a number of corruption charges). However, Putin's decisive character won over the Russian people, and he was elected president of Russia on March 26, 2000, in the first round of balloting. He was inaugurated as president on May 7 and immediately began planning for an early summit meeting with President Clinton in order to get the U.S.-Russian relationship back on a positive track. And as a gift for President Clinton, Vladimir Putin was able to deliver what Boris Yeltsin could not: a ratified START-2, which was positively voted on by the Russian parliament on April 17.[71]

In early June the two presidents—one just starting his term, the other nearing the end of his—met in Moscow. While there were hopes that the two leaders would be able to reach an agreement on missile defense and a START-3 agreement that reduced the nuclear warheads on each side to between 2,000 and 2,500, in the end all that could be accomplished were two minor agreements on the control of Russian plutonium and a joint U.S.-Russian military effort to monitor against accidental missile launches. Clinton was under pressure not to agree to any further cuts in the U.S. nuclear arsenal without first securing a missile defense agreement. The U.S. nuclear strategy was built to accommodate a 2,000 to 2,500 warhead figure. Any reduction beyond this level placed the United States at risk, according to the Pentagon, especially if it did not have a missile defense shield to fall back on. As for Putin, he pushed for even greater warhead cuts but was uncompromising on the issue of missile defense. While begrudgingly acknowledging that there could be a future threat from a "rogue nation," Putin declared that missile defense was "a cure worse than the disease itself."[72]

The summer of 2000 saw the U.S. presidential elections in full swing. While Clinton was in Moscow, Republican hard-liners, including Senator Jesse Helms and the Republican Party candidate, Governor George W. Bush of Texas, warned Clinton not to undertake any obligations that would tie the hands of the next president. With the Moscow summit a failure, Clinton had little choice but to acknowledge that the issue of a U.S. missile defense system was one that would be handled by the next administration, headed by either Al Gore or Bush.

On September 6, 2000, presidents Clinton and Putin met for the last time as national leaders, at a summit held in New York City. The two men signed the "Strategic Stability Cooperation Initiative," a document that recommitted both nations to undertaking, and in some cases extending, existing bilateral arms control and nonproliferation agreements and initiatives. All existing bilateral arms control treaties were reaffirmed, including the ABM treaty, as was the NPT. The initiative also called for continued work on achieving a START-3, as well as working jointly to address the issue of emerging ballistic missile threats. In addition the initiative supported joint U.S.-Russian cooperation on the early ratification of the CTBT. But few people were paying serious attention to what was transpiring in New York. All eyes were on the upcoming elections in November 2000. Whoever won would have to deal with the mixed bag of arms control successes and miscues that marked the Clinton presidency. One thing was certain: the future of U.S.-Russian arms control and nonproliferation cooperation would hinge on the issue of missile defense. The prospects of sustaining the viability of the ABM treaty seemed slim. It would be up to the next president to define the path America would take with regard to its arms control policy.[73]

Russia wasn't the only nation the Clinton administration was racing the clock with in terms of wrapping up unresolved arms control issues prior to the end of President Clinton's term in office. There was the open issue of Iraq's disarmament obligation, left in limbo when UN weapons inspectors were pulled out on Clinton's instructions in December 1998. In the fall of 1998, under pressure from Republicans in Congress and right-wing advocacy groups such as the American Enterprise Institute and the Project for a New American Century, President Clinton had signed the Iraq Liberation Act, which established as official American policy the removal of Saddam Hussein from power. The United Nations's stated disarmament objectives had been hijacked by American regime-change policy. With neither the United States nor Iraq pressing for the return of UN inspectors (the United States was satisfied with the continuation of economic sanctions as a vehicle for undermining Saddam Hussein's hold on power, and Iraq no longer trusted the inspection process as a means of achieving an end to the sanctions), the question of the status of Iraq's WMD programs remained open, enabling no end of alarmist speculation about what the Iraqi government might be up to now that inspectors were no longer monitoring its industrial facilities. Saddam's continued defiance had turned into a political nightmare for the Clinton administration, and the issue of removing him from power through the use of force, as opposed to resuming the disarmament of Iraq, became a central theme of the Republican Party as the 2000 presidential election approached.

The last pressing arms control matter confronting President Clinton was that of North Korea and its nuclear and ballistic missile programs. The Rumsfeld Commission report on 1998 had highlighted North Korea as the one "rogue state" that would possess the means to strike the territory of the United States with a ballistic missile in the not so distant future. There was also concern that North Korea was selling its missile technology to Iran, in exchange for hard currency and oil. As early as January 1996, the United States and North Korea had entered into talks about missile proliferation issues. The Clinton administration had offered to ease economic sanctions in exchange for North Korean cooperation on the issue of ballistic missile proliferation. The two sides met in Berlin in April 1996, but the talks went nowhere, as the United States pushed for North Korean adherence to the missile technology control regime (MTCR), and North Korea demanded that the United States provide financial compensation for revenue lost through lost sales. In response, the Clinton administration imposed largely symbolic economic sanctions in May 1996. Tensions were increased further in October, when North Korea undertook preparations to test a long-range missile. North Korea canceled the test after a series of meetings between U.S. and North Korean officials in New York City. A second round of talks in the summer of 1997, also in New York, made no progress on the issue of North Korean missile sales. In June 1998 North Korea formally announced that it would not end missile exports until it was properly compensated for lost revenue, heightening tensions on the eve of the release of the Rumsfeld Commission report. As if to underscore the analysis of the report, in August 1998 North Korea launched a three-stage rocket, ostensibly to place a small satellite in orbit. Analysts assess that the missile, named the Taepo-Dong-1, would possess a range of 2,000 kilometers if used in a surface-to-surface role.[74]

All efforts to establish a meaningful dialogue between the United States and North Korea on the issue of ballistic missiles failed until November 1998, when President Clinton appointed former secretary of defense William Perry as his North Korea policy director. Perry's role took on added importance when, in December 1998, the United States detected suspicious activity at an underground nuclear facility, and in January 1999, CIA Director George Tenet testified before Congress that the Taepo-Dong-1 missile could be modified to deliver small payloads to Hawaii and Alaska. Tenet went on to say that a follow-on missile, the Taepo-Dong-2, would be able to do the same to targets on the West Coast of the United States. This alarmist testimony served to underscore, in the eyes of hard-liners in and out of the Clinton administration, the pressing need for a missile defense shield.[75]

Building on momentum created through the combination of talks be-tween U.S. and North Korean officials in Pyongyang in late March 1999, and a U.S. inspection of the suspect underground nuclear facility (the team found no evidence of nuclear activity), Perry traveled to North Korea May 25–28, 1999. Perry carried a letter from President Clinton to North Korea's leader, Kim Jong Il, in which Clinton proposed the lifting of U.S. economic sanctions, the normalization of relations, and the provision of a U.S. security guarantee in exchange for North Korea agreeing to be more open about its nuclear activities, especially those that fell outside the Agreed Framework, and its ballistic missile programs. In response, in September 1999, North Korea agreed to a moratorium on ballistic missile testing. Building on this slim foundation, Perry, in a report to Congress in Octo-ber, recommended a completely new approach toward dealing with North Korea, which involved improving diplomatic relations and lifting eco-nomic sanctions as a means of encouraging North Korean cooperation.[76]

While nothing substantive was produced as a result of Perry's ideas, the improvement in relations between North Korea and the West facilitated a summit meeting in June 2000 between North and South Korea in which the issue of unification was discussed. Building on this momentum, Clin-ton ordered economic sanctions to be eased, causing North Korea to ex-tend its moratorium on ballistic missile testing. North Korea, while continuing to demand economic compensation for its lost missile sales, also suggested that it would halt its ballistic missile program altogether if it were able to receive assistance from other nations in launching satellites into orbit. The United States responded by sending a diplomat to North Korea for the purpose of "studying" the proposal. Relations between the United States and North Korea had improved so much that when Secre-tary of State Albright visited North Korea in late October 2000, there was talk about a possible visit by President Clinton prior to his leaving office. However, a follow-on round of negotiations held in Kuala Lumpur, Malaysia, collapsed with no agreement, dashing any chance of a Clinton visit to Pyongyang. Prior to leaving office, on January 2, 2001, President Clinton ordered the imposition of economic sanctions against North Korea for its failure to rein in its missile proliferation activities. After so much hope for a breakthrough, U.S.-North Korean relations were once again frozen in place, waiting for a new president to facilitate a thaw.[77]

CHAPTER 15

THE END OF ARMS CONTROL

The 2000 presidential election was like no other in modern American history. Although the Democratic candidate, Vice President Al Gore, won the overall popular vote, the electoral college vote, which constitutionally decides the election, came down to the state of Florida and some contested ballots from a handful of counties. In a legal showdown worthy of a Greek drama, the final decision on the disposition of the votes was made by the United States Supreme Court, which after a delay of over a month, ruled that Governor George W. Bush had won the Florida election, and with it the presidency.

The accession of George W. Bush to the position of president of the United States represented a political victory for the Republican-dominated hard-liners, who had, since before the administration of President Reagan, opposed arms control (ironically, they were sustaining a policy position that, in its modern embodiment, was first embraced by Democrats such as Scoop Jackson). The global viewpoint of these conservative thinkers was best captured by the abortive Defense Policy Guidance document prepared by the Pentagon in 1992, when Dick Cheney was serving as the secretary of defense. Cheney was now the vice president and had established a working relationship with newly elected President Bush that gave the vice president's office unprecedented influence and control over the national security policies of the United States. The two drafters of the 1992 DPG were likewise ensconced in influential positions—Scooter Libby as Cheney's chief of staff and Paul Wolfowitz as the deputy secretary of defense.

President Bush rounded out his national security team by selecting Donald Rumsfeld, the former secretary of defense under President Ford and the author of the 1998 Rumsfeld Commission report on the threat posed by ballistic missiles, as the new secretary of defense, a clear signal the missile defense was going to be a major priority of the new Bush administration. His choice for national security advisor was Condoleezza Rice, who had served on the National Security Council of President George H. W. Bush as the director of Soviet and East European affairs and had been deeply involved in the issues pertaining to the dissolution of the Warsaw Pact and the Soviet Union as well as German reunification. Until her selection as national security advisor, Rice had served as the provost for Stanford University. The sole moderate on the Bush national security team was Colin Powell, whom Bush selected to be secretary of state. Powell had an extensive national security résumé, having served previously as the national security advisor to President Reagan from 1987 until 1991, and later as the chair of the Joint Chiefs of Staff during the administrations of both President George H. W. Bush and President Clinton.

The national security policy of the United States under the presidency of George W. Bush was designed from the outset to represent a break from the past. The confused multilateralism of the Clinton era was to be replaced by a more streamlined, decisive unilateralism that, in the mind of its framers, was designed by intent to exploit the preeminent position held by the United States in international affairs. Philosophically this meant avoiding the entanglement of complicated arms control agreements and instead doing what was required to better promote American national interests. Operating from the simplistic view that the United States was imbued with a moral right of assertiveness and equipped with a natural inclination to do good, the Bush team set out to redefine how America would operate in relation to the rest of the world. Multilateral institutions such as the United Nations were viewed with suspicion or even outright derision, while traditional alliances such as NATO were addressed from the standpoint of how they could best support the policies and interests of the United States.[1]

The Bush administration took as its operating instructions the words of the newly elected president during his inaugural address of January 20, 2001:

We will build our defenses beyond challenge, lest weakness invite challenge. We will confront weapons of mass destruction, so that a new century is spared new horrors. The enemies of liberty and our country should make no mistake: America remains engaged in the world by history and by choice, shaping a balance of power that favors freedom. We will defend our allies and our interests. We will meet aggression and bad faith with resolve and strength. And to all nations, we will speak for the values that gave our nation birth.[2]

The new Bush team entered office with a sense of certainty on what direction it wanted to take on a number of critical issues, including the matter of arms control. As a candidate, George W. Bush had stated that, if elected president, he would "offer Russia the necessary amendments to the ABM Treaty so as to make our deployment of effective missile defenses consistent with the treaty."[3] However, shortly after coming into office, the Bush administration began pushing for a series of new missile defense plans, including the construction of a missile defense "test bed" in Alaska (designed to counter a North Korean missile attack as postulated by the Rumsfeld Commission report) that would directly challenge the terms of the 1972 ABM treaty. As early as May 1, 2001, President Bush, in a speech delivered at the National Defense University, was talking not about remaining "consistent" with the ABM treaty but rather about moving "beyond" that treaty.[4]

The missile defense system that the Bush administration was proposing to field was a far cry from the space-based, advanced technology–driven "Star Wars" system that had been proposed by President Reagan. Instead, the Pentagon was envisioning a more limited system, at least at the start, which combined ground-based interceptors with advanced surface-to-air missiles based on U.S. Navy ships to create a "shield" that could shoot down a small number of missiles launched from any potential rogue nation. On the surface, the concept was attractive: an insurance policy against the irrational acts of nations operating outside the framework of international law and human decency. But in embracing this moralistic argument, the Bush administration ran up against the reality that a missile defense shield had long been viewed as a force of destabilization, a modern-day Maginot Line that would compel potential adversaries threatened by the notion of a nuclear-armed America hiding behind a missile defense system to find the means of overcoming that shield, thereby setting off an expensive arms race. The fact that the technology the Bush administration was planning to deploy, even in its scaled-down version, was still untested only further underscored the arguments of those opposed.

But the Bush team, headed by Secretary of Defense Rumsfeld, and backstopped behind the scenes by Deputy National Security Advisor Stephan Hadley (who had worked on ABM issues during the presidency of George H. W. Bush), firmly believed that some form of defense shield was better than no defense shield at all. The ABM treaty was a flawed product of times long past, they noted, and Russia today was not the Soviet Union of the past, in terms of either intent or capability. New threats were emerging, manifested in the present by nations such as North Korea and Iran, with no guarantees that even greater threats would not emerge in the future. As such, the United States should no longer be constrained by Cold War thinking.[5]

President Bush, in his first meeting with Russian President Vladimir Putin at the G-8 Summit in Genoa, Italy, held in July 2001, drove home this point of view, advocating reworking the ABM treaty in exchange for even greater strategic force reductions. The two leaders quickly expressed a sense of mutual admiration for one another, referring to each other as "friend." But behind the warm rhetoric lay ideological differences that made it clear that the Bush ABM policy would not be warmly received in Moscow. The Russian president continued to call the ABM treaty the "cornerstone" of arms control. Another issue of great sensitivity was that of NATO expansion. In a June 2001 tour of European nations, including several Eastern European stops, Bush made a series of speeches in which he spoke of NATO expansion. Such expansion, Bush said, was no longer a question of whether but a question of when. "Russia should not fear the expansion of freedom-loving people towards her borders," Bush declared.[6] The former Warsaw Pact nations of Hungary, Poland, and the Czech Republic were already in line to become NATO members, and talks were under way with the three former Soviet Baltic Republics (Lithuania, Estonia, and Latvia) for their membership as well.

For his part, Putin put the United States on notice that Russia would not look favorably toward any continued expansion of NATO, which the Russian president said had outlived its usefulness. "There is no more Warsaw Pact, no more Soviet Union, but NATO continues to exist and develop," Putin said. The expansion of NATO into Eastern Europe was "not caused by any political or military necessity" and created a security situation that put pressure on both Europe and Russia—pressure that was counterproductive in the post–Cold War era. The Russian president made clear his preference for either the disbandment of NATO or the creation of a new framework that had Russia joining as an equal partner.[7]

Led by Condoleezza Rice, who argued that Russia no longer carried the influence it did when it was part of the Soviet Union, the Bush administration shrugged off the Russian protests as largely irrelevant, since in their view Russia was not in a position economically or militarily to challenge the United States. This mind-set was clearly demonstrated during the visit of the Russian deputy chief of staff, General Yuri Baluevski, to the United States in August 2001, for the purpose of discussing possible amendments to the ABM treaty that would enable the United States to test a limited missile defense system. Baluevski continued to propose a solution that was linked to the conditions and restrictions set forth in the ABM treaty. His U.S. counterparts responded by stating bluntly that in order to accomplish what it wanted, the United States viewed the ABM treaty, if it was to continue to be referred to, as existing in name only.[8]

The ABM treaty was not the only arms control regime coming under closer scrutiny by the Bush administration. An effort by the Biological and Toxins Weapons Convention (BTWC), undertaken from 1994 through 2001, to strengthen its capability to detect violations with a level of confidence equal to that of verification systems in place for comparable nuclear and chemical weapons treaties and accords ran afoul of unilateral American interests. An ad hoc committee was formed to create a mechanism of declarations and on-site inspection, in the form of a BTWC Protocol, which would provide greater information about, and improved access to, dual-capable biological facilities so that they could not be misused for the production of biological weapons. While not seamless, the proposed protocol was designed to deter illicit biological weapons activities by making it more complicated for potential proliferators to operate outside of their BTWC obligations.[9]

The primary problem was that while the United States was comfortable in demanding increased access to facilities and personnel operating in other nations, it would not permit the kind of reciprocity required of multilateral agreements. The United States was engaged in a whole host of classified defense-related work in biological defense, involving the actual manufacture of live biological agent, which would have to be declared (and which technically was a violation of the BTWC itself). Likewise, American industries that were involved in biological research, such as pharmaceutical companies, were loath to allow international inspectors access to their proprietary information. The United States demanded a double standard that would close American companies and activities but open up the rest of the world, including Europe, to inspection. When the BTWC balked at this double standard, the Bush administration withdrew from the BTWC

Protocol negotiations and demanded that the effort to produce a protocol cease and desist.[10]

On September 11, 2001, a terrorist attack on the United States of America forever changed how the Bush administration would approach issues pertaining to national security, including arms control. An Islamic fundamentalist organization known as Al Qaeda, led by a Saudi Arabian named Osama Bin Laden and his Egyptian deputy, Ayman al-Zuwahiri, operating from Afghanistan but employing support cells in Germany and the United States, orchestrated the simultaneous hijacking of four U.S. airliners, which were then taken under control by hijackers who had received rudimentary flight training and flown into the Twin Towers of the World Trade Center in New York City (two aircraft) and the Pentagon (one aircraft). The fourth aircraft, which was targeting the U.S. Capitol, crashed into a field in southwest Pennsylvania after passengers attempted to regain control. Nearly 3,000 people lost their lives in the attacks, and the administration of President Bush found itself engaged in a war that was unprecedented in American history.

The September 11, 2001, attacks were not the first conducted by Al Qaeda on American targets. In August 1998 Al Qaeda orchestrated the bombings of U.S. embassies in Kenya and Tanzania and was behind the suicide attack on a U.S. Navy ship, the USS *Cole*, in Yemen on October 12, 2000. But the September 11 attacks were the first carried out by Al Qaeda on the soil of the United States, and that fact, coupled with the horrific scale of the damage done, combined to create a psychological impact on America that had not been seen since the 1941 bombing of Pearl Harbor. The major difference between the two events, however, was that in 1941 the United States was able to clearly define who would be held accountable for the attack—Imperial Japan, followed by Nazi Germany, when it joined Japan in declaring war against the United States. President Roosevelt asked Congress to declare war against Japan (and later Germany), and the United States subsequently mobilized to wage global war against a well-defined enemy.

In 2001, forty years later, the enemy was not so well defined. Other than a few thousand Al Qaeda Islamic extremists operating inside Afghanistan, there was no physical manifestation of an enemy for the United States to declare war on. Rather than confronting the physical reality of a nation-state, or groups of nation-states, the Bush administration found itself squaring off against an ideology, Islamic fundamentalism, which in itself was nebulous and lacked physical form beyond the bands of fighters operating in Afghanistan. Within a month the United States had deployed forces into Southwest Asia to begin the process of destroying Al Qaeda and bringing Osama Bin Laden and his lieutenants to justice ("dead or alive," according to President Bush). The target list was expanded to include bringing down the Islamic fundamentalist regime of the Taliban, a coalition of fundamentalist religious clerics who were able to seize power in the aftermath of the chaos and anarchy that had gripped Afghanistan following the withdrawal of Soviet forces in the late 1980s. By December 2001 the Taliban had been evicted from power, and the Al Qaeda forces in Afghanistan either destroyed or scattered. Osama Bin Laden had narrowly escaped capture and was believed to have escaped to a sanctuary in the lawless expanse of Pakistan's Northwest Territories.

The impact of the terrorist attacks of September 11 on U.S. foreign relations and national security policy was sweeping and manifested itself almost immediately. In a speech before a joint session of the U.S. Congress on September 20, 2001, President Bush declared war on terrorism not just in Afghanistan but around the world. "Our enemy is a radical network of terrorists and every government that supports them. Our war on terror begins with al-Qaeda, but it does not end there. It will not end until every terrorist group of global reach has been found, stopped and defeated." Invoking the memory of the Second World War, when America and its allies fought the forces of world fascism, President Bush proclaimed that "we will direct every resource at our command—every means of diplomacy, every tool of intelligence, every instrument of law enforcement, every financial influence and every necessary weapon of war—to the destruction and to the defeat of the global terror network."[11] In response, Congress passed sweeping legislation, in the form of the USA PATRIOT Act, which gave the president the tools he claimed he needed to wage this war. NATO also responded, by invoking Article V of its charter, declaring that the attack on the United States was an attack on all of NATO. The United States and NATO were now inextricably linked in combating the war on terror. In the simplistic formulation of President Bush, who pointedly told Congress and the world, "Every nation in every region now has a decision to make: Either you are with us, or you are with the terrorists," U.S. national security prerogatives were now not only paramount but sacrosanct.[12] Waging the global war on terror had become a crusade, with all of the intensity and fervor of past crusades. Woven into this crusade was a whole host of complicated topics, including missile defense and NATO expansion, which were now considered part and parcel of the global war on terror, and as such no longer subject to debate and discussion.

The first opportunity to observe how the new post–September 11 mind-set of the United States would affect U.S.-Russian relations came on

November 13–15, 2001, when Russian President Putin visited President Bush in Washington and later at the Bush family ranch in Crawford, Texas. The two leaders discussed a wide range of issues, including the ongoing situation in Afghanistan, U.S.-Russian economic relations, and Russia's relationship with NATO. But the main focus of the meetings was on the issue of missile defense, coupled with new strategic force reductions. While Putin had come into the meetings still holding out that a compromise could be reached that permitted the United States to test its missile defense system within the framework of the 1972 ABM treaty, the Bush administration, led by National Security Advisor Rice, made it clear that it was, in the opinion of the United States, time to "move on," beyond the ABM treaty. Noting that the ABM treaty no longer represented a foundational role in defining U.S.-Russian relations, Rice, together with Secretary of State Colin Powell, signaled that its demise was all but certain.[13]

On the issue of strategic force reductions, the Bush administration made it clear that it not only sought deep cuts in the numbers of deployed nuclear warheads (from the 7,000 currently deployed to a level of 1,700 to 2,200 within ten years) but also wanted to avoid the complicated and drawn-out processes normally associated with arms control agreements of this nature. President Bush told Putin he was looking for an informal, nonbinding arrangement that would reduce the strategic arsenals of each nation but provide flexibility for each nation to adapt to unforeseen developments in the future. A treaty structure, such as provided for under START, was no longer desirable or needed because the United States and Russia, according to Bush, had "a new relationship based on trust."

For his part, Putin, while embracing the strategic force reductions (and committing Russia to levels on par with the U.S. force structure), made it clear that Russia would prefer a more formal arrangement codified in the form of a treaty. "The world is far from having international relations that are built solely on trust, unfortunately," Putin responded. "That's why it is so important today to rely on the existing foundation of treaties and agreements in the arms control and disarmament areas." Putin was commenting not just on START, but also on the ABM treaty.[14]

But it was too late to save the ABM treaty. On December 13, 2001, President Bush announced that the United States would withdraw from the 1972 ABM treaty, triggering the six-month notification process called for by that agreement. "I have concluded the ABM treaty hinders our government's ability to develop ways to protect our people from future terrorist or rogue state missile attacks," the president said.[15] Bush had hinted as much to Putin during their meetings in November, so the Russian president was not taken completely by surprise. Putin, in response, labeled the U.S. decision a "mistake" and urged the United States and Russia to move quickly to create a "new framework of our strategic relationship." Putin also addressed the Russian people, assuring them that the U.S. decision "presents no threat to the security of the Russian Federation."[16]

President Bush's articulation of deep strategic reductions was enabled by the results of a Nuclear Posture Review conducted by the National Security Council, the Department of Defense, and the Joint Chiefs of Staff. This review was ordered by National Security Presidential Directive 4 (NSPD-4). In seeking a nuclear force of around 2,000 warheads, the Bush administration had made a decision to sustain the force level structure put in place by President Clinton. The United States would get rid of the MX missile and limit the number of B-2 bombers to twenty. The *Minuteman* III missile force would be kept at five hundred, and the number of *Trident* submarines armed with D-5 missiles reduced from eighteen to fourteen (the other four were to be converted to cruise-missile launch platforms). The B-1 bomber would be retained, but its nuclear mission was eliminated. The B-52 bomber fleet would be maintained at seventy-six, all of which were nuclear capable.[17]

But although the Bush administration sustained the nuclear force structure it inherited from the Clinton presidency, it changed the nuclear posture of the United States away from the concept of adaptive strategy, in which nuclear weapons were de-targeted while placed in a state of operational readiness, with the ability to target as required either in accordance with the existing nuclear war plan or in response to contingencies as they developed. Based on the 2001 Nuclear Posture Review, which was updated following the September 11 attacks, the United States put forward new nuclear weapons planning guidance, in the form of National Security Presidential Directive 14 (NSPD-14), published in early 2002, which resulted in the publication of SIOP-03. But rather than an actual single integrated operations plan, the new SIOP-03 was a series of seven separate nuclear war plans, one each for Russia, China, North Korea, Iran, Libya, Syria, and Iraq. And while nuclear weapons were no longer actively targeting either Russia or China, after September 11, given the heightened concern over WMD and rogue states, nuclear weapons and delivery resources were allocated to each of the five "rogue state" plans.[18]

In addition to a radically new nuclear weapons war plan, the Bush administration, as part of its review, initiated a program to study the need for a new "responsive infrastructure" for the design and deployment of a new generation of nuclear weapons in significantly shorter time periods than in the past. These weapons would "augment" existing nuclear weapons already deployed and would be designed for use against hardened targets and underground facilities. While the Bush administration was touting the fact that it was reducing the U.S. nuclear weapons arsenal to the lowest level in decades, in fact it was integrating nuclear weapons into the military response profile in a manner not seen since the early days of the Reagan administration. Rather than heading away from the edge of the nuclear abyss, the Bush administration was taking a giant step forward toward making the horror of nuclear weapons employment not only a possibility but a reality.[19]

In February 2002, in recognition of the need to respond to Russian sensitivities over formalizing strategic arms reductions, the Bush administration announced that the United States and Russia would begin a process to codify the agreed-on arms cuts. This process would result in a "legally binding" agreement, either in the form of a treaty or in the form of an Executive Agreement that could be commented on by the U.S. Congress. The Bush administration argued that the United States had no interest in dictating the size and composition of Russia's strategic forces, and given the fact that America could be facing new dangers in the future, it wasn't prudent to solidify the size and makeup of the U.S. nuclear arsenal as well. Russia continued to insist that whatever forms such an agreement took, it would have to be subject to the approval of the legislative branches of both countries. Both sides were looking for an agreement of ten years' duration, which would use the verification mechanisms in place under START. In response to President Putin's threats to reequip Russian missiles with MIRVs if the United States went ahead with its plans to withdraw from the ABM treaty, Secretary of State Colin Powell indicated that such a move was of no concern to the Bush administration, which no longer viewed Russia as a threat and therefore would not interfere with whatever moves Russia deemed necessary to defend itself.[20]

On May 24, 2002, President Bush traveled to Moscow, where he met with President Putin to sign a new treaty, the Strategic Offensive Reductions Treaty, or SORT, which represented the codification that Russia had been seeking. The SORT document consisted of only five hundred words, as opposed to the hundreds of pages comprising START. The document was vague on what kind of warheads were to be covered and how warheads would be counted. However, by referring to past statements by Bush and Putin, SORT clearly only covered warheads actually mated on operational missiles, not warheads held in reserve. SORT also failed to specify whether the warheads removed under the agreement should be destroyed or not. Russia wanted them destroyed in a verifiable fashion, while the United States wanted to keep the warheads in storage, thereby retaining the ability to upload them if the strategic situation warranted.[21]

Although SORT was touted as a "reduction" treaty, critics in Congress noted that it did not require the destruction of a single warhead. So while the Bush administration claimed that it had reduced the operational nuclear warheads in the U.S. inventory to 2,200, the fact was that another 2,400 warheads would be retained in reserve, some of which could be returned into service within weeks of a decision, with the entire arsenal made operational within a three-year period. It appeared that the Bush administration was using arms control as a cover for maintaining a larger, more robust nuclear capability than publicly advertised. Adding to the concerns that SORT was simply a vehicle to disguise a more capable nuclear war plan, the treaty had a three-month withdrawal clause, as opposed to the six-month clause in START. This time period coincided with the time it would take to make ready substantial portions of the reserve nuclear stockpile. The Bush administration approached SORT with a sense of finality. While the Russians continued to press for follow-on negotiations to clarify the many outstanding issues not covered by SORT, the Bush administration made it clear that any additional negotiations designed to apply even more constraints on the U.S. nuclear arsenal would not be welcome.[22]

The timing of SORT was not an accident. On June 13, 2002, the United States formally withdrew from the ABM treaty, as promised by President Bush. The next day, June 14, Russia declared that it would not longer abide by START-2, meaning that Russia would seek to build new missiles and equip those and their current inventory with MIRVs as they saw fit. The Bush administration was not concerned by the Russian moves. By design, SORT provided the United States with the ability to wait and see which direction the Russians took on rearmament. If at any time the Russian capability became worrisome, the United States could, at relatively low expense, simply pull its reserve warheads out of storage and upload its *Minuteman* III and *Trident* D-5 missiles, rapidly offsetting any moves the Russians might make. In any event, many inside the Bush administration believed that the Russian economy would not be able to sustain the expense of a new arms race, and thus felt that Putin's threats were empty.[23]

By the summer of 2002, the issue of the ABM treaty was rapidly overtaken by the growing crisis in the Middle East concerning Iraq. In the aftermath of September 11, the Bush administration had made the case that removing Saddam Hussein from power was consistent with the goals and objectives of the global war on terrorism. In their thinking, Saddam's continued refusal to permit the return of UN weapons inspectors created the conditions for Iraq's reacquisition of WMD. Since the United States had labeled Iraq a "state sponsor of terror" and had accused Saddam Hussein of collaborating with Al Qaeda (although with vague and unsubstantiated information), the Bush administration claimed that an unacceptable nexus had been created whereby Saddam Hussein would be able to produce WMD for use by Al Qaeda to attack the United States and its allies. Even when Iraq agreed, in September 2002, to permit the return of UN weapons inspectors in an effort to demonstrate that it was in compliance with its disarmament obligation, the Bush administration continued to allege that Iraq maintained a stockpile of chemical and biological weapons and long-range missiles to deliver them and that it was actively pursuing a nuclear weapons program.

On September 20, 2002, President Bush released the National Security Strategy of the United States, and in doing so introduced the world to how America viewed itself in the post–September 11 era. In keeping with the theme that the Cold War was finished, the new strategy abandoned the traditional concepts of deterrence and instead embraced a forward-leaning strategy that emphasized preemption of problems before they could manifest themselves into actions that harmed the United States or its allies. America's Cold War opponents were no longer the enemy. President Bush stated that the new threat came in the form of radical terrorists and rogue states that sought to acquire weapons of mass destruction with which to attack the American homeland. This required a new strategy, which had the United States identifying and destroying any terrorist threat before it reached the United States. The tools the Bush administration was bringing to bear against this new problem included law enforcement, intelligence, diplomacy, and the military. It was on the military solution that the president focused the most, declaring that America must maintain its position as the sole remaining superpower on earth by deploying an armed force so powerful and advanced that potential threats and rivals would not even contemplate competing with, or confronting, the United States.[24]

This newly defined supremacy was more than simple rhetoric, as the situation with Iraq demonstrated. The return of UN weapons inspectors was delayed while the United States pushed for a new UN Security Council resolution that would set the conditions of Iraqi compliance and that could serve as the justification for military action against Iraq should the United States deem Iraq to be in violation of that resolution. In this effort the United States was joined by the United Kingdom. However, the remaining three permanent members of the Security Council—Russia, France, and China—were not in support of creating an automatic "trigger" for war and instead insisted that any resolution passed by the Security Council defining Iraqi disarmament obligations would have to be followed by a second resolution specifically authorizing the use of force against Iraq, if such a move was deemed necessary. In the give-and-take negotiations that followed, a resolution was crafted, SCR 1441, which, while not explicitly authorizing the use of force if Iraq failed to comply, remained ambiguous on the issue of a second resolution.

While the Security Council debated the issue of a resolution on Iraq, the United States worked with its NATO allies to gather support for any future military move against Iraq. NATO was decidedly split on the issue, with the governments of France, Germany, and Belgium firmly opposed to a conflict with Iraq, and those of the United Kingdom and Spain supportive. But NATO had three new members—Hungary, Poland, and the Czech Republic—that were loath to go against the United States on the issue of Iraq. When UN weapons inspectors finally returned to Iraq, in November 2002, they quickly undermined many of the U.S. claims about Iraq's reconstitution of WMD capability by inspecting facilities named by the Pentagon as being actively involved in WMD work, only to find that the facilities in question were derelict or clearly involved in nonproscribed activity. By the end of 2002, France and Germany were siding with Russia and China in insisting that UN weapons inspectors be given all the time they needed to verify Iraqi compliance. Secretary of Defense Donald Rumsfeld, who assumed a very public role in defending the Bush administration's claims against Iraq, derided the null findings of the UN inspectors in Iraq, declaring that "the absence of evidence is not evidence of absence," and noting that "the fact that the inspectors have not yet come up with new evidence of Iraq's WMD program could be evidence, in and of itself, of Iraq's non-cooperation." Rumsfeld went on to explain: "We do know that Iraq has designed its programs in a way that they can proceed in an environment of inspections and that they are skilled at denial and deception."[25]

In December 2002 Rumsfeld pushed NATO to support any U.S. effort against Iraq. Faced with continued obstruction by France and Germany, Rumsfeld observed, "Germany has been a problem, and France has been a problem. But you look at vast numbers of other countries in Europe. They're not with France and Germany on this, they're with the United States."[26] Germany and France, Rumsfeld said, represent "old Europe." NATO's recent expansion meant that "the center of gravity is shifting to the east," Rumsfeld said. It wasn't just Hungary, Poland, and the Czech

Republic that Rumsfeld was referring to. NATO had extended invitations to Bulgaria, Slovakia, and Slovenia, as well as Latvia, Lithuania, and Estonia. These nations were looking to join NATO as early as 2004 and were more than prepared to back the United States on Iraq as the price of admission. This new direction for NATO was ominous from a Russian point of view. Not only was NATO expanding to the borders of Russia and, in the case of the Baltic Republics, into the territory of the former Soviet Union, it was assuming a worldwide militaristic stance. NATO was in active negotiation with the United States and the Afghan government about the prospects of NATO taking command of the International Security Assistance Force (ISAF), which had been created by UN Security Council resolution in December 2001. This action would represent a major new role and mission for NATO, one that took it out of Europe and into a nation that bordered the former Soviet Union. Now NATO was expanding further and talking about the potential of military involvement in Iraq. The concept of NATO as a defensive alliance was rapidly fading, especially from Russia's perspective.

The situation in Iraq was viewed as a defining moment by the Bush administration. From their perspective, Iraq was a prime example of how WMD in the hands of a hostile state, or terrorists, could threaten the United States and its allies. The multilateral approach for resolving a situation like Iraq, via the United Nations Security Council, was unsatisfactory in the view of the Bush national security team. What was needed was an American plan to deal with this emerging threat. In December 2002 the Bush administration published such a plan, in the form of NSPD-17, the "National Strategy to Combat Weapons of Mass Destruction." The United States, NSPD-17 announced, "will not permit the world's most dangerous regimes and terrorists to threaten us with the world's most destructive weapons. We must accord the highest priority to the protection of the United States, our forces, and our friends and allies from the existing and growing WMD threat."[27]

NSPD-17 set forth a three-tiered plan for dealing with the global WMD threat, which focused on counter-proliferation actions by the U.S. military and "appropriate civilian agencies"; enhanced "traditional measures," such as diplomacy, arms control, and multilateral agreements; and what they called "consequence management" within the United States itself—the ability to effectively respond to any use of WMD within America's borders. NSPD-17 sought to ensure global compliance with the Nuclear Nonproliferation Treaty (NPT), the Chemical Weapons Convention (CWC), and the Biological and Toxins Weapons Convention (BTWC).[28]

The call for the embrace of multilateral institutions inherent in NSPD-17 clashed with the Bush administration's lack of support for the UN weapons inspection process in Iraq. Rather than embrace multilateralism, the Bush administration aggressively pursued its unilateral objective of regime change in Iraq, using the threat of WMD as a facilitating device. By mid-March 2003, the U.S. preparations for war with Iraq were in place, and President Bush instructed the UN to remove its inspectors from Iraq, citing Iraqi noncompliance despite the fact that the UN inspectors had found no evidence of Iraqi retention or reconstitution of WMD. Even though the United States was unable to secure a second Security Council resolution explicitly authorizing the use of force against Iraq, President Bush, backed by British Prime Minister Tony Blair, ordered the invasion of Iraq. Saddam Hussein's government collapsed in early April 2003, and by May 2003 the United States had installed a provisional occupation government. Russia strongly condemned the invasion and subsequent occupation. By the end of May, with all of Iraq under the control of the U.S. and British military, no WMD had been uncovered. The primary argument cited by President Bush in support of his decision to invade had turned out to be wrong. Contrary to the claims made by the Bush administration and others, Iraq had in fact disposed of the totality of its viable WMD stocks in the summer of 1991, just as Saddam Hussein had claimed to the UN weapons inspectors. Not only were there no WMD in Iraq, but the claims of a link between Saddam Hussein's Iraq and Al Qaeda were likewise found to be false. There was no nexus between Iraqi WMD and the forces of terror after all.

The stunning speed at which the United States was able to oust Saddam Hussein at first provided substance to the rhetoric put forward by the Bush administration in the 2002 National Security Strategy of the United States. Fresh from their ouster of the Iraqi dictator, the Bush administration set its eyes on resolving the issue of the remaining "rogue states"—Iran, North Korea, Syria, and Libya. Of the four nations, North Korea was perhaps the most problematic. In October 2002 the Bush administration began pressuring North Korea about its nuclear and missile programs. In particular, the Bush administration claimed that North Korea had a secret uranium-enrichment program operating outside of the 1994 Agreed Framework. On November 14, 2002, President Bush declared that the oil shipments to North Korea would be suspended if Pyongyang did not halt its nuclear ambitions. By December 2002 North Korea threatened to restart its nuclear power plants, claiming it had no choice given the halting of oil shipments. North Korea ordered the IAEA to begin dismantling its monitoring system at the Yongbyon power plant; when the IAEA refused, North Korea dismantled them itself. North Korea evicted the two IAEA inspectors who were in charge of the monitoring effort and began moving nearly 1,000 nuclear fuel rods to Yongbyon, where they could be used to manufacture plutonium for a nuclear weapon.[29]

In early January 2003 the IAEA demanded that North Korea readmit the IAEA inspectors and cease its nuclear weapons activities. North Korea, in response, announced on January 10 that it would withdraw from the NPT, a replay of the scenario that brought the United States and North Korea on the verge of war in 1994. However, in 2003 the United States had its sights set on Baghdad, not Pyongyang, and the Bush administration was forced to limit its response to diplomatic maneuvering and rhetoric. Tensions between North Korea and the United States continued to rise, and in April 2003 North Korea admitted it had reprocessed spent fuel rods at the Yongbyon plant and was able to extract enough plutonium for an atomic bomb. America's new nonproliferation policy was being put to the test, especially as it grew increasingly apparent that the United States had deployed its military to confront a threat (Iraq) that had no WMD programs, while another threat (North Korea), which appeared to be working toward a nuclear weapons capability, was dealt with diplomatically.[30]

Another looming proliferation problem appeared to be building with Iran. In August 2002 reports from an Iranian opposition group, the National Council of Resistance, indicated that Iran had constructed a uranium enrichment plant outside the framework of its safeguards agreement with the IAEA. The IAEA immediately demanded that its inspectors be granted access to this site, and Iran agreed. It soon became apparent that Iran was embarked on a major program for the enrichment of uranium. Iran contended that this program was for peaceful nuclear energy. The Bush administration, on the other hand, contended that given the secrecy in which Iran had surrounded its nuclear program, the only reasonable conclusion that could be drawn was that Iran was pursuing an illicit nuclear weapons capability. Iran was also pursuing its own indigenous ballistic missile program and had deployed a missile, the *Shahib*-2, which possessed a range of 750 kilometers. Another missile, the *Shahib*-3, was in the final stages of testing and could achieve ranges of around 2,000 kilometers. These missiles gave Iran the ability to reach targets throughout the Middle East, including Israel. If the missiles were armed with nuclear warheads, as the Bush administration feared was Teheran's objective, then the entire region could be destabilized. Iran denied having a nuclear weapons program and contended its missiles were for self-defense only.[31]

Flush from the perceived military victory in Iraq, and with the issues of North Korea and Iran looming on the near horizon, President Bush traveled to St. Petersburg, Russia, for a short summit meeting with Russian President Putin. The two presidents exchanged the instruments of ratification of the Strategic Offensive Reductions Treaty, or SORT, also known as the Moscow Treaty. The treaty thus went into force at that time. The treaty itself had been signed in May 2002 but had gone through a lengthy and tumultuous ratification process in the legislative bodies of both Russia and the United States, where both sides were concerned about the brevity of the treaty and the lack of detail. In the end, the U.S. Senate voted in favor of ratification on March 6, 2003, unwilling to confront the president on the eve of the Iraq conflict. The Russian Parliament followed suit on May 24, wanting to give Putin a vehicle to smooth over relations with the United States, which had soured because of the invasion of Iraq.[32]

In his comments to the media following the exchange of documents, President Bush declared his intent to pursue constructive joint projects with Russia in the field of ballistic missile defense, while proclaiming that the United States and Russia would "intensify efforts to confront the global threats of terrorism, and the proliferation of weapons of mass destruction and their means of delivery, that threaten our peoples and freedom-loving peoples around the world." Bush in particular pressed Putin for Russian assistance on the issues of North Korea and Iran. For his part, Putin was more muted, simply noting, "This current summit meeting yet again confirmed the fact that there is no alternative for the cooperation between Russia and the United States, both in terms of ensuring our domestic national agendas and in terms of cooperation for the sake of enhanced international strategic stability."[33]

While Russia and the United States agreed to reduce the size of their respective nuclear arsenals, the Bush administration was moving forward with a new nuclear weapons employment doctrine, derived from the criteria established in NSPD-17, the "National Strategy to Combat Weapons of Mass Destruction." One of the major new aspects to this doctrine was that it did away with the SIOP concept of integrated planning for nuclear war, replacing it instead with an operational planning process that focused on "conflicts." The difference was more than just semantic. The military rationale behind this decision was that a nuclear "war" implied an exchange of nuclear weapons between two opponents. In a nuclear "conflict," only one side—the United States—would be employing nuclear weapons. Nuclear war involved the complementary processes of "deliberate planning" and "adaptive planning," in which a war would be waged in accordance with a set plan for weapons release (deliberate), followed up by intelligence-generated targets (adaptive). However, "adaptive" planning was always preceded by "deliberate" planning. The new U.S. doctrine for nuclear war placed an emphasis not on adapting to an existing plan, but rather on developing operational plans in response to an imminent crisis, a process known as "crisis action planning."[34]

The Bush administration contended that the new reality of the post–Cold War era created a multipolar world that was more unpredictable and dangerous than what the United States confronted when all it had to deal with was the Soviet Union. "Crisis action" planning lowered the threshold for the employment of nuclear weapons by creating an operational framework that could envision the preemptive use of nuclear weapons in a nonnuclear environment, even one involving nonstate players such as terrorist organizations. In the post–September 11 world, the United States was not going to wait for terrorists to strike again before responding, especially if the terrorists were armed with WMD capability. Instead, the United States would seek to identify the terrorist threat early on and preempt it, even if the weapon used for preemption was nuclear. The new nuclear war plan, known as OPLAN 8022, identified four conditions where the preemptive employment of nuclear weapons could occur: if an enemy intended to use WMD against Americans or allied forces of civilians; if there were an imminent attack expected in the form of biological weapons that only the effects of a nuclear detonation could destroy; if there were a need to strike at buried or hardened bunkers or facilities involved in the production of WMD, or the command and control of weapons so armed; and to demonstrate America's will and intent to use nuclear weapons. While recognizing that the preemptive use of nuclear weapons would lead to widespread condemnation of the United States, the Bush administration had determined that there was no legal obstacle to such use if a determination was made that the situation was warranted.[35]

In the end, the reduction of nuclear warheads as a result of the Moscow Treaty did not reduce the likelihood of a nuclear conflict, but rather increased it. In a bipolar situation such as existed during the Cold War, any use of nuclear weapons would have triggered a catastrophic chain of events that would have devastated each nation and the rest of the world. In a perverse way, the larger numbers of warheads actually made war less likely, given the consequences. In the post–September 11 era, especially after the reductions ordered by SORT, the Bush administration was convinced that the United States was the only viable nuclear power remaining in the world. The Russian nuclear arsenal was no longer capable of delivery of a first-strike, knockout blow. However, given the hard-kill capabilities of both the *Minuteman*-III and the *Trident* D-5, the same could not be said about U.S. nuclear capability. The American nuclear capability was robust enough to deal effectively with Russia and China while still retaining enough of a reserve to handle any emerging threat that might exist. With the consequences of employing nuclear weapons all but eliminated in terms of physical damage to the United States, all that mattered was whether a given situation warranted a nuclear response. The weak link in this thinking was the "crisis action" aspect of the planning process. Accurate intelligence data and astute assessments were required. Whether this would actually be the case in terms of the input provided to the nuclear planners was very much an open question, given the precedent of Iraq (where the Bush administration got it completely wrong on the issue of WMD).

The new OPLAN 8022 nuclear war plan brought with it the inherent need for a new generation of nuclear weapons designed not for massive Cold Ward hardened-silo destruction, but rather for precision-based attacks against smaller, buried facilities. OPLAN 8022 defined a need. Now the Bush administration sought to fill the requirement. In the aftermath of the September 11 terror attacks, the U.S. military assessed its options for attacking what it believed were "vast underground complexes" inside Afghanistan, where Al Qaeda was thought to be hiding. One of the options considered was to design and field a new generation of nuclear warhead, the so-called Robust Nuclear Earth Penetrator, or RNEP. Afghanistan gave way to Iraq, where Saddam Hussein was accused of burying secret WMD factories deep underground. Again, in the aftermath of the March 2003 invasion of Iraq, these allegations turned out to be false. But there were plenty of real underground facilities in the targeted "rogue nations," from the underground nuclear facilities in North Korea and Iran to the buried chemical weapons plant in Libya. There was a role for the RNEP. The main problem was that the United States had, since 1992, been engaged in a moratorium on nuclear weapons testing, and without the ability to test, RNEP would remain a dream.[36]

The comprehensive test ban treaty (CTBT) remained tied up in the Senate Foreign Relations Committee, where the chair, Jesse Helms, made sure it would never see the light of day. The CTBT was viewed by its proponents as a foundational element of any viable nuclear nonproliferation effort. At the 2000 NPT Review Conference in April–May 2000, all participating nations, including the United States, had agreed to a thirteen-point plan that sought, among its objectives, the total elimination of their nuclear arsenals, ratification of the CTBT, continued observation of a moratorium on nuclear testing until the CTBT entered into force, and "the principle of irreversibility to apply to nuclear disarmament, nuclear and other related arms control and reduction measures."[37]

The 2000 NPT Review Conference took place during the administration of President Clinton. Under President Bush, the United States backed away altogether from the road map put together in 2000, undermining the 2005 NPT Review Conference, which closed without even being able to assemble an agreed statement. The Bush administration made it clear that it would not support ratification of the CTBT. One of the reasons for this was that, by 2005, President Bush was giving serious consideration not only to the development and deployment of an RNEP weapon, but also to an entirely new class of nuclear weapons known as the Reliable Replacement Warhead, or RRW. The concept behind the RRW was to design a new family of nuclear weapons that are highly reliable, easy, and safe to manufacture, monitor, and test. The RRW would make use of a common design and shared components that could then be adapted to various implementation requirements, depending on delivery vehicle and desired effects.[38]

A major argument put forward by the Bush administration for the RRW was the need to guarantee the safety and reliability of the U.S. nuclear warhead stockpile. While the 2002 SORT had the United States reducing its operational nuclear warheads to around 2,200, when one counted nondeployed warheads and spares, the total number of available nuclear warheads expected to be retained numbered 6,000, comprising seven separate designs. The RRW would utilize one basic design that could then be rapidly adapted, repaired, or modified as requirements evolved, providing the U.S. nuclear arsenal the flexibility needed to respond to changing military needs without maintaining a large number of additional warheads. Bush asked for, and received, funding in 2005 for the RRW. Nevertheless, many in Congress recognized the slippery slope toward undermining the NPT and CTBT if the RRW were allowed to proceed unrestrained, so instead Congress specified that "any weapons design under the RRW program must stay within the military requirements of the existing deployed stockpile and any new weapon design must stay within the design parameters validated by past nuclear tests."[39]

While the Bush administration pursued the concept of a new nuclear weapons design, the issue of global nuclear weapons proliferation continued to grow. The situation in Iraq had deteriorated badly in the aftermath of the initial period of invasion and occupation, and the U.S. experiment in preemption had stalled. There were some successes in the field of non-proliferation, including the unraveling of a black market network run by the father of the Pakistani nuclear bomb, Dr. A. Q. Khan, which supplied the enrichment programs of Iran and Libya and was suspected of helping North Korea as well. Dr. Khan was arrested by Pakistani officials in early 2004. Likewise, a U.S. military operation conducted in October 2003 as part of the Bush administration's so-called proliferation security initiative uncovered a shipment of nuclear weapons–related production materials shipped from A. Q. Khan to Libya. In the aftermath of the resulting investigation, and in light of the reality of the U.S. policy of preemption as practiced in Iraq, Libya acknowledged having nuclear, chemical, and biological weapons programs and opened these programs to inspection and dismantlement by the international community. In exchange, the United States agreed to end its economic embargo and work to facilitate Libya's reentry into the world community as a member in good standing.[40]

The situation concerning the nuclear programs of Iran and North Korea was not nearly so positive. Iran continued to insist that its uranium enrichment program was intended for peaceful nuclear energy, and it refused to comply with the U.S.-backed decision of the IAEA to permanently suspend enrichment activities. The United States tried to make a case against Iran by citing traces of highly enriched uranium detected by the IAEA in Iran, but the case collapsed when the IAEA determined that these traces were linked back to Pakistan's nuclear program, not Iran's. Despite finding no evidence to sustain the allegations put forward by the Bush administration that Iran was pursuing a nuclear weapons program, the IAEA Board of Governors voted in February 2006 to have the Iran issue transferred to the Security Council, where the United States hoped it would be able to levy even harsher punishment on Iran if it continued to insist on operating its own indigenous enrichment capability.[41]

North Korea was a much more dangerous situation. After withdrawing from the NPT in 2003, North Korea continued to threaten to make a nuclear weapon. Many in the Bush administration viewed this as a gambit on the part of Pyongyang to pressure the United States into giving North Korea greater concessions as part of a diplomatic deal to get North Korea to agree to return to the NPT. In early October 2006, North Korea made good on its promise and carried out an underground test of a nuclear device. After a flurry of threats about the possibility of a war with the United States, North Korea's leaders reversed course, and by December 2006 they were once again seated at a negotiation table, participating in the six-party talks involving the two Koreas, Japan, Russia, China, and the United States.[42]

As the Bush administration sought to shore up its policies targeting the nuclear programs of Iran and North Korea, and in doing so citing the importance of both these nations complying with the NPT, it carried out completely contradictory policy directions when dealing with the nuclear weapons programs of both Pakistan and India. The Clinton administration had imposed economic sanctions on both India and Pakistan in the aftermath of their respective nuclear tests in 1998, but within a year these sanctions had all but disappeared, having been eased incrementally by the United States in order to help improve diplomatic relations (Pakistan) and economic ties (India). The danger represented by these two adversaries having nuclear weapons came to a head in 1999, when Pakistan launched a military offensive against Indian positions in the disputed territory of Kashmir. A summit between Pakistan and India on the issue of Kashmir collapsed in the summer of 2001, and shortly after the September 11 attacks on the United States, an Islamic fundamentalist terrorist attack on the Indian parliament, backed by Pakistani intelligence, brought the two South Asian nations on the verge of a nuclear exchange.[43]

The Bush administration viewed Pakistan as a critical ally in the global war on terror, especially in terms of prosecuting military operations in Afghanistan, and as such it moved to assist Pakistan in securing its nuclear arsenal in the aftermath of September 11. This action created U.S. recognition of Pakistan as a nuclear weapons power, greatly undermining the legitimacy of the NPT. With India, the Bush administration was interested in improving economic ties with one of the world's largest developing economies. It was also interested in using India as a counter to Chinese growth in the region. India was facing an economic crisis driven by its insatiable appetite for energy to feed its growing economy. Continued U.S. sanctions on nuclear-related technology hurt India. The United States was required by the NPT, as a nuclear weapons state, to supply nuclear technology only to those nations who were signatories to the NPT. India was not, and furthermore, India had developed a nuclear weapons capability. At the same time that the Bush administration pushed the NPT as a vehicle to punish Iran and North Korea, it conveniently forgot about the NPT when it came to India. President Bush, in July of 2006, pledged to supply India with the nuclear technology it desired. India was to be treated with the same benefits as befitting a signatory to the NPT, even though it refused to sign that treaty. This action violated not only the spirit of the NPT but the letter of the law. Nevertheless, faced with the potential of $100 billion in increased trade between the United States and India, the U.S. Congress approved the deal in October 2008.[44]

November 2006 witnessed important midterm elections in the United States, which saw the Democratic Party win back control of the House of Representatives. Plagued by a growing debacle in Iraq, an unresolved conflict in Afghanistan, and a scandal·over the torture of people detained by the United States as part of the global war on terror, Secretary of Defense Rumsfeld resigned from office. His departure represented the final shuffle in the national security team of President Bush, which began following the 2004 presidential election with the resignation of Colin Powell as secretary of state. Condoleezza Rice was appointed as Powell's replacement, and Stephen Hadley, Rice's deputy at the NSC, was made national security advisor. President Bush appointed Robert Gates, the former CIA director under President George H. W. Bush, as the new secretary of defense. President Bush now had a team that would not only prosecute the war on terror but also move to implement other programs that his administration had previously committed to, such as missile defense, but that had been overwhelmed by the events in Iraq and Afghanistan.

In early January 2007 the Bush administration announced that it would be seeking to deploy a missile defense system into Eastern Europe, basing interceptor missiles in Poland and associated radar systems in the Czech Republic. This action was explained as necessary in order to protect the United States and Europe from the growing threat presented by Iranian missiles, in particular the *Shahib*-3. While governments of both Poland and the Czech Republic endorsed the proposal, Russia strongly condemned it. Moscow warned that any missile defense system deployed so close to the borders of Russia would alter the strategic balance in a decisive fashion. The Russian military disputed the claim that the missile defense system was designed to deal with an Iranian threat, and noted that if the United States were to go through with the proposal it would be treated as a military threat against Russia.[45]

The extent to which the proposed missile defense shield irritated Russia became clear when, in February 2007, President Putin addressed a conference in Munich, Germany, declaring that President Bush had embarked on a policy of "almost unconstrained use of military force," which increased the proliferation of nuclear weapons rather than curtailed it. Putin strongly condemned the U.S. decision to deploy a missile defense system in Eastern Europe. But he saved his strongest criticism for the expansion of NATO, noting that NATO nations were quick to charge Russia with violations of the Adapted CFE treaty of 1999 based on the presence of Russian troops in the Republics of Georgia and Moldova, but ignored the fact that the United States had created so-called flexible frontline bases in

Eastern Europe, holding up to 5,000 troops in each. These actions put NATO frontline troops right on the border with Russia, Putin noted. The Russian president questioned the reasoning behind NATO expansion, expressing doubt that it had anything to do with securing Europe. NATO had violated the guarantees made when Germany was unified that it would not seek to deploy NATO forces outside the borders of NATO. "Where are those guarantees now?" Putin asked.[46]

The Russian president's harsh upbraiding of the United States and NATO represented a growing frustration within Russia that the United States was behaving more and more like a global hegemon and that NATO was being used as a tool to facilitate American objectives. Putin described the U.S.-Russian disarmament effort as "stagnating" and criticized the United States for failing to be transparent about its intentions regarding its sizable reserve of nuclear warheads. All of these actions served to put Russia on the defensive, at a time when the Russian economy, fueled by a massive infusion of income brought in by Russia's sale of oil and natural gas, was improving. Russia's status as the major supplier of natural gas to Europe also factored into Moscow's growing sense of entitlement when it came to garnering the respect of NATO and the United States.

The Bush administration largely downplayed Putin's remarks and likewise shrugged off a warning from senior Russian military officials that not only would Russia deploy short-range missiles into the Russian European enclave of Kaliningrad to target any missile shield deployed in Poland and the Czech Republic, but also Russia might be compelled to unilaterally withdraw from the INF treaty, creating conditions under which Russia might once again develop and deploy intermediate nuclear forces that threatened Europe. And in a speech to the Russian parliament in April 2007, Putin indicated that he was considering a "moratorium" on the CFE treaty.[47] At the G-8 Summit in Germany in June 2007, Putin offered Bush an alternative to the proposed radar installation in the Czech Republic, offering up a Russian radar system in Azerbaijan that was closer to Iran and thus more in conformity with the stated objective of the proposed missile defense shield. The United States brushed the Russian offer aside.[48] With U.S.-Russian relations plummeting to their lowest levels since the end of the Cold War, Putin traveled to Kennebunkport, Maine, in early July 2007. There he offered up another Russian radar for use in the missile shield, this one located in southern Russia. Bush didn't reject the Russian offer outright but reiterated his objective of deploying the missile defense system as planned in Eastern Europe.[49]

On July 14, 2007, President Putin formally announced Russia's intent to withdraw from the CFE treaty, triggering the 150-day notification period required by the treaty. Putin cited the failure of NATO to abide by the terms of the Adapted CFE treaty, together with the U.S. decision to deploy a missile defense shield in Eastern Europe, as the primary reasons for his action.[50] In October Putin continued to put pressure on the United States regarding the missile defense shield, reiterating a threat to withdraw from the INF treaty during a visit by Secretary of State Rice and Secretary of Defense Gates to Moscow to discuss the proposed European missile defense system. The United States insisted that the system as designed posed no threat to Russia. Putin and his military disagreed, stating that there could only be one target for the proposed missile defense system, and that was Russia. In November President Putin formally suspended Russia's observance of the CFE treaty.[51] Piece by piece, the framework of arms control treaties that had secured peace and stability in Europe was collapsing. With NATO continuing to press for expansion, indicating that it was considering extending invitations to Georgia and Ukraine, it was only a matter of time before it ran up against Russian opposition that took a more substantive form than rejecting Cold War–era treaties.

Recognizing that the current situation with Russia was untenable, President Bush pushed for one last summit with Vladimir Putin, held in early April in the southern Russian city of Sochi. Bush unveiled a plan for a "strategic framework" with Russia that would seek to alleviate Russian concerns over his administration's plans to deploy a missile defense shield in Eastern Europe. Included in the framework was a plan that would allow for the deployment of the missile interceptors but not activate them unless Iran developed a long-range missile that could threaten Europe. Putin responded cautiously to the proposal. Another issue discussed between the two presidents was the looming December 2009 expiration of START. While the provisions of START had long ago been complied with by both sides, the treaty brought with it an extensive verification regime that was being used to monitor the new round of arms reductions carried out in accordance with the 2002 SORT. The two presidents also discussed Russia's decision to suspend its observance of the CFE treaty. Bush lauded the summit as a success, although nothing of substance had in fact been agreed to.[52]

In August 2008 the Republic of Georgia sent its troops into the breakaway territory of South Ossetia, allegedly in response to provocations carried out by South Ossetian paramilitary forces. While advancing into South Ossetia, the Georgian forces came into contact with Russian peacekeeping forces, and in the fighting that followed the Russians suffered numerous casualties. This fighting triggered a major Russian military response, with tens of thousands of Russian troops, backed by thousands of armored vehicles, pouring into South Ossetia, evicting the Georgian forces, and then moving into Georgia proper, occupying the port city of Poti and threatening the Georgian capital of Tbilisi. The Russian navy sortied from its bases in Sevastopol, Ukraine, to implement a naval blockade of the Georgian coast.[53]

The United States and its NATO allies condemned the Russian assault on Georgia. The fighting took place during the height of the 2008 presidential campaign, and both the Democratic candidate, Illinois Senator Barack Obama, and his Republican opponent, Arizona Senator John McCain, spoke critically of the Russian action. In a move designed to send a signal to Russia, Secretary of State Condoleezza Rice traveled to Poland, where she signed a formal agreement with the Polish government about the basing of missile interceptors on Polish soil. This action prompted a stern rebuke by the Russian military, which warned that Poland was "exposing itself to a strike—100 percent." Russian military doctrine, General Anatoly Nogovitsin warned, permitted the use of nuclear weapons in such a situation. Exacerbating the situation further, NATO dispatched a small naval task force into the Black Sea for the purpose of delivering humanitarian supplies to Georgia in defiance of the Russian blockade. Both President Bush and NATO expressed their intent to work toward making both Georgia and Ukraine members of NATO in the future.[54]

In November 2008 Senator Barack Obama won his bid to become president of the United States. He did so in convincing fashion, decisively beating John McCain in both the popular vote and the electoral vote. The situation President Obama inherited from George W. Bush was grim. America was at war on two fronts, in Iraq and Afghanistan. The standoffs with Iran and North Korea concerning their respective nuclear programs remained unresolved. U.S.-Russian relations were at an all-time low, with important discussions concerning the future of the soon-to-be-expired START at a standstill. And while the Bush administration articulated the importance of continued arms reductions, Secretary of Defense Gates still pushed Congress for a revitalization of the U.S. nuclear weapons complex and argued the need for a new generation of U.S. nuclear weapons—the Reliable Replacement Warhead, or RRW. Failure to fund the RRW, Gates warned, could lead to a situation in which the United States would be forced to resume nuclear testing in order to verify the safety and reliability of the U.S. nuclear warhead stockpile.[55]

In addition to seeking a new generation of nuclear weapons, Gates also released the report of a special panel, headed by former Secretary of Defense James Schlesinger, which addressed the issue of nuclear weapons management. "The presence of US nuclear weapons in Europe remains a pillar of NATO unity," the report noted. "As long as NATO members rely on US nuclear weapons for deterrence—and as long as they maintain their own dual-capable aircraft as part of that deterrence—no action should be taken to remove them without a thorough and deliberate process of consultation." The United States maintained a force of some four hundred nuclear bombs in storage facilities located in Germany, Italy, Turkey, and the United Kingdom.[56]

The talk of NATO nuclear deterrence, coupled with Russian rhetoric about a potential nuclear response to the U.S. decision to deploy a missile defense system in Eastern Europe, was being backed up by a decision to retain U.S. tactical nuclear weapons in Europe while Russia deployed nuclear-capable short-range missiles into the Russian territory of Kaliningrad, nestled between Poland and Lithuania. Far from stabilizing European security, the actions of the United States, combined with the counteractions of the Russians, were putting nuclear forces face-to-face at a time of increased tension. The Russia recognition of the independence of two breakaway Georgian territories, Abkhazia and South Ossetia, only complicated matters further by bringing volatile ethnic tension into the mix of Georgia's bid for NATO membership.

The Bush administration legacy, from an arms control perspective, is one of arrogance and incompetence, which combined to create incoherence, resulting in the virtual destruction of the framework of disarmament and nonproliferation that was supposed to enhance U.S. and world security in the post–Cold War era. The path of America's failed arms control policy, stretching from the decision to drop the atomic bomb on Japan in 1945 to the decision to deploy a missile defense shield in Eastern Europe in 2008, has placed the United States on very dangerous ground indeed. What the future holds in the form of future arms control policy articulated by future American presidential administrations is unknown. What is certain is that the presidency of George W. Bush did more harm to arms control and nonproliferation policy than the actions of all the administrations that preceded his. Contrary to the opinions of those whose ideological leanings might view such a statement as faint praise, the opposite is in fact the case: It is the harshest indictment one can offer of a failed leader of a failed administration.

CONCLUSION

TOWARD A NUCLEAR WEAPONS–FREE WORLD

On July 4, 2008, a reunion took place that garnered little or no attention from around the world, other than from those who were in attendance. The twentieth anniversary of the INF treaty coming into force was held on the grounds of the Votkinsk Machine Building Plant, some seven hundred miles east of Moscow in the heart of the Russian Federation. Former inspectors mingled with former factory employees on the same ground where, in March 1990, the so-called Missile Crisis took place. In the background the massive concrete structure housing the CargoScan X-ray machine loomed. There was a barbeque and the standard protocol of speeches from officials, both American and Russian, but for the most part the affair consisted of people gathering in clusters, reminiscing about the past and catching up on two decades of life experience.

Even while the former inspectors and their Russian factory colleagues celebrated the success of their efforts to rid the world of dangerous and destabilizing weapons, new missiles possessing even greater destructive force were being assembled nearby, with no treaty framework in place to restrict or constrain them. Furthermore, given the fact that the United States was seeking to deploy a missile defense shield in Europe, there was a real potential that the Votkinsk factory could be retooled to begin manufacturing a new generation of SS-20-type intermediate-range missiles if

Russia followed through with its threat to withdraw from the INF treaty, once again placing Europe at risk of imminent nuclear destruction.

Just a stone's throw away from where this gathering took place are the gates to the factory facility, which once produced the mighty SS-20 missile that terrified Europe. That missile, because of the work done by those gathered outside the factory, was no longer in existence. The Votkinsk factory continues to build missiles to this day, including the SS-27 "Topol-M" ICBM (at a rate of ten to fifteen missiles per year), capable of delivering three nuclear-armed MIRVs to targets around the world, including the United States. The SS-27 was supposed to be configured as a single-warhead missile under the provisions of START-2, but the collapse of that agreement in the aftermath of President Bush's decision to withdraw from the ABM treaty paved the way for the SS-27 to be transformed into its current MIRV-capable configuration, ostensibly to better overwhelm the new generation of missile defense systems the United States plans to build in the post–ABM treaty period.

In addition to the SS-27, the Votkinsk factory is involved in the manufacture of a completely new generation of ICBM, the RS-24/SS-X-29, which will begin being deployed with an operational status in December 2009. Armed with four MIRVs, the RS-24/SS-X-29 was specifically designed with U.S. missile defense systems in mind, repeating the historical examples of the U.S.-Soviet arms race of the 1960s and 1970s. The link between one side fielding an ABM system and another side developing missiles designed to defeat it is clear. At a time when the United States and Russia should be gravitating away from any form of strategic arms race, it appears that the opposite is occurring. If left untouched by diplomatic intervention in the way of meaningful arms control, it is only a matter of time before the United States, sensing strategic vulnerability, begins reequipping its ICBMs with MIRVs and seeking to develop its own new generation of missiles to counter the "Russian threat."

The final vestige of a meaningful arms control framework that existed between the United States and Russia was the Cold War–era START, scheduled to expire by the end of 2009. President Obama made negotiating a replacement agreement that retained, or even expanded on, the existing verification mechanisms contained in START, while cutting the respective nuclear arsenals of both sides by a significant amount, one of the top priorities of his July 2009 summit with the Russians in Moscow. Obama arrived in Moscow seemingly anxious to repair U.S.-Russian relations, which had soured significantly over the course of the previous administration of George W. Bush. Obama was able to get the Russians to agree to a "framework agreement" designed to replace START, in which both sides agreed to reduce their respective nuclear stockpiles by between 1,500 and 1,675 warheads and to cut back on their strategic delivery vehicles (heavy bombers, ICBMs, and submarine-launched missiles) by between 500 and 1,100 each.[1]

But Obama's Moscow summit was plagued by the same issues that generated U.S.-Russian tension before his term. The primary roadblock remained the matter of missile defense, and the refusal of the Obama administration to reject the deployment of a ballistic missile defense system in Europe out of hand. When his Russian counterparts insisted that there could be no new arms control agreement so long as the United States continued with its plans to deploy interceptors in Poland and missile radars in the Czech Republic, all the new American president could offer was a meek promise to review the U.S. policy regarding missile defense and an assurance that the two sides would be able to "reconcile" their differences in due course. The reality is that there will be no such reconciliation. Obama made it clear to the Russians that he was married to the concept of missile defense, and instead of rejecting a path that America had stumbled down three times since the 1960s (*Safeguard*, *Sentinel*, and "Star Wars"), all he could muster was an offer to share missile defense technology with the Russians and apply Kissinger-like "linkage" between any European-based ABM shield and Russia's willingness to join the United States in confronting Iran, noting that "if the threat from Iran's nuclear and ballistic missile program is eliminated, the driving force for missile defense in Europe will be eliminated, and that is in our mutual interests."[2]

Nevertheless, the Russians in turn made it clear that there could be no agreement to cut back on nuclear weapons and renew any arms control framework so long as the United States continued with its plans to deploy the European-based ABM shield, and that any effort to link an ABM shield Moscow believed was oriented toward Russia with an Iranian missile threat that was largely illusory was likewise unworkable. And while Obama may have publicly committed the United States to a "resetting" of relations with Russia, the sort of post–Cold War arrogance that has defined the U.S. approach toward Russia since the collapse of the Soviet Union reared its ugly head in dramatic fashion when Vice President Joe Biden undiplomatically noted that it was Russia's "withering economy" more than any genuine desire to achieve arms reductions that drove it to seek a disarmament agreement with the United States, noting that Russia could no longer afford its nuclear arsenal and therefore needed a new disarmament agreement more than America, and as such would agree to the terms set by the Obama administration.[3]

The hubris that produced Joe Biden's less-than-helpful comments on the heels of what had been a largely positive summit for President Obama was not unique to the vice president, but rather representative of a mind-set of U.S. superiority evident in the American approach toward disarmament since the dawn of the nuclear era. Far from resetting relations between the United States and Russia, the Obama administration increasingly finds itself trapped by the reality of America's own history and an inability and/or unwillingness to break free of the prejudices that emerge from that history. Pressures from this history run counter to any new thinking in regard to disarmament, as well as the threats to U.S. national security that have to be dealt with. The intellectual environment the Obama administration finds itself operating in politically is perhaps best illustrated by a report produced by former senators Bob Graham (a Democrat from Florida) and Jim Talent (a Republican from Missouri), together with Dr. Graham Allison, the director of the Belfer Center at Harvard University, as part of the Commission on the Prevention of Weapons of Mass Destruction Proliferation and Terrorism (the Graham Commission), which they chaired. Titled "World at Risk: Nuclear and Biological Weapons Pose Greatest Peril," the Graham Commission's report, released in December 2008, just prior to Obama taking office, was a response to Congress's post–September 11 fear that "the world's most dangerous terrorists" might acquire "the world's most dangerous weapons" and attack the United States.[4]

There was no mention of Votkinsk, or its ongoing work to produce weapons that will target American (and European) cities and facilities with the most destructive force known to humankind—a nuclear bomb—in the Graham Commission's report. Instead, the report laid out its case that America's "margin of safety against WMD terrorism is shrinking," and that "a terrorist attack involving a weapon of mass destruction—nuclear, biological, chemical, or radiological—is more likely than not to occur somewhere in the world in the next five years." The Graham Commission emphasized as its greatest concern the threat posed not by nuclear attack, but rather by biological attack, citing the proliferation of "relevant dual-use materials, equipment, and know-how." In an assessment full of inherent contradictions, the Graham Commission assessed that the most likely source of a future terrorist attack would come from the lawless regions of Pakistan's Northwest Frontier—not from the people living in that region (the Graham Commission rightly noted that "given the difficulty of weaponizing and disseminating significant quantities of a biological agent as an aerosol cloud . . . no terrorist group has the operational capability to carry out a mass casualty attack"), but rather from outside "experts" who would base themselves out of Pakistan's wild tribal region. The commission concluded that "the United States should be less concerned that terrorists will become biologists and far more concerned that biologists will become terrorists."

Ignoring the example of history, in which no modern terrorist group has successfully employed a self-made biological agent (the example of Japan's Aum Shinrikyo attempting, and failing, to produce and disseminate anthrax and botulinum toxin in the 1990s stands out), the Graham Commission warned that terrorists could overcome the difficulties of science "if they were able to recruit technical experts with experience in national bioweapons programs." The level of threat would expand exponentially if the scientists who were so recruited were experts in "synthetic genomics," with access to automated machines capable of DNA synthesis so that they could "synthesize nearly any virus whose DNA sequence has been decoded, such as the smallpox virus." The question of how such machinery would make its way to, and be successfully operated from, Pakistan's Northwest Frontier was not addressed. Nor did the Graham Commission more fully explore the one example of a recent biological terror event in the United States, the anthrax letter events of October 2001. If they had, they would have found that the biggest threat in the form of biological weapons comes not from terrorists operating out of Pakistan but rather from the scientists operating from within the Defense Department's own biological weapons laboratories.

Almost as disturbing as the threat assessment model put forward by the Graham Commission was its solution, which focused on everything except the strengthening of the one multilateral institution in existence designed to deal with precisely the kind of biological threat the Graham Commission warns about: the Biological and Toxins Weapons Convention (BTWC). The commission concluded that the decision undertaken by the Bush administration in June 2001 was "fundamentally sound," and that the effort to produce a BTWC Protocol for verification should not be resumed. This was, and is, a strange conclusion for a commission that defined the threat of biological weapons attack against the United States, emanating from the very dual-use technologies the BTWC Protocol was targeting, as the "greatest peril" for America in the coming years.

The Graham Commission's assessment of the threat posed by nuclear terrorism was likewise flawed. The commission correctly noted that "al Qaeda probably does not currently have the nuclear materials or the technical expertise necessary to produce a nuclear weapon," and then repeated its threat construction model used in its assessment of a biological weapons threat by warning that "the terrorists' ability to produce such a device could increase dramatically should they recruit just one or two individuals with access to nuclear materials and knowledge of nuclear weapons designs." The heart of the solution proposed by the commission was a mix of improved multilateral safeguard functions defined in the NPT carried out under the auspices of the IAEA, combined with unilateral counter-proliferation efforts conducted by the United States. The Graham Commission focused on the nuclear program of Pakistan as being problematic, as well as the efforts of Iran and North Korea to pursue their own nuclear capability. Left unmentioned were the consequences of the Bush administration's outreach to India in terms of undermining the credibility of the NPT, or the failure of the United States and the other nuclear weapons states to follow through with their obligations under Article VI of the NPT to disarm themselves of nuclear weapons.

Examined in isolation, the Graham Commission's report created a disturbing picture of an imminent threat requiring immediate and decisive action. However, when examined within the context of America's post–Second World War experience with arms control, it became just another inflammatory tract designed to manipulate public opinion and governmental policy. The commission postulated a "Biological Terror" gap in the same way past assessments described a "Bomber Gap," a "Missile Gap," and an "ABM Gap." The flawed analysis contained in the report brings to mind the work of Team B of the 1970s in defining a Soviet threat that didn't exist (or doing the same in regard to the illusory Iraqi WMD threat two decades later). And the rejection of legitimate arms control–based solutions to resolve difficult proliferation issues was nothing more than a continuation of the unilateralism embraced by the United States since the dawn of the nuclear age.

The Graham Commission downplayed the threat from chemical weapons, noting that they are difficult to make and employ in a manner that produces "mass casualty" events. The absurdity of this argument is underscored by the ready availability of toxic industrial chemicals and the history of mass casualty events derived from industrial accidents. The 1984 release of methyl isocyanate by Union Carbide in Bhopol, India, which killed nearly 20,000 people, and the 2005 Graniteville train derailment in South Carolina, which released chlorine gas that killed 9 people and injured more than 250 others, are but two of many such instances. By comparison, the 2001 anthrax attack killed 5 people and infected 17 others, and the sarin nerve agent attack on the Tokyo subway system in 1995 killed 8 and seriously injured 275.

But it is difficult to create mass hysteria by referring to events that transpire on a daily basis in and around every town and city in America. Terror is a psychological condition derived from fear. The Graham Commission, like similar panels before it, helped manufacture fear by exploiting the ignorance of their target population, in this case the American people. The real purpose of such a commission's work is to create a secondary distraction that either diverts public attention away from, or serves to manufacture legitimacy for, the principal issue at hand. This is true when dealing with the current focus of attention given to terrorism, especially in the aftermath of the September 11 terror attacks on the United States (which didn't use classic weapons of mass destruction but nonetheless managed to kill nearly 3,000 people). The principal issue, left unstated in the Graham Commission's report, isn't international terror but rather the need to find a new justification for American arms control policy that continues to seek to undermine or exploit disarmament regimes for unilateral advantage, as well as makes legitimate the only true weapons of mass destruction to exist in the world today: nuclear weapons.

The fact is that the greatest threat to America derived from a weapon of mass destruction (chemical, biological, or nuclear) does not come from a terrorist group hiding in the mountains of Pakistan or from rogue nuclear and biological scientists peddling their knowledge to the highest bidder. It comes from an American national security posture that continues to view nuclear weapons as a legitimate deterrent to the threats facing the United States and its allies. It is sometimes easy to forget that the United States continues to field thousands of nuclear weapons on a daily basis that are tied to active war plans targeting nations and populations around the world. And when this inconvenient reality is broached, the principal justification of the American nuclear arsenal is to deter "rogue nations" and nonstate terrorists from using WMD against the United States and its allies. This is the real shame of the Graham Commission, and others like it, since they do not advance any real solution to the problem of WMD proliferation other than to cite a threat, thereby justifying, even in an unstated manner, the need for American nuclear deterrence.

The concept of nuclear deterrence is, at least from the perspective of the American experience, a fraud. General Lee Butler, the former commander of U.S. Strategic Air Command and as such responsible for implementing U.S. nuclear deterrence in the 1990s, called deterrence in the Cold War setting "fatally flawed at the most fundamental level of human psychology in its projection of western reason through the crazed lens of a paranoid foe," a "dialogue of the blind with the deaf."[5] The first atomic bombs were built not to deter Japan or Germany, but rather to win a war. When it became clear that victory was assured without the need to resort to the use of nuclear weapons, they were used anyway (against Hiroshima and Nagasaki), not for the purpose of compelling the surrender of Japan, but rather to demonstrate American superiority of arms over the Soviet Union and thus contain postwar Soviet expansion. As with the case of the Graham Commission and its assessment of the threat posed by terrorism, however, the analysis that postulated a Soviet threat to American interests in the immediate aftermath of the Second World War was inaccurate and misleading.

The root cause of the problem between the Soviet Union and the United States wasn't a drive by Moscow to dominate the world, but rather a drive by Washington to dominate the Soviet Union. This is a lesson of history that Vice President Biden would do well to dwell on when considering the larger framework of U.S.-Russian relations today. The American nuclear monopoly was used solely as a device to intimidate and contain (i.e., deter) the Soviet "threat," but there really wasn't a Soviet threat worthy of a nuclear bomb. Cause-and-effect analysis of the postwar period clearly demonstrates a cause-and-effect pattern of events traceable to American overreaching derived from the false security of its nuclear monopoly. Soviet reaction manifested itself in an American counter, and so events unfolded. If one removes the artificial sense of "supremacy" created by the American nuclear monopoly, it becomes clear that the history of East-West relations would have proceeded in a far less confrontational manner.

Since 1945, America has rejected every effort made, from within and without, to voluntarily surrender its nuclear monopoly. But the drive for global supremacy (repackaged as "freedom and democracy"), an inherent by-product of a nation built on the concept of manifest destiny, dictated that America keep the bomb for itself. Once the Soviet Union acquired its own nuclear capability, the goal of American nuclear policy was never parity or deterrence, but rather supremacy and victory. Each time the Soviet Union attempted to achieve equality with the United States in terms of nuclear capability, the United States manufactured an excuse to continue to build its own arsenal, extending the arms race and expanding its nuclear weaponry. This expansion reached outrageous proportions. In a situation in which 400 nuclear bombs can destroy a nation, and 2,000 the world, the United States built its arsenal to over 10,000 weapons. The Soviets, of course, strived to match this capability. The focus on the East-West nuclear competition created conditions ideal for nuclear proliferation, and today the world is witness to the existence of not only five "declared" nuclear weapons states (the United States, France, China, Russia, and the United Kingdom), but at least four other "nondeclared" nuclear powers (Israel, Pakistan, India, and North Korea), and dozens of nations that possess the ability to become nuclear weapons states if they so choose.

Some speak of the proliferation of nuclear weapons as if their existence in and of itself promotes stability through implied deterrence. This might hold true if the deterrence model was in fact applied, meaning that the use of a nuclear bomb by one party would bring about a similar devastation, or worse, from the nuclear bombs of another power. But the American model of deterrence theory, put forward by the likes of Albert Wohlstetter and others, never accepted the concept of nuclear parity as the basis of deterrence, but rather nuclear supremacy. The problem with a supremacy-based deterrence model is that it is but a short step toward embracing the concept of the viability of nuclear victory. An examination of how American deterrence theory went from Assured Destruction, to Mutually Assured Destruction, to Countervailing, and then to Prevailing is a case in point. As General Lee Butler sagely noted, American deterrence theory "was largely a bargain we in the West made with ourselves."[6]

When one speaks of nuclear capability, it can never be forgotten that what is being discussed is a nuclear *weapon*, an instrument of war. Weapons are built to be used, not to be put on display. To use a weapon, one must have a war plan. And since war plans are linked to real activities and places, there is always a possibility that these plans might turn into reality, resulting in the employment of nuclear weapons. The development of the American nuclear war plan (from SIOP to OPLAN 8022 and beyond) illustrates this. As the American deterrence model progressed from Assured Destruction to Prevailing, each step was marked by a reworking of the nuclear war plan to meet the new objectives. And in the rush to rationalize nuclear war by providing a president with nuclear employment options beyond Armageddon, these war plans became less and less threatening. "Major" objectives were reduced to "limited" options, in an effort to constrain the pressures of escalation.

But the semantics of nuclear war planning could never cover up the reality that, once employed, nuclear weapons would create a self-destructive pattern of escalation that would ultimately manifest itself in general nuclear war—Armageddon. A counter to this thinking was the notion of nuclear preemption, sometimes disguised by the terms *first strike* and *launch on warning*. This was done without specifying what kind of "warning" one was speaking about—an actual enemy launch, or simply preparations thereof? Preemption always carried with it the risk of some residual nuclear capability surviving, which in the nuclear age meant a retaliatory strike resulting in millions of deaths among the population of the nation originating the attack (not to mention the possibility of hundreds of millions of deaths in the nation or nations originally attacked). To guard against such a retaliatory capability, the concept of a defense against nuclear-armed ballistic missiles was pursued, until one had an ABM defense shield. Of course, possession of such a shield created the conditions for nuclear supremacy by the nation possessing it, so the other nation either builds its own ABM system—threatening the offensive capability of the first—or devises an offensive solution to the ABM defense to begin with, or does both. This cycle of cause-and-effect relationships quickly evolves into the kind of arms race the United States and the Soviet Union engaged in for forty-five years and are threatened with today.

There is a tendency today to downplay the threat of nuclear conflict between Russia and the United States, especially in light of the end of the Cold War. But the reality is that the Cold War never really ended. Many of the institutions that dominated the Cold War (U.S. and NATO nuclear weapons, NATO itself, and the Russian nuclear arsenal) still exist. After the rapid expansion of NATO into Eastern Europe following the collapse of the Warsaw Pact, a situation exists now in which NATO and Russia are nose to nose along an extensive border that possesses past tension that could lead to present-day friction. The United States may have brushed off Russian threats against Poland in 2008, but the Poles did not.

NATO still operates with nuclear war plans that are relatively unchanged since the Cold War. These plans link any use of nuclear weapons by NATO with the strategic nuclear capabilities of the United States. The Russian military inherited a doctrine for the use of tactical nuclear weapons from the former Soviet military. As with their approach toward strategic nuclear weapons, Russia does not want to use tactical nuclear weapons but believes that if they were to be employed, it has to be as part of a viable military doctrine and not just for show. This is why the Russian reference to "doctrine" when speaking of a nuclear strike against any American missile defense shield based in Poland should not be taken lightly. And once nuclear weapons are used in Europe, the Russians and/or America and its NATO allies could easily transition to general nuclear war.

This is the fundamental flaw with American nuclear strategy when applied to Russia today. The analysis used to justify procuring weapons systems such as the missile defense shield only further Russian paranoia of an American nuclear first strike. When these weapons procurement efforts combine with an embrace of "flexible" nuclear strategy intended to provide an American president with increased options in case of nuclear conflict, it only assures the rapid transition from crisis to all-out nuclear warfare. No matter how elegant American nuclear strategists want to get in crafting "limited" and "selective" strike options, there would be no such luxury of controlled escalation in any nuclear exchange with Russia, just massive annihilation.

Based on this reality, the only logical conclusion one can draw is that it is the nuclear arsenal of the United States, attached to a nuclear weapons employment strategy permitting "limited" nuclear strikes, that threatens the world, and by extension the United States itself, more so than any other threat in existence today or one that can be postulated in the future. Given the history of America's nuclear experience, dominated as it is with themes of global supremacy, one must question any proposed solution to this problem that speaks of "containment" or "reductions" when addressing the nuclear arsenal of the United States. There can be no meaningful reduction of the American nuclear arsenal so long as it is attached to a national security strategy based on global dominance, which has been, and continues to be, the case. Since the United States neither will, nor should, voluntarily cede its position of world leadership, then the only rational solution to the problem of American nuclear weapons is their elimination.

The concept of the elimination of America's nuclear weapons arsenal is not as revolutionary as it might sound. From the moment American scientists built the atomic bomb, there have been rational thinkers, in and out of government, inclusive of the bomb designers themselves, who have articulated in favor of doing away with nuclear weapons. From J. Robert Oppenheimer, the father of the American atomic bomb, to General Lee Butler, the former commander of SAC, rational voices of people fully cognizant of the reality of nuclear weapons have been calling for their elimination. In an opinion piece published in the *Wall Street Journal* on January 5, 2007, Henry Kissinger, George Shultz, William Perry, and Sam Nunn, all former U.S. government officials with experience in nuclear weapons and nuclear strategy, made an articulate, intelligent, and bipartisan call for the abolition of nuclear weapons.[7]

Recently a new name has been added to this list: Barack Obama. The less than satisfactory results of the July Moscow Summit confronted President Obama with the reality that he needed to match his disarmament rhetoric with similar action. While his Prague speech in April 2009 presented his vision of a nuclear weapons–free world, Cold War–driven programs, such as missile defense, were an insurmountable obstacle when it came to moving this vision forward. Although the Obama administration had signaled its dissatisfaction with the Bush-era European-based "missile shield", planned for installation in Poland and the Czech Republic by severely cutting funding of this program in the spring of 2009, his unwillingness to formally terminate the missile defense plan proved to be a poison pill for any hopes of a new arms control initiative between the United States and Russia. And if there was no U.S.-Russian rapprochement, then there would be no global embrace of Obama's far-reaching vision for nuclear nonproliferation and disarmament.

Determined to move his disarmament agenda forward, President Obama took the politically risky step, on September 18, 2009, of terminating the missile defense plan that had been approved by President Bush, a move that immediately won praise from the Russians and condemnation from conservative elements within the United States. But instead of completely scrapping the concept of missile defense, the Obama administration simply replaced the unproven technology of the Bush-era system with a new missile defense plan making use of ship-based missile interceptors. Ground variants of these ship-based missiles could be eventually deployed to Poland and the Czech Republic, among other nations, along with new radar installations that could be installed in Georgia or Ukraine. Not surprisingly, this new missile defense shield was viewed with great suspicion by the Russians and, as of October 2009, was a major reason behind the failure of U.S. and Russian negotiators to conclude a new arms control agreement that would keep the verification inspection regime of START in place once that treaty expired on December 5, 2009. The Russians were insisting on linking restrictions on missile defense with any new arms reduction treaty, something the Obama administration refused to accept.[8]

The delay in reaching a replacement agreement for START means that unless some sort of executive agreement can be reached between Russia and the United States to extend the presence of inspectors on each other's soil until a new arms control treaty can be crafted to replace START, the era of on-site inspection-based verification will end. There is every reason to believe that such a bridging mechanism will be agreed to. Nevertheless, ratification of any new arms control treaty by either the Senate or the Russian Parliament is not guaranteed, especially if the impasse over missile defense cannot be resolved. This is an unfortunate reality brought on by the Cold War–era thinking that continues to prevail in Washington and represents President Obama's greatest challenge in his effort to bring about meaningful disarmament, inclusive of the elimination of nuclear weapons.

The path toward nuclear abolition is a difficult one, made more so by the level of nuclear proliferation in existence today. Obama need only turn to the pages of America's tortured arms control history to find examples of past efforts to disarm that, with his inspired leadership, might serve as a blueprint for a future effort. One of the best plans that could be recommended for review and revision, to adapt it for the realities of the present day, would be the findings put forward by the Gilpatric Committee back in 1964 (or the Foster Panel in 1961 or the Acheson-Lilianthal Report in 1945). President Lyndon Johnson ignored the Gilpatric Committee's informed recommendations, and the result was forty-five years of continued nuclear proliferation. With America, Russia, and the world at a critical crossroads in modern history, the sage advice of the Gilpatric Committee to foreswear nuclear weapons in all forms should not be forgotten.

Drafting a detailed plan for creating a regime of nuclear abolition is best left to those who would be charged with formulating and implementing such a plan. However, after examining the history of America's failed arms control experience, I have several foundational suggestions:

- Nuclear abolition must be global in scale. All nations of the world must be involved, without exception. The benchmarks of nuclear disarmament can be adjusted as required so that no nation, or group of nations, feels vulnerable to nuclear blackmail during this disarmament period. But the bottom line is that all nuclear weapons, throughout the world, will be eliminated.
- Eliminating the viability of nuclear weapons is an important precursor toward global abolition. The United States must take the lead in working with all nuclear weapons states to remove their nuclear weapons from operational service as soon as possible. As long as the nuclear sword hangs over the heads of any nation or nonnation entity, terrorist or nonterrorist alike, the perception of the legitimacy of nuclear deterrence—or worse, nuclear war—exists. Nuclear weapons must be eliminated as an option for dealing with any circumstance, however dire.
- Verification and compliance must be universal and equally binding on all parties. The United States has long enjoyed exclusionary status brought on by its standing as the world's sole remaining superpower. There can be no exceptions made to any aspect of a global nuclear weapons abolition regime. The United States must be subjected to the same level of verification inspection as will be required of all other nuclear weapons states.
- Nuclear energy, and its related technology, must be regulated and controlled in the strictest manner. This holds especially true for any technology or process that produces fissile material (i.e., the

nuclear fuel cycle). Fissile material must become a fully accountable material, subjected to tight international controls. Universal
"safe" nuclear reactor designs ("light water" reactors or properly
safeguarded "heavy water" reactors of the CANDU design), optimized for energy production rather than weapons manufacture,
must be certified, and all nations must be provided equal access to
such reactors without prejudice.

- The NPT, in whatever new form it takes, must become universal.
For nuclear abolition to work there can be no exceptions. The
trade-off for the United States and other nuclear weapons states
forgoing their nuclear weapons arsenal must be mandatory entry
and compliance with the terms of an appropriately drafted NPT
for all nations in the world, even if this means compelled entry
and compliance through strict diplomatic isolation and economic
sanctions.

- In addition to eliminating nuclear weapons, the most dangerous
means of delivering such weapons must also be eliminated. There
must be a global elimination of ballistic missiles, inclusive of long-
range cruise missiles (i.e., any system capable of ranges greater than
five hundred kilometers). To facilitate international acceptance of
such a regime, the United States must work with the other nations
possessing ballistic missile programs and space launch capability to
ensure that any nation seeking access to space launch capability
will be able to do so at a reasonable cost and in a reasonable manner. The Missile Technology and Control Regime (MTCR) must
be renegotiated and restructured to become a global treaty on par
with other international agreements and accords. Hand in hand
with a new MTCR agreement must be the renouncement of missile defense. Far from providing any form of realistic protection
from the threat of ballistic missiles, missile defense has historically
only served as a force of destabilization by facilitating an arms race
born of the need to develop missiles capable of overcoming any
such defense. The impasse between Russia and the United States
over a replacement treaty for START is but the most current manifestation of the destabilizing character of missile defense systems.

- To organize, formulate, and implement the kind of sweeping arms
control policies involved in the abolition of nuclear weapons, the
United States needs a bureaucracy and policy process that can survive multiple administrations and is beyond ideological manipulation. A new permanent arms control bureaucracy, in the model
of ACDA, needs to be created. The history of ACDA shows that

the best advocates for arms control are those who are solely tasked with this job. A limited mandate produced limited results. As such, the appropriate laws must be passed to empower it to carry out its task. Mechanisms of executive and legislative control and oversight need to be constructed that protect this new arms control bureaucracy from both individual and/or partisan abuse. Any new bureaucracy must be accountable to both the president and Congress. Congressional control should be in the form of a standing bipartisan committee organized solely for the purpose of nuclear weapons abolition and appropriately mandated to deal not only with disarmament issues but also with those matters involving the administration of the U.S. nuclear infrastructure, in terms of both energy and military, that affect any nuclear weapons abolition effort.

- Finally, and perhaps most importantly, America needs to reinvent itself in terms of how it interacts with the rest of the world. National security strategies that speak of global domination must become things of the past. America's tortured relationship with the United Nations and international law must likewise be reexamined, even if this means restructuring the Security Council in a manner that represents the realities of the present, not the history of the past. The continued isolation of nations such as India, Japan, and Germany, and regions such as Africa and South America, is not conducive to any international forum claiming a global security mandate. If the United States seeks to help build a viable multilateral institution to verify compliance with any global abolition of nuclear weapons, then it must learn to become a multilateral player on the world stage. This does not imply a reduction in America's role as a world leader. It just demands a different kind of leadership. Eliminating nuclear weapons will go a long way in freeing up a new American mind-set in this regard.

These are not trivial tasks. They are vitally important ones. The study of history often serves as the best means of ascertaining a solution to a present-day problem. This is why an examination of America's relationship with nuclear weapons, and the interaction of this relationship with arms control policy over the years, is so critical. America, and the world, stands at the crossroads of history when it comes to the issue of nuclear weapons. Having survived the Cold War era without resorting to the use of nuclear weapons, the American people once again find themselves in a situation in which they perceive themselves to possess nuclear supremacy and likewise the obligation to use this supremacy to contain the myriad threats facing the United States and its allies today. Traditional arms control mechanisms and methodologies, when applied to these new threats, do not work, because the American model of arms control quickly devolves into situational manipulation designed to retain the status of American nuclear supremacy.

One cannot speak of solving a problem unless the problem has, first and foremost, been properly defined. Void of such definition, any "solution" is merely an exercise in frustration and futility, since it is solving nothing and in the process making matters worse. In seeking a solution to America's arms control problem, the root of the problem needs to be recognized: the cause-and-effect relationship between America's acquisition of the atomic bomb and our collective unwillingness and/or inability to free ourselves from the addictive lure of power that comes from possessing such a weapon. Defining our relationship with nuclear weapons as an addiction goes a long way toward being able to decipher the lessons learned from studying the history of our involvement with nuclear weapons and to understand how this involvement has manifested itself in how we construct national security policy and how we participate in arms control and disarmament.

Once we recognize the addiction, then the cycle of repetitive behavior stemming from our need for nuclear weapons–based security begins to make sense. Past patterns of behavior tend to repeat themselves, especially if nothing is done to change the parameters that govern the behavior. We get the atomic bomb, we incorporate the atomic bomb into our defense culture, we learn to love the power attributed to possessing the atomic bomb, we begin to fear the consequences of having the atomic bomb, we seek ways to control and/or eliminate the atomic bomb, and then we feel threatened by outside powers and realize that we have the atomic bomb, it is incorporated into our defense culture, its existence gives us power, etc. This cycle has played out repeatedly over the past sixty-five years, with different players operating in differing cultures that have incorporated different technologies and norms. The single constant throughout was the existence of the nuclear weapon, which fed an addictive behavior pattern that is timeless. The only way to break this cycle is to recognize the addiction and its root cause and eliminate that cause. America is addicted to power. The ultimate symbol/source of this power is our nuclear weapons. To free ourselves, and the world, from the ramifications of our addiction, we must wean ourselves from the narcotic of nuclear weapons.

If history teaches us anything about America's nuclear weapons, it is this: we will use them, and in order to maintain our superior position, we will continue to build them. This is very dangerous ground to be treading on. Under these circumstances, arms control will never be undertaken to eliminate nuclear weapons, but rather it will be used to manipulate the international balance of power so that America's nuclear weapons reign supreme. This is why every meaningful attempt at arms control and disarmament undertaken by the United States has ultimately failed. Having stumbled down the path of failed arms control policy for over sixty years, America must choose a new direction, one that leads away from the addiction of nuclear weapons, and the perceived status derived from possessing them, and toward the liberation of a world free of nuclear weapons. If this happens, then there is a good possibility that, when the fortieth anniversary of the INF treaty is celebrated on the grounds of the Votkinsk Machine Building Plant, the gates of the factory will be open, a reflection of the reality that missiles used to deliver nuclear weapons are no longer needed. If it does not happen, then there is every possibility that the Votkinsk factory will be building new generations of missiles that threaten not only the United States but the entire world, including—indirectly— Russia itself. Or it will mean that the addiction to nuclear weapons finally manifested itself in its logical conclusion, and the Votkinsk factory has been reduced to a radioactive wasteland as a result of an American nuclear attack.

President Obama must not allow himself and his administration to fall victim to the mistakes of the past. The Cold War is over. It ended in 1991, with the dissolution of the Soviet Union. Successive administrations, starting with President George H. W. Bush, through President Clinton, and on to President George W. Bush, failed to craft foreign and national security policies that recognized this reality. Instead they pursued Cold War policies in a unilateral fashion. President Obama has a chance to correct this historical mistake by embracing policies that divorce the United States from the constraints of Cold War thinking. Nuclear disarmament represents by far the most dramatic manifestation of this opportunity. In charting out his bold yet incomplete vision of a nuclear weapons–free world, through his Prague speech of April 2009, Obama has set forth a challenge for his administration that must seize on the motto that has come to define his presidency—"Yes, We Can"—and transform it into "Yes, We Will." Yes, we will disarm, not in theory, but in reality, and not tomorrow, but now, in the present, during this administration. If the study of the history of America's relationship with nuclear weapons and arms control teaches us anything, it is that any disarmament vision that is put off for the future will never happen. The time for bold action is now. This is truly one of those decisive moments in a nation's history when the opportunity for change exists. One only needs to take that first step toward achieving it. The choice is ours to make.

ACKNOWLEDGMENTS

Books do not happen in a vacuum, especially ones as complex as this. When I first sat down with Carl Bromley, my fantastic editor at Nation Books, and John Sherer at Basic Books, to discuss the vision for this effort, we had agreed on a far more contemporary theme involving disarmament, and in particular the dangers that arose from what we all viewed as a failure of U.S. arms control policy.

However, as I began to carry out the initial phases of the research, it became clear to me that the only way one could make sense of any contemporary telling of America's shortcomings in arms control policy was to trace the tale back to its very beginning. The more I was compelled to do this, the more I realized that the real story of America's failed arms control policy centered not around a technical analysis of the present and future, but rather a deeper understanding of our past, especially the psychological impact of the advent of the nuclear age. In short, I was writing a very different book than the one originally agreed to.

I would like to thank Carl and John for embracing this new vision and allowing me to proceed down the path which ultimately produced this effort. Carl gets special kudos for patiently helping pare back what had rapidly grown into a massive volume of research into a more focused final product. I would also like to thank the professionals at the Perseus production staff, especially Sandra Beris and her team of outstanding copyeditors, who helped put the final polish on this project.

Writing a book is a very lonely process, and unless one has family, friends, and colleagues to turn for support, it couldn't get done. I would especially like to thank Sy Hersh, for his friendship and example, and Raja

385

Sidawi, for his faith and unwavering support. The Delmar Fire Department has provided me with a solid foundation of community involvement that helped me keep things in perspective when I would get too wrapped up in research and writing. A finer team of volunteers couldn't be found. Having a network of longtime friends is also a great help, none more so than Bob and Amy Murphy, who were always there, in good times and bad.

But at the end of the day, nothing gets done without family. My parents, Bill and Pat Ritter, and my three sisters (Shirley, Suzanne, and Amy) together with their respective spouses and children, have been a constant source of encouragement and support. So have the many members of our extended family. But ultimately it comes down to the ones I share my life with, my loving wife, Marina, and our twin daughters, Patty and Vicka, and Marina's father, Bidzina Khatiashvili. Thank you for providing me with a love-filled home from which to work and live. More than anyone else, this book could not have been written without you.

—*Scott Ritter*
DELMAR, NEW YORK
NOVEMBER 2009

NOTES

INTRODUCTION

1. Jan Pottker, *Janet and Jackie: The Story of a Mother and Her Daughter, Jacqueline Kennedy Onassis* (New York: Macmillan, 2002), 184.

2. White House Office of the Press Secretary, "Remarks by President Barack Obama, Hradcany Square, Prague, the Czech Republic," press release, April 5, 2009.

PROLOGUE

1. Rowland Evans and Robert Novak, "Missile Crisis," *Washington Post*, March 16, 1990, 23.

2. Letter from Senator Jesse Helms to President Ronald Reagan, January 11, 1989.

3. Letter from Senator Jesse Helms to President George H. W. Bush, January 12, 1990.

4. OSIA Portal Monitoring Memorandum S69-Jan 90, January 22, 1990.

5. *Local Understanding Concerning Interim Procedures for Operating the CargoScan Radiographic Imaging System*, February 5, 1990.

6. Department for the Cooperation with the U.S. Inspection Group, *Memorandum for the U.S. Site Commander*, February 7, 1990.

7. OSIA Portal, *Memorandum for the Record*, February 28, 1990.

8. OSIA Portal, "Results of the Technical Experts Negotiations in Votkinsk," *Monitoring Memorandum for the Director*, March 23, 1990.

CHAPTER ONE

1. Arthur Holly Compton, *Atomic Quest: A Personal Narrative* (New York: Oxford University Press, 1967), 237.

2. Gar Alperovitz, *The Decision to Use the Atomic Bomb and the Architecture of an American Myth* (New York: Vintage Books, 1996), 364.

3. John Ray Skates, *The Invasion of Japan: Alternative to the Bomb* (Columbia: University of South Carolina Press, 2000), 25.

4. Donald L. Miller, *Masters of the Air: America's Bomber Boys Who Fought the Air War Against Nazi Germany* (New York: Simon & Schuster, 2006), 112.

5. Michael B. Stoff, ed., *The Manhattan Project: A Documentary Introduction to the Atomic Age* (Philadelphia: Temple University Press, 1991), 95–96.

6. Townsend Hoopes and Douglas Brinkley, *Driven Patriot: The Life and Times of James Forrestal* (Annapolis, MD: Naval Institute Press, 2000 [1992]), 210.

7. Walter Isaacson and Evan Thomas, *The Wise Men: Six Friends and the World They Made* (New York: Simon & Schuster, 1997), 293–294.

8. Silvan S. Schweber, *Einstein and Oppenheimer: The Meaning of Genius* (Cambridge, MA: Harvard University Press, 2008), 335n31.

9. Spencer Weart and Gertrud Szilard, eds., *Leo Szilard: His Version of the Facts* (Cambridge, MA: MIT Press, 1980), 184.

10. Robert Maddox, *Weapons for Victory: The Hiroshima Decision 50 Years Later* (Columbia: University of Missouri Press, 1995), 49.

11. Joseph Albright and Marcia Kunstel, *Bombshell: The Secret Story of America's Unknown Atomic Spy Conspiracy* (New York: Times Books, 1997), 86.

12. Alperovitz, 442.

13. Dan Kurzman, *Day of the Bomb: Countdown to Hiroshima* (New York: McGraw-Hill, 1986), 494.

14. Wilson D. Miscamble, *From Roosevelt to Truman: Potsdam, Hiroshima, and the Cold War* (Cambridge: Cambridge University Press, 2007), 201.

15. Richard Rhodes, *Dark Sun: The Making of the Hydrogen Bomb* (New York: Simon & Schuster, 1995), 365.

16. Georgii Konstantinovich Zhukov, *The Memoirs of Marshal Zhukov* (New York: Delacorte Press, 1971), 674–675.

17. Rhodes, 23.

18. Ibid., 204.

19. Isaacson and Thomas, 319.

20. John Lewis Gaddis, *The United States and the Origin of the Cold War, 1941–1947* (New York: Columbia University Press, 2000), 255.

21. Rhodes, 279.

22. Gaddis, 254.

23. Lawrence Wittner, *The Struggle Against the Bomb* (Stanford, CA: Stanford University Press, 1993), 249.

24. Chalmers M. Roberts, *The Nuclear Years: The Arms Race and Arms Control, 1945–70* (New York: Praeger, 1970), 12.

25. Rhodes, 214.

26. F. G. Gosling, *The Manhattan Project: Making the Atomic Bomb* (Washington, DC: Department of Energy History Division, 1999), 57.

27. Schweber, 171.

28. Robert L. Beisner, *Dean Acheson: A Life in the Cold War* (Oxford: Oxford University Press, 2006), 34.

29. Isaacson and Thomas, 352.

30. Rhodes, 236.

31. James Patterson, *Grand Expectations: The United States, 1945–1974* (New York: Oxford University Press, 1997), 107.

32. Gaddis, 333–334.

33. Rhodes, 277.

34. Gaddis, 351.

35. Greg Behrman, *The Most Noble Adventure: The Marshall Plan and the Time When America Helped Save Europe* (New York: Simon & Schuster, 2007), 163.

36. Christopher Gacek, *The Logic of Force: The Dilemma of Limited War in American Foreign Policy* (New York: Columbia University Press, 1994), 32–33.

37. Rhodes, 320.

38. Ibid., 353.

39. Keith D. McFarland and David L. Roll, *Louis Johnson and the Arming of America: The Roosevelt and Truman Years* (Bloomington: Indiana University Press, 2005), 219.

CHAPTER TWO

1. Thomas Finletter, *Survival in the Air Age: A Report* (Washington, DC: U.S. Government Printing Office, 1948), 10.

2. Ibid., 20.

3. Air University Review 1981 (Recurring Publication 50–2) (Colorado Springs, CO: United States Air Force, 1981), 20.

4. Steven Usdin, *Engineering Communism: How Two Americans Spied for Stalin and Founded the Soviet Silicon Valley* (New Haven, CT: Yale University Press, 2005), 89.

5. Michael J. Ybarra, *Washington Gone Crazy: Senator Pat McCarran and the Great American Communist Hunt* (Hanover, NH: Steerforth Press, 2004), 450.

6. Geoffrey R. Stone, *Perilous Times: Free Speech in Wartime from the Sedition Act of 1798 to the War on Terrorism* (New York: W. W. Norton, 2004), 331.

7. Fred Kaplan, *The Wizards of Armageddon*, Stanford Nuclear Age Series (Stanford, CA: Stanford University Press, 1991 [1983]), 139.

8. Paul H. Nitze, *NSC-68: Forging the Strategy of Containment*, ed. S. Nelson Drew (Washington, DC: National Defense University, 1994), 50–58.

9. Ibid., 52.

10. Wilson D. Miscamble, *George F. Kennan and the Making of American Foreign Policy, 1947–1950* (Princeton, NJ: Princeton University Press, 1992), 311.

11. Robert L. Beisner, *Dean Acheson: A Life in the Cold War* (Oxford: Oxford University Press, 2006), 241.

12. Robert Donovan, *Tumultuous Years: The Presidency of Harry S. Truman, 1949–1953* (Columbia: University of Missouri Press, 1996), 149.

13. Zuoyue Wang, *In Sputnik's Shadow: The President's Science Advisory Committee and Cold War America* (New Brunswick, NJ: Rutgers University Press, 2008), 28.

14. Richard Rhodes, *Dark Sun: The Making of the Hydrogen Bomb* (New York: Simon & Schuster, 1995), 402.

15. Ibid., 405–406.

16. Ibid., 406.

17. Ibid., 407.

18. Ibid.

19. Vladislav Zubok and Konstatin Pleshakov, *Inside the Kremlin's Cold War: From Stalin to Khrushchev* (Cambridge, MA: Harvard University Press, 1996), 63.

20. Ibid., 64.

21. Callum MacDonald, "The Atomic Bomb and the Korean War, 1950–53," in *Decisions and Diplomacy: Essays in Twentieth Century International History: In Memory of George Grün and Esmonde Robertson*, ed. Dick Richardson and Glyn Stone (New York: Routledge, 1995), 179.

22. Stanley Weintraub, *MacArthur's War: Korea and the Undoing of an American Hero* (New York: Free Press, 2000), 252.

23. Ibid., 253.

24. David Halberstam, *The Coldest Winter: America and the Korean War* (New York: Hyperion, 2007), 478.

25. Weintraub, 333–334.

26. Steve Neal, *Harry and Ike: The Partnership That Remade the Postwar World* (New York: Simon & Schuster, 2002), 175.

27. David Callahan, *Dangerous Capabilities: Paul Nitze and the Cold War* (New York: HarperCollins, 1990), 134.

28. Alonzo Hamby, *Man of the People: A Life of Harry S. Truman* (New York: Oxford University Press, 1995), 553.

29. Herbert Romerstein and Eric Breindel, *The Venona Secrets: Exposing Soviet Espionage and America's Traitors* (Washington, DC: Regnery Publishing, 2001), 248.

30. James Carroll, *House of War: The Pentagon and the Disastrous Rise of American Power* (Boston: Houghton Mifflin, 2006), 186.

31. Senate Committee on Foreign Relations, United States Congress, *Control and Reduction of Armaments, Final Report* (Washington, DC: Government Printing Assistance, 1958), 146.

32. Gregg Herken, *The Winning Weapon: The Atomic Bomb in the Cold War, 1945–1950* (New York: Knopf, 1980), 333.

33. Michael Hopkins, *Oliver Franks and the Truman Administration: Anglo-America Relations, 1948–1952* (New York: Routledge, 2003), 219.

34. Stephan I. Schwartz, ed., *Atomic Audit: The Costs and Consequences of Nuclear Weapons Since 1940* (Washington, DC: Brookings Institution Press, 1998), 4.

35. Rhodes, 421.

36. Ibid., 423–424.

37. Ibid., 493.

38. Ibid., 497.

39. Ibid., 662.

CHAPTER THREE

1. David Barash, *The Survival Game: How Game Theory Explains the Biology of Human Cooperation and Competition* (New York: Macmillan, 2003), 190–191.

2. Jonathan Schell, *The Seventh Decade: The New Shape of Nuclear Danger* (New York: Macmillan, 2007), 168.

3. John Wilson Lewis and Xue Litai, *China Builds the Bomb* (Stanford, CA: Stanford University Press, 1991), 14.

4. Stephen E. Ambrose, *Eisenhower: Soldier and President* (New York: Simon & Schuster, 1990), 320–322.

5. Richard Rhodes, *Dark Sun: The Making of the Hydrogen Bomb* (New York: Simon & Schuster, 1995), 365.

6. Jacek Kugler, ed., *Parity and War: Evaluations and Extensions of the War Ledger* (Ann Arbor: University of Michigan Press, 1996), 231–232.

7. Bernard Brodie, *The Absolute Weapon: Atomic Power and World Order* (New York: Harcourt Brace, 1946), 74.

8. Fred Kaplan, *The Wizards of Armageddon*, Stanford Nuclear Age Series (Stanford, CA: Stanford University Press, 1991 [1983]), 97–98.

9. Ibid., 174.

10. John Lewis Gaddis, *Strategies of Containment: A Critical Appraisal of American National Security Policy During the Cold War*, rev. and exp. ed. (New York: Oxford University Press, 2005), 148.

11. Martin Windrow, *The Last Valley: Dien Bien Phu and the French Defeat in Vietnam* (Cambridge, MA: Da Capo Press, 2005), 569.

12. Gaddis, 176.

13. Robert Accinelli, *Crisis and Commitment: United States Policy Toward Taiwan, 1950–1955* (Chapel Hill: University of North Carolina Press, 1996), 196.

14. Christopher M. Gacek, *The Logic of Force: The Dilemma of Limited War in American Foreign Policy* (New York: Columbia University Press, 1994), 125.

15. Dwight D. Eisenhower, *The White House Years*, vol. 1, *Mandate for Change, 1953–1956* (Garden City, NY: Doubleday, 1963), 463–464.

16. David Holloway, *Stalin and the Bomb: The Soviet Union and Atomic Energy, 1939–1956* (New Haven, CT: Yale University Press, 1996), 313.

17. Richard L. Miller, *Under the Cloud: The Decades of Nuclear Testing* (New York: Free Press, 1986), 192.

18. J. Robert Oppenheimer, "Atomic Weapons and American Policy," *Foreign Affairs* 31, no. 4 (July 1953): 529.

19. Gregg Herken, *Brotherhood of the Bomb: The Tangled Lives and Loyalties of Robert Oppenheimer, Ernest Lawrence, and Edward Teller* (New York: Henry Holt, 2002), 290–293.

20. Ibid., 295.

21. Thomas Doherty, *Cold War, Cool Medium: Television, McCarthyism and American Culture*, Film and Culture (New York: Columbia University Press, 2005), 204.

22. Kaplan, 163.

23. Ibid., 113.

24. Nathan F. Twining, *Neither Liberty nor Safety: A Hard Look at U.S. Military Policy and Strategy* (New York: Holt, Rinehart and Winston, 1966), 291.

25. Matt Bille and Erika Lishock, *The First Space Race: Launching the World's First Satellites* (College Station: Texas A&M University Press, 2004), 74.

26. Twining, 249.

27. Peter J. Roman, *Eisenhower and the Missile Gap*, Cornell Studies in Security Affairs (Ithaca, NY: Cornell University Press, 1995), 24.

28. Eugene Jarecki, *The American Way of War: Guided Missiles, Misguided Men, and a Republic in Peril* (New York: Free Press, 2008), 150.

29. Wilfried Loth, *Stalin's Unwanted Child: The Soviet Union, the German Question, and the Founding of the GDR*, trans. Robert F. Hogg (New York: St. Martin's, 1998), 169–171.

30. Norman Polmar, *Spyplane: The U-2 History Declassified* (Osceola, WI: MBI, 2001), 92–94.

CHAPTER FOUR

1. Linda McFarland, *Cold War Strategist: Stuart Symington and the Search for National Security* (Westport, CT: Praeger, 2001), 78.

2. Fred Kaplan, *The Wizards of Armageddon*, Stanford Nuclear Age Series (Stanford, CA: Stanford University Press, 1991 [1983]), 163.

3. Michael D'Antonio, *A Ball, a Dog, and a Monkey: 1957, the Space Race Begins* (New York: Simon & Schuster, 2007), 11–14.

4. Victor Rosenberg, *Soviet-American Relations, 1953–1960: Diplomacy and Cultural Exchange During the Eisenhower Presidency* (Jefferson, NC: McFarland, 2005), 118.

5. Daniel Patrick Moynihan, *Secrecy: The American Experience* (New Haven, CT: Yale University Press, 1999), 193–194.

6. Peter J. Roman, *Eisenhower and the Missile Gap*, Cornell Studies in Security Affairs (Ithaca, NY: Cornell University Press, 1995), 32–33.

7. Ibid., 173–174.

8. Albert Wohlstetter, "The Delicate Balance of Terror," *Foreign Affairs* 37, no. 1 (1959): 212.

9. Ibid., 218.

10. Ibid., 232.

11. Dwight Eisenhower, address to the UN General Assembly, on December 8, 1953, *Congressional Record* 100 (January 7, 1954): 62.

12. Ibid., 63.

13. Richard L. Miller, *Under the Cloud: The Decades of Nuclear Testing* (New York: Free Press, 1986), 197.

14. Gregg Herken, *Cardinal Choices: Presidential Science Advising from the Atomic Bomb to SDI* (New York: Oxford University Press, 1992), 84.

15. Benjamin P. Greene, *Eisenhower, Science Advice, and the Nuclear Test-Ban Debate, 1945–1963*, Stanford Nuclear Age Series (Stanford, CA: Stanford University Press, 2007), 82–83.

16. Ibid., 209–210.

17. Ibid., 163.

18. Ibid., 165–166.

19. Michael S. Sherry, *In the Shadow of War: The United States Since the 1930's* (New Haven, CT: Yale University Press, 1995), 220.

20. Glenn T. Seaborg, *Kennedy, Khrushchev, and the Test Ban* (Berkeley: University of California Press, 1983), 16.

21. Ibid., 21–22.

22. Ibid., 22.

23. Dimitris Bourantonis, *The United Nations and the Quest for Nuclear Disarmament* (Brookfield, VT: Dartmouth, 1993), 62.

24. Seaborg, 39.

25. George E. Lowe, *The Age of Deterrence* (Boston: Little, Brown, 1964), 182.

26. Roman, 130.

27. Robert M. Slusser, *The Berlin Crisis of 1961: Soviet-American Relations and the Struggle for Power in the Kremlin, June-November 1961* (Baltimore: Johns Hopkins University Press, 1973), 221.

28. George B. Kistiakowsky, *A Scientist at the White House: The Private Diary of President Eisenhower's Special Assistant for Science and Technology* (Cambridge, MA: Harvard University Press, 1976), 251.

29. Norman Polmar, *Spyplane: The U-2 History Declassified* (Osceola, WI: MBI, 2001), 127–128.

30. Ibid., 130.

31. Hope M. Harrison, *Driving the Soviets up the Wall: Soviet-East German Relations, 1953–1961*, Princeton Studies in International History and Politics (Princeton, NJ: Princeton University Press, 2003), 100.

32. Saki Dockrill, *Eisenhower's New-Look National Security Policy, 1953–61* (New York: St. Martin's, 1996), 253.

33. Mark Monmonier, *Spying with Maps: Surveillance Technologies and the Future of Privacy* (Chicago: University of Chicago Press, 2004), 22.

34. Jonathan Schell, *The Seventh Decade: The New Shape of Nuclear Danger* (New York: Metropolitan Books, 2007), 63.

35. Roger D. Launius and Dennis R. Jenkins, eds., *To Reach the High Frontier: A History of U.S. Launch Vehicles* (Lexington: University Press of Kentucky, 2002), 56.

36. Christoph Bluth, *Britain, Germany and Western Nuclear Strategy*, Nuclear History Program 3 (New York: Oxford University Press, 1995), 64.

37. Roman, 167.

38. Ibid., 130.

39. Alex Abella, *Soldiers of Reason: The Rand Corporation and the Rise of the American Empire* (Orlando, FL: Harcourt, 2008), 158.

40. Roman, 131–132.

41. Stephen E. Ambrose, *Eisenhower: Soldier and President* (New York: Simon & Schuster, 1990), 537.

42. Jeffrey A. Engel, ed., *Local Consequences of the Global Cold War*, Cold War International History Project Series (Stanford, CA: Stanford University Press, 2007), 256.

CHAPTER FIVE

1. Walter Isaacson and Evan Thomas, *The Wise Men: Six Friends and the World They Made* (New York: Simon & Schuster, 1997), 599.

2. Harold Brown, "Is Arms Control Dead?" *Washington Quarterly* 23, no. 2 (Spring 2000): 173.

3. Kai Bird, *The Chairman: John J. McCloy, the Making of the American Establishment* (New York: Simon & Schuster, 1992), 469.

4. Glenn T. Seaborg, *Kennedy, Khrushchev, and the Test Ban* (Berkeley: University of California Press, 1983), 36–42.

5. Maxwell D. Taylor, *Swords and Plowshares* (New York: Da Capo Press, 1990), 174–175.

6. Henry G. Gole, *General William E. DePuy: Preparing the Army for Modern War*, American Warriors (Lexington: University Press of Kentucky, 2008), 106–107.

7. Taylor, 179–180.

8. Melvin Small, *Democracy & Diplomacy: The Impact of Domestic Politics on U.S. Foreign Policy, 1789–1994*, The American Moment (Baltimore: Johns Hopkins University Press, 1996), 106.

9. James Srodes, *Allen Dulles: Master of Spies* (Washington, DC: Regnery Publishing, 2000), 507–508.

10. Lawrence Freedman, *Kennedy's Wars: Berlin, Cuba, Laos, and Vietnam* (New York: Oxford University Press, 2002), 130–132.

11. Rockefeller Brothers Fund, *The Power of the Democratic Idea*, Special Studies Project Report 6 (Garden City, NY: Doubleday, 1960).

12. Deborah Hart Strober and Gerald S. Strober, *The Kennedy Presidency: An Oral History of the Era* (Washington, DC: Brassey's, 2003), 130–131.

13. Fred Kaplan, *The Wizards of Armageddon*, Stanford Nuclear Age Series (Stanford, CA: Stanford University Press, 1991 [1983]), 288.

14. John Prados, *The Soviet Estimate: U.S. Intelligence Analysis & Russian Military Strength* (New York: Dial Press, 1982), 112.

15. Jeffrey T. Richelson, *A Century of Spies: Intelligence in the Twentieth Century* (New York: Oxford University Press, 1992), 299.

16. Samuel F. Wells Jr. and Robert S. Litwak, eds., *Strategic Defenses and Soviet-American Relations* (Cambridge, MA: Ballinger, 1987), 17.

17. Lauren Holland, *Weapons Under Fire*, Garland Reference Library of Social Science 1047 (New York: Garland, 1997), 33.

18. Andreas Wenger, *Living with Peril: Eisenhower, Kennedy, and Nuclear Weapons* (Lanham, MD: Rowman & Littlefield, 1997), 186.

19. Kaplan, 269.

20. Paul N. Edwards, *The Closed World: Computers and the Politics of Discourse in Cold War America* (Cambridge, MA: MIT Press, 1996), 127.

21. Ibid., 127–128.

22. Alex Abella, *Soldiers of Reason: The Rand Corporation and the Rise of the American Empire* (Orlando, FL: Harcourt, 2008), 160.

23. Kaplan, 279.

24. Ibid., 297–298.

25. Freedman, 145.

26. Ibid., 115.

27. Richard Reeves, *President Kennedy: Profile of Power* (New York: Simon & Schuster, 1993), 137.

28. Peter Wyden, *Wall: The Inside Story of Divided Berlin* (New York: Simon & Schuster, 1989), 55.

29. Reeves, 171.

30. James Carroll, *House of War: The Pentagon and the Disastrous Rise of American Power* (Boston: Houghton Mifflin, 2006), 245.

31. Deborah Welch Larson, *Anatomy of Mistrust: U.S.-Soviet Relations During the Cold War* (Ithaca, NY: Cornell University Press, 2000), 126.

32. Richard K. Betts, *Nuclear Blackmail and Nuclear Balance* (Washington, DC: Brookings Institution, 1987), 107.

33. William F. Buckley Jr., *The Fall of the Berlin Wall* (Hoboken, NJ: John Wiley & Sons, 2004), 18–20.

34. Douglas Brinkley, *Dean Acheson: The Cold War Years, 1953–71* (New Haven, CT: Yale University Press, 1992), 119–121.

35. Arthur M. Schlesinger Jr., *A Thousand Days: John F. Kennedy in the White House* (Boston: Houghton Mifflin, 2002), 388.

36. Walter Isaacson, *Kissinger: A Biography* (New York: Simon & Schuster, 2005), 111–113.

37. Kaplan, 296.

38. Diane B. Kunz, ed., *The Diplomacy of the Crucial Decade: American Foreign Relations During the 1960s* (New York: Columbia University Press, 1994), 123.

39. Buckley, 44.

40. Seaborg, 74.

41. Robert M. Slusser, *The Berlin Crisis of 1961: Soviet-American Relations and the Struggle for Power in the Kremlin, June–November 1961* (Baltimore: Johns Hopkins University Press, 1973), 90.

42. Seaborg, 74.

43. Schlesinger, 456–457.

44. Hope M. Harrison, *Driving the Soviets up the Wall: Soviet-East German Relations, 1953–1961*, Princeton Studies in International History and Politics (Princeton, NJ: Princeton University Press, 2003), 168–169.

45. William T. Lee and Richard F. Staar, *Soviet Military Policy Since World War II* (Stanford, CA: Hoover Institution Press, Stanford University, 1986), 28–29.

46. Buckley, 50–51.

47. Larson, 132.

48. Frank Costigliola, "The Pursuit of the Atlantic Community: Nuclear Arms, Dollars, and Berlin," in *Kennedy's Quest for Victory: American Foreign Policy, 1961–1963*, ed. Thomas G. Paterson (New York: Oxford University Press, 1989), 41–43.

49. Bird, 510.

50. Matthew Evangelista, *Unarmed Forces: The Transnational Movement to End the Cold War* (Ithaca, NY: Cornell University Press, 2002), 71–72.

51. Schlesinger, 448.

52. Lawrence S. Wittner, *Cold War America: From Hiroshima to Watergate* (Westport, CT: Praeger, 1974), 218.

53. Dan Cohen, *Undefeated: The Life of Hubert H. Humphrey* (Minneapolis: Lerner Publications, 1978), 236.

54. Schlesinger, 478.

55. Freedman, 98–99.

56. Ibid., 100.

57. Bird, 515.

58. Carroll, 315–316.

59. George Bunn, *Arms Control by Committee: Managing Negotiations with the Russians* (Stanford, CA: Stanford University Press, 1992), 29.

60. General Lemnitzer, "Memorandum for General Taylor (Subject: Strategic Air Planning and Berlin)," October 11, 1961, in *First Strike Options and the Berlin Crisis*, National Security Archive, Washington, DC.

61. James E. Goodby, *At the Borderline of Armageddon: How American Presidents Managed the Atomic Bomb* (Lanham, MD: Rowman & Littlefield, 2006), 45–46.

62. Slusser, 371.

63. Pavel Podvig, ed., *Russian Strategic Nuclear Forces* (Cambridge, MA: MIT Press, 2001), 466, 498.

CHAPTER SIX

1. Kai Bird, *The Color of Truth: McGeorge Bundy and William Bundy, Brothers in Arms—A Biography* (New York: Simon & Schuster, 1998), 216.

2. Lawrence Freedman, *Kennedy's Wars: Berlin, Cuba, Laos, and Vietnam* (New York: Oxford University Press, 2002), 106–107.

3. Arthur M. Schlesinger Jr., *A Thousand Days: John F. Kennedy in the White House* (Boston: Houghton Mifflin, 2002), 851.

4. Dirk Stikker, "Final Communiqué on the Athens Guidelines," NATO Conference, Berlin, May 4, 1962.

5. Peter R. Beckman et al., *The Nuclear Predicament: An Introduction* (Englewood Cliffs, NJ: Prentice Hall, 1989), 90.

6. Joseph Lepgold, *The Declining Hegemon: The United States and European Defense, 1960–1990* (Westport, CT: Greenwood Press, 1990), 122.

7. Fred Kaplan, *The Wizards of Armageddon*, Stanford Nuclear Age Series (Stanford, CA: Stanford University Press, 1991 [1983]), 283–285.

8. William W. Kaufmann, *The McNamara Strategy* (New York: Harper & Row, 1964), 114.

9. Walter LaFeber, *America, Russia, and the Cold War, 1945–1992*, 7th ed. (New York: McGraw-Hill, 1993), 225.

10. Cristoph Bluth, *Soviet Strategic Arms Policy Before SALT* (Cambridge: Cambridge University Press, 1992), 9–10.

11. Michael McGwire, *Perestroika and Soviet National Security* (Washington, DC: Brookings Institution, 1991), 49–50.

12. Aleksandr Fursenko and Timothy Naftali, *One Hell of a Gamble: Khrushchev, Castro, and Kennedy, 1958–1964* (New York: W. W. Norton, 1998), 155.

13. Stephan I. Schwartz, ed., *Atomic Audit: The Costs and Consequences of Nuclear Weapons Since 1940* (Washington, DC: Brookings Institution Press, 1998), 123.

14. Graham Spinardi, *From Polaris to Trident: The Development of US Fleet Ballistic Missile Technology* (Cambridge: Cambridge University Press, 1994), 76.

15. Philip Nash, *The Other Missiles of October: Eisenhower, Kennedy, and the Jupiters, 1957–1963* (Chapel Hill: University of North Carolina Press, 1997), 108–110.

16. Raymond L. Garthoff, *Reflections on the Cuban Missile Crisis*, rev. ed. (Washington, DC: Brookings Institution Press, 1989), 12.

17. Fursenko and Naftali, 213.

18. Glenn T. Seaborg, *Kennedy, Khrushchev, and the Test Ban* (Berkeley: University of California Press, 1983), 20–21.

19. Timothy Naftali, ed., *John F. Kennedy: The Great Crises*, vol. 1, *July 30–August 1962*, The Presidential Recordings (New York: W. W. Norton, 2001), 82.

20. Richard Dean Burns, ed., *Encyclopedia of Arms Control and Disarmament* (New York: Scribner's, 1993), 232.

21. Anatoly Dobrynin, *In Confidence: Moscow's Ambassador to America's Six Cold War Presidents (1962–1986)* (New York: Times Books, Random House, 1995), 68.

22. Naftali, 62–64.

23. Richard K. Betts, *Nuclear Blackmail and Nuclear Balance* (Washington, DC: Brookings Institution, 1987), 113.

24. Naftali, 573.

25. Sheldon M. Stern, *Averting the "Final Failure": John F. Kennedy and the Secret Cuban Missile Crisis Meetings*, Stanford Nuclear Age Series (Stanford, CA: Stanford University Press, 2003), 144–146.

26. Naftali, 91.

27. Garthoff, 42.

28. Nasuh Uslu, *The Turkish-American Relationship Between 1947 and 2003: The History of a Distinctive Alliance* (New York: Nova Science Publishers, 2003), 141–144.

29. Ibid., 150.

30. Fursenko and Naftali, 112.

31. Michael R. Beschloss, *The Crisis Years: Kennedy and Khrushchev, 1960–1963* (New York: Edward Burlingame Books, 1991), 501.

32. Betts, 118.

33. Stern, 85.

34. Naftali, 335.

35. Freedman, 209–210.

36. Dobrynin, 87–88.

CHAPTER SEVEN

1. Timothy Naftali, ed., *John F. Kennedy: The Great Crises*, vol. 1, *July 30–August 1962*, The Presidential Recordings (New York: W. W. Norton, 2001), 93.

2. Pavel Podvig, ed., *Russian Strategic Nuclear Forces* (Cambridge, MA: MIT Press, 2001), 451.

3. Nish Jamgotch, *Sectors of Mutual Benefit in US-Soviet Relations* (Durham, NC: Duke University Press, 1985), 183.

4. William Baugh, *The Politics of Nuclear Balance: Ambiguity and Continuity in Strategic Policies* (Reading, MA: Longman, 1984), 126.

5. Allan Winkler, *Life Under a Cloud: American Anxiety About the Atom* (Urbana: University of Illinois Press, 1999), 179.

6. Douglas Brinkley and Richard Griffiths, eds., *John F. Kennedy and Europe* (Baton Rouge: Louisiana State University Press, 1999), 78.

7. Alan Milward, *The Rise and Fall of a National Strategy, 1945–1963* (London: Routledge, 2002), 462–465.

8. Glenn T. Seaborg with Benjamin S. Loeb, *Stemming the Tide: Arms Control in the Johnson Years* (Lexington, MA: Lexington Books, 1987), 194.

9. John Wilson Lewis and Xue Litai, *China Builds the Bomb* (Stanford, CA: Stanford University Press, 1991), 62.

10. Itty Abraham, *The Making of the Indian Atomic Bomb: Science, Secrecy and the Post-Colonial State* (London: Zed Books, 1998), 152.

11. Lawrence Freedman, *Kennedy's Wars: Berlin, Cuba, Laos, and Vietnam* (New York: Oxford University Press, 2002), 272.

12. Seaborg with Loeb, 181.

13. Ibid.

14. Aleksandr Fursenko and Timothy Naftali, *One Hell of a Gamble: Khrushchev, Castro, and Kennedy, 1958–1964* (New York: W. W. Norton, 1998), 156.

15. James C. Olson, *Stuart Symington: A Life*, Missouri Biography Series (Columbia: University of Missouri Press, 2003), 372.

16. Seaborg with Loeb, 211.

17. Fursenko and Naftali, 337.

18. Ibid.

19. Albert Carnesale and Richard N. Haass, eds., *Superpower Arms Control: Setting the Record Straight* (Cambridge, MA: Ballinger, 1987), 239.

20. Seaborg with Loeb, 227.

21. James E. Goodby, *At the Borderline of Armageddon: How Presidents Managed the Atom Bomb* (Lanham, MD: Rowman & Littlefield, 2006), 67.

22. Seaborg with Loeb, 257.

23. William Taubman, *Khrushchev: The Man and His Era* (New York: Norton, 2003), 605.

24. April Carter, *Success and Failure in Arms Control Negotiations* (Oxford: Oxford University Press, 1989), 73.

25. Ronald Terchek, *The Making of the Test Ban Treaty* (Leiden: Brill Archive, 1973), 163.

26. Stephen Schwartz, ed., *Atomic Audit: The Costs and Consequences of Nuclear Weapons Since 1940* (Washington, DC: Brookings Institution Press, 1998), 26.

27. John Clearwater, *Johnson, McNamara and the Birth of SALT and the ABM Treaty, 1963–1969* (Boca Raton, FL: Universal Publishers, 1996), 13.

28. Eric Mlyn, *The State, Society and Limited Nuclear War* (Albany: State University of New York Press, 1995), 70.

29. James Douglas, *JFK and the Unspeakable: Why He Died, and Why It Matters* (Maryknoll, NY: Orbis Books, 2008), 241.

30. Anatoly Dobrynin, *In Confidence: Moscow's Ambassador to America's Six Cold War Presidents (1962–1986)* (New York: Times Books, Random House, 1995), 106–107.

31. Taubman, 604.

32. John Drumbell, *President Lyndon Johnson and Soviet Communism* (Manchester, UK: Manchester University Press, 2004), 60.

33. Clearwater, 71.

34. Deborah Welch Larson, *Anatomy of Mistrust: U.S.-Soviet Relations During the Cold War* (Ithaca, NY: Cornell University Press, 2000), 152.

35. Peter Pry, *Israel's Nuclear Arsenal* (Boulder, CO: Westview Press, 1984), 39.

36. Avner Cohen, *Israel and the Bomb* (New York: Columbia University Press, 1999), 117.

37. William Burr and Jeffrey Richelson, "A Chinese Puzzle," *Bulletin of the Atomic Scientists*, July 1997, 42.

38. Stephen Philip Cohen, *India: Emerging Power* (Washington, DC: Brookings Institution Press, 2001), 157.

39. ACDA, *Documents on Disarmament* 126 (1964): 352.

40. "The US Tries Again," *Time*, October 6, 1961.

41. William Safire, *Safire's Political Dictionary* (New York: Oxford University Press, 2008), 229.

42. Rick Perlstein, *Before the Storm: Barry Goldwater and the Unmaking of the American Consensus* (New York: Nation Books, 2009), 391.

43. Harold Hinton, *Communist China in World Politics* (Boston: Houghton Mifflin, 1966), 472.

44. Burr and Richelson, 42.

45. Harold Faber, *The Road to the White House: The Story of the 1964 Election* (New York: McGraw-Hill, 1965), 247.

46. William Hyland and Richard Shyrock, *The Fall of Khrushchev* (New York: Funk & Wagnalls, 1968), 134.

47. Edwin Bacon and Mark Sandle, *Brezhnev Reconsidered* (New York: Palgrave Macmillan, 2002), 90.

48. Robert Spero, *The Duping of the American Voter: Dishonesty and Deception in Presidential Television Advertising* (New York: Lippincott & Crowell, 1980), 80.

CHAPTER EIGHT

1. Thomas Alan Schwartz, *Lyndon Johnson and Europe: In the Shadow of Vietnam* (Cambridge, MA: Harvard University Press, 2003), 53.

2. Raymond L. Garthoff, *A Journey Through the Cold War: A Memoir of Containment and Coexistence* (Washington, DC: Brookings Institution Press, 2001), 193.

3. Glenn T. Seaborg with Benjamin Loeb, *Stemming the Tide: Arms Control in the Johnson Years* (Lexington, MA: Lexington Books, 1987), 143–144.

4. Roswell Gilpatric, *A Report to the President by the Committee on Nuclear Proliferation*, January 21, 1965, 3.

5. Ibid.

6. Ibid., 4–5.

7. Ibid., 5.

8. Ibid., 7–8.

9. Ibid, 20–21.

10. Seaborg with Loeb, 144.

11. President Lyndon Johnson, *State of the Union Addresses* (Whitefish, MT: Kessinger Publishing, 2004), 13.

12. Ibid., 14.

13. Memorandum to the president, June 25, 1965, "McGeorge Bundy, vol. 11, June 1965 [1 of 2]" folder, Memos to the President, NSF, Box 3, Lyndon Johnson Presidential Library.

14. Memorandum to the secretary of state and the secretary of defense, March 27, 1965, "Presidential Task Force, Committee on Nuclear Proliferation" folder, Subject File, NSF, Box 35, Lyndon Johnson Presidential Library.

15. Ibid.

16. Ibid.; Memorandum for Bundy from Keeny, March 26, 1965, "Presidential Task Force Committee on Nuclear Proliferation" folder, Subject Files, NSF, Box 35, Lyndon Johnson Presidential Library.

17. National Security Action Memorandum 335, *Preparation of Arms Control Program*, June 28, 1965.

18. Memorandum for the president, July 3, 1965, "McGeorge Bundy, vol. 12, July 1965" folder, Memos to the President, Box 4, Lyndon Johnson Presidential Library.

19. National Intelligence Estimate, *Prospects for West German Foreign Policy*, April 22, 1965.

20. Seaborg with Loeb, 277.

21. John P. S. Gearson and Kori Schake, eds., *The Berlin Wall Crisis: Perspectives on Cold War Alliances* (New York: Palgrave MacMillan, 2002), 76.

22. International Peace Academy, *South Africa in Crisis: Regional and International Responses* (Leiden: Brill, 1988), 74–75.

23. Avner Cohen, *Israel and the Bomb* (New York: Columbia University Press, 1999), 232.

24. George Perkovitch, *India's Nuclear Bomb: The Impact on Global Proliferation* (Berkeley: University of California Press, 1999), 94–95.

25. Ashton B. Carter and David N. Schwartz, eds., *Ballistic Missile Defense* (Washington, DC: Brookings Institution, 1984), 334–336.

26. Nigel Hey, *The Star Wars Enigma: Behind the Scenes of the Cold War Race for Missile Defense* (Washington, DC: Potomac Books, 2006), 20.

27. Pavel Podvig, ed., *Russian Strategic Nuclear Forces* (Cambridge, MA: MIT Press, 2001), 415.

28. Trevor Dupuy, *A Documentary History of Arms Control and Disarmament* (Ann Arbor: University of Michigan Press, 1973), 549.

29. Alain C. Enthoven and K. Wayne Smith, *How Much Is Enough? Shaping the Defense Program, 1961–1969*, new ed. (Santa Monica, CA: RAND Corporation, 2005), 207.

30. Gregg Herken, *Counsels of War* (New York: Knopf, 1985), 154–155.

31. Graham Spinardi, *From Polaris to Trident: The Development of US Fleet Ballistic Missile Technology* (Cambridge: Cambridge University Press, 1994), 72.

32. Robert Ehrlich, *Waging Nuclear Peace: The Technology and Politics of Nuclear Weapons* (Albany: State University of New York Press, 1984), 54.

33. John Clearwater, *Johnson, McNamara, and the Birth of SALT and the ABM Treaty 1963–1969* (Boca Raton, FL: Universal Publishers, 1996), 53.

34. Ibid., 55.

35. United States Department of the Army, *History of Strategic Air and Ballistic Missile Defense, Volume II (1956–1972)* (San Diego: U.S. Military Press, 1975), 201.

36. Glenn A. Kent, *Thinking About America's Defense: An Analytical Memoir* (Santa Monica, CA: RAND Corporation, 2008), 51.

37. Glenn A. Kent, *Damage Limiting: A Rationale for the Allocation of Resources by the U.S. and the U.S.S.R.* (Washington, DC: Directorate of Defense Research & Engineering, 1964).

38. Clearwater, 8.

39. Morton H. Halperin, with Priscilla Clapp and Arnold Kanter, *Bureaucratic Politics and Foreign Policy* (Washington, DC: Brookings Institution Press, 1974), 298.

40. Ibid., 300.

41. Memorandum from the deputy secretary of defense to President Johnson, December 10, 1966, "Washington National Records Center, OSD," files, FRC 330 71 A 3470, ABM Memo and JCS View Folder 103.

42. United States Department of the Army, 203–204.

43. Clearwater, 82.

44. Ibid., 83–84.

45. Ibid., 87–88.

46. "Satellite Spying Cited by Johnson," *New York Times*, March 17, 1967.

47. George Bunn, *Arms Control by Committee: Managing Negotiations with the Russians* (Stanford, CA: Stanford University Press, 1994), 72–73.

48. News conference, *Weekly Compilation of Presidential Documents, Vol. II*, no. 27 (July 11, 1966).

49. Bunn, 76–77.

50. John Wilson Lewis and Xue Litai, *China Builds the Bomb* (Stanford, CA: Stanford University Press, 1991), 202–210.

51. John Dumbrell, *President Lyndon Johnson and Soviet Communism* (Manchester: Manchester University Press, 2004), 76–77.

52. Robert S. McNamara, *Blundering Toward Disaster: Surviving the First Century of the Nuclear Age* (New York: Pantheon Books, 1986), 65.

53. Rob de Wijk, *Flexibility in Response? Attempts to Construct a Plausible Strategy for NATO, 1959–1989* (Berkeley: University of California Press, 2007), 83.

54. Podvig, 127.

55. Ibid.

56. Renata Fritsch-Bournazel, *Europe and German Unification* (New York: Berg, 1992), 48.

57. Kevin Pollpeter, *U.S.-China Security Management: Assessing the Military-to-Military Relationship* (Santa Monica, CA: RAND Corporation, 2003), 53.

58. Roger Trask, *The Secretaries of Defense: A Brief History, 1947–1985* (Washington, DC: Historical Office, Office of the Secretary of Defense, 1985), 33.

59. John Prados, *Keepers of the Keys: A History of the National Security Council from Truman to Bush* (New York: William Morrow, 1991), 193.

60. Larry Berman, *Lyndon Johnson's War: The Road to Stalemate in Vietnam* (New York: W. W. Norton, 1991), 176.

61. Seaborg with Loeb, 432.

62. Letter from President Johnson to Chairman Kosygin, May 2, 1968, "Department of State, Pen Pal Correspondence," lot 77 D 163, Special U.S.-U.S.S.R. File, Pen-Pal Series, 1968.

63. Ibid.

64. Message from A. Kosygin to President Johnson, June 21, 1968, "Papers of Clark Clifford," Box 12, Soviet Union, Talks, Lyndon Johnson Presidential Library.

65. *Public Papers of the Presidents of the United States: Lyndon B. Johnson, 1968–69, Book II*, 765.

66. Paper Prepared by Interagency Working Group, Strategic Missile Talk Proposal, July 31, 1968, "Clifford Papers, Kosygin-Talks with Soviet Union (2)," Box 22, Lyndon Johnson Presidential Library.

67. Glenn Seaborg, *The Journal of Glenn T. Seaborg* (Berkeley: University of California: 1990), pp. 132–133.

68. Memorandum from Secretary of State Rusk and director of the Arms Control and Disarmament Agency to President Johnson, August 15, 1968, "National Security File, Intelligence File, Arms Limitation Talk," Box 11, Lyndon Johnson Presidential Library.

69. Memorandum of conversation between Secretary of State Rusk and the Soviet ambassador, August 15, 1968, "National Security File, Rostow Files, Rusk-Dobrynin," Lyndon Johnson Presidential Library; H. W. Brands, *The Foreign Policies of Lyndon Johnson: Beyond Vietnam* (College Station: Texas A&M University Press, 1999), 28.

70. Telegram from the president's special assistant to president Johnson, August 19, 1968, "National Security File, Rostow Files, Trip to Soviet Union," Lyndon Johnson Presidential Library.

71. Brands, 29–30.

72. Notes of Emergency Meeting of the National Security Council, August 20, 1968, "Tom Johnson's Notes of Meetings," Lyndon Johnson Presidential Library.

73. Memorandum of Conversation, September 20, 1968, "National Security File, Rostow Files, Rusk-Dobrynin," Lyndon Johnson Presidential Library.

CHAPTER NINE

1. Elizabeth Drew, *Richard M. Nixon* (New York: Times Books, 2007), 63.

2. Jussi Hanhimäki, *The Flawed Architect: Henry Kissinger and American Foreign Policy* (New York: Oxford University Press, 2004), 9.

3. David Kunsman and Douglas Lawson, *A Primer on US Nuclear Strategy* (Albuquerque: Sandia National Laboratories, 2001), 110.

4. Richard Nixon, inaugural address, January 20, 1969.

5. Ibid.

6. Margaret MacMillan, *Nixon and Mao: The Week That Changed the World* (New York: Random House, 2007), 7.

7. Yukinori Komine, *Secrecy in US Foreign Policy: Nixon, Kissinger and the Rapprochement with China* (Burlington, VT: Ashgate Publishing, 2008), 73.

8. Yafeng Xia, *Negotiating with the Enemy: US-China Talks During the Cold War, 1949–1972* (Bloomington: Indiana University Press, 2006), 132–133.

9. Anatoly Dobrynin, *In Confidence: Moscow's Ambassador to America's Six Cold War Presidents (1962–1986)* (New York: Times Books, Random House, 1995), 198–199.

10. William Burrow, ed., *The Kissinger Transcripts: The Top-Secret Talks with Beijing and Moscow* (New York: New Press, 1999), 25.

11. Henry Kissinger, *The White House Years* (Boston: Little, Brown, 1979), 266–268.

12. Raymond L. Garthoff, *Détente and Confrontation: American-Soviet Relations from Nixon to Reagan*, rev. ed. (Washington, DC: Brookings Institution Press, 1994), 82.

13. Alex F. Dowlah and John E. Elliott, *The Life and Times of Soviet Socialism* (Westport, CT: Praeger, 1997), 146.

14. Deborah Welch Larson, *Anatomy of Mistrust: US-Soviet Relations During the Cold War* (Ithaca, NY: Cornell University Press, 2000), 162.

15. Anne Hessing Cahn, *Killing Detente: The Right Attacks the CIA* (University Park: Pennsylvania State University Press, 1998), 96.

16. Larson, 161.

17. Garthoff, 151.

18. Gregg Herken, *Cardinal Choices: Presidential Scientific Advising from the Atomic Bomb to SDI*, rev. and exp. ed. (Stanford, CA: Stanford University Press, 2000), 172–173.

19. William Burr, "The Nixon Administration, the 'Horror Strategy,' and the Search for Limited Nuclear Options, 1969–1972," *Journal of Cold War Studies* 7, no. 3 (Summer 2005): 34–35.

20. Ibid., 44–48.

21. Ibid., 48–50.

22. Ibid., 51.

23. Ibid., 52–54.

24. Ibid., 56.

25. Robert McNamara, "Mutual Deterrence," speech, San Francisco, California, September 18, 1969.

26. April Carter, *Success and Failure in Arms Control Negotiations* (Oxford: Oxford University Press, 1989), 129.

27. Ernest Yanarella, *The Missile Defense Controversy: Technology in Search of a Mission* (Lexington: University Press of Kentucky, 2002), 172–175.

28. Memorandum for Dr. Kissinger, NSC Review Group Meeting, May 29, 1969, p. 17.

29. Henry A. Kissinger, "Memorandum for the President, Modified Sentinel System," March 5, 1969, cover page (handwritten comments by the president).

30. Garthoff, 164.

31. Yanarella, 156.

32. Robert S. Litwak, *Détente and the Nixon Doctrine: American Foreign Policy and the Pursuit of Stability, 1969–1976* (Cambridge: Cambridge University Press, 1984), 40.

33. Dobrynin, 202.

34. Raymond L. Garthoff, *A Journey Through the Cold War: A Memoir of Containment and Coexistence* (Washington, DC: Brookings Institution Press, 2001), 264.

35. Gerard Smith, *Doubletalk: The Story of the First Strategic Arms Limitation Talks* (Garden City, NY: Doubleday, 1980), 75–80.

36. Garthoff, *Détente and Confrontation*, 168.

37. Ibid., 159.

38. Smith, 174–175.

39. Ibid., 146.

40. Charles Cannon, *The Military-Industrial Complex in American Politics, 1953–1970* (Stanford, CA: Stanford University, 1974), 51.

41. Garthoff, *Détente and Confrontation*, 94.

42. Dobrynin, 207.

43. Smith, 149.

44. National Security Decision Memorandum 69, "Strategic Arms Limitations Talks," July 9, 1970, 2–5.

45. Seymour M. Hersh, *The Price of Power: Kissinger in the Nixon White House* (New York: Summit Books, 1983), 338.

46. Jonathan Tucker, "A Farewell to Germs: The US Renunciation of Biological and Toxin Warfare, 1969–1970," *International Security* 27, no. 1 (Summer 2002): 118.

47. "Willy Brandt," *Time*, January 4, 1971.

48. Hanhimäki, 89.

49. Ibid., 84.

50. Ibid.

51. Smith, 185.

52. Ibid., 225.

53. Garthoff, *Détente and Confrontation*, 167.

54. Smith, 232.

55. Mason Willrich and John B. Rhinelander, ed., *SALT: The Moscow Agreements and Beyond* (New York: Free Press, 1974), 29.

56. Smith, 351.

57. Garthoff, *Détente and Confrontation*, 176.

58. Smith, 449.

CHAPTER TEN

1. Gerard Smith, *Doubletalk: The Story of the First Strategic Arms Limitation Talks* (Garden City, NY: Doubleday, 1980), 228.

2. Robert Kaufman, *Henry M. Jackson: A Life in Politics* (Seattle: University of Washington Press, 2000), 213–214.

3. United States Congress, Senate Armed Services Committee, *Hearings and Reports* (Washington, DC: Government Printing Office, 1976), 186.

4. April Carter, *Success and Failure in Arms Control Negotiations* (Oxford: Oxford University Press, 1989), 131.

5. Kaufmann, 255–258.

6. Raymond L. Garthoff, *Détente and Confrontation: American-Soviet Relations from Nixon to Reagan*, rev. ed. (Washington, DC: Brookings Institution Press, 1994), 911.

7. Smith, 443.

8. Strobe Talbott, *The Master of the Game: Paul Nitze and the Nuclear Peace* (New York: Knopf, 1988), 136.

9. Robert D. Schulzinger, *American Diplomacy in the Twentieth Century* (New York: Oxford University Press, 1984), 329.

10. Ronald E. Powaski, *March to Armageddon: The United States and the Nuclear Arms Race, 1939 to the Present* (New York: Oxford University Press, 1987), 146.

11. William Burr, "The Nixon Administration, the 'Horror Strategy,' and the Search for Limited Nuclear Options, 1969–1972: Prelude to the Schlesinger Doctrine," *Cold War Studies* 7, no. 3 (Summer 2005): 40–45.

12. Fred Kaplan, *The Wizards of Armageddon*, Stanford Nuclear Age Series (Stanford, CA: Stanford University Press, 1991 [1983]), 369–370.

13. Fred Iklé, "Can Nuclear Deterrence Last Out the Century?" *Foreign Affairs* 51, no. 2 (January 1973): 267–285.

14. Raymond L. Garthoff, *A Journey Through the Cold War: A Memoir of Containment and Coexistence* (Washington, DC: Brookings Institution Press, 2001), 288.

15. Garthoff, *Détente and Confrontation*, 377.

16. Raymond L. Garthoff, *Deterrence and the Revolution in Soviet Military Doctrine* (Washington, DC: Brookings Institution Press, 1990), 86.

17. Garthoff, *Détente and Confrontation*, 424.

18. Robert Kleiman, "The Real Question . . . Europe's Security, VII. Preventing Nuclear War," Allicia Patterson Foundation, 1973.

19. Kaplan, 342.

20. Burr, 46–48.

21. Elizabeth Drew, *Richard M. Nixon* (New York: Times Books, 2007), 3.

22. Terry Terriff, *The Nixon Administration and the Making of U.S. Nuclear Strategy* (Ithaca, NY: Cornell University Press, 1995), 204–205.

23. Graham Spinardi, *From Polaris to Trident: The Development of US Fleet Ballistic Missile Technology* (Cambridge: Cambridge University Press, 1994), 152.

24. Rob de Wijk, *Flexibility in Response? Attempts to Construct a Plausible Strategy for NATO, 1959–1989* (Berkeley: University of California Press, 1989), 189.

25. Edward L. Rowny, *It Takes One to Tango* (Washington, DC: Brassey's, 1992), 268.

26. William Vogele, *Stepping Back: Nuclear Arms Control and the End of the Cold War* (Westport, CT: Praeger, 1994), 78.

27. Thomas Wolfe, *The SALT Experience* (Santa Monica, CA: RAND, 1979), 327.

28. Vogele, 40.

29. Powaski, 159.

30. Wolfe, 88.

31. Talbott, 138.

32. Powaski, 147.

33. Richard Burt, ed., *Arms Control and Defense Postures in the 1980s* (Boulder, CO: Westview Press, 1982), 167.

34. Jussi Hanhimäki, *The Flawed Architect: Henry Kissinger and American Foreign Policy* (New York: Oxford University Press, 2004), 352.

35. Bob Woodward, *Shadow: Five Presidents and the Legacy of Watergate* (New York: Simon & Schuster, 1999), 23.

36. Yanek Mieczkowski, *Gerald Ford and the Challenges of the 1970s* (Lexington: University Press of Kentucky, 2005), 283.

37. Garthoff, *Détente and Confrontation*, 494.

38. Carter, 146.

39. Garthoff, *Détente and Confrontation*, 496–497.

40. Ibid., 501.

41. Ibid., 502.

42. John Prados, *Lost Crusader: The Secret Wars of CIA Director William Colby* (Oxford: Oxford University Press, 2003), 281–282.

43. Gerald Haines and Robert Leggit, *Watching the Bear: Essays on CIA Analysis of the Soviet Threat* (Alexandria, VA: Central Intelligence Agency, 2003), 158.

44. Anne Hessing Cahn, *Killing Détente: The Right Attacks the CIA* (University Park: Pennsylvania State University Press, 1998), 107.

45. Ibid., 113.

46. Ibid., 117.

47. Ibid., 118.

48. Ibid., 118–119.

49. Garthoff, *Détente and Confrontation*, 502.

50. John Newhouse, *War and Peace in the Nuclear Age* (New York: Vintage Books, 1990), 261.

51. Garthoff, *Détente and Confrontation*, 502.

52. Walter Isaacson, *Kissinger: A Biography* (New York: Simon & Schuster, 2005), 669.

53. Newhouse, 260.

54. Andrew Crain, *The Ford Presidency: A History* (Jefferson, NC: McFarland, 2009), 200.

55. Mieczkowski, 288.

CHAPTER ELEVEN

1. William Bennett, *America: The World's Last Great Hope, Volume 2* (Nashville: Thomas Nelson, 2007), 455.

2. Ibid., 516.

3. Joseph Nogee and Robert Donaldson, *Soviet Foreign Policy Since World War II* (New York: Macmillan, 1992), 306.

4. John Diamond, *The CIA and the Culture of Failure: U.S. Intelligence from the End of the Cold War to the Invasion of Iraq*, Stanford Security Series (Stanford, CA: Stanford University Press, 2008), 436.

5. Andrew Kopkind and JoAnn Wypijewski, *The Thirty Years' War: Dispatches and Diversions of a Radical Journalist, 1965–1994* (London: Verso, 1995), 335–336.

6. Anne Hessing Cahn, *Killing Détente: The Right Attacks the CIA* (University Park: Pennsylvania State University Press, 1998), 139.

7. Raymond L. Garthoff, *A Journey Through the Cold War: A Memoir of Containment and Coexistence* (Washington, DC: Brookings Institution Press, 2001), 328.

8. Diamond, 50.

9. Cahn, 176.

10. Sidney Blumenthal, *The Strange Death of Republican America: Chronicles of a Collapsing Party* (New York: Sterling Publishing, 2008), 160.

11. Philip Burch, *Reagan, Bush and Right-Wing Politics: Elites, Think-Tanks, Power and Policy, Part 1* (Greenwich, CT: JAI Press, 1997), 136.

12. Lawrence Wittner, *Toward Nuclear Abolition: A History of the World Disarmament Movement, 1971–Present* (Stanford, CA: Stanford University Press, 2003), 108.

13. Phillip J. Morledge, *"I Do Solemnly Swear": Presidential Inaugurations from George Washington to George W. Bush* (Sheffield, UK: PJM Publishing, 2008), 240.

14. Anatoliy Dobrynin, *In Confidence: Moscow's Ambassador to America's Six Cold War President's (1962–1986)* (New York: Random House, 1995), 423.

15. April Carter, *Success and Failure in Arms Control Negotiations* (Oxford: Oxford University Press, 1989), 197–198.

16. Strobe Talbott, *Endgame: The Inside Story of SALT II* (New York: Harper & Row, 1979), 53.

17. Raymond L. Garthoff, *Détente and Confrontation: American-Soviet Relations from Nixon to Reagan*, rev. ed. (Washington, DC: Brookings Institution Press, 1994), 868.

18. Terence Garvey, *Bones of Contention: An Enquiry into East-West Relations* (London: Routledge & Kegan Paul, 1978), 94.

19. Garthoff, *Détente and Confrontation*, 755.

20. Talbott, 74.

21. Carter, 88.

22. Fred Kaplan, *The Wizards of Armageddon*, Stanford Nuclear Age Series (Stanford, CA: Stanford University Press, 1991 [1983]), 383.

23. David Walsh, *The Military Balance in the Cold War: US Perceptions and Policies, 1976–85* (New York: Routledge, 2007), 22–24.

24. David Skidmore, *Reversing Course: Carter's Foreign Policy, Domestic Politics, and the Failure of Reform* (Nashville: Vanderbilt University Press, 1996), 49–50.

25. Douglas Lackey, *Moral Principles and Nuclear Weapons* (Lanham, MD: Rowman & Littlefield, 1984), 65–66.

26. Donald MacKenzie, *Inventing Accuracy: A Historical Sociology of Nuclear Missile Guidance* (Cambridge, MA: MIT Press, 1993), 215–217.

27. Lackey, 65.

28. Tom Sauer, *Nuclear Inertia: US Weapons Policy After the Cold War* (London: I. B. Tauris, 2005), 120–121.

29. Brian Auten, *Carter's Conversion: The Hardening of American Defense Policy* (Columbia: University of Missouri Press, 2008), 128.

30. Ibid., 205.

31. Robert Ehrlich, *Waging Nuclear Peace: The Technology and Politics of Nuclear Weapons* (Albany: State University of New York Press, 1985), 109.

32. Carter, 153.

33. Walter Goldstein, ed., *Fighting Allies: Tensions Within the Atlantic Alliance* (Washington, DC: Brassey's, 1986), 42.

34. Eric A. Croddy and James J. Wirtz, eds., *Weapons of Mass Destruction: An Encyclopedia of Worldwide Policy, Technology, and History* (Santa Barbara, CA: ABC-CLIO, 2005), 283.

35. Auten, 176.

36. Stephen Flanagan and Fen Osler Hampson, *Securing Europe's Future* (London: Routledge, 1986), 31.

37. Ronald Huisken, *The Origin of the Strategic Cruise Missile* (Greenwood, CT: Praeger, 1981), 3.

38. James Martin, "How the Soviet Union Came to Gain Escalation Dominance: Trends and Assymetrics in the Theater Nuclear Balance," in *Soviet Power and Western Negotiating Policies*, ed. Uwe Nerlich (Cambridge, MA: Ballinger Publishing, 1983), 92–98.

39. David Rothkopf, *Running the World: The Inside Story of the National Security Council and the Architects of Power* (New York: Public Affairs, 2005), 195.

40. Garthoff, *Détente and Confrontation*, 900.

41. Talbott, 87.

42. Auten, 123.

43. Rothkopf, 490.

44. Talbott, 81.

45. Garthoff, *Détente and Confrontation*, 897.

46. Carter, 154.

47. Garthoff, *Détente and Confrontation*, 937.

48. Thomas Graham Jr., *Disarmament Sketches: Three Decades of Arms Control and International Law* (Seattle: Institute for Global and Regional Security Studies, University of Washington Press, 2002), 79–81.

49. Jimmy Carter, *Keeping Faith: Memoirs of a President* (New York: Bantam, 1983), 232.

50. Ronald E. Powaski, *March to Armageddon: The United States and the Nuclear Arms Race, 1939 to the Present* (New York: Oxford University Press, 1987), 172.

51. Richard Gabriel, *To Serve With Honor: A Treatise on Military Ethics and the Way of the Soldier* (Westport, CT: Greenwood Press, 1982), 184.

52. Powaski, 174.

53. A. Carter, 157.

54. Adam Ulam, *Understanding the Cold War: A Historian's Personal Reflection* (Edison, NJ: Transaction Publishers, 2002), 266.

55. Cyrus Vance, *Hard Choices: Critical Years in America's Foreign Policy* (New York: Simon & Schuster, 1983), 136.

56. J. Carter, 234.

57. Ibid., 243.

58. Auten, 276.

59. Ibid., 279.

60. William C. Potter, *Verification and SALT: The Challenge of Strategic Deception* (Boulder, CO: Westview Press, 1980), 120.

61. J. Carter, 255.

62. Vance, 138.

63. Garthoff, *Détente and Confrontation*, 950.

64. Richard Scribner, Theodore Ralston, and William Metz, *The Verification Challenge: Problems and Promise of Strategic Nuclear Arms Control Verification* (Basel, Switzerland: Birkhäuser, 1985), 205.

65. Theodore Windt, *Presidential Rhetoric: 1961 to Present* (Dubuque, IA: Kendall/Hunt Publishing, 1987), 272.

66. Jerry Sanders, *Peddlers of Crisis: The Committee on the Present Danger and the Politics of Containment* (Cambridge, MA: South End Press, 1983), 254.

67. Richard Stubbing and Richard Mendel, *The Defense Game: An Insider Explores the Astonishing Realities of America's Defense Establishment* (New York: Harper & Row, 1986), 17–18.

68. Senate Committee on Foreign Relations, *The SALT II Treaty Hearings*, 96th Congress (Washington, DC: Government Printing Office, 1979).

69. Garthoff, *Détente and Confrontation*, 1084.

70. Michael Mandelbaum, *The Other Side of the Table: The Soviet Approach to Arms Control* (New York: Council on Foreign Relations, 1990), 104.

71. Barry Goldwater, *With No Apologies: The Personal and Political Memoirs of United States Senator Barry M. Goldwater* (New York: William Morrow, 1979), 298.

72. John Moore, ed., *U.S. Defense Policy: Weapons, Strategy, and Commitments* (Washington, DC: Congressional Quarterly, 1980), 54.

73. Ibid., 54.

CHAPTER TWELVE

1. Allan M. Winkler, *Life Under a Cloud: American Anxiety About the Atom* (Urbana: University of Illinois Press, 1999), 39–41.

2. Steven Hayward, *The Real Jimmy Carter: How Our Worst Ex-President Undermines American Foreign Policy, Coddles Dictators and Created the Party of Clinton and Kerry* (Washington, DC: Regnery Press, 2004), 65.

3. Jimmy Carter, *State of the Union Addresses of Jimmy Carter* (Middlesex, UK: Echo Library, 2007), 22.

4. Fred Kaplan, *The Wizards of Armageddon*, Stanford Nuclear Age Series (Stanford, CA: Stanford University Press, 1991 [1983]) 384.

5. Eric Mlyn, *The State, Society, and Limited Nuclear War* (Albany: State University of New York Press, 1995), 116.

6. Scott Sagan, *Moving Targets: Nuclear Strategy and National Security* (Princeton, NJ: Princeton University Press, 1990), 49.

7. Robert Banis, *Inaugural Addresses: Presidents of the United States from George Washington to 2008* (Science & Humanitarian Press, 2008), 331.

8. David Rothkopf, *Running the World: The Inside Story of the National Security Council and the Architects of Power* (New York: Public Affairs, 2005), 215.

9. Jerry Sanders, *Peddlers of Crisis: The Committee on the Present Danger and the Politics of Containment* (Cambridge, MA: South End Press, 1983), 8.

10. Keith Shimko, *Images and Arms Control: Perceptions of the Soviet Union in the Reagan Administration* (Ann Arbor: University of Michigan Press, 1991), 64.

11. Raymond L. Garthoff, *The Great Transition: American-Soviet Relations and the End of the Cold War* (Washington, DC: Brookings Institution Press, 1994), 8.

12. Ronald Reagan, *Dear Americans: Letters from the Desk of President Ronald Reagan*, ed. Ralph E. Weber (New York: Doubleday, 2003), 12.

13. Beth Fisher, *The Reagan Reversal: Foreign Policy and the End of the Cold War* (Columbia: University of Missouri Press, 2000), 25.

14. Ibid., 27.

15. J. Peter Scoblic, *U.S. Versus Them: How a Half Century of Conservatism Has Undermined America's Security* (New York: Viking, 2008), 119.

16. Ibid., 126.

17. April Carter, *Success and Failure in Arms Control Negotiations* (Oxford: Oxford University Press, 1989), 197.

18. Scoblic, 127.

19. Stefan Halper and Jonathan Clarke, *America Alone: The Neo-Conservatives and the Global Order* (Cambridge: Cambridge University Press, 2005), 61–62.

20. Peter L. Hays, Brenda J. Vallance, and Alan R. Van Tassel, eds., *American Defense Policy*, 7th ed. (Baltimore: Johns Hopkins University Press, 1997), 223.

21. James A. Nathan and James K. Oliver, *United States Foreign Policy and World Order*, 4th ed. (Glenview, IL: Scott, Foresman, 1989), 396.

22. Steve Breyman, *Why Movements Matter: The West German Peace Movement and U.S. Arms Control Policy* (Albany: State University of New York Press, 2001), 257.

23. Scoblic, 119.

24. Ted Carpenter, *Collective Defense or Strategic Independence? Alternative Strategies for the Future* (Washington, DC: Cato Institute, 1989), 54.

25. Laurence Barrett, *Gambling with History: Ronald Reagan in the White House* (New York: Doubleday, 1983), 310.

26. Strobe Talbott, *Deadly Gambits: The Reagan Administration and the Stalemate of Nuclear Arms Control* (New York: Knopf, 1984), 70.

27. Ibid., 72.

28. Richard Shearer, *On-Site Inspection for Arms Control: Breaking the Verification Barrier* (Washington, DC: National Defense University, 1984), 41.

29. Talbott, 157.

30. Michael Mandelbaum, *The Other Side of the Table: The Soviet Approach to Arms Control* (New York: Council on Foreign Relations, 1990), 91.

31. Paul Lettow, *Ronald Reagan and His Quest to Abolish Nuclear Weapons* (New York: Random House, 2006), 71.

32. A. Carter, 184.

33. Lou Cannon, *Reagan* (New York: G. P. Putnam, 1982), 400.

34. Strobe Talbott and Paul Nitze, *The Master of the Game: Paul Nitze and the Nuclear Peace* (New York: Knopf, 1988), 174.

35. Mandelbaum, 110.

36. Talbott, 144.

37. Garthoff, 523.

38. Scoblic, 124.

39. Ian Bellany, Coit D. Blacker, and Joseph Gallacher, eds., *The Nuclear Non-Proliferation Treaty* (London: Cass, 1985), 63).

40. Ronald E. Powaski, *March to Armageddon: The United States and the Nuclear Arms Race, 1939 to the Present* (New York: Oxford University Press, 1987), 207.

41. Philip L. Cantelon, Richard G. Hewlett, and Robert C. Williams, eds., *The American Atom: A Documentary History of Nuclear Policies from the Discovery of Fission to the Present*, 2nd ed. (Philadelphia: University of Pennsylvania Press, 1991), 218.

42. Lettow, 84.

43. Ronald E. Powaski, *Return to Armageddon: The United States and the Nuclear Arms Race, 1981–1999* (Oxford: Oxford University Press, 1984), 36.

44. Garthoff, 86.

45. Martin Ebon, *The Andropov File: The Life and Ideas of Yuri V. Andropov, General Secretary of the Communist Party of the Soviet Union* (New York: McGraw-Hill, 1983), 261.

46. Breyman, 135.

47. John Lewis Gaddis, *The Cold War: A New History* (New York: Penguin Books, 2006), 224.

48. Francis Fitzgerald, *Way Out in the Blue: Reagan, Star Wars and the End of the Cold War* (New York: Simon & Schuster, 2000), 147.

49. Lou Dubose and Jake Bernstein, *Vice: Dick Cheney and the Hijacking of the American Presidency* (New York: Random House, 2006), 51.

50. Lou Cannon, *President Reagan: The Role of a Lifetime* (New York: Simon & Shuster, 1991), 742.

51. Garthoff, 129.

52. Paul Bennett, *Russian Negotiating Strategy: Analytic Case Studies from SALT to START* (Hauppauge, NY: Nova Science Publishers, 1997), 99.

53. Garthoff, 136.

CHAPTER THIRTEEN

1. Mikhail A. Alexseev, *Without Warning: Threat Assessment, Intelligence and Global Struggle* (New York: St. Martin's Press, 1997), 207–208.

2. Paul Kengor and Patricia Clark Doerner, *The Judge: William P. Clark, Ronald Reagan's Top Hand* (San Francisco: Ignatius Press, 2007), 200.

3. Beth Fisher, *The Reagan Reversal: Foreign Policy and the End of the Cold War* (Columbia: University of Missouri Press, 2000), 133.

4. Raymond L. Garthoff, *The Great Transition: American-Soviet Relations and the End of the Cold War* (Washington, DC: Brookings Institution Press, 1994), 188.

5. Ibid., 159.

6. Lou Cannon, *President Reagan: The Role of a Lifetime* (New York: Simon & Schuster, 1991), 473.

7. Robert Cowley, *The Cold War: A Military History* (New York: Random House, 2005), 449.

8. Dev Murarka, *Gorbachov: The Limits of Power* (London: Hutchinson, 1988), 125.

9. Robert Daniels, *The End of the Communist Revolution* (London: Routledge, 1993), 12.

10. Fred Holyrod, *Thinking About Nuclear Weapons: Analyses and Prescriptions* (New York: Routledge, 1990), 146.

11. Leonard S. Spector, *Nuclear Proliferation Today* (New York: Vintage Books, 1984), 129.

12. Scott Kennedy, ed., *China Cross Talk: The American Debate over China Policy Since Normalization: A Reader* (Lanham, MD: Rowman & Littlefield, 2003), 75–76.

13. George P. Shultz, "Address to United Nations Association of the United States," *Current Policy* 631 (1984).

14. Harald Müller, David Fischer, and Wolfgang Kötter, *Nuclear Non-Proliferation and Global Order* (Oxford: Oxford University Press, 1994), 31.

15. Cannon, 746.

16. Thomas Graham Jr., *Disarmament Sketches: Three Decades of Arms Control and International Law* (Seattle: Institute for Global and Regional Security Studies, University of Washington Press, 2002), 122.

17. J. Peter Scoblic, *U.S. Versus Them: How a Half Century of Conservatism Has Undermined America's Security* (New York: Viking, 2008), 123.

18. Robert Kaiser, *Why Gorbachev Happened: His Triumphs and His Failure* (New York: Simon & Schuster, 1991), 95.

19. Jay Winik, *On the Brink: The Dramatic, Behind-the-Scenes Saga of the Reagan Era and the Men and Women Who Won the Cold War* (New York: Simon & Schuster, 1996), 353.

20. Ronald Reagan, *An American Life* (New York: Simon & Schuster, 1990), 622.

21. Lloyd S. Fischel, ed., *Dear Mr. Gorbachev* (Edinburgh, UK: Canongate, 1990), 275.

22. Jack Matlock, *Reagan and Gorbachev: How the Cold War Ended* (New York: Random House, 2004), 140.

23. Thomas Risse-Kappen, *The Zero Option: INF, West Germany and Arms Control* (Boulder, CO: Westview Press, 1988), 107.

24. Alan Weisman, *Prince of Darkness, Richard Perle: The Kingdom, the Power and the End of Empire in America* (New York: Union Square Press, 2007), 88.

25. Martin Anderson, *Reagan's Secret War: The Untold Story of His Fight to Save the World from Nuclear Disaster* (New York: Crown Publishers, 2009), 235.

26. Garthoff, 520.

27. Ibid., 521.

28. Weisman, 87.

29. John Lewis Gaddis, *The Cold War: A New History* (New York: Penguin Books, 2006), 231.

30. Fred Kaplan, *Daydream Believers: How a Few Grand Ideas Wrecked American Power* (Hoboken, NJ: John Wiley & Sons, 2008), 95.

31. Raymond L. Garthoff, *Policy Versus the Law: The Reinterpretation of the ABM Treaty* (Washington, DC: Brookings Institution Press, 1987), 9.

32. Garthoff, *The Great Transition*, 523.

33. Scoblic, 121.

34. Kaiser, 125.

35. James Mann, *The Rebellion of Ronald Reagan: A History of the End of the Cold War* (New York: Viking, 2009), 41.

36. Donald M. Snow, *The Necessary Peace: Nuclear Weapons and Superpower Relations* (Lexington, MA: Lexington Books, 1987), 67.

37. Hedrick Smith, *The Power Game: How Washington Works* (New York: Random House, 1988), 614.

38. George Rueckert, *Global Double Zero: The INF Treaty from Its Origins to Implementation* (Westport, CT: Greenwood Press, 1993), 63.

39. George Shultz, *Turmoil and Triumph: My Years as Secretary of State* (New York: Scribner's, 1993), 728.

40. Anderson, 284.

41. Smith, 576.

42. Winik, 589.

43. Strobe Talbott, *Master of the Game: Paul Nitze and the Nuclear Peace* (New York: Knopf, 1988), 316.

44. Anderson, 293.

45. Talbott, 316.

46. Ibid., 363.

47. Ibid., 324.

48. Matlock, 291.

49. Paul Lettow, *Ronald Reagan and His Quest to Abolish Nuclear Weapons* (New York: Random House, 2006), 294.

50. Max Kampelman, *Entering New Worlds: The Memoirs of a Private Man in Public Life* (New York: Harper Collins, 1991), 320.

51. Lynn Eden and Steven Miller, *Nuclear Arguments: Understanding the Strategic Nuclear Arms and Arms Control Debates* (Ithaca, NY: Cornell University Press, 1989), 300.

52. Mann, 179.

53. Rueckert, 76.

54. W. R. Smyser, *Restive Partners: Washington and Bonn Diverge* (Boulder, CO: Westview Press, 1990), 72.

55. Garthoff, *The Great Transition*, 244.

56. Talbott, 354.

57. Mann, 288.

58. Cannon, 403.

59. Matlock, 327.

60. Mann, 298.

61. Garthoff, *The Great Transition*, 358.

62. Mikhail Gorbachev, *Memoirs* (New York: Doubleday, 1996), 702.

63. Dusko Doder and Louise Branson, *Gorbachev: Heretic in the Kremlin* (New York: Viking, 1990), 356.

64. Kaiser, 249.

65. Christopher Maynard, *Out of the Shadow: George H. W. Bush and the End of the Cold War* (College Station: Texas A&M University Press, 2008), 28–29.

66. Tom Harkin with C. E. Thomas, *Five Minutes to Midnight: Why the Nuclear Threat Is Growing Faster than Ever* (New York: Carol Publishing, 1990), 168.

67. Lawrence Wittner, *Confronting the Bomb: A Short History of the World Nuclear Disarmament Movement* (Stanford, CA: Stanford University Press, 2009), 197.

68. Vilho Harle and Pekka Sivonen, eds., *Nuclear Weapons in a Changing Europe* (London: Pinter, 1991), 183.

69. Garthoff, 380.

70. John G. Tower, James Brown, and William K. Cheek, eds., *Verification: The Key to Arms Control in the 1990s* (Washington, DC: Brassey's, 1992), 5.

71. Garthoff, *The Great Transition*, 383.

72. Ibid., 404.

73. William Newmann, *Managing National Security Policy: The President and the Process* (Pittsburgh: University of Pittsburgh Press, 2003), 154–156.

74. Appu K. Soman, *Double-Edged Sword: Nuclear Diplomacy in Unequal Conflicts: The United States and China, 1950–1958* (Westport, CT: Praeger, 2000), 226.

75. Stephen J. Cimbala, ed., *Clinton and Post–Cold War Defense* (Westport, CT: Praeger, 1996), 54–55.

76. Newmann, 155.

77. Richard J. Krickus, *Showdown: The Lithuanian Rebellion and the Breakup of the Soviet Empire* (Washington, DC: Brassey's, 1997), 224.

78. Rudolf Avenhaus, Victor Kremenyuk, and Gunnar Sjöstedt, eds., *Containing the Atom* (Lanham, MD: Lexington Books, 2002), 36.

79. James M. Goldgeier and Michael McFaul, *Power and Purpose: U.S. Policy Toward Russia after the Cold War* (Washington, DC: Brookings Institution Press, 2003), 45.

CHAPTER FOURTEEN

1. Amy Woolf, ed., *The Nunn-Lugar Cooperative Threat Reduction Programs: Issues for Congress* (New York: Novinka Books, 2003), 2–3.

2. Karen Dawisha and Bruce Parrot, *Russia and the New States of Eurasia: The Politics of Upheaval* (Cambridge: Cambridge University Press, 1994), 260.

3. Ted Carpenter and Barbara Conry, *NATO Enlargement: Illusions and Reality* (Washington, DC: Cato Institute, 1998), 110.

4. Katherine A. S. Sibley, *The Cold War* (Westport, CT: Greenwood Press, 1998), 177.

5. Clifford Thompson, ed., *Russia & Eastern Europe* (New York: H. W. Wilson, 1998), 58.

6. James Goldgeier and Michael McFaul, *Power and Purpose: U.S. Policy Toward Russia After the Cold War* (Washington, DC: Brookings Institution Press, 2003), 52.

7. Strobe Talbott, *The Russia Hand: A Memoir of Presidential Diplomacy* (New York: Random House, 2002), 42.

8. Lloyd Jenson, *Bargaining for National Security: The Postwar Disarmament Negotiations* (Columbia: University of South Carolina Press, 1988), 252.

9. Hugh Gusterson, *Nuclear Rites: A Weapons Laboratory at the End of the Cold War* (Berkeley: University of California Press, 1998), 145–146.

10. Lawrence Wittner, *Toward Nuclear Abolition: A History of the World Nuclear Disarmament Movement, 1971–Present* (Stanford, CA: Stanford University Press, 2003), 439.

11. Philip Schrag, *Global Action: Nuclear Test Ban Diplomacy at the End of the Cold War* (Boulder, CO: Westview Press, 1992), 75.

12. Darryl Howlett, John Simpson, and Philip Acton, ed., *Nuclear Non-Proliferation: A Reference Handbook* (Harlow, Essex, UK: Longman Group, 1992), 27.

13. Stuart Croft, *Strategies of Arms Control: A History and Typology* (Manchester: Manchester University Press, 1996), 99.

14. Mitchell Reiss, *Bridled Ambition: Why Countries Constrain Their Nuclear Capabilities* (Washington, DC: Woodrow Wilson Center Press, 1995), 97–98.

15. Adrian Levy and Catherine Scott-Clark, *Deception: Pakistan, the United States, and the Secret Trade in Nuclear Weapons* (New York: Walker, 2007), 95.

16. Jonathan B. Tucker, *War of Nerves: Chemical Warfare from World War I to Al Qaeda* (New York: Pantheon Books, 2007), 438.

17. Michael Brown, *Grave New World: Security Challenges in the 21st Century* (Washington, DC: Georgetown University Press, 2003), 43–44.

18. Hal Gardner, *American Global Strategy and the "War on Terrorism"* (Burlington, VT: Ashgate Publishing, 2007), 34–35.

19. Peter Nolan, *Capitalism and Freedom: The Contradictory Character of Globalisation* (London: Anthem Press, 2008), 180–181.

20. Stefan Halper and Jonathan Clarke, *America Alone: The Neo-Conservatives and the Global Order* (Cambridge: Cambridge University Press, 2005), 145.

21. David Halberstam, *War in a Time of Peace: Bush, Clinton, and the Generals* (New York: Scribner, 2001), 243.

22. Philip Auerswald, Christian Duttweiler, and John Garufano, eds., *Clinton's Foreign Policy: A Documentary Record* (New York: Kluwer Law International, 2003), 21–22.

23. Hans Blix, *Disarming Iraq* (New York: Pantheon Books, 2004), 17.

24. Jim A. Kuypers, *Presidential Crisis Rhetoric and the Press in the Post–Cold War World* (Westport, CT: Praeger, 1997), 57.

25. Warren Christopher, *In the Stream of History: Shaping Foreign Policy for a New Era* (Stanford, CA: Stanford University Press, 1998), 193.

26. Scott Ritter, *Iraq Confidential: The Untold Story of the Intelligence Conspiracy to Undermine the UN and Overthrow Saddam Hussein* (New York: Nation Books, 2005), 290.

27. Ryan Hendrickson, *The Clinton Wars: The Constitution, Congress, and War Powers* (Nashville: Vanderbilt University Press, 2002), 75.

28. Ibid., 192.

29. Ashton Carter and William Perry, *Preventive Defense: A New Security Strategy for America* (Washington, DC: Brookings Institution Press, 1999), 194–195.

30. Andrew Krepinevich, *The Bottom-Up Review: An Assessment*, The Defense Budget Project, Washington, DC, February 1994.

31. Tom Sauer, *Nuclear Inertia: U.S. Weapons Policy after the Cold War* (London: I. B. Tauris, 2005), 124.

32. Goldgeier and McFaul, 110.

33. Eric A. Croddy and James J. Wirtz, *Weapons of Mass Destruction: An Encyclopedia of Worldwide Policy, Technology, and History* (Santa Barbara, CA: ABC-CLIO, 2005), 217.

34. Paul Podvig, *START and the ABM Treaty: Is a Compromise Possible?* PONARS Policy Memo 132, Center for Arms Control, Moscow Institute of Physics and Technology, April 2000.

35. Marco De Andreis and Francesco Calogero, *The Soviet Nuclear Weapon Legacy* (Oxford: Oxford University Press, 1995), 15.

36. Jae Hyung-Lee, *China and the Asia-Pacific Region: Geostrategic Relations and a Naval Dimension* (Bloomington, IN: iUniverse, 2002), 65.

37. Mohamed Bin Huwaidin, *China's Relations with Arabia and the Gulf, 1949–1999* (London: RoutledgeCurzon, 2002). 78.

38. Richard N. Haas and Meghan L. O'Sullivan, eds., *Honey and Vinegar: Incentives, Sanctions, and Foreign Policy* (Washington, DC: Brookings Institution Press, 2000), 82.

39. Ritter, 127–128.

40. Hendrickson, 79.

41. Tony Judt, *Postwar: A History of Europe Since 1945* (New York: Penguin, 2005), 150.

42. Robert J. Leiber, ed., *Eagle Rules? Foreign Policy and American Primacy in the Twenty-First Century* (Upper Saddle River, NJ: Prentice Hall, 2001), 66.

43. Peter Truscott, *Russia First: Breaking with the West* (London: I. B. Tauris, 1997), 159–161.

44. S. Victor Papacosma and Mary Ann Heiss, eds., *NATO in the Post-Cold War Era: Does It Have a Future?* (New York: St. Martin's Press, 1995), 119–120.

45. Sauer, 150.

46. Harald Müller, David Fischer, and Wolfgang Kötter, *Nuclear Non-Proliferation and Global Order* (Oxford: Oxford University Press, 1994), 94.

47. David Shambaugh and Richard H. Yang, eds., *China's Military in Transition* (New York: Oxford University Press, 1997), 302.

48. Christopher, 338.

49. Croddy and Wirtz, 68.

50. Rebecca K. C. Hersman, *Friends and Foes: How Congress and the President Really Make Foreign Policy* (Washington, DC: Brookings Institution Press, 2000), 94.

51. Michael Krepon, Amy E. Smithson, and John Parachini, *The Battle to Obtain U.S. Ratification of the Chemical Weapons Convention* (Washington, DC: Henry L. Stimson Center, 1997), 8.

52. Thomas Graham Jr., *Disarmament Sketches: Three Decades of Arms Control and International Law* (Seattle: Institute for Global and Regional Security Studies, University of Washington Press, 2002), 307.

53. Sauer, 58.

54. Hersman, 92.

55. Goldgeier and McFaul, 293.

56. Frank Columbus, *Russia in Transition*, vol. 1 (Hauppauge, NY: Nova Science Publishers, 2003), 119.

57. William J. Clinton, *The State of the Union Addresses of William J. Clinton* (Middlesex, UK: Echo Library, 2007), 87.

58. Sauer, 40.

59. Ibid., 52.

60. Nathan E. Busch, *No End in Sight: The Continuing Menace of Nuclear Proliferation* (Lexington: University Press of Kentucky: 2004), 320.

61. Sumit Gangulay and Devin Hagerty, *Fearful Symmetry: India-Pakistan Crises in the Shadow of Nuclear Weapons* (Seattle: University of Washington Press, 2006), 116.

62. Graham, 295.

63. George Bunn and Christopher F. Chyba, eds., *U.S. Nuclear Weapons Policy: Confronting Today's Threats* (Stanford, CA: Center for International Security and Cooperation, 2006), 83.

64. Leiber, 290.

65. Barry R. Schneider and Jim A. Davis, eds., *Avoiding the Abyss: Progress, Shortfalls, and the Way Ahead in Combating the WMD Threat* (Westport, CT: Praeger Security International, 2006), 138.

66. Columbus, 124.

67. Joseph Black, *Vladimir Putin and the New World Order: Looking East, Looking West?* (Lanham, MD: Rowman & Littlefield, 2004), 188.

68. Columbus, 132.

69. Black, 224.

70. Andrew Felkay, *Yeltsin's Russia and the West* (Westport, CT: Greenwood Publishing, 2002), 228.

71. Columbus, 89.

72. James Lindsay and Michael O'Hanley, *Defending America: The Case for a National Missile Defense* (Washington, DC: Brookings Institution Press, 2002), 118.

73. James F. Forest, ed., *Countering Terrorism and Insurgency in the 21st Century: International Perspectives*, vol. 1, *Strategic and Tactical Considerations* (Westport, CT: Praeger Security International, 2007), 437.

74. Dinshaw Mistry, *Containing Missile Proliferation: Strategic Technology, Security Regimes, and International Cooperation in Arms Control* (Seattle: University of Washington Press, 2003), 135.

75. John Diamond, *The CIA and the Culture of Failure: U.S. Intelligence from the End of the Cold War to the Invasion of Iraq* (Stanford, CA: Stanford Security Series, 2008), 275.

76. Hal Brands, *From Berlin to Baghdad: America's Search for Purpose in the Post–Cold War World* (Lexington: University Press of Kentucky, 2008), 166–167.

77. Ibid., 168.

CHAPTER FIFTEEN

1. Alexander Moens, *The Foreign Policy of George W. Bush: Values, Strategy, and Loyalty* (Burlington, VT: Ashgate, 2004), 87–88.

2. Scott Ritter, *Frontier Justice: Weapons of Mass Destruction and the Bushwhacking of America* (New York: Context Books, 2003), 75.

3. Arms Control Association, "ABM Treaty Withdrawal Neither Necessary Nor Prudent," Press Conference, December 13, 2001.

4. Wade Boese, "Bush Pushes New Strategic Framework, Missile Defenses," *Arms Control Today*, June 2001.

5. Stephen J. Hadley, "A Call to Deploy," *Washington Quarterly* 23, no. 3 (2000): 95–108.

6. George W. Bush, Press Conference with Poland's President Aleksander Kwasniewski, Warsaw, Poland, June 15, 2001.

7. Vladimir Putin, Press Conference, July 18, 2001.

8. Nikolai Sokov, *US Withdrawal from ABM Treaty: Post-Mortem and Possible Consequences*, Center for Non-Proliferation Studies Report, December 14, 2001.

9. Malcolm R. Dando, *Preventing Biological Warfare: The Failure of American Leadership* (New York: Palgrave, 2002), 166–167.

10. Ibid., 168–169.

11. Patrick Hayden, Tom Lansford, and Robert P. Watson, eds., *America's War on Terror* (Burlington, VT: Ashgate, 2003), 60.

12. Chris Dolan, *In War We Trust: The Bush Doctrine and the Pursuit of Just War* (Burlington, VT: Ashgate, 2005), 5.

13. Joseph Black, *Vladimir Putin and the New World Order: Looking East, Looking West?* (Lanham, MD: Rowman & Littlefield, 2004), 148.

14. J. Peter Scoblic, *U.S. Versus Them: How a Half Century of Conservatism Has Undermined America's Security* (New York: Viking, 2008), 175.

15. Stefan Halper and Jonathan Clarke, *America Alone: The Neo-Conservatives and the Global Order* (Cambridge: Cambridge University Press, 2005), 126.

16. Strobe Talbott, *The Russia Hand: A Memoir of Presidential Diplomacy* (New York: Random House, 2002), 419.

17. Norman Polmar, *The Naval Institute Guide to the Ships and Aircraft of the U.S. Fleet* (Annapolis, MD: Naval Institute Press, 2005), 62.

18. Nick Ritchie, *US Nuclear Weapons Policy after the Cold War: Russians, "Rogues," and Domestic Division* (New York: Routledge, 2008), 118.

19. Amy F. Woolf, *U.S. Nuclear Weapons: Changes in Policy and Force Structure* (New York: Novinka, 2005), 33.

20. Black, 207.

21. Tom Sauer, *Nuclear Inertia: U.S. Weapons Policy after the Cold War* (London: I. B. Tauris, 2005), 28.

22. "Treaty on Strategic Offensive Reduction: The Moscow Treaty," Hearings before the Committee on Foreign Relations, United States Senate, 107th Congress, 2nd Session, July 9, 17, 23, and September 12, 2002, vols. 107–622, 252.

23. Sarah Diehl and James Moltz, eds., *Nuclear Weapons and Non-Proliferation: A Reference Book* (Santa Barbara, CA: ABC-CLIO, 2002), 158.

24. M. Kent Bolton, *U.S. National Security and Foreign Policymaking after 9/11: Present at the Re-Creation* (Lanham, MD: Rowman & Littlefield, 2008), 22.

25. Glen Segell, *Disarming Iraq* (London: Glen Segell Publishers, 2004), 117.

26. Russ Hoyle, *Going to War: How Misinformation, Disinformation, and Arrogance Led America into Iraq* (New York: Thomas Dunne Books, 2008), 308.

27. *National Strategy to Combat Weapons of Mass Destruction* (Unclassified Version), NSPD-17/HSPD-17 (Department of Homeland Security), December 2002.

28. Ibid.

29. Hall Gardner, *American Global Strategy and the "War on Terror"* (Burlington, VT: Ashgate Publishing, 2005), 95.

30. Ibid., 96.

31. Stephen J. Cimbala, *Nuclear Weapons and Cooperative Security in the 21st Century: The New Disorder* (New York: Routledge, 2009), 68.

32. Peter Truscott, *Putin's Progress: A Biography of Russia's Enigmatic President, Vladimir Putin* (New York: Simon & Schuster, 2004), 293.

33. Joint Statement by President George W. Bush and President Vladimir V. Putin on the New Strategic Relationship, St. Petersburg, Russia, June 1, 2003.

34. Hans Kristensen, "The Role of U.S. Nuclear Weapons: New Doctrine Falls Short of Bush Pledge," *Arms Control Today* (September 2005).

35. Ritchie, 66.

36. Scoblic, 181.

37. John Francis Murphy, *The United States and the Rule of Law in International Affairs* (Cambridge: Cambridge University Press, 2004), 223.

38. William J. Perry, Charles D. Ferguson, and Brent Scowcroft, *U.S. Nuclear Weapons Policy* (Washington, DC: Council on Foreign Relations, 2009), 78.

39. Los Alamos Study Group, "The Reliable Replacement Warhead (RRW) Can't Meet Congressional Objections," Abbreviated Talking Points, April 16, 2004.

40. Scott Ritter, *Target Iran: The Truth About the White House's Plans for Regime Change* (New York: Nation Books, 2006), 113.

41. Ibid., 132.

42. Patrick M. Cronin, ed., *Double Trouble: Iran and North Korea as Challenges to International Security* (Westport, CT: Praeger Security International, 2008), 129.

43. Gardner, 118.

44. Diehl and Moltz, 64.

45. Ibid., 89.

46. Stephen Blank, "Towards a New Russian Policy," Strategic Studies Institute, U.S. Army War College, February 2008.

47. Foreign Affairs Committee, House of Commons, "Global Security: Russia, Second Report of Session 2007–2008, Report," Parliament of Great Britain, 2007, 102.

48. Richard Ragaini, ed., *International Seminar on Nuclear War and Planetary Emergencies, 38th Session* (Hackensack, NJ: World Scientific, 2008), 212.

49. Richard Weitz, *China-Russia Security Relations: Strategic Parallelism Without Partnership or Passion?* (Carlisle, PA: Strategic Studies Institute, U.S. Army War College, 2008), 44.

50. Foreign Affairs Committee, 102.

51. G. P. Geoghegan, *Republicanism: The Dark Night of the American Dream* (Raleigh, NC: Lulu.com, 2008), 25.

52. Foreign Affairs Committee, 58.

53. Jeffrey Mankoff, *Russian Foreign Policy: The Return of Great Power Politics* (Lanham, MD: Rowman & Littlefield, 2009), 294.

54. Jim Heintz, "Russia Warns Poland on U.S. Missile Base," *Boston Globe*, August 16, 2008.

55. Mark Thompson, "Obama's Showdown over Nukes," *Time*, January 26, 2009.

56. Walter Pincus, "Panel Urges Keeping U.S. Nuclear Arms in Europe," *Washington Post*, January 9, 2009.

CONCLUSION

1. Julian Borger and Luke Harding, "US and Russia Agree to Nuclear Disarmament Roadmap," *Guardian* (London), July 6, 2009, 1.

2. "Remarks by the President at the New Economic School Graduation," Office of the Press Secretary, The White House, July 7, 2009.

3. Peter Spiegel, "Biden Says Weakened Russia Will Bend to U.S.," *Wall Street Journal*, July 25, 2009, 1.

4. Bob Graham, Jim Talent, et al., *World at Risk: The Report of the Commission on the Prevention of WMD Proliferation and Terrorism* (New York: Vintage Books, 2008), digital book.

5. General Lee Butler (Ret.), "The Risks of Nuclear Deterrence: From Superpowers to Rogue Leaders," speech given to National Press Club, Washington, DC, February 2, 1998.

6. Ibid.

7. George P. Shultz, William J. Perry, Henry A. Kissinger, and Sam Nunn, "A World Free of Nuclear Weapons," *Wall Street Journal*, January 4, 2007, A15.

8. Thom Shanker and Peter Baker, "U.S. Seeks 'Bridge' on Russian Arms Pact," *New York Times*, October 20, 2009.

INDEX